World

ADVENTURES IN TIME AND PLACE

James A. Banks

Barry K. Beyer

Gloria Contreras

Jean Craven

Gloria Ladson-Billings

Mary A. McFarland

Walter C. Parker

NATIONAL
GEOGRAPHIC
SOCIETY

THIS GOLDEN MASK WAS FOUND

IN THE TOMB OF TUTANKHAMUN,

WHO RULED ANCIENT EGYPT

MORE THAN 3,000 YEARS AGO.

HE IS ONE OF THE MANY PEOPLE

WHO HELPED SHAPE THE

WORLD WE LIVE IN.

Macmillan McGraw-Hill

New York   Farmington

PROGRAM AUTHORS

Dr. James A. Banks
Professor of Education and Director of the Center for Multicultural Education
University of Washington
Seattle, Washington

Dr. Barry K. Beyer
Professor Emeritus, Graduate School of Education
George Mason University
Fairfax, Virginia

Dr. Gloria Contreras
Professor of Education
University of North Texas
Denton, Texas

Jean Craven
District Coordinator of Curriculum Development
Albuquerque Public Schools
Albuquerque, New Mexico

Dr. Gloria Ladson-Billings
Professor of Education
University of Wisconsin
Madison, Wisconsin

Dr. Mary A. McFarland
Instructional Coordinator of Social Studies, K–12, and Director of Staff Development
Parkway School District
Chesterfield, Missouri

Dr. Walter C. Parker
Professor and Program Chair for Social Studies Education
University of Washington
Seattle, Washington

NATIONAL GEOGRAPHIC SOCIETY
Washington, D.C.

PROGRAM CONSULTANTS

Daniel Berman
Asian Studies Specialist
Coordinator of Social Studies
Bedford Central Schools
Bedford, New York

Dr. Khalid Y. Blankinship
Affiliated Scholar, Council on Islamic Education
Fountain Valley, California
Assistant Professor of Religion
Temple University
Philadelphia, Pennsylvania

Dr. John Bodnar
Professor of History
Indiana University
Bloomington, Indiana

Dr. Roberto R. Calderón
Department of Ethnic Studies
University of California at Riverside
Riverside, California

Dr. Sheilah Clarke-Ekong
Asst. Professor, Department of Anthropology and Research Associate, Center for International Studies
University of Missouri, St. Louis
St. Louis, Missouri

Dr. John L. Esposito
Professor of Religion and International Affairs
Georgetown University
Washington, D.C.

Dr. Darlene Clark Hine
John A. Hannah Professor of History
Michigan State University
East Lansing, Michigan

Paulla Dove Jennings
Project Director
The Rhode Island Indian Council, Inc.
Providence, Rhode Island

Dr. Henrietta Mann
Professor of Native American Studies
University of Montana, Missoula
Missoula, Montana

Dr. Gary Manson
Professor, Department of Geography
Michigan State University
East Lansing, Michigan

Dr. Juan Mora-Torrés
Professor of Latin American History
University of Texas at San Antonio
San Antonio, Texas

Dr. Valerie Ooka Pang
Professor, School of Teacher Education
San Diego State University
San Diego, California

Dr. Joseph R. Rosenbloom
Professor, Classics Department
Washington University
St. Louis, Missouri

Dr. Joseph B. Rubin
Director of Reading
Fort Worth Independent School District
Fort Worth, Texas

Dr. Robert M. Seltzer
Professor of Jewish History
Hunter College of The City University of New York
New York, New York

Dr. Peter N. Stearns
Dean, College of Humanities and Social Studies
Carnegie Mellon University
Pittsburgh, Pennsylvania

GRADE-LEVEL CONSULTANTS

Dianne C. Baker
Sixth Grade Teacher
Ingleside Middle School
Phoenix, Arizona

Maureen F. Barber
Sixth and Seventh Grade Social Studies Teacher
Center Based Gifted Program
Manchester Middle School
Chesterfield, Virginia

David H. Delgado
Sixth Grade Social Studies Teacher
Rogers Middle School
San Antonio, Texas

Martha Doster
Sixth Grade Teacher
Northwest Rankin Attendance Center
Brandon, Mississippi

Joyce Garbe Orland
Sixth–Eighth Grade Teacher and Chairperson, Social Studies Department
Pershing School
Berwyn, Illinois

CONTRIBUTING WRITERS

Ruth Akamine Wassynger
Winston-Salem, North Carolina

Spencer Finch
Brooklyn, New York

Linda Scher
Raleigh, North Carolina

Acknowledgments

The publisher gratefully acknowledges permission to reprint the following copyrighted material:

From **Lost Civilizations: Sumer: Cities of Eden** by the editors of Time-Life Books. Copyright 1993 Time-Life Books, Inc. Reprinted by permission.
From **Tropical Rainforests** by Arnold Newman. Text copyright 1990 Arnold Newman. Reprinted with permission of Facts On File, Inc., New York.
From **The Iliad of Homer: The Wrath of Achilles,** translated by I.A. Richards, Translation copyright 1950 by W.W. Norton & Company, Inc., renewed 1978 by I.A. Richards. Reprinted with permission of W.W. Norton & Company, Inc.
Excerpts from **Corpus of Early Arabic Sources for West African History.** Copyright University of Ghana, International Academic Union, Cambridge University Press 1981. Reprinted with the permission of Cambridge University Press.

(continued on page R79)

Macmillan/McGraw-Hill

A Division of The McGraw·Hill Companies

Macmillan/McGraw-Hill
1221 Avenue of the Americas
New York, New York 10020

Printed in the United States of America

ISBN 0-02-146561-4

6 7 8 9 RRW 02 01 00 99 98 97

CONTENTS

xiv   *Your Textbook at a Glance*

G2   ☐   NATIONAL GEOGRAPHIC
      Five Themes of Geography

G4   *Reviewing Geography Skills*
     G4   **PART 1**   **Using Globes**
     G6   **PART 2**   **Using Maps**
     G9   **PART 3**   **Different Kinds of Maps**

UNIT ONE
2

Understanding the World

4   ☐   ADVENTURES WITH NATIONAL GEOGRAPHIC
     Stony Silence

6   **CHAPTER 1** ● *Regions of the World*

     8   **LESSON 1**   **World Regions**
     12   **GEOGRAPHY SKILLS**   **Working with Latitude and Longitude**
     14   **LESSON 2**   **Regions and Culture**
     20   **CHAPTER 1 REVIEW**

22   **CHAPTER 2** ● *A Look into the Past*

     24   **LESSON 1**   **Understanding History**
     30   **THINKING SKILLS**   **Decision Making**
     32   **LESSON 2**   **Iceman of the Alps**
     38   **CITIZENSHIP** **Viewpoints** **When Should Cultural Sites Around the World Be Protected?**
     40   **CHAPTER 2 REVIEW**

42   **CHAPTER 3** ● *Early Cultures*

     44   **LESSON 1**   **Early People**
     50   **LEGACY**   **Artists and Their Environments**
     52   **LESSON 2**   **Agriculture Changes the World**
     58   **STUDY SKILLS**   **Reading Time Lines**
     60   **CHAPTER 3 REVIEW**
     62   **UNIT 1 REVIEW**

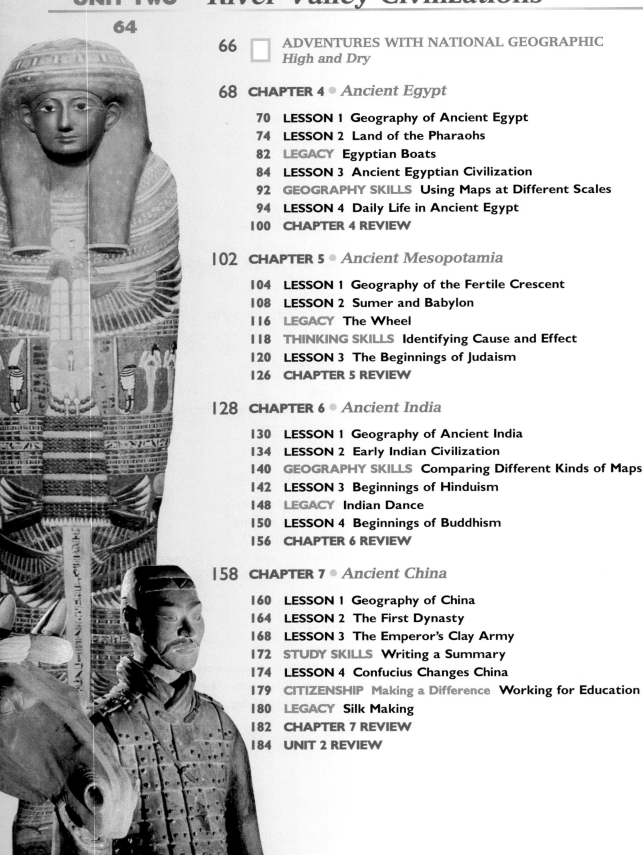

UNIT TWO *River Valley Civilizations*
64

66 ADVENTURES WITH NATIONAL GEOGRAPHIC
High and Dry

68 CHAPTER 4 ● *Ancient Egypt*

   70 LESSON 1 Geography of Ancient Egypt
   74 LESSON 2 Land of the Pharaohs
   82 LEGACY Egyptian Boats
   84 LESSON 3 Ancient Egyptian Civilization
   92 GEOGRAPHY SKILLS Using Maps at Different Scales
   94 LESSON 4 Daily Life in Ancient Egypt
   100 CHAPTER 4 REVIEW

102 CHAPTER 5 ● *Ancient Mesopotamia*

   104 LESSON 1 Geography of the Fertile Crescent
   108 LESSON 2 Sumer and Babylon
   116 LEGACY The Wheel
   118 THINKING SKILLS Identifying Cause and Effect
   120 LESSON 3 The Beginnings of Judaism
   126 CHAPTER 5 REVIEW

128 CHAPTER 6 ● *Ancient India*

   130 LESSON 1 Geography of Ancient India
   134 LESSON 2 Early Indian Civilization
   140 GEOGRAPHY SKILLS Comparing Different Kinds of Maps
   142 LESSON 3 Beginnings of Hinduism
   148 LEGACY Indian Dance
   150 LESSON 4 Beginnings of Buddhism
   156 CHAPTER 6 REVIEW

158 CHAPTER 7 ● *Ancient China*

   160 LESSON 1 Geography of China
   164 LESSON 2 The First Dynasty
   168 LESSON 3 The Emperor's Clay Army
   172 STUDY SKILLS Writing a Summary
   174 LESSON 4 Confucius Changes China
   179 CITIZENSHIP Making a Difference Working for Education
   180 LEGACY Silk Making
   182 CHAPTER 7 REVIEW
   184 UNIT 2 REVIEW

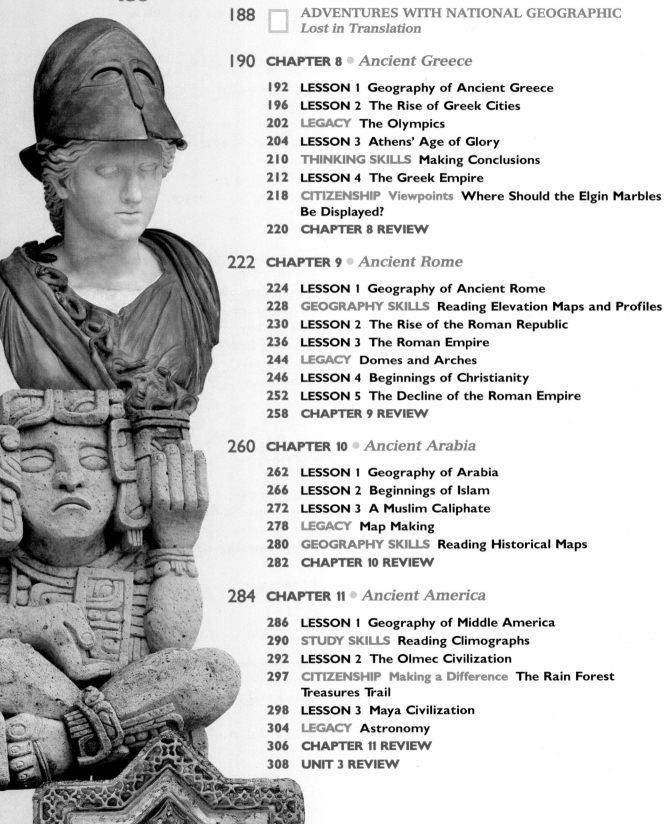

UNIT THREE *New Ideas and New Empires*

186

188 ADVENTURES WITH NATIONAL GEOGRAPHIC
Lost in Translation

190 **CHAPTER 8** ● *Ancient Greece*

192 **LESSON 1** Geography of Ancient Greece
196 **LESSON 2** The Rise of Greek Cities
202 LEGACY The Olympics
204 **LESSON 3** Athens' Age of Glory
210 THINKING SKILLS Making Conclusions
212 **LESSON 4** The Greek Empire
218 CITIZENSHIP Viewpoints Where Should the Elgin Marbles Be Displayed?
220 **CHAPTER 8 REVIEW**

222 **CHAPTER 9** ● *Ancient Rome*

224 **LESSON 1** Geography of Ancient Rome
228 GEOGRAPHY SKILLS Reading Elevation Maps and Profiles
230 **LESSON 2** The Rise of the Roman Republic
236 **LESSON 3** The Roman Empire
244 LEGACY Domes and Arches
246 **LESSON 4** Beginnings of Christianity
252 **LESSON 5** The Decline of the Roman Empire
258 **CHAPTER 9 REVIEW**

260 **CHAPTER 10** ● *Ancient Arabia*

262 **LESSON 1** Geography of Arabia
266 **LESSON 2** Beginnings of Islam
272 **LESSON 3** A Muslim Caliphate
278 LEGACY Map Making
280 GEOGRAPHY SKILLS Reading Historical Maps
282 **CHAPTER 10 REVIEW**

284 **CHAPTER 11** ● *Ancient America*

286 **LESSON 1** Geography of Middle America
290 STUDY SKILLS Reading Climographs
292 **LESSON 2** The Olmec Civilization
297 CITIZENSHIP Making a Difference The Rain Forest Treasures Trail
298 **LESSON 3** Maya Civilization
304 LEGACY Astronomy
306 **CHAPTER 11 REVIEW**
308 **UNIT 3 REVIEW**

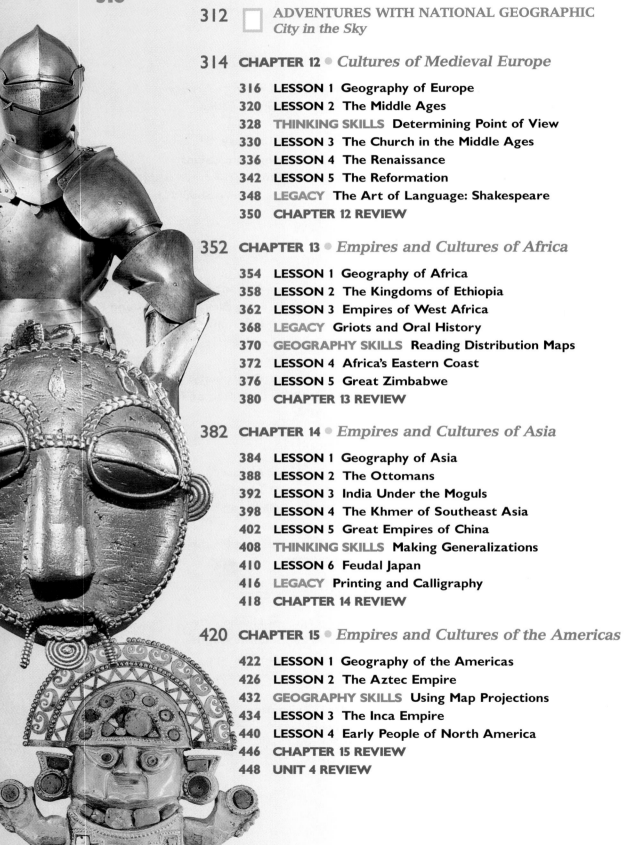

UNIT FOUR   *World Regions in Transition*

310

312 ADVENTURES WITH NATIONAL GEOGRAPHIC
City in the Sky

314 **CHAPTER 12** ● *Cultures of Medieval Europe*

316 **LESSON 1 Geography of Europe**
320 **LESSON 2 The Middle Ages**
328 **THINKING SKILLS Determining Point of View**
330 **LESSON 3 The Church in the Middle Ages**
336 **LESSON 4 The Renaissance**
342 **LESSON 5 The Reformation**
348 **LEGACY The Art of Language: Shakespeare**
350 **CHAPTER 12 REVIEW**

352 **CHAPTER 13** ● *Empires and Cultures of Africa*

354 **LESSON 1 Geography of Africa**
358 **LESSON 2 The Kingdoms of Ethiopia**
362 **LESSON 3 Empires of West Africa**
368 **LEGACY Griots and Oral History**
370 **GEOGRAPHY SKILLS Reading Distribution Maps**
372 **LESSON 4 Africa's Eastern Coast**
376 **LESSON 5 Great Zimbabwe**
380 **CHAPTER 13 REVIEW**

382 **CHAPTER 14** ● *Empires and Cultures of Asia*

384 **LESSON 1 Geography of Asia**
388 **LESSON 2 The Ottomans**
392 **LESSON 3 India Under the Moguls**
398 **LESSON 4 The Khmer of Southeast Asia**
402 **LESSON 5 Great Empires of China**
408 **THINKING SKILLS Making Generalizations**
410 **LESSON 6 Feudal Japan**
416 **LEGACY Printing and Calligraphy**
418 **CHAPTER 14 REVIEW**

420 **CHAPTER 15** ● *Empires and Cultures of the Americas*

422 **LESSON 1 Geography of the Americas**
426 **LESSON 2 The Aztec Empire**
432 **GEOGRAPHY SKILLS Using Map Projections**
434 **LESSON 3 The Inca Empire**
440 **LESSON 4 Early People of North America**
446 **CHAPTER 15 REVIEW**
448 **UNIT 4 REVIEW**

UNIT FIVE   Dawn of the Modern World

450

452 ☐ **ADVENTURES WITH NATIONAL GEOGRAPHIC**
Golden Voyage

454 **CHAPTER 16** ● *European Expansion*

456 **LESSON 1** The Beginning of Modern Science
461 **CITIZENSHIP** Making a Difference **Making History in Space**
462 **LESSON 2** An Age of Exploration
466 **LESSON 3** Europeans in the Americas
472 **THINKING SKILLS** Analyzing the Credibility of a Source
474 **LESSON 4** Africans in the Americas
478 **LESSON 5** A European Colony in Canada
482 **CHAPTER 16 REVIEW**

484 **CHAPTER 17** ● *Revolutions Change the World*

486 **LESSON 1** The French Revolution
492 **LESSON 2** Independence in the Americas
498 **LEGACY** The United States Constitution
500 **LESSON 3** The Industrial Revolution
506 **GEOGRAPHY SKILLS** Using Cartograms
508 **LESSON 4** The Rise of Industrial Japan
514 **CITIZENSHIP** Viewpoints **1853: What Did the Japanese Think About Opening Their Country to the West?**
516 **CHAPTER 17 REVIEW**
518 **UNIT 5 REVIEW**

UNIT SIX
520

A Century of Conflict

522 ☐ **ADVENTURES WITH NATIONAL GEOGRAPHIC**
The Last Unknown Place

524 CHAPTER 18 ● *A World at War*

526 LESSON 1 The Great War
532 LESSON 2 The Russian Revolution
540 LESSON 3 World War II
548 GEOGRAPHY SKILLS Time Zone Maps
550 LESSON 4 Communism in China
556 LESSON 5 Cold War
562 CHAPTER 18 REVIEW

564 CHAPTER 19 ● *New Nations*

566 LESSON 1 Independence in Africa
572 STUDY SKILLS Political Cartoons
574 LESSON 2 New Nations in the Middle East
579 CITIZENSHIP Making a Difference
Building Bridges to Friendship
580 LESSON 3 India's Struggle for Independence
586 LESSON 4 New Nations in Southeast Asia
592 CHAPTER 19 REVIEW

594 CHAPTER 20 ● *A Changing World*

596 LESSON 1 A Changing Europe
604 THINKING SKILLS Evaluating Information for Accuracy
606 LESSON 2 A Changing Africa
613 CITIZENSHIP Making a Difference
A More Equal Chance for Justice
614 LESSON 3 A Changing Asia
622 LESSON 4 The Changing Americas
630 CITIZENSHIP Viewpoints
Why Is International Trade Important?
632 CHAPTER 20 REVIEW
634 UNIT 6 REVIEW

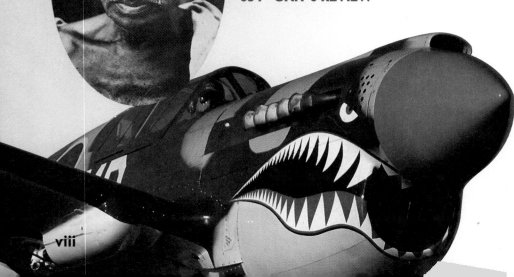

REFERENCE SECTION

R4 ATLAS
R20 COUNTRIES OF THE WORLD
R36 WORLD HISTORY TIME LINES
R46 DICTIONARY OF GEOGRAPHIC TERMS
R48 GAZETTEER
R55 BIOGRAPHICAL DICTIONARY
R60 GLOSSARY
R70 INDEX

FEATURES

SKILLS LESSONS

Geography Skills
Working with Latitude and Longitude / 12
Using Maps at Different Scales / 92
Comparing Different Kinds of Maps / 140
Reading Elevation Maps and Profiles / 228
Reading Historical Maps / 280
Reading Distribution Maps / 370
Using Map Projections / 432
Using Cartograms / 506
Time Zone Maps / 548

Thinking Skills
Decision Making / 30
Identifying Cause and Effect / 118
Making Conclusions / 210
Determining Point of View / 328
Making Generalizations / 408
Analyzing the Credibility of a Source / 472
Evaluating Information for Accuracy / 604

Study Skills
Reading Time Lines / 58
Writing a Summary / 172
Reading Climographs / 290
Political Cartoons / 572

CITIZENSHIP

Making a Difference
Working for Education / 179
The Rain Forest Treasures Trail / 297
Making History in Space / 461
Building Bridges to Friendship / 579
A More Equal Chance for Justice / 613

Viewpoints
When Should Cultural Sites Around the World Be Protected? / 38
Where Should the Elgin Marbles Be Displayed? / 218
1853: What Did the Japanese Think About Opening Their Country to the West? / 514
Why Is International Trade Important? / 630

LEGACIES
Artists and Their Environments / 50
Egyptian Boats / 82
The Wheel / 116
Indian Dance / 148
Silk Making / 180
The Olympics / 202
Domes and Arches / 244
Map Making / 278
Astronomy / 304
The Art of Language: Shakespeare / 348
Griots and Oral History / 368
Printing and Calligraphy / 416
The United States Constitution / 498

MANY VOICES

Primary Sources

Michael Winship, 1988 / **26**

The Rosetta Stone, 196 B.C. / **79**

Code of Hammurabi, c. 1800 B.C. / **113**

The Ten Commandments / **123**

Song from the *Rig Veda*, about 1000 B.C. / **143**

Verses on the Law, around 100 B.C. / **154**

The Analects of Confucius, c. 400 B.C. / **175**

Iliad, Homer, c. 700 B.C. / **200**

Stories of Rome, Livy, 494 B.C. / **231**

Satires, Juvenal, c. A.D. 100 / **238**

Gospel of Luke, New Testament, c. A.D. 60 / **248**

Chapter One, The Quran, about A.D. 650 / **269**

Copán Stela A, about A.D. 750 / **302**

Magna Carta, A.D. 1215 / **327**

The 95 Theses, Martin Luther, 1517 / **343**

Queen Elizabeth I, 1588 / **347**

Al-'Umari, about 1337–1338 / **366**

Painting from Mogul India, 1570 / **395**

Olaudah Equiano, 1789 / **476**

Charles Quinnell, 1916 / **529**

The Diary of Anne Frank, 1944 / **546**

Mohandas Gandhi, 1982 / **582**

Music

"Fung Yang Song" / **405**

"My Bark Canoe" / **442**

"La Marseillaise" / **489**

"N'kosi Sikelel'i Afrika" / **609**

INFOGRAPHICS

Cultures Around the World / **18**

Old Stone Age Technology Around the World / **48**

Treasures of an Ancient Tomb / **88**

Seven Wonders of the Ancient World / **216**

Daily Life in Pompeii / **242**

Life in the Caliphate / **276**

The Spread of the Renaissance / **340**

Timbuktu / **365**

Trade on the Silk Road / **406**

Native North Americans / **444**

Inventions of the Industrial Revolution / **503**

Weapons of World War I / **530**

Economy of Europe / **602**

Economy of Africa / **611**

Economy of Asia / **620**

Economy of the Americas / **628**

LINKS

Links to Mathematics / **55**

Links to Mathematics / **73**

Links to Science / **91**

Links to Current Events / **107**

Links to Language Arts / **114**

Links to Music / **275**

Links to Art / **333**

Links to Art / **511**

Links to Current Events / **603**

Links to Current Events / **627**

DID YOU KNOW?

What language is spoken in India today? / **17**

How did archaeologists figure out how old the Iceman was? / **37**

Why is the Huang River often called "China's Sorrow"? / **163**

What did ancient Greeks do for entertainment? / **206**

How were Roman architects able to build large, lasting structures? / **241**

How hot WAS it? / **289**

What trade good from Zanzibar is commonly in demand today? / **375**

How did Süleyman's gardens change life in the Netherlands? / **391**

How did the Inca keep records of trade throughout the empire? / **437**

How have telescopes changed since Galileo's time? / **459**

Who was Uncle Sam? / **531**

What is the origin of the word *boycott*? / **568**

How did Hong Kong get its name? / **621**

CHARTS, GRAPHS, & DIAGRAMS

Graphic Organizer: Summing Up
Chapter 1 / **21**

Diagram: The Iceman of the Alps / **36**

Graphic Organizer: Summing Up
Chapter 2 / **41**

Diagram: Rooftop Living in Catal
Huyuk / **54**

Chart: New Stone Age Agriculture
Around the World / **57**

Graphic Organizer: Summing Up
Chapter 3 / **61**

Diagram: Three Crowns of Egypt / **75**

Diagram: Building the Great Pyramid
/ **80**

Diagram: Treasures of an Ancient
Tomb / **88**

Diagram: Egyptian Social Pyramid / **95**

Graphic Organizer: Summing Up
Chapter 4 / **101**

Diagram: Water Control in
Mesopotamia / **106**

Chart: How Cuneiform Developed
/ **109**

Graphic Organizer: Summing Up
Chapter 5 / **127**

Graphic Organizer: Summing Up
Chapter 6 / **157**

Diagram: Development of Chinese
Writing / **166**

Graphic Organizer: Summing Up
Chapter 7 / **183**

Diagram: The Golden Age of Athens
/ **207**

Graphic Organizer: Summing Up
Chapter 8 / **221**

Chart: Roman Government about 287
B.C. / **232**

Chart: Development of the Modern
Alphabet / **256**

Graphic Organizer: Summing Up
Chapter 9 / **259**

Graphic Organizer: Summing Up
Chapter 10 / **283**

Climograph A: Acapulco / **290**

Climograph B: Mexico City / **291**

Climograph C: Veracruz / **291**

Graphic Organizer: Summing Up
Chapter 11 / **307**

Chart: Europe at a Glance / **319**

Diagram: Manor Life / **323**

Diagram: A Medieval Town / **325**

Graphic Organizer: Summing Up
Chapter 12 / **351**

Chart: Africa at a Glance / **357**

Graphic Organizer: Summing Up
Chapter 13 / **381**

Chart: Asia at a Glance / **387**

Graphic Organizer: Summing Up
Chapter 14 / **419**

Chart: The Americas at a Glance / **425**

Graphic Organizer: Summing Up
Chapter 15 / **447**

Graphic Organizer: Summing Up
Chapter 16 / **483**

Chart: The Three Estates / **487**

Graph: Japan's GDP, 1885–1910 / **513**

Graphic Organizer: Summing Up
Chapter 17 / **517**

Graphic Organizer: Summing Up
Chapter 18 / **563**

Graphic Organizer: Summing Up
Chapter 19 / **593**

Bar Graph: GDP: Europe, 1993 / **602**

Pie Graph: Rural/Urban Population,
Europe / **602**

Bar Graph: GDP: Africa, 1993 / **611**

Pie Graph: Rural/Urban Population,
Africa / **611**

Bar Graph: GDP: Asia, 1993 / **620**

Pie Graph: Rural/Urban Population,
Asia / **620**

Chart: The World's Five Largest Cities
/ **625**

Bar Graph: GDP: The Americas, 1993
/ **628**

Pie Graph: Rural/Urban Population,
The Americas / **628**

Graphic Organizer: Summing Up
Chapter 20 / **633**

Chart: Countries of the World / **R20**

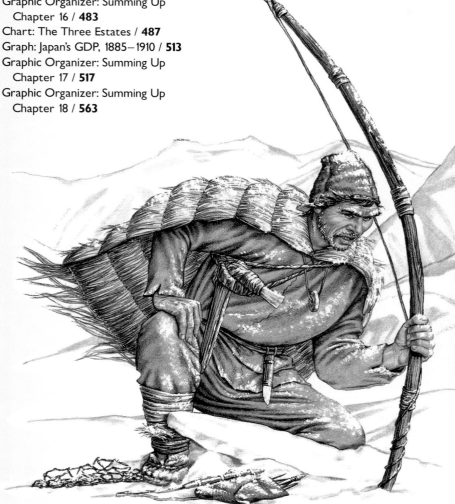

TIME LINES

Early Cultures / **42**
Early People / **44**
Agriculture Changes the World / **52**
Agriculture Time Line / **58**
Technology Time Line / **59**
Major Events of Chapter 3 / **60**
Ancient Egypt / **68**
Land of the Pharaohs / **74**
Ancient Egyptian Civilization / **84**
Daily Life in Ancient Egypt / **94**
Major Events of Chapter 4 / **100**
Ancient Mesopotamia / **102**
Sumer and Babylon / **108**
The Beginnings of Judaism / **120**
Major Events of Chapter 5 / **126**
Ancient India / **128**
Early Indian Civilization / **134**
Beginnings of Hinduism / **142**
Beginnings of Buddhism / **150**
Major Events of Chapter 6 / **156**
Ancient China / **158**
The First Dynasty / **164**
The Emperor's Clay Army / **168**
Confucius Changes China / **174**
Major Events of Chapter 7 / **182**
Ancient Greece / **190**
The Rise of Greek Cities / **196**
Athens' Age of Glory / **204**
The Greek Empire / **212**
Major Events of Chapter 8 / **220**
Ancient Rome / **222**
The Rise of the Roman Republic / **230**
The Roman Empire / **236**

Beginnings of Christianity / **246**
The Decline of the Roman Empire / **252**
Major Events of Chapter 9 / **258**
Ancient Arabia / **260**
Beginnings of Islam / **266**
A Muslim Caliphate / **272**
Major Events of Chapter 10 / **282**
Ancient America / **284**
The Olmec Civilization / **292**
Maya Civilization / **298**
Major Events of Chapter 11 / **306**
Cultures of Medieval Europe / **314**
The Middle Ages / **320**
The Church in the Middle Ages / **330**
The Renaissance / **336**
The Reformation / **342**
Major Events of Chapter 12 / **350**
Empires and Cultures of Africa / **352**
The Kingdoms of Ethiopia / **358**
Empires of West Africa / **362**
Africa's Eastern Coast / **372**
Great Zimbabwe / **376**
Major Events of Chapter 13 / **380**
Empires and Cultures of Asia / **382**
The Ottomans / **388**
India Under the Moguls / **392**
The Khmer of Southeast Asia / **398**
Great Empires of China / **402**
Feudal Japan / **410**
Major Events of Chapter 14 / **418**
Empires and Cultures of the Americas / **420**

The Aztec Empire / **426**
The Inca Empire / **434**
Early People of North America / **440**
Major Events of Chapter 15 / **446**
European Expansion / **454**
The Beginning of Modern Science / **456**
An Age of Exploration / **462**
Europeans in the Americas / **466**
Africans in the Americas / **474**
A European Colony in Canada / **478**
Major Events of Chapter 16 / **482**
Revolutions Change the World / **484**
The French Revolution / **486**
Independence in the Americas / **492**
The Industrial Revolution / **500**
The Rise of Industrial Japan / **508**
Major Events of Chapter 17 / **516**
A World at War / **524**
The Great War / **526**
The Russian Revolution / **532**
World War II / **540**
Communism in China / **550**
Cold War / **556**
Major Events of Chapter 18 / **562**
New Nations / **564**
Independence in Africa / **566**
New Nations in the Middle East / **574**
India's Struggle for Independence / **580**
New Nations in Southeast Asia / **586**
Major Events of Chapter 19 / **592**
World History Time Lines / **R36**

MAPS

Northern Hemisphere / **G5**
Southern Hemisphere / **G5**
Western Hemisphere / **G5**
Eastern Hemisphere / **G5**
Global Grid / **G5**
Australia / **G6**
Map A: Trinidad and Tobago / **G7**
Map B: Trinidad and Tobago / **G7**
Argentina: Resources / **G8**
Switzerland: Physical / **G8**

South Asia: Political / **G9**
Tanzania: Elevation / **G10**
Tanzania: Relief / **G10**
The Growth of the United States, 1789–1898 / **G11**
Russia: Vegetation / **G11**
The World: Continents and Oceans / **9**
Regions in the Western Hemisphere / **11**
Lines of Latitude / **12**

Lines of Longitude / **12**
Global Grid / **13**
India: Political / **15**
Cultures Around the World / **18**
Lines of Longitude / **21**
The Aegean Region / **30**
Archaeological Discovery Site / **33**
The Aegean Region / **41**
Early Cultures / **43**
Border Cave / **47**

Old Stone Age Technology Around the World / **48**

Catal Huyuk / **53**

Ancient Egypt / **69**

Nile River Valley / **71**

Egypt: Old Kingdom / **76**

New Kingdom Trade / **86**

Map A: Nile Valley / **92**

Map B: Thebes, c. 1100 B.C. / **93**

Ancient Mesopotamia / **103**

The Fertile Crescent: Physical / **105**

Mesopotamia, 2500 B.C.–1800 B.C. / **110**

Beginnings of Judaism in the Fertile Crescent / **121**

Ancient India / **129**

Indian Subcontinent: Physical / **131**

Indus Valley Civilization, c. 2000 B.C / **135**

Indus Valley Trade and Migration, c. 1500 B.C / **138**

Map A: Pakistan: Political / **140**

Map B: Pakistan: Physical / **140**

Map C: Pakistan: Agriculture / **141**

Ancient China / **159**

China: Physical / **161**

Lands of the Shang Dynasty, 1200 B.C / **165**

Lands of the Qin Dynasty, 221 B.C / **169**

The Walls of China / **172**

Lands of the Han Dynasty, A.D. 100 / **176**

Ancient Greece / **191**

Ancient Greece: Physical / **193**

Greek City-States, c. 500 B.C. / **198**

The Peloponnesian War, 431–404 B.C / **208**

Empire of Alexander the Great, c. 323 B.C. / **214**

Seven Wonders of the Ancient World / **216**

Ancient Rome / **223**

Italy, c. 700 B.C. / **225**

Map A: Rome: Elevation / **228**

Map B: Rome: A Profile / **229**

The Punic Wars, 264–202 B.C / **234**

Roman Empire, A.D. 14 / **240**

Judea, in the time of Jesus / **247**

Division of the Roman Empire, A.D. 330 / **254**

Ancient Arabia / **261**

The Arabian Peninsula: Physical / **263**

Arabian Trade Routes, c. A.D. 500 / **267**

The Caliphate, c. A.D. 760 / **273**

Growth of the Caliphate, A.D. 711–732 / **280**

Ibn Battuta's Travels / **281**

Ancient America / **285**

Middle America: Physical / **287**

Middle America, 500 B.C. / **293**

The Maya, A.D. 250–900 / **299**

Cultures of Medieval Europe / **315**

Europe: Physical / **317**

Frankish Empire, A.D. 800 / **321**

Religion in the Middle Ages, c. 1300 / **334**

The Spread of the Renaissance / **340**

Christianity in Western Europe, c. 1550 / **345**

Empires and Cultures of Africa / **353**

Africa: Physical / **355**

Kingdom of Aksum, c. A.D. 700 / **359**

Empires of West Africa / **364**

Map A: Africa: Population Density, 1991 / **370**

Map B: Africa: Population Density, 1991 / **371**

Swahili Cities, c. 1400 / **373**

Great Zimbabwe, c. 1400 / **377**

Empires and Cultures of Asia / **383**

Asia: Physical / **385**

The Ottoman Empire of Süleyman I, 1520–1566 / **390**

Mogul Empire, c. 1700 / **393**

Khmer Kingdom, c. 1150 / **399**

Mongol Empire, c. 1200–1400 / **403**

Ming China, 1368–1644 / **404**

Japan, 1200–1700 / **411**

Empires and Cultures of the Americas / **421**

The Americas: Physical / **423**

Aztec Empire, c. 1450 / **427**

Map A: Equal-Area Projection / **432**

Map B: Equal-Area Projection / **432**

Map C: Mercator Projection / **433**

Map D: Polar Projection / **433**

Inca Empire, c. 1530 / **435**

Peoples of the Great Lakes, c. 1500 / **441**

Native North Americans / **444**

European Expansion / **455**

European Voyages of Exploration, 1487–1522 / **464**

Conquest of the Americas / **467**

European Colonies Around the Caribbean Sea, 1650 / **475**

St. Lawrence River Valley / **479**

European Claims in Eastern North America, 1648 / **481**

Revolutions Change the World / **485**

Middle America and the Caribbean, 1805 / **493**

Routes of Bolívar and San Martín, c. 1810–1821 / **496**

World Cartogram: Gross Domestic Product / **506**

Growth of Japan, 1870–1905 / **512**

A World at War / **525**

Europe, 1914 / **528**

Growth of Russia, 1360–1917 / **533**

World War II / **544**

The World: Time Zones / **548**

The Long March, 1934–1935 / **552**

Europe, 1948–1989 / **558**

New Nations / **565**

Independence in Africa, 1951–1993 / **570**

New Nations in the Middle East, 1923–1977 / **576**

Israel and Territories / **578**

New Nations in South Asia, 1947–1972 / **583**

New Nations in Southeast Asia, 1948–1984 / **587**

A Changing World / **594**

Countries of the Former Soviet Union / **599**

Europe: Political / **601**

Africa: Political / **607**

Asia: Political / **616**

The Americas: Political / **623**

MAP BUILDER The World: Climate and Population / **R4**

The World: Climates / **Overlay 1**

The World: Climate and Latitude Zones / **Overlay 2**

The World: Climate and Population / **Overlay 3**

Europe: Political / **R6**

Europe: Physical / **R7**

Africa: Political / **R8**

Africa: Physical / **R9**

Asia: Political / **R10**

Asia: Physical / **R11**

The Americas: Political / **R12**

The Americas: Physical / **R13**

The United States: Political / **R14**

The World: Political / **R16**

The World: Physical / **R18**

YOUR TEXTBOOK
at a glance

Your textbook is called *World: Adventures in Time and Place*. It has 20 chapters, each with two or more lessons. There are also many special features for you to study and enjoy.

NATIONAL GEOGRAPHIC

Five Themes of Geography

Location
How do these bicyclists know they are entering another country?

Place
What makes the Netherlands different from other places?

Special pages right after these two pages and before each unit bring you ideas and **Adventures** in geography with **National Geographic**.

---

reaches the forest floor. In the cooler rain forests of tierra templada, clouds sometimes blanket the entire forest.

People in Middle America

The first people in Middle America probably arrived about 11,000 years ago. Small knives and arrow points have been found in the Central Plateau. These stone tools were left in caves by early hunter-gatherers. [...] gathered onions, squash [...] and hunted rabbits and [...] people in other parts of [...] moved around in search [...]

WHY IT MA[...]

After the first people ca[...] Beringia to North Amer[...] moved southward to Mi[...] The diverse lands of this [...] ed a warm climate and [...] These resources made [...] ideal for human settlem[...] lesson you will read ab[...] many groups of people [...] civilization on this land.

✔ Reviewing Fact[...]

SUM IT UP
- The first people in th[...] have come from Asia[...] Beringia land bridge [...] 25,000 years ago.
- Middle America has [...] rolling hills, and coas[...] has three main climat[...]

DID YOU KNOW?

How hot WAS it?

To learn about recent changes in climate, scientists often look at written records. By studying records, such as the dates of cherry blossom festivals in Japan or har-[...]

WHY IT MATTERS

The region called Mesopotamia is not naturally an inviting place to live. Yet it was here that one of the world's earliest civilizations developed. Water and soil brought by the Tigris and the Euphrates helped to make this civilization possible. Even more important were the farmers of ancient Mesopotamia. These early farmers figured out how to use the two rivers to make the land more fertile.

As in some other early cultures, the farmers of Mesopotamia produced surplus crops. These surpluses allowed for specialization, which in turn led to the growth of towns and cities. The early cities formed a great civilization. As you will see, the legacy of early Mesopotamian civilization reaches even into our own times.

Links to CURRENT EVENTS

High Water!

Do floods still destroy people's homes and property today?

Unfortunately, the answer is yes. Although dams now help to control river flow in many parts of the world, floods are also caused by storms and earthquakes. In January 1995 heavy rains caused terrible flooding in Sacramento, California. This flood killed 11 people, washed away hundreds of homes, and caused about $300 million in damages.

Find another example of a flood in modern times. When and where did this flood occur? Your teacher can show you how to research recent newspapers to learn more about current events.

FLOODS!

✔ Reviewing Facts and Ideas

SUM IT UP
- Mesopotamia is the region between the Tigris and Euphrates rivers. It is divided into a rugged plateau to the north and fertile plains to the south.
- Like the Nile River, the Tigris and Euphrates flooded each year. These [...] water and silt to

THINK ABOUT IT

1. What were the main crops grown in ancient Mesopotamia? What other foods were grown there?

2. Why was the timing of spring floods so important to farmers in ancient Mesopotamia? What could happen to crops if the floods came a little earlier than expected?

LESSON 2

509 B.C.   100 B.C.   A.D. 1   A.D. 250   A.D. 500

THE RISE OF THE ROMAN REPUBLIC

READ ALOUD

The Roman leader Cicero declared that Rome should be governed by its "best" citizens. But just who were Rome's "best" citizens? Were they the city's small circle of nobles? Or did they also include the many other citizens, poor and rich, who contributed to life in Rome? The way Romans answered this question would shape their lives and ours.

Focus Activity

READ TO LEARN
What kind of government did the Romans establish?

VOCABULARY
plebeian
patrician
republic
representative
Senate
tribune
consul
Twelve Tables
Punic Wars

PEOPLE
Livy
Hannibal
Scipio

PLACES
Forum
Carthage
Zama

THE BIG PICTURE

Almost 3,000 years ago, when the city of Anyang in China was losing power, Rome was only a cluster of mud huts on the hills overlooking the Tiber River. From the hilltops, farmers could enjoy a view of two small lakes that rippled in the valley below. The sound of lowing cattle drifted across the marshland at the river's edge.

By 509 B.C. Romans had overthrown their king, Tarquinius. They began setting up a new government in which citizens played a larger part. Their community became a city. A wooden bridge now crossed the Tiber River. The valley's marshland was drained and served as a busy market and meeting place.

High atop one of Rome's hills stood a stone temple as big as any in Greece. On other hilltops, fine brick homes housed Rome's wealthy. Some Romans clearly had become richer than others. The division between rich and poor, powerful and not so powerful, would affect the shape of the new government Romans were creating for themselves.

230

◀ Some lessons have features called **Links** or **Did You Know**—activities to try and interesting information to share.

Look for a variety of lessons and features. **Infographics** bring you information with pictures, charts, graphs, and maps. You will build your **Skills**, learn about **Legacies** that connect us to the past, and meet people who show what **Citizenship** is. ▶

Three **DIFFERENT** Viewpoints

LORD II NAOSUKE
Feudal lord, Excerpt from a letter, 1847

The condition of foreign states is not what it once was: they have invented the steamship and introduced radical changes in the art of navigation, they have also built up their armies to a state of great efficiency and they are possessed of war implements of great power and precision; in short, they have risen to be imposing powers. If we cling to our outdated systems, heaven only knows what mighty calamity may befall our empire.

One of Shakespeare's most popular plays, "Romeo and Juliet" (left), inspired the creators of the Broadway musical and hit movie, "West Side Story" (below). The stories of romantic love and the troubles of youth are just as important to people today as they were in the 1500s.

Legacy
LINKING PAST AND PRESENT
THE ART OF LANGUAGE:
SHAKESPEARE

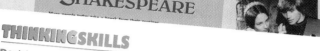

THINKING SKILLS

Decision Making

THE AEGEAN REGION
BULGARIA

bloody battles. You will learn more about these legends when you study ancient

HELPING Yourself

"A decision is choice between

Schliemann decided that this mound on a plain overlooking the blue Aegean Sea

Infographic

Treasures of an Ancient Tomb

West of ancient Thebes, under the piercing blue sky and scorching sun of the Egyptian desert, steep cliffs plunge into a rocky valley. This is the _____, resting place of 30 New Kingdom pharaohs.

One of the pharaohs buried in the valley was a very young man. He ruled Egypt from the time he

FRONT HALL

ENTRANCE

When Carter and Carnarvon first peered into the tomb, this is what they saw (right). Imagine their surprise!

BURIAL CHAMBER

This beautiful golden mask (below) shows what Tutankhamun looked like when he was alive.

TREASURY

89

THE CITIZENS OF ROME

As in Greece, society in Rome was divided into two groups: those who were citizens and those who were not. At first, Rome had few slaves. The city did have many women, but none of them were citizens.

The body of citizens included two groups. Most Roman citizens were plebeians (plih BEE unz). Plebeians were men who farmed, traded, and made things for a living. The second group was made up of Rome's handful of patricians (puh TRISH unz). Patricians were members of Rome's noble families. They owned large farms and had plebeians work the land for them.

Plebeians Protest

After Rome's last king was overthrown in 509 B.C., the patricians took power. As they did this they remade the city's government. Only patricians could belong to a ruling assembly or become government leaders.

Rome's many plebeians reacted to the patricians' rules with protest. According to the Roman historian Livy,

A patrician woman had no voice in Rome's government.

plebeians rebelled in 494 B.C., demanding changes in the government. To calm them down, Livy wrote, the patricians sent a popular leader to speak with the plebeians. He told them this story. How do you suppose the plebeians reacted?

MANY VOICES
PRIMARY SOURCE

Excerpt from
Stories of Rome, Livy, 494 B.C.

Once upon a time, the different parts of the human body were not all in agreement. . . . And it seemed very unfair to the other parts of the body that they should worry and sweat away to look after the belly. After all, the belly just sat there . . . doing nothing, enjoying all the nice things that came along. So they hatched a plot. The hands weren't going to take food to the mouth; even if they did, the mouth wasn't going to accept it. . . . They went into a sulk and waited for the belly to cry for help. But while they waited, one by one all the parts of the body got weaker and weaker. The moral of this story? The belly too has its job to do. It has to be fed, but it also does feeding of its own.

sulk: to be in a bad mood and stay silent

A New Government

According to Livy both sides in time agreed to work together to improve Rome's government. The new government was called a republic, which means "public things" in Latin. Latin was the language of ancient Rome. In a republic citizens choose their leaders.

231

Use the **Reference Section** at the end of your book to look up words, people, and places. This section includes the **World History Time Lines** and a table of **Countries of Our World.** ▼

Biographical Dictionary

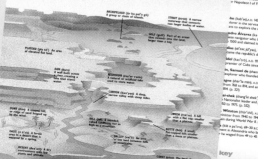

The Biographical Dictionary tells you about the people you have learned about in this book. The Pronunciation Key tells you how to say their names. The page numbers tell you where each person first appears in the text.

B

Ben-Gurion, David (ben gūr'ē ən), A.D. 1886–1973 Israeli prime minister from 1949 to 1953 and from 1955 to 1963; he proclaimed Israel to be a separate and independent country on May 14, 1948. (p. 577)

(ben'i dikt), A.D. 480?–547 Italian monk; _____ of the Benedictine order. (p. 331)

_____ämón (bō lē'vär, sē món'), A.D. 1783–1830 _____ of the struggle for independence in South _____; his armies freed Colombia, Venezuela, and _____ from Spanish rule. (p. 496)

_____te, Napoleon (bō'nə pärt, nə pō'lē ən), A.D. ____–1821 French revolutionary general who became _____ _____; crowned Napoleon I of France in 1804. (p. 490)

_____ (kab'ōt), A.D. 1450?–1499? Italian navigator _____ explorer in the service of England; one of the first _____ to explore the coast of Canada. (p. 478)

_____edro Álvarez (ka bräl'), A.D. 1467?–1520? _____ese navigator who landed on the coast of _____ 1500 and claimed it for Portugal. (p. 467)

_____lius (kas'ē əs), 100?–44 B.C. Roman general _____came the republic's dictator in 45 B.C. (p. 237)

_____idel (kas'trō), A.D. 1926– Cuban revolutionary _____came the premier of Cuba since 1959. (p. 560)

_____in, Samuel de (sham plān'), A.D. 1567?–1635 _____ explorer who founded Quebec in 1608. (p. 479)

_____-shek (chäng'kī shek'), A.D. 1887–1975 _____ Nationalist leader and president of Taiwan _____ 1950 to 1975. (p. 552)

_____ Winston (chûr'chil), A.D. 1874–1965 British _____ minister from 1940 to 1945 and 1951 to 1955. He _____ during World War II. (p. 542)

_____ (klē ə pa'trə), 69–30 B.C. Ruler of the Egyptian _____ ment at Alexandria who backed Caesar in the _____; he waged from 49 to 46 B.C. (p. 237)

Dictionary of
GEOGRAPHIC TERMS

ARCHIPELAGO (är ka pel'a gō) A group or chain of islands.

STRAIT (strāt) A narrow waterway that connects two larger bodies of water.

GULF (gulf) Part of an ocean that extends into the land, larger than a bay.

PLATEAU (pla tō') An area of elevated land.

DAM (dam) A wall built across a river, creating a lake or storing water.

RESERVOIR (rez'ər vwär) A natural or artificial lake used to store water.

CANYON (kan'yən) A deep, narrow valley with steep sides.

DUNE (dün) A mound, hill, or ridge of sand heaped up by the wind.

HILL (hil) A rounded, raised area of land, lower than a mountain.

MESA (mā'sə) A hill with a flat top, smaller than a plateau.

OASIS (ō ā'sis) A fertile area in a desert that is watered by a spring.

VALLEY (val'ē) An area of low land between hills or mountains.

BUTTE (būt) A small, flat-topped hill, smaller than a mesa.

DESERT (dez'ərt) A dry environment with few plants and animals.

COAST (kōst) The land along an ocean.

_____ (sē) Part of an ocean or _____ take that extends deeply into _____ land.

Key

Lessons begin with a **Read Aloud** selection and **The Big Picture**. Study the **Read to Learn** question and list of words, people, and places. Enjoy **Many Voices**—writings, songs, and art by various people.

NATIONAL GEOGRAPHIC

Five Themes of Geography

Location
How do these bicyclists know they are entering another country?

Place
What makes the Netherlands different from other places?

Human/Environment Interactions
How have people changed this landscape in Indonesia?

Region
What are some things that help make the Middle East a special region?

Movement
How do goods travel from place to place?

PART 1
Using Globes

VOCABULARY

continent	meridian
hemisphere	prime meridian
equator	latitude
longitude	parallel

What do globes show?

- A globe is a model that shows Earth as it looks when seen from outer space.

- A globe shows Earth's seven continents, or large bodies of land. They are Africa, Antarctica, Asia, Australia, Europe, North America, and South America. Which continents are shown on this globe?

- Much of Earth is covered by four oceans, or large bodies of salt water. They are the Atlantic, Arctic, Indian, and Pacific oceans. Which oceans do you see on the globe? Which continents and oceans are not shown?

What is a hemisphere?

- A globe, much like Earth, is in the shape of a ball or sphere. Looking at a globe from any direction, you can see only half of it. *Hemi* is a Greek word for "half." Hemisphere means "half a sphere."

- Geographers divide Earth into the four hemispheres shown at the top of the next page.

- An imaginary line dividing the world into the Northern Hemisphere and Southern Hemisphere is called the equator. It lies halfway between the North Pole and South Pole. Which continents are in the Northern Hemisphere? In the Southern Hemisphere?

- Geographers divide Earth into the Eastern and Western hemispheres. Which hemi-

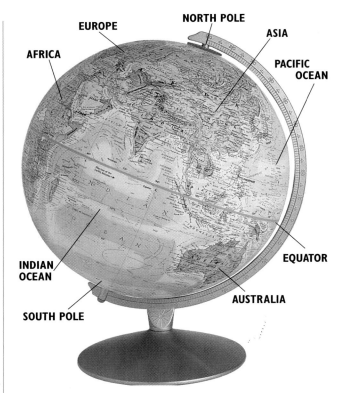

sphere includes all of Africa? Which hemisphere does not include Antarctica?

How are longitude and latitude useful?

- You can locate places on a map or globe by using a grid of imaginary lines.

- Running north to south are longitude lines, or meridians. These imaginary lines measure the distance east and west of the prime meridian. The unit of measurement is degrees. Look at the map at the bottom of the next page. What is the longitude of Cape Town?

- Running east to west are latitude lines, or parallels. These show distance in degrees north and south of the equator. What are the latitude and longitude of Mexico City?

More Practice

You can find longitude and latitude lines on many maps in this book. For examples, see pages 9, 12, and 13.

THE HEMISPHERES

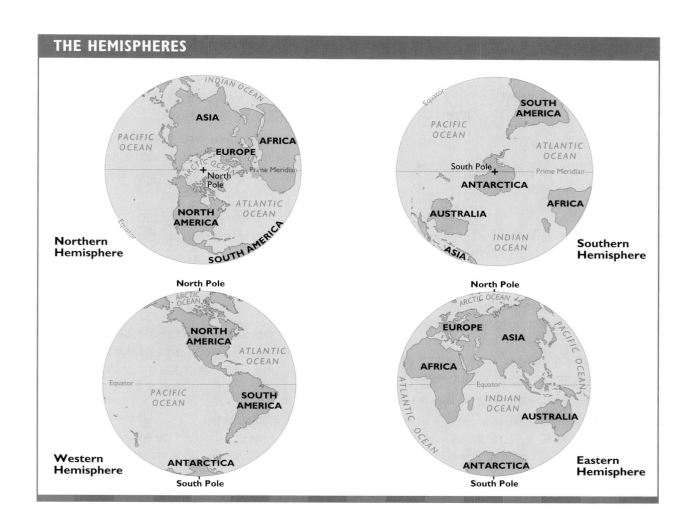

Northern Hemisphere

Southern Hemisphere

Western Hemisphere

Eastern Hemisphere

GLOBAL GRID

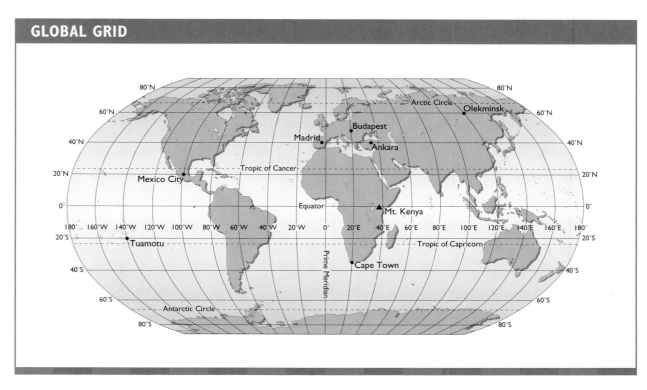

PART 2
Using Maps

VOCABULARY
cardinal directions
intermediate directions
compass rose
scale
symbol
map key
locator

What are cardinal directions?

- When you face in the direction of the North Pole, you are facing north. Behind you is south. East is to your right and west is to your left. If you turn to face east, what direction is now behind you? What direction is now to your left?

- There are four cardinal directions–north, south, east, and west.

- The letters **N**, **S**, **E**, and **W** are often used to represent the cardinal directions. What does **W** stand for?

How can you determine intermediate directions?

- Northeast (**NE**), southeast (**SE**), southwest (**SW**), and northwest (**NW**) are called intermediate directions.

- The intermediate directions are halfway between the cardinal directions. Northeast is the direction halfway between north and east. Where does **SE** lie?

How can you find directions on maps that do not include the North Pole?

- Most maps are drawn with north toward the top of the map. Many also include a compass rose, a drawing that shows directions.

- In this book, the compass rose usually shows both cardinal and intermediate directions. Look at the map of Australia. Which cities are southwest of Canberra?

More Practice

You can practice finding directions and using a compass rose on most maps in this book. For examples, see pages 105, 225, and 355.

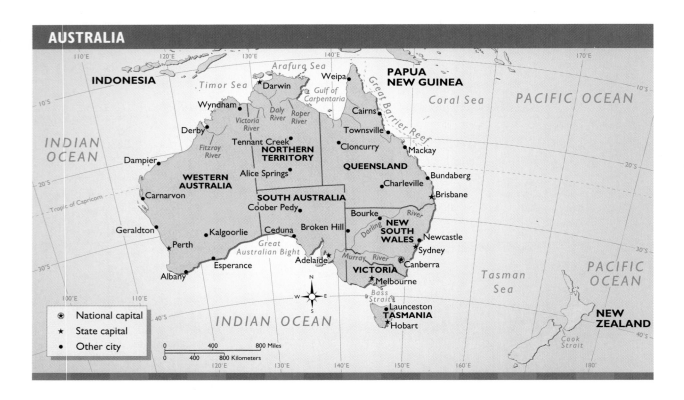

AUSTRALIA

MAP A: TRINIDAD AND TOBAGO

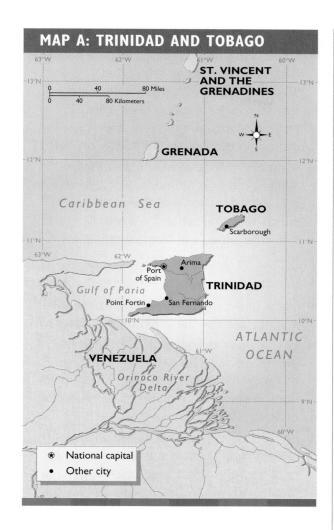

MAP B: TRINIDAD AND TOBAGO

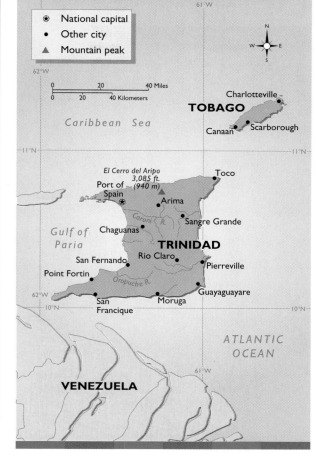

What is a map scale?

- Maps are always smaller than the actual places they show. The scale tells you how much smaller the distance on a map is compared with the actual distance.

- Map scales in this book include two lines for measuring distances. Which unit of measurement does each line show?

How do you use a scale? Why are map scales sometimes different?

- You can use a ruler to measure distances on a map.

- To determine the distance in miles between San Fernando and Scarborough, measure the length on the scale that represents 80 miles on Map A. The length is one inch. Now measure the distance between San Fernando and Scarborough in inches. Multiply the result by 80 to determine the distance. What is the distance between the two cities?

- Different maps often show the same area using different scales. Map A and Map B both show the Caribbean country of Trinidad and Tobago. However, the islands look larger on Map B. They look larger because one inch stands for fewer miles on the Map B scale than on the A scale. The larger scale allows more details to be shown. What kinds of details are shown on Map B that are not on Map A?

More Practice

Most of the maps in the book show map scales. For example, see pages 76, 135, and 403.

ARGENTINA: Resources

PARAGUAY

PbZn

CHILE

PbZn

Córdoba

PbZn

Santa Fe

Rosario

BRAZIL

URUGUAY

Buenos Aires

ARGENTINA

Rio de la Plata

Viedma • Carmen de Patagones

ATLANTIC OCEAN

PbZn

Falkland Is. (Islas Malvinas) (U.K.)

Strait of Magellan

PACIFIC OCEAN

Cape Horn

	National capital
•	Other city
▲	Oil
⬡	Natural gas
PbZn	Lead and Zinc

0   200   400 Miles
0   200   400 Kilometers

What information does a map key give?

- Maps often use symbols to give information. A symbol is anything that stands for something else. On many maps a black dot stands for a city. Other symbols include triangles, squares, and lines. What are some other symbols found on maps?

- Symbols do not always stand for the same things on all maps. For this reason it is important to read the map key, which tells you what the symbols stand for. What does the triangle stand for on each map on this page?

How do locators help in studying maps?

- Maps use locators to show where the subject area of the main map is located.

- In this book the locator is a small map in the shape a globe or a rectangular portion of Earth's surface. The area of the main map is shown in red. What is the shape of Switzerland's locator?

- Some locators show a hemisphere. Others may show a continent, a region, or a country. What area does Argentina's locator show?

More Practice

You will see many keys and locators. For examples of map keys, see pages 172, 280, and 281. For examples of locators, see pages 287, 385, and 601.

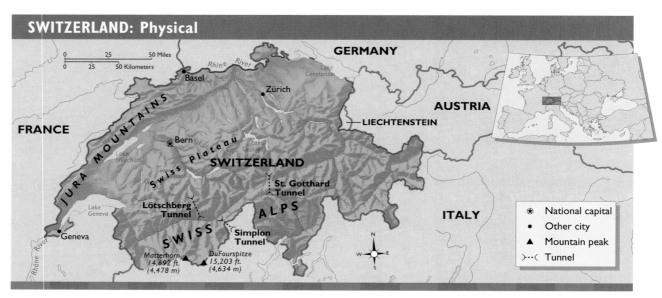

SWITZERLAND: Physical

0   25   50 Miles
0   25   50 Kilometers

GERMANY

Rhine River

Basel

Lake Constance

Zürich

AUSTRIA

FRANCE

LIECHTENSTEIN

JURA MOUNTAINS

Bern

Swiss Plateau

Lake Neuchâtel

SWITZERLAND

Lake Lucerne

St. Gotthard Tunnel

Lötschberg Tunnel

Lake Geneva

ALPS

Simplon Tunnel

ITALY

SWISS

Geneva

Rhône River

Matterhorn 14,692 ft. (4,478 m)

DuFourspitze 15,203 ft. (4,634 m)

	National capital
•	Other city
▲	Mountain peak
⟩⋅⋅⟨	Tunnel

PART 3

Different Kinds of Maps

VOCABULARY

political map	relief map
physical map	historical map
elevation map	distribution map

Why are there different kinds of maps?

- Maps differ in the kinds of information they give. This section will cover four kinds of maps.

- When studying a map, first look at the map title. It will tell you the subject area and the type of information provided. What subject area does the map below show?

- A map may include areas that are not part of its subject area. In this book such areas are shown in gray. What countries are not in the subject area of the map below?

What is a political map?

- A political map shows information such as countries, states, cities, and other important political features. Although many maps include national or state boundaries, a political map may also use colors to highlight countries or states.

- Look at the map below. What color is used to show Nepal? How many different colors are used to show countries? What countries have disputed borders? What are the capital cities of those countries?

More Practice

You can find other political maps in this book. For examples, see pages 528, 576, and 623.

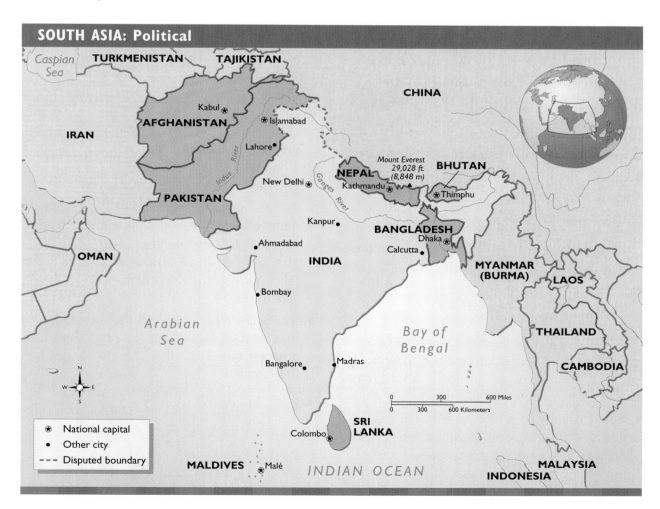

SOUTH ASIA: Political

- National capital
- Other city
- - - Disputed boundary

Caspian Sea
TURKMENISTAN
TAJIKISTAN
CHINA
Kabul ⊛
AFGHANISTAN
⊛ Islamabad
IRAN
Lahore •
Indus River
Mount Everest 29,028 ft. (8,848 m) ▲
NEPAL
BHUTAN
New Delhi ⊛
Ganges River
Kathmandu ⊛
⊛ Thimphu
PAKISTAN
Kanpur •
BANGLADESH
Dhaka ⊛
Calcutta •
OMAN
• Ahmadabad
INDIA
MYANMAR (BURMA)
LAOS
• Bombay
Arabian Sea
Bay of Bengal
THAILAND
Bangalore •
• Madras
CAMBODIA
0   300   600 Miles
0   300   600 Kilometers
SRI LANKA
Colombo •
MALDIVES • Malé
INDIAN OCEAN
MALAYSIA
INDONESIA

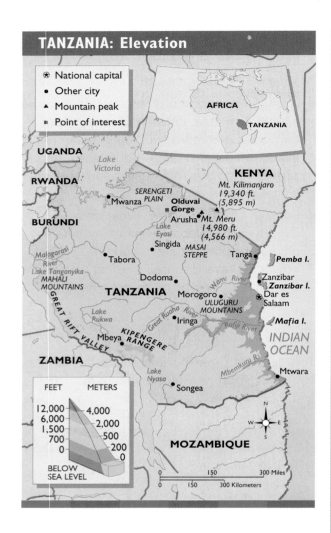

TANZANIA: Elevation

- ⊛ National capital
- • Other city
- ▲ Mountain peak
- ■ Point of interest

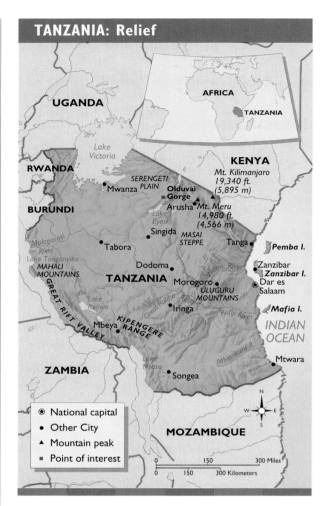

TANZANIA: Relief

- ⊛ National capital
- • Other City
- ▲ Mountain peak
- ■ Point of interest

What do different kinds of physical maps show?

- **Physical maps** show Earth's natural features. This section will cover two different kinds of physical maps.

- One type of physical map is an **elevation map**. Elevation maps use color to show the height of land above sea level. In this book elevation is measured in feet and in meters.

- Look at the maps above. On the elevation map of Tanzania, what color represents the elevation of 0 to 700 feet? What areas of Tanzania have this elevation?

- **Relief maps** are a kind of physical map that show changes in elevation. Areas with no shading represent places where there are no changes in elevation. Lightly shaded areas show places where changes are

very gradual. Dark shading represents areas with sharp changes in elevation, such as a steep hill.

- An area can show a lot of relief, or dramatic changes in elevation, without being very high above sea level. An area can be at a high elevation but have very little relief, as a flat plateau high above sea level does.

- Study the relief map and the elevation map of Tanzania. What area has the greatest relief? What is the elevation of this area?

More Practice

There are other physical maps in this book. For examples, see pages 71, 131, and 317.

What is an historical map?

- Maps that show information about the past or where past events took place are called historical maps.

- The map title tells you the subject of the map. Many of the historical maps in this book include dates in the title or in the key. Study the map of the United States' expansion below, in the middle of the page. Between what dates did the expansion shown in this map occur? By what year did the United States own land west of the Mississippi River?

What is a distribution map?

- Distribution maps show how things such as language, religion, population, and rainfall are distributed throughout an area.

- The map key on the distribution map below shows colors that represent kinds of plants found in Russia. What kind of plants cover the largest area of land?

More Practice

You can find many different kinds of maps in this book. For historical maps, see pages 280, 281, and 464. For distribution maps, see pages 345, 370, and 371.

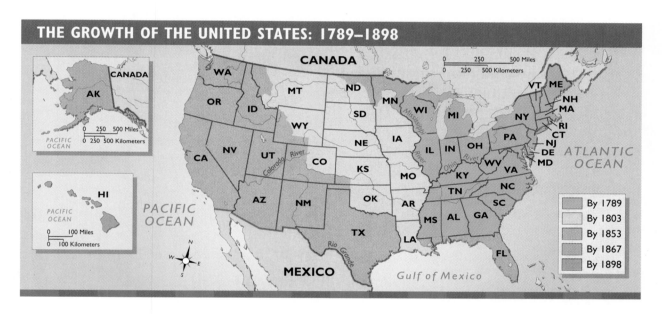

THE GROWTH OF THE UNITED STATES: 1789–1898

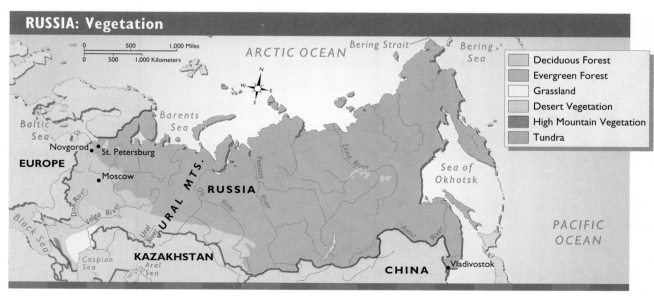

RUSSIA: Vegetation

NEAR LIFE-SIZED CHESS PIECES, INDIA
OLMEC SCULPTURE, MEXICO
PYRAMID AND SPHINX, EGYPT

Understanding the World

"My imagination was caught by the great age of the world."

from *Self Made Man* by Jonathan Kingdon
See page 44.

WHY DOES IT MATTER?

These are the words of scientist Jonathan Kingdon, who was born and grew up in East Africa. They could also be the thoughts of anyone who has imagined what life was like hundreds or even thousands of years ago. How did people live? What did they eat? What was their land like? People have always wanted to know what things were like for those who lived before them.

Thanks to historians and other scholars, answers to many of these questions are being discovered. Objects made by ancient people have been uncovered all over the world. These objects reveal mysteries of the distant past. They also help us to better understand who we are.

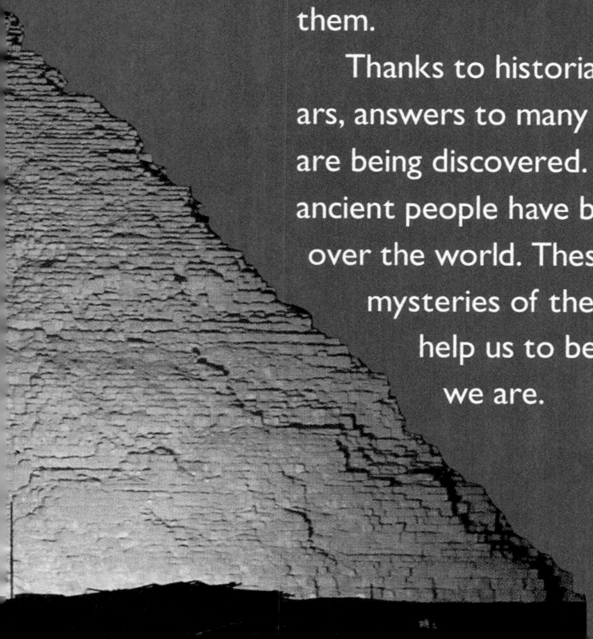

STONEHENGE, ENGLAND
PREHISTORIC BONE NEEDLE, FRANCE

3

Adventures
with
NATIONAL GEOGRAPHIC

Stony Silence

Some of the stones have toppled. But others still stand, tall and mysterious, on this plain in southern England—just as they have for thousands of years. Who built Stonehenge? How were the 50-ton stones transported to this place and raised up by prehistoric people using only simple tools? And, perhaps more mysterious, why? Some archaeologists suggest that Stonehenge may have been a temple that marked the movements of the sun. But we may never know for sure.

GEO JOURNAL

If you could talk to one of the workers who helped build Stonehenge long ago, what questions would you ask?

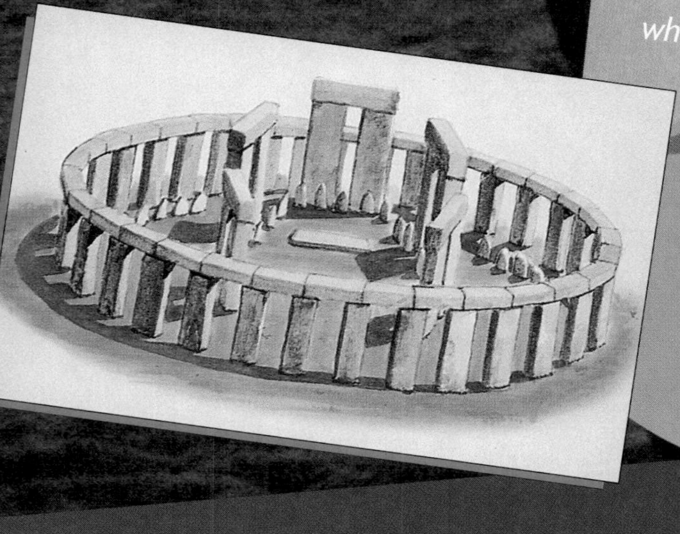

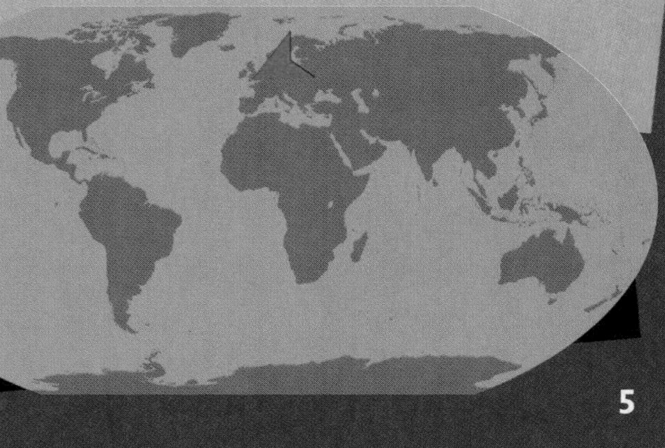

CHAPTER 1

Regions of the World

THINKING ABOUT GEOGRAPHY AND CULTURE

What do you think of when you see a photo of Earth from outer space? Try imagining a world of over 4 billion people, living in thousands of places. Some may have lives much like yours. People's lives may be as different as night and day. These differences, as well as the similarities, tell the great story of the world's regions and cultures.

China
ASIA

Farmers in China have long used terraces like these in Guangxi to farm in hilly areas. The rice grown in these southern terraces feeds millions of people.

Namibia
AFRICA

Southern Africa has many busy harbors like this one at Lüderitz. People along Africa's coasts have traveled and traded by sea for hundreds of years.

Austria
EUROPE

The town of Sankt Gallen lies high in the southern Alps. The people who settled these fertile mountain valleys have long been famous for their herding and dairy farms.

Canada
THE AMERICAS

This icy plain in the Arctic is part of a vast area of awesome beauty. Plants and animals like this polar bear have had to adapt to the Arctic's unique environment.

WORLD REGIONS

READ ALOUD

How many different living areas do you pass through each day? Bedroom, bathroom, kitchen, classroom, gym, lunchroom . . . all of these areas serve different purposes in your life. When you stop and think about them, these areas, or regions, also reveal a great deal about who you are. The world, too, is divided into many different regions. They can tell us much about what life is like all across planet Earth.

THE BIG PICTURE

Learning about life on planet Earth—that's what geography is all about. Geography is the study of Earth, how it shapes people's lives and is shaped in turn by people's activities. In fact, the word *geography* comes from a Greek word that means "Earth writing," or "writing about Earth."

You don't have to be in a classroom to learn about geography. Geography is a part of almost everything you do. When you coast down a hill on your bike, splash in a pool on a hot summer day, or wipe frost from a window in winter, you are experiencing part of geography. Each time you read a road sign on a highway or listen to the weather report on the radio, you become, for a moment, a geographer. You are using the tools of geography to study planet Earth.

Focus Activity

READ TO LEARN
What does studying regions tell us about the world?

VOCABULARY
geography
region
landform
climate
culture

8

WHAT IS A REGION?

Geographers divide Earth's surface into different kinds of regions. A **region** is an area with common features that set it apart from other areas. By studying different regions we can learn more about the world, more about ourselves, and more about people in other parts of the world.

Regions can be huge. Some are as big as half of Earth's surface. You have learned about these kinds of regions, called hemispheres, on pages G4–G5. Regions can also be very small. Your school's playground, for example, is an "exercise region" of your school.

Physical Regions

Regions that are defined by Earth's natural environment are called physical regions. Physical regions often have common **landforms**, such as mountains or plains.

As you can see from the map on this page, continents are the biggest kind of physical region. Continents can be divided into many smaller physical regions. In the region of South America, for example, the Andes Mountains make up a physical region.

Climate Regions

Physical regions can also be organized by **climate**, or the weather pattern that an area has over a long period of time. For example, the climate around Earth's central part, near the equator, is hot and humid. This is the world's tropical region. Around the North Pole, by contrast, the average winter temperature is -30°F. The North Pole is located in one of the two polar regions of the world.

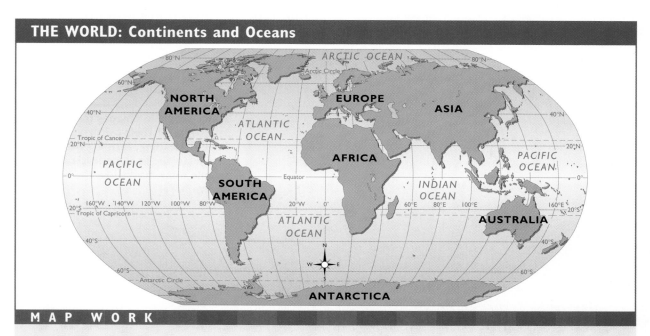

THE WORLD: Continents and Oceans

MAP WORK

Continents are the largest land **regions**.

1. How many continents are there?
2. What is the largest continent?
3. On which continent do you live?
4. What is the smallest continent?

LOOKING AT REGIONS

If you were to fly in an airplane, you would see many landforms that make up the world's physical regions. Another type of region, however, is invisible from an airplane. These regions are based on culture. Culture is the way of life of a group of people, including their daily habits, beliefs, and arts.

Cultural Regions

To learn about cultural regions, you must come down to Earth and meet the people who live in a place. Language, religion, and ethnic heritage are some of the parts of culture that make up cultural regions. For example, South America, Central America, and most of the Caribbean Islands form the cultural region of Latin America. Most people there speak Spanish, Portuguese, or French—all offshoots of an old language called Latin. Religion also ties Latin America together, since many Latin Americans are Roman Catholics.

Within Latin America are many smaller cultural regions, such as the region of Chiapas (chee AH pus) in the southeastern corner of Mexico. In Chiapas, unlike in the rest of Mexico, most people are Indians. Many speak a Mayan Indian language rather than Spanish. They eat traditional foods such as *tamales de frijol* (tuh MAH leez duh FREE hohl), a dish made of corn, black beans, and hot peppers.

Other Regions

Most places are part of more than one type of region. For example, Chiapas is a cultural region, but it is a political region as well. Political regions are

Many people in Chiapas follow traditions of their culture. These include clothing, farming methods, and festivals. In some festivals, people wear masks like the ones shown here.

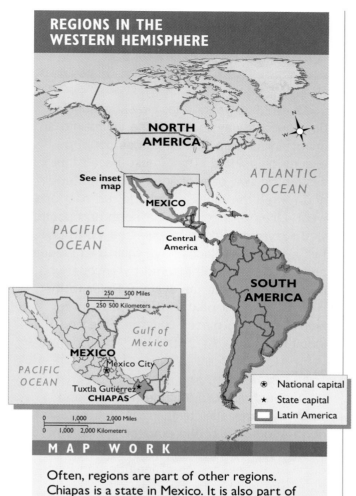

REGIONS IN THE WESTERN HEMISPHERE

NORTH AMERICA

ATLANTIC OCEAN

See inset map

MEXICO

PACIFIC OCEAN

Central America

SOUTH AMERICA

0   250   500 Miles
0   250 500 Kilometers

Gulf of Mexico

MEXICO

Mexico City

PACIFIC OCEAN

Tuxtla Gutiérrez
CHIAPAS

⊛ National capital
★ State capital
☐ Latin America

0   1,000   2,000 Miles
0   1,000 2,000 Kilometers

MAP WORK

Often, regions are part of other regions. Chiapas is a state in Mexico. It is also part of North America, which in turn is part of the Western Hemisphere.

Is Chiapas a physical or cultural region?

set up by governments. Just as Texas is one state of the 50 United States, Chiapas is one of the 31 states in Mexico.

Many of the people in Chiapas work as farmers. They live in the state's rugged countryside, in rural regions. Their lives are very different from the 20 million Mexicans who live 500 miles away in one of the world's largest urban regions—Mexico City.

By looking at Chiapas you can see that different kinds of regions often overlap. Look at the map on this page. How many different regions is Chiapas a part of?

WHY IT MATTERS

Throughout this book you will be learning about life in different regions. You will discover how the environment has shaped life in each region. You will explore the physical and cultural features that make regions similar to and different from each other. You will study how these regions have interacted over time. Finally, you will learn how certain cultural forces have, over time, tied all of Earth's regions into one interdependent world.

✓/ Reviewing Facts and Ideas

SUM IT UP

- Geographers use regions to help them understand planet Earth.
- Physical regions are often defined by landforms and climate.
- Cultural regions are often defined by language and religion.
- There are many different kinds of regions, and they often overlap.

THINK ABOUT IT

1. What is geography? How is riding downhill on a bike an example of geography in action?

2. Why is it helpful to meet the people in a place when learning about their region?

3. **FOCUS** Why do geographers divide the world into regions?

4. **THINKING SKILL** List different regions of your community and then *classify* them as physical or cultural regions.

5. **WRITE** Suppose that you are flying around the earth in an airplane. Describe the large bodies of water and landforms you see.

GEOGRAPHYSKILLS

Working with Latitude and Longitude

VOCABULARY

latitude	parallel
longitude	meridian
degree	global grid

WHY THE SKILL MATTERS

The people of the world are separated by many differences in language, religion, and customs. One skill that most of us share today, however, is the ability to read maps.

People around the world have long made maps. Yet not all maps were the same. Some people drew their maps so that east, rather than north, was at the top of the map. Others made their own region huge and outlying areas tiny. It was not always easy for people to understand each other's maps.

Over 2,000 years ago, Greek scientists developed a way to divide the world into an imaginary grid so that all places could be exactly pinpointed. The Greeks based their system on two sets of lines called latitude and longitude. Lines of latitude run east and west. Lines of longitude run north and south.

Today mapmakers all over the world use this system. All places have their own unique address and can be located by anyone who knows how to use the system. Refer to the Helping Yourself box on the next page for help in locating places using latitude and longitude.

USING THE SKILL

Although lines of latitude run east and west, they measure distance in degrees north and south of the equator. A degree is a unit of measurement that describes the distance between lines of latitude and longitude. The symbol for degrees is °. As you can see on Map A, the equator is the starting line for measuring latitude.

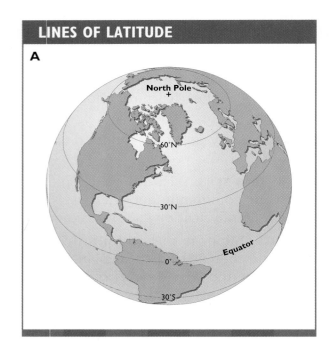

LINES OF LATITUDE

A

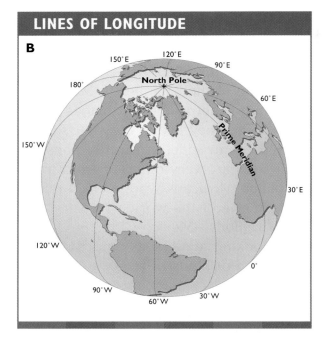

LINES OF LONGITUDE

B

Lines of latitude are also known as **parallels**. Parallels are lines that run in the same direction and are always the same distance apart.

If you imagine that the earth were an apple, lines of latitude would cut the apple into a stack of rings. Lines of longitude, by contrast, would cut the apple into equal wedges. Lines of longitude run north and south, and measure distance in degrees east and west of the prime meridian.

Look at Map B on page 12. The prime meridian is marked 0°, meaning zero degrees longitude, and it separates east from west. All lines east and west of the prime meridian are called **meridians**.

Look at Map B on page 12.

HELPING Yourself

- ● Lines of **latitude** measure the distance north and south of the equator.
- ● Lines of **longitude** measure the distance east and west of the prime meridian.
- ● Lines of longitude and latitude cross to form a grid that can be used to locate any place.

TRYING THE SKILL

On Map C the parallels and meridians cross each other to form a **global grid**. This grid makes it possible to pinpoint exact locations. Which line of latitude is New Delhi, India, closest to? Which line of longitude is it closest to?

REVIEWING THE SKILL

Now find the correct latitude and longitude of Oslo, Norway, on Map C.

1. Starting from the equator, in which direction do you travel to get to Oslo?

2. Which line of latitude does Oslo lie on?

3. How might latitude and longitude be helpful to travelers?

GLOBAL GRID

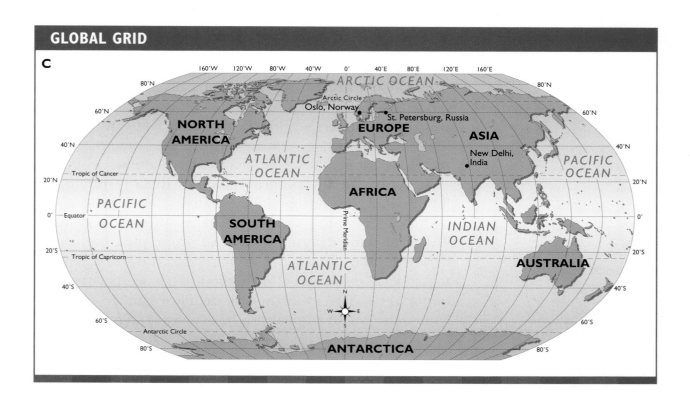

C

Focus Activity

READ TO LEARN
What is daily life like for a boy in India?

VOCABULARY
custom
values
interaction

PLACES
New Delhi

REGIONS AND CULTURE

READ ALOUD

Azeez Narain (uh ZHEEZ nuh RAHN) is an eleven-year old boy who lives in New Delhi, India. Azeez begins each day with prayers in his family's temple room and then heads to the kitchen for breakfast. Sometimes he eats toast and cereal. More often he eats poha, which is puffed rice with nuts and coconut roasted in butter and spices. Then Azeez rides a bus to school, where he studies 11 subjects six days a week. Four of those subjects are different languages.

THE BIG PICTURE

Do parts of Azeez's life sound familiar to you? Some probably do, like eating cereal for breakfast and riding a bus to school. Many such customs are shared by people around the world. Customs are ways of living that people practice regularly over time. Some of Azeez's customs, however, may not be familiar to you. That is because the cultural region of India is very different from that of the United States.

All cultures are made up of many different customs. Those customs determine how we dress, play, eat, learn, live with other people, and understand the world. Customs can reveal a great deal about what we believe is important in life. In fact, every detail of our life says something about the culture in which we live.

This is a typical street scene in New Delhi, India. How is it similar to an American city?

LIVING IN INDIA

Azeez Narain lives with his parents and six-year-old brother in New Delhi, India. The Narains share many customs with people in other parts of the world. Both parents work, for example. Azeez's mother teaches at a university and his father works as a journalist. Azeez and his friends like to ride their bikes and play computer games.

Many of the Narains' other customs are unique to the culture of India. Before you can understand these customs, however, you need to know a bit about India's past.

Culture and History

Throughout history people have brought new customs and ideas to India. Thousands of years ago the religion of Hinduism began shaping Indian culture. It remains a very important influence on Indian culture.

About 1,000 years ago Muslims began to settle in India. Muslims are people who follow the religion of Islam. Hinduism and Islam call for different ways of thinking and living. These differences in culture have caused conflicts between these groups in India.

About 250 years ago British traders arrived in India and brought their own customs with them. Britain took over

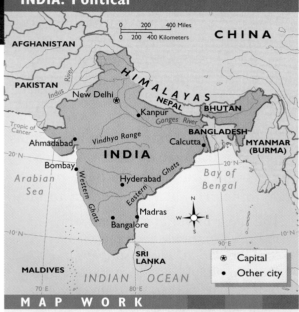

INDIA: Political

0   200   400 Miles
0   200   400 Kilometers

CHINA
AFGHANISTAN
PAKISTAN
Indus River
HIMALAYAS
New Delhi
NEPAL
Kanpur
BHUTAN
Ganges River
Tropic of Cancer
Ahmadabad
Vindhya Range
BANGLADESH
Calcutta
MYANMAR (BURMA)
20°N
INDIA
20°N
Bombay
Western Ghats
Eastern Ghats
Hyderabad
Bay of Bengal
Arabian Sea
Madras
Bangalore
10°N
10°N
90°E
80°E
SRI LANKA
MALDIVES
INDIAN OCEAN
70°E

⊛ Capital
• Other city

MAP WORK

The country of India is located in the southern part of Asia.

1. What bodies of water surround India on three sides?
2. Which countries border India?
3. What is the capital of India?

India's government in 1858 and ruled India for nearly 100 years. Today, some Indians still speak English.

The lives of Azeez and his family reflect the different cultures that are part of India's rich past. The Narains speak both Hindi and English. Azeez loves to play cricket, a game invented in Britain that is a bit like baseball. The Narains are Hindu, as are most Indians. However, the name *Azeez* is a combination of Muslim and Hindu words that means "community-harmony."

CULTURE HAS MANY PARTS

As you can see, a culture is made up of customs that are passed down through time. Azeez's life shows that the ways we speak, play, and view others can reveal clues about our culture.

Values and Beliefs

One of the most important parts of any culture is its values, or the things people believe are most important in life. Many people's values are shaped by their religious beliefs.

As a Hindu, for example, Azeez believes that all living things have souls and are "a fraction of God." Azeez's parents and grandparents have passed many other Hindu values down to him.

The most important lessons which my grandparents have taught me are that we should live a simple life and that we should not be attracted by money. We should not hurt anyone, including the animals. That's why we are strict vegetarians and don't even eat eggs.

Think about how the values or religious beliefs that you have been taught affect the way you live from day to day.

Culture at Home

You can get many hints about what a culture is like by seeing how people live at home. The Narains live in a six-room apartment. Their living room is filled with books, sofas, a television with 15 channels, and carvings and pictures of Indian leaders and Hindu gods. Mainly traditional Indian food is cooked in the kitchen, including Azeez's favorite dish—*uttapam* (OOT uh pam). Azeez describes this as "a sort of south Indian pizza made of rice with vegetables, coconut, and dried fruit."

A temple room honors the Hindu god Krishna. Each morning and evening Azeez goes there to offer his prayers. On Sundays the Narains travel to the local temple to worship.

Think about how the way you live at home reflects your family's beliefs and customs.

Cultures Change

Cultures do not stay the same forever. They constantly change through their interaction with other cultures. Interaction is the exchange of ideas and customs.

The Narains, for example, do not cook only Indian food. Sometimes they make Chinese or American food as well. Once in a while Azeez plays chess, a game probably invented in India

over 1,000 years ago. The style of chess Azeez plays today, though, was created through interaction between Asian and European cultures.

Another part of Indian culture that has changed is the role of women. Today women in India, especially in cities, have much more freedom and many more rights than in the past. In fact, Indians elected a woman, Indira Gandhi, as head of their government in 1966. Azeez's 11-year-old cousin Kalayani (ka luh YAH nee) says of her future, "I can do anything I want to do."

Azeez at School

Just as home life reveals much about a culture, so does life at school. Azeez attends school six days a week and must wear a uniform. Because so many different languages are spoken in India, Azeez studies four different languages: Hindi, English, Bengali, and Sanskrit, which is an ancient written language. Classes are taught in Hindi and English. Besides languages, Azeez also studies history, geography, math, science, government, and music.

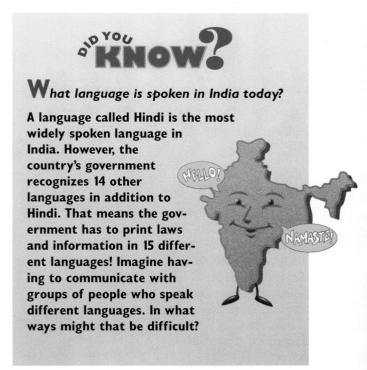

DID YOU KNOW?

What language is spoken in India today?

A language called Hindi is the most widely spoken language in India. However, the country's government recognizes 14 other languages in addition to Hindi. That means the government has to print laws and information in 15 different languages! Imagine having to communicate with groups of people who speak different languages. In what ways might that be difficult?

HELLO!

NAMASTE!

Other Parts of Culture at School

One instrument Azeez plays in music class at school is the *mridanga* (mri DAHNG guh), a two-headed drum used in Indian music. Every day Azeez eats in the school lunchroom with his friends. No meat or egg dishes are served. Instead, the students have spicy vegetables and lentils with rice, and flat breads fried in butter.

Government

New Delhi, where Azeez lives, is the capital of India. India's government is similar to that of the United States. Indians vote for leaders to represent them in government. This form of government, called a representative democracy, is an important part of India's culture. It gives all Indians a say in how they are ruled. When Azeez turns 18, he, too, will be able to vote for the leaders of his government. How old will you have to be to vote in elections in the United States?

Azeez enjoys playing chess and making music with friends. Here, he is playing the mridanga, a traditional Indian two-headed drum.

Infographic

Cultures Around the World

You have met Azeez Narain in this lesson. Now meet five more young people in this Infographic. What do they have in common? What are some differences in their lives?

Rachel Dennis, age 11
Halifax, Nova Scotia, Canada

HOME: Lives in a house on the Atlantic coast with her parents, brother, and dog
LANGUAGE: English
SCHOOL SUBJECTS: Social studies, science, English, math, art, health, music, physical education
HOBBIES: Gymnastics, horseback riding
FAVORITE FOOD: Waffles

Anna Patricia de Martinez, age 12
Lima, Peru

HOME: Lives in a brick house with her mother, brother, and grandparents
LANGUAGE: Spanish
SCHOOL SUBJECTS: Science, math, Spanish, social studies, English, physical education, music, gardening
HOBBIES: Swimming, volleyball, aerobics
FAVORITE FOOD: Pastelle de Manzanas (pie)

Olanike Olakunri, age 10
Lagos, Nigeria

HOME: Lives in a cinder block house with her parents
LANGUAGES: Yoruba, English
SCHOOL SUBJECTS: Math, English, Citizenship, music
HOBBIES: Board games, mystery books, school running team
FAVORITE FOOD: Eba (a porridge made of cassava flour and dipped in okra)

Brian Lawlor, age 11
County Tipperary, Ireland

HOME: Lives in a farm cottage with his parents and sister
LANGUAGE: English
SCHOOL SUBJECTS: Math, English, geography, music, science, Gaelic studies, physical education
HOBBIES: Hurling (like field hockey), and playing the accordion
FAVORITE FOOD: Apple tart

Harry Tan, age 10
Singapore

HOME: Lives in an apartment with his parents, brother, sister, and dog
LANGUAGE: Mandarin Chinese
SCHOOL SUBJECTS: English, Chinese, social studies, math, science, art, physical education
HOBBIES: Video games, skateboarding, baseball
FAVORITE FOOD: Rice with chicken in curry gravy

WHY IT MATTERS

Whenever and wherever people have lived, their lives have been shaped by the culture around them. A culture's language, government, values, foods, and entertainment make people who they are. Cultures also change as they interact with others over time.

This process of interaction is a big part of the story you will read in this book. In the chapters to come you will read about the world's many different cultures. Interaction between these cultures over the years has created the fascinating and complex world that we live in today.

✓ Reviewing Facts and Ideas

SUM IT UP

- All cultures are made up of similar parts, such as religion, government, and education.
- Values affect not only what people believe, but also how they live.
- Cultures change as people of different cultures interact with one another.

THINK ABOUT IT

1. What are some clues you can study to learn about a culture?

2. How has religion shaped life for people in India?

3. **FOCUS** What has Azeez Narain's life taught you about the many parts of Indian culture?

4. **THINKING SKILL** What are two *generalizations* that you could make about Azeez's family?

5. **WRITE** Write an article for visitors from other countries. Describe how culture in the United States has been shaped by interaction with other cultures.

CHAPTER 1 REVIEW

THINKING ABOUT VOCABULARY

Number a sheet of paper from 1 to 10. Beside each number write the word from the list below that best matches the statement.

climate	landform
culture	latitude
custom	longitude
degree	region
geography	values

1. The things that people believe are most important in life

2. The distance east or west of the prime meridian measured by imaginary lines that run north and south on a map or globe

3. An area with common features that set it apart from other areas

4. The way of life of a group of people at a particular time that includes their daily habits, beliefs, and arts

5. The distance north or south of the equator measured by imaginary lines that run east and west on a map or a globe

6. The study of Earth

7. A weather pattern of an area over a long period of time

8. A physical feature such as a mountain range, plain, or plateau

9. A unit of measurement describing the distance between lines of latitude and longitude

10. A way of living that people practice regularly over time

THINKING ABOUT FACTS

1. What is geography and what can we learn by studying it?

2. Why do geographers use the concept of regions?

3. What are three types of regions?

4. What defines a physical region?

5. What do the equator and the prime meridian have in common?

6. How does a global grid make it possible to find locations?

7. What makes up a culture?

8. Explain one way in which culture influences a country.

9. What is the role that religion plays in a culture?

10. How is India's government an example of cultural interaction?

THINK AND WRITE

WRITING A PARAGRAPH OF DESCRIPTION

Write a paragraph about the region where you live. In it describe the region's major landforms, its climate, and some important features of its culture.

WRITING A LETTER

Write a letter to Azeez Narain in India. Tell him about the culture and values of the community in which you live. Also tell him about some of the ways you think your life is similar to or different from his.

WRITING A TRAVEL PAMPHLET

Write a brief pamphlet about an interesting place you have visited. Suppose you are writing it for people from another country who will be visiting the place you describe.

APPLYING GEOGRAPHY SKILLS

LONGITUDE

Use the map on this page to answer the following questions.

1. What are lines of longitude?

2. What is the prime meridian?

3. What is the first line of longitude shown west of the prime meridian? What is the first line of longitude shown east of the prime meridian?

4. How far apart are the lines of longitude shown on the globe?

5. What is useful about having lines of longitude on a map?

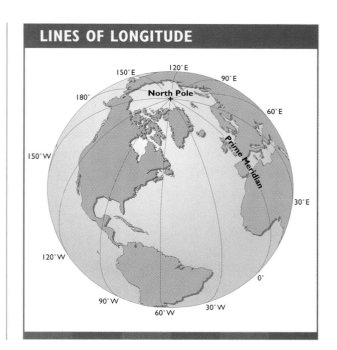

LINES OF LONGITUDE

Summing Up the Chapter

Copy the main idea table below on a separate sheet of paper. Then place each item in the feature list in the correct category below. Think of other features you might want to add. When you have completed the table, write a paragraph answering the question "How might the land, water, and climate of a region help shape the culture of the people who live there?"

MAIN IDEA	The geographical features of a region—land, water, climate—help shape the culture of the people who live there.		
Features	landforms, temperature, religion, education, bodies of water, vegetation, humidity, rainfall, music, natural resources, air currents, government, soil, latitude, values, altitude		
PHYSICAL		**CLIMATE**	**CULTURAL**
landforms		rainfall	religion

CHAPTER
2

A Look Into the Past

**THINKING ABOUT
GEOGRAPHY AND CULTURE**

These photographs show places built by people many centuries ago. While the places or their ruins remain, the people who built them are gone. Read Chapter 2 to begin your journey into the mystery of the very distant past.

India
ASIA

The Taj Mahal in Agra, India, is among the world's most beautiful buildings. A ruler had it built to honor his wife.

Mesa Verde
THE AMERICAS

In what is now south-western Colorado, Native Americans began building their homes right into the area's cliffs about 1,400 years ago.

Athens
EUROPE

Ruins at the Acropolis hint at the glory of Ancient Greece. Its people developed a great civilization and formed the first democratic government.

Egypt
AFRICA

Thousands of years ago traders made their way across the dry lands of northern Africa. Their journey was made easier by camels.

23

UNDERSTANDING HISTORY

READ ALOUD

How has your life changed from the way it was five years ago? You're probably playing different games and have long outgrown your old clothes. Your family may have moved into a new home. Your life will continue to change as you grow older. Look around carefully. Ten years from now, everything around you—every object you use, every song you enjoy listening to—will help tell the story of what your life was like today.

THE BIG PICTURE

As the story of your life unfolds, it becomes part of an even bigger story of human **history**. History is the story of the past. People who study what has happened in the past are called historians. They may study details of daily life, or they may examine events that have changed the world. Historians have learned, for example, that people in Central America first enjoyed what we now call bubble gum hundreds of years ago. Historians have also learned how terrible wars brought huge changes for these same people in Central America.

Whether they study life-changing events or interesting details, historians use different kinds of sources, from books to bones, to discover what life was like in the past. Sources are an historian's most important tools. Like all tools, they need to be used carefully and skillfully.

Focus Activity

READ TO LEARN
What do historians do to look into the past?

VOCABULARY
history
oral tradition
artifact
primary source
secondary source

HISTORY ALL AROUND

Nina was so excited that she forgot to say hello as she burst through her grandfather's front door.

"Grandpa, guess what? We're getting a new computer tonight!"

"Why, hello Nina," Grandpa Joe replied, putting down his magazine. "What is all this I hear about a new computer?"

An attic or storeroom (above) can be an excellent place to find artifacts from the past. An old camera is an example of an artifact.

"It's a lot more powerful, so my friends and I can play CD-ROMs on it."

"Whoa, Nina," laughed Grandpa Joe. "I still don't understand that much about computers. See, back when I was your age, we didn't even have television. Most people didn't."

"What?" gasped Nina.

"It's true," her grandfather continued. "Back in 1950 our family was the first in our neighborhood to get a TV. That was a big deal! I'll never forget how our neighbors crowded around that TV wanting to see all the new shows. . . ."

Grandpa Joe was describing the past using oral tradition—passing on history by word of mouth. Oral tradition is an important way that people remember the past. This was how history was kept alive before writing was invented.

"You know," mused Grandpa Joe, "I kept that old TV set. It's up in the attic. You should see it! It's nothing like what we have today."

"Hmmm . . . OK," answered Nina, her curiosity getting the better of her.

Learning from Artifacts

The old TV was definitely an artifact (AHR tuh fakt) from another time. An artifact is an object made by someone in the past. The TV's small screen was housed in a big, bulky, wooden cabinet. It was hard to imagine that such a homely machine had once been the center of so much attention. Propped up against the TV was another artifact—a large plastic ring that rattled when Nina picked it up. What did it do? Nina shook it, rolled it, then looped it around her shoulder. She decided to take it with her and figure it out later.

DIFFERENT SOURCES

On the shelf next to the TV lay other interesting artifacts: a dusty model of an old car, a big scrapbook filled with newspaper clippings, and a yellowing stack of magazines.

Nina scooped up as many items as she could, along with a newer-looking book called *God's Country: America in the Fifties.* Then she headed back downstairs to examine her finds.

Using Primary Sources

Except for the book, all of the items that Nina picked up in the attic were primary sources from the 1950s. Primary sources are materials that were created during the time under study. They can be written things, such as magazine articles or advertisements. They can also be nonwritten things, such as toys or tools or pictures.

Read the following excerpt from one of Nina's written sources. It describes a time in America's past when televisions were a novelty. What clues in the text tell you this is a primary source?

MANY VOICES
PRIMARY SOURCE

Excerpt from an interview published in *Television*, by Michael Winship, 1988.

I first saw television when I was a kid growing up in Brooklyn. . . . We didn't own a television set—most people didn't. But the Texaco Star Theater with Milton Berle was on Tuesday nights. So we all stood on the street, and the people who had a television set on my block would put it in the window facing the street. Half the block would gather—maybe 50 people would watch the show.

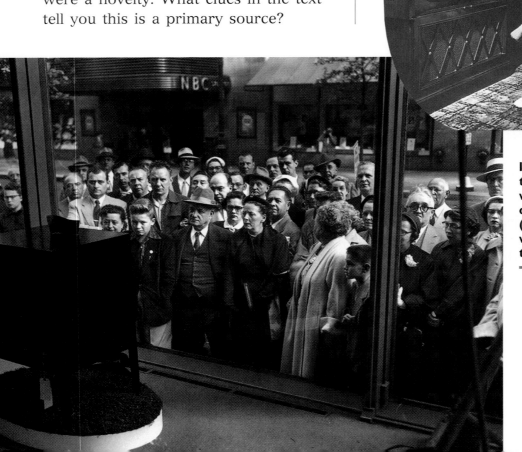

In the early days of television, not everyone was lucky enough to own their own set (above). Often, people would crowd sidewalks to watch (left).

A Secondary Source

Secondary sources are records of the past that are based on studies of primary sources. Nina's secondary source was the book *God's Country: America in the Fifties*. This is a study of life in the 1950s written by J. Ronald Oakley in 1986. Read the following excerpt from *America in the Fifties*.

> *In the America of 1950, almost 90 percent of all families did not have a television set. . . . By the early 1960s, 90 percent of all American homes had at least one television set. Never had a new product expanded so rapidly or so quickly become an essential part of American life.*

How does the information given in this secondary source differ from the information given in the primary source on the previous page?

Different Viewpoints

Nina could appreciate the old TV in the attic much more now that she knew how rare TVs were in 1950. But what could she make of the cars from the 1950s?

"They were so *huge*, so different from the cars we have today," Nina marveled as she picked up the old car model. "They couldn't have been very practical—and they must have been real gas guzzlers, too."

"But people didn't *care* that much about being practical back then," Grandpa Joe answered. "We wanted comfort and grandness, and those cars delivered!" To support his opinion, Grandpa Joe turned to an old car advertisement in his scrapbook. Look at the advertisement on this page.

Nina and her grandfather looked at the model car from different viewpoints. Nina noticed how the car contrasted

An advertisement in a scrapbook can show what was important to car buyers in the 1950s.

with today's cars. On the other hand, Grandpa Joe was reminded of people's attitudes about cars during the 1950s. These different viewpoints brought them to different conclusions.

Historians often disagree about how sources should be interpreted, or how life in a past time should be remembered. Since their own viewpoints shape the way they view the past, historians can end up constructing different pictures of the same historical period.

Historians also have trouble reconstructing the past. The further back in time something happened, the harder their job becomes. In addition, many important sources from the past have been destroyed or lost. This makes it impossible to understand certain past cultures and events.

PUTTING IT ALL TOGETHER

Based on the sources she had to work with, Nina was beginning to put together a picture of what life was like in the 1950s. In some ways the 1950s were similar to the 1990s. People worked hard and enjoyed relaxing with their families and friends. There were major differences, too. Television was still a new invention, so it was just starting to become the basic part of American life it is today. Cars were larger and used more gasoline. Conserving natural resources such as oil was not as much of a concern then as it is now.

Looking at an Artifact

But what purpose did the big plastic ring serve? The answer came as Nina flipped through a 1958 issue of *Life* magazine. A photograph in an article caught her eye. It showed teenagers swinging the rings around their waists.

A library is a good place to find primary and secondary sources. **Your local library probably has sections for books and magazines from the past. Many modern libraries now also have computers and CD-ROMs.**

The article called the rings "hula hoops" and said they were "the newest national craze. . . bigger than anything that ever hit the toy business." You can see a page from that article on page 28.

Combining Sources

Nina's article shows why written sources can be so valuable to historians. They can speak for people and things from another time. The article, a written source, helped explain the hula hoop, an artifact.

Without realizing it Nina had done work similar to that of a true historian. She used primary and secondary sources to shed light on her topic, life in the United States in the 1950s. She also examined artifacts to learn their purpose and importance in a culture. Lastly, she used and interpreted written sources to try to understand one of a culture's customs.

WHY IT MATTERS

The work of an historian is like that of a detective. Clues to an historical period or event may be deeply buried. So historians have to rebuild the past as accurately as possible, using the evidence that is available to them. Sometimes key evidence has been lost or destroyed, making the job even harder.

Historians are not alone in their task, however. They have skilled partners—scientists—who help them uncover written and unwritten sources from the past. You will read about these scientists and the work they do in the next lesson.

SUM IT UP

- History is the study of what happened in the past.
- Before writing was invented, history was passed down through oral tradition, or word of mouth.
- Artifacts, or objects made in the past, can also tell how people lived.
- Historians use primary and secondary sources to interpret what life was like in the past.
- The sources that historians use, the way they use these sources, and their points of view, shape the way the past is remembered.

THINK ABOUT IT

1. How does oral tradition differ from a written source? How can both help to preserve history?

2. What is a secondary source? Give an example of a secondary source you use at school.

3. **FOCUS** How do sources help us to learn about the past?

4. **THINKING SKILL** What *effects* do the sources available to a historian have on the ways she or he understands the past? How might a historian's point of view affect the way she or he understands history?

5. **WRITE** Use your imagination to write about how the artifacts in your classroom might be viewed by an historian 100 years from now. What are three conclusions the historian could make from these artifacts about life in the 1990s?

THINKINGSKILLS

Decision Making

VOCABULARY
decision

WHY THE SKILL MATTERS

One of the most important parts of an historian's job is making choices. Every historian chooses which sources to study and how to interpret those sources. When historians make these choices, they are making decisions. A decision is a choice arrived at after thought.

USING THE SKILL

One of the most thrilling historical studies ever made involved the search for the ancient city of Troy by Heinrich Schliemann (HĪN rihk SHLEE mahn) in 1870. Many legends told of a great walled city called Troy, where heroic warriors long ago had fought fierce and

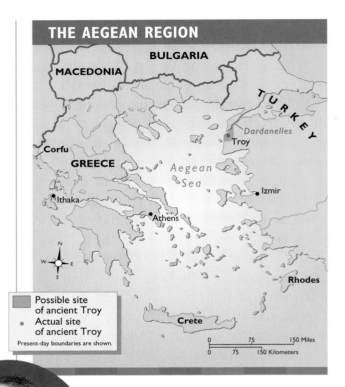

THE AEGEAN REGION

MACEDONIA
BULGARIA
GREECE
TURKEY
Dardanelles
Troy
Corfu
Aegean Sea
Ithaka
Izmir
Athens
Rhodes
Crete

Possible site of ancient Troy
Actual site of ancient Troy
Present-day boundaries are shown.

| 0 | 75 | 150 Miles |
| 0 | 75 | 150 Kilometers |

Heinrich Schliemann located the site of ancient Troy (left and above).

bloody battles. You will learn more about these legends when you study ancient Greece in Chapter 8.

No one knew for sure whether Troy had been a real city or whether it had been created in the imaginations of ancient poets. Many historians believed that Troy had flourished in a part of western Asia near the Aegean (ih JEE un) Sea more than 3,000 years ago. Schliemann was fascinated by the stories of this old city, and he was determined to find its location and learn its secrets.

Now that Schliemann had set his goal, he had to identify different alternatives, or ways, of reaching the goal. Then he had to decide, or choose, the best places to look for the lost city. Schliemann examined many different sources to learn as much as he could about the location of Troy. He carefully studied the descriptions of Troy in a book called the *Iliad,* by the Greek poet Homer. Schliemann believed that this book was the most accurate source because it was the oldest one, written about 2,800 years ago. Schliemann also studied the landforms of Greece and Turkey in hopes of finding more clues about Troy.

Finally Schliemann had enough information to identify the different alternatives, or likely places to search for Troy. Some historians thought that Troy could be found on the island of Corfu, northwest of mainland Greece. Others believed that the city was located on the west coast of Turkey. Schliemann noticed that a small mound located a few miles south of the Dardanelles Strait seemed to match a description of Troy given by Homer in the *Iliad.*

HELPING Yourself

- A **decision** is a choice between alternatives.
- Identify the **goal** you want to reach.
- Consider the different alternatives for reaching the goal.
- Choose the best alternative.

Schliemann decided that this mound on a plain overlooking the blue Aegean Sea was the best alternative. This mound was called Hissarlik (hih sur LIK), and it was there that he began his search for Troy. In 1870 Schliemann began digging at Hissarlik with his wife, Sophia. Soon they found stone walls and other remains of an ancient city. As they dug deeper and deeper they found gold and silver artifacts and other evidence of the magnificent city that had once been Troy. Eventually, the remains of nine cities, newer ones built upon the ruins of older ones, were uncovered. Today historians believe that the sixth city was the one that Homer had written about in the *Iliad.*

TRYING THE SKILL

Refer to the Helping Yourself box for help in making a decision. Imagine that you are trying to learn about the history of your hometown. Your goal is to find the best historical source about the first people who lived there. What are three sources that you could choose to find out more about the first people in your hometown? Decide which of these sources is the best one. Why?

REVIEWING THE SKILL

1. How is making a decision similar to making a choice?
2. Why is it important to set a goal when making decisions?
3. Why is it important to identify alternatives for reaching a goal?
4. When might it be useful to be able to make good decisions?

ICEMAN OF THE ALPS

READ ALOUD

It was warm and sunny in the Alps on September 19, 1991—a perfect day for hiking. As Erika and Helmut Simon moved along a mountain ridge, they spotted something in the melting ice. At first they thought it was trash, or maybe a doll. When they got closer Erika cried out, "It's a man!" The leathery-brown body was indeed human, lying half-buried in the snow. Shocked, the Simons hurried down the mountain to tell the police. They would not learn until several days later that the body they stumbled upon was over 5,000 years old.

THE BIG PICTURE

History is full of mysteries. It is the job of historians to do the detective work needed to solve these mysteries. As you learned in the last lesson, written sources can be a big help to historians trying to interpret past events. Artifacts are helpful clues, too.

The science of archaeology (ahr kee AHL uh jee) is the study of the remains of past cultures. Archaeologists carefully dig up and explore historical sites. They use modern instruments to discover, identify, and save these remains. They take X rays to see what is inside an object and how it was made. They do tests to determine the age of artifacts. Above all, archaeologists must link different clues to figure out what artifacts and remains might say about how people lived in past cultures.

Focus Activity

READ TO LEARN
What can artifacts tell us about the ancient past?

VOCABULARY
archaeology
prehistory

PEOPLE
Konrad Spindler

PLACES
Alps

A DISCOVERY IN THE ALPS

The **Alps** are Europe's highest mountain range. They contain dozens of snow-covered peaks and massive slabs of ice called glaciers. On some days the Alps are a beautiful and safe place to hike. On other days the Alps can be deadly. In fact, each year more than 100 people die in sudden snowstorms there.

Thus police and local reporters were not too surprised when the Simons found a body in the Alps. Two days after the discovery, a local newspaper reported:

Judging by the dead man's equipment, he was a mountaineer. It seems that the accident occurred some decades ago. The body has not yet been identified.

The article was accurate in many ways, but very wrong in one. Soon it would become clear that this "mountaineer" had been frozen for far more than 40 or 50 years.

A Mystery in the Ice

A few days after the Simons made their discovery, the police set out to recover the body. Look at the map on this page to see where the body was found. The police also saved some items scattered around the area. These included a knife, some bits of rope and leather, and an ax. After a closer look they realized that this ax was no ordinary hiking tool. Its metal blade was lashed to a wooden handle with strips of leather. The ax looked hundreds of years old!

The story of the "Iceman" now became big news, especially to archaeologists. Five days after the Iceman was found, German archaeologist **Konrad Spindler** came to investigate. When he

saw the Iceman's belongings, Spindler's eyes widened. "This [was] something any first-year archaeology student could identify," he later wrote. Spindler estimated the Iceman's age by observing that his ax was made of copper and his knife-blade of chipped stone. Looking up, Spindler announced his conclusion: "Roughly 4,000 years old!"

Later on, detailed testing would prove that the Iceman was actually about 5,300 years old. From these results, archeologists realized that the Iceman had lived in Europe in the age of **prehistory**, or the time before writing was developed there. "A fully equipped prehistoric man—nothing like it had ever been seen by an archaeologist," Spindler wrote.

ARCHAEOLOGICAL DISCOVERY SITE

Site of the "Iceman" discovery.

MAP WORK

The site of the Iceman discovery lies high in Europe's Alps mountains.

1. The Iceman was found very near the border of which two countries?

2. In what direction did archaeologist Konrad Spindler travel to get from Germany to the site?

When hikers in the Alps stumbled upon his body, the "Iceman" (left and above) had been frozen for over 5,000 years!

AN AMAZING FIND

Archaeologists have uncovered axes and knives and prehistoric graves before. What made the discovery of the Iceman so interesting? He was found with the tools and clothes he used every day. The Iceman brought a price-less treasure of artifacts into the 1990s.

Tools of the Archaeologist

Several archaeologists rushed to the Alps to recover as many of the Ice-man's belongings as possible. They were able to work only a few days, however, before the first winter snows buried the site. The following summer, these archaeologists shoveled away over 600 tons of snow before they could pick up where they had left off.

The archaeologists' first task was to make a detailed map of the location. They also took photographs showing where each artifact was found. Next, they used steam blowers and even hair dryers to melt snow and ice around the artifacts. The melted water was filtered three times. Archaeologists wanted to make sure that even the tiniest specks of evidence were not lost.

The archaeologists found flecks of wheat. This proved that the Iceman must have had contact with a village where grain was grown. Archaeologists also recovered over 2,000 grains of pollen, or plant dust. Study of the pollen with a microscope showed that most of the grains came from alder and pine trees. Scientists reasoned that the

Iceman probably died in autumn, the season when pine and alder trees give off the most pollen.

Equipped for Survival

Near the Iceman, archaeologists found all sorts of survival gear, such as knife-blades, rope, and hunting arrows. They also recovered a small net. Was the net used to carry things? Was it a fishing net? The wide spaces in the mesh seemed to rule out both of these possibilities. Then Konrad Spindler compared the net to modern nets used by European farmers to catch birds. They matched exactly. The question of the net's purpose seemed to be answered.

In a leather belt-pouch the Iceman carried needed tools, such as small flint blades and a bone needle probably used to repair equipment. There was also a handful of a black fungus. Chemical study showed that tiny crystals of sulfur and iron were attached to the fungus. These are ingredients in today's matches. Archaeologists concluded that the Iceman used the fungus as a kind of fire-starter.

The Iceman also carried two small beads of a different kind of fungus on a leather strap. Close comparison of samples with those in a huge fungus collection showed that the Iceman's beads were made from birch fungus. Birch fungus contains an ingredient that helps fight disease. Therefore, archaeologists believe that this was the Iceman's "medicine chest."

Artifacts found near the Iceman tell archaeologists much about life in prehistoric Europe. It seems that people then had survival skills possessed by few people today.

Examining the Evidence

The Iceman was moved from the Alps to a special refrigerated room in Innsbruck, Austria. There scientists determined that he was about 5 feet 2 inches tall. From the amount of wear on his teeth, they reasoned that he was 35 to 40 years old when he died. Pieces of his hair showed that he had wavy dark-brown hair and a beard.

X rays indicated that the Iceman had some broken ribs on his right side. Some archaeologists believe that the Iceman was somehow injured before he died, because he was found lying on his left side. Shortly after his death, he was covered by snowfall. Glacier ice gradually encased him. It would imprison— and preserve—him for 5,000 years.

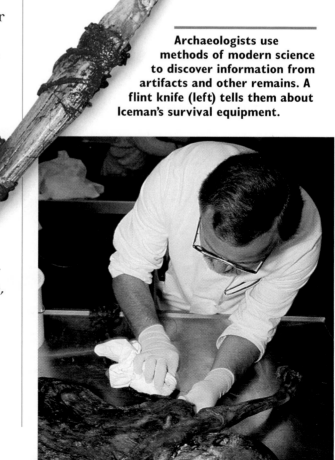

Archaeologists use methods of modern science to discover information from artifacts and other remains. A flint knife (left) tells them about Iceman's survival equipment.

WHO WAS THE ICEMAN?

From the body of one man and a few of his belongings, archaeologists have learned much about what life was like in the Alps during prehistoric times. Many mysteries have been solved, but some still remain.

Living 5,000 Years Ago

We now know at least the following about the Iceman's world. The people of the Iceman's time were experts at interacting with their environment. Archaeologists concluded this because as many as 17 different kinds of trees and 8 different kinds of animals were used to make the Iceman's belongings. These prehistoric people were also skilled metalworkers. They were able to shape copper into tools. And the Iceman must have had contact with farmers. We know this because traces of grain were found in his belongings.

The Mystery Remains

What about the Iceman himself? Who was he and what did he do for a living? Why did he hike up into the high mountains of the Alps just before

THE ICEMAN OF THE ALPS

The Iceman's clothes and tools help archaeologists to figure out what his life may have been like.

BOW
Six-foot bow for hunting game

AX
Copper ax for chopping firewood

CAPE
Woven grass cape for extra warmth

COAT
Deerskin coat for protection from the cold

LEGGINGS
Leather pants of animal skins

SHOES
Leather boots insulated with grass

NET
Net similar to modern European bird nets

KNIFE
Flint knife with leather case

winter set in? Spindler believes that the Iceman may have been a shepherd who spent long periods of time in the mountains, away from his village below. We may never know for certain what he was doing high in the mountains that long-ago autumn day. Whatever the reason, the Iceman's misfortune has proven to be history's great gain.

WHY IT MATTERS

We can sometimes learn facts about an entire culture by focusing on one individual, such as the Iceman. Archaeologists looked carefully at artifacts that the Iceman used every day. They discovered much about how people lived in the highlands of prehistoric Europe.

In chapters to come, you can use some of the same methods you learned about in this lesson. You will read about great ideas and events that changed the world. But you will also have the opportunity to think about individuals like the Iceman. These individuals add fullness and detail to the big picture of history.

DID YOU KNOW?

How did archaeologists figure out how old the Iceman was?

Tiny skin samples were sent to four laboratories for carbon-dating tests. All living things contain carbon, and when they die a special type of carbon called carbon-14 slowly begins to break down at a known rate. By measuring the amount of carbon-14 that has broken down in a sample, scientists can then determine its age.

All four test results concluded that the Iceman lived between 5,000 to 5,300 years ago.

 Reviewing Facts and Ideas

SUM IT UP

- Archaeologists use science to study and interpret the remains of past cultures.

- Our understanding of prehistory, or the time before writing was invented, is often based on the work done by archaeologists.

- Archaeologists and historians can sometimes make conclusions about life in past cultures. One of the ways they do this is by looking closely at information about one or two individuals.

THINK ABOUT IT

1. What made Spindler realize that the Iceman was actually very old?

2. What was the Iceman's net probably used for? How did Spindler find out?

3. **FOCUS** How do archaeologists help to uncover secrets of the past?

4. **THINKING SKILL** What are two _facts_ and two _opinions_ presented about the Iceman in this lesson?

5. **GEOGRAPHY** Describe how the Iceman's belongings tell the different ways in which he interacted with his environment.

CITIZENSHIP
VIEWPOINTS

Rather than let them be flooded, workers took apart and moved the temples at Abu Simbel, in Egypt.

WHEN SHOULD CULTURAL SITES AROUND THE WORLD BE PROTECTED?

Many places have ruins of ancient temples and palaces. These ruins provide clues to ancient cultures. Both in the past and today, people have not always protected such places. Wars and pollution damaged some. Other sites became overgrown. Still others have been destroyed to make room for new buildings.

Serious efforts to protect archaeological sites began in 1959. Archaeologists learned that a huge dam being built at Aswan in Egypt would flood temples thousands of years old. The United Nations Educational, Scientific, and Cultural Organization (UNESCO) worked with the Egyptian government to save these temples.

Along with archaeologists and officials from many nations, UNESCO has drawn up a list of almost 400 "World Heritage sites" to be preserved. The list includes Southeast Asian temples, Mexican pyramids, European cathedrals, and ancient African cities. Sites in the United States are in danger of being destroyed as well. Some people think such sites should be preserved. Nancy Marzulla explains other factors that should be considered, such as the use and value of property. Consider the viewpoints on this issue and answer the questions that follow.

Three DIFFERENT Viewpoints

1 **GUSTAVO ARAOZ**
Architect, Washington, D.C.
Excerpt from Interview, 1995

We need to protect our global cultural heritage, because if such places are not properly kept up, they can be changed beyond recognition or destroyed. Once you lose a cultural site, you can never get it back. It's like losing a book and all the information in it. It's gone forever. When the tombs of ancient Egypt were looted and the artifacts stolen, the world lost a significant source of information about the past.

"It's gone forever."

2 **NANCY MARZULLA**
Lawyer, Washington, D.C.
Excerpt from Interview, 1995

Historic preservation is fine as long as we also protect the rights of property owners. In the United States the Constitution guarantees these rights. The owner of a house or building has the right to be paid a fair amount for any property to be preserved if it results in the destruction of private property rights. Preservation laws may require the owner to keep a site or building exactly as it is, which could destroy the value of the property.

"... protect the rights of property owners."

3 **BREDA PAVLIC**
International Relations Specialist, Paris, France
Excerpt from Interview, 1995

Today our global cultural resources are threatened in many ways. Among these threats are industrial pollution, urban growth, war, natural disasters such as earthquakes, floods, hurricanes, and too much tourism. The loss of any one of these unique sites is irreplaceable. These sites are a link between the past and the present, and, if we manage to preserve them, a link with the future. They give us a feeling of belonging to the world as a whole.

"... a link between the past and the present ..."

BUILDING CITIZENSHIP

1. Explain how each person supports her or his view.

2. In what ways are some of the viewpoints alike? In what ways are they different?

3. What other viewpoints might people have on this issue? How could you find out about historical sites in your community?

SHARING VIEWPOINTS
Discuss what you agree with or disagree with about these and other viewpoints. Discuss why you think the speakers might feel as they do. Then, as a class, write two statements that all of you can agree with about preserving historical sites.

39

CHAPTER 2 REVIEW

THINKING ABOUT VOCABULARY

Number a sheet of paper from 1 to 10. Beside each number write the word or term from the list below that best completes the sentence. You will need to use some words more than once.

archaeology
artifact
decision
history
oral tradition
prehistory
primary source
secondary source

1. Before written records were kept, people passed on their history by word of mouth or _____.

2. A written study of the past that is based on a primary source is called a _____.

3. An object made by someone in the past is an _____.

4. The scrapbook that Nina found in her grandfather's attic is an example of a _____.

5. _____ is the study of the remains of past cultures.

6. To make a choice between two or more alternatives is to make a _____.

7. _____ can be identified as the story of the past.

8. The time before the development of writing is called _____.

9. _____ often involves the search for artifacts.

10. Stories and legends were passed on during prehistory through _____.

THINKING ABOUT FACTS

1. What sources do historians use to study the past?

2. What is the difference between primary and secondary sources?

3. How is an historian like a detective?

4. What do artifacts show about the past?

5. How is history different from prehistory?

6. What do archaeologists study?

7. What conclusions did the archaeologist Konrad Spindler make about the frozen man found in the Alps?

8. What belongings of the Iceman were discovered, and what did archaeologists learn from examining them?

9. Name at least one method the archaeologists used to find information about the Iceman.

10. What mysteries still remain to be solved about the Iceman?

THINK AND WRITE

WRITING A SUMMARY

Write a paragraph summarizing what you know about the history of your community.

WRITING AN ARTICLE

Suppose you are writing an article for your school newspaper about "The Iceman of the Alps." Describe the discovery and what archaeologists learned from it.

WRITING AN INTERVIEW

Suppose you were able to interview the Iceman. Write at least three questions you would ask him, and provide the answers you think he might give.

APPLYING THINKING SKILLS

DECISION MAKING

Suppose you are Heinrich Schliemann in 1870. You are fascinated by stories of an ancient city called Troy. No one knows for sure if the city is real or imaginary. You decide to find out.

1. What goal do you set for yourself?

2. What alternatives do you consider to reach your goal?

3. What are the possible consequences of each alternative?

4. Will a map like this one help you to set your goal?

5. Do you think you made a good decision?

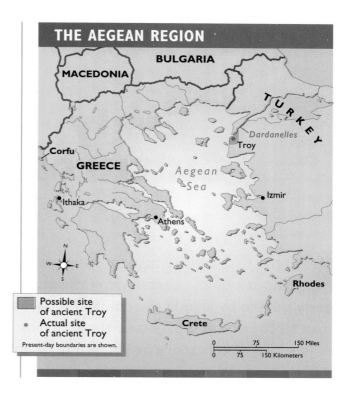

THE AEGEAN REGION

| | Possible site of ancient Troy |
| • | Actual site of ancient Troy |

Present-day boundaries are shown.

Summing Up the Chapter

Copy the main-idea diagram below on a separate sheet of paper. Then review the chapter to find at least two details that support the main ideas. When you have filled in the diagram, answer the question "How do we learn about past cultures?"

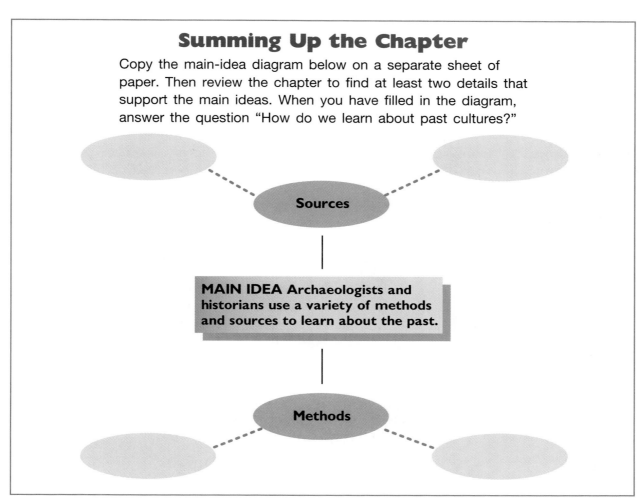

Sources

MAIN IDEA Archaeologists and historians use a variety of methods and sources to learn about the past.

Methods

CHAPTER 3

Early Cultures

THINKING ABOUT HISTORY AND GEOGRAPHY

Most scientists believe humans have walked Earth for many thousands of years. Follow the story of these early people by linking the colored squares on the map to the colored panels of the time line. You will read more of this story as you study Chapter 3.

ATLANTIC OCEAN

45,000 YEARS AGO

OLDUVAI GORGE, TANZANIA

Early people hunt and gather their food

40,000 YEARS AGO

BORDER CAVE, SOUTH AFRICA

People make tools from stone

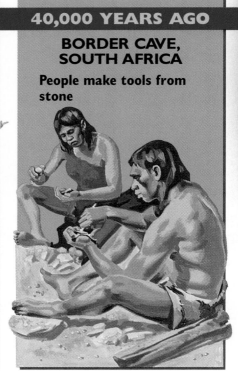

30,000 YEARS AGO

AVIGNON, FRANCE

People create paintings on the walls of caves

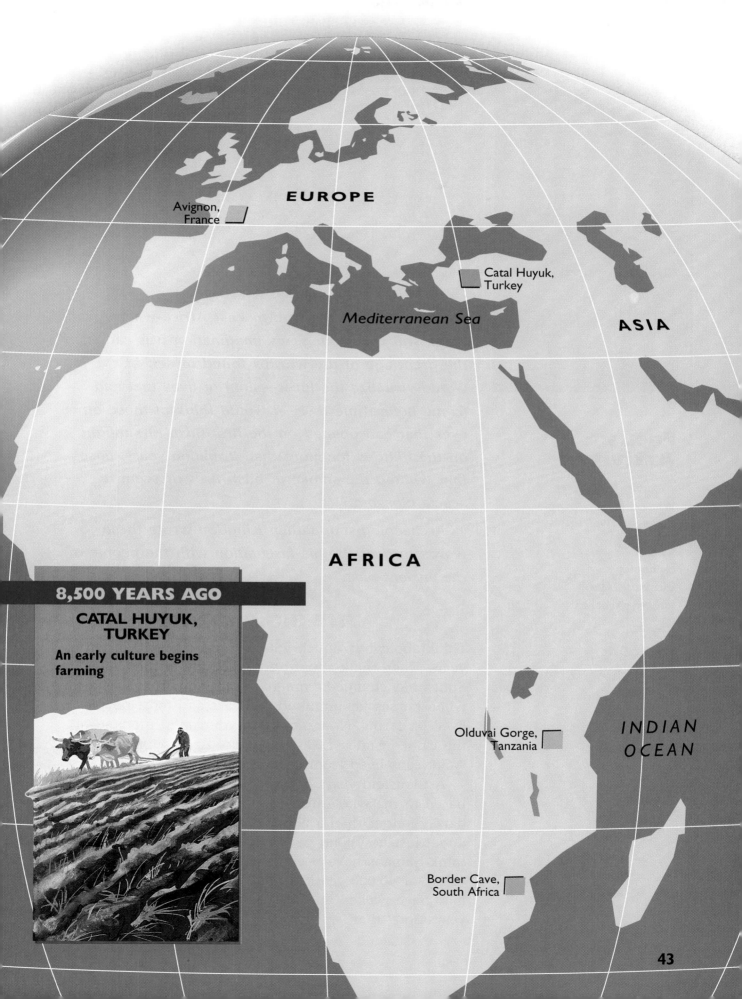

EUROPE

Avignon,
France

Catal Huyuk,
Turkey

ASIA

Mediterranean Sea

AFRICA

8,500 YEARS AGO

CATAL HUYUK, TURKEY

An early culture begins farming

Olduvai Gorge,
Tanzania

INDIAN OCEAN

Border Cave,
South Africa

43

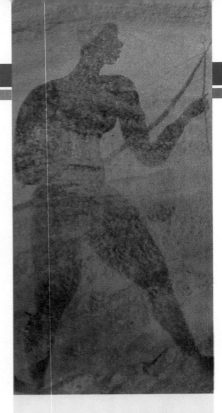

EARLY PEOPLE

READ ALOUD

"I was born and grew up in East Africa where, while I was still very young, my imagination was caught by the great age of the world I found myself in. . . . I would visualize the [procession] of lives that had [come before] me there. I would think of those other eyes that had opened on the first flush of sunlight on the hilltops for more than 2 million years, noses that whiffed the smoke of bush fires or scent of acacia blossom."

Archaeologist Jonathan Kingdon wrote these words to describe his fascination with the people of the ancient past.

THE BIG PICTURE

Think about how much your life has changed in ten years. Then think about how much life in the United States has changed from 100 years ago. That was a time when horses far outnumbered cars and most people lived on farms. Now picture in your mind the land of the United States 1,000 years ago. At this time Native Americans lived from coast to coast.

A thousand years is a very long time. When compared to the whole history of the world, however, it is hardly longer than a blink of the eye. Scientists disagree about just how long people have been around. Many think humans have been around for over 40 times 1,000 years, or 40,000 years. Some scientists think that people may have walked on Earth as long as *2,000* times 1,000 years ago—that is, 2 *million* years ago!

Focus Activity

READ TO LEARN
What did early people do to survive?

VOCABULARY
technology
Old Stone Age
hunter-gatherer

PLACES
Border Cave

44

LIFE LONG AGO

When did human life begin, and what was life like for the world's early people? These are big questions for historians and archaeologists. Many different answers have been given over time.

Discoveries in Africa

Scientists do not agree about where or when human life began. Some scientists today think that human life may have begun in Africa over 2 million years ago and then spread throughout the rest of the world. This conclusion is based on remains found by archaeologists in East Africa. Ancient remains uncovered there are the oldest of their kind ever found.

At one site in the country of Tanzania, a long canyon cuts deeply through the surrounding plains. In this canyon are dry beds of big prehistoric lakes. In those ancient lakebeds archaeologists have found remains that some think may be about 2 million years old.

Tools from Long Ago

Along with these remains, archaeologists have found what may have been the world's first tools. Viewed under a microscope, stones like the ones on this page reveal edges that were pounded to create a knife-like sharpness. They may not look like much to us, but the stones could cut through the hides of animals and chop through wood. These simple but useful tools mark the start of **technology** in culture. Technology is the use of skills and tools to meet practical needs. Stone tools were the most common technology until about 12,000 years ago. That period of time is called the Old Stone Age.

Remains of ancient animal bones found with the stone tools suggest that the early people hunted for survival. During the Old Stone Age, people learned another skill besides hunting and tool-making. This new skill was using fire, and it changed their lives. The technology of fire-building made it possible to cook food for the first time. It also meant people could move into colder climates. Warmth from fires helped people survive through the long winter months.

Early people in Peru made this firestarter (above right). Many stone tools (above) have been found in the Great Rift Valley, Tanzania (right).

Archaeologists probe the darkness of the Border Cave. History's treasures, in the form of artifacts, await.

LIFE IN THE OLD STONE AGE

Many scientists believe that before 40,000 years ago, stone-age technology gradually became more complex. Smaller, finer blades were crafted, for example. Some blades were tied to wooden handles to make small axes. From about 40,000 years ago, changes came more rapidly. This also marked the time when people began to work more closely together and to develop cultures.

Hunting and Gathering

What was it like to live on Earth about 40,000 years ago? Families that once lived in a cave in South Africa have left behind enough clues to give us an idea.

Border Cave is located in Zululand, the northeastern tip of South Africa. Look at the map on the following page to see where Border Cave is. Back then, much like now, the cave nestled in the side of a cliff. It overlooked a grassy river valley dotted with buffalo-thorn trees and other shrubs. Herds of eland (EE lund), a type of antelope, moved into the valley each year. There they ate grass and drank from the river. Border Cave was an excellent base for people who followed the herds and hunted them for survival.

Remains show that the people of Border Cave made their home as comfortable as possible. They lined its cool dirt floor with grass for bedding. They made campfires to cook on and to light the cave's darkness.

From the opening of the cave high on the cliff, the people of the Border Cave could keep watch over the animals' movement. These people probably traveled many miles to hunt the eland herds. Small, arrowhead-like blades suggest that these people may have used bows and arrows to kill animals for food.

The people of Border Cave were not just hunters, though. They knew a great deal about the plants around them. They knew which ones were tasty, useful as medicine, or filled with dangerous poisons. Ancient remains of seeds and leaves show that they gathered wild plums, oranges, and starchy plants for food. They also may have used seeds from nearby trees to help soothe coughs and upset stomachs. Since these people met their needs by hunting and by gathering plants, they are known as hunter-gatherers.

A Changing Culture

At some point many thousands of years ago, a small baby was buried along with a seashell bead towards the back of the cave. This act reveals several important things about life among the people of Border Cave.

It suggests that the baby was deeply cared for. Otherwise people would not have bothered to bury it. It also suggests that the people believed the child would somehow live on after death, or it would not have mattered that the child be buried with the bead. Many archaeologists think that such thoughts about life and death marked the beginning of religious belief in the world.

The seashell bead says other things about the everyday lives of the people of Border Cave. At times they must have traveled to the shores of the Indian Ocean, some 50 miles away. Additionally, the bead shows that these early people valued beauty. Why else would they take the time to make something otherwise "useless" out of the shell?

The earliest signs of art in human culture date back about 40,000 years. Amazing rock paintings in France and Spain date back to about 30,000 years ago. Many other breathtaking rock paintings and carvings dating back

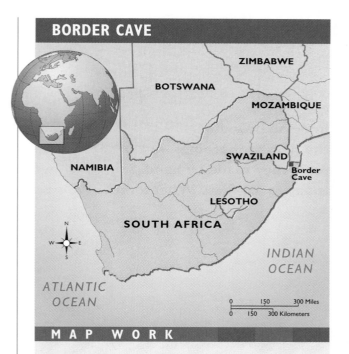

BORDER CAVE

ZIMBABWE
BOTSWANA
MOZAMBIQUE
NAMIBIA
SWAZILAND
Border Cave
LESOTHO
SOUTH AFRICA
INDIAN OCEAN
ATLANTIC OCEAN

| 0 | 150 | 300 Miles |
| 0 | 150 | 300 Kilometers |

M A P   W O R K

Border Cave is an important archaeological site in South Africa.

1. What bodies of water lie on either side of Africa?
2. Which of them is Border Cave closer to?

10,000 years have been found on every continent inhabited by humans. The exact purpose of these pieces of artwork is not known. It is clear, however, that the makers of each had something they wanted to say. The ancient artists found a way to express themselves through their artwork.

Early hunters made these rock paintings (left) showing great herds of eland in South Africa.

Infographic

Old Stone Age Technology Around the World

Imagine how difficult it would be for people to build things without the help of machines. As you read in Lesson 1, Stone Age people used tools they made by hand. Some of the things they created still survive today as artifacts. What kind of skills were needed to create these objects?

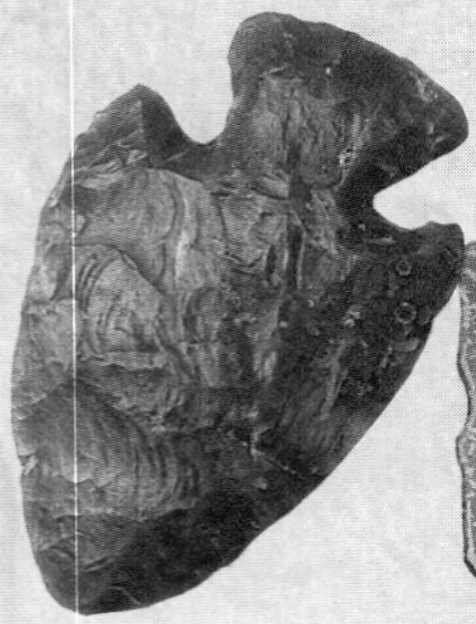

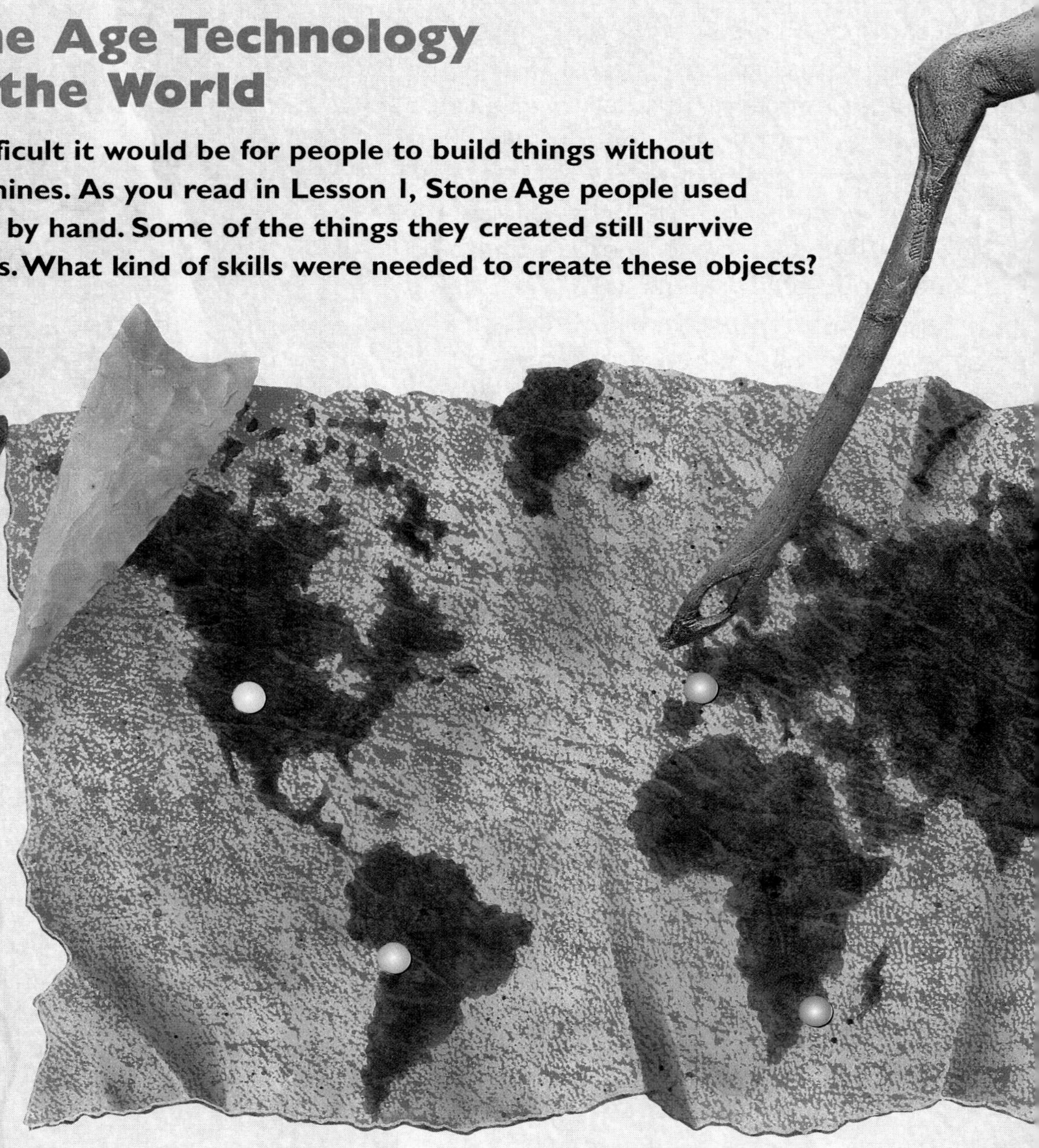

●NORTH AMERICA
Arrowheads, United States, about 12,000 years ago

●SOUTH AMERICA
Firestarter, Peru, about 11,000 years ago

●AFRICA
Fishing sinkers, South Africa, 40,000 years ago

EUROPE
Spearthrower, France, about 14,000 years ago

ASIA
Bead necklace, China, about 30,000 years ago

AUSTRALIA
Rock art, Australia, about 20,000 years ago

WHY IT MATTERS

From about 40,000 years ago until the end of the Old Stone Age roughly 12,000 years ago, human beings spread throughout the world.

During the next 6,000 years, life would change rapidly. For the first time in the long history of the world some people would live in small cities. Their homes would not be caves, but apartment-like buildings packed side by side. In the next lesson you will read about the changes that made such developments possible.

✓✓ Reviewing Facts and Ideas

SUM IT UP

- Early people survived by hunting animals and gathering plants.
- Technology began with the creation of tools out of stone.
- At the end of the Old Stone Age, art and religious beliefs were a part of human life.

THINK ABOUT IT

1. How did the Old Stone Age get its name?

2. How did life on earth change during the Old Stone Age, beginning around 40,000 years ago?

3. **FOCUS** What kinds of technology did the people of Border Cave use in order to survive?

4. **THINKING SKILL** Based on what evidence can we make the _conclusion_ that human life became more complex at the close of the Old Stone Age?

5. **WRITE** Write a paragraph that compares your life today with what it might have been like to live in Border Cave in the Old Stone Age.

ARTISTS
AND THEIR ENVIRONMENTS

Try to picture a world without art—no paintings, no sculpture, no photographs, or music. It would be a less interesting world!

Art has been here from very early times. Although art has changed much since then, there are many similarities between ancient and modern artists.

Artists from ancient times drew their world as they saw it. They painted objects and events that were important to them and their cultures. Modern artists also respond to their environments. They create art that reflects today's concerns.

Art from ancient times becomes especially important when there are no written records. Often historians study this art to discover early people's concerns and beliefs.

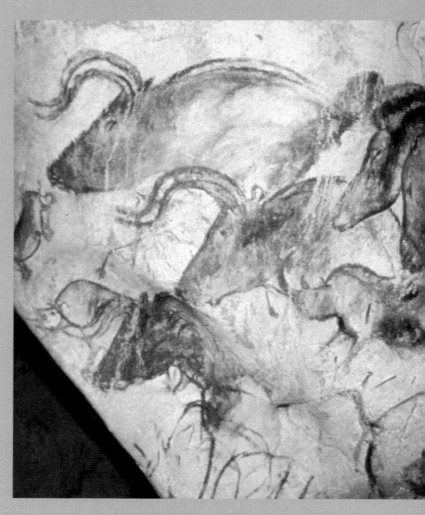

In 1994 hikers discovered cave paintings near Avignon (a vee NYAWN), France. These paintings are believed to be 20,000 years old. The artists used iron dust, sand, and clay to paint these images. Looking at art tells us some of what was important to the people who created it. What do you think was important to the artist who painted the animals here?

This Chinese painting was created around A.D. 1000. The artist painted this scene on silk cloth.

Dutch painter Pieter Brueghel (BROY gul) painted this agricultural scene in the mid-1500s. What does this painting show about life in Europe in the 1500s?

Similar to artists in ancient France, modern artists use materials available to them to give their impressions of the world. American artist Hima Pamoedjo used a computer to create the image shown here.

AGRICULTURE CHANGES THE WORLD

Focus Activity

READ TO LEARN
What was life like in an early farming community?

VOCABULARY
agriculture
New Stone Age
domesticate
surplus
specialization
civilization
trade

READ ALOUD

What would you do if there were no markets or restaurants from which to buy food? How would you find something to eat? You learned in the last lesson that early people faced this challenge by hunting and gathering their food from the wild. However, you can probably think of another way people get food from Earth.

THE BIG PICTURE

About 12,000 years ago Earth's cool climate began to warm. This change caused the number of plants and animals on Earth to soar. The number of people grew as well, as hunters and gatherers around the world took advantage of Earth's new bounty.

Many archaeologists think that some hunters and gatherers began building permanent homes in places rich with wild grains and animals. In time, these early people started to experiment with agriculture. Agriculture is the raising of crops and animals for human use. These experiments changed life on Earth forever.

The period beginning about 12,000 years ago and ending roughly 6,000 years ago is called the New Stone Age. During this time people all around the world still depended on stone tools, but began experimenting with agriculture. Agriculture continues to shape the ways we live today. It is the reason you can go to a supermarket. It is also the reason you may live on a farm—or in a town or city.

CATAL HUYUK

On the grassy banks of the Carsamba (chahr SHAHM bah) River in southern Turkey sits a large mound. The mound covers over 32 acres, an area the size of 21 football fields. Underneath this big but ordinary-looking hill rests one of the world's first cities: Catal Huyuk (CHAH tul HOO yook). Parts of this city on the Carsamba River plain existed over 8,500 years ago.

Catal Huyuk is the largest city this old ever uncovered by archaeologists. The city once housed about 5,000 people. How could so many people live close together at a time when most still lived as hunters and gatherers? The answer is agriculture.

Agriculture Brings Change

Agriculture provided a way for people to live in large groups without the need to travel great distances to gather food. To use agriculture, people first had to **domesticate** (duh MES tih kayt) plants and animals. To domesticate means to train something to be useful to people. For example, people at Catal Huyuk learned to plant seeds and care for edible plants like wheat, barley, peas, and lentils.

The world's first farmers also learned to domesticate animals such as wild goats, cattle, and sheep. Domestica-

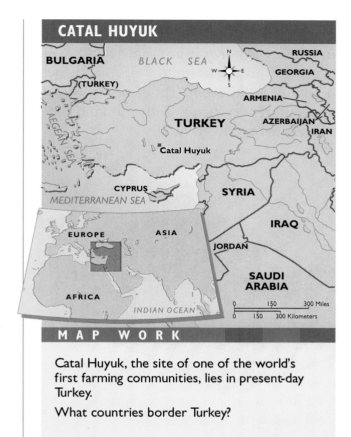

MAP WORK

Catal Huyuk, the site of one of the world's first farming communities, lies in present-day Turkey.

What countries border Turkey?

tion involved more than taming the animals. It meant breeding them to be most useful to humans. Wild sheep, for example, have very little wool. In contrast, domestic sheep have been bred to grow thick layers of the useful material.

The ruins of Catal Huyuk were not discovered until 1958. Today many tourists visit these extensive ruins.

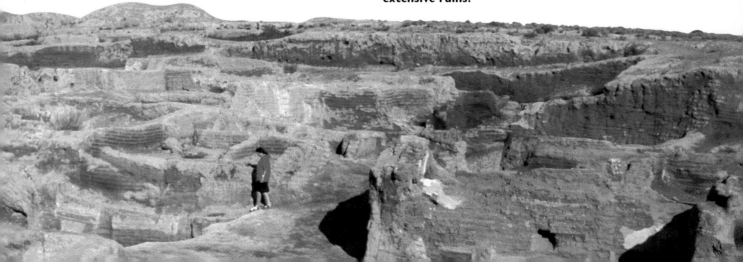

LIVING IN CATAL HUYUK

In some ways living in Catal Huyuk was like living in a city today. In other ways it was very different. The similarities and differences begin with the kinds of houses people lived in.

A New Kind of Home

The homes of Catal Huyuk were built to last. Houses had brick walls coated with white plaster. The large, flat reed roofs were supported by wooden beams. Houses were built right against each other, perhaps to defend the city from attack. There were no streets in Catal Huyuk and no doors on the houses. People entered their homes from the roof, by climbing down ladders!

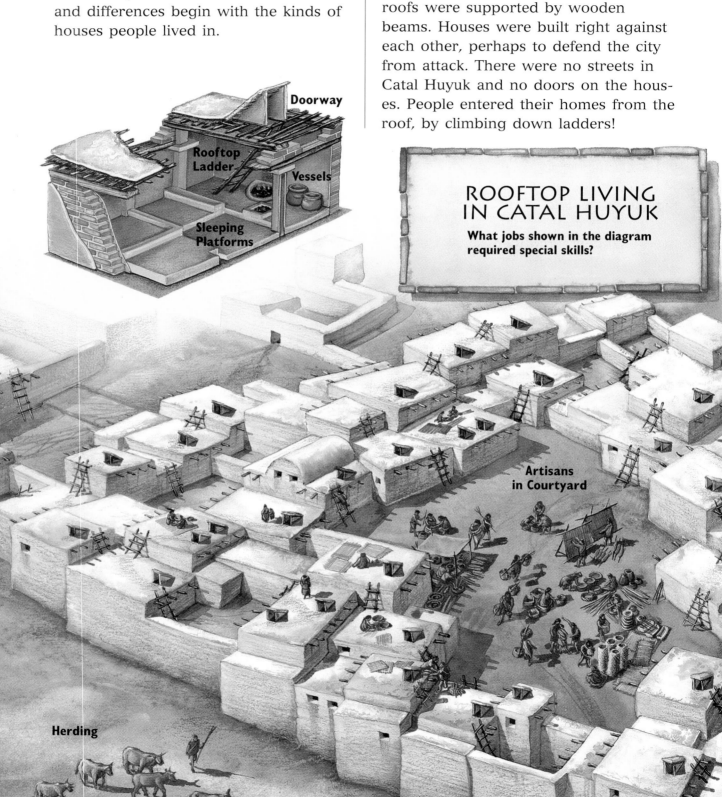

Doorway

Rooftop Ladder

Vessels

Sleeping Platforms

ROOFTOP LIVING IN CATAL HUYUK

What jobs shown in the diagram required special skills?

Artisans in Courtyard

Herding

About one out of every three buildings in the city was probably a temple. Therefore, archaeologists think that religion played a big role in daily life. And what may have been the world's first wall paintings—of cattle, leopards, and other things—filled these rooms. Historians believe that religion in Catal Huyuk may have focused on the success of domestic crops and animals. These were important to the survival of people of the city.

Like many apartment buildings today, homes in Catal Huyuk were all about the same size and shape. Coming down from the roof, people entered a home's main living room. Near the base of the ladder were a fireplace and an oven for heating and cooking. Built into the walls were raised platforms covered with reed mats. These platforms served as all-purpose sofas and beds. A tiny doorway led to the family's storage room. There, large clay pots held stores of wheat and barley.

New Ways of Life

People in Catal Huyuk depended on the grain stores kept in these pots. Agriculture created a new food surplus that hunters and gatherers never had. A surplus is an extra supply of something. Enough crops could be harvested to provide food for the whole year. Cattle provided a steady supply of milk and meat.

The people who worked as farmers were able to provide food for all of the people of Catal Huyuk. There was even some left over for winter. But farming for a whole community was a demanding job. It left little time for other tasks.

The demands on farmers' time led to specialization, or people training to do particular kinds of work. Thus, while some people farmed, other people made wheat into bread flour. Others specialized in making things like tools, bricks, and pots. Since farmers could produce more food than their families needed, they could exchange their surplus food with workers who made other products.

Agriculture changed everyday chores in the city as well. Taking out the trash, for example, was not as simple as burying it in a nearby field. People had to carry it up to the roof, across other people's roofs, and over to the nearest empty courtyard. Courtyards, spaces often left by broken-down homes, served as local garbage dumps.

These changes in community life sparked the growth of a complex new civilization (sihv uh luh ZAY shun) at Catal Huyuk. A civilization is a culture that has developed systems of specialization, religion, learning, and government. The busy town grew until it had about 1,000 homes.

Links to MATHEMATICS

That's a Lot of Wheat!

How much more wheat can we produce now than people could during the New Stone Age?

It's impossible to know exactly how much wheat people were able to grow in Catal Huyuk. But one thing is certain. Agriculture has come a long way since the New Stone Age. In the United States today, modern farming methods help to provide wheat for everyone in America—with surplus to sell to other countries.

In the modern United States, each acre of farmland yields about 35 bushels of wheat per year. If each bushel weighs 60 pounds, how many pounds of wheat are produced on each acre of farmland?

A BUSY CITY

In its time, Catal Huyuk was probably widely known for its arts, crafts, and tools. The city's workers used new kinds of technology to make wonderful assortments of clay pots, woven cloth, and copper jewelry. These were among the first of their kind in the world. By about age 12, girls and boys probably helped to make these products, since they were taught the skills of their mothers and fathers.

Although people in Catal Huyuk depended on stone tools, they began to work with a new material: copper. After gathering pieces of copper, craftworkers made their fires burn hot enough to soften the metal. Once softened, the copper was hammered into the shapes of rings, beads, or pins.

It also took several steps to produce fine wool cloth. First, wool was sheared from domestic sheep. Next, the material was separated and twisted into thread. Finally, the thread was carefully woven into cloth on wooden looms.

Artifacts from Catal Huyuk include necklaces and artwork of a hunt dance.

Signs of Movement

Catal Huyuk's crafts attracted many people to the city. They wanted to own some of the useful and beautiful new products. People in Catal Huyuk wanted to see the things others had to offer. **Trade**, or the exchange of goods, boomed between city residents and visitors to the city.

One thing that people in Catal Huyuk traded was obsidian (ub SIHD ee un). Obsidian is a glassy, black rock used to make beautiful mirrors and razor-sharp knives. City residents probably traveled to a nearby volcano to gather the black stones. Cattle were used to carry back the heavy loads. Craftworkers then made the obsidian into goods to trade with people from all around the region.

People from Near and Far

The people of Catal Huyuk probably traded obsidian knives and arrowheads with people who lived in forests miles away. In return, they received oak wood needed for house-building, along with such treats as apples and nuts.

Traders from nearby areas probably brought many other popular goods to Catal Huyuk. These goods included red paint used in temples and raw copper to be made into tools and jewelry.

Traders also came to Catal Huyuk from faraway places. Archaeologists have found remains of the city's special obsidian goods in ancient settlements as far away as modern Syria. They have also found pieces of Syrian pottery in Catal Huyuk, along with shells from the Red Sea.

People, as well as goods, were on the move, both to and from Catal Huyuk. Archaeologists have found evidence that people from far and wide

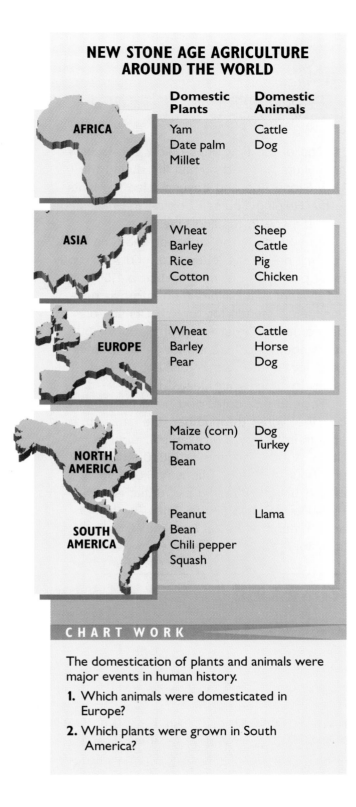

NEW STONE AGE AGRICULTURE AROUND THE WORLD

	Domestic Plants	Domestic Animals
AFRICA	Yam Date palm Millet	Cattle Dog
ASIA	Wheat Barley Rice Cotton	Sheep Cattle Pig Chicken
EUROPE	Wheat Barley Pear	Cattle Horse Dog
NORTH AMERICA	Maize (corn) Tomato Bean	Dog Turkey
SOUTH AMERICA	Peanut Bean Chili pepper Squash	Llama

CHART WORK

The domestication of plants and animals were major events in human history.

1. Which animals were domesticated in Europe?
2. Which plants were grown in South America?

moved to and lived in the city. They brought with them their own skills and traditions. This may be part of the reason for the growth of this rich and complex civilization.

WHY IT MATTERS

As the chart on this page shows, many groups began to develop agriculture during the New Stone Age. The relatively complex civilization of Catal Huyuk showed just how much agriculture could change life. Even bigger changes were yet to come. In the next chapter you will read about another civilization based on agriculture. It, too, rose up along the banks of a river. Unlike the people of Catal Huyuk, the people there developed ways to tell their secrets to others through the ages.

✓/// Reviewing Facts and Ideas

SUM IT UP

- Agriculture made it possible for a few people to raise food for an entire group. Others could specialize, or concentrate on other tasks.

- People of Catal Huyuk were among the first to make pottery and obsidian and metal products. They also traded.

THINK ABOUT IT

1. What is involved in domesticating plants and animals?

2. How did trade help people, both outside and within Catal Huyuk? How did trade help the city to grow?

3. **FOCUS** How did the development of agriculture change the way people lived?

4. **THINKING SKILL** Suppose that you are a visitor to Catal Huyuk. *Decide* whether you want to become a farmer or craftworker for the city, or to remain a hunter and gatherer in the forests nearby.

5. **GEOGRAPHY** Explain how agriculture changed the way people interacted with their environments.

STUDY SKILLS

Reading Time Lines

VOCABULARY

time line
circa

WHY THE SKILL MATTERS

During the New Stone Age, agriculture became a worldwide development. People in North Africa began domesticating cattle and barley, while people in Central and South America raised corn, beans, and animals called llamas. Farmers in other regions domesticated other plants and animals.

One of the easiest ways to keep track of when events happened is to use a time line. A time line is a diagram that shows when things took place in a given period of time. Its words tell what happened and when. The spaces between descriptions indicate how much time passed between events.

USING THE SKILL

One of the time lines below shows how agriculture affected human life during the New Stone Age and beyond. Use the hints in the Helping Yourself box on the next page to guide you in reading time lines.

As you study the labels on the time lines, you will notice the letters B.C. and A.D. Today most people in our country use a 1,500-year-old system that divides time into two periods. "B.C." stands for "before Christ," or before Jesus Christ was born (about 2,000 years ago). "A.D." stands for "anno Domini"—Latin for "in the year of our Lord"—and refers to years since Jesus' birth.

To read B.C. dates you need to remember: the *higher* the number, the *earlier* that time is in history. For example, the New Stone Age began about 10,000 B.C. and ended about 4000 B.C. This was 6,000 years after it began. Reading A.D. dates is easier because we do it all the time. The *higher* an A.D. number is, the *later* that time is in history.

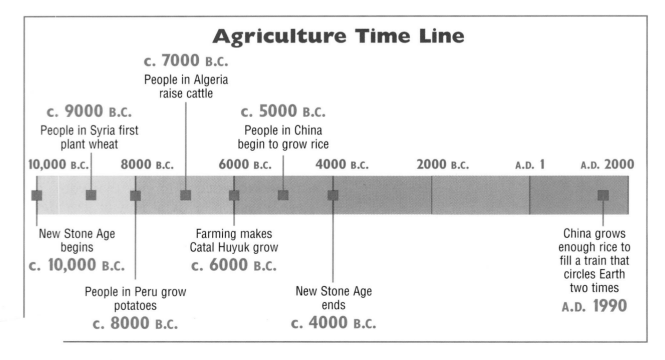

Agriculture Time Line

c. 7000 B.C.
People in Algeria raise cattle

c. 9000 B.C.
People in Syria first plant wheat

c. 5000 B.C.
People in China begin to grow rice

10,000 B.C.   8000 B.C.   6000 B.C.   4000 B.C.   2000 B.C.   A.D. 1   A.D. 2000

New Stone Age begins
c. 10,000 B.C.

Farming makes Catal Huyuk grow
c. 6000 B.C.

New Stone Age ends
c. 4000 B.C.

China grows enough rice to fill a train that circles Earth two times
A.D. 1990

People in Peru grow potatoes
c. 8000 B.C.

You will also notice that some dates on the time lines have the letter *c.* before them. The lowercase *c.* stands for circa, another Latin word. Circa means "about" or "around." If historians are not sure exactly when something happened, they use the term *circa.*

Study the agriculture time line on the opposite page. On what period of time does it focus? Is most of that time A.D. or B.C.? About how many years passed between the time people in China began to grow rice and the end of the New Stone Age?

TRYING THE SKILL

After you have practiced reading the agriculture time line, try studying the time line about the growth of technology. Each entry describes how people used materials from

HELPING Yourself

- **A time line shows when things happened in the past.**
- **Look at the first and last dates to see how much time is being covered.**
- **Read the title and each entry.**
- **Examine the spaces that separate events.**

their environments to make useful tools or crafts. With what material did people in Peru make nets and baskets in 8000 B.C.? What sorts of materials are people using in A.D. 1997?

REVIEWING THE SKILL

Use the technology time line on this page to answer the following questions:

1. What sort of information do time lines show?

2. About how many years does the time line below cover?

3. How many years passed between the time Japanese people first began making clay pots and the time people in Iraq began painting pottery?

4. How does using the time line help you to understand the development of agriculture?

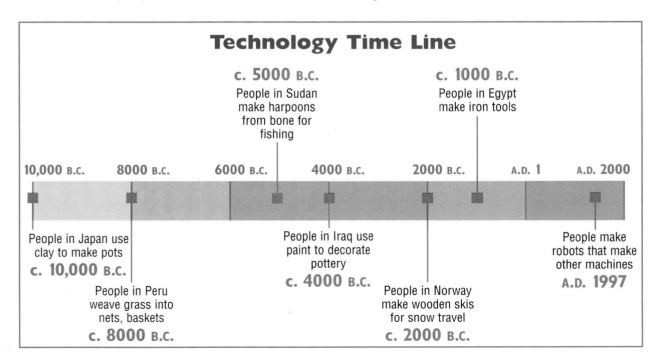

Technology Time Line

c. 5000 B.C.
People in Sudan make harpoons from bone for fishing

c. 1000 B.C.
People in Egypt make iron tools

| 10,000 B.C. | 8000 B.C. | 6000 B.C. | 4000 B.C. | 2000 B.C. | A.D. 1 | A.D. 2000 |

People in Japan use clay to make pots
c. 10,000 B.C.

People in Iraq use paint to decorate pottery
c. 4000 B.C.

People make robots that make other machines
A.D. 1997

People in Peru weave grass into nets, baskets
c. 8000 B.C.

People in Norway make wooden skis for snow travel
c. 2000 B.C.

CHAPTER 3 REVIEW

Major Events

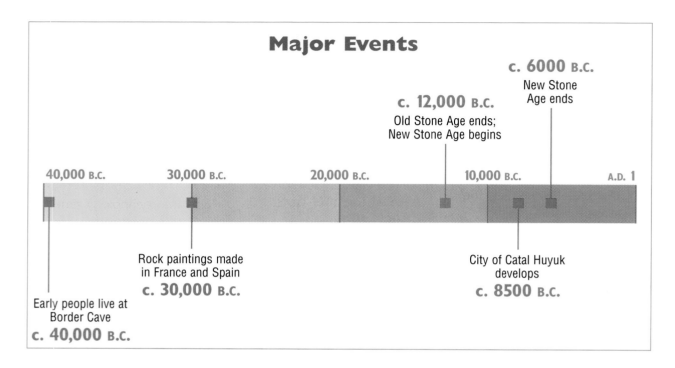

c. 6000 B.C.
New Stone Age ends

c. 12,000 B.C.
Old Stone Age ends;
New Stone Age begins

40,000 B.C.   30,000 B.C.   20,000 B.C.   10,000 B.C.   A.D. 1

Rock paintings made
in France and Spain
c. 30,000 B.C.

City of Catal Huyuk
develops
c. 8500 B.C.

Early people live at
Border Cave
c. 40,000 B.C.

THINKING ABOUT VOCABULARY

Number a sheet of paper from 1 to 10. Beside each number write the word or term from the list below that best matches the definition.

agriculture   Old Stone Age
circa   specialization
civilization   surplus
domesticate   time line
New Stone Age   trade

1. An exchange of goods
2. The period until about 12,000 years ago when the use of stone tools was wide-spread
3. The raising of crops and animals for human use
4. To train plants or animals to be useful to people
5. An extra supply of something
6. The doing of particular kinds of work

7. The period from 12,000 to 6,000 years ago when people developed agriculture and used stone tools
8. A Latin word that means "about" or "around"
9. A diagram that shows when things took place in a certain period of time
10. A culture with developed systems of religion, learning, and government

THINKING ABOUT FACTS

1. What are the earliest signs of human life that scientists have found?
2. How was the New Stone Age different from the Old Stone Age?
3. What changes in the way people lived did agriculture make possible?
4. What is Catal Huyuk, and where is it located? What did archaeologists learn after they uncovered it?
5. What is obsidian? Why was it important to the people of Catal Huyuk?

WRITING A PARAGRAPH OF CONTRAST

Write a paragraph about the differences between the Old Stone Age and the New Stone Age. Discuss methods of obtaining food, types of shelter, and tools.

WRITING A JOURNAL ENTRY

Suppose that you have gone back in time to live in the New Stone Age. Using the diagram of Catal Huyuk on page 54, write a journal entry about your life there. Include details about the way you live, the work you do, and the people you see.

WRITING ABOUT PERSPECTIVES

We are different in many ways from people who lived in the Old Stone Age. However, we also have much in common. Describe three ways you think you are like a person of your age who lived near Border Cave about 40,000 years ago.

APPLYING STUDY SKILLS

READING TIME LINES

1. What is a time line?

2. Look at the time line on page 60. Add the following event in its correct place on the time line: People in Peru weave grass into nets and baskets.

3. Look at the time line on page 60. Add the following event in its correct place: People in China begin to grow rice.

4. On the time line on page 60, add the following event in its correct place: Earth's cool climate began to warm.

5. In what ways are time lines useful?

Summing Up the Chapter

Copy the compare-and-contrast chart below on a separate piece of paper. Then review the chapter to find some of the things that changed during the Old and the New Stone Ages. When you have filled in the chart, use the information to write a paragraph that answers the question "How did early people use their environment to improve their lives?"

MAIN IDEA	Early people developed innovative ways of adapting to their environment in order to meet their basic survival needs.

Old Stone Age	New Stone Age
. . . .	. . . .
. . . .	. . . .
. . . .	. . . .

UNIT 1 REVIEW

THINKING ABOUT VOCABULARY

archaeology

artifact

civilization

climate

degree

geography

Old Stone Age

oral tradition

time line

values

Number a sheet of paper from 1 to 10. Beside each number write the word or term from the list above that best matches the definition.

1. A culture with developed systems of religion, learning, and government

2. The study of the earth, including its land, water, weather, and plants

3. The study of the remains of past cultures

4. The things people believe in and think are important

5. The passing of stories, history, and information passed on by word of mouth

6. The weather pattern over a long period of time

7. The period from 2 million to about 12,000 years ago when people used mostly stone tools

8. A diagram that shows when things happened during a certain period of time

9. A unit of map measurement that describes distance between lines of latitude and longitude

10. An object made by somebody in the past

THINK AND WRITE

WRITING A LETTER

Write to somebody who lives far away. Describe the climate and two or three interesting geographical features of your area. Also tell about some of the customs of the people who live in your community.

WRITING ABOUT PERSPECTIVES

Suppose that you are asked to bury three things that belong to you. These objects should help some future historian learn about the way you lived. Write a paragraph about what you would choose and why.

WRITING AN INTERVIEW

Suppose you could interview one person from the Old Stone Age and one person from the New Stone Age. Write a set of questions you would ask each person and the answers you think they would give.

BUILDING SKILLS

1. **Latitude and longitude** Look at the map on page 15. What is the approximate latitude and longitude of Sri Lanka?

2. **Latitude and longitude** Look at an atlas of the United States and find a map that shows your area. What is the latitude and longitude of your community? Find a community on the other side of the world that has the same latitude. What is the longitude of that community?

3. **Decision making** What is a good first step in making a decision?

4. **Decision making** How would you go about deciding what book to read for an end-of-unit book report? What are the steps you would take?

5. **Time lines** Using events from Unit 1, make a civilizations time line. Put the events in their correct places. Keep this time line so you can add more events.

YESTERDAY, TODAY &
TOMORROW

Historians learn about past civilizations from the artifacts and records that have been left behind. Our civilization will leave large numbers of artifacts and records. Which ones do you think will be most valuable for future historians? Explain your choices.

READING ON YOUR OWN

Here are some books you might find at the library to help you learn more.

INDIA
Ed. by MaryLee Knowlton
This book describes the daily life of a young boy in Rajasthan, India.

DIG THIS!
by Michael Avi-Yonah
This discussion highlights archaeological excavations of ancient cities.

THE GREAT ANCESTOR HUNT; THE FUN OF FINDING OUT WHO YOU ARE
by Lila Perl
This book explains how to trace one's family history.

UNIT PROJECT

Design Your Own Region

1. Suppose you could create your own region.
2. With your group, decide which landforms from this unit you want to include in your region. Perhaps you want to include valleys and streams.
3. Draw a sketch of what you want your region to look like.
4. Create your region out of clay. You may want to start with a sturdy cardboard base and use different colored clay for the different landforms.
5. Make a label for each landform. Then cut out each label, glue it onto a toothpick and place it by its landform.
6. Give your region a name and write a description of it on an index card.
7. Present your region to the class.

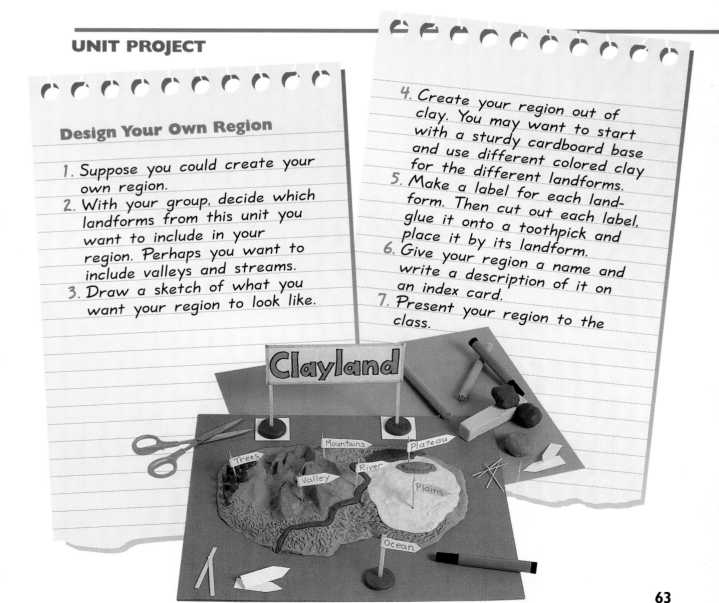

SEDER PLATE, SPAIN
ANCIENT COFFIN, EGYPT
TILE WALL, BABYLON

Israel Museum

Metropolitan Museum of Art

The Granger Collection

LIFE-SIZED HORSEMAN,
CHINA

River Valley Civilizations

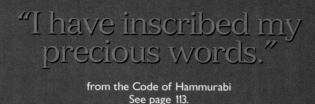

"I have inscribed my precious words."

from the Code of Hammurabi
See page 113.

WHY DOES IT MATTER?

Hammurabi, the king of the ancient empire of Babylonia, had these words inscribed in stone about 4,000 years ago. His words introduced the laws he had created for the people of his empire. This is one of the earliest recorded examples of written laws. Even before Hammurabi lived, people in that part of the world had developed systems of writing. They recorded important information about their lives. By studying texts like this, historians have learned about languages, laws, and customs of ancient civilizations.

Babylonia was a powerful civilization that grew in the fertile river valleys of Mesopotamia, in western Asia. Other river valley civilizations developed in Egypt, India, and China. In this unit you will read about legacies left by these ancient peoples that continue to influence the world today.

CUNEIFORM TABLET, IRAQ
STATUE OF BRAHMA, INDIA

Adventures
with
NATIONAL
GEOGRAPHIC

HIGH AND DRY

Around 1270 B.C., an Egyptian pharaoh named Ramses II had two temples built along the banks of the Nile. Four colossal statues of Ramses himself—each more than 60 feet high—marked the entrance to the larger temple. For 3,000 years, the statues sat on their enormous stone thrones. Then, in the 1960s, the Egyptians built a dam on the Nile, and water started rising behind the dam. Soon, the water would cover the temples! Many nations got together for a massive rescue effort. Workers cut the temples into more than a thousand pieces, lifted them to a place above the level of the water, and put the pieces together again. Now the statues again sit high and dry.

GEO JOURNAL

You're an Egyptian official in the 1960s. Write a letter to the United Nations, explaining why the world should help save the temples of Ramses II.

CHAPTER 4

Ancient Egypt

THINKING ABOUT
HISTORY AND GEOGRAPHY

The story of ancient Egypt begins with farmers along the Nile River. They formed communities that grew into cities. In 3100 **B.C.** Menes united Egypt. Rulers who came after him ordered the building of large, stone monuments such as the pyramids. They also led trading expeditions south and east and increased their land. By 1200 **B.C.** goods and ideas spread from Egypt's capital city, Thebes, to three continents.

5000 B.C.
NILE RIVER DELTA
Egyptians begin to farm

3100 B.C.
MEMPHIS
Menes unites Egypt

2600 B.C.
GIZA
Khufu orders the building of the Great Pyramid

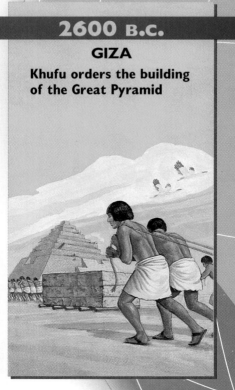

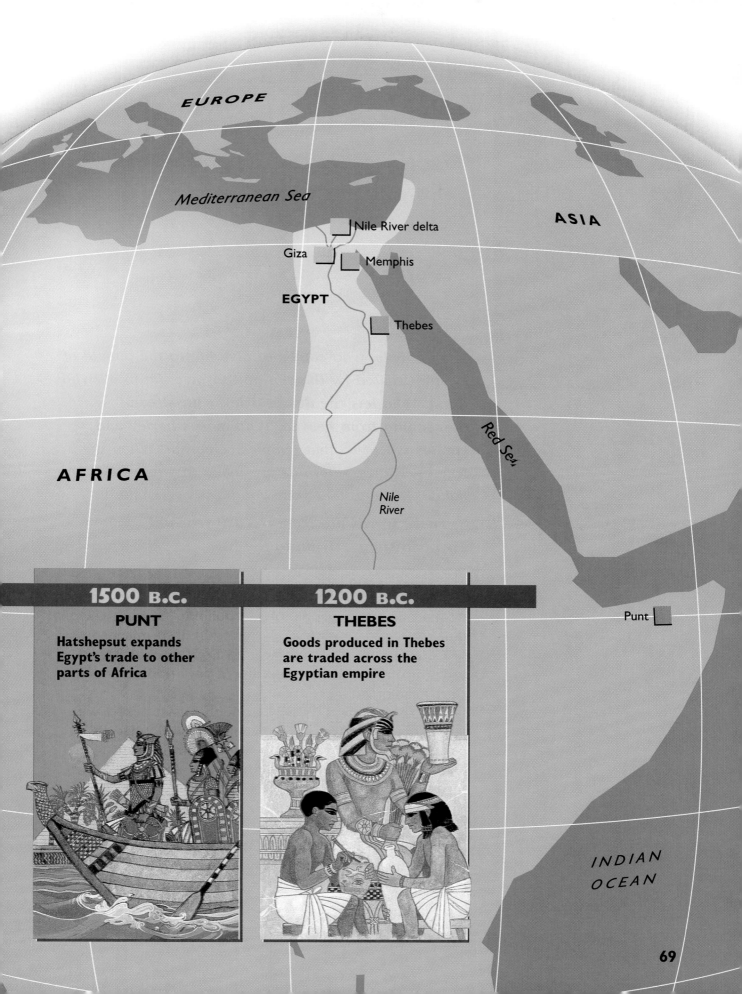

EUROPE

Mediterranean Sea

ASIA

Nile River delta

Giza

Memphis

EGYPT

Thebes

Red Sea

AFRICA

Nile
River

Punt

INDIAN
OCEAN

1500 B.C.

PUNT

Hatshepsut expands Egypt's trade to other parts of Africa

1200 B.C.

THEBES

Goods produced in Thebes are traded across the Egyptian empire

Focus Activity

READ TO LEARN
In what ways did the ancient Egyptians depend upon the Nile River?

VOCABULARY
silt
delta
irrigation

PLACES
Nile River
Lower Egypt
Upper Egypt

GEOGRAPHY OF ANCIENT EGYPT

READ ALOUD

"Hail O Nile, who comes to give life to the people of Egypt. Created by the sun-god to give life to all who thirst. Who lets the desert drink with streams descending from heaven. Who makes barley and creates wheat so that temples celebrate. When the Nile overflows, offerings are made to you, cattle are [killed] for you, that your goodness be repaid."

These words are from a 3,000-year-old Egyptian song, "Hymn to the Nile."

THE BIG PICTURE

Around 5000 B.C. people began building farming villages in a river valley in Africa, several hundred miles south of Catal Huyuk. The area around Egypt's Nile River valley probably did not look like a very good place to start farming.

The river wound its way through a vast desert with few signs of life. Yet every year the Nile flooded its banks. The river swamped everything in its path with water and mud for four solid months—from July through October.

This yearly flood made the Nile Valley lush and green. It also allowed people to make use of the land. With the help of water from the Nile River, ancient farmers turned the Nile Valley into a productive agricultural region.

THE GIFT OF THE NILE

In many ways, Egyptian civilization owes its life to the Nile River. The Nile provided water and food in the desert. This seemed like a blessing from the gods of the ancient people. For that reason, Egypt has often been called the "Gift of the Nile."

A Mighty River

The Nile is the world's longest river. It flows over 4,000 miles north from the snowcapped mountains of East Africa. It passes through the present-day countries of Uganda, Ethiopia, Sudan, and Egypt. Then the Nile empties into the warm Mediterranean Sea.

Much of East Africa has a rainy season that lasts from May until September. During that time the Nile swells with rainwater and rushes northward with extra power. The river carries off silt as it goes. Silt is a mixture of tiny bits of soil and rock.

Over time, much of the silt has been deposited where the Nile empties into the Mediterranean. There the river divides into several branches, forming a vast, fan-shaped delta. A delta is very fertile, flat land made of silt left behind as a river drains into a larger body of water. Look at the map on this page. Use the map scale to find the width of the Nile Delta at its widest point.

The Nile Delta region is in northern Egypt, and appears nearer the top on maps that have north at the top. This makes the Delta seem to be "higher." However, the Delta is called Lower Egypt, because it is the lower, or downstream, part of the Nile.

In Upper Egypt, to the south, the Nile cuts through stone cliffs and desert sands. This landscape is very different from the mild, fertile Delta.

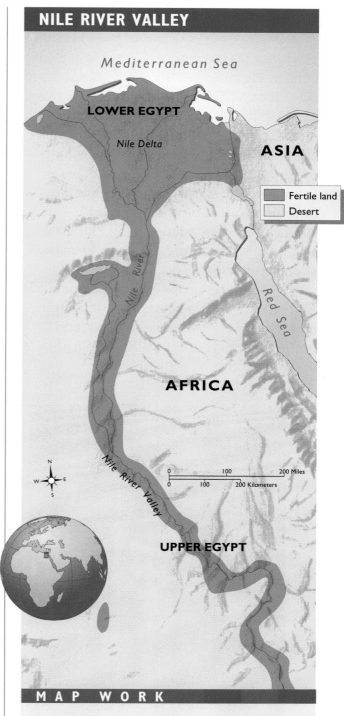

NILE RIVER VALLEY

Mediterranean Sea

LOWER EGYPT

Nile Delta

ASIA

Fertile land
Desert

Nile River

Red Sea

AFRICA

Nile River Valley

0   100   200 Miles
0   100   200 Kilometers

UPPER EGYPT

MAP WORK

The mighty Nile River winds its way through the northeastern part of Africa.

1. In which direction would you travel to get from the Nile River to the Red Sea?
2. The Nile **Delta** is near the division between which two continents?
3. Where is the largest fertile region along the Nile?

A LAND OF DROUGHT AND FLOOD

Egyptian farmers almost always welcomed the mud left by each summer's Nile flood. This silt-filled mud was rich in minerals needed by plants. The black soil brought by the Nile contrasted sharply with the dry, yellow sand of Egypt's desert. In many places a farmer could stand with one foot on farmland and the other on sand!

Farmers depended on the right amount of flooding each year to grow successful crops. Too little flooding meant farmers' crops failed and people went hungry. Too much meant people and cattle could be swept away and homes destroyed. Life was a delicate balance in the Nile River valley.

A System of Agriculture

In October the flooded land began to dry. Then farmers planted wheat and barley. They also planted garden vegetables such as cucumbers, lettuce, onions, and beans. Farmers also grew flax, a plant used to make cloth.

To water their newly planted crops, Egypt's farmers used a form of technology called irrigation. Irrigation is the watering of land by means of canals or pipes. At first, farmers simply built dirt walls around their farmland to hold the Nile floodwaters in the fields. Later, they dug small channels, or canals, to bring water from the Nile directly to their farmland. Farmers scooped water from the canals and poured it into the fields, using a bucket-lifter called a shadouf (shah DOOF). The photograph on this page shows how this tool is still used today.

By March the crops were ready for harvesting. In good years the fields were filled with ripe vegetables and grains. Then farm families had more food than they needed. Their surplus, or extra supply of goods, was then gathered up and carried off to storehouses. As in Catal Huyuk, these grain stores made specialization and community life possible.

Travel Along the Nile

Harvest-time ended in late June, before the Nile once again began to flood. During the four-month flood

Ancient Egyptians found ways to make farming easier and more productive. A shadouf, shown in the picture (above), helped distribute water to the fields. Farmers also built plows, like the one in the model (left), which animals pulled through the fields.

The British Museum

season, farmers could not work in their fields. Instead, many used the time to visit neighboring villages.

Flood season was one of the busiest times for travel on the Nile. Yet river traffic was heavy all year. The Nile was the main way that people and goods moved from place to place. The 600-mile journey between Upper and Lower Egypt would take over a month to walk. In a reed boat it took only about half that time.

WHY IT MATTERS

By 5000 B.C. life in the early farming communities of ancient Egypt centered around the Nile River. The river provided the Egyptian people with fertile soil, water for irrigation, and a means of transportation.

Throughout Egypt's long history, the world's longest river has played a key role. In time, the ancient Egyptians would use the Nile to build the largest civilization the world had ever seen. The following lessons will introduce you to this rich civilization.

The Trusty Nilometer!

How did Egyptians measure the yearly level of the Nile flood?

Ancient Egyptians built special staircases along the river to measure the height of the Nile as it rose. Each step was one "cubit" high—the distance from a person's elbow to the tip of the thumb. One cubit is about 20 inches.

In a good flood year, the Nile rose 16 steps on the Nilometers. How many feet does this equal? In a bad flood year, the Nile rose only 7 steps or less. How many feet is this?

✓// **Reviewing Facts and Ideas**

SUM IT UP

- The Nile is the world's longest river. It is more than 4,000 miles long.

- Farmers' understanding of the yearly Nile floods made community life in Egypt possible.

- Mineral-rich silt deposits and irrigation technology made farming in ancient Egypt very productive.

- People used boats to get from place to place along the Nile.

THINK ABOUT IT

1. Describe the irrigation methods used by the ancient Egyptians.

2. How did the Nile's yearly floods help ancient Egyptian farmers?

3. **FOCUS** Name three ways the people of ancient Egypt used the Nile River.

4. **THINKING SKILL** As an ancient farmer, _decide_ whether Upper Egypt or Lower Egypt is a better place for farming.

5. **GEOGRAPHY** Look at the map on page 71. Describe three different types of physical regions that the Nile flows through.

LESSON 2

3100
B.C.

2000
B.C.

1500
B.C.

1000
B.C.

LAND OF THE PHARAOHS

READ ALOUD

About 3100 B.C. two mighty kings met in battle. One king wore a white crown and ruled over a long stretch of the Nile River in Upper Egypt. The other king had a red crown and controlled a large area in Lower Egypt. The outcome of the battle was of enormous importance. Whoever won it would control the biggest kingdom in the world.

THE BIG PICTURE

You have already read that farming towns began appearing in different parts of the world during the New Stone Age. Some towns grew into small cities, as people specialized and developed trade with neighboring towns.

These communities created rules to promote peace and fairness among neighbors. Village leaders were usually in charge of creating these rules and making sure that the rules were followed. As the communities grew larger, their governments changed to meet their many new needs.

Along the Nile River in Egypt, groups of villages joined together under the leadership of kings. These larger communities developed complex systems of government. Soon the people of the Nile River valley would see even greater changes in the way their communities were run.

Focus Activity

READ TO LEARN
What role did the pharaohs play in ancient Egypt?

VOCABULARY
unification
pharaoh
economy
hieroglyphics
scribe
papyrus

PEOPLE
Menes
Khufu

PLACES
Memphis
Thebes

UNION OF TWO CROWNS

Along the Nile River 5,000 years ago, Egypt's villages were thriving. Farmers were learning how to produce more surplus crops. Craftworkers in villages were using new technology to make tools, pottery, and jewelry. How do you think this affected trade? As you may have guessed, the Nile River became crowded with boats as trade increased between towns.

Egyptians Join Together

In the midst of all this activity, there were also terror and fear. Ruins of walls around early towns and paintings of bloody battle scenes suggest that there were many wars between villages. To better protect themselves and their belongings, the people along the Nile banded together into two separate kingdoms. Towns in Upper Egypt supported a king who wore a white crown. Towns in Lower Egypt followed a king who wore a red crown.

Then, about 3100 B.C., this changed. Forces led by Menes (MEE nees), the king of Upper Egypt, swept north into the Nile Delta. Menes's army overthrew the king of Lower Egypt. To show his victory, Menes wore a double crown. It combined his white crown with the red crown of Lower Egypt. This change stood for the unification of Egypt. Unification is the joining of separate parts into one.

Following this unification of the two kingdoms, Menes became the first pharaoh (FAY roh) of Egypt. The word pharaoh actually refers to the "great palace" in which the rulers lived. Later it became the name given to all the rulers of Egypt. The time when Egypt's early pharaohs worked to build unity within the country is called the Old Kingdom. It lasted from about 2686 B.C. until 2181 B.C. Two other major periods in ancient Egypt's history, the Middle Kingdom and the New Kingdom, would follow.

These Egyptian carvings show rulers and the crowns they wore. The middle crown represents a unification of the other two.

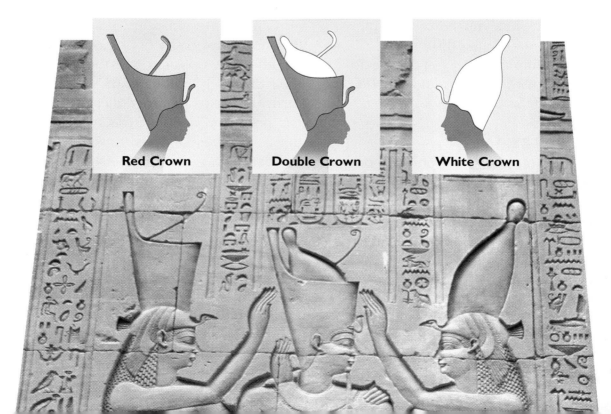

Red Crown   **Double Crown**   **White Crown**

LIFE IN THE OLD KINGDOM

At first, Egypt's pharaohs did not greatly change the civilization that they ruled. They mainly added to the practices of local government, trade, and religion that had existed for hundreds of years along the Nile.

In time, though, the pharaoh became the center of the civilization. His or her actions shaped the fate of all Egypt.

Government Under the Pharaohs

After unification, the most powerful local leaders in Egypt were made area governors for the new government. They performed some of the same services as your local leaders. They were in charge of collecting taxes in their areas and served as local judges. They had different duties as well. Ancient Egyptian governors made sure that precious flood waters were shared fairly among farmers through the use of canals and storage pools.

The area governors reported to the pharaoh's headquarters in Memphis, Egypt's capital city. Memphis was located between Upper and Lower Egypt, near present-day Cairo. From the palace in Memphis, the pharaoh decided how Egypt's affairs should be run, from the highest to the lowest levels.

Religion in Egypt

The pharaoh had great political power in Egypt. He or she had great religious powers as well. In fact, Egyptians believed that the pharaoh was a child of their sun god Ra (RAH). Just as Egyptians believed that Ra gave life to Earth, so they believed that the pharaoh gave life to Egypt and its people. Just as Ra deserved to be worshiped, so, too, did the pharaoh.

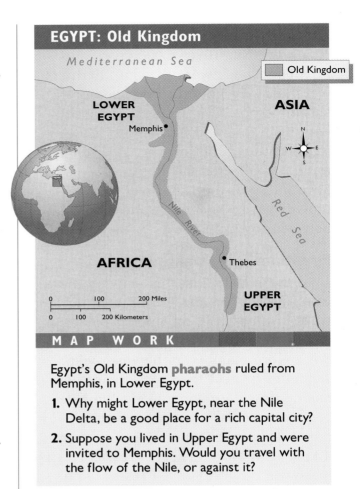

EGYPT: Old Kingdom

Mediterranean Sea

LOWER EGYPT

Memphis

ASIA

Nile River

Red Sea

AFRICA

Thebes

UPPER EGYPT

Old Kingdom

0   100   200 Miles
0   100   200 Kilometers

MAP WORK

Egypt's Old Kingdom **pharaohs** ruled from Memphis, in Lower Egypt.

1. Why might Lower Egypt, near the Nile Delta, be a good place for a rich capital city?

2. Suppose you lived in Upper Egypt and were invited to Memphis. Would you travel with the flow of the Nile, or against it?

Ra was the most important of the many gods whom ancient Egyptians worshiped. Egyptians believed different gods had different roles. For example, one god caused the flooding of the Nile. Another gave potters and metalworkers their creativity. Other gods took the form of snakes or crocodiles. The god Isis protected people from sickness and harm. Her husband Osiris represented the dead who awaited rebirth.

Osiris was important because belief in the afterlife was central to the religion of Egypt. Egyptians believed that after a person died, he or she would go on to the "Next World." Egyptians believed that the dead could take food and objects into the "Next World." Thus, food and belongings were buried with the dead.

Ancient Egyptians preserved the bodies of dead royalty with a process called *mummification*. The bodies were dried and wrapped in strips of cloth. Sometimes pets such as cats were also mummified to accompany their owners into the afterlife.

Egypt's Economy

Since the pharaoh was considered a god, all things in Egypt belonged to him or her. This put the pharaoh at the center of Egypt's economy. The economy of a country is the way its people manage money and resources for the production of goods and services.

Egypt's economy was based on agriculture. Farmers produced a surplus of food, which fed the whole country. How was that surplus divided? The main way was through taxes. The pharaoh collected a large part of every farmer's crops each year as taxes. The grain, eggs, meat, fruits, and olive oil were then used to feed the pharaoh's family and servants. The goods were also used to pay for any other items the pharaoh wanted.

The pharaoh also took taxes on everything else made in Egypt, such as leather goods, linen cloth, and baskets. The pharaoh even taxed people's time. During flood season, for example, Egyptians from priests to potters to farmers were called upon to build canals or buildings for the government.

Egypt's craftworkers and artists depended on the pharaohs for their jobs. These people spent most of their time working to keep Egypt's many temples supplied. For example, temples needed golden bowls and stone statues.

Since the pharaoh owned all of Egypt's temples, it was the government's job to pay for all the supplies they used. No money changed hands, since money did not exist in Egypt at that time. Rather, goods of equal value were traded. For their efforts, craftworkers received clothes and food.

Mummies were wrapped in cloth and covered with masks before being put in coffins. Portraits and scenes of daily life were painted on the tomb walls.

The British Museum

The Granger Collection

A SYSTEM OF WRITING

How was it possible for the pharaoh's government to keep track of all of its business details? How could it make sure, for example, that a farmer in Upper Egypt was paying taxes or that a temple in the Delta had enough linen?

The pharaoh's local governors helped by communicating with the pharaoh's government in Memphis. What made this communication possible was a system of writing.

Ancient Egyptians developed a system of writing sometime before unification. This system, called hieroglyphics (hi roh GLIF ix), was made up of about 800 picture-signs. These individual picture-signs, or symbols, were called *hieroglyphs*. Hieroglyphs could stand for objects, such as bread, or for sounds, such as *s*. Hieroglyphics are the reason why we now know so much about the lives of ancient Egyptians.

The Life of a Scribe

Pharaohs depended on written records to keep their government in order. A number of writers called scribes traveled throughout Egypt to keep records of details great and small. They went out into the fields with local leaders to record how much grain farmers harvested. Scribes also determined how much farmers owed to the government. Scribes drafted letters and marriage contracts for townspeople. Because writing was taught to only a few, scribes were highly respected in Egyptian culture. It was a great honor to become a scribe.

Only boys could become scribes, and they began training when they were about 10 years old. Each day in school they chanted passages aloud to improve their reading skills. Then they spent hours writing out lessons and

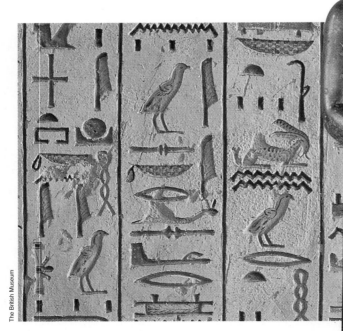

This statue shows Imhotep, a doctor who later was worshiped as the god of medicine. The hieroglyphics are from a king's tomb.

stories over and over. If their attention wandered, they ran the risk of being beaten. Junior scribes used broken pottery as their "scrap paper."

Writing on Paper

After the boys mastered a simple type of hieroglyphics used for record keeping, they graduated to writing on papyrus (puh PĪ rus). Papyrus is a reed plant that grows along the Nile. Ancient Egyptians used these reeds to make a kind of paper, also called papyrus. Papyrus paper was not very different from the paper we use today. Did you notice how similar the words *papyrus* and *paper* are? Our modern word comes from the ancient one!

Scribes used sharpened reeds as pens. They dipped the reeds into small disks of red or black ink. Then the scribes carefully wrote the information they needed to record on their rolls of papyrus paper.

Scribes had to have good penmanship. They also needed to be good at math. After all, they had to keep correct records of the pharaoh's many goods. Scribes also figured out the number of workers and the amount of materials needed to complete building projects.

The Key to a Lost Language

By about A.D. 400, hieroglyphics fell out of use and their meaning was lost. The ancient symbols found on Egyptian tombs and walls were a mystery to people who came upon them many centuries later.

In 1799 a French soldier was digging in the Nile Delta town of Rosetta. There, he found a large, black stone with writing on it. This stone was later called the Rosetta Stone, after the place where it was found. It contained a pas-

sage written three times, in hieroglyphics, Greek, and another type of Egyptian writing called *demotic*. By comparing the three languages, a French scholar named Jean François Champollion (shahm pohl YON) worked to solve the mystery of hieroglyphics. By 1822 he had succeeded. Look at the photograph of the Rosetta Stone. How has its writing helped historians?

MANY VOICES PRIMARY SOURCE

The Rosetta Stone
196 B.C.

Champollion recognized the symbols for Ptolemy (TAH luh mee), a later Egyptian pharaoh. His name is shown here in its hieroglyph symbols. The Rosetta Stone records many of Ptolemy's deeds. For example, the pharaoh lowered taxes, rebuilt certain temples, and freed prisoners!

The stone has the same message in three languages: (from the top) hieroglyphics, late Egyptian (demotic), and Greek.

The British Museum

BUILDING THE GREAT PYRAMID

GREAT PYRAMID OF KHUFU

Average weight of blocks: 2.5 tons
Total number of blocks: 2,300,000
Number of blocks added each day: 285

Air Shaft

King's chamber

Air Shaft

Queen's chamber

Underground Room

BUILDING THE PYRAMIDS

No project could have been more challenging to scribes than keeping track of the building of the pyramids. These huge stone structures were built as tombs, or burial places, for pharaohs.

The Great Pyramid is the Old Kingdom's most spectacular monument. It is by far the biggest of all pyramids built in Egypt's history. Pharaoh Khufu (KOO foo) ordered construction to begin about 2600 B.C. This mountain of stone was to be his tomb. It would bring glory not only to himself but to all of Egypt. He would be buried inside with many belongings that he would take into the afterlife.

The 20-year project involved as many as 100,000 people and took a huge amount of Egypt's resources. Few families escaped the call to work at the site. Large amounts of Egyptian taxes went to feed and clothe the project's workers. Even the Nile River landscape changed. Entire cliffs of stone were cut into blocks to make up the pharaoh's great stone monument! Look at the diagram on page 80 to see the construction of the Great Pyramid.

WHY IT MATTERS

Khufu was not the only pharaoh who demanded such massive building projects. Other rulers during the Old Kingdom called for similar, if smaller, monuments. The huge projects took their toll on Egypt's economy and people. Anger against the pharaohs probably began to grow.

Egypt's hard-won unity started breaking down. Local governments began resisting the orders of the pharaohs. In about 2000 B.C. leaders in Upper Egypt revolted and eventually set up a new pharaoh. They based their new capital in the southern town of Thebes. With this division of the country, the Old Kingdom came to an end.

The breakdown of the Old Kingdom, however, led to the rise of an even greater civilization in ancient Egypt. The next lesson tells how the pharaohs learned from their mistakes. They stopped building pyramids. Instead, they built the richest and most powerful civilization the world had ever known.

Reviewing Facts and Ideas

SUM IT UP

- Menes united the kingdoms of Upper and Lower Egypt to form the largest government in the world at that time.

- The pharaoh was central to Egypt's government, economy, and religion.

- The writing system of Egypt, called *hieroglyphics,* provided a way for government workers to communicate over long distances.

- Ordinary people worked to build huge, government building projects like the Great Pyramid. This strained both Egypt's economy and its people.

THINK ABOUT IT

1. How did local governors help the pharaoh to rule all of Egypt?

2. Why was Memphis a good place to build Egypt's capital city?

3. **FOCUS** How did the pharaohs' government affect the lives of Egyptians?

4. **THINKING SKILL** What *effects* did hieroglyphic writing have on Egypt? Explain why these were effects.

5. **WRITE** Create your own hieroglyph symbols that represent objects or sounds. See if a partner can read your message.

EGYPTIAN BOATS

People have been living along the Nile, the first "superhighway of Egypt," for thousands of years. We may never know when they first tied together bundles of papyrus plant stems to build boats. We do know that boat-building technology was developed very early in ancient Egypt. Egyptians today still sail the Nile, and they see some of the same sights their ancestors saw over 5,000 years ago. As you look at the photos and art on these pages, think about why advances in boat building have played an important part in history.

The British Museum

Models like this were put in Egyptian tombs. Ancient Egyptians believed they would use them in the afterlife. Note the jobs performed by the crew as the boat's owner rests under a canopy. The man on the bow is measuring the water's depth with a plumb line.

River travel was so important to the ancient Egyptians, even their written language showed it. The hieroglyphic sign for "traveling south" was a boat with sails, because the winds in Egypt usually blow from the north. The sign for "traveling north" was a boat with oars. These signs were used even when the travel was by land!

This boat is made of papyrus stalks tied together. It is similar to boats built by the ancient Egyptians. In 1970 explorer Thor Heyerdahl (HAY air dahl) sailed this papyrus boat from Africa to America. Heyerdahl proved that ancient Egyptians could have made this trip!

This modern Egyptian sailboat, or felucca (fuh LUK uh), is not that different from boats used on the Nile thousands of years ago. Many historians believe that ancient Egyptians invented the sail. Most boats on the Nile today, however, use diesel engines.

3000 B.C.   2500 B.C.   2100 B.C.   1300 B.C.   1000 B.C.

ANCIENT EGYPTIAN CIVILIZATION

Focus Activity

READ TO LEARN
What made Egypt's civilization a rich one?

VOCABULARY
empire
expedition

PEOPLE
Ahmose
Hatshepsut
Tutankhamun

PLACES
Nubia
Kush
Punt
Valley of Kings

READ ALOUD

If you took ancient Egypt's two major trade routes and put them in the United States, one would stretch from Washington, D.C., to Chicago and the other from Washington, D.C., to the northern tip of Maine. These were large distances to travel by boat and caravan. But those distances did not keep Egypt from bringing in a fortune along those roads, as you will see.

THE BIG PICTURE

While Egyptian civilization was spreading along the Nile, neighboring cultures were also growing. To the north, people in Europe were developing the islands and peninsulas across the Mediterranean Sea. To the west, other Africans were finding ways to survive in the harsh desert environment of the Sahara. To the south, the kingdoms of Nubia were thriving, due to gold mines and trade networks. To the east, Asian communities large and small were forming in what are today Israel, Jordan, Lebanon, Syria, and Iraq.

Trade and movement of people and ideas helped to shape development in all of these cultures. Each culture had different resources, products, and ideas to exchange. Egyptian civilization affected neighboring areas. Other cultures had their effects on Egypt as well.

NEW RULERS IN EGYPT

Following the collapse of the Old Kingdom, a new era began in Egyptian history. Historians call this period, from about 2100 B.C. until about 1700 B.C., Egypt's Middle Kingdom.

During this time Egypt's contact with other parts of the world increased. For example, the pharaoh's armies conquered kingdoms in Nubia and made use of the area's gold mines. The name *Nubia,* in fact, may come from the Egyptian word *nub,* for gold. Find Nubia on the map on page 86.

Meanwhile Egyptian traders increased their business with cities in western Asia. As trade grew, people also began moving. People from Asia came to live in Egypt's Delta region. By 1650 B.C. these new settlers from the hills of western Asia, called Hyksos (HIK sohs), were powerful enough to challenge the pharaoh.

War with the Hyksos

For the next 100 years, the Hyksos—Greek for "rulers of hill-lands"—ruled Lower Egypt. The Hyksos people used horses, chariots, strong bronze weapons, and bows and arrows to defeat Egyptian armies in battle. However, Egyptian leaders at Thebes continued to control Upper Egypt.

Although they lost Lower Egypt, the Egyptians learned from their war with the Hyksos. In 1550 B.C., about 100 years after the Hyksos gained control of the Delta, Egypt rallied behind Pharaoh Ahmose (AH mohs). This time, with the help of weapons and chariots copied from the Hyksos, the Egyptians succeeded in taking back the Delta.

The defeat of the Hyksos began the period in Egyptian history called the New Kingdom. Pharaoh Ahmose vowed that outsiders would never again control any part of Egypt. Ahmose and later pharaohs set out to make Egypt the strongest military power in its part of the world.

Tomb walls often had paintings like this scene of the Egyptians fighting the Hyksos. At right is a model Egyptian army.

EXPANSION AND TRADE

During the New Kingdom period, Egypt's leaders worked to win back the lands lost in war. Nubia had gained its independence, but now the armies of the New Kingdom conquered the valuable territory once more.

Egyptian armies also marched northeast, into what is today Israel, and took over that territory. They even pushed as far as the Euphrates River, the edge of another powerful civilization that you will read about in Chapter 5.

During the New Kingdom period, Egypt became an empire. An empire is a group of lands and peoples ruled by one government. Egypt's economy no longer revolved around farming along the Nile. The Egyptian empire now had other valuable resources from conquered lands.

Across Land and Sea

Egypt's New Kingdom traders spread far and wide. Egyptian ships loaded with golden jewelry, linen cloth, and papyrus sailed to what are today Lebanon and Syria. The ships returned carrying silver, timber, and wine—rare treasures in the land of the pharaoh. Remains of oil jars and paintings from what is now Greece have been found in Lower Egypt. These artifacts suggest that Egypt also traded with its neighbors across the Mediterranean Sea.

Egypt's most important trading partner, however, lay to the south. When the pharaoh's armies conquered Nubia, they also gained control of the ancient and wealthy kingdom of Kush (KUSH). Kush controlled rich trade routes to other African kingdoms. Trade goods came from parts of Africa even farther south. The kingdom of Kush traded ebony, leopard skins, and elephant

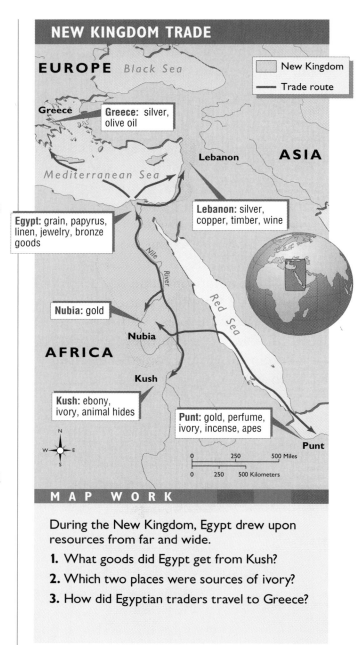

NEW KINGDOM TRADE

EUROPE *Black Sea*

Greece

Greece: silver, olive oil

Mediterranean Sea

Lebanon   ASIA

Lebanon: silver, copper, timber, wine

Egypt: grain, papyrus, linen, jewelry, bronze goods

Nile River

Red Sea

Nubia: gold

Nubia

AFRICA

Kush

Kush: ebony, ivory, animal hides

Punt: gold, perfume, ivory, incense, apes

Punt

New Kingdom

Trade route

0   250   500 Miles

0   250   500 Kilometers

M A P   W O R K

During the New Kingdom, Egypt drew upon resources from far and wide.

1. What goods did Egypt get from Kush?

2. Which two places were sources of ivory?

3. How did Egyptian traders travel to Greece?

ivory. Elephant ivory is ivory from elephant tusks. Kush also owned reserves of gold, copper, and precious stones.

Caravans of men and pack animals brought these treasures out of Kush and back to Egypt. On some trading trips, it took 150 men just to carry all of the gold bars that were being sent to Egypt. Soldiers traveled with trading caravans to keep the pharaoh's treasures safe from bandits. Large, castle-like forts were also built along the Upper Nile to scare away robbers.

Back in Egypt, craftworkers made raw materials into beautiful objects. These included furniture, jewelry, and other fine goods for the pharaoh and Egypt's wealthy families.

Hatshepsut

One pharaoh expanded Egyptian trade well beyond the boundaries of the Egyptian empire. That pharaoh was one of Egypt's few female rulers. Her name was Hatshepsut (hat SHEP soot), "Foremost [first] of the Noble Ladies."

Hatshepsut was a princess and the wife of a pharaoh. She seized the chance to become pharaoh herself when her husband died. Her young stepson was supposed to become the new pharaoh of Egypt. Hatshepsut proclaimed, however, that the ten-year-old boy was too young to rule on his own. In this way she succeeded in being named co-ruler.

Hatshepsut's Trading Journey

In the eighth year of her reign, Hatshepsut organized the biggest trading expedition of her career. An expedition is a group of people who go on a trip for a set reason. The goal of Hatshepsut's expedition was to trade with Egypt's neighbors to the south in Punt. Historians think Punt may have been in what is today Ethiopia or Somalia. Look at the map on page 86. Find the place where the kingdom of Punt is believed to have been located.

The huge caravan of scribes, soldiers, artists, and attendants set off along a dusty road that led east to the Red Sea. There they loaded their cargo onto five sleek ships for the long journey south.

When they finally arrived in Punt, the ships were welcomed by the king and queen. Hatshepsut's scribes then displayed the jewelry, papyrus, and bronze weapons the Egyptians had brought to trade. In exchange the pharaoh received gold, perfume, ivory, leopard skins, and even live apes. Hatshepsut's traders also received rare incense trees. Incense trees produce a perfumelike smell.

After touring the kingdom of Punt, the Egyptians began to prepare for their return home. Scribes carefully recorded the exact numbers of goods loaded aboard the ships. Then the members of the expedition climbed aboard. They also brought with them several leaders from Punt who wanted to visit Egypt, which they knew as Khmet, to meet Pharaoh Hatshepsut. The expedition had lasted two years.

Craftworkers made beautiful jewelry (above) and other items. Hatshepsut (right) organized trade of such objects.

Infographic

Treasures of an Ancient Tomb

West of ancient Thebes, under the piercing blue sky and scorching sun of the Egyptian desert, steep cliffs plunge into a rocky valley. This is the Valley of the Kings, resting place of 30 New Kingdom pharaohs.

One of the pharaohs buried in the valley was a very young man. He ruled Egypt from the time he was about 9 years old until he died at about age 19. This pharaoh, Tutankhamun (too tahng KAH mun), is best-known today for his magnificent tomb.

Tutankhamun's tomb remained untouched for over 3,000 years. It was finally found in 1922 by two British archaeologists, Howard Carter and Lord Carnarvon. Fabulous treasures from the tomb tell a great deal about ancient Egyptian trade and values. The beautiful materials and crafting of the artifacts also show just how rich Egypt had become in the New Kingdom.

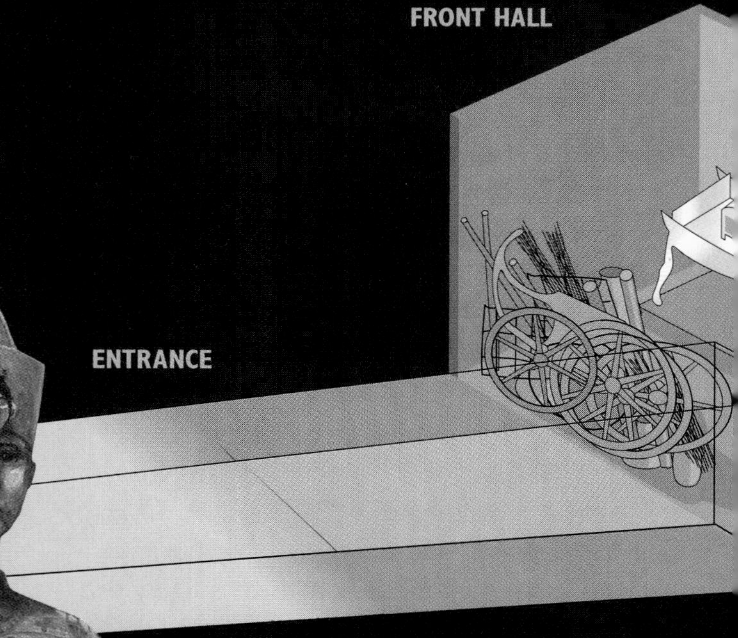

FRONT HALL

ENTRANCE

Among the artifacts found in the tomb were more than 300 articles of Tutankhamun's clothing. The clothes are teaching archaeologists much about how ancient Egyptians really looked. For example, ancient Egyptian "underwear" was a triangle-shaped piece of cloth tied around the waist. Since the only fasteners used in ancient Egypt were string ties, the young king probably had to adjust his clothing constantly.

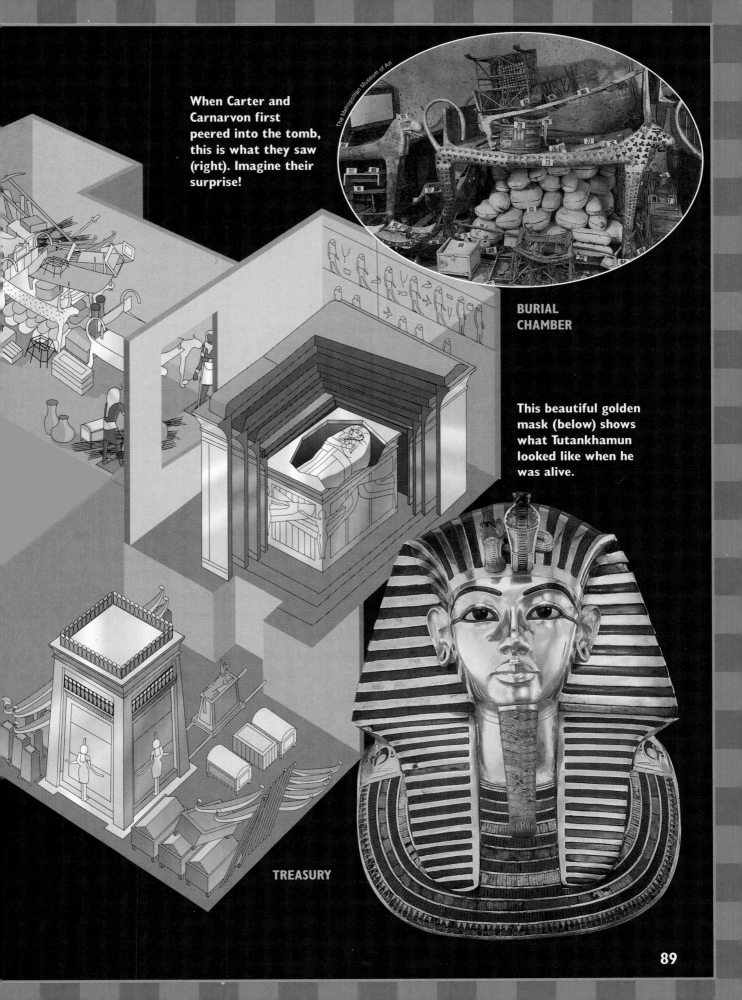

When Carter and Carnarvon first peered into the tomb, this is what they saw (right). Imagine their surprise!

The Metropolitan Museum of Art

BURIAL CHAMBER

This beautiful golden mask (below) shows what Tutankhamun looked like when he was alive.

TREASURY

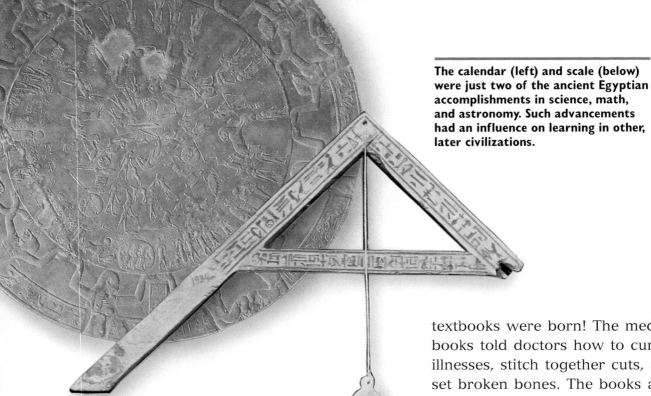

The calendar (left) and scale (below) were just two of the ancient Egyptian accomplishments in science, math, and astronomy. Such advancements had an influence on learning in other, later civilizations.

MOVING IDEAS

In the time of the Egyptian empire, trade goods were not the only things that moved from place to place. Ideas and skills spread too.

You have already read how the Egyptians learned about new weapons from their old enemy, the Hyksos. Other cultures, in turn, learned from Egypt. Egyptian understanding of medicine, mathematics, and astronomy became famous in other countries. Records tell of a king in Lebanon who became sick. He insisted on being treated only by an Egyptian doctor.

Medicine in Egypt

Most Egyptian doctors were actually priests who learned their skills in temple schools. The storehouse of medical knowledge in temple schools was vast and old. For thousands of years priests had noted different kinds of illnesses and injuries and what worked best in treating them. When writing was invented, scribes wrote down this knowledge. The world's first medical textbooks were born! The medical books told doctors how to cure illnesses, stitch together cuts, and set broken bones. The books also explained how to "measure the heart" to see if it was beating too quickly or slowly. Do you know how to measure your own pulse?

Many ancient Egyptian cures centered around treatments that are no longer used. Many other cures, however, introduced ingredients that we still use today. Chamomile, an herb used to make tea, was used to calm upset stomachs. Moldy bread was often placed on wounds. This sounds terrible until we remember that modern antibiotics, or germ-killing drugs, are often made from certain kinds of molds!

Math and Science

Along with medicine, Egyptian priests knew a great deal about mathematics. They developed the mathematical rules needed in building the pyramids, for example.

The priest-scientists also used their knowledge of math to understand the stars. Without telescopes, Egyptians identified five of the solar system's planets, which they called the "stars that know no rest." The mysterious darkness of eclipses did not scare priests. They had figured out that such events were just "meetings of the Sun and Moon."

WHY IT MATTERS

These ideas and others spread throughout the Egyptian empire. In chapters to come you will learn how Egyptian culture influenced other civilizations.

The creation of an empire made Egypt one of the largest civilizations the world had ever known. With resources gained through new territories and trade, Egypt also became incredibly rich. Pharaoh Tutankhamun's tomb has taught archaeologists much about the empire's riches. In the next lesson you will learn how the growth of the empire affected everyday life.

How Many Days Off Is That?

How did ancient Egyptians invent a 365-day calendar?

They based the calendar on the yearly rising and setting of a star named Sirius. Each year Sirius shines in the sky for about 295 nights. Then the star disappears for 70 days. On the day it reappeared in the sky—just before the Nile began flooding—the Egyptians celebrated the start of a new year.

The Egyptian calendar was broken into 12 months of 30 days each. How many "leftover" days did Egyptians have as holidays each year?

✓/ Reviewing Facts and Ideas

SUM IT UP

- Trade and war helped to link Egypt with its neighbors in the Sahara, Nubia, western Asia, and the Mediterranean.

- Egypt became an empire when it conquered Nubia, Syria, and Lebanon. These new lands gave Egypt a wealth of new resources upon which to draw.

- Pharaoh Hatshepsut expanded trade to a region of eastern Africa called Punt.

- The discovery of Tutankhamun's tomb in 1922 yielded hundreds of New Kingdom artifacts.

- The Egyptians' knowledge of medicine, math, and science became famous among their neighbors. Hyksos skills in metalworking became part of life in Egypt.

THINK ABOUT IT

1. Why were Egypt's leaders interested in conquering Nubia?

2. When was Tutankhamun's tomb discovered? What did archaeologists find there?

3. **FOCUS** In what ways was ancient Egypt a rich civilization?

4. **THINKING SKILL** Think about the different ways Egypt "grew" during the New Kingdom. What *effects* did this growth have on Egypt? How did Egypt affect its neighbors?

5. **GEOGRAPHY** Use the map on page 86 to trace an outline of Egypt and its trading partners during the New Kingdom. Then write in the resources of each territory.

GEOGRAPHYSKILLS

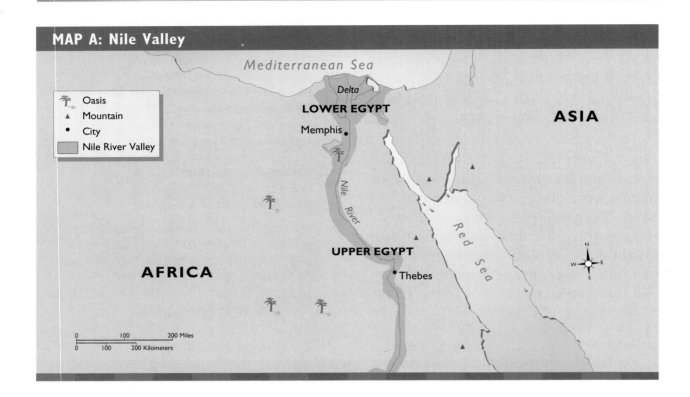

Legend:
- Oasis
- Mountain
- City
- Nile River Valley

Mediterranean Sea

Delta

LOWER EGYPT

Memphis

ASIA

Nile River

Red Sea

UPPER EGYPT

AFRICA

Thebes

0   100   200 Miles
0   100   200 Kilometers

Using Maps at Different Scales

VOCABULARY

scale
small-scale map
large-scale map

WHY THE SKILL MATTERS

As the Egyptian empire grew during the New Kingdom, so did the new capital city at Thebes. Beautiful palaces sprang up along the banks of the Nile. More than a dozen massive temples were built in the surrounding desert to honor gods and pharaohs. Throughout the New Kingdom, Thebes was a symbol of the power of the pharaohs.

Mapmakers can show Thebes up close or in relation to the rest of Egypt. Mapmakers can do this with any other place on Earth by using different map scales. A map scale is a unit of measure, such as an inch, used to represent a distance on Earth.

USING THE SKILL

Map scales can be large or small. Mapmakers use small-scale maps to give viewers the "big picture" of a place. Large-scale maps provide more details about smaller areas. Of course, the real distances on Earth stay the same! Both types of maps are useful, however. Depending on the kind of information needed, you might use one or both types.

Look at Map A. On this small-scale map, one inch stands for 200 miles. Compare this map with Map B, on the next page. Map B shows a smaller area and more details than Map A. Because one inch represents different distances on the two maps, they have different scales. What distance does one inch stand for on Map B?

Suppose you wanted to figure out how to get from Tutankhamun's tomb to Hatshepsut's temple. First, you need to decide which map to use. Which map shows the detail you need? As you can see, Map B, a large-scale map, better shows the detailed information of a small area. Now measure the distance using the map's scale.

TRYING THE SKILL

Suppose that you are writing a book about places near Thebes. Use the Helping Yourself box to answer these questions. Which map would you use to find the oasis, or watered area within a desert, nearest to Thebes? Find the Red Sea. How far is ancient Egypt's capital, Thebes, from the Red Sea? Which type of map gives a "big picture" of this place?

HELPING Yourself

- **A map's scale is a unit of measure that relates distance on the map to distance on Earth.**
- **Maps use different scales to show places up close or at great distances from each other.**
- **Remember that large-scale maps measure distance in *smaller* units. Small-scale maps measure distance in *larger* units.**

REVIEWING THE SKILL

1. What are the differences between small-scale and large-scale maps?
2. From which map could you find the width of the Nile Delta region?
3. About how wide did the Nile River become near Thebes? Which map gave you the answer to that question?
4. How might using large- and small-scale maps help you in planning a trip?

MAP B: Thebes, c. 1100 B.C.

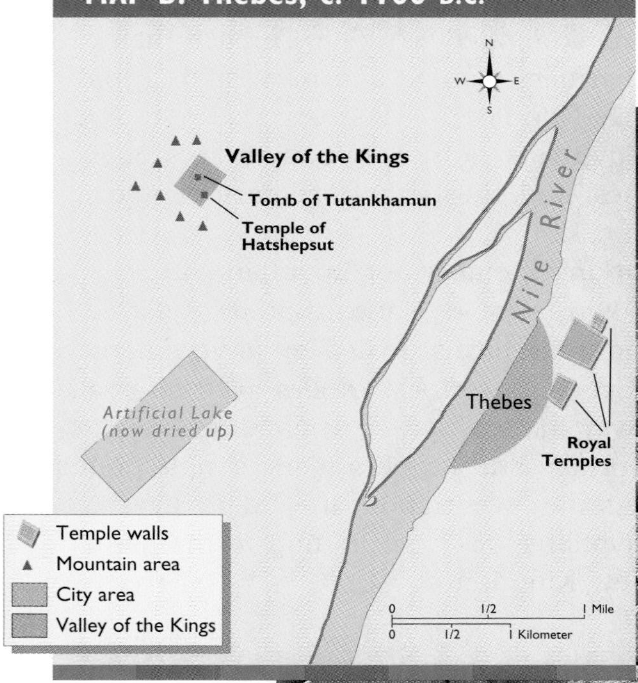
N
W
E
S
Valley of the Kings
Tomb of Tutankhamun
Temple of Hatshepsut
Nile River
Thebes
Royal Temples
Artificial Lake (now dried up)
Temple walls
Mountain area
City area
Valley of the Kings
0
1/2
1 Mile
0
1/2
1 Kilometer

Huge temples, like this one for Hatshepsut, were built to honor Egyptian gods and pharaohs.

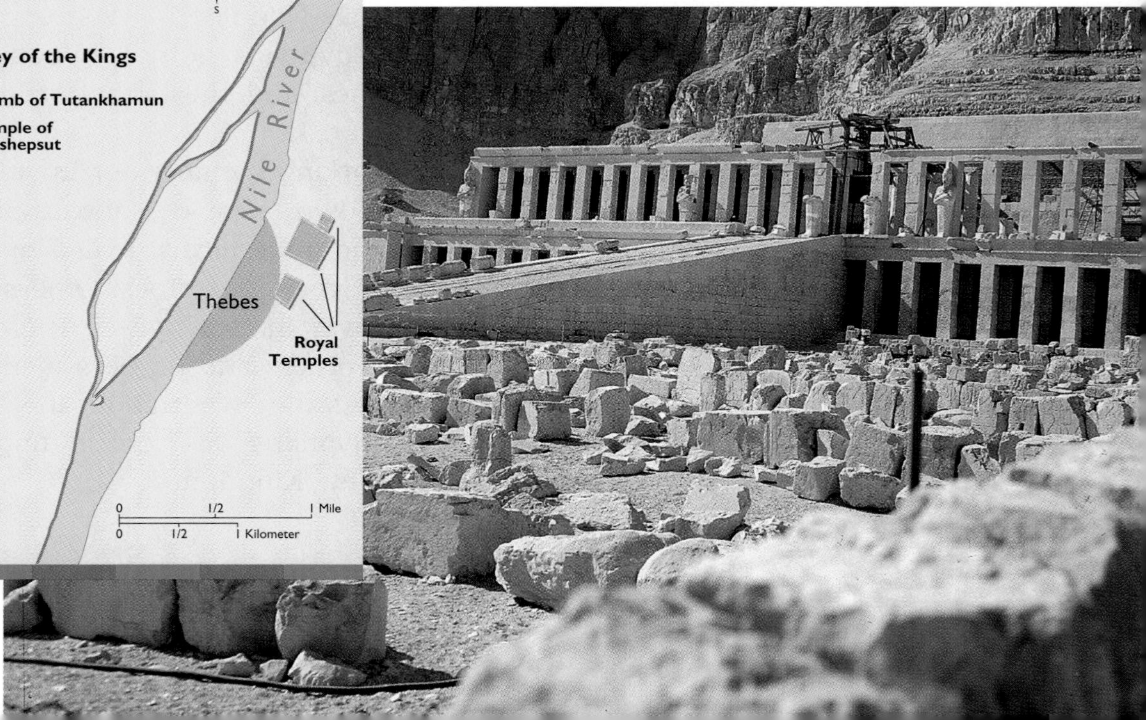

The Granger Collection

DAILY LIFE IN ANCIENT EGYPT

Focus Activity

READ TO LEARN
How did people of the New Kingdom live and work?

VOCABULARY
social pyramid
slavery

READ ALOUD

Under the pharaohs of the New Kingdom, Egypt became the largest and most powerful empire in the world. As you have read, the empire spread eastward into western Asia. Egypt also conquered Nubia, to the south. You have also read how Egyptian goods and ideas spread far from the Nile Valley. How did this growing wealth and power affect the ordinary people who lived in the Egyptian empire?

THE BIG PICTURE

While Egypt's armies and traders traveled far and wide, Egyptians at home continued working to make their country strong. Farmers planted and harvested crops between the yearly Nile floods. Weavers made the linen cloth that kept Egyptians clothed. Woodworkers built the plows, benches, and chests that ordinary people used every day.

These hardworking members of Egyptian society rarely had their own farms or shops. Rather, most people worked on huge farms owned by government leaders, army officers, or scribes. Others lived in small houses tucked away in crowded city neighborhoods. There the craftworkers and farmers made simple goods in their homes. As they went about their daily lives, each of these Egyptians was contributing to the great success of the New Kingdom.

A SOCIAL PYRAMID

From the earliest days of Egypt's history, a person's position in society depended on what he or she did for a living. As a result the shape of Egyptian society was similar to that of a pyramid. The most powerful person, the pharaoh, was at the top of this social pyramid. Below the pharaoh ranked government officials, and below them, craftworkers. At the pyramid's base were farmers and captured people who made up the largest part of society.

Egyptians were not the only people who filled the empire's social pyramid. Nubian soldiers made up a large part of the pharaoh's army and police force. Syrian princes joined the ranks of Egypt's government officials. Syrian and Nubian craftworkers worked side by side with Egyptian craftworkers.

Slavery in Egypt

The people at the lowest level of this social pyramid were those who lived under slavery. Slavery is the practice of one person owning another person. When Egypt conquered Nubia and part of western Asia, Egyptians captured prisoners of war and enslaved them. Most of these people were Syrians, though many were Nubians.

Slaves did some of the hardest work that had to be done in Egypt. They worked in the heat of the desert to mine gold in Nubia. They worked alongside free farmers in the flood-waters of the Nile. They dug canals and prepared land for planting. Enslaved people also worked as house servants to wealthy Egyptians.

Egyptians bought enslaved Syrians and Nubians like they did cattle or cloth. One Syrian girl, for example, was sold for the price of four big sacks of grain and a piece of silver. However, enslaved people did have some basic rights in Egypt. They had the right to be treated fairly under the law and even to own property.

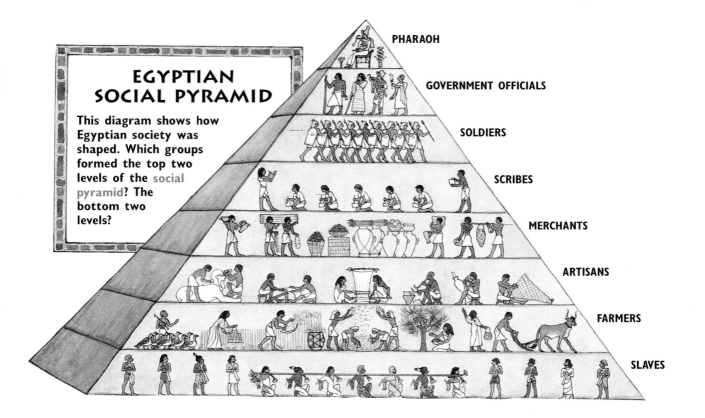

EGYPTIAN SOCIAL PYRAMID

This diagram shows how Egyptian society was shaped. Which groups formed the top two levels of the social pyramid? The bottom two levels?

PHARAOH

GOVERNMENT OFFICIALS

SOLDIERS

SCRIBES

MERCHANTS

ARTISANS

FARMERS

SLAVES

FARMS AND CITIES

During the New Kingdom huge farms and busy cities dotted the shores of the Nile River. Life was very different in the two settings, but some things were similar. In both places ordinary people worked long hours for few rewards. Both in cities and on farms, people also enjoyed simple pleasures, such as celebrating holidays and playing games.

Farm Life

As you have read, most Egyptians lived on big farms owned by powerful people from the top of the social pyramid. These farms were run by loyal scribes. Farmers, craftworkers, and slaves did most of the work. Farms were like small worlds of their own. They produced most of the goods the people living there needed.

Farms bustled with many different kinds of activities. Farmers grew and harvested crops. Herders tended cattle and chickens. Bakers ground wheat from the fields and baked bread. Brewers made beer from wheat and barley, and fishers caught fish in the Nile. Brickmakers shaped bricks from river mud for workers' houses.

As many as half of these products went to the pharaoh as taxes. Most of what remained went to the owner of the farm. Workers and slaves divided the little that was left.

Planting and Harvesting

None of the jobs were easy, but farming was perhaps the hardest of all. To prepare the soil for planting, farmers dug up large fields with cattle-drawn wooden plows and hoes. To

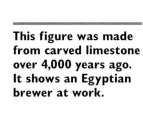

This figure was made from carved limestone over 4,000 years ago. It shows an Egyptian brewer at work.

The Granger Collection

bring water to the fields, farmers dug irrigation canals and hauled water using shadoufs. In addition farmers were often called upon by the government to help build canals, temples, or tombs for the pharaoh. It seemed like a farmer's work never ended!

At harvesttime women, men, and children headed out to the fields to cut, stack, and carry grain. As they worked in the blazing sun, a song leader chanted out songs and everyone sang along. Singing helped to make the time pass more quickly.

Farmers loaded the cut stalks into baskets and took them to threshing, or separating, areas. There, oxen or donkeys were walked over the stalks to separate the grain from the straw. Once again people sang songs, like this one, to make the hard work more fun:

> Strike [sort grain] for yourselves,
> Strike for yourselves, oxen!
> Straw to eat for yourselves
>   and barley for your masters.
> Don't let your hearts grow weary!

Once the grain was separated, girls tossed it into the air using wooden shovels so the wind would blow the remaining straw away. Scribes measured and took away the shares claimed by the pharaoh and the farm owner. Despite the hard work harvest was a time for celebration. During this time special offerings were made to Ra and Rennunet, the gods of the harvest.

Cities in Egypt

In Egypt's cities craftworkers and artists worked under similar conditions. Most lived in small, mud-brick homes crowded along narrow, winding streets. Archaeologists have uncovered the home of one family that lived in Memphis during Tutankhamun's rule. This house tells us much about life in Egypt's cities during the New Kingdom.

A Busy Neighborhood

The house in which this family lived opened onto a busy, noisy alley. The entrance room served as a workshop where the parents made baskets or leather products. Behind the workshop were a small living room with a fireplace and two tiny rooms that may have been bedrooms. A stairway led up to the flat roof—a cool place to sleep on hot summer nights.

The family also had "everyday" chores to do. Every morning the women of the house went down to the local canal to get water. As the sun rose they chatted with friends who also were getting water. They returned home with clay water pots balanced on their heads. Women also had to bake bread. Bread was an important part of the ancient Egyptians' diet.

Each day the family probably went to market to sell their wares. At local markets the family could buy wheat, grapes, olives, fresh fish, beef, pork, and chicken. They may have bought linen cloth from the woman next door. Archaeologists think she made her living as a weaver. A toolmaker also lived nearby. Imagine the clang of his hammer above the sounds of the city.

Townspeople worked hard at their jobs, but they liked to have fun too. Among the artifacts found in the house in Memphis were board games, for moments of free time.

These statues and walls are the remains of a temple in Luxor, Egypt. Note the size of the statues compared to the people standing nearby.

Tomb paintings show many animals living along the Nile River. Tombs also contained mummies of pets, such as dogs and cats.

CHILDREN IN EGYPT

Adults were not the only Egyptians who played games. Children rich and poor loved to spin tops, make cloth dolls, wrestle, run, and play games. Favorite pets included dogs, cats, and monkeys. Young boys and girls often played in the canals that flowed through the farms and villages. The children of pharaohs swam in their own swimming pools!

The amount of time children had to play depended on what their family did for work. Farmers' children had little time to play since they were often needed to help in the fields. Besides working at harvest time, farm children helped

scatter seeds during planting time. Farm children also did daily chores, such as carrying water or feeding the family's many farm animals.

From about age five the children of craftworkers began working alongside their parents. In this way children learned the trade they would work at as adults. At an early age potters' children helped their parents put a smooth finish on their pots. At about age 12 girls studying to become weavers started training. This training could sometimes last up to five years.

Sons of government leaders became assistants to their fathers. They, too, would become leaders one day. Sons of scribes knew that from age ten they would be going to scribe school. That was a skill usually passed down from father to son as well.

WHY IT MATTERS

The Egyptian empire went through great changes around the end of the New Kingdom. New armies from the west and northeast challenged the pharaoh's hold on the empire. The Egyptian army began to lose its firm control over the region. Finally, around 1100 B.C., united Egypt collapsed. The fall of the New Kingdom ended one of the richest civilizations in history.

Still, the "Gift of the Nile" would live on and affect people everywhere for centuries to come. Ancient Egypt's legacy extends even to our own time. Think about this legacy the next time you see a sailor harnessing the wind. You may think of another Egyptian legacy as you answer the Think About It questions on a sheet of *paper!*

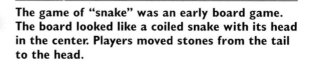

The game of "snake" was an early board game. The board looked like a coiled snake with its head in the center. Players moved stones from the tail to the head.

Reviewing Facts and Ideas

SUM IT UP

- While Egypt became a mighty empire, ordinary people continued to work in much the same ways as they had for thousands of years.
- Enslaved Syrians and Nubians became key workers in Egypt's empire. They worked alongside farmers and craftworkers to produce needed crops and goods.
- Most farmers worked on large farms owned by powerful families.
- Most people in Egypt's towns and cities lived in crowded neighborhoods and crafted goods for a living.

THINK ABOUT IT

1. How did Egypt's social pyramid shape life in the New Kingdom?

2. How did the growth of Egypt's empire play a role in the growth of slavery along the Nile? How did enslaved people add to the empire's economy?

3. **FOCUS** What was everyday life like for ancient Egyptians of the New Kingdom?

4. **THINKING SKILL** Make a *conclusion* about the variety of goods available in ancient Egyptian cities. What evidence can you find in the lesson to support your conclusion?

5. **WRITE** Suppose you are a scribe in ancient Thebes. Write a letter to the owner of a large farm. Tell him or her what goods to send to your city.

CHAPTER 4 REVIEW

Major Events

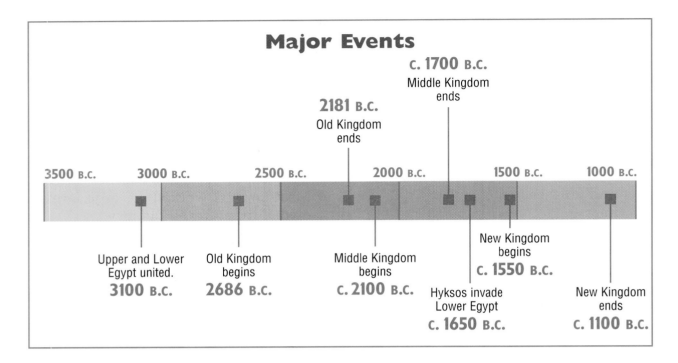

c. 1700 B.C.
Middle Kingdom ends

2181 B.C.
Old Kingdom ends

3500 B.C.　3000 B.C.　2500 B.C.　2000 B.C.　1500 B.C.　1000 B.C.

Upper and Lower Egypt united.
3100 B.C.

Old Kingdom begins
2686 B.C.

Middle Kingdom begins
c. 2100 B.C.

Hyksos invade Lower Egypt
c. 1650 B.C.

New Kingdom begins
c. 1550 B.C.

New Kingdom ends
c. 1100 B.C.

THINKING ABOUT VOCABULARY

Number a sheet of paper from 1 to 10. Decide whether the underlined word in each of the following statements correctly completes the sentence. If the word is correct, write **C** beside the number. If the word is incorrect, write **I** and then write the word that completes the sentence.

delta	hieroglyphics	slavery
economy	irrigation	unification
empire	scale	
expedition	scribe	

1. Irrigation is the joining of parts into one.
2. Slavery is the owning of one person by another.
3. A scribe is a writer of records, letters, and contracts.
4. An empire is the flat, fertile land made of silt left behind as a river drains into a larger body of water.
5. The watering of land by means of canals or pipes is called scale.

6. An economy is the way people manage money and resources.
7. Delta is the ancient Egyptian system of writing.
8. A group of lands or peoples ruled by one government is called an expedition.
9. Hieroglyphics is a unit of measure used on a map to represent a distance.
10. A group of people who go on a trip for a set reason is called a unification.

THINKING ABOUT FACTS

1. What was the role of the Nile River in the development of Egyptian civilization?
2. How did its first pharaoh unify Egypt?
3. How has the Rosetta Stone helped historians to understand Egypt's past?
4. Where did Egypt get its slaves? Who were above slaves on the Egyptian social pyramid?
5. Look at the time line above. How many years after Egypt was united did the Middle Kingdom begin?

THINK AND WRITE

WRITING A LIST
Make a list of three things about ancient Egypt that you think mark it as an important civilization.

WRITING AN EXPLANATION
Explain how the shape of Egyptian society was similar to that of a pyramid. Then describe the groups that made up the Egyptian social pyramid.

WRITING A PARAGRAPH OF ANALYSIS
Write a paragraph about the effect of the Nile River on ancient Egyptian civilization. Tell about the problems the Nile caused and what people did to solve them.

APPLYING GEOGRAPHY SKILLS

USING MAPS AT DIFFERENT SCALES
1. What is meant by the term *scale*?
2. What does a small-scale map show?
3. What does a large-scale map show?
4. Which kind of map can show the most information? How is that possible? Explain.
5. What are the advantages of knowing how to use maps at different scales?

Summing Up the Chapter

Copy the main-idea pyramid below on a separate piece of paper. Then review the chapter to find at least two pieces of information that support each part of the main idea. Add these to the bottom of the pyramid. When you have filled in the pyramid, use it to write a paragraph titled "How did the ancient Egyptians create their complex civilization?"

Ancient Egypt

Ancient Egyptians used their environment.

Organization helped the Egyptians to unite.

CHAPTER 5

Ancient Mesopotamia

THINKING ABOUT HISTORY AND GEOGRAPHY

Around 4000 B.C. farmers living between the Tigris and Euphrates rivers built canals to try to control flooding. They also built cities and developed a system of writing. Eventually, a strong ruler, Sargon, united the region into a kingdom called Sumer. Much later Hammurabi conquered Sumer and wrote a code of laws. The movement of the Hebrews into Canaan led to the development of Judaism.

AFRICA

4000 B.C.	3000 B.C.	2300 B.C.
MESOPOTAMIA	**UR**	**KISH**
Farmers build irrigation ditches to control river floods	Schools are built in Sumer to teach writing	Sargon unites Sumer

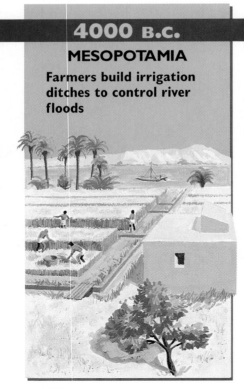

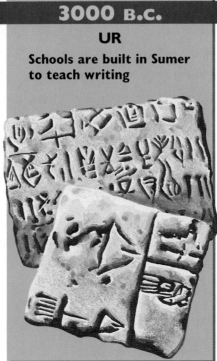

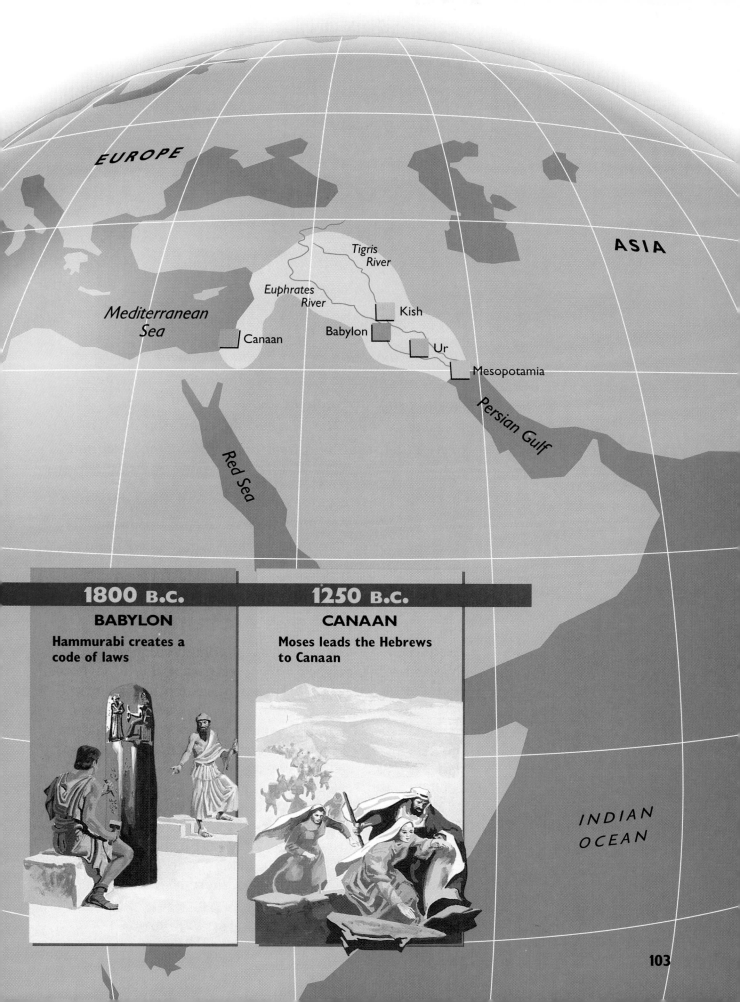

EUROPE

ASIA

Tigris
River

Euphrates
River

Kish

Mediterranean
Sea

Babylon

Canaan

Ur

Mesopotamia

Persian Gulf

Red Sea

INDIAN
OCEAN

1800 B.C.

BABYLON

Hammurabi creates a code of laws

1250 B.C.

CANAAN

Moses leads the Hebrews to Canaan

GEOGRAPHY OF THE FERTILE CRESCENT

Focus Activity

READ TO LEARN
In what ways did two great rivers affect life in this region?

VOCABULARY
plateau
drought

PLACES
Fertile Crescent
Tigris River
Euphrates River
Mesopotamia

READ ALOUD

"For six days and seven nights the wind blew, flood and tempest [storm] overwhelmed the land; when the seventh day arrived, the tempest [and] flood . . . blew themselves out. The sea became calm, the . . . wind grew quiet, the flood held back. . . . Silence reigned, for all mankind had returned to clay."

These words come from an ancient western Asian story about a flood that destroyed most of humanity. Ancient stories like this one later influenced people all around the world.

THE BIG PICTURE

Around 4000 B.C. Egyptian farm communities were growing along the Nile River in Africa. Another civilization was also developing in a vast region to the northeast. This region, in western Asia, was later called the Fertile Crescent. A crescent shape looks like a quarter moon. Find the Fertile Crescent on the map on the next page. It covers the present-day countries of Iraq, Syria, Lebanon, and Israel.

Much of this land was either rocky mountains or desert. Parts of the Fertile Crescent, however, were lush and green. Two rivers, the Tigris (TĪ grihs) and the Euphrates (yoo FRAY teez), made life in these areas possible. Like the Nile in Egypt, these rivers affected the people living along the banks. As you can see from the story above, the rivers' effects were not always positive.

BETWEEN TWO RIVERS

The region between the Tigris and the Euphrates is known as Mesopotamia (mes uh puh TAY mee uh). In Greek, *Mesopotamia* means "Land Between Two Rivers." This area is now known as Iraq. Mesopotamia included several types of physical regions. Follow the course of the two rivers on the map. Let's see how Mesopotamia's northern and southern regions differ.

From Mountains to the Sea

Both the Tigris and Euphrates rivers begin in the snow-capped Taurus Mountains of what is today Turkey. The rivers rush down narrow canyons to the valleys below. Then the Tigris and Euphrates reach the plateau (pla TOH) of present-day northern Iraq. A plateau is an area of elevated flatland. In southern Iraq the rivers continue to flow to lower land. Here they make their way to the Persian Gulf.

Flood!

As in Egypt, early communities in Mesopotamia depended on river deposits of silt. Silt made the region a good place for farming. Early farmers had to meet several challenges, though.

Mesopotamia's yearly floods did not come as regularly as those in Egypt. In fact, they often came at just the wrong time for farmers. The Tigris and the Euphrates did not flood during planting season, when dry fields needed to be softened and prepared for new growth. Instead, the floods often burst through fields just as crops were about to be harvested. Such deadly floods cost not only crops, but lives and homes as well.

Farmers had to protect their fields from flood damage. They also had to keep their crops watered in the hot, dry climate. Southern Mesopotamia rarely received more than a few sprinkles of rain each year. Droughts, or long periods of dry weather, were a constant threat to farmers and their crops in southern Mesopotamia.

Northern Mesopotamia, in contrast, usually had enough rain to make some farming possible. Yet the rocky earth of the northern plateau had only pockets of fertile soil. The flooding rivers did not leave behind as much silt here in the north as to the south. For this reason southern Mesopotamia became better known for its fertile fields than northern Mesopotamia.

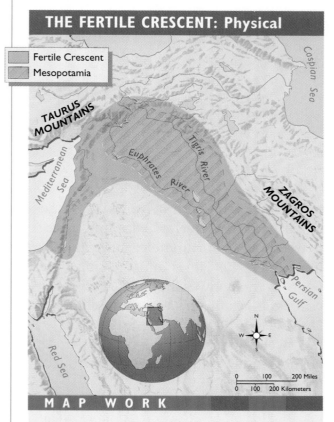

THE FERTILE CRESCENT: Physical

Legend:
Fertile Crescent
Mesopotamia

TAURUS MOUNTAINS · Mediterranean Sea · Euphrates River · Tigris River · Caspian Sea · ZAGROS MOUNTAINS · Persian Gulf · Red Sea

0   100   200 Miles
0   100   200 Kilometers

MAP WORK

The Fertile Crescent extends from the Persian Gulf to the Mediterranean Sea.

1. Is Mesopotamia larger or smaller than the Fertile Crescent?

2. What mountain range lies east of the Fertile Crescent?

WATER CONTROL IN MESOPOTAMIA

Like the ancient Egyptians, Mesopotamians also adapted rivers for farming.

Tigris River

Artificial Lake

Gate

Irrigation Canal

Gate

FROM RIVER TO FIELD

In the fall farmers in southern Mesopotamia needed water to plant and raise new crops. Unfortunately, fall was the time when the Tigris and the Euphrates were at their lowest. Spring was harvest time in ancient Mesopotamia. However, it was also the time when the rivers flooded their banks. Then farmers often got more water than they wanted.

To solve these difficulties, ancient farmers learned to build water-control and irrigation systems. Look at the diagram shown above to see how these systems worked.

Farming in Ancient Mesopotamia

Early Mesopotamian farmers grew many different crops. If you were able to go back there in time, you would see fields of wheat and barley. These were the region's most important crops. You would also see gardens of beans, onions, lettuce, cucumbers, and spice plants. Ancient farmers also grew date palm, apple, and pomegranate trees. Because crops and trees need plenty of water, Mesopotamian farmers often planted them along canal banks.

In the distance, on the edges of village farmland, you might see shepherds caring for sheep and goats. Shepherds also had to ward off attacks from wild animals such as lions and jackals. Sheep were especially prized in Mesopotamia for their milk and wool. Ancient Mesopotamians also valued cattle. Cattle were good work-animals, besides being used for milk, leather, and meat.

WHY IT MATTERS

The region called Mesopotamia is not naturally an inviting place to live. Yet it was here that one of the world's earliest civilizations developed. Water and soil brought by the Tigris and the Euphrates helped to make this civilization possible. Even more important were the farmers of ancient Mesopotamia. These early farmers figured out how to use the two rivers to make the land more fertile.

As in some other early cultures, the farmers of Mesopotamia produced surplus crops. These surpluses allowed for specialization, which in turn led to the growth of towns and cities. The early cities formed a great civilization. As you will see, the legacy of early Mesopotamian civilization reaches even into our own times.

Reviewing Facts and Ideas

SUM IT UP

- Mesopotamia is the region between the Tigris and Euphrates rivers. It is divided into a rugged plateau to the north and fertile plains to the south.

- Like the Nile River, the Tigris and the Euphrates flooded each year. These floods brought water and silt to Mesopotamia.

- Unlike those in Egypt, floods in Mesopotamia were often destructive and badly timed for farmers.

- Mesopotamian farmers used canal systems to control dangerous flooding, making their land productive.

THINK ABOUT IT

1. What were the main crops grown in ancient Mesopotamia? What other foods were grown there?

2. Why was the timing of spring floods so important to farmers in ancient Mesopotamia? What could happen to crops if the floods came a little earlier than expected?

3. **FOCUS** In what ways did Mesopotamian farmers adapt to and change their environment?

4. **THINKING SKILL** Suppose you lived in ancient Mesopotamia. Write a poem about the Tigris and Euphrates rivers from a farmer's _point of view_.

5. **GEOGRAPHY** Where is the Fertile Crescent located?

The British Museum

4000 B.C.　3500 B.C.　689 B.C.　A.D. 1

SUMER AND BABYLON

READ ALOUD

This is an ancient Mesopotamian riddle. See if you can solve it.

> *"He whose eyes are not open enters it.*
> *He whose eyes are wide open comes out of it.*
> *What is it?*
> *The solution is: It's a school."*

How might school "open your eyes"?

THE BIG PICTURE

You have read about southern Mesopotamia's large surpluses. These allowed an increasing number of people to live as skilled workers in cities. By 3000 B.C.—around the time that Menes unified Egypt—about a dozen small cities dotted southern Mesopotamia. This region was also known as Sumer (SOO mur).

The people of Sumer's cities valued their independence highly. They often fought against being ruled by other cities. However, all Sumerians shared a rich cultural heritage. They worked hard to control the Tigris and Euphrates rivers to produce food crops. They worshiped similar gods. The Sumerians made some of the world's first wheeled vehicles and sailboats. They also made simple machines, such as pottery wheels. In addition, early Sumerians explored new ideas in math and science.

The invention of writing helped to bring the ancient cities together. Laws, letters, records, stories, instructions, riddles, and proverbs could all be widely shared, thanks to cuneiform (kyoo NEE uh fawrm). Cuneiform was the system of writing invented in Sumer.

Focus Activity

READ TO LEARN
What changes did the development of writing bring to ancient Mesopotamia?

VOCABULARY
cuneiform
city-state
ziggurat
polytheism
code of law

PEOPLE
Sargon
Hammurabi

PLACES
Sumer
Babylonia

A SYSTEM OF WRITING

Some historians believe that cuneiform was first developed to record farm surpluses. Ancient Sumerians used sharp reeds to scratch the records into wet clay tablets. The dried tablets became permanent records.

In 3500 B.C.—the time of the oldest tablets that have been found—cuneiform symbols looked like the things they described. Over time, however, Sumerian scribes developed faster ways to write. They simplified their figures so they could be formed more quickly. Look at the chart on this page for examples.

About 500 signs were regularly used! These signs could also be combined to form more complex words. Like Egyptian hieroglyphs, cuneiform signs represented sounds and ideas as well as objects. The sign for "arrow," called *ti* (TEE), looked like this: ➤◁◁. Since *ti* also meant "life," the symbol could stand for this word too.

School in Sumer

As in ancient Egypt few people could write. Even kings usually could not. It was an honor to be able to go to school and learn to be a scribe. Boys and, very rarely, girls spent years studying in local schools. First they learned how to make clay tablets and reed "pens." Then students practiced over and over how to write the basic signs of cuneiform. Scribes in Sumer also had to study mathematics so they would be able to keep accurate records.

Trained scribes could and did write almost anything. They even wrote love letters for people and sealed them in clay "envelopes"! Scribes also recorded stories, laws, and songs.

The sturdy ancient tablets have survived thousands of years. They have helped historians to piece together a detailed picture of early Mesopotamia.

Scribes (left) filled an important role in ancient Sumer. They were record keepers, since most people could not write.

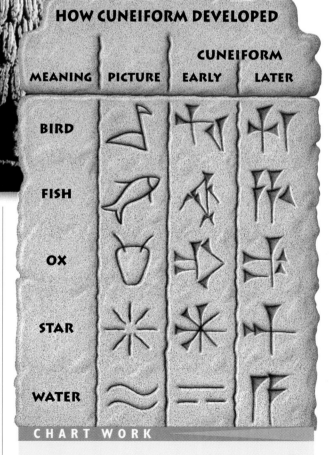

HOW CUNEIFORM DEVELOPED

MEANING	PICTURE	CUNEIFORM EARLY	LATER
BIRD			
FISH			
OX			
STAR			
WATER			

CHART WORK

This chart shows how some Sumerian symbols changed over time.

The photo on page 108 shows a **cuneiform** symbol found on this chart. What is this symbol? Is it early or later cuneiform?

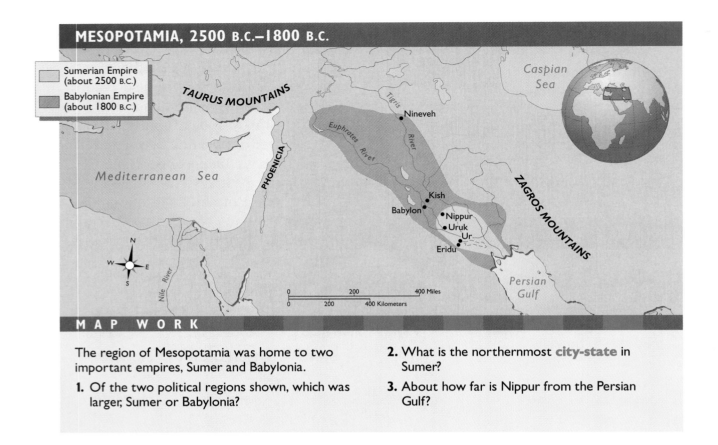

MESOPOTAMIA, 2500 B.C.–1800 B.C.

Sumerian Empire (about 2500 B.C.)
Babylonian Empire (about 1800 B.C.)

TAURUS MOUNTAINS

Caspian Sea

Mediterranean Sea

PHOENICIA

Nineveh

Euphrates River

Tigris River

ZAGROS MOUNTAINS

Kish

Babylon

Nippur

Uruk

Ur

Eridu

Persian Gulf

Nile River

0   200   400 Miles
0   200   400 Kilometers

MAP WORK

The region of Mesopotamia was home to two important empires, Sumer and Babylonia.

1. Of the two political regions shown, which was larger, Sumer or Babylonia?

2. What is the northernmost **city-state** in Sumer?

3. About how far is Nippur from the Persian Gulf?

CITY-STATES OF SUMER

Cuneiform writing first appeared in about 3500 B.C. Over the next thousand years, Sumerian life centered around the **city-states** of southern Mesopotamia. A city-state is a self-governing city that also governs surrounding villages. Find the city-states Ur, Uruk, and Eridu on the map.

Through cuneiform we know about an early Sumerian mythical hero named Gilgamesh (GIHL guh mesh). Read the following passage about Gilgamesh. Think about what made him a hero to the ancient Sumerians.

The great Gilgamesh was one who knew everything. He had seen all there was to see and done all there was to do. He had built the walls of the city, Uruk. Look at its brickwork! Nobody could build a better wall. It was made of copper and burnt brick, and was wide enough to walk upon.

Gilgamesh was part god and part [man], and as strong as an ox. He was the strongest in the land, and the best fighter.

Living in a Sumerian City

City-states often went to war to gain control of precious river water. For this reason strong walls were built to protect against attack. Large gateways in city walls allowed people and goods to get into and out of cities. City gates were also where people gathered to buy fresh vegetables and other goods. Goods were brought to the cities by farmers and traders.

The king's palace could be seen from almost everywhere in a city. The palace was where a city-state's planning and decision-making took place. Kings served as generals, judges, and canal overseers. Unlike Egyptian pharaohs, though, Sumerian kings were not considered to be gods.

Religion in Ancient Sumer

In the center of most ancient Sumerian cities stood a towering mud-brick building. That building was a **ziggurat** (ZIHG oo rat). A ziggurat was a large building with a temple on its peak.

Since these temples were located in the center of cities, historians believe that religion was very important in Sumer. Like the Egyptians', Sumerians' religious beliefs involved **polytheism**. Polytheism is belief in many gods and goddesses. Each city-state had a special god or goddess. That god or goddess was worshiped at the city's ziggurat. People also worshiped other gods and goddesses at home. One favorite was Ishtar, the goddess of love and war. Another was Enki, the god of water.

Uniting the City-States

In time the city-states were united under one ruler—**Sargon**, king of the city-state Kish. Sargon rose to power about 2300 B.C. His rule began a new period in Mesopotamia's history. Sargon expanded his empire to the northern end of the Fertile Crescent, in what is present-day Syria.

Along the Mediterranean Sea, Sumerians traded with the ancient seafaring people called Phoenicians (fih NEE shunz). The Phoenicians also traded with merchants from Egypt. Phoenicians sent wine and timber to Sargon's city-states. In return they received Mesopotamian farm products and other goods.

Cuneiform writing spread through the Fertile Crescent along with trade goods. Other cultures began using cuneiform to write out their own languages. Because cuneiform was used throughout his empire, Sargon could send instructions and govern over great distances.

Sargon, king of Kish, led the world's first empire. Ziggurats (below) dominated most Sumerian cities around 2000 B.C.

THE RISE OF BABYLON

Sargon's rule lasted about 56 years, until about 2279 B.C. Then the city-states rebelled against the empire. Almost 500 years would pass before another empire controlled Mesopotamia.

During those years a group of people from the Syrian desert moved into northern Mesopotamia. They created a small kingdom centered around a city-state called Babylon.

A Northern Empire

About 1800 B.C. Babylon's king, Hammurabi (hah moo RAH bee), began a drive to gain control over the old city-states of Sumer. Hammurabi and the Babylonians dammed key parts of the Euphrates. This gave them the power to cut off the flow of water or cause terrible floods downstream. Next, Hammurabi's armies attacked the weakened Sumerians. Hammurabi also won control of the city-states around Babylon. He created a huge empire. Find Babylon and the Babylonian empire on the map on page 110.

The empire of Babylonia under Hammurabi became rich and powerful. Shipments of silver, copper, timber, and wine poured into Babylonia. These goods came from people in what are today Turkey, Iran, and Syria. In exchange people in Babylonia sent grain and fruits. Servants even floated ice from distant mountains down rivers to refrigerate food and drink.

Under Hammurabi Mesopotamia's center of power shifted north to Babylon. Yet many Sumerian traditions remained. Babylonians used cuneiform to communicate in writing. In fact the world's first dictionaries were created so Babylonians could adopt Sumerian culture and language.

This dagger and sheath are typical of the weapons used by soldiers in Mesopotamia. The mosaic (below), known as the Standard of Ur, was found in a king's grave in the city of Ur.

A CODE OF LAW

When Hammurabi gained control of Sumer, he set out to act as the Sumerian kings had done. He oversaw projects to build and repair canals. Hammurabi also acted as a judge. He used some of the laws that Sumerians had written down hundreds of years before him.

In 1901 archaeologists found a large stone pillar from ancient Babylon. The pillar was inscribed with over 200 laws written in cuneiform. Imagine historians' excitement when they realized that the laws had actually been formed by Hammurabi himself. They had been written almost 4,000 years before they were discovered!

The Code of Hammurabi is one of the world's oldest codes of law. A code of law is a written set of laws that apply to everyone under a government.

The pillar shows that slavery existed in Babylonia and that not everyone was treated equally under the law. Copies of the pillar were also found outside of Babylon. This suggests that Hammurabi meant for his laws to be followed throughout the empire. Cuneiform made this possible. How important is writing in our own civilization? What other ways do we have to communicate over long distances?

Read the following excerpt from the Code of Hammurabi. What does it tell you about what justice meant to Hammurabi and other Babylonians?

Excerpt from
The Code of Hammurabi, c. 1800 B.C.

[So] that the strong may not [abuse] the weak, to give justice to the orphan and the widow, I have inscribed my precious words. . . .

If a Freeman has put out the eye of another Freeman, they shall put out his eye.

If he breaks the bone of another Freeman, they shall break his bone.

If he puts out the eye of a Poor Man, or breaks the bone of a Poor Man, he shall pay 1 mina [17.5 ounces] of silver. If he puts out the eye of the Slave of another Freeman . . . , he shall pay half his price.

THE "NEW" BABYLONIA

After Hammurabi died, about 1750 B.C., Babylonia began to fall apart. The city-states in the south rebelled again, much as they had against Sargon. Powerful armies from the mountains to the north and east began taking the empire's territory. Throughout western Asia new powers overthrew old ones.

During this time of change, however, Babylon remained one of the most powerful cities in the Fertile Crescent. Just as Hammurabi had used Sumerian ideas, new rulers respected the history of "Old Babylonia." They worshiped its gods and passed down its legends— many of which had begun in Sumer.

In 689 B.C. Babylon was destroyed by powerful rulers from a northern Mesopotamian city called Nineveh. About 60 years later the Babylonians were able to rebuild Babylon and make it the capital of an even stronger empire.

Links to LANGUAGE ARTS

What Did You Call Me?!

Words are often "borrowed" when different cultures come into contact. Some historians think modern English may have been affected by ancient Mesopotamian languages! On an ancient cuneiform tablet, one student insults another, calling him a "clever fool." Ancient Greeks probably borrowed the phrase for their compound word *sophos-moros*—clever fool. Modern English takes the word from the Greeks. When you reach your second year of high school, you will be known as a *sophomore!*

Most dictionaries show how some English words came from other languages. Look up the English meaning of *sophomore*. What are the meanings and origin of *cuneiform*?

The "New" Babylon

The new Babylon soon became the world's largest city. It grew famous for its great beauty and technology. Two massive walls and a moat now protected Babylon. The city was split in two by the Euphrates River but was connected by a movable bridge and an underwater tunnel! At the center of the city stood a huge ziggurat. It was 200 yards wide and rose 100 yards into the sky. Elsewhere were grid-style streets, sewer and water systems, and three- and four-story homes. Babylon was also known for its marvelous "hanging gardens." Unfortunately, we do not know exactly what they looked like.

Sorrow in Babylon

Not everyone thought of Babylon as a wonderful place. To some who were brought to the great city, Babylon was anything but beautiful and certainly not home. One poet wrote:

> By the rivers of Babylon,
> there we sat,
> sat and wept,
> when we thought of [home].

These newcomers were prisoners. They were brought from what is today Israel.

The carving shows a Sumerian husband and wife. The ruins (above) are all that remain of the ziggurat of Ur. It was dedicated to the storm god, Enlil.

Oriental Institute of Chicago

WHY IT MATTERS

One cuneiform tablet reads:

The gods alone live forever under the divine sun. But as for [humans], their days are numbered. All their activities will be nothing but wind.

It is hard to believe that the ruins of an ancient Mesopotamian city-state were once home to thousands of people. Yet this land was covered with green fields and bustling cities. The people who lived here shared many of the same concerns that we have today.

The ancient Sumerians and Babylonians left records of their civilizations in cuneiform writing. Ideas formed in ancient times—about schools, literature, science, and law—echo into our own time. Despite the ancient scribe's prediction, the legacy of Mesopotamia has not been lost.

The modern countries of the Fertile Crescent are Iraq, Syria, Lebanon, and Israel. Like the ancient empires, these countries are also covered with farms and cities.

SUM IT UP

- Cuneiform probably developed as a way to keep track of farm supplies and surplus. The system was later expanded to communicate more complex ideas as well.

- Mesopotamia was not always unified into a single empire. Both government and religion greatly shaped life on a local level.

- Cuneiform writing helped Sargon, king of Kish, to rule over great distances.

- The rise to power of Hammurabi made Babylon one of the world's richest and most powerful cities in ancient times.

THINK ABOUT IT

1. Why was it an honor to become a scribe in Mesopotamia?

2. How was Egyptian culture similar to the culture of Mesopotamia? How was it different?

3. **FOCUS** How did cuneiform help Sargon to create and rule an empire in Mesopotamia?

4. **THINKING SKILL** Look at the excerpt from the story of Gilgamesh on page 110. *Make conclusions* about what was important in ancient Sumer.

5. **WRITE** Write a one-paragraph response to the laws found in the Code of Hammurabi. How did they protect the people of Babylon?

115

THE WHEEL

How did you get to school this morning? If you did not walk, you probably used a vehicle with wheels. Can you imagine what life would be like if the wheel had never been invented?

Most archaeologists believe that ancient Mesopotamians invented the wheel. Some of the first wheels were used on farm carts and war chariots. Over time, people found other uses for the wheel.

The wheel still plays an important role in transportation. There are wheels turning in machines in our homes and factories, too. You can find them winding the film on a movie projector or spinning a compact disc. The wheel has proven to be one of the most important inventions in human history!

Some of the earliest wheels found were used on Sumerian war chariots like this one. This 6,000-year-old chariot was pulled by a donkey. The solid wood wheels made it very heavy and difficult to steer.

The turning motion of inter-locking wheels, or *gears*, is a key part of many machines. The gears in this watch turn at just the right speeds to keep accurate time. What other machines can you think of that use gears?

The wheel can be put to practical use or it can be used for fun. Originally called a *pleasure wheel*, this ride is named after the man who built the largest one ever for the Chicago World's Fair in 1893: George Ferris.

Countries all over the world have built vast networks of roads and highways. Millions of people travel these roads each day. Bicycles and cars share this street in Beijing, China.

THINKINGSKILLS

Identifying Cause and Effect

VOCABULARY

cause
effect

WHY THE SKILL MATTERS

By about 3000 B.C. Sumerians had built their first city-states on the plains of southern Mesopotamia. At about the same time, craftworkers in what is today Syria learned how to make a useful and beautiful new material. They mixed together and then heated sand and a certain kind of plant ash. In this way they created the world's first known glass.

The development of glass brought many changes in the ways people lived. These changes interest historians, who analyze cause and effect connections. A cause is something that makes something else happen. What happens as a result of a cause is called an effect. Historians study causes and their effects to understand why events happened the way they did.

USING THE SKILL

Now practice tracing a cause, such as the invention of glassmaking, to its effects.

By Hammurabi's time glassmaking was just being introduced in Mesopotamia. As time passed, craftworkers figured out how to make elegant vases and other containers from glass. These beautiful glass products attracted the eyes of the empire's rich people. Remember, up until now they had seen only clay and metal containers.

People began buying the new glass goods and using them. The glass items also became popular outside the empire. They

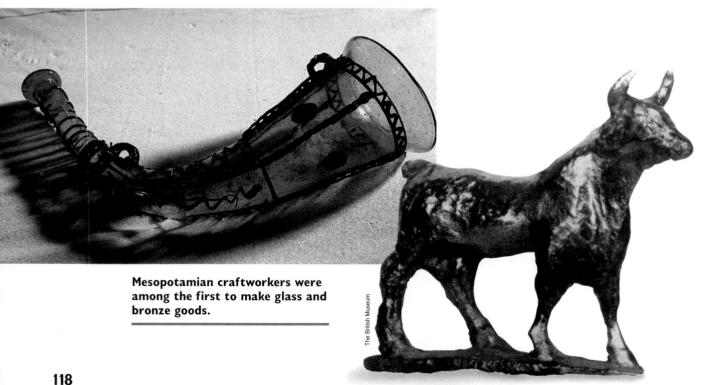

Mesopotamian craftworkers were among the first to make glass and bronze goods.

The British Museum

118

were traded in such faraway places as what are today Iran and Greece. Some historians also think that glassmakers from the Fertile Crescent may have gone to work in Egyptian workshops. There they introduced their skill to Egyptian craftworkers. It is thought that the art of glassmaking spread from Egypt and Mesopotamia to areas in India, Russia, Spain, and China.

Do you see a cause in the above paragraphs? It is the invention of glass in Mesopotamia. One effect, in this case, was the development of different uses for the new material. Another effect was the spread of glassmaking technology to other parts of the world. As you can see, one cause can have more than one effect. It works the other way around too—an effect can have more than one cause.

Can you trace a cause to all of its effects in this example? Try numbering the events in the order in which they happened. The invention of glass happened first—it is a cause. Related events that happened later are effects of that cause.

TRYING THE SKILL

As you read the following passage, look for causes and effects. Refer to the Helping Yourself box for help in finding the connections between events.

Glass was not the only material that craftworkers in ancient Mesopotamia experimented with. Around 2000 B.C. Mesopotamians were among the first in the world to blend copper and tin to make bronze.

HELPING Yourself

- A **cause** makes something else happen. The result of a cause is an **effect.**
- Arrange events in the order in which they happened.
- Look for connections between events.
- Look for clue words, such as *because, since,* and *as a result.* They indicate cause-effect connections.

Bronze brought many changes to life in Mesopotamia. For one thing, bronze was much harder than the copper products that were used until that time. Because it was harder, bronze made better tools and sharper weapons. This improvement in technology was a help to farmers, craftworkers, and soldiers alike.

Molten [melted] bronze was also easier to pour than the metals used earlier. Craftworkers could pour the hot liquid metal into more varied and detailed molds. As a result, these craftworkers were able to make finer arrows, ax-heads, statues, bowls, and other objects.

More and more tin was needed as the demand for products made from bronze increased. Historians believe that traders brought the tin needed to make bronze from distant regions.

How did trade affect Mesopotamia and its neighbors?

REVIEWING THE SKILL

1. What effect did the invention of bronze have on Mesopotamian farming?

2. In what ways did the invention of bronze affect trade between Mesopotamia and its neighbors?

3. Was there any connection between the invention of bronze and the development of the arts in ancient Mesopotamia?

4. How do cause-effect connections help you to understand why things happen the way they do?

Gemäldegalerie Berlin

| 4000 B.C. | 3000 B.C. | 2000 B.C. | 1700 BC. | 586 B.C. | A.D. 1 |

THE BEGINNINGS OF JUDAISM

Focus Activity

READ TO LEARN
How did the writings in the Torah shape Judaism?

VOCABULARY
Judaism
Torah
monotheism
Ten Commandments
Sabbath
Diaspora

PEOPLE
Abraham
Moses

PLACES
Jerusalem

READ ALOUD

"Hear, O Israel! The Lord is our God, the Lord alone." This short passage from the Bible expresses the basis of Jewish religious belief. In this lesson you will read about the great meaning it would have for the ancestors of the Jewish people in the changing world of the Fertile Crescent.

THE BIG PICTURE

Hammurabi ruled the Babylonian empire in the late 1700s B.C. Meanwhile people were on the move throughout the Fertile Crescent. Phoenician port cities along the Mediterranean Sea were expanding their trade with Egypt and cities across the sea. Merchants were traveling along the dusty roads that connected Egypt and Mesopotamia.

Some information about this exciting time comes from a source that millions of people continue to read today. That source is the collection of books known as the Hebrew Bible. Its original language was Hebrew. It has been translated into almost every language on Earth. Its writings are sacred to more than 17 million Jews today. Christians and Muslims also read and honor the Hebrew Bible.

The Hebrew Bible is the Jewish people's record of their history and their religion, which is called Judaism. In this lesson you will follow the Bible's account of Judaism's beginnings.

ABRAHAM OF UR

The first book of the Bible tells of a family that lived in Mesopotamia. This family came from the city-state of Ur. In this city people worshiped the Sumerian moon goddess. However, this family worshiped a different god. The Bible tells about a man named Abraham and his wife Sarah:

The Lord said to Abraham: "Go forth from your native land and from your father's house to the land that I will show you. I will make of you a great nation, and I will bless you. . . ." [So] Abraham took his wife, Sarah . . . and they set out for the land of Canaan.

The Covenant

To reach the land of Canaan from Mesopotamia, the travelers would have set out on the trade routes that linked major cities of the Fertile Crescent. Look at the map on this page to see their route. The journey would have taken months, and it would have been hard to be a stranger in a new place. When Abraham arrived in Canaan, the Bible says that God made a covenant, or special agreement, with him.

I am God Almighty. Walk in My ways and be blameless. I will establish My covenant with you, and I will make you exceedingly numerous. . . . I assign the land you sojourn [rest] in to you and your offspring to come . . . I will be their God.

This covenant is considered by the Jewish people to be the beginning of their history. Later, their descendants would become known as people of Israel, or Israelites, after Abraham's grandson Israel. They also came to be known as Jews.

Going to Egypt

As time passed, the Bible says, Abraham's children and grandchildren prospered as shepherds in Canaan. Then came a time of poor crops and terrible hunger. The people of Israel went to Egypt, where food could be found.

Here the people of Israel were welcomed. As time passed, things changed. "A new king arose over Egypt," the Bible says. This pharaoh "set taskmasters over [the people of Israel] to oppress them with forced labor." Like others in ancient Egypt, the people of Israel had become slaves.

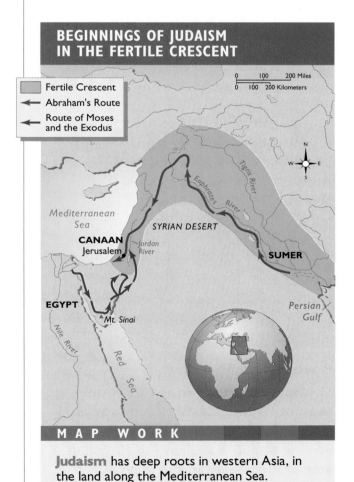

BEGINNINGS OF JUDAISM IN THE FERTILE CRESCENT

Fertile Crescent
Abraham's Route
Route of Moses and the Exodus

0 100 200 Miles
0 100 200 Kilometers

Mediterranean Sea
SYRIAN DESERT
Euphrates River
Tigris River
CANAAN
Jerusalem
Jordan River
SUMER
EGYPT
Persian Gulf
Mt. Sinai
Nile River
Red Sea

MAP WORK

Judaism has deep roots in western Asia, in the land along the Mediterranean Sea.

1. Abraham and Moses both reached which river?

2. Moses' route passed a famous mountain. What is it?

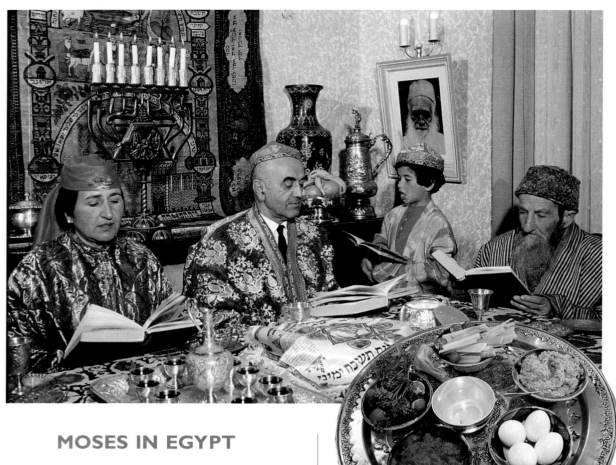

This family celebrates Passover by reading the Bible and sharing a traditional meal. The foods on the plate are symbolic of an ancient story.

MOSES IN EGYPT

Fortunately for the Israelites, a man named **Moses** rose to leadership. According to the Bible, Moses was born to Israelite parents but was adopted as a baby by the pharaoh's daughter. Raised in the royal household, Moses experienced all the wealth and power of Egypt. Yet he would someday become leader and teacher to enslaved Israelites who lived all around him.

Becoming a Prophet

One day, the Bible says, Moses saw an Egyptian beating an Israelite slave. Moses looked around, and seeing no one about, he killed the Egyptian and hid the body in the sand.

Moses was wanted for murder by the pharaoh. He fled to the land of Midian, which was probably in present-day Saudi Arabia. There he remained for years until God called to him,

"Come . . . I will send you to Pharaoh, and you shall free My people, the Israelites, from Egypt."

At first Moses protested, saying, "Please, O Lord, I have never been a man of words. . . . I am slow of speech and slow of tongue." In the end, however, the Bible says, he obeyed God and made the long trek back to Egypt. Moses was now seen as a *prophet,* or a person who speaks for God. Moses walked the halls of the pharaoh's court once again. There he tried to convince the pharaoh to free the Israelite slaves. Moses wanted to lead them to safety.

The Bible describes how Moses, with the help of God, led the Israelite captives from Egypt. To this day Jews celebrate the Passover festival each year to remember their freedom from slavery.

The Torah

According to the Bible, Moses led the Israelites into the wilderness of eastern Egypt. There they wandered for 40 difficult years. Early in their journey the Israelites traveled to a mountain called Mount Sinai. There, the Bible says, God gave Moses five books of laws and teachings. These five books are the first books of the Bible. In Hebrew they are known as the Torah, which comes from the word meaning "to teach."

Some of these laws are very similar to laws that were common in Babylonia. Like the Code of Hammurabi, for example, the Torah also had laws that forbade stealing and hurting others. In one very important way, however, the Torah was different. The God of the Hebrews forbade them to worship any other gods. This belief in only one God became known as monotheism. It set the Israelites apart from the other peoples living in the Fertile Crescent.

Among the laws that God gave to Moses at Mount Sinai were the Ten Commandments. These commandments became the core of the Jewish religion and teachings. In what ways do the Ten Commandments differ from Hammurabi's laws?

The Ten Commandments (Exodus 20:1–14).

I the Lord am your God. . . . You shall have no other gods besides Me.

You shall not make for yourself a sculptured image, or any likeness of what is in the heavens above, or on the earth below. . . . You shall not bow down to them or serve them.

You shall not swear falsely by the name of the Lord your God.

Remember the Sabbath [day of rest] and keep it holy.

Honor your father and your mother.

You shall not murder.

You shall not commit adultery.

You shall not steal.

You shall not bear false witness against your neighbor.

You shall not covet [desire] . . . anything that is your neighbor's.

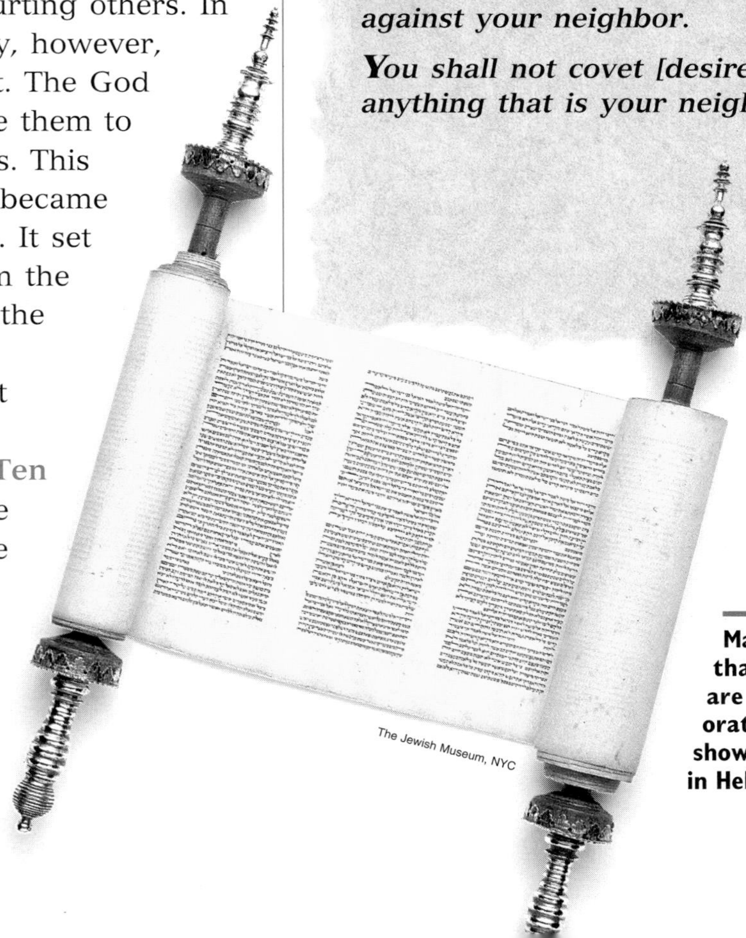

The Jewish Museum, NYC

Many of the scrolls that hold the Torah are beautifully decorated. The Torah shown here is written in Hebrew.

Jerusalem is the capital of Israel and a religious center. Jews gather at the Western Wall to pray.

THE KINGDOM OF ISRAEL

After 40 years in the wilderness, the Israelites prepared to enter Canaan. The Bible says that Moses spoke to his people one last time before he died.

> *This is the Instruction—the laws and the rule—that the Lord your God has commanded me to impart to you . . . so that you, your children, and your children's children may revere [worship] the Lord your God . . . to the end that you may long endure [survive].*

The Bible says that after hearing Moses' final words, the Israelites crossed the Jordan River into the land of Canaan. There they defeated several kings and set up a nation of their own, called Israel. Now the Israelites were not only a people defined by their religious beliefs. They were a nation with a land, as well.

A Nation of Israel

For the people of Israel, the Torah was the basis of life and faith. It commanded people, for example, to "remember the Sabbath, and keep it holy." The Sabbath is the weekly day of rest, prayer, and study. It falls on Saturday. The instructions of the Torah reminded Israelites of their closeness to God. They continue to do so today.

According to the Bible, Israel became a powerful kingdom under the leadership of King David. He made the city of Jerusalem his capital about 1000 B.C. Jerusalem became even more important to Israel when David's son Solomon built a great temple there. Jerusalem became a center of both religious and political life.

Exile to Babylonia

After Solomon's death, about 928 B.C., the kingdom of Israel split into two kingdoms. The northern kingdom, Israel, was conquered by the Assyrians in 721 B.C. The southern kingdom was called Judah. This is where the name Jews comes from. The kingdom of Judah survived until 586 B.C. When Babylonian armies destroyed Jerusalem and Solomon's temple, many Jews were led away to Babylon. This would not be the last time the Jews were exiled, or forced to leave their homeland. The scattering of the Jews to many parts of the world is called the Diaspora (di AS pur uh).

WHY IT MATTERS

Alas!
Lonely sits the city
Once great with people! . . .
Take us back, O Lord, to Yourself,
And let us come back;
Renew our days as of old!

These words from the Bible record the despair felt by the Jews. However, even in the Diaspora, many Jews would continue to live by the Torah. They would also remember the covenant described in the Bible so many lifetimes earlier.

A Jewish boy studies the Torah in preparation for his bar mitzvah. After this ceremony he will be recognized as an adult.

SUM IT UP

- Trade and movement of people in the 1700s B.C. helped link major cities of the Fertile Crescent and Egypt.
- The Bible says Moses led the Israelites out of slavery in Egypt and passed on laws from God regarding how they should live.
- Monotheism—the belief in one God—set the Hebrews apart from other groups around them.
- Sacred writings, called the Torah, form the heart of Judaism.

THINK ABOUT IT

1. What role did Abraham play in the history of Judaism?
2. Why do Jews still celebrate Passover?
3. **FOCUS** How were Moses and the teachings of the Torah important to the beginnings of Judaism?
4. **THINKING SKILL** According to the Bible, what was the *cause* of the Israelites' move to Egypt?
5. **WRITE** Briefly compare and contrast polytheism and monotheism.

CHAPTER 5 REVIEW

Major Events

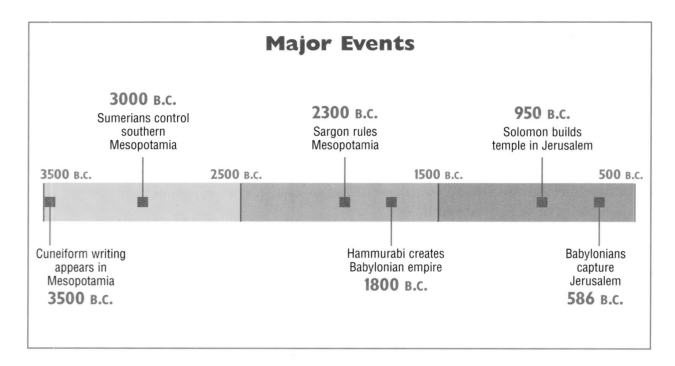

3000 B.C.
Sumerians control southern Mesopotamia

2300 B.C.
Sargon rules Mesopotamia

950 B.C.
Solomon builds temple in Jerusalem

3500 B.C.   2500 B.C.   1500 B.C.   500 B.C.

Cuneiform writing appears in Mesopotamia
3500 B.C.

Hammurabi creates Babylonian empire
1800 B.C.

Babylonians capture Jerusalem
586 B.C.

THINKING ABOUT VOCABULARY

Each of the following statements contains an underlined vocabulary word. Number a sheet of paper from 1 to 5. Beside each number write **T** if the statement is true and **F** if the statement is false. If the statement is false, rewrite the sentence using the vocabulary word correctly.

1. Monotheism is a belief in many gods.
2. A ziggurat is a long, pointed weapon used by Sumerian warriors.
3. The system of writing invented in Sumer is cuneiform.
4. The Diaspora is the trip Jews made to live in Israel.
5. An area of fertile land near the coast that is good for farming is called a plateau.

THINKING ABOUT FACTS

1. What is the Fertile Crescent?
2. Who were two of the Sumerian gods?
3. How did Hammurabi create his powerful empire?
4. Where was Nineveh? Why was it famous?
5. According to the Bible, what was the covenant with Abraham? Why is it important in Jewish history?
6. Who invented the wheel? How was it used?
7. What did early Mesopotamian farmers grow?
8. What is the Hebrew Bible? Why is it important?
9. Who was Sargon and what did he accomplish?
10. According to the time line above, about how many centuries before Solomon did Hammurabi live? How many centuries before Hammurabi did Sargon live?

THINK AND WRITE

WRITING COMPARISONS
Write a comparison of the governments and rulers of ancient Egypt and Sumer. How were they similar? How were they different?

WRITING AN EXPLANATION
Write two or three paragraphs about the Code of Hammurabi and the Ten Commandments. Explain why they are regarded as important steps forward in civilization.

WRITING BIOGRAPHICAL PARAGRAPHS
Write one paragraph about two of the following people: (1) Sargon, (2) Hammurabi, (3) Abraham, and (4) Moses.

APPLYING THINKING SKILLS

IDENTIFYING CAUSE AND EFFECT

1. What is a cause? What is an effect?
2. Can you think of an example from the chapter of an effect having two or more causes?
3. Name as many causes as you can for the rise of civilization in Mesopotamia.
4. Name two or more effects of the invention of the wheel. Can you think of another example from the chapter of a cause having more than one effect?
5. How do cause-effect connections help historians understand the past?

Summing Up the Chapter

Copy the main idea chart below on a separate piece of paper. Then review the chapter to find information for each category on the chart. When you have filled in the chart, use the information to answer the question "What contributions did the peoples of the Fertile Crescent make to civilization?"

MAIN IDEA	People of the Fertile Crescent made many contributions to civilization.		
People	**Writing Systems**	**Government/Law**	**Type of Religion**
Sumerians	cuneiform records		
Babylonians			polytheism
Israelites		Torah Ten commandments	

CHAPTER 6

Ancient India

THINKING ABOUT
HISTORY AND GEOGRAPHY

Indian civilization begins around 6000 **B.C.** in the Indus River valley, in what is today Pakistan. Mohenjo-Daro and Harappa were the most powerful cities in the valley until the arrival of horse-riding herders from the north. Their meeting changed both cultures and led to the development of a religion called Hinduism. India later became the birthplace of Buddhism as well.

6000 B.C.
INDUS RIVER VALLEY
People begin growing rice

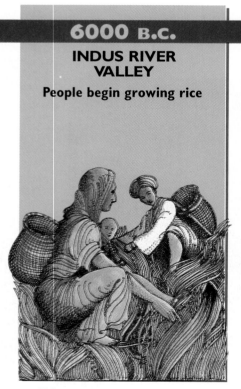

2500 B.C.
MOHENJO-DARO
Craftworkers have the time and skill to make beautiful pottery

1900 B.C.
KHYBER PASS
After crossing the Hindu Kush, Aryans win control of the Indus Valley

Khyber Pass

Indus River

Indus Valley

Mohenjo-Daro

ASIA

HIMALAYAS

Bodh-Gaya

INDIAN SUBCONTINENT

ARABIAN SEA

Bay of Bengal

INDIAN OCEAN

540s B.C.

BODH-GAYA

Siddharta Gautama, later known as Buddha, teaches new religious ideas

GEOGRAPHY OF ANCIENT INDIA

Focus Activity

READ TO LEARN
What did the Indus River contribute to a new civilization?

VOCABULARY
subcontinent

PLACES
Indus River
Himalayas
Indus Plain

READ ALOUD

Boulders [ground] to silt by water . . .
deep, round valleys, robed in cloud
against the crag-carving sunlight on
[mountain] peaks . . .
And centuries of cloud have melted, valleys
have sweated froth-white cascades
to draw that long, brown line down to the sea.

This is how Pakistani poet Salman Tarik Kureshi describes the Indus River.

THE BIG PICTURE

As the poem above describes, the Indus River begins in the snow-covered mountains of South Asia. It flows through what are today China, India, and Pakistan. In India and Pakistan other rivers join the Indus as it flows south. The silt it carries makes the river the color of cocoa. During spring floods this silt is spread throughout the Indus Valley.

The silt deposits and river water make farming possible in the otherwise dry environment of western South Asia. For this reason the Indus is similar to the Nile, Tigris, and Euphrates rivers. They have all been great givers of life to people for thousands of years. In fact, the Indus Valley was one of the first places in the world where farming developed. Archaeologists have found evidence of farming communities there that have been dated to around 6000 B.C.

A GREAT RIVER IS BORN

The Indus River begins as an icy stream high in the world's tallest mountains. These mountains are the Himalayas (hihm uh LAY uz). You have probably heard of their highest peak, Mount Everest. It stands 29,028 feet tall. The towering Himalayas separate the Indian subcontinent from much of Asia. A subcontinent is a large landmass that is geographically separated from the rest of a continent. Find the Indian subcontinent, the Himalayas, and the Indus River on the map on this page.

Long Journey of the Indus

In the spring the Indus swells with melting snow. It flows south to the Arabian Sea on an 1,800-mile journey through what is today mainly Pakistan. As the river passes through the Himalayas, it rushes through vast canyons. Some of these canyons are three miles deep! Imagine dropping a coin straight from the top of one canyon. It would take about 90 seconds for it to hit the river below. That same coin would hit the floor of America's Grand Canyon in 30 seconds.

The Indus flows swiftly down the mountains until it is joined by other rivers. Locate these on the map. These rivers join the Indus in the northern part of the dry, desert-like Indus Plain. During the spring flood season, the enlarged river spills across the plain, spreading fertile silt.

The Indus actually carries twice as much silt as the mighty Nile in Egypt. Like the Nile, the Indus branches into a huge delta before it reaches the sea.

Think about what you have learned about other river valleys. How do you think the river might have affected people centuries ago in the Indus Valley?

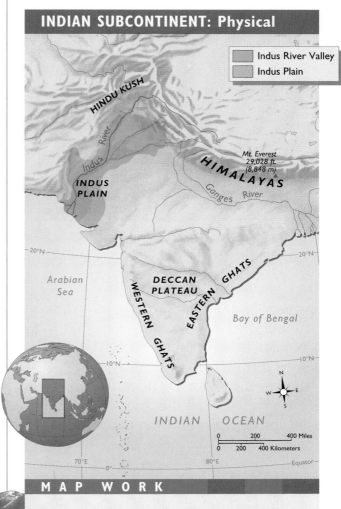

INDIAN SUBCONTINENT: Physical

- Indus River Valley
- Indus Plain

HINDU KUSH

Indus River

Mt. Everest 29,028 ft. (8,848 m)

HIMALAYAS

INDUS PLAIN

Ganges River

20°N

Arabian Sea

DECCAN PLATEAU

WESTERN GHATS

EASTERN GHATS

Bay of Bengal

20°N

10°N

10°N

INDIAN OCEAN

0   200   400 Miles
0   200   400 Kilometers

70°E   80°E   Equator   0°

M A P   W O R K

The Indian **subcontinent** extends south from the continent of Asia.

1. What bodies of water surround the Indian subcontinent?
2. Is Mt. Everest located east or west of the Indus River?

This palace at Stok, in Northern India, nestles in the Himalayas.

131

The Indus is still an important source of water for agriculture. These children (left) are washing domestic water buffaloes. A woman in the Indus Valley harvests vegetables (above).

AGRICULTURE AND THE INDUS RIVER

Farmers began planting crops in the rich soil of the Indus Valley around 6000 B.C. This was about 1,000 years before farming began in Egypt. Indus Valley farmers grew wheat, barley, beans, and sesame. Sesame is a seed used for cooking and for making oil. These farmers also grew some of the world's first rice, banana, black pepper, mustard, and cotton crops. In time they domesticated cattle and water buffalo. With animals to pull plows and wagons, farmers could plant larger fields.

Farmers built irrigation canals to bring water from the river to their crops. Thanks to the Indus Valley's hot climate, crops grew quickly. Archaeologists believe that this made it possible for farmers to plant and harvest twice a year.

In the fall, farmers planted wheat and barley. They harvested just before the melting snow caused spring floods. Then farmers quickly planted fields of cotton and sesame. Dirt walls were constructed to protect these crops from the Indus flood. By the next fall, crops were ready for another harvest.

Working with the Environment

Successful harvests did not always come easily in the Indus River valley. Earth and rock walls could not always hold back the floodwaters. Fields and entire villages could sometimes be swept away.

Wildlife in the valley also brought problems. Tigers, jackals, and wild pigs could threaten lives. Deer and such birds as wild parakeets often ate farmers' crops. Archaeologists think that ancient Indus farmers used slings and clay balls to scare birds from fields and fruit trees. Farm children in India and Pakistan today often have the chore of scaring away birds. Perhaps children in ancient times had this job too.

WHY IT MATTERS

As in ancient Egypt and Mesopotamia, civilization in the Indus River valley developed along a river. The civilization could not have survived without the crops that farmers grew in the fertile valley soil. By about 3000 B.C. villages and small towns had grown throughout the valley. Within 300 years cities would develop along the mighty river. In the next lesson you will read about life in one of those cities.

SUM IT UP

- The Indus River brings water and silt that make farming possible.
- The Indus begins in the Himalayas and crosses desert-like plains before reaching the Arabian Sea.
- Ancient Indus Valley farmers irrigated their fields and built dirt walls to protect their crops and homes from terrible floods.

THINK ABOUT IT

1. Compare the Indus and the Nile rivers. How are they similar?

2. What made it possible for Indus Valley farmers to harvest crops two times a year?

3. **FOCUS** In what ways did the Indus River help farmers? In what ways could it hurt them?

4. **THINKING SKILL** You have now learned about three early river-valley civilizations. Based on what you have read, make a _generalization_ about how rivers shaped the lives of early people. On what facts did you base your generalization?

5. **GEOGRAPHY** Draw a map of the Indian subcontinent and the Himalayas. Trace the routes of the Indus and Ganges rivers.

Chili peppers are an important crop in India. Millions are bought and sold in markets like this one.

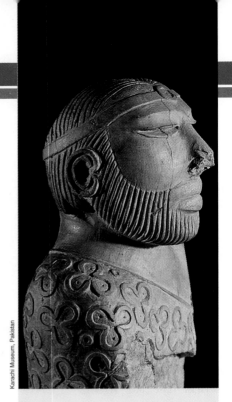

Karachi Museum, Pakistan

2500 B.C.   1500 B.C.   1000 B.C.   500 B.C.

EARLY INDIAN CIVILIZATION

Focus Activity

READ TO LEARN
What was life like in the ancient cities of the Indus River valley?

VOCABULARY
citadel
migrate

PLACES
Harappa
Mohenjo-Daro

READ ALOUD

In 1921 archaeologists gathered around a huge dirt mound on the southern plains of the Indus Valley. They knew remains of the past lay hidden beneath the mound. Earlier visitors had found artifacts there. But how old were the remains? What would they reveal about how Indian people lived long ago?

As the archaeologists dug down, the ruins of a great city began to appear. A new understanding about India's ancient past had begun.

THE BIG PICTURE

Over 1,000 miles separate the Indus River valley from Iraq, the region once known as Mesopotamia. This distance did not keep people from traveling between the two regions over 4,000 years ago, though. Like merchants from Egypt, Indian merchants traded goods in Mesopotamian cities.

Of these three ancient civilizations—Mesopotamia, Egypt, and the Indus River valley—the least is known about the Indus River valley civilization. One reason that historians know less about this culture is that experts have not been able to figure out how to read ancient Indian writing. Another reason is that few Indus artifacts and remains have been found. Despite these limits, historians have pieced together a picture of what ancient life may have been like for the people along the Indus River.

A CIVILIZATION IN THE INDUS VALLEY

The city described in the Read Aloud is called Harappa (huh RAH puh). The people who lived nearby named the ruins after an Indian god. Archaeologists have no way of knowing what early people living along the Indus called themselves. Therefore, the entire ancient Indus Valley civilization is called Harappan civilization. It lasted for almost 1,000 years, from about 2500 B.C. until about 1600 B.C.

One year after the city of Harappa was uncovered, archaeologists found a city almost exactly like it about 400 miles to the south. The local name for it was Mohenjo-Daro (moh HEN joh DAH roh), which means "Mound of the Dead" in Sanskrit. Sanskrit is an ancient Indian language. Locate the ancient cities of Harappa and Mohenjo-Daro on the map on this page.

A City Along the Indus

The city of Mohenjo-Daro was not small. Archaeologists believe that as many as 40,000 people once lived there! Dozens of streets crisscrossed each other. Larger avenues were paved with tan-colored bricks. The streets that crossed them were narrower and were usually left unpaved.

Hundreds of sturdy brick houses lined the streets of Mohenjo-Daro. Most homes were small, one-room buildings. Others were several stories high. Some even had such luxuries as airy courtyards or balconies.

At the west end of the city stood a massive fort, or citadel (SIT uh dul). Surrounding this citadel were thick walls that protected against both floods and enemy attacks. Next to the citadel was an enormous grain warehouse.

Judging from its size, farmers around Mohenjo-Daro must have been very successful at growing barley and wheat.

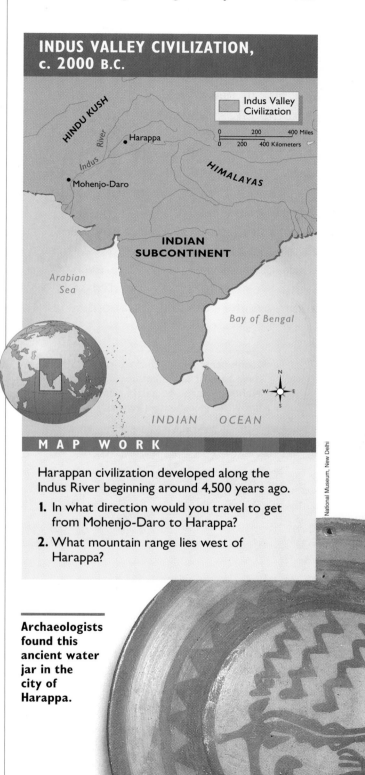

INDUS VALLEY CIVILIZATION, c. 2000 B.C.

HINDU KUSH

Indus River

• Harappa

Indus

HIMALAYAS

Indus Valley Civilization

0   200   400 Miles
0   200   400 Kilometers

• Mohenjo-Daro

INDIAN SUBCONTINENT

Arabian Sea

Bay of Bengal

N
W   E
S

INDIAN   OCEAN

National Museum, New Delhi

MAP WORK

Harappan civilization developed along the Indus River beginning around 4,500 years ago.

1. In what direction would you travel to get from Mohenjo-Daro to Harappa?

2. What mountain range lies west of Harappa?

Archaeologists found this ancient water jar in the city of Harappa.

LIFE IN MOHENJO-DARO

Suppose that you are an archaeologist living 4,000 years in the future. You have just stumbled upon the ruins of a small North American city dating back to the A.D. 1990s. You uncover buildings and dusty artifacts. You find machines and bits of plastic labels. You cannot read the city's languages, though. How much will you be able to understand about everyday life in this city? How many conclusions will you be able to make about the culture of the North American civilization?

Archaeologists studying ancient Harappan civilization have faced these kinds of challenges since the early 1900s. Yet they have succeeded in making some conclusions about what life was like for ancient Harappans. Many of their conclusions are based on remains found in Mohenjo-Daro.

City Planning

One of the most striking things about Mohenjo-Daro is the exactness of the measurements used in making and building things. Bricklayers used thousands of same-sized bricks to pave streets and build homes. City engineers dug wells throughout the city. They also created a sewer system, complete with "manholes," to keep the city clean.

Projects like this need much planning. Therefore, historians believe

Stone seals (right) and other artifacts have taught archaeologists about Mohenjo-Daro. An artist depicted daily life in the city (below).

Mohenjo-Daro must have had a strong government. Harappa had almost the same layout as Mohenjo-Daro. Therefore, historians conclude that the Indus River valley also must have had a strong central government.

On top of Mohenjo-Daro's citadel are the remains of a large, pillar-supported building. Archaeologists think it may have served as a "city hall," because it overlooked the city. Next door was a building that housed a pool-sized bath. The bath may have had religious importance. Cleansing practices later became a key part of Indian religions. The artwork at left shows what Mohenjo-Daro may have looked like in 2000 B.C.

Working in Mohenjo-Daro

Harappan builders, engineers, and craftworkers were highly skilled. Archaeologists have found remains of their work in the workshops that lined city avenues.

Skilled workers carved beautiful figures into small squares of stone. These stone squares were probably used as seals for marking belongings. Potters made water jars, cooking bowls, and other containers. These were covered with colorful paintings. Metalworkers made everything from copper fish hooks to razors. They also made fine statues of people cast in bronze. Perhaps for the first time anywhere, weavers made cloth from cotton.

As in other ancient cities, such specialization meant that Harappan farmers produced surplus food. Surplus grain was stored in a great warehouse. Perhaps, as in ancient Egypt, government workers collected grain from farmers as taxes. The stored grain could later be measured out again, possibly as payment to city workers.

The once-busy city of Mohenjo-Daro is empty today. These women climb steps that are thousands of years old.

Harappan Trade

Historians are not sure of the exact trade routes used by ancient Harappans. However, historians do know that Harappan merchants traded with neighbors both near and far.

From artifacts, archaeologists know that Harappans sold stone seals in what is today Iran. They brought home blue stones called lapis lazuli from what is today Afghanistan. Beadmakers made necklaces from stones brought from what is today India. These and other goods were then traded in faraway Mesopotamia.

The long journey to Mesopotamia was probably made in small sailboats. From the Indus River delta, the boats headed west along the southern coast of Asia. The sailors may have taken along field birds such as crows and swallows. When set free, the birds would fly toward land.

NEWCOMERS

Sometime around 1600 B.C. the city of Mohenjo-Daro was totally abandoned. So was the city of Harappa. Why?

Unfortunately we may never know for sure why these ancient cities were abandoned. One possible answer, archaeologists say, is that an earthquake caused the Indus to change its course. Without river water, farming would have become very difficult in this area. This earthquake may also have created massive floods. Floods may have destroyed the region's two largest cities. Life went on in the Indus Valley after the disaster. Harappan civilization, however, was never the same again.

Life in the Indus Valley changed even more, beginning around 1500 B.C. At that time newcomers began crossing the icy passes of the Hindu Kush Mountains. The Aryan (AYR ee un) people, originally from central Asia, herded cattle and sheep on horseback. Perhaps due to natural disasters or wars at home, they migrated (MĪ gray tud). To migrate means to move from one place to another to live. The Aryans migrated both to Europe and India. Follow their routes to India on the map.

Aryans means "noble ones" in Sanskrit. The Aryan people brought this language to the Indus Valley and the rest of the subcontinent. They also

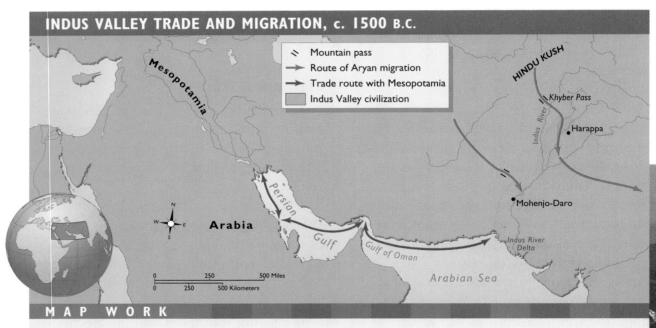

INDUS VALLEY TRADE AND MIGRATION, c. 1500 B.C.

Mesopotamia

HINDU KUSH

Khyber Pass

Indus River

Harappa

Mountain pass
Route of Aryan migration
Trade route with Mesopotamia
Indus Valley civilization

Persian

Arabia

Gulf

Gulf of Oman

Mohenjo-Daro

Indus River Delta

Arabian Sea

0   250   500 Miles
0   250   500 Kilometers

MAP WORK

Aryan peoples **migrated** to the Indian subcontinent through mountain passes.

1. What is the name of a mountain pass through which Aryans probably migrated?

2. About how far is Mesopotamia from the city of Mohenjo-Daro?

3. Through which large bodies of water would traders have to sail to get from the Indus River to Mesopotamia?

Narrow passes through the Hindu Kush Mountains continue to be useful in modern transportation of goods.

brought new religious ideas, which you will read about in the next lesson.

WHY IT MATTERS

Harappan civilization existed in the Indus River valley for almost 1,000 years. During that time farmers produced a large surplus of food. This surplus fed the populations of the great cities that developed along the fertile plains. Workers in cities like Mohenjo-Daro created items unknown in other parts of the world at that time. These included cotton cloth, stone seals, and citywide drainage systems.

In the end, Harappan civilization may have been destroyed by the very thing that made it possible—the Indus River. Yet parts of that civilization would continue in new forms. New peoples would come to control the Indian subcontinent. In time their cultures would blend with the culture of the Harappans to create a new, rich culture.

Reviewing Facts and Ideas

SUM IT UP

- Little is known about Harappan civilization because its writing system has not yet been figured out.

- The city of Mohenjo-Daro included many brick buildings and a huge citadel. The city also had a sewer system more advanced than any other of its time.

- The orderly layout of the city and its large grain warehouse suggest that Mohenjo-Daro was ruled by a strong local government.

- Harappan merchants traded goods in many places, some of which were as far away as Mesopotamia.

- In about 1500 B.C. people called Aryans migrated to the Indian subcontinent. They brought new ideas to the region.

THINK ABOUT IT

1. Why is ancient Indus Valley civilization called Harappan civilization?

2. What have historians learned about Harappan civilization from written sources? What have they learned from building remains in cities like Mohenjo-Daro?

3. **FOCUS** What do we know about the early culture of Mohenjo-Daro?

4. **THINKING SKILL** Based on the information in this lesson, what *conclusions* can you make about the people who lived in Mohenjo-Daro? What evidence supports your conclusions?

5. **GEOGRAPHY** Sketch a map of southern and western Asia. Draw the routes of the Aryan migration and the trade route between Harappa and Mesopotamia. Be sure to include physical features like mountains, rivers, and seas in your sketch.

GEOGRAPHYSKILLS

Comparing Different Kinds of Maps

WHY THE SKILL MATTERS

In Lesson 1 you read that yearly floods and deposits of silt made farming possible in the ancient Indus River valley. Farming, in turn, led to the development of city life in the valley.

Today farming is still an important part of life in the Indus River valley. This area is now a part of Pakistan. The success of present-day farmers there still depends on the Indus River.

To better understand the ties between land and human life in the Indus River valley, it helps to compare different kinds of maps.

Comparing maps showing the same area allows you to discover new information that you would not be able to get by looking at maps separately. Different types of maps show different information. For example, look at Map A and Map B, both on this page.

USING THE SKILL

As you can see from the map titles, Map A shows Pakistan's borders and major cities, while Map B shows Pakistan's physical features. What kinds of features does Map B highlight?

When you compare the information on both maps, you can learn different things about Pakistan. For example, you can see that there are no large cities in most of the southwestern part of Pakistan. What are the physical features of that region? How do you think they affect the way in which people settled there?

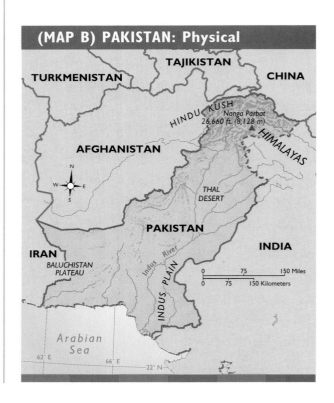

(MAP A) PAKISTAN: Political

TAJIKISTAN
TURKMENISTAN
CHINA
AFGHANISTAN
Peshawar
Islamabad
Rawalpindi
Gujranwala
Faisalabad
Lahore
Multan
PAKISTAN
INDIA
IRAN
Indus River
Hyderabad
Karachi
Arabian Sea

0   75   150 Miles
0   75   150 Kilometers

62° E   66° E   22° N

• City
✳ National capital

(MAP B) PAKISTAN: Physical

TAJIKISTAN
TURKMENISTAN
CHINA
HINDU KUSH
Nanga Parbat 26,660 ft. (8,128 m)
HIMALAYAS
AFGHANISTAN
THAL DESERT
PAKISTAN
INDIA
IRAN
BALUCHISTAN PLATEAU
Indus River
INDUS PLAIN
Arabian Sea

0   75   150 Miles
0   75   150 Kilometers

62° E   66° E   22° N

TRYING THE SKILL

In the first lesson you also learned that ancient Indus farmers planted wheat as well as some of the world's first crops of rice. As you can see from Map C on this page, those two crops are still important in the Indus Valley area today.

Use the Helping Yourself box on this page to compare Maps B and C. This study will

help you to gain more information about modern farming in Pakistan. What kind of physical features does the land have where most wheat and rice farming are done?

REVIEWING THE SKILL

1. How can comparing maps help you to better understand a place?
2. Look at maps B and C. Which natural features are needed to support agriculture for a large population? How did you reach your conclusion?
3. What might you learn about where you live by studying and comparing different kinds of maps?

(MAP C) PAKISTAN: Agriculture

TURKMENISTAN
TAJIKISTAN
CHINA
AFGHANISTAN
Islamabad
PAKISTAN
Indus River
INDIA
IRAN
Karachi
Arabian Sea
62° E   66° E   22° N

0   75   150 Miles
0   75   150 Kilometers

Wheat
Rice
Canal

In Pakistan today, oxen are sometimes used to draw well water. The water irrigates crops.

2500 B.C.   2000 B.C.   1500 B.C.   500 B.C.

BEGINNINGS OF HINDUISM

READ ALOUD

Ancient Hindu writings tell the story of a father who used simple examples to teach his son about the meaning of life. One day he told his son to bring him a fig from a fig tree. The boy did so, and his father told him to split the fruit open.

"What do you see?"

"These fine [tiny] seeds," replied the son.

"Break one open! What do you see?"

"Nothing at all, sir!"

His father said, "This finest element, which you cannot see—out of this finest element comes this big fig tree!" The boy was similar to the tree, he said. The father was teaching his son the Hindu belief that all life is connected by an invisible force.

Focus Activity

READ TO LEARN
How did the Vedas shape Indian culture?

VOCABULARY
Hinduism
Vedas
caste system
reincarnation
dharma

THE BIG PICTURE

This belief in a link between a powerful, invisible force and everything in the world is a key part of Hinduism (HIHN doo ihz um). Hinduism, one of the world's oldest religions, grew out of the beliefs of the Aryans, whom you read about in the last lesson. Today it has nearly 800 million followers. As is the case with most religions, Hinduism is practiced in many different ways. Yet all Hindus share some basic beliefs. Hindus also share a history that stretches back to the ancient past of the Indian subcontinent.

WRITINGS OF A NEW RELIGION

When Aryans migrated to the Indian subcontinent around 1500 B.C., they had little in common with Harappans. The two peoples spoke different languages and had different cultures. Many Harappans lived in great cities like Mohenjo-Daro. As herders, the Aryan people were used to moving around more. They lived in smaller villages and moved often.

As time passed, the two cultural groups began to learn from each other. Aryans began farming and specializing in crafts like their Harappan neighbors.

Harappans, meanwhile, learned ancient Aryan songs about how the world works. These songs, believed to be holy, were passed down by oral tradition. Around 600 B.C. the sacred songs were finally collected. The books containing them were called the Vedas (VAY duz), or "Books of Knowledge."

The Vedas

The Vedas were the first building blocks of Hinduism. They told Hindus how they should live, and explained life. The oldest Veda has more than 1,000 hymns. It says that the world is run by many gods and goddesses. Which Hindu goddess does this hymn praise? What are her "twinkling eyes"?

Victoria and Albert Museum

MANY VOICES
PRIMARY SOURCE

Song from the *Rig Veda*, first written down in about 1000 B.C.

Goddess Night, with all her
  twinkling eyes,
To different points in splendor she
  comes.
Immortal, she **broods over** the
  high and low;
The Goddess, with her gaze, lightens
  the dark.

In her trail, her sister Dawn follows,
And with her the darkness
  vanishes. . . .
The villagers, all that flies and walks
Are closed in their homes. Even
  vultures ignore their **prey**.

O [Night], fence off the wolf and its
  mate;
Fence off the thief. Be easy for us to
  pass.

Bright, she has come near me, the
  darkness **subdued**
With light's promise. Dawn, cancel
  darkness.

---

immortal: never dying
broods over: thinks about
prey: animal hunted for food
subdued: conquered

Many Hindu temples are decorated with statues of gods and goddesses.

HINDUISM AND CULTURE

The Vedas explain how Hindus believe people were created and what is the proper way to live. The following hymn explains the Hindu belief that four different kinds, or classes, of people were created. These first humans were said to be born from the different parts of a god's body.

> The Priest was his mouth;
> The Princes became his arms;
> His [legs] produced the
> Professionals and Merchants;
> His feet gave birth to the [Servant].

The Caste System

These four classes of people developed into India's caste system (KAST SIHS tum). The caste system is a way of organizing people into hundreds of different levels.

In a Hindu caste system a person's place in society is determined by the rank of the family she or he is born into. People born into the priestly caste of India have the highest rank and respect. Their main job is to study and

Bathing in the Ganges is an important Hindu ceremony. Caste is often shown with a mark on the forehead. There are as many as 3,000 castes in India.

teach people about the Vedas. People of the servant caste are said to be born to serve the other castes.

According to the Vedas, people do have some control over the caste they are born into. The Vedas state that people move in a constant circle of birth, death, and rebirth. This cycle is called reincarnation (ree ihn kahr NAY shun).

Hindus believe that bad deeds done in one lifetime must be paid for in a person's next life. According to this belief, people born as servants, then, are paying for wrongs done in the past. Priests, on the other hand, have done many good things in past lives.

The Importance of Duty

How did Hindus know what was right and good? They followed the **dharma** (DAHR muh) of their caste, described in the Vedas. Dharma means laws and duties. It includes hundreds of rules that instruct Hindus how to live.

For example, part of the dharma of servants was to do their jobs cheerfully. Professionals and merchants were responsible for producing and selling goods and services. Priests also had to spend some of their time working to support their families. The Vedas told which jobs people in each caste could and could not do.

Following dharma helped to keep Hindu society running in an orderly fashion. When people broke the rules of dharma, the Vedas warned, disorder would be the result. One of the sacred writings said:

If a person is engaged in doing his proper work, he reaches the highest end.

People who married against the rules of their caste, or who did a job their caste was not allowed to do, were forced to live outside all castes. These "outcastes" were looked down upon by others and said to be "impure." Some Hindu priests performed a "cleansing" ceremony if they were touched by even the shadow of an outcaste.

Outcastes had few rights. Because their children were born outside all castes, they too, had to live their lives as "untouchables."

Many Paths to Truth

Over time, Hinduism developed hundreds of different forms. Some Hindus believed their dharma called them to become priests or to perform special exercises. Others felt it was important to eat no meat, eggs, or fish. Still others explored non-Hindu beliefs in their search to understand the meaning of life and the proper way to live.

These different approaches did not upset Hindu priests. Hinduism allows for the existence of more than one god and more than one way to truth. In a very popular Hindu book—called the *Bhagavad Gita* (BUG uh vud GEE tah)—the god Vishnu says:

Howsoever people approach me, even so do I accept them; for on all sides, whatever path they may choose is mine.

Today Hindu priests read from the sacred Vedas, just as their ancestors have for hundreds of years.

HINDUISM TODAY

As in ancient times, Hindus of today worship many different gods and goddesses. Some gods, however, have become special favorites. The god Vishnu is worshiped as "The One that is the All" by millions of Hindus. Millions more honor Shiva, "The God of Time and Destruction." Still other believers prefer the goddess Devi, "The Mother of All Creation."

Most Hindu families today worship their favorite gods at home, at temples, and at special festivals.

A Changing Religion

Many Hindus still consider the Vedas the most holy books of their religion. Other books of adventure-filled stories, or *epics*, are also considered to be holy guides to living. Some of these stories have even been made into films.

Although Hinduism has roots in the ancient past, it has changed over the years. Some important changes have had to do with the caste system. In 1950, for example, the Indian government made it illegal to mistreat or to show disrespect for Hindu "outcastes."

Karachi Museum, Pakistan

Art of Hindu gods and goddesses shows (clockwise from left) Krishna and his wife Radha, Vishnu, and Ganesh.

Many Hindus observe traditional customs for important occasions, such as weddings. At this wedding ceremony in India, garlands of flowers surround a happy couple.

WHY IT MATTERS

Hinduism, one of the world's oldest religions, is followed by hundreds of millions of people today. Hinduism began in the blending of two cultures and honors many gods and goddesses. Today Hinduism continues to combine beliefs from different cultures. Most modern Hindus live in present-day India and Pakistan.

The legacy of Hinduism has influenced the arts, science, and society for great numbers of Hindus. As you will read in the next lesson, it also affected millions of others. Hinduism became the starting point for another world religion.

As you will read in the next lesson,

Reviewing Facts and Ideas

SUM IT UP

- Hinduism is practiced in many different ways. It is one of the world's oldest religions and has nearly 800 million followers today.

- Aryan newcomers to the Indian subcontinent introduced sacred songs written in the Vedas. They became the foundation of Hinduism.

- The Vedas supported a way of dividing Hindu society into four major classes of people. These four classes developed into the caste system.

- An important theme in Hinduism is reincarnation. This is the idea that people live in a constant circle of birth, death, and rebirth.

- By following the dharma, or instruction, of their caste, Hindus believe that people can break free of the cycle of reincarnation.

THINK ABOUT IT

1. What is dharma? Is it the same for all Hindus?

2. Why was it important for Hindus to do the duties expected of their caste?

3. **FOCUS** What are the Vedas? What role did they play in the shaping of Indian culture?

4. **THINKING SKILL** Make three _generalizations_ about what can happen when different cultures come into contact. Base your generalizations on what you have learned about each of the ancient river-valley civilizations.

5. **WRITING** Suppose you are interviewing a Hindu for a newspaper article. On a sheet of paper, write a list of questions you would ask.

INDIAN DANCE

The ancient Hindus believed that dance was given to them by the gods and goddesses. From the earliest times dance has been an important part of Indian life.

Indian dances vary greatly. Some of them tell a story without words. Other dances were created for their own sakes. In fact the people of ancient India used the same word, *natya* (NAH tyah), for both dance and drama. Both art forms told stories of Hindu gods and heroes.

Many Indian dances require great skill. Today dancers learn rules taught by Bharata (BAH ruh tuh), a teacher who lived some 1500 years ago. He even told dancers how to move their eyelashes!

In Hindu legend the god Shiva created the world by destroying his monster enemies. From then on the gods and goddesses danced. This sculpture shows Shiva performing his dance of destruction.

Dance is still an important part of life in India. These dancers are acting out a Hindu story. This ancient sculpture shows that if you had lived in India 1,000 years ago, you might have seen the very same dance performed in a temple.

Museum of Oriental Art, Rome

Bharata natyam is the oldest dance in the world that is still performed today. Hand gestures, or mudras (MOO drus), are an important part of this solo dance. Mudras often stand for animals, plants, or feelings.

149

BEGINNINGS OF BUDDHISM

Focus Activity

READ TO LEARN
What did the Buddha teach?

VOCABULARY
Buddhism
monk
karma
Four Noble Truths
Eightfold Path
Middle Way

PEOPLE
Siddhartha Gautama

PLACES
Kosala

READ ALOUD

According to its followers, the founder of one of the world's major religions began his life as a prince in a mountain kingdom of northern India. He enjoyed all the best the world had to offer him—the finest clothes, many servants, and a beautiful palace for each season of the year. As a young man, though, the prince gave up his fame and fortune to seek the true meaning of life. His followers believe he found the answer. The man would become known as "the Buddha."

THE BIG PICTURE

Between about 1500 B.C. and 500 B.C., Aryan settlers spread eastward across the Indian subcontinent. They conquered many towns and cities as they went. By around 500 B.C. Aryan princes were in control of much of the Indian subcontinent.

In the far north, at the base of the Himalayas, some kingdoms held onto their independence. To keep their freedom, however, they had to make yearly payments to Aryan rulers to the south. In spite of this, conflict and struggle remained a part of their lives. Some Indians began to look for answers to life's problems beyond the Vedas. One was the prince described in the Read Aloud. His name was Siddhartha Gautama (sih DAHR tuh GOW tah muh). The answers he found would become Buddhism (BOOD ihz um), a religion that continues to attract followers. Today there are more than 330 million Buddhists.

LIFE OF THE BUDDHA

Siddhartha Gautama is traditionally said to have been born around 563 B.C. His parents were the king and queen of Kosala, a northern kingdom near the Himalayas. Siddhartha means "He Who Has Reached His Goal" in Sanskrit.

The Young Prince

Ancient Buddhist writings say that Siddhartha's mother dreamed about her son's future. The dreams predicted that if Siddhartha stayed at home, he would rule a great kingdom. If he left home, he would become a wise teacher and monk. A monk is a man who devotes his life to a religious group. Monks often give up all they own and live only a religious way of life.

Siddhartha's father wanted the boy to be a king. From that point on, Buddhist texts state, the king did all he could to keep his son happy at home. He had the best singing groups entertain his son and arranged for the prince to marry the woman of his dreams. He built stunning gardens around the royal palace so Siddhartha would be surrounded by beauty.

Discovery in the Garden

Even in his own garden, though, the king could not shelter Siddhartha from sorrow forever. One day the prince went for a ride in the royal gardens. There he spotted an elderly man hobbling painfully along with a cane. Siddhartha asked his chariot driver what was wrong with the man. He learned that all people grow old someday and said, "Shame on birth, since to everyone that is born, old age must come!"

During another ride through the gardens, Siddhartha saw someone

The young Siddhartha was introduced to sickness, old age, and death in his daily rides through his father's gardens.

who was very ill. It troubled him to find out that sickness was part of life. On yet another day the prince came upon a funeral procession. He learned that death was a part of life.

Finally Siddhartha spotted a man in the park who seemed to be at peace with the world. The man was calm even though he was asking people for help in getting his next meal. Siddhartha asked his driver who the man was and learned that the man was a monk. The prince was amazed that someone could be so at peace in a world filled with sorrow and suffering.

That day, Buddhist texts state, the prince made a difficult decision. He chose to give up all he had and become a monk. After saying good-bye to his wife and newborn son, he left the palace. His journey to find the meaning of life had begun.

THE TRAVELS OF THE BUDDHA

For the next six years, Siddhartha traveled throughout northern India as a monk. In his search for wisdom, he talked at length with Hindu priests, but felt their answers were not enough. To clear his mind, he stopped eating, but began again when he nearly starved himself to death.

At last, Buddhist texts say, an understanding came to the former prince one day as he sat under a fig tree. The wisdom it is said he received that day would later earn him the title *the Buddha,* which means "Awakened One."

The Teachings of Buddhism

Some of the Buddha's ideas were not new to India. He used some Hindu ideas and changed others. Like Hindus, the Buddha believed that all people went through a circle of birth, death, and rebirth, or reincarnation. Also like Hindus, he believed in karma. Karma is described by both Hindus and Buddhists as a force caused by a person's good and bad acts. Karma is said to affect future lives.

Buddhist prayer flags (top) float in the breeze near Kanchenjunga, India, the world's third-highest mountain. Buddhist monks (above) in Thailand wear traditional robes.

Unlike Hindus, the Buddha did not search for the one powerful force believed to connect all of life. Instead, the Buddha believed that the most important thing in life was to reach peace by ending suffering. How did he reach his conclusion, and how did he hope to reach this end?

The Way to End Suffering

Buddhist texts say that as he sat under the tree that day, the Buddha concluded that life is ruled by **Four Noble Truths**.

1. Life is filled with suffering.
2. Suffering is caused by people's wants. People may want more pleasure, more power, or a longer life.
3. Suffering can be ended if people stop wanting things.
4. To stop wanting things, people must follow eight basic laws.

The Buddha explained these Four Noble Truths to his followers, but they were not written down until later. He called the way to end suffering the **Eightfold Path**. The Eightfold Path is a set of instructions on the proper way to live. By following the Eightfold Path, the Buddha taught, people could end the suffering in their lives.

The Middle Way

The laws of the Eightfold Path were meant to represent a **Middle Way** of living for Buddhists. This way of life was meant to be neither too strict nor too easy. The Buddha compared the Middle Way to playing a stringed instrument. If the strings are kept too loose, they will not make a sound. On the other hand, if they are too tight, they will break when they are played. Only those strings that are kept at just the right amount of tightness will make beautiful sounds. Life works the same way, the Buddha concluded.

The Buddha's Final Journeys

The Buddha spent the rest of his life traveling around India and sharing his message with people of all castes. One of the first places he went to was his father's palace.

At first the elderly king was shocked. His son looked no different from any other humble monk he had met. But after listening to his son's message, Buddhists believe that the king, too, became a follower of the Buddha. So did the Buddha's wife and son.

By the time the Buddha died at age 80, there were thousands of Buddhists in northern India. They lived according to his Four Noble Truths. Like the Buddha, Buddhist monks gave up all they owned and depended on other Buddhist followers to give them food each day. They worked to live peacefully among all living things and to love others.

Special prayers are written in Sanskrit on "Mani" stones (below). The stones are left along roadsides. Scenes from the Buddha's life are painted in the Ajanta caves in India (right).

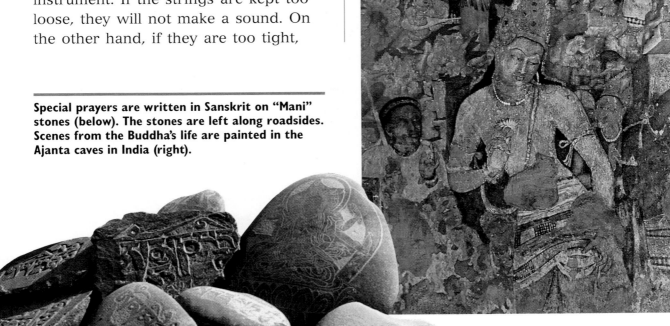

THE GROWTH OF BUDDHISM

After the Buddha's death in 483 B.C., Buddhism spread throughout southern and eastern Asia. Traveling monks introduced the Buddha's teachings in other places. These included what are today China, Tibet, Sri Lanka, Japan, Korea, Thailand, and Vietnam.

Buddhists everywhere lived by the Buddha's teachings, which were written down as proverbs. According to the proverbs that follow, what qualities do Buddhists value and believe to be the most important in life?

MANY VOICES PRIMARY SOURCE

Verses on the Law,
an ancient Buddhist text,
written down around 100 B.C.

*Hatreds never **cease** by hatred in this world; by love alone they cease. This is an ancient law.*

*The reputation of him who is energetic, mindful, pure in deed, considerate, self-controlled, right-living, and **heedful** steadily increases.*

Calm is his mind, calm is his speech, calm is his action, who, rightly knowing, is wholly freed, perfectly peaceful, and self-controlled.

Irrigators lead the waters; carpenters bend the wood; the wise control themselves.

As a solid rock is not shaken by the wind, even so the wise are not ruffled by praise or blame.

---

cease: stop
heedful: aware

Changing Buddhism

As in Hinduism, many different schools of thought developed in Buddhism over the years. Some suggested that the Buddha was a god. Others thought that the Buddha was an ordinary person who discovered a way to end suffering. Buddhists differed with each other on what it meant to live according to the Middle Way. Buddhists also disagreed about how people reached peace and truth and freedom from suffering.

These differences of opinion continue today among Buddhists around the world. Yet some basic teachings continue to be shared by all Buddhists. These include honoring the Buddha and his teachings and helping others to end suffering.

WHY IT MATTERS

Buddhism developed in ancient India. From the beginning, it centered around the life and thoughts of Siddhartha Gautama. This man had much wealth as a prince, but left it all behind when he chose to become a penniless monk.

The teachings of the Buddha would have a big impact on Indian civilization for a time. However, Buddhism gained even greater influence in other parts of Asia. You will read about more of this story in chapters to come.

✔ Reviewing Facts and Ideas

SUM IT UP

- Between about 1500 and 500 B.C., Aryan rulers gained control over much of India and spread Hinduism.
- Siddhartha Gautama founded Buddhism. He gave up all he owned to search for a way to end suffering.
- The Buddha borrowed beliefs from Hinduism. He also taught the Four Noble Truths, the Eightfold Path, and the Middle Way.
- Buddhism spread after the Buddha's death. This religion has 330 million followers today.

THINK ABOUT IT

1. What were the two ways of life that the young prince Siddhartha was said to have to choose between?

2. What might a Buddhist hope to achieve by following the Buddha's Eightfold Path?

3. **FOCUS** How did the Buddha say people should live? What guidelines did he offer?

4. **THINKING SKILL** What _caused_ Siddhartha Gautama to become a monk? What _effects_ did his becoming the Buddha have on life in India?

5. **WRITE** Write a paragraph comparing and contrasting Hindu and Buddhist beliefs. What do they share?

In China this giant statue of "sleeping Buddha" (left) is visited by Buddhists and tourists. The smaller statues are other ancient sculptures of the Buddha. A father and son (above, left) share a Buddhist candle ceremony.

CHAPTER 6 REVIEW

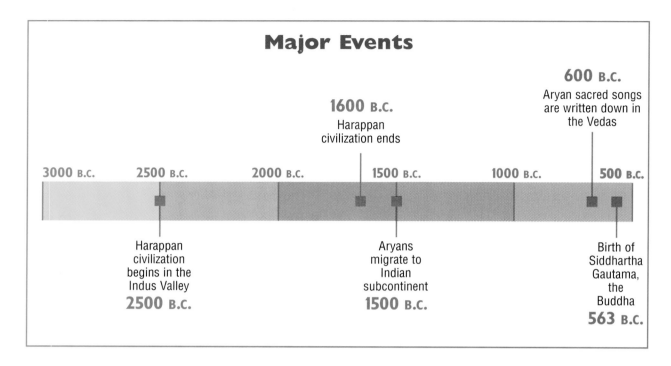

Major Events

600 B.C.
Aryan sacred songs are written down in the Vedas

1600 B.C.
Harappan civilization ends

3000 B.C.   2500 B.C.   2000 B.C.   1500 B.C.   1000 B.C.   500 B.C.

Harappan civilization begins in the Indus Valley
2500 B.C.

Aryans migrate to Indian subcontinent
1500 B.C.

Birth of Siddhartha Gautama, the Buddha
563 B.C.

THINKING ABOUT VOCABULARY

Number a sheet of paper from 1 to 5. Beside each number write the word or term from the list below that best completes each sentence.

karma   subcontinent
Middle Way   Vedas
reincarnation

1. The constant cycle of life, death, and rebirth is called _____.

2. A _____ is a large landmass that is geographically separated from the rest of a continent.

3. The sacred songs of the ancient Aryans were written down about 600 B.C. in books called the _____.

4. According to Hindu belief, _____ is the force created by a person's good and bad deeds that affects his or her future life.

5. According to Buddhist belief, the laws of the Eightfold Path lead to the _____.

THINKING ABOUT FACTS

1. What made Siddhartha Gautama give up all he had and become a monk?

2. How did Siddhartha Gautama become the Buddha?

3. How has Hinduism changed recently?

4. What are the Four Noble Truths?

5. What four groups of people make up the Indian caste system?

6. How does the caste system shape the lives of Indians?

7. What was the role of the Indus River in the creation of Indian civilization?

8. Why do historians know less about the Indus River valley civilization than about ancient Egypt and Mesopotamia?

9. What did Harappan workers create that was unknown to other cultures?

10. According to the time line above, how long after the Aryans migrated to the Indian subcontinent were their sacred songs written down?

THINK AND WRITE

WRITING A LETTER

Suppose that you are one of the archaeologists who had uncovered the remains of Mohenjo-Daro. In a letter to a friend, describe the most interesting artifacts you found and what they reveal about the lives of the people who lived there.

WRITING A REPORT

Write a class report about the Hindu belief that people live in a constant cycle of birth, death, and rebirth. Explain this cycle and how it affects the way Hindus live.

WRITING AN ESSAY

Write a short essay about India's caste system. Describe what it is and discuss the beliefs that created it. Finally describe how the caste system is changing.

APPLYING GEOGRAPHY SKILLS

COMPARING DIFFERENT KINDS OF MAPS

1. Look back at "Applying Geography Skills" on page 140. What did you learn by comparing Maps A and B?

2. What do you learn about Islamabad by comparing the three maps in the skill?

3. What conclusions can you make by comparing the maps on page 131 and page 135?

4. Look at the map on page 138. Can you learn anything by comparing it with the maps on pages 131 and 135?

5. What kind of information might one map show that another might not?

Summing Up the Chapter

Copy the word map below on a separate piece of paper. Then review the chapter and fill in details that support the main idea. After you have filled in the details, use the word map to write a paragraph that answers the question "How did civilization develop in India?"

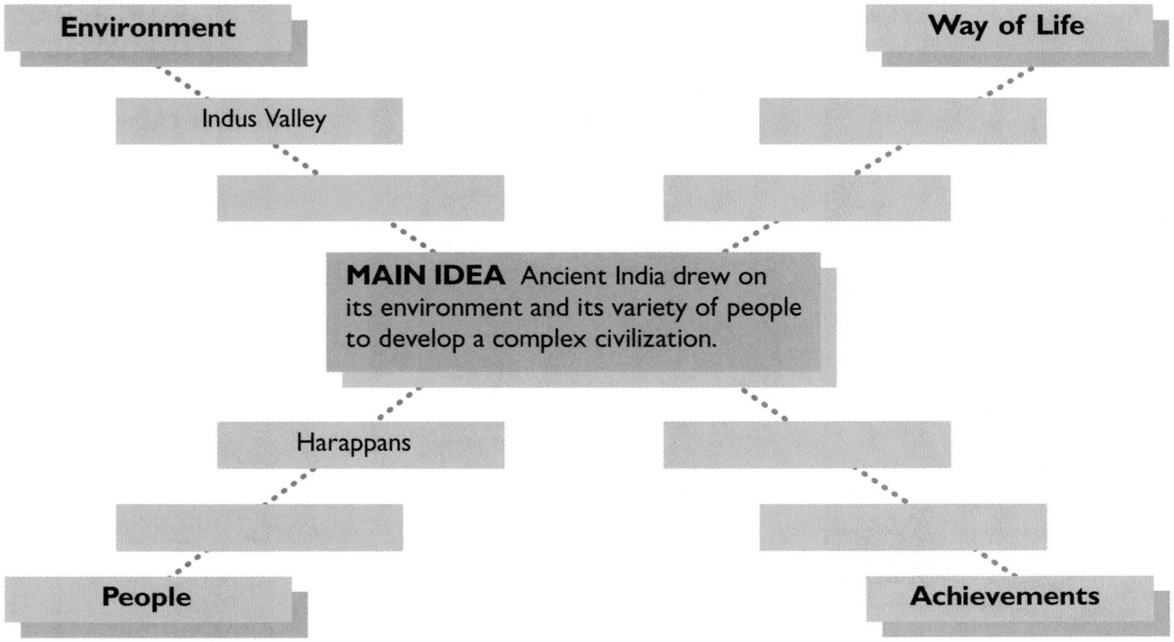

Environment

Indus Valley

Way of Life

MAIN IDEA Ancient India drew on its environment and its variety of people to develop a complex civilization.

Harappans

People

Achievements

CHAPTER 7

Ancient China

THINKING ABOUT HISTORY AND GEOGRAPHY

Around 3000 B.C. farmers in the Huang River valley learned to control the river's floods in order to grow food. A group that ruled over a large area of the valley developed a written language around 1100 B.C. This was the beginning of modern Chinese writing. China grew into a large area. Within it, the teachings of a great scholar shaped life from about 500 B.C. to the present.

3000 B.C.
HUANG RIVER VALLEY

Farmers use levees to control floods

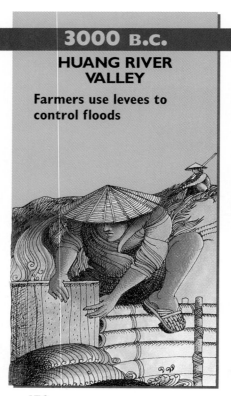

1100 B.C.
ANYANG

Priests use a writing system to record events and make predictions

221 B.C.
XIANYANG

A powerful leader creates the first Chinese empire

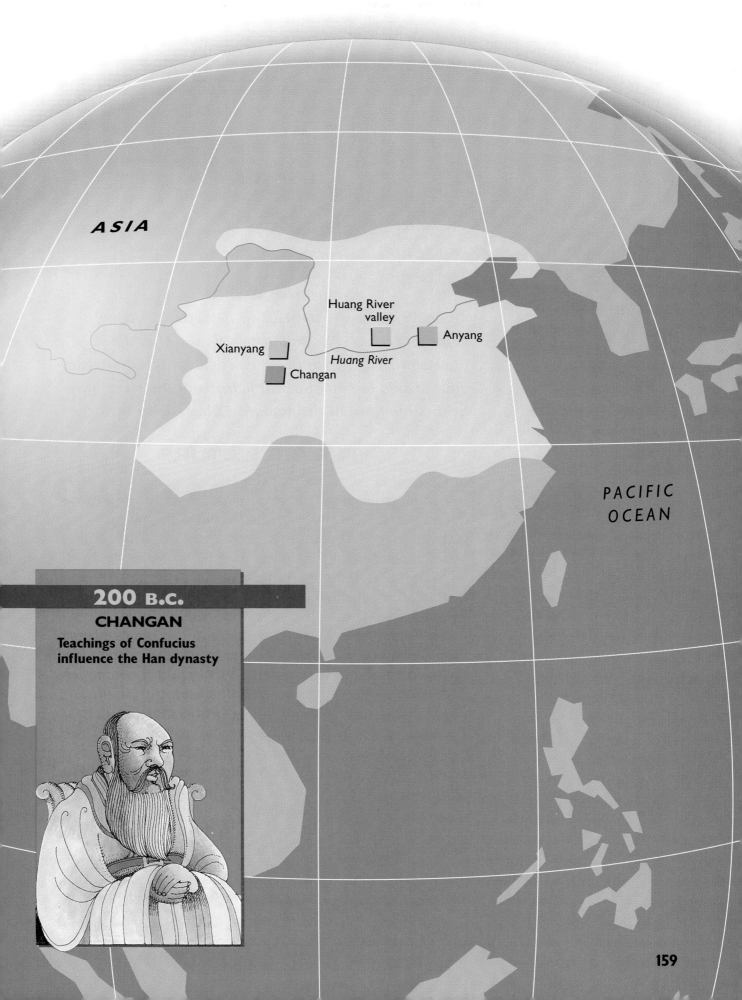

ASIA

Huang River
valley

Xianyang

Huang River

Changan

Anyang

PACIFIC
OCEAN

200 B.C.

CHANGAN

**Teachings of Confucius
influence the Han dynasty**

GEOGRAPHY OF CHINA

READ ALOUD

"Whoever controls the Huang (HWAHNG) River controls China." According to Chinese tradition a powerful ruler spoke these words almost 4,000 years ago. In this lesson you will learn why the river has been so important throughout China's long history.

Focus Activity

READ TO LEARN
How did the Huang River affect ancient Chinese civilization?

VOCABULARY
loess
levee
erosion
famine
steppe

PLACES
Huang River
North China Plain

THE BIG PICTURE

In Chapter 6 you read that the Himalayas separate the Indian subcontinent from the rest of Asia. Within those mountains is "The Roof of the World"—the huge plateau, or raised plain, that forms most of Tibet. This plateau sits higher than most mountaintops in the United States. The Indus and many of Asia's largest rivers begin on this plateau. It is here that the Huang River begins its 3,000-mile trip across northern China.

The Huang has been a major force in China's history. Like the Indus, it starts as a clear stream but grows and picks up silt along its winding journey. During summer floods the Huang spreads enough silt on the North China Plain to create one of the world's largest deltas. The river also creates miles of fertile marshland.

About 4000 B.C. farming communities developed along the lower part of the Huang River. China's oldest civilization grew from these farming communities. This civilization later spread to include many regions and groups of people. Find the Huang River and the North China Plain on the map on the next page.

Loess washes into the Huang River, giving it a yellow color. The word *Huang* means "yellow" in Chinese.

THE HUANG RIVER VALLEY

At one point along its journey, the Huang makes a giant curve around the edge of the Ordos Desert. Find this curve on the map below. As it turns, the Huang cuts through a hilly region. The hills are made almost entirely out of **loess** (LES). Loess is a dusty, yellow soil that has been deposited in this region by wind.

Working with the Environment

Loess has been a blessing and a curse to Chinese farmers. During summer rains, huge amounts of it are washed into the Huang. In fact, the Huang is the world's muddiest river.

When the Huang floods the North China Plain, the silt deposits create a unique environment. This loess-silt helps farmers because it is fine, rock-free, and very fertile. Because it is so light and fluffy, however, loess is easily carried away by storms. When this happens farmers are left with poor soil.

Like farmers in the Indus Valley, ancient farmers made use of the Huang Valley's fertile soil. They also fought to control river floods. This battle with nature has been going on since China's earliest days. It continues to this day.

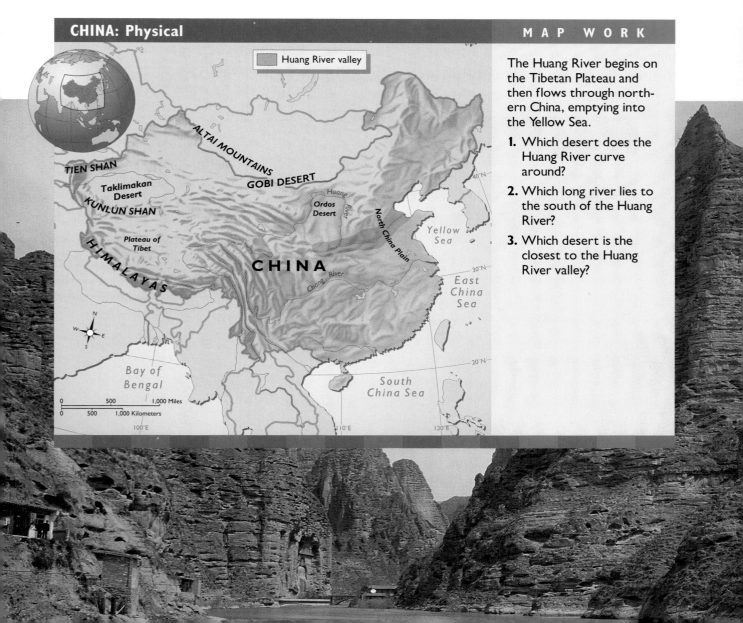

CHINA: Physical

Huang River valley

ALTAI MOUNTAINS
TIEN SHAN
Taklimakan Desert
KUNLUN SHAN
GOBI DESERT
Huang River
Ordos Desert
North China Plain
Yellow Sea
Plateau of Tibet
HIMALAYAS
CHINA
Chong River
East China Sea
Bay of Bengal
South China Sea

40°N
30°N
20°N
100°E
110°E
120°E

N W E S

0   500   1,000 Miles
0   500   1,000 Kilometers

MAP WORK

The Huang River begins on the Tibetan Plateau and then flows through northern China, emptying into the Yellow Sea.

1. Which desert does the Huang River curve around?

2. Which long river lies to the south of the Huang River?

3. Which desert is the closest to the Huang River valley?

AGRICULTURE ALONG THE HUANG

Do you remember how Egypt's farmers usually welcomed the Nile's summer floods? China's farmers could not afford to let the Huang overflow freely. Their fields could be washed away. Huang Valley farmers needed to control floods.

Controlling the River

About 3,000 years ago, farmers began building earth levees (LEV eez) to hold back the Huang. A levee is a wall that keeps a river within its banks. Over time, though, a thick layer of mud built up along the riverbed. As the mud deposits grew, the river eventually spilled over the farmers' levees.

Like the Sumerians, ancient Chinese farmers also built canals to bring water to their fields. Yet loess once again caused problems. It constantly clogged the canals and had to be cleared away.

Crops Grow in Loess Soil

In spite of the problems it caused, loess also provided a rich soil. Many kinds of plants could grow in it. Huang farmers grew rice, millet (a type of grain), wheat, green onions, and ginger. They harvested grapes, peaches, plums, and wild chestnuts.

Because Huang Valley farmers were successful, the area's population grew. More farmable land became needed to feed people. Farmers had to clear trees from rich loess-lands to plant crops. One result was erosion. Erosion is the wearing away of soil by wind or water. This loss of soil occurs in areas where trees and shrubs are removed. Erosion of fertile soil sometimes makes it difficult for farmers to grow successful crops. If too much soil washes away and crops fail, a famine can happen. Famine is a time when very little food is available and people starve.

Other Regions in Ancient China

Not all of China was as suitable for farming as the Huang River valley. Growing crops is very difficult or impossible in many parts of China. To the north of the Huang Valley are windswept **steppes** (STEPS). A steppe is a dry, treeless plain. In this region people used another type of agriculture. Here, instead of planting crops, they herded sheep and cattle on horseback.

Lifestyles were very different along the Huang and on the steppes. How might a typical daily meal on the steppes have been different from a meal in the river valley?

WHY IT MATTERS

The hard work of China's ancient farmers paved the way for powerful kingdoms to develop throughout China. Many of those kingdoms grew along the Huang River. You will read about one of the earliest and most powerful of these kingdoms in the next lesson.

DID YOU KNOW?

Why is the Huang River often called "China's Sorrow"?

The flooding of the Huang has cost millions of lives throughout China's history. Famine, as much as drowning, has been a cause of these deaths. When the river washes away crops, it leaves people with little or nothing to eat.

Chinese generals have also used the power of the river as a deadly weapon. In World War II, for example, one general blew up key levees during flood season to stop the Japanese army. His plan worked—but it also took the lives of almost one million farmers. Many more died during the famine that followed.

Reviewing Facts and Ideas

SUM IT UP

- Loess has made the Huang River valley extremely fertile, but it causes many problems too.

- Ancient Chinese farmers built dirt levees along the Huang to try to keep the river on its course.

- Like people in other river valleys, farmers along the Huang raised crops. On China's northern steppes, people herded animals.

The farmer (far left) is harvesting rice. China produces 41 percent of the world's rice each year. Herders who live on China's steppes often live in tents (left). The herders move to new grazing land each season.

THINK ABOUT IT

1. What does the Huang River share in common with the Indus River?

2. How has loess helped China's farmers? How has it caused problems?

3. **FOCUS** Why was it important for ancient farmers to control the Huang River? What made it hard for them to achieve their goal?

4. **THINKING SKILL** What *caused* ancient farmers to strip loess-lands of their trees and shrubs? What *effects* did this have on life along the Huang?

5. **GEOGRAPHY** Why is the big curve of the Huang an important part of the river? What happens here?

THE FIRST DYNASTY

Focus Activity

READ TO LEARN
What do the remains at Anyang tell us about life in early China?

VOCABULARY
dynasty
nobles
oracle bones

PEOPLE
Fu Hao

PLACES
Anyang

READ ALOUD

In 1899 a Chinese scholar became ill and asked his doctor for help. He was given a packet of animal bones that, when ground up, would make a popular medicine. When the scholar looked closely at the bones, he noticed that they were covered with mysterious ancient writing. He became determined to find out where the bones came from and what they meant. Later the scholar led archaeologists to a site along the Huang River. What they found would change history books about ancient China.

THE BIG PICTURE

By 3000 B.C. Egypt was being united and city-states and towns were expanding in the Fertile Crescent and the Indus Valley. At the same time farms along China's Huang River were growing larger and more productive. Towns grew too, and the largest of these became capitals of states.

By about 1700 B.C. one kingdom had won control over the large Huang River delta. One of its earliest capitals was a city called Shang. That name also became the state's name. Since it was ruled by one family for a long period of time, the government became known as the Shang dynasty. A dynasty is a line of rulers who belong to the same family. Control is passed from one generation to the next. For 600 years the Shang dynasty would shape the lives of people along the Huang River.

TOWNS ALONG THE HUANG RIVER

The Shang state spread along the Huang River until it ruled hundreds of towns. The Shang kings created new towns by giving land to their relatives, or **nobles**. These nobles oversaw the construction of the new towns and became their rulers.

Think of what it might have been like to rule a town during the Shang dynasty. You would have been very busy. The towns were important centers of production. They supplied food, clothing, and other products for the king and the nobles. These towns also helped to keep enemy states from invading the vast Shang lands. People from the towns often were part-time soldiers. They were sent to war whenever they were needed.

An Ancient City

Near the end of the Shang dynasty's 600-year rule, the capital was moved. Its new site was near the town that is today **Anyang** (AHN YAHNG). Find Anyang on the map on this page. The writing on the bones described

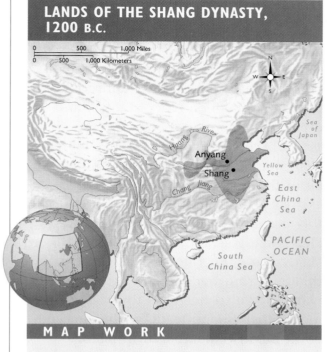

LANDS OF THE SHANG DYNASTY, 1200 B.C.

MAP WORK

The Shang dynasty controlled lands along the Huang River.

1. How far from the Yellow Sea is Anyang?

2. Where was the city of Anyang located— north or south of the Huang River?

in the lesson introduction led archaeologists to the ancient city. Its ruins have taught much about life in Shang China.

Shang society was organized like a pyramid. At the top were the king and his family. Below them were nobles, then craftworkers, then farmers. Prisoners of war were at the bottom.

Archaeologists at Anyang have uncovered many huts. Dug halfway into the ground, these "pithouses" served as homes and workshops for metalworkers, potters, and servants. Remains of what seem to be palaces lie in the city's center. Bronze cups, stone carvings, and magnificent chariots were found in nearby royal tombs.

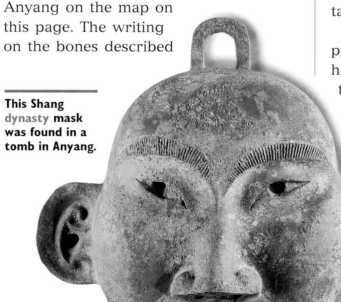

This Shang dynasty mask was found in a tomb in Anyang.

BURIED TREASURES

The finds at Anyang are a treasure for archaeologists and historians. One royal tomb found at Anyang contained more artifacts than any other. Hundreds of bronze containers, ivory statues, and other valuable objects were in the grave. Artifacts from this tomb tell how rich Shang rulers were. For whom were all of these riches made?

Archaeologists have determined that this grave belonged to a king's wife. Her name was Fu Hao (FOO HOW), or "Lady Hao." Fu Hao succeeded at many things during her life. She led troops to war. She ruled her own town. Unlike most other Shang leaders, she succeeded at being remembered in history. That is because records about her life have been preserved in her tomb.

A Written Record

A writing system had developed along parts of the Huang River before the Shang dynasty. Like early cuneiform, the earliest Chinese signs looked like pictures of objects. By the time of the Shang dynasty, though, characters were simpler. Symbols could stand for objects or ideas. Look at the diagram on this page to see one way this writing system developed over time.

One ancient Chinese historian mentioned that many records of the Shang were "written on bamboo and silk." Unfortunately, no bamboo tablets or silk cloth have survived from Shang times. However, writing has been found on bronze pots and stone.

More writing has been discovered on the thousands of "dragon bones" found

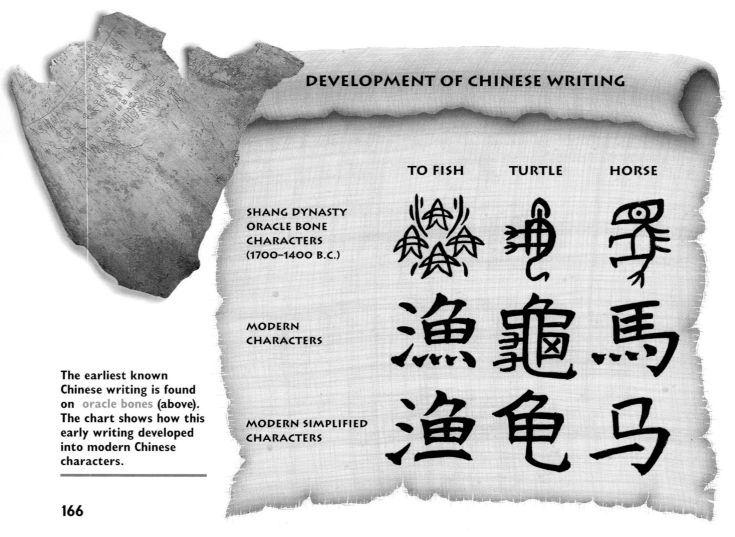

DEVELOPMENT OF CHINESE WRITING

	TO FISH	TURTLE	HORSE
SHANG DYNASTY ORACLE BONE CHARACTERS (1700–1400 B.C.)			
MODERN CHARACTERS			
MODERN SIMPLIFIED CHARACTERS			

The earliest known Chinese writing is found on oracle bones (above). The chart shows how this early writing developed into modern Chinese characters.

WHY IT MATTERS

The Shang dynasty of the Huang River valley created a legacy that would shape life in China for centuries. Shang religious beliefs and style of government would live on for hundreds of years. The writing system developed during this time is similar to the system that is still used in China today. In the next lesson you will read about a man who spread many Shang ideas about religion and government throughout China.

at Anyang. Most of these bones came from cattle or sheep. They were used by special priests who the Shang believed were oracles (AWR uh kulz), or people who could predict the future. The bones became known as "oracle bones." Priests heated the oracle bones over a fire until they cracked. The pattern of cracks was used to answer questions about the future.

Like most Shang kings, Fu Hao's husband, Wu Ding, depended on priests to read oracle bones and predict the future. Would Fu Hao recover from an illness? Would farmers have a good harvest? Should Wu Ding go to war? It was believed that the pattern of cracks in the oracle bones gave the answers to his questions.

Religion of the Shang

Shang Chinese believed that their ancestors lived in another world and controlled human life. If an oracle's prediction came true, they believed that the king was being helped by his ancestors. This, they believed, proved that he was the right person to be king.

The people of the Shang dynasty worshiped many different gods. They believed these gods controlled nature. The ancient people also believed that when they died, they would join their ancestors and the gods.

Reviewing Facts and Ideas

SUM IT UP

- Around 1700 B.C. the Shang state won control over the Huang Valley region. This area was ruled by the Shang dynasty until about 1100 B.C.

- The Shang used writing to record and predict important events.

THINK ABOUT IT

1. Describe the social pyramid of China during the Shang dynasty.

2. What were oracle bones? How were they used in ancient China?

3. **FOCUS** What were three artifacts found at Anyang? What do they tell us about the people who lived there?

4. **THINKING SKILL** *Compare* the Shang system of government with that of the pharaohs' government in Egypt.

5. **GEOGRAPHY** Imagine you are a noble who is building a town in Shang China. Where would you decide to build? What would you consider in making your decision?

| 2000 B.C. | 1500 B.C. | 1000 B.C. | 500 B.C. | 221 B.C. | 206 B.C. | A.D. 1 |

THE EMPEROR'S CLAY ARMY

Focus Activity

READ TO LEARN
How did Shihuangdi build an empire in China?

VOCABULARY
emperor
province

PEOPLE
Shihuangdi

PLACES
Qin
Qinling Mountains
Xianyang
Great Wall of China

READ ALOUD

In 1974 farmers living near the southern curve in the Huang River began digging a new well. Imagine their surprise when they began to uncover life-sized clay soldiers! Archaeologists were called to the site. Since that day an entire clay army—more than 8,000 soldiers, horses, and chariots—has been unearthed. No two of the soldiers look alike. Each one once held a real weapon to fight off some unknown enemy. Who built this amazing clay army and why? Following is the story of China's Qin (CHIN) dynasty.

THE BIG PICTURE

The Shang dynasty came to an end around 1100 B.C. For many years afterward the Huang River valley was a place of conflict and turmoil. Slowly one region, called Qin, built up its strength. Qin's ruler was a general who would one day order the making of the great clay army described above. In 221 B.C. this general led a real army in a bold drive to take control of the Huang River delta. He and his army won battle after battle, eventually conquering all of northern China.

When his victory was complete, the Qin general declared himself China's emperor. An emperor is the supreme ruler of an empire. He celebrated his new role by taking the name Shihuangdi (SHEE hwahng dee), or "First Grand Emperor." Shihuangdi boasted that his Qin dynasty would last for 10,000 generations.

THE RISE OF AN EMPIRE

What made it possible for Shihuangdi and the Qin armies to win control and hold an empire together? Geography played a part in their victory. The original Qin region was protected by the Qinling (CHIN LING) Mountains on one side and by the Huang River on the other. From this central point, soldiers were able to march out and expand the Qin empire.

A New Kind of Government

Shihuangdi had new ideas about how a government should be run. These ideas were even more important than his armies in strengthening Qin's power. Shihuangdi split the empire into 36 provinces (PRAHV in sez), or political divisions of land.

The emperor also let farmers own land. This weakened the power of the nobles. Shihuangdi also forced many nobles to move to the capital city, Xianyang (shee AHN yang). There he took away their bronze weapons.

As in ancient Egypt, new ideas about communication helped to unify China. Shihuangdi set up a single system of writing throughout the empire. Local leaders used this writing system to report to the capital. Written language also helped the government to record and collect taxes.

Shihuangdi also created a single system of money to be used throughout the empire. Craftworkers made coins out of bronze. Holes in the coins allowed people to keep their money on a string. These changes were strictly enforced by the emperor's soldiers.

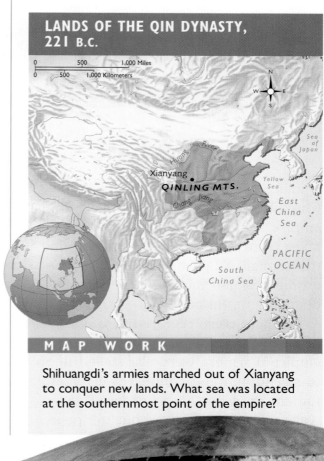

LANDS OF THE QIN DYNASTY, 221 B.C.

0   500   1,000 Miles
0   500   1,000 Kilometers

Sea of Japan

Huang River

Xianyang
QINLING MTS.
Chang Jiang

Yellow Sea

East China Sea

PACIFIC OCEAN

South China Sea

MAP WORK

Shihuangdi's armies marched out of Xianyang to conquer new lands. What sea was located at the southernmost point of the empire?

A bronze chariot and horses were in Shihuangdi's tomb.

FARMERS BUILD THE EMPIRE

Under Shihuangdi's leadership, unified China grew bigger and stronger. The empire also became increasingly rich as taxes from China's farmers flowed into the capital. As time went by, the government began making ever greater demands on its people.

Farmers were required to build the highways that linked the cities of the empire. Farmers were also called upon to strengthen and connect walls along the empire's northern border. These walls were built to keep out the people of the northern steppes. Much later, similar walls would be built across these same mountains and valleys. The later walls made up the Great Wall of China that we can see today. The Great Wall of China eventually grew to be more than 1,500 miles long!

Farmers were the backbone of the Qin empire. Their hard work as farmers, soldiers, and builders kept the empire strong. Still, their lives mostly centered around the seasonal floods of the Huang. As before, they continued to grow the wheat, rice, and other crops needed to feed an empire.

Building the Emperor's Tomb

One of the greatest building projects in the Qin empire was the construction of a tomb for Shihuangdi. The emperor wanted his tomb to be a spectacular mirror of the real world. The clay army, which you read about in the lesson introduction, was just one part of this "mirror world." Its many soldiers and

Shihuangdi ordered that these clay soldiers be set up in formation. They stood with their backs to the emperor in order to protect him from attack.

horses stood guard, ready to protect the emperor from attack.

Shihuangdi's burial place lies under a giant mound near the clay army. Archaeologists have not yet uncovered the contents of the tomb. However, an ancient Chinese historian once told what lay inside.

The treasure-filled tomb, the historian wrote, was laid out like a giant map of the empire. Models of the Huang and other rivers, he said, flowed with mercury pumped by machines. On the ceiling sparkled bright stars. To keep out robbers, crossbows were set up that would shoot arrows if the tomb's entrance was disturbed. One day archaeologists may be able to compare the ancient historian's description with the actual remains in the tomb.

WHY IT MATTERS

In 221 B.C. Shihuangdi had boasted that the Qin dynasty would rule China for 10,000 generations. It actually lasted only 15 years. After Shihuangdi's death in 210 B.C., farmers and nobles alike revolted against his dynasty's harsh rule. However, China's first emperor would leave a lasting legacy. The centralized systems of writing, government, and money that he created would live on for centuries.

Reviewing Facts and Ideas

SUM IT UP

- Around 221 B.C. Shihuangdi unified China with his powerful armies and by strengthening government. He created standard writing and money systems across the empire.

- Farmers were the backbone of the Qin economy. They also served as part-time soldiers and builders.

THINK ABOUT IT

1. How did farmers help make Shihuangdi's empire strong?

2. What qualities might have been admired in the first emperor? What qualities were probably feared?

3. **FOCUS** How was Shihuangdi able to gain control over China?

4. **THINKING SKILL** Suppose you are a noble governing your own town in Qin China. Emperor Shihuangdi has just called you to his capital at Xianyang. Write a letter in response to the emperor's request from the noble's *point of view*.

5. **GEOGRAPHY** Look at the map on page 169. How did geographical features help Shihuangdi's army to conquer northern China?

STUDYSKILLS

Writing a Summary

VOCABULARY
summary
topic sentence

WHY THE SKILL MATTERS

Soon after Shihuangdi became China's first emperor in 221 B.C., he sent his army to strengthen the northern border of his empire. The story of how and why he did this is complicated, but it is an important part of China's early history. Many stories from history are long and complicated. They usually contain much information. However, people can present the important information in a story by creating a **summary**. A summary briefly states the main ideas contained in a piece of writing or group of ideas.

USING THE SKILL

Read the following paragraph about Shihuangdi and the herders of northern China.

After Shihuangdi won the battle for control over China in 221 B.C., one challenge remained. Herders who lived on the steppes of northern China had crossed the Huang River and set up their tents on the plains near the river's big curve. This narrowed the distance between these two very different cultures. Because they were expert riders and hunters, the herders were a threat to the empire. Shihuangdi feared that the herders would decide to invade China, taking its land and crops. He ordered his army to push the herders back beyond the Huang.

To prepare for writing a summary, find the **topic sentences**, or the sentences that contain the main ideas. Often a topic sentence is the first sentence of the paragraph. However, it may also be at the end of the paragraph. The topic sentences in the previous paragraph tell that the people of the steppes became a threat to Shihuangdi. How he responded is also important.

Other sentences give supporting details, such as information about the herders being expert riders and hunters.

After you identify the main ideas and supporting details, you can write a short summary. What main ideas are expressed in the paragraph on Shihuangdi and the herders? What are some supporting details?

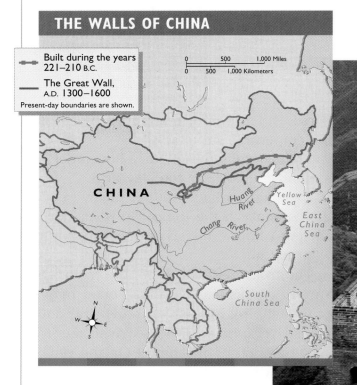

THE WALLS OF CHINA

Built during the years 221–210 B.C.

The Great Wall, A.D. 1300–1600

Present-day boundaries are shown.

0   500   1,000 Miles
0   500   1,000 Kilometers

CHINA

Huang River

Yellow Sea

Chang River

East China Sea

South China Sea

N W E S

Little remains of Shihuangdi's wall (far right). The Great Wall (right) is about 1,500 miles in length.

TRYING THE SKILL

Now read the story below and use the Helping Yourself box to write a summary.

In about 215 B.C. Shihuangdi's army succeeded in driving the herders out. To help keep them out, more than 300,000 workers strengthened a 100-year-old wall along China's northern border. It was just rock-hard mounds of earth. Lookouts posted on the wall would signal an invasion by waving flags or by lighting fires. The army would then come to chase the herders away. China's leaders carried on this idea of wall building. Most famous of all was the Great Wall. This wall was mostly built between A.D. 1300 and 1600. It was much larger than the previous earthen walls and was made of bricks. Even the Great Wall was not a very effective barrier. Invaders continued to make their way over or around the wall.

What is the main idea that runs through this entire paragraph? What are the supporting details?

REVIEWING THE SKILL

1. How does writing a summary differ from simply rewriting an entire piece in your own words?

2. If you had to write a single summary of both paragraphs about Shihuangdi in this lesson, what would that summary include?

3. How did you choose what would go into your summary? Could you use the map?

4. When might writing a summary be a helpful skill?

Bibliotheque Nationale

| 2000 B.C. | 1500 B.C. | 1000 B.C. | 500 B.C. | 206 B.C. | A.D. 220 |

CONFUCIUS CHANGES CHINA

Focus Activity

READ TO LEARN
What effects did the teachings of Confucius have on China?

VOCABULARY
Confucianism
Mandate of Heaven
Grand School
seismograph

PEOPLE
Han Gaozu
Confucius
Wudi

READ ALOUD

"When a prince's personal conduct is correct, his government is effective without the issuing of orders. If his personal conduct is not correct, he may issue orders, but they will not be followed."

These words were spoken by Confucius, an important Chinese philosopher, teacher, and scholar.

THE BIG PICTURE

In 206 B.C. Shihuangdi's Qin dynasty was overthrown by rebel armies. These armies were led by a farmer-turned-general called **Han Gaozu** (HAHN GOW ZOO). His family began the mighty Han dynasty, which would rule China for over 400 years. During the Han dynasty, China expanded north to what are today North and South Korea and south to the country of Vietnam.

Shihuangdi had lived by the idea that a ruler should be able to do whatever he chooses. Later, Han rulers developed different ideas about government. Their thoughts were based on the teachings of a man named Confucius, who lived between 551 B.C. and 479 B.C.

Like the Buddha, who was teaching in India during this time, Confucius lived through an age of warfare and conflict. In this time of conflict, Confucius suggested a different, more peaceful way of living. Also like the Buddha, he won many followers during and after his lifetime. Unlike the Buddha, Confucius's ideas would not start a new religion. However, Confucius's ideas would reshape entire civilizations.

CONFUCIUS

Both of his parents died when he was young, so Confucius had to make his own way in life. He had a passion for learning. He mastered subjects such as writing, mathematics, history, and archery. This helped Confucius to get a job in government. In later years, though, he devoted his life to teaching.

The Followers of Confucius

Confucius's ideas, later called Confucianism, taught that Chinese culture had lost its traditions. According to Confucius, ancient traditions had once made society just and good. Through education, Confucius said, people from rulers to farmers could learn how to become good people once again. Good people would make a good civilization.

A central idea of Confucianism was to have respect within the family. This idea also applied to government. Just as a child must respect a parent, a subject must respect the ruler. However, the ruler had a duty to be wise and good. Some followers of Confucius said that emperors did not have the right to rule just because they came from a certain family. Rather, each emperor received a right to rule from the gods, called the Mandate of Heaven. This mandate, or command, echoed the Shang belief that the gods spoke to kings through oracle bones.

Confucius's thoughts were recorded by his students in a book called *The Analects.* Analects are selected writings. What does a good person do, according to Confucius?

Excerpt from
The Analects of Confucius,
c. 400 B.C.

Do not do unto others what you would not want others to do to you.

If you make a mistake and do not correct it, this is called a mistake.

Be dutiful at home, brotherly in public; be discreet and trustworthy, love all people, and draw near to humanity. If you have extra energy as you do that, then study literature.

If leaders are courteous, their people will not dare to be disrespectful. If leaders are just, people will not dare to be [ungovernable]. If leaders are trustworthy, people will not dare to be dishonest.

A certain pupil asked Confucius about government: "What qualifies one to participate in government?"

Confucius said, "Honor five refinements. . . . Then you can participate in government."

The pupil asked, "What are the five refinements?"

Confucius said, "Good people are generous without being wasteful; they are hardworking without being resentful; they desire without being greedy; they are at ease without being [proud]; they are dignified without being fierce."

---

refinements: improvements
participate: take part in

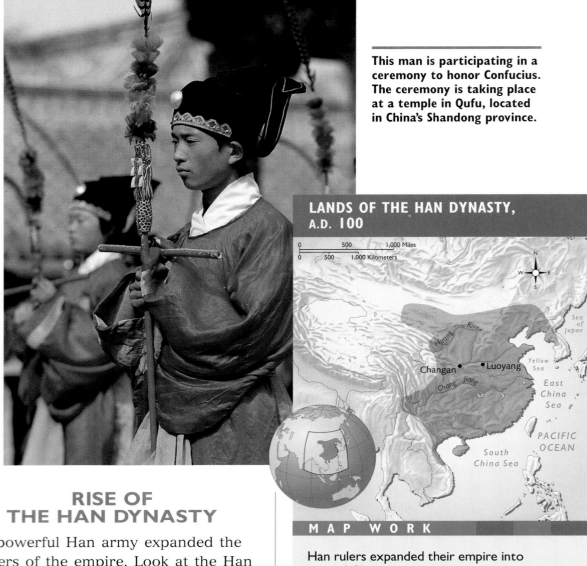

This man is participating in a ceremony to honor Confucius. The ceremony is taking place at a temple in Qufu, located in China's Shandong province.

LANDS OF THE HAN DYNASTY, A.D. 100

Changan • Luoyang

Sea of Japan

Yellow Sea

East China Sea

PACIFIC OCEAN

South China Sea

MAP WORK

Han rulers expanded their empire into central China.

1. What two cities were located on the Huang River?
2. Which city was farther west?

RISE OF THE HAN DYNASTY

The powerful Han army expanded the borders of the empire. Look at the Han dynasty lands on the map on this page. Controlling the huge empire was a difficult job. During the Qin dynasty Shihuangdi had many people who disagreed with him killed. Some of them were Confucianists. He did not want anyone to question his right to rule. During the Han dynasty, however, Confucianism became accepted again. Han emperors wanted to find ways to rule more fairly. They also wanted to lessen the power of the nobles.

Han rulers kept the Qin dynasty's system of government. However, they gave government jobs to educated people, rather than just to nobles. **Wudi** (WOO DEE), was the first strong emperor of the Han dynasty. His rule lasted from 140 B.C. to 87 B.C. Wudi created schools to prepare students for government service. These schools were run by Confucian teachers.

The Grand School

Under Wudi's government, schools were set up in each province, or state. The schools taught Chinese literature to students who would serve in local government. Very good students sometimes were sent to the empire's best school, the Grand School.

During Wudi's rule only 50 students were allowed to study at the Grand School. By A.D. 200 it had more than 30,000 students. For one year they learned about ancient China's poetry, history, proper behavior, and folk songs. These had all been preserved by Confucius. The teachers were China's most brilliant Confucian scholars. At the end of the year, students at the Grand School took a long test. If they passed, they earned jobs as government workers or as teachers in province schools. They also won great respect in society because they were so well educated.

During the Han dynasty, learning of many different kinds blossomed throughout the empire. Like the ancient Egyptians, Chinese scientists and mathematicians learned to predict eclipses of the sun. Doctors discovered new kinds of medicines, and poets wrote about the beauty of the land. In fact, during the course of the Han dynasty, the Chinese language grew from 3,000 to 9,000 characters. In A.D. 100 scholars wrote the first Chinese dictionary.

The Invention of Paper

Confucian emphasis on education brought increased knowledge and discovery in the Han dynasty. This can be seen in the many inventions that appeared during this time. For example, Han craftworkers invented paper. Like Egyptian papyrus, paper provided a way to keep written records. The Chinese made paper by pounding bark of mulberry trees. These are the same trees that feed China's silkworms.

An Amazing Instrument

One of the most remarkable achievements of Han inventors was the seismograph (SĪZ muh graf). This is a machine used to detect earthquakes. Although this ancient seismograph looks like a bronze vase covered with dragons and toads, it is actually a complicated scientific instrument.

Inside the vase swung a long metal pendulum. When the ground shook ever so slightly, the pendulum would swing in the direction in which the earthquake occurred. The pendulum would hit a rod inside the vase. This rod, in turn, would knock a ball out of a dragon's mouth. The ball came out in the direction in which the earthquake had occurred.

In this way Han rulers could learn about an earthquake as soon as it happened. They could immediately send food and supplies to the damaged area.

This is a model of the seismograph invented by Zhang Heng. The original detected an earthquake hundreds of miles away.

LIFE DURING THE HAN DYNASTY

As you have read, the Han empire stretched across thousands of miles and achieved many things. Still, farming continued to be the center of China's economy and society. Most people lived on farms and in small villages. China's farmers grew food for the entire empire. The economy was based on customs handed down for generations. This is an example of a traditional economic system.

The lives of farmers during the Han dynasty centered around their families and the endless work in the fields. This has remained relatively unchanged through much of China's long history.

WHY IT MATTERS

Confucius wanted China to become a civilization of good and dutiful people. He believed it had once been that way. During the Han dynasty China's government adopted some of Confucius's ideas. Despite this, however, conflict and hardship remained part of life in ancient China. The Han dynasty ended around A.D. 220. It broke down under the strain of failed military campaigns beyond China and fights among its leaders. In the centuries to come, many Chinese looked to the teachings of Confucius to renew their civilization. The legacy of Confucian ideas of fairness and learning continues in China today.

Reviewing Facts and Ideas

SUM IT UP

- Confucian ideas about duty and education influenced life during the Han dynasty.
- The Han emperor Wudi started Confucian schools in order to educate government workers.
- The Han dynasty produced many great achievements in science, mathematics, the arts, and trade.
- As in earlier dynasties, farmers during the Han dynasty produced the food and goods that brought China great wealth.

THINK ABOUT IT

1. What did Confucius believe was the duty of a ruler?

2. What are three ways Confucius defined goodness in people?

3. FOCUS How did Confucianism affect life during the Han dynasty?

4. THINKING SKILL Imagine that you are Emperor Wudi. _Decide_ which aspects of Confucianism you can use to help you govern the empire. Explain how you made your choices.

5. GEOGRAPHY Compare the maps on pages 165, 169, and 176. How did China's empire change in the Shang, the Qin, and the Han dynasties?

This model of a house came from a Han dynasty tomb.

CITIZENSHIP
MAKING A DIFFERENCE

Working for Education

GUIZHOU (GWEE JOH), CHINA—In this small village in rural China, a group of six women come together once a week. They sit in a circle listening intently to a seventh woman. She reads slowly and clearly from a small magazine. Sometimes she stops and points to pictures on the page.

Except for the woman holding the magazine, none of these women can read. Yet they would like to learn. The magazine, called in English "Rural Women Knowing All," is helping these six women and many thousands more all over China to do just that. The magazine has articles that teach reading and writing. It also has articles about women who have become leaders in their villages and towns.

Ever since the days of the Han dynasty, education has been an important part of Chinese culture. Unfortunately it has not always been easy for girls to receive an education. For much of Chinese history, it was considered more important for boys to go to school. Girls often stayed at home. It is now the law in China that all children, boys and girls, must attend school for at least six years.

Wu Qing (WOO CHING), who teaches at Beijing Foreign Studies University, helped start this magazine in 1993. She is its chief adviser and fundraiser. "The need to educate rural women is great," she says, "because girls, especially in rural areas, have had fewer chances than boys to go to school. If a poor family could only afford to educate one child, the boy almost always would be chosen."

The magazine, which in American money costs about 12¢ a copy, is growing rapidly. It has over 200,000 subscribers and many thousands more readers. As a fundraiser, Wu convinced several large companies to donate cars, televisions, and other prizes for those women's groups that sell large numbers of subscriptions.

Wu believes in educating rural women because "Once rural women know how to read and write, . . . it will make a lot of difference for China." Helping others comes naturally to Wu. "I feel it is up to me to help change China," she says. "That is why I have the energy to work hard."

"I feel it is up to me to help change China."

Wu Qing

SILK MAKING

Bibliothèque Municipale, Poitiers

Have you ever watched a caterpillar spin a cocoon? One kind of caterpillar, the silkworm, spins a cocoon that can be used to create a special cloth. This cloth is called silk. Ancient Chinese farmers discovered how to make silk around 2700 B.C.

In the spring women cut leaves from mulberry trees to feed the silkworms. After several weeks of noisy eating, the silkworms spun their cocoons. Women unwound the cocoons and twisted the strands into threads. These threads were then woven to make cloth. In China today silk is made the same way, except for the added help of machines.

Silk is a strong, beautiful, smooth fabric. It stretches easily and is light and warm. The legacy of making silk enables people all over the world to enjoy the special qualities of this cloth.

This Chinese painting from the 1800s shows a farm family making silk. Women and girls made most of the silk.

Chinese emperors decided to keep silk making a secret from other civilizations. Rulers threatened people with death if they told the secret. This threat worked for over 3,000 years!

Modern factories produce millions of yards of silk cloth. The source of the silk, however, is the same as ever: the cocoon of the silkworm. Today people around the world wear silk to work and to school. It is often used to make suits, shirts, ties, and dresses.

CHAPTER 7 REVIEW

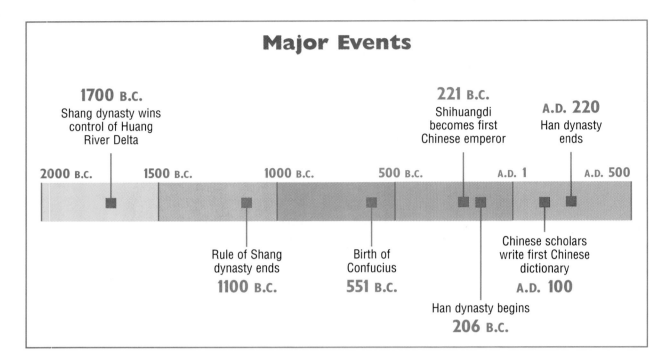

Major Events

1700 B.C.
Shang dynasty wins control of Huang River Delta

221 B.C.
Shihuangdi becomes first Chinese emperor

A.D. 220
Han dynasty ends

2000 B.C.   1500 B.C.   1000 B.C.   500 B.C.   A.D. 1   A.D. 500

Rule of Shang dynasty ends
1100 B.C.

Birth of Confucius
551 B.C.

Chinese scholars write first Chinese dictionary
A.D. 100

Han dynasty begins
206 B.C.

THINKING ABOUT VOCABULARY

Number a sheet of paper from 1 to 10. Beside each number write the word or term from the list below that matches the definition.

dynasty   Mandate of Heaven
emperor   province
erosion   seismograph
famine   steppe
levee   topic sentence

1. A dry, treeless plain

2. A wall that keeps a river within its banks

3. A special machine used to detect earthquakes

4. The wearing away of soil by wind or water

5. A time when food is scarce and people starve

6. A line of rulers who belong to the same family

7. A sentence that contains the main idea

8. The supreme ruler of an empire

9. A division of land

10. A special right to rule that the emperor is thought to receive from the gods

THINKING ABOUT FACTS

1. In what ways did the Huang River help early Chinese farmers?

2. How have discoveries made at Anyang helped historians to understand ancient China?

3. Who was China's first emperor? What did he do to unify China?

4. What is Confucianism?

5. Look at the time line above. How long were the reigns of the Shang and Han dynasties?

THINK AND WRITE

WRITING A JOURNAL

Suppose you live in the time of the Han Dynasty and are a student in the Grand School. Write an entry in your journal describing your thoughts about your studies and the long test you have to take at the end of the year.

WRITING AN ARTICLE

Write a short article for your school newspaper about ancient Chinese civilization. Describe the contributions it has made to world history.

WRITING ABOUT PERSPECTIVES

Suppose you live in ancient China and your teacher asks you to write about what you learned about the Huang River from books and from your parents' experiences. Write three paragraphs about your impressions.

APPLYING STUDY SKILLS

WRITING A SUMMARY

1. What is a summary?
2. How is writing a summary different from rewriting something entirely?
3. What are topic sentences? How can they be useful in writing a summary?
4. After rereading "Silk Making" on page 180, write a three-sentence summary of what you read.
5. How are summaries useful?

Summing Up the Chapter

Copy the main-idea diagram below on a separate piece of paper. Then review the chapter to find at least two pieces of information that support each part of the main idea. After you have filled in the information, use it to write a paragraph that answers the question "What developments of China's Huang River civilization continue to affect China today?"

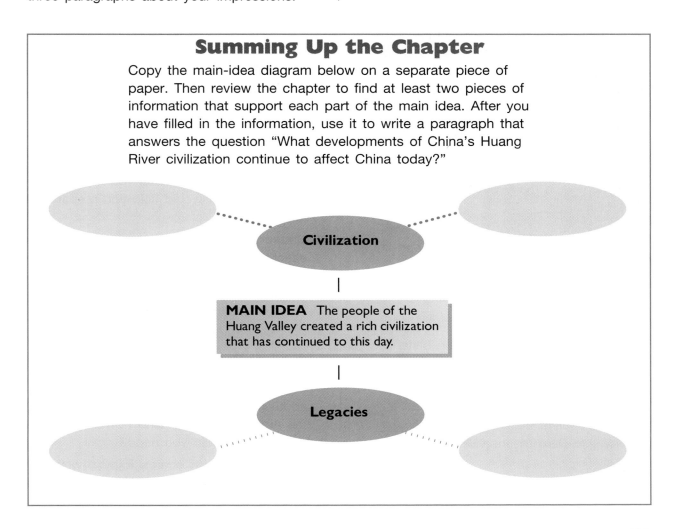

Civilization

MAIN IDEA The people of the Huang Valley created a rich civilization that has continued to this day.

Legacies

UNIT 2 REVIEW

THINKING ABOUT VOCABULARY

dynasty   Sanskrit

empire   summary

hieroglyphics Torah

polytheism   Vedas

reincarnation ziggurat

Number a sheet of paper from 1 to 10. Beside each number write the word from the list above that best completes each sentence.

1. A large religious building with a temple on its peak that stood at the center of most ancient Sumerian cities is called a _____.

2. A brief statement of the main ideas in a piece of writing or group of ideas is a _____.

3. Egypt became an _____ during the New Kingdom period.

4. The books that contain the ancient Aryan sacred songs are called the _____.

5. The belief of the ancient Egyptians and Sumerians in many gods and goddesses is called _____.

6. The Shang _____ of the Huang River valley created a legacy that shaped life in China for centuries.

7. The first five books of the Hebrew Bible are called the _____.

8. Government workers in ancient Egypt could communicate over long distances using a writing system called _____.

9. _____ is what Hindus call a cycle of life, death, and rebirth.

10. In the ancient Indian language of _____, *Mohenjo-Daro* means "Mound of the Dead."

THINK AND WRITE ◄ ▶

WRITING ABOUT PERSPECTIVES
Write a comparison of the ancient civilizations of Egypt, Sumer, and China. What were their main features? How were they similar? How were they different?

WRITING A TRAVEL PAMPHLET
Suppose you lived in Han China. Write a pamphlet describing some of the things visitors might see there. Describe the geography as well as the people.

WRITING AN INTERVIEW
Interview a person from this unit—for example, Hammurabi, Shihuangdi, or Siddhartha Gautama. Write down your questions and the answers you receive.

BUILDING SKILLS

1. **Summarizing** Reread the section "Children in Egypt" on page 98. Then write four sentences that summarize the section.

2. **Summarizing** Do you think that having summaries of the material you need to know for a test would help you prepare for it or not? Explain.

3. **Cause and effect** Explain the causes and effects of Moses' leading the Hebrews out of Egypt. Tell about the events leading to the departure of the Hebrews from Egypt. What resulted from it?

4. **Different kinds of maps** Look at the map showing the Alps on page 33. Why would knowing only the latitude and longitude of the Alps not be enough to inform you about the temperature and precipitation in the Alps? What other kind of map or information would you need?

5. **Maps at different scales** Explain why it would be helpful to have maps of different scales for a car trip across the country.

YESTERDAY, TODAY & *TOMORROW*

Writing helped in the development of ancient civilizations. Writing is also important to us today. Do you think writing will continue to be as important in the future? Will there be as many books and magazines? Do you think something else will take their place? Explain your answers.

READING ON YOUR OWN

Here are some books you might find at the library to help you learn more.

STREET SMART! CITIES OF THE ANCIENT WORLD
by Geography Dept. of Lerner Publications
This discussion of ancient cities tells how archaeology uncovers clues to past civilizations.

MUMMIES MADE IN EGYPT
by Aliki
This illustrated book describes mummification in ancient Egypt.

GILGAMESH THE KING
by Ludmilla Zeman, reteller
First created by Sumerians, the story of Gilgamesh tells of literature's first hero in a beautifully illustrated picture book.

UNIT PROJECT

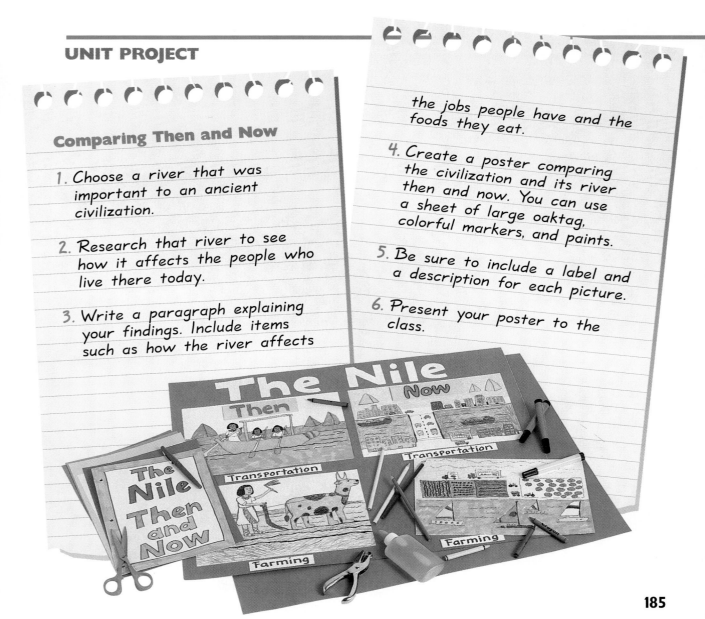

Comparing Then and Now

1. Choose a river that was important to an ancient civilization.

2. Research that river to see how it affects the people who live there today.

3. Write a paragraph explaining your findings. Include items such as how the river affects the jobs people have and the foods they eat.

4. Create a poster comparing the civilization and its river then and now. You can use a sheet of large oaktag, colorful markers, and paints.

5. Be sure to include a label and a description for each picture.

6. Present your poster to the class.

ISLAMIC TILE, SPAIN;
STATUE OF GODDESS OF WISDOM, ROME;
STATUE OF MAYA GODDESS, HONDURAS;
THE COLOSSEUM, ROME

New Ideas and New Empires

"The armor upon their bodies flashed in the sun."

from the *Iliad*, by Homer
See page 200.

WHY DOES IT MATTER?

A poet in ancient Greece wrote these words to describe a great battle. Today people around the world are familiar with Homer's words as well as many other achievements of his time. People of the world today owe much to the early peoples of Greece, Rome, Arabia, and the Americas. Their ideas about government, law, beauty, education, science, and religion continue to influence us today. Such accomplishments are only a few of the reasons for calling certain periods "Classic."

VASE WITH BATTLE SCENE, GREECE

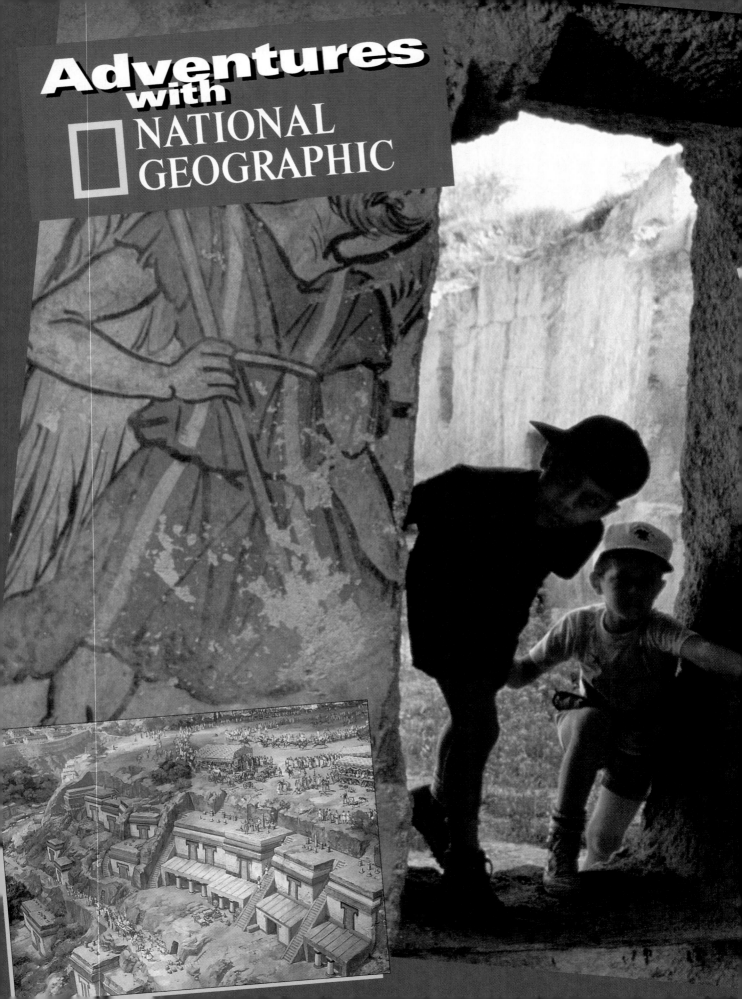

Adventures
with
NATIONAL
GEOGRAPHIC

Lost In Translation

You poke your head into the doorway of a ruined tomb, and you wonder about the people who painted the walls more than 2,000 years ago. You're not alone. Archaeologists also wonder about the Etruscans, who lived in Italy about the same time that the ancient Greeks were flourishing nearby. The Etruscans built great cities and elaborate tombs. But unlike the Greeks, they left few written records. And the records they *did* leave— well, no one can read them now, for no one knows the language. So archaeologists hunt through the ruins, looking for other clues about the mystery people of the ancient world.

Geo Journal

List some ways you might find out about a culture even if you couldn't read its language.

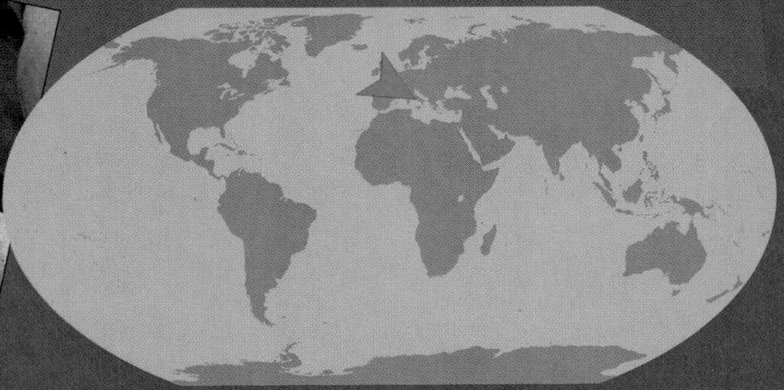

CHAPTER 8

Ancient Greece

THINKING ABOUT
HISTORY AND GEOGRAPHY

In this chapter you will read about a civilization that developed in the rocky landscape by the Aegean Sea more than 3,000 years ago. Following the time line, you see how the ancient Greeks built cities with unique ways of life. In time, interaction and conflict among the cities and peoples of the region led to a period of tremendous creativity. Greek civilization eventually spread to areas around the Mediterranean Sea.

1400 B.C.
AEGEAN SEA
Seagoing people trade among the islands of Greece

800 B.C.
SPARTA
Boys and girls train to build a strong city

450 B.C.
ATHENS
Pericles encourages poor and rich citizens to take part in government

EUROPE

ASIA

Black Sea

Caspian Sea

GREECE   Aegean Sea

Athens

Sparta

Tigris River

Euphrates River

Mediterranean Sea

Alexandria

AFRICA

Red Sea

390 B.C.

ATHENS

Socrates teaches students philosophy

331 B.C.

ALEXANDRIA

Alexander expands the Greek empire to North Africa

GEOGRAPHY OF ANCIENT GREECE

Focus Activity

READ TO LEARN
What effects did the sea have on life in ancient Greece?

VOCABULARY
peninsula
harbor

PLACES
Mediterranean Sea
Crete
Rhodes
Attica
Peloponnesus
Phoenicia

READ ALOUD

"The good Odysseus (oh DIHS ee us) gladly spread his sail: seated, he steered. . . . Seventeen days he sailed across the sea; on the eighteenth he saw that he'd drawn close to shadowed peaks: he now was near the coast of [an] island; in the mist that land took on the likeness of a shield."

About 2,700 years ago Greeks first began listening to the exciting tales, like the one above, of a poet named Homer. Homer's stories about Odysseus helped the ancient Greeks imagine a distant age much different from their own. They also expressed the strong connection the people of ancient Greece felt with the sea.

THE BIG PICTURE

In 1500 B.C. the Shang dynasty ruled much of the land along the Huang River. In Egypt the pharaohs of the New Kingdom were building an empire along the southeastern shores of the Mediterranean Sea. Along the Mediterranean's northeastern shores, meanwhile, another civilization was growing. It was that of ancient Greece, a civilization that had been developing for more than 1,000 years.

No great river carrying thick layers of silt flowed through this land. Rather than being located in a fertile river valley, ancient Greek civilization was rooted in a rocky landscape surrounded by the sea.

MOUNTAINS AND SEA

The land of ancient Greece was made up of a part of the southern European mainland along with over 400 islands. This is the same area that makes up Greece today. As you can see on the map, the biggest of the islands is Crete. Crete lies about one day's sail south of the Greek mainland. East of Crete lies Rhodes, an island near what is today Turkey. Rhodes provides an ideal rest stop for ships sailing between Greece and western Asia.

Mountains and hills cover about nine out of every ten acres in Greece. The most mountainous region, however, is located in western Greece. There, travel by land is difficult, and little farmable land exists. Herds of sheep and goats live on wild plants that grow on the rugged hillsides.

Land Along the Coast

Larger plains suitable for farming lie in eastern Greece, near the coast. A few of these plains are on Attica, a wedge-shaped peninsula that juts into the Mediterranean Sea. A peninsula is an area of land nearly surrounded by water. Attica also contains excellent natural harbors for ships. A harbor is a sheltered place along a coast.

A large peninsula called the Peloponnesus (pel uh puh NEE sus) lies to the southwest of Attica. Shaped like a giant hand reaching toward Crete, the Peloponnesus is a mountainous region ringed by a thin band of fertile land. Like the rest of Greece, the Peloponnesus contains several rivers. Many of the region's rivers, however, dry up in the summertime, unlike rivers in Egypt or Mesopotamia.

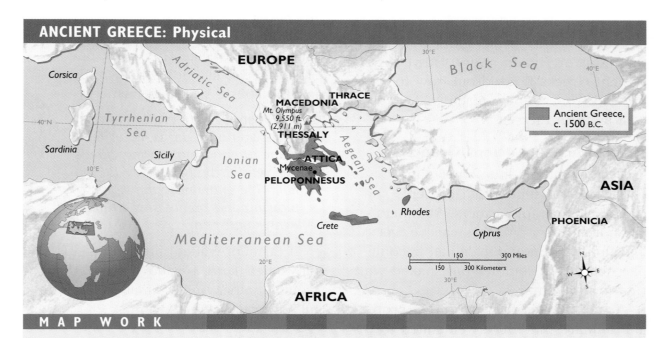

ANCIENT GREECE: Physical

MAP WORK

For its size, the land of ancient Greece had a very long coastline. Much of the land is also mountainous. This geography had a great impact on life in the region.

1. What method of transportation do you suppose was quickest in ancient Greece?

2. About how long is the island of Crete? Use the map scale to find this answer.

3. What body of water lies east of Attica?

4. In which direction would you travel to get from Crete to Rhodes?

Like their ancestors in ancient times, many farmers in Greece today herd sheep (left) and raise olives (above).

EARLY ECONOMY IN GREECE

Greece is not as fertile as the valleys of the Indus or Huang rivers. However, ancient Greeks figured out how to make a living from the few fertile valleys as well as from the sea.

Agriculture in Ancient Greece

Besides having little fertile land, Greece has a climate that presents special challenges for farmers. Summers are hot and dry. Winters can be wet and fiercely windy. Fields can become parched in the summer but soaked with rain in the winter.

Ancient Greek farmers raised crops and animals that were well suited to this environment. They grew some wheat and barley to make bread, which was important to the Greek diet. Olives and grapes became Greece's other major crops. Both grew well in rocky and hilly areas. Shrubs on Greece's many hills and mountains provided food for herds of sheep, goats, and cattle.

Timing was important to successful farming in Greece. The Greek poet Hesiod (HEE see ud), who wrote during the 700s B.C., urged farmers:

Take careful note of the time when you hear the voice of the crane uttering high in the clouds her yearly trumpeting cry [in the fall]. She announces the signal for plowing and points to the time of winter and rain.

If farmers waited until winter to plow their land, Hesiod warned, they would "gather only a small little handful" of grain in the spring.

Crossing the Seas

Because farmers could not produce huge grain surpluses, and because travel on the hilly land was difficult, sailing became an important part of life in Greece. Sailors traveled as far as ancient Egypt to trade. Greek merchants competed with traders from Phoenicia (fuh NEE shuh), in what is today Lebanon. Phoenician sailors were as skilled as the Greeks and traveled to ports all across the Mediterranean Sea.

For many years olive oil was one of the most prized of Greek exports. People loved the flavor it gave food as well as its usefulness as lamp fuel and body lotion. The sale of olive oil made it possible for Greeks to buy much-needed grain for their markets at home.

WHY IT MATTERS

In the lessons to come, you will read the story of Greek civilization. Beginning around 800 B.C., great changes would take place on these rocky islands and peninsulas. Some things, however, would never change. Farming and sailing would always be lifelines for the people of ancient Greece.

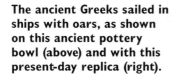

The ancient Greeks sailed in ships with oars, as shown on this ancient pottery bowl (above) and with this present-day replica (right).

Reviewing Facts and Ideas

SUM IT UP

- Unlike the Nile or Huang River valleys, Greece has land that is hilly and rocky, making farming difficult in most areas.

- Ancient Greeks used the Mediterranean Sea as a "highway" to trade for goods they could not produce themselves.

- Olive oil—a product of a crop that grows well in Greece's rocky soil— became valuable to trade for grain.

THINK ABOUT IT

1. Why was farming a challenge in Greece? Why was timing important?

2. Contrast the geography of Greece with that of an ancient river valley civilization such as Mesopotamia or the Indus Valley.

3. **FOCUS** How did ancient Greeks use the sea to spread their products and culture to other regions?

4. **THINKING SKILL** What *effects* did geography have on the ways ancient Greeks met their needs?

5. **GEOGRAPHY** Draw a map of the Mediterranean Sea region. Draw in arrows to show where ancient Greeks sailed.

700 B.C. 600 B.C. 500 B.C. 400 B.C. 300 B.C.

THE RISE OF GREEK CITIES

Focus Activity

READ TO LEARN
What was life like in the ancient Greek cities of Sparta and Athens?

VOCABULARY
polis
acropolis
agora
citizen
oligarchy
monarchy
democracy
colony

PEOPLE
Homer

PLACES
Athens
Sparta
Mount Olympus

READ ALOUD

"Shared blood, shared language, shared religion, and shared customs." Long ago a Greek historian named Herodotus (hih RAHD uh tus) used these words to describe what it meant to be Greek. Greeks were very proud of what they shared. However, they prized just as highly those things that made them different from one another. Those differences began in the many city-states that dotted the mainland and islands of ancient Greece.

THE BIG PICTURE

By 1100 B.C. both Egypt's New Kingdom empire and China's Shang dynasty had lost their power. Historians know little about how people in Greece lived during this period or during the next 400 years. Very few artifacts from Greece at this time have been found. However, many artifacts dating from about 700 B.C. onward have been found. They show that life had changed greatly since the earliest days of ancient Greece. In many cities, groups of powerful men worked together to make decisions for their communities. Each community usually revolved around one city. The Greek word for this kind of city-state was **polis** (POH lihs).

A GREEK POLIS

Most city-states were laid out according to a similar plan. Most were built around an acropolis (uh KROP uh lihs). An acropolis was a large hill where city residents could seek shelter and safety in times of war. In a nearby clearing farmers would gather to trade with each other and with craftworkers. The clearing, called an agora (AG ur uh), often served both as a marketplace and as a meeting place.

Developing Governments

Although city-states often looked similar, each one had a different type of government. In each type, however, leaders had to be citizens of their polis. Today a citizen is a person who has certain rights and responsibilities in his or her country or community. In ancient Greece, though, only men could be citizens. Women and slaves were not allowed to be citizens and had few rights. Slaves, or *helots* (HEL uts), in ancient Greece were usually conquered neighbors. Slavery was common throughout ancient Greece.

Being a citizen did not automatically give men a role in their government. In many city-states a small group of the richest, most powerful citizens controlled decision making. This type of government is called an oligarchy (OL ih gahr kee). By 600 B.C. the Greek city-state of Athens was governed by an oligarchy. One Athenian said:

Oligarchy is a government resting on the value of property, in which the rich have power and the poor have none.

Before the oligarchy Athens had another form of government. Like other Greek city-states, it was ruled by one ruler, or king. This type of government is called a monarchy. In fact the word *monarchy* comes from two Greek words meaning "rule by one."

The Acropolis in Athens is the best known of the many acropolises built in Greece.

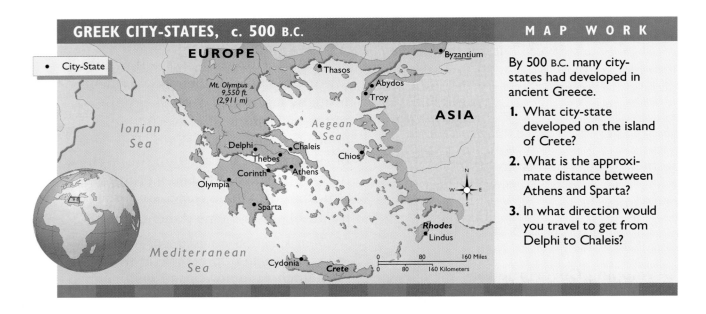

EUROPE

Byzantium

Thasos

Mt. Olympus
9,550 ft.
(2,911 m)

Abydos
Troy

ASIA

Ionian
Sea

Aegean
Sea

Delphi

Chaleis

Thebes
Corinth
Olympia

Chios

Athens

Sparta

N
W   E
S

Rhodes
Lindus

Mediterranean
Sea

Cydonia

Crete

City-State

0   80   160 Miles
0   80   160 Kilometers

By 500 B.C. many city-states had developed in ancient Greece.

1. What city-state developed on the island of Crete?

2. What is the approximate distance between Athens and Sparta?

3. In what direction would you travel to get from Delphi to Chaleis?

TWO GREEK CITIES

Of Greece's many city-states, historians know most about Athens and Sparta. Many documents and artifacts from those cities have been preserved. Like all Greek city-states, they had much in common. The way people lived in the two powerful city-states from day to day, however, differed a great deal.

Sparta

In 700 B.C. Sparta covered much of the southern Peloponnesus and was Greece's largest city-state. Dozens of villages belonged to this polis. Sparta's central "city" was a cluster of villages that lay almost 30 miles from the Mediterranean Sea. A low mountain nearby formed Sparta's acropolis. Near its base lay the polis agora, or meeting place. Here Sparta's leaders made the decisions that shaped life in this polis.

As in other city-states, farmers gathered at Sparta's agora to do business. Most of Sparta's farm workers, however, were slaves. Sparta had many more slaves than other city-states. At some times, there were as many as seven slaves for every one Spartan.

The Spartan Military

Around 600 B.C. Sparta's slaves revolted. The Spartans, however, managed to overpower their slaves. Polis leaders then set out to make Sparta the strongest military power in Greece. They wanted to make sure that neither slaves nor another polis could ever gain control of Sparta.

Sparta's people dedicated much of their lives to making their polis strong. Spartan children, too, were expected to do their part for the polis. At about age seven, boys and girls began training. Although they spent some time learning to read and write, boys spent even more time training to be soldiers. Girls practiced running, throwing spears called javelins, and playing ball games. In Sparta, girls trained not to become soldiers but rather to be strong mothers of strong children.

Athens

Life for girls and boys was very different in the city of Athens. Athens lay on the peninsula of Attica, northeast of Sparta. Athenian girls did not practice sports. Rather, they were told to "see little, hear little, and ask no more questions than are absolutely necessary." Girls stayed at home to help their mothers. They carried out such duties as weaving cloth from sheep's wool. Girls who lived on farms helped in the fields at harvesttime.

Many Athenian boys worked each day with their fathers in the fields, or in pottery or stoneworking shops. If their parents could afford to send them to school, boys studied reading and writing. After classes they would practice wrestling or boxing at a local gymnasium before returning home.

Government in Athens

Life in Athens was different from that in Sparta. Athenians did not spend as much time and energy building a strong army. Yet Athens had challenges of its own.

Remember, Athens' government around 600 B.C. was an oligarchy. Most of Athens' early leaders belonged to noble families that were both rich and powerful. In time the poorer citizens of Athens demanded to have more say in how their government was run. The nobles were forced to share some of their power with other citizens.

Power to the People

The developing new government featured large meetings where all the citizens could take part in making decisions for the polis. This form of government is today called a **democracy**. The word *democracy* combines two Greek words meaning "rule by the people." It means that citizens vote to make government decisions.

The beginnings of democracy marked an important time in world history. Some historians, in fact, trace our own ideas of democracy back to ancient Greece. In the next lesson you will read about further developments in Greece's new democratic system.

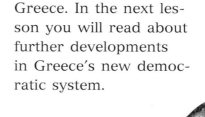

Spartan women trained vigorously (right) while women in Athens led more gentle lives (below).

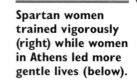

SHARED CULTURE

The citizens of Athens did not meet to discuss government policies every day. Like the people of the other Greek cities, Athenians reserved a few days of every month for religious celebrations to honor gods and goddesses.

Ancient Greeks believed that many gods and goddesses ruled the world. The most powerful were said to live on **Mount Olympus**. Mount Olympus is a mountain in northern Greece.

Special Festivals

Each polis honored at least one god or goddess as its special protector and provider. In Athens people worshiped *Athena,* the goddess of wisdom. Every summer they held a huge festival in her honor. After singing and dancing all night, Athenians walked to the top of the city's acropolis. There, as the sun rose in the sky, priests killed cattle in honor of Athena.

People from all over Greece also gathered at temples to worship Zeus (ZOOS), the most powerful god in the ancient Greek religion. The city-states also came together to compete in athletic competitions. You will read more about the most well known of these games, the Olympics, in this chapter's Legacy on pages 202–203. At the Olympic Games crowds cheered athletes from many city-states.

A Greek Poet

People in all city-states loved to hear the stories of the poet **Homer**. Many of these stories described Greece's past. Homer is thought to have lived sometime between 800 and 700 B.C. His most famous epic poems, the *Iliad* and the *Odyssey,* tell stories of war and adventure. The *Iliad* describes what happened when a prince from Troy, an ancient city in what is today Turkey, kidnapped Helen, a Greek queen. The poem also describes how the gods created Greek cities. How does Homer describe the Greek army?

Excerpt from the *Iliad*, by Homer, c. 700 B.C.

As when, at the edge of the sounding sea, wave after wave comes up under the driving of the West Wind—out on the deep it lifts its crest and is broken on the land with a noise like thunder, and far over the headlands shoots its salt foam—so did the Greek lines then go into battle. Each chief gave his men their orders, but the rest said not a word. You would not have thought that all that great army had a voice among them, in such silence they all went through fear of their chiefs. And as they moved, the armor upon their bodies flashed in the sun.

Beyond Greece

Not long after the Greek festivals and Olympics were begun, athletes from faraway Greek colonies came to participate. The colonies were made up of groups of people who lived apart from, but kept ties with, Greece. Colonies were founded by Greeks in the 700s B.C. Many colonies became important trading partners because they grew grains that were much in demand in Greece. Greek ships also traveled south to Egypt's Nile Delta.

By 500 B.C. Greek city-states ringed the Mediterranean "like frogs around a pond," as a teacher named Plato put it. Some of Greece's eastern territories, however, were being taken over by a growing empire that was already vastly larger than Greece. At its height this empire of Persia—based in what is today Iran—was bigger than any that had yet existed in the world. It included all lands from Egypt and the western edge of the Mediterranean Sea to the Indus Valley.

Ancient Greeks worshiped Apollo, their god of the sun.

WHY IT MATTERS

The city-states of ancient Greece had their differences and valued their independence. Many of the Greek cities even had different types of government. One of these cities, Athens, began to develop a new kind of government called democracy. The idea of democracy is important in the United States.

Despite their differences, the cities of ancient Greece shared many cultural ties. In 499 B.C. a Greek colony on the edge of what is today Turkey wanted to break free from Persian control. People of the colony asked the Greek city-states for help. Athens, Sparta, and other city-states joined together to fight Persia. The war that followed would change Greece forever.

✓// Reviewing Facts and Ideas

SUM IT UP

- Life in most of the Greek city-states revolved around an agora and an acropolis.

- Spartans spent much of their time working to strengthen their bodies and their army. In Athens free women and girls worked at home. Boys and men worked, went to school, or took part in government.

THINK ABOUT IT

1. What did city-states have in common? What made them different?

2. Who was allowed to vote in the developing democracy of Athens?

3. **FOCUS** Why was life in Sparta so different from life in Athens?

4. **THINKING SKILL** What *effects* did slavery have on life in Sparta?

5. **GEOGRAPHY** What made the agora a center for cultural interaction?

THE OLYMPICS

Have you ever dreamed of competing in the Olympic Games? You may have imagined yourself crossing the finish line at the end of a race. Perhaps you simply enjoy watching the events on television.

The Olympic Games were first held nearly 3,000 years ago in ancient Greece. City-states cooperated to make the games an important part of Greek culture.

By about A.D. 400 the ancient Olympics had faded away. The tradition was revived in 1896. Today the international games take place every four years. Most nations of the world send their best athletes to take part in the Summer and the Winter Olympic Games.

Look at the pictures on these pages. Think about how the modern Olympic Games help people to remember an important legacy of the past.

Disabled athletes compete in Special Olympic Games. The first Special Olympic Games were held in Chicago in 1968. Today athletes from more than 100 different countries participate in these events.

Unlike ancient Olympic Games, women now compete in most sports. American speed skater Bonnie Blair won two gold medals during the 1994 Winter Olympics. Also new to the Winter Olympics are cold-weather sports, such as skiing, ice hockey, and bobsledding. Those events became part of Olympic competition in 1924.

The modern games begin with a parade of Olympic athletes from every participating nation. Today many of the athletes take part in team competitions. Such team events were not part of ancient Olympic Games.

ATHENS' AGE OF GLORY

Focus Activity

READ TO LEARN
What did the Athenians achieve during Athens' "Golden Age"?

VOCABULARY
assembly
jury
philosophy
Peloponnesian Wars

PEOPLE
Pericles
Socrates
Plato

PLACES
Acropolis
Parthenon

READ ALOUD

If Athenians living in 500 B.C. could somehow have traveled 65 years into the future, they would have been amazed by what they saw. In the city's harbor many ships would be tied at a long dock leading straight to a huge trading area. People could buy a wide range of goods, from Egyptian papyrus to Italian cheese, with coins from Athens or Persia. Walking up the road to the city—now surrounded by walls—they would have seen grand stone temples where far simpler ones had once stood. Athens, clearly, was flourishing.

THE BIG PICTURE

What happened to bring about the success of Athens? As you read in the last lesson, the city-states of Greece went to war against the empire of Persia in 499 B.C. Understanding the importance of sea power, the Athenians built a mighty naval fleet. Over the next 20 years they joined forces with the armies of Sparta and other city-states. Together they defeated the Persians.

Many Greek colonies were still in danger of Persian attack, however. Some of them began paying money for protection by the Athenian navy. Athens became rich from these payments. Some of that money went toward building an even more powerful navy. Much of the rest went to improve life in the city itself.

Around 460 B.C. Athens entered a period of rich culture. Some historians call the next 30 years the "Golden Age" of Athens. It was a time of great achievement.

GOLDEN AGE OF ATHENS

In the middle 400s B.C. Athens was the same in many ways as it had been 65 years earlier. Life still revolved around the agora and the acropolis. Citizens still voted on issues that shaped life in the city. Festivals honoring Athena were still held every summer. Much, however, had changed.

Beautifully made vases (left) and the Parthenon (below) were among the many achievements of the ancient Greeks.

A Walk Through Athens

The Acropolis, high above the city, was the religious center of Athens. Many Greek cities had their own acropolises. The one at Athens, however, was larger than others—that is why it is generally spelled with a capital *A*. Here a group of buildings displayed the city's new wealth and power. At their center rose a temple to Athena made of marble cut from a nearby mountain. This stunning temple was the Parthenon (PAHR thuh nahn). It still sits on the highest point of the Acropolis and can be seen from all over the city.

Looking down from the Acropolis, one could see many buildings. About 100,000 people lived in Athens, making it the largest city in Greece.

Activity in the Agora

Following the winding road down from the Acropolis, one might see crowds of people. Many had come to do business at the agora. There were shopkeepers, students, and lawyers heading for the market or government buildings. In one corner of the agora, citizens gathered at a monument that served as the city's "bulletin board." Here people could leave messages or read postings about upcoming matters to be voted on.

Merchants sold perfume, vegetables, and clothing or offered haircuts. In nearby workshops, potters crafted vases and bowls. The diagram on page 207 shows what Athens may have looked like.

ATHENIAN GOVERNMENT

In the early 400s B.C. a small council of powerful citizens made all of the city's important decisions. Later in the century, though, the council's powers had been taken over by an assembly of citizens. An assembly is a lawmaking body of a government. The assembly voted on issues that helped to shape the future of the city.

Do you remember from the last lesson who were considered citizens in Athens and who were not? No women and no enslaved men had a voice in Athens' government. In fact they did not enjoy any of the rights of citizenship, such as land ownership. However, the people of ancient Athens took a big step toward creating a government that represented the people.

DID YOU KNOW?

What did ancient Greeks do for entertainment?

Famous people such as Socrates and Pericles were made fun of by writers such as Aristophanes (ar uh STOHF uh neez). He wrote funny plays called comedies. Comedies, along with serious plays called tragedies, were performed at festivals. Another playwright, Aeschylus (ES kuh lus), wrote tragedies about events in Greek history.

Over 13,000 people crowded into outdoor theaters to watch the popular plays. Actors played their parts with the help of big masks. A group called the "chorus" sang, danced, and acted in the plays.

A Great Statesman

Pericles (PER ih kleez), an Athenian leader around 450 B.C., explained his city's government this way:

> Our city is called a democracy because it is governed by the many, not the few. . . . No one, moreover, if he has it in him to do some good for the city, is barred because of poverty or humble origins.

Pericles made sure poor as well as rich citizens could take part in government.

Citizens served on the assembly and sat on juries. A jury is a group of citizens chosen to hear evidence and make decisions in a court of law. Pericles arranged for citizens to be paid when they held office or served on a jury. This meant that farmers and other poor citizens could afford to take the time to become involved in government.

Philosophy in Athens

While citizens debated government issues, famous teachers like Socrates (SAHK ruh teez) led discussions about the right way to live. Socrates lived around the middle 400s B.C. He taught his students philosophy, or the search for wisdom and the right way to live. They discussed what makes the best kind of government or what it means to love or to be a good citizen.

Shortly before 400 B.C. Socrates began questioning Athenian values, such as laws, customs—even religion. It made some Athenians angry that he would doubt anything about the polis. In 399 B.C. Socrates was brought to trial for "urging Athens' young people to revolt." The jury decided he was guilty and sentenced him to death. His teachings, however, were written down by a student, Plato (PLAY toh), who also became a famous philosopher.

DORIC   IONIC   CORINTHIAN

Ancient Greeks developed three types of columns.

PARTHENON

ACROPOLIS

AGORA

THE GOLDEN AGE OF ATHENS

In the 400s B.C. Athens was flourishing. Many daily activities took place at the Acropolis. What do you see going on?

WAR AND CONFLICT

The Golden Age of Athens did not last, however. Sparta and other Greek city-states were jealous of the power and wealth of Athens. They formed what they called the Peloponnesian League. You can see where the allies of Sparta and the allies of Athens were located on the map on this page. In 431 B.C. the two sides began what became known as the Peloponnesian (pel uh puh NEEZH un) Wars.

Battles on Land and Sea

The wars began with an attack by the Spartan army. Pericles knew that his army was no match for Sparta's. He called for Athenians living outside the city to move inside the city walls. The walls protected the city, but Sparta's army destroyed the farmland around Athens. The Athenians did not starve, however, because their navy controlled the Aegean Sea. Ships were able to bring in grain from other areas.

In fact the powerful Athenian navy kept the wars in a deadlock for many years. Athens was able to win most of the battles at sea while Sparta won more often on land. However, the course of the wars worsened for Athens. A terrible disease swept through the crowded city. At least one third of the population died from it. One of its victims was Pericles. Meanwhile the wars continued, taking many more lives.

A Final Blow

In 404 B.C. Sparta was able to cut off the Athenian grain supply from the Black Sea. The starving Athenians had to surrender. All of Greece had suffered great losses from the Peloponnesian

THE PELOPONNESIAN WAR, 431–404 B.C.

MACEDONIA

411 B.C.

THESSALY

Ionian Sea

429 B.C.

Aegean Sea

404 B.C.

406 B.C.

418 B.C.

Athens

PERSIAN EMPIRE

Athens surrenders

Sparta

Mediterranean Sea

Rhodes

Athens and allies
Sparta and allies
Other Greek areas
Athenian victory
Spartan victory

0   75   150 Miles
0   75   150 Kilometers

MAP WORK

The **Peloponnesian Wars** cost many lives.

1. How long did the Peloponnesian Wars last?

2. Which side, Athens or Sparta, controlled more coastal areas? Why do you suppose that might have been?

3. How many battles shown on this map took place on the island of Rhodes?

4. What northern region did Sparta control?

5. In what year did Athens finally surrender?

Ancient Greek soldiers went into battle protected by bronze helmets and chest plates.

Wars. The Greek historian Thucydides (thoo SIHD ih deez), who lived during the time, concluded that war "is a violent teacher."

The End of a Golden Age

Following the Peloponnesian Wars, Sparta was once again the leading polis in Greece. Yet its victory was short-lived. For the next 50 years no city-state was able to maintain control for long before others challenged it. These unsettled times would leave Greece open to threat from a new power to the north.

WHY IT MATTERS

Between 500 B.C. and 400 B.C. Athens gave the world some of ancient Greece's most enduring legacies. Athenians improved their democracy and built splendid temples. They searched for wisdom through philosophy and created new dramatic forms. After 400 B.C. a young warrior-king from another land would spread those legacies far and wide. His name was Alexander. You will read about him in the following lesson.

Reviewing Facts and Ideas

SUM IT UP

- In the 400s B.C., during their "Golden Age," Athenians discussed philosophy, wrote plays, and built many grand buildings.

- Though democracy was still limited to male citizens, Pericles worked to give poorer citizens a voice in Athenian government.

- The Peloponnesian Wars ended the "Golden Age" of Athens. Afterward no single polis dominated Greece.

THINK ABOUT IT

1. How did the war against Persia bring new wealth and power to Athens?

2. What changes did Pericles introduce in Athens?

3. **FOCUS** List three things that reflect how the century before 400 B.C. was a "golden age" for Athens.

4. **THINKING SKILL** Make a *generalization* about the changes that occurred in Athenian government between 500 B.C. and 400 B.C.

5. **WRITE** Write a paragraph comparing democracy in Athens with democracy in the United States.

THINKINGSKILLS

Making Conclusions

The painting *School of Athens* by Raphael shows Socrates with other philosophers. Plato (left), shown in another part of the painting, takes notes.

VOCABULARY

conclusion

WHY THE SKILL MATTERS

In the last lesson you read about a type of government that developed in Athens. While you read, you may have made certain conclusions about democracy. Making a conclusion involves putting together information. This skill helps you to make sense of new knowledge. Use the Helping Yourself box for some hints that will help you to make conclusions.

The skill of making conclusions is an especially important one to students of history. It helps you to see the "big picture" created by facts and dates, and it gives that information meaning.

USING THE SKILL

Practice making a conclusion by reading through the paragraph on the next page. Look for ideas that can be put together into a general picture. Then make a statement that makes sense of the ideas.

In the 400s B.C. more schools were created in Athens than ever before—though none were for girls or slaves. Families who could afford the cost began sending their boys to school at age seven. There they learned to read, write, and memorize the poems of Homer. Math and science were rarely taught. Most students left school after learning basic skills. The sons of wealthy families kept studying until they were teenagers. Their teachers worked to make them good thinkers and speakers so they would be respected in the city's assembly.

This sculpture shows Aristotle, a student of Plato, thinking. Aristotle is considered to be one of the greatest Greek philosophers.

HELPING
Yourself

- The making of **conclusions** involves finding a meaning by combining facts or information.

- Think about what each piece of information means.

- Think about what all the information means when it is linked together.

- Make a statement that sums up the meaning of all the information.

The paragraph provides information about education in Athens. Because many schools were created and some students attended until they were teenagers, you might conclude that education became more important in Athens during the 400s B.C. You might also conclude that the sons of wealthy families were given more opportunities to learn. You can often make more than one conclusion from the same information.

TRYING THE SKILL

Read the following paragraph. What is the paragraph mostly about?

Most teachers of wealthy students in Athens charged fees to teach public speaking. A few philosophers like Socrates, though, taught students for free. To those thinkers, understanding the proper way to live was more important than money or the skills that made money. Thanks to Socrates and his fellow philosophers, the search for knowledge and truth would become an important part of life in Athens for years to come.

REVIEWING THE SKILL

1. What conclusion did you make from the paragraph above?

2. What evidence can you give to support your conclusion?

3. How does making a conclusion help you to better understand something that you've just read?

THE GREEK EMPIRE

READ ALOUD

Stadium. Gymnasium. Museum. Democracy. These words represent things that are important in our lives today. All of them had beginnings in ancient Greece. The story of Greek civilization continues with a young man named Alexander.

THE BIG PICTURE

In the late 400s B.C. the Peloponnesian Wars raged in Greece. During this time the Persian empire, which you read about in the last lesson, still controlled a huge part of the world. Egyptians, Phoenicians, Jews, Babylonians, and Indians all lived under the rule of Persian kings. Connecting this empire was a network of roads and messenger services.

The Greek historian Herodotus may have traveled those roads around 450 B.C. He once made a 1,500-mile journey in about 90 days. He was amazed by the relay of royal messengers who traveled the same roads in just nine days! "Neither snow nor rain nor heat nor night holds back [the messenger from] the accomplishment of the course that has been assigned him," he marveled. Today the United States Postal Service uses similar words to describe the task of letter carriers as they transport mail across the country and around the world.

A man named Alexander traveled the roads of the Persian empire between 334 and 323 B.C., a little over 100 years after Herodotus. He conquered many areas and eventually became known as "Alexander the Great." As a result of his victories, Greek language and traditions spread as far as Egypt in Africa and the Indus Valley in Asia.

Focus Activity

READ TO LEARN
What did Alexander the Great do to spread legacies of Greek civilization?

PEOPLE
Alexander
Aristotle

PLACES
Macedonia
Alexandria

ALEXANDER OF MACEDONIA

Although the Peloponnesian Wars ended in 404 B.C., conflict continued to weaken the Greek city-states. This left them open to attack from Macedonia (mas ih DAHN nee uh), a powerful kingdom to the north. By 336 B.C. Macedonia's army had conquered most of Greece.

Macedonia's king at this time was a 20-year-old man named Alexander. He had already proven that he was a bold commander. He was also well educated. Aristotle (AR uh staht ul), one of the most famous philosophers in Athens, had been his private teacher. Because of Aristotle's teachings, Alexander developed a deep respect for Greek culture and traditions.

Expanding the Empire

In 334 B.C. Alexander and his armies set out to conquer Persia. Find their route on the map on the next page. For three years they fought their way along the eastern coast of the Mediterranean. Everywhere they went, they seized food and whatever else they needed to continue their journey.

The powerful Macedonian army never lost a battle. In 331 B.C. Alexander proclaimed, or publicly declared, himself ruler of Persia's vast empire as well as of Greece. To secure his power, Alexander pushed his army farther east.

In a few more years his troops had entered the Indus River valley. There they defeated an army that used elephants. Many of Alexander's soldiers had never seen such animals before. After his victory, though, the young emperor became sick. Unable to complete the journey, he died in June 323 B.C., in Babylon.

Alexander the Great was a brilliant military leader. These works of art show Alexander in battle.

A CITY IN THE EMPIRE

About nine years before he died, Alexander planned the creation of a city in Egypt, on the western edge of the Nile Delta. Alexandria, named after the emperor, soon became one of the most important cities in the Greek empire. The city of Alexandria was an example of how Greek civilization and ideas were carried far beyond Greece.

A Blending of Cultures

Like the many cities that Alexander had built, Alexandria's basic layout mirrored a Greek polis. It had an agora, a theater, several temples, a stadium, and a gymnasium. Alexandria's harbor became a major hub of Mediterranean trade. At the mouth of the harbor stood a gigantic lighthouse. This was one of the first lighthouses in the world. Its beam was a guide for sailors many miles away at sea.

The mixture of peoples and cultures in Alexandria created an unusual community. Besides building temples to Greek gods, Alexander planned a temple to the Egyptian goddess Isis. The Greek and Macedonian citizens of Alexandria took part in democratic assemblies. Egyptians in Alexandria had courts of their own. So did the city's Jews, who lived in their own section of the city. Craftworkers made Greek-style pottery. Papermakers continued to practice their ancient craft.

A Legacy of Learning

Not far from Alexandria's busy agora stood the city's museum. At the museum, scholars studied the world and how it worked. To help with their research,

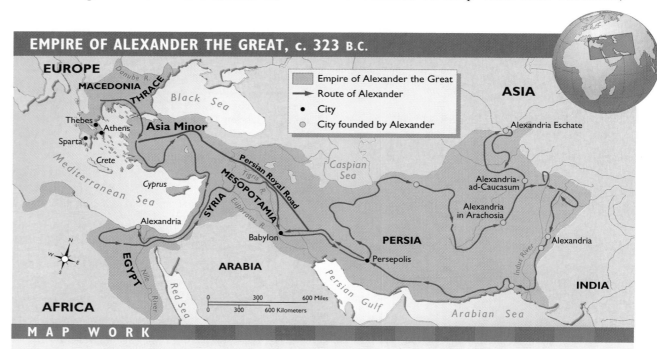

EMPIRE OF ALEXANDER THE GREAT, c. 323 B.C.

Empire of Alexander the Great
Route of Alexander
• City
○ City founded by Alexander

EUROPE
MACEDONIA
THRACE
Danube R.
Black Sea
Thebes
Athens
Asia Minor
Sparta
Crete
Cyprus
Mediterranean Sea
Alexandria
SYRIA
MESOPOTAMIA
Tigris R.
Euphrates R.
Persian Royal Road
Babylon
Persepolis
Caspian Sea
PERSIA
ASIA
Alexandria Eschate
Alexandria-ad-Caucasum
Alexandria in Arachosia
Indus River
Alexandria
INDIA
EGYPT
Nile River
Red Sea
ARABIA
Persian Gulf
Arabian Sea
AFRICA

0   300   600 Miles
0   300   600 Kilometers

M A P   W O R K

Alexander the Great controlled enormous territories with the help of a very powerful army.

1. Alexander's vast empire included land on three continents. What are they?

2. What region south of Mesopotamia did Alexander not gain control of?

3. What is the easternmost river within Alexander's empire?

4. What river marks the northernmost border of Alexander's empire?

5. In which direction did Alexander travel along the coast of the Arabian Sea?

Alexander (left) founded Alexandria, one of the most important cities in the Greek empire. Today it is the second largest city in Egypt.

they used the books in the library nearby. Alexandria's library had almost 500,000 books written on papyrus rolls, and librarians were always searching for more! Inspectors at the harbor searched newly arrived ships to see if they carried any books. They kept whatever they found until copies could be made for the city's library.

An Alphabet

Scholars from many countries visited the library in Alexandria to study the books there. The skills of reading and writing had become important for preserving information. Unlike Egyptian hieroglyphics, Mesopotamian cuneiform, and Chinese characters, written Greek used a simple alphabet. Each symbol represented a sound. Learning to read required mastering less than 30 letters, rather than hundreds of symbols. The alphabet made it easier for more people to learn to read and write.

Math and Science

The library in Alexandria contained many books on mathematics. Ancient Greece produced brilliant mathematicians. They had learned a great deal from earlier Egyptian scholars, whose achievements in math and science you learned about in Chapter 4. Today many of the things you do in math class are legacies of their work. *Arithmetic, geometry,* and *mathematics* are all words that have Greek origins.

Infographic

Seven Wonders of the World

Around the time of Alexander, travelers told of the "Seven Wonders of the World." They were called wonders because of their size, beauty, craftwork, or all three. Today only the pyramids still stand, but many people try to imagine the other ancient wonders. This is an artist's idea of what they may have looked like.

Are there Seven Wonders of the modern world? What list would you give a traveler today?

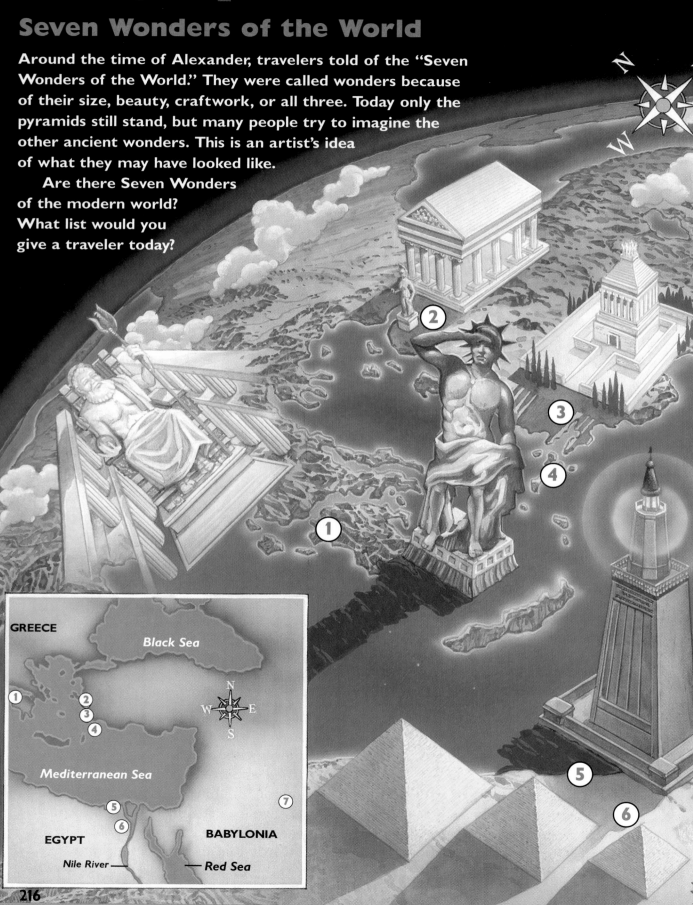

GREECE

Black Sea

Mediterranean Sea

EGYPT

BABYLONIA

Nile River ——— Red Sea

1 Statue of Zeus at Olympia
about 435 B.C.

The statue of Zeus showed the god on his throne. It is said to have been about 40 feet high. Historians say it was probably the most famous statue in the ancient world.

2 Temple of Artemis at Ephesus
about 550 B.C.

This temple is said to have been more than 40 feet high. It was made almost entirely of marble and was dedicated to the Greek god Artemis.

3 Mausoleum at Halicarnassus
about 353 B.C.

This tomb was built for a Persian ruler called Mausolus. It was decorated with a pyramid. The tomb was so famous that all large tombs are now called *mausoleums*.

4 Colossus of Rhodes
about 200 B.C.

The Colossus was a bronze statue built to honor the sun god Helios. A Greek sculptor is said to have worked for 12 years to create the statue.

5 Lighthouse of Alexandria
about 283-246 B.C.

This lighthouse stood over 400 feet high. A fire that burned at the top of it guided ships into the harbor of Alexandria for about 1,500 years.

6 Pyramids of Egypt at Giza
about 2600-2500 B.C.

The pyramids were built as tombs for Egyptian kings. The largest one, called the Great Pyramid, stands about 450 feet high.

7 Hanging Gardens of Babylon
about 605-562 B.C.

These gardens were probably laid out on a large terrace about 75 feet above the ground. They were watered by the Euphrates River.

WHY IT MATTERS

After Alexander died, no one person was able to control the vast empire. By 300 B.C. Alexander's generals had divided it up.

Although Alexander's empire did not last, his short rule had far-reaching effects. One of the most important was the mixing of cultures throughout North Africa and western and central Asia.

Many legacies of ancient Greece continue to influence cultures today. You can see Greek influence in classes on such subjects as math, philosophy, and science. Perhaps most important, Greek ideas live on in the way our government operates—as a democracy.

Reviewing Facts and Ideas

SUM IT UP

- When Alexander the Great conquered the Persian empire, he spread Greek culture from Egypt to India.

- Alexandria, one of the empire's most powerful cities, reflected the great mix of cultures within the empire.

- Legacies from ancient Greece influence today's education, government, philosophy, sports, and drama.

THINK ABOUT IT

1. How was Alexander influenced by Greek culture?

2. What did Alexandria have in common with a polis? How was it influenced by a variety of cultures?

3. **FOCUS** How did Alexander change life around the Mediterranean region?

4. **THINKING SKILL** What *conclusions* can you *make* about Greece's importance to history?

5. **WRITE** In one paragraph describe how a Greek legacy affects your life.

CITIZENSHIP
VIEWPOINTS

WHERE SHOULD THE ELGIN MARBLES BE DISPLAYED?

The famous "Elgin Marbles" (above) were designed by the ancient Greek artist, Phidias.

More than 2,400 years ago, ancient Greeks built the Parthenon, a temple to the goddess Athena. Today many people visit the ruins of this once-magnificent building in Athens. Over a thousand miles away in London, England, people visit the British Museum to see 83 marble statues that once were a part of the Parthenon. The "Elgin Marbles," as the statues are called today, were shipped to England in the early 1800s. Since 1830 the government of Greece has twice requested that the statues be returned.

Some people, such as Robert Anderson, say that the marbles were properly removed from the Parthenon, and are best preserved and displayed in the British Museum. Martin Krause, who opposes returning the Elgin Marbles, says that museums would soon be empty if they returned the treasures in their collections to the people and nations who claim them. Melina Mercouri points out that Greece is not asking for the return of all Greek artifacts, only those taken from the Parthenon. Consider viewpoints on this issue and answer the questions that follow.

Three DIFFERENT Viewpoints

1 **ROBERT ANDERSON**
Museum Curator, London, England
Excerpt from interview

The sculptures were rescued by Lord Elgin from the ruins of the Parthenon with the approval of the appropriate authorities. The entire collection was purchased from Elgin by the British Government in 1816 and entrusted to the British Museum to be preserved and kept together. The Parthenon sculptures are one of the Museum's greatest and best-loved treasures. It is appropriate that they should remain in a Museum which is international in its scope.

"... Museum's greatest and best-loved treasures"

2 **MARTIN KRAUSE**
Museum Curator, Indianapolis, Indiana
Excerpt from interview

Taking the Elgin Marbles helped preserve them in much better condition than if they had remained in Athens exposed to the elements. If every country reclaimed the art from its country, the only art that would remain in American museums would be American art. However, these sculptures were made for the Parthenon and should not have been detached. They are the greatest sculptures of Greece's greatest century so naturally Greece would want them back.

"... these sculptures were made for the Parthenon."

3 **MELINA MERCOURI**
Former Greek Minister of Culture, Athens, Greece
Excerpt from interview

The Parthenon marbles are our pride, our noblest symbol of excellence. . . . Greece has never ceased to ask for their return. [Some say] that more people could see the marbles if they were kept by the British Museum. By such logic, why not place them in permanent exhibit at Disneyland? Is it right that 95 percent of the Greek people might never see the finest of Greek creation?

"... our pride, our noblest symbol of excellence"

BUILDING CITIZENSHIP

1. What is the viewpoint of each person? How does each support his or her views?
2. In what ways are some of the viewpoints alike? In what ways are they different?
3. What other viewpoints might people have on this issue? What other examples of this type of issue might exist in the United States?

SHARING VIEWPOINTS

Discuss what you agree with or disagree with about these and other viewpoints. Discuss why you think each speaker might feel as he or she does. Then as a class, write three statements that all of you can agree with about the display of the Elgin Marbles.

CHAPTER 8 REVIEW

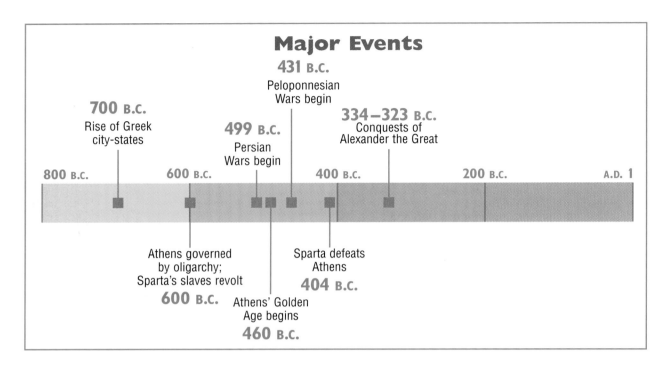

Major Events

431 B.C.
Peloponnesian Wars begin

700 B.C.
Rise of Greek city-states

499 B.C.
Persian Wars begin

334–323 B.C.
Conquests of Alexander the Great

800 B.C.   600 B.C.   400 B.C.   200 B.C.   A.D. 1

Athens governed by oligarchy; Sparta's slaves revolt
600 B.C.

Athens' Golden Age begins
460 B.C.

Sparta defeats Athens
404 B.C.

THINKING ABOUT VOCABULARY

Number a sheet of paper from 1 to 10. Beside each number write the word from the list below that matches the statement.

acropolis	monarchy
assembly	oligarchy
democracy	peninsula
harbor	philosophy
jury	polis

1. A government of one ruler

2. A law-making body of government

3. Rule by the people

4. A group of citizens chosen to decide in court cases

5. A large hill where city residents went for safety

6. An area of land nearly surrounded by water

7. A sheltered place along a coast

8. A Greek city-state

9. The search for wisdom and the right way to live

10. Rule by a small, rich group

THINKING ABOUT FACTS

1. What were two main crops of the ancient Greeks?

2. What was the largest city-state in Greece in 700 B.C.? What made this city-state strong?

3. What did Socrates teach? Why was he put to death?

4. How did Alexander the Great affect the history of his time?

5. Look at the time line above. What important events happened between 500 and 400 B.C? Why was the century such an important one for Athens?

THINK AND WRITE

WRITING ABOUT CONTRASTS
Reread pages 198–199. Then write a paragraph describing the main differences between Athens and Sparta.

WRITING ABOUT PERSPECTIVES
Suppose you live in ancient Athens. Write a paragraph about why you think women should or should not participate fully in Athenian democracy.

WRITING BIOGRAPHIES
Write one paragraph about two of the following people: (1) Homer, (2) Socrates, (3) Pericles, and (4) Alexander the Great.

APPLYING THINKING SKILLS

MAKING CONCLUSIONS

1. What is a conclusion?
2. Reread "Did You Know?" on page 206 and make a conclusion about why the Greeks liked drama. What information did you use to come to your conclusion?
3. If you were asked to make a conclusion about how successful drama is today in America, what facts would you need to know?
4. When in your life have you made a conclusion about something but later made a different conclusion about the same thing?
5. Why is the ability to make conclusions important for studying history?

Summing Up the Chapter

Review the chapter, then copy the word map below on a separate sheet of paper. Next, fill in each box with at least two related details. After you have filled in the details, use the word map to write a paragraph that answers the question "What did the ancient Greeks contribute to world civilization?"

Geography
....
peninsula

Sparta
....

Athens
....

ANCIENT GREECE

Wars
....

Legacy
....

Greek Empire
....
Spread of Greek learning

CHAPTER 9

Ancient Rome

THINKING ABOUT HISTORY AND GEOGRAPHY

About 700 B.C. people of the Italian peninsula founded a city called Rome. Within 200 years, Rome would develop a government ruled by its citizens. Under later rulers, Rome grew into a vast empire that stretched across Europe, touching Africa and western Asia. The influence of this great empire, including its laws, language, technology, and religion, spread far and wide and has lasted into modern times.

509 B.C.

ROME

Roman citizens start a republic

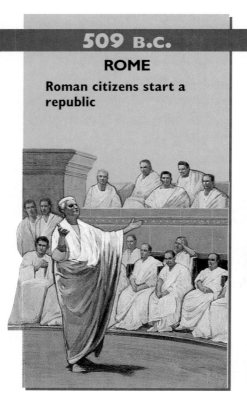

48 B.C.

ALEXANDRIA

Julius Caesar and Cleopatra join forces

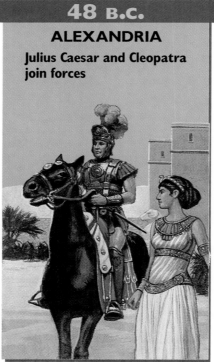

27 B.C.

ROME

Augustus becomes the first Roman emperor and continues expansion of the empire

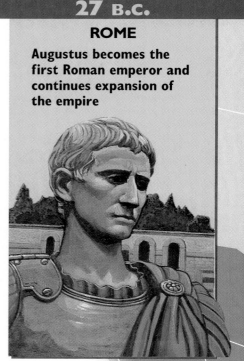

EUROPE

ASIA

Black Sea

Rome

Constantinople

Caspian Sea

Mediterranean Sea

Galilee

Alexandria

AFRICA

Red Sea

A.D. 31

GALILEE

Jesus teaches religious ideas that are the beginning of Christianity

A.D. 306

CONSTANTINOPLE

Constantine founds a new capital

GEOGRAPHY OF ANCIENT ROME

READ ALOUD

"The countryside round here is very beautiful. . . . The broad, spreading plain is ringed by mountains, their summits topped by ancient woods of tall timber. . . . Below these the vineyards extend on every side, weaving their uniform pattern far and wide. . . . Then come the meadows and grainfields, which can only be broken by huge oxen and the most powerful plows."

A Roman named Pliny the Younger wrote these words in a letter to a friend almost 2,000 years ago. As you will see, they describe the land around ancient Rome well.

THE BIG PICTURE

Around 700 B.C. people from Sparta and other city-states began leaving Greece to start new colonies in other parts of the Mediterranean region. Many sailed west to present-day Italy, where the land was rich and fertile. There the Greek colonists settled among several groups of peoples who spoke different languages and followed different customs. The communities shared in common their ways of making a living from the land.

While Sparta and Athens rose to power in Greece, another city was growing strong in Italy. That city was Rome. In time, Rome would unify all of Italy's many communities under its rule and eventually conquer Greece itself.

Focus Activity

READ TO LEARN

In what ways did Rome's geography help it to grow strong?

PLACES

Rome
Sicily
Alps
Apennine Mountains
Latium
Tiber River

A BOOT INTO THE SEA

The Italian peninsula is part of the European continent. It juts out into the the Mediterranean Sea like a kicking boot. Find the "toe" of the boot on the map on this page. The island to the west of the toe is called Sicily. It was a popular destination for ancient Greek colonists because of its rich farmland.

Mountains of Italy

At the northern border of present-day Italy stand the craggy Alps. The Alps are Europe's highest mountain range. Do you remember how the Himalayas separate the Indian subcontinent from the rest of Asia? The Alps wall off the Italian peninsula from the rest of Europe in a similar way.

Another mountain range has had an even greater effect on life in Italy. The Apennine (AP uh nin) Mountains form a giant "backbone" through the Italian peninsula. Their towering height makes it difficult to travel across the peninsula. The Apennines also lack rich soil, so there is more sheep herding than farming on the mountainsides.

Fertile Plains

Italy, like Greece, has much mountainous land. Also like Greece, Italy has a number of fertile plains. One important plain, Latium (LAY shee um), is located on the west coast of central Italy. The Tiber River runs through the center of this plain. Archaeologists have found remains of ancient communities on the Latium plain that date back about 3,000 years. Eventually, a great city called Rome would also arise on the plain along the Tiber River.

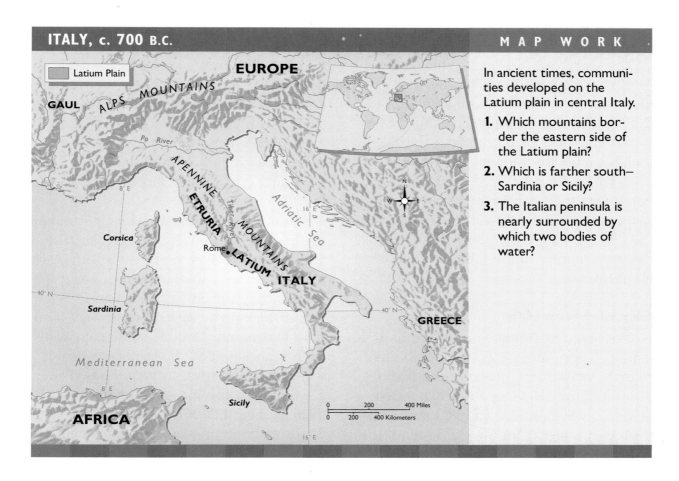

ITALY, c. 700 B.C.

Latium Plain

EUROPE
GAUL
ALPS MOUNTAINS
Po River
APENNINE
ETRURIA
Tiber River
LATIUM MOUNTAINS
Corsica
Rome
ITALY
Adriatic Sea
Sardinia
GREECE
Mediterranean Sea
Sicily
AFRICA

MAP WORK

In ancient times, communities developed on the Latium plain in central Italy.

1. Which mountains border the eastern side of the Latium plain?

2. Which is farther south—Sardinia or Sicily?

3. The Italian peninsula is nearly surrounded by which two bodies of water?

0   200   400 Miles
0   200   400 Kilometers

A CITY ALONG THE TIBER

Today Rome is a large, modern city beside the Tiber River, on the northern edge of the Latium plain. Rome was also a great city over 2,000 years ago. How did this city come into being?

The Legend of Romulus and Remus

According to Roman legend, a king ruled a small city near the Tiber River over 2,700 years ago. His younger brother overthrew him and drove away the rest of the royal family. Later the older brother's daughter gave birth to twin boys, Romulus and Remus. The new king was afraid these boys would try to claim the throne. He gave orders to throw the twins into the flooded Tiber River. This was done—but miraculously the boys did not drown. They were both washed up on a hilltop where a wolf happened along and rescued them.

The story goes on to say that a shepherd came upon the wolf's den and took the boys home. Romulus and Remus grew up to be strong and brave. In the end they helped their grandfather become king again. Then Romulus and Remus founded a new city on the hill where they had been rescued. The two brothers fought over the naming of the city, and Romulus killed Remus. The city was named Rome after its first king, Romulus.

City of Seven Hills

The story of Romulus and Remus is a legend. There are, however, many good reasons why Rome grew where it did. First, as Rome developed, it expanded across seven hills. These hills helped to protect the city from attack. Second, the Tiber River made a fine "highway" for

An ancient Roman bridge spans the Tiber River (above). Grapes remain a major crop in Italy (right).

travel between the mountains and the Mediterranean coast. Boats brought goods from faraway seaports as well as news from communities upriver. Last but not least, the Latium plain was surrounded by inactive volcanoes. Ash from earlier eruptions had created a thin but rich soil. As a result, farmers were able to produce large surpluses on the Latium plain.

Latium farmers grew wheat to make bread. They also grew beans, cabbage, and lettuce, as well as figs and other fruits. Perhaps most important were the grapes they raised to make wine. Grapevines grow best in rocky soil, and Italy had plenty of that. Wine sold well in the marketplace. Most people drank watered-down wine at mealtimes. People poured wine into cuts and wounds to help them heal. In time, Italy's fine wines became one of the peninsula's most valued trade goods.

WHY IT MATTERS

During the period of Etruscan rule, Rome continued to grow and develop. However, the people of the small city on the Tiber River could not have known what the future would hold. As you will soon see, Rome would one day become the center of a mighty empire. Roman laws, language, and achievements would affect not only all of Italy, but in time, much of the world.

Reviewing Facts and Ideas

SUM UP

- At the base of Italy's two mountain ranges—the Alps and the Apennines—lie fertile regions, such as the Latium plain.

- Italy's fertile plains were well used by local farmers as well as colonists from ancient Greece.

- The city of Rome was founded on seven hills. They helped to protect it from attack. The nearby Latium plain provided fertile farmland.

- Etruscan kings ruled Rome and other regions of Italy before being overthrown by Romans in 509 B.C.

THINK ABOUT IT

1. Why did grapes become an important crop in ancient Italy?

2. How did Rome come to be founded, according to legend? What role does geography play in this story?

3. **FOCUS** Why was the location of Rome a good place for a city?

4. **THINKING SKILL** What were the _causes_ of farmers' success at growing grapevines in Italy?

5. **GEOGRAPHY** How did the mountains of Italy affect communication and transportation?

Peoples of the Peninsula

Before the founding of Rome, there were other peoples who developed civilizations in Italy. One group, called the Etruscans, settled on the plain northwest of the Tiber River. Find this plain, called Etruria (ih TRUR ee uh), on the map on page 225.

Around 575 B.C. the Etruscan army conquered much of the Italian peninsula, including Rome. Etruscan kings led the city to victory over many of its neighbors in Latium. However, in about 509 B.C., the leading families of Rome overthrew their Etruscan king.

GEOGRAPHYSKILLS

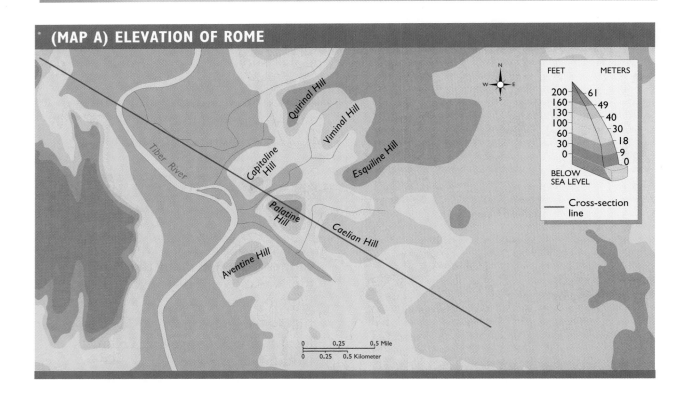

Reading Elevation Maps and Profiles

VOCABULARY

elevation
profile

WHY THE SKILL MATTERS

The geography of the region around Rome includes a variety of landforms, ranging from jutting hills to flat plains. You can see the height of such landforms on maps. Mapmakers show differences in the height of land in several ways. For example, the varying heights of Rome can be shown using an elevation map. Elevation means height above sea level. Elevation can also

be shown in another way. Mapmakers can take an imaginary slice of the land through a place such as Rome and make a profile map of the area. Profile means to view something from the side. Another term for *profile* is "cross section."

USING AN ELEVATION MAP

Study Map A. This is an elevation map of Rome and the region around it. According to the map key, elevation is measured in feet and in meters on the map. What color shows the highest elevation? What color shows the lowest elevation? Look for the part of the city with the lowest elevation. Notice that it is the area around the Tiber River, shown on the left of the map. According to the map key, the elevation here is almost at sea level. Notice that the seven hills of Rome are east of the river. One of the purposes of elevation maps is to show relative location—or, how one place in a region relates to another.

228

USING A PROFILE MAP

Now study Map B. This is a profile map of the same region. Find the Palatine hill on the map. This hill was where the richest people in ancient Rome lived. Based on the map key, how many feet high is this hill? Look at the height of the Palatine Hill as compared to the height of the Caelian (SEE lee un) Hill. You might find that it is often easier to see differences in elevation using a profile map like Map B. Because profile maps show only a "slice" of land, however, they do not show an area's relative location as well as elevation maps do.

TRYING THE SKILL

Now try to find other information using the elevation map and the profile map. Refer to the Helping Yourself box if you need help answering questions.

In the last lesson you read that, according to the story about the founding of Rome,

the twins Romulus and Remus were thrown into the flooded Tiber River. They were saved when they washed up on a hill. The story says the twins built the city of Rome on the spot where they were saved. Assuming that the twins washed up on the highest hill in Rome, which hill was it? How many meters higher is it than the land along the Tiber River? You can see this well on the profile map below. Find that same hill on the elevation map of Rome.

REVIEWING THE SKILL

1. What facts about these maps let you know that they are elevation and profile maps?

2. What is the difference in elevation between the Aventine Hill and the Latium plain? How did you arrive at this answer?

3. When might it be helpful to be able to read elevation and profile maps?

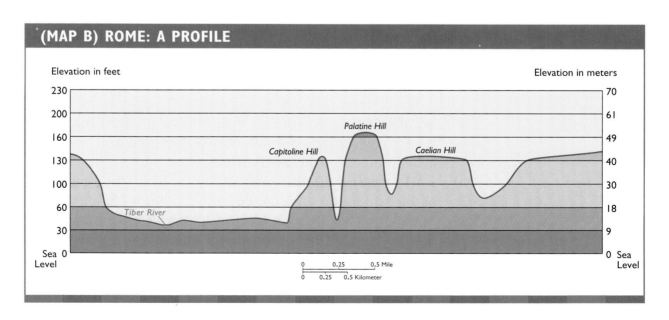

(MAP B) ROME: A PROFILE

Elevation in feet · Elevation in meters

Palatine Hill · Capitoline Hill · Caelian Hill · Tiber River

509 B.C.   100 B.C.   A.D. 1   A.D. 250   A.D. 500

THE RISE OF THE ROMAN REPUBLIC

Focus Activity

READ TO LEARN
What kind of government did the Romans establish?

VOCABULARY
plebeian
patrician
republic
representative
Senate
tribune
consul
Twelve Tables
Punic Wars

PEOPLE
Livy
Hannibal
Scipio

PLACES
Forum
Carthage
Zama

READ ALOUD

The Roman leader Cicero declared that Rome should be governed by its "best" citizens. But just who were Rome's "best" citizens? Were they the city's small circle of nobles? Or did they also include the many other citizens, poor and rich, who contributed to life in Rome? The way Romans answered this question would shape their lives and ours.

THE BIG PICTURE

Almost 3,000 years ago, when the city of Anyang in China was losing power, Rome was only a cluster of mud huts on the hills overlooking the Tiber River. From the hilltops, farmers could enjoy a view of two small lakes that rippled in the valley below. The sound of lowing cattle drifted across the marshland at the river's edge.

By 509 B.C. Romans had overthrown their king, Tarquinius. They began setting up a new government in which citizens played a larger part. Their community became a city. A wooden bridge now crossed the Tiber River. The valley's marshland was drained and served as a busy market and meeting place.

High atop one of Rome's hills stood a stone temple as big as any in Greece. On other hilltops, fine brick homes housed Rome's wealthy. Some Romans clearly had become richer than others. The division between rich and poor, powerful and not so powerful, would affect the shape of the new government Romans were creating for themselves.

THE CITIZENS OF ROME

As in Greece, society in Rome was divided into two groups: those who were citizens and those who were not. At first, Rome had few slaves. The city did have many women, but none of them were citizens.

The body of citizens included two groups. Most Roman citizens were plebeians (plih BEE unz). Plebeians were men who farmed, traded, and made things for a living. The second group was made up of Rome's handful of patricians (puh TRISH unz). Patricians were members of Rome's noble families. They owned large farms and had plebeians work the land for them.

Plebeians Protest

After Rome's last king was overthrown in 509 B.C., the patricians took power. As they did this they remade the city's government. Only patricians could belong to a ruling assembly or become government leaders.

Rome's many plebeians reacted to the patricians' rules with protest. According to the Roman historian Livy,

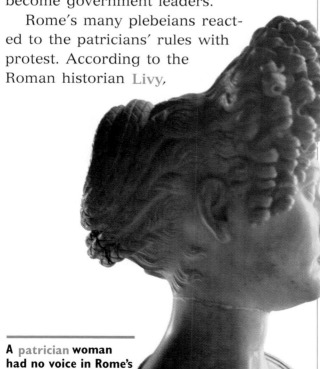

A patrician woman had no voice in Rome's government.

plebeians rebelled in 494 B.C., demanding changes in the government. To calm them down, Livy wrote, the patricians sent a popular leader to speak with the plebeians. He told them this story. How do you suppose the plebeians reacted?

MANY VOICES
PRIMARY SOURCE

Excerpt from
***Stories of Rome*, Livy, c. 20 B.C.**

*Once upon a time, the different parts of the human body were not all in agreement. . . . And it seemed very unfair to the other parts of the body that they should worry and sweat away to look after the belly. After all, the belly just sat there . . . doing nothing, enjoying all the nice things that came along. So they hatched a plot. The hands weren't going to take food to the mouth; even if they did, the mouth wasn't going to accept it. . . . They went into a **sulk** and waited for the belly to cry for help. But while they waited, one by one all the parts of the body got weaker and weaker. The moral of this story? The belly too has its job to do. It has to be fed, but it also does feeding of its own.*

---

sulk: to be in a bad mood and stay silent

A New Government

According to Livy both sides in time agreed to work together to improve Rome's government. The new government was called a republic, which means "public things" in Latin. Latin was the language of ancient Rome. In a republic citizens choose their leaders.

GOVERNING THE REPUBLIC

Unlike in the democracy of Athens, not all Roman citizens participated in the assembly that ran their city. Instead, they elected representatives, people who acted for them.

Does this sound familiar? The government of the United States is often called a republic. Citizens elect representatives who serve in Congress or in state legislatures. Unlike in the United States, however, not all the votes of Roman citizens were equal. In Rome the more powerful a man was, the greater influence his vote had.

Rome's republic lasted for nearly 500 years. During that time, three different government branches ran the city's affairs. Each of these branches had decision-making powers that allowed it to have some control over the actions of the other branches. What were the three branches?

The oldest and most powerful branch of the republic was the Senate. The Senate was controlled by Rome's patricians. Like the Senate of the United States, the Roman Senate determined how Rome would act toward other governments. It also had control of all the money collected and spent by the Roman Republic.

Power for the Plebeians

To make their voices heard in Rome, plebeians formed a citizen assembly. Beginning in 494 B.C., the citizen assembly elected tribunes (trih BYOONZ) who worked to gain rights for the plebeians of Rome. The tribunes were the leaders of the large citizen assembly.

The Consuls

Early tribunes worked to make sure plebeians got fair trials. They brought plebeian complaints before the Senate and the consuls. The consuls were the third branch of Rome's republic.

Each year the citizen assembly elected two men to become consuls. Consuls served as Rome's army commanders and the city's most powerful judges. They could order anyone to be arrested. The consuls could also propose new laws for Rome. The citizen assembly, however, could veto, or stop, any of the consuls' actions.

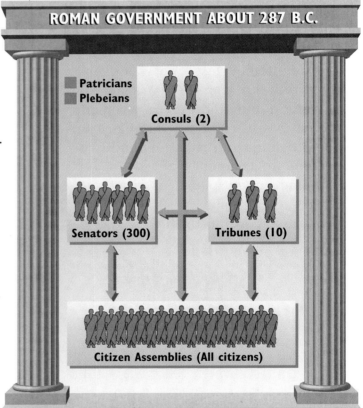

ROMAN GOVERNMENT ABOUT 287 B.C.

- Patricians
- Plebeians

Consuls (2)

Senators (300)   Tribunes (10)

Citizen Assemblies (All citizens)

CHART WORK

Both patricians and plebeians had a role in the government of Rome.

1. Which citizens served as Rome's consuls?
2. How many citizens served as Senators?
3. In which parts of government could plebeians participate?

Power in Rome was shared, if very unevenly, among the different branches of the republic. Study the chart to see how power was divided.

Plebeian Influence Grows

The citizens in the assembly often met to vote in a large field along the Tiber River. The field was also the headquarters of Rome's mostly plebeian army. Rome's patricians depended heavily on the army. In its early years Rome was constantly at war.

The plebeian army protected both the city of Rome and its patrician leaders. This role gave plebeians added power to change Rome's government in an important way.

For many years patrician leaders had ruled Rome according to laws that were unwritten. Only the patrician leaders had knowledge of those laws. As a result, plebeians had no way of knowing just what was and was not against the law. If brought to court, plebeians could only hope that the patrician judges would give them a fair trial.

About 450 B.C. the plebeians protested the unfairness of Rome's unwritten laws. Finally the patricians agreed to write a collection of laws on twelve wooden tablets, or tables. These became known as the Twelve Tables.

The Laws of the Republic

Historians today know little about what the Twelve Tables actually said. They do know, though, that the laws governed everything from marriage to slavery. Plebeians could not marry patricians. People who did not pay their debts could be made slaves. Like Hammurabi's Code in Babylon, the Twelve Tables were an important step in the development of written laws.

The Twelve Tables were posted in the city's crowded Forum. In the late 400s B.C. the Forum was a gravel clearing not much bigger than a soccer field. This clearing was the center of life in Rome. Here senators met and citizens pleaded their cases before judges. Women sometimes joined in the debates that took place there, hoping to influence those who could vote.

This painting shows a Roman trial by law. The Twelve Tables developed into a code of laws that influenced the laws of many future governments.

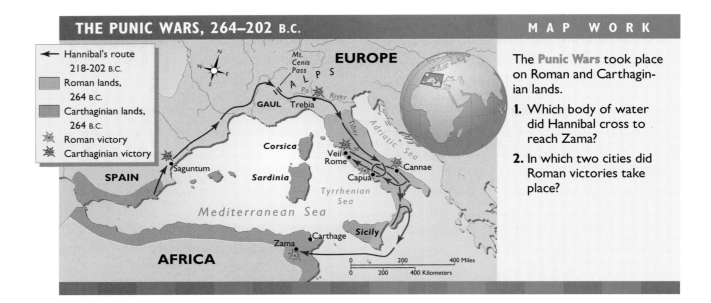

Legend:
- Hannibal's route 218–202 B.C.
- Roman lands, 264 B.C.
- Carthaginian lands, 264 B.C.
- Roman victory
- Carthaginian victory

EUROPE

Mt. Cenis Pass

ALPS

GAUL

Po River

Trebia

Corsica

Veii
Rome

Sardinia

Capua

Cannae

Adriatic Sea

Tiber R.

Tyrrhenian Sea

Mediterranean Sea

Saguntum

SPAIN

Carthage

Sicily

Zama

AFRICA

0   200   400 Miles
0   200   400 Kilometers

The **Punic Wars** took place on Roman and Carthaginian lands.

1. Which body of water did Hannibal cross to reach Zama?

2. In which two cities did Roman victories take place?

THE REPUBLIC EXPANDS

The Roman army moved out across the peninsula to conquer other areas. By 265 B.C. Rome controlled all of the Italian peninsula.

A Rival Across the Sea

In 264 B.C. Roman soldiers landed on the island of Sicily. Their arrival sparked a long conflict with the powerful empire of **Carthage**. Carthage was a city based in present-day Tunisia, on the northern coast of Africa. This city controlled much of the land around the western Mediterranean, including Sicily. Since Carthage had once been a colony of Phoenicia, Romans named their conflicts with that city the **Punic Wars**. *Punic* comes from the Latin word for Phoenicia.

In 241 B.C., after more than 20 years of fighting, Carthage surrendered control of Sicily to Rome. Rome then seized even more of the lands controlled by Carthage. The leaders of Carthage were outraged! One general asked his son **Hannibal** to seek revenge. In 218 B.C., when he was 29 years old, Hannibal led an army against the forces of Rome.

Hannibal's Plan

Hannibal came up with a daring plan. Since Rome's navy controlled the waters around Italy, he decided to attack by land. Hannibal marched from Spain to Rome with an army of about 90,000 men. He also brought elephants, which scared the Romans, who had never before seen these huge animals. In front of Hannibal, though, lay 1,000 miles of enemy territory.

More than 15 soldiers could ride atop one of Hannibal's elephants.

The army from Carthage actually carried out much of this plan, though thousands died along the way. Hannibal won major battles in Italy and caused great destruction there. Hannibal's success, however, did not win victory for Carthage. In Rome a 25-year-old general, **Scipio** (SIHP ee oh), was elected as consul. Scipio's large army defeated Hannibal outside Carthage in the Battle of **Zama** in 202 B.C. The defeat of Hannibal gave Rome control over Carthage's vast territory. Rome became the most powerful nation in the Mediterranean region.

The Changing Republic

All of these changes upset the workings of the republic. Patricians and plebeians struggled for government control. Slaves and conquered peoples revolted against their Roman leaders. Roman generals used their troops to take control of the government. By about 100 B.C. the republican government of Rome was fighting for its life.

WHY IT MATTERS

When the Roman republic was first set up, participation was limited to those who lived in and around the city. By 100 B.C., though, the republic was huge. It extended around the Mediterranean Sea and included millions of people.

The republic would not long survive. However, the ideas about how people could govern themselves—using a Senate, a people's assembly, and elected officials—would inspire the creators of the United States government over 2,000 years later.

✓ Reviewing Facts and Ideas

SUM IT UP

- After about 509 B.C. Rome's citizens created a republic in which citizens elected leaders to run the government. Wealthy patrician citizens had more power than plebeian citizens.

- The republic of Rome was divided into three main branches—the Senate, the citizen assembly, and the consuls.

- Defeating Carthage in the Punic Wars made Rome the leading power in the Mediterranean region by 202 B.C.

THINK ABOUT IT

1. Describe the differences between patricians and plebeians.

2. Why was it important for Rome's laws to be written down?

3. **FOCUS** How did the struggle between the plebeians and patricians affect Roman government?

4. **THINKING SKILL** *Make conclusions* about the importance of the Punic Wars to Rome's history.

5. **WRITE** In a paragraph, explain the branches of Rome's republic.

THE ROMAN EMPIRE

Focus Activity

READ TO LEARN
What events led to the Pax Romana?

VOCABULARY
Pax Romana
civil war
dictator
aqueduct
census
gladiator

PEOPLE
Julius Caesar
Cleopatra
Augustus

PLACES
Gaul
Colosseum
Pantheon
Pompeii

READ ALOUD

"He found Rome built of brick and left it in marble." About 2,000 years ago, the biographer Suetonius (swih TOH nee us) wrote these words to describe how greatly Rome had changed under the leadership of one man. That leader was Augustus (aw GUS tus), the first Roman emperor.

THE BIG PICTURE

About 100 B.C. the leaders of the Han dynasty were ruling a unified China. Around the Mediterranean, meanwhile, the struggle for power in Rome grew. Patricians and plebeians each tried to win control for themselves. As problems in Rome increased, conquered peoples rebelled against their Roman governors.

By the century's end, though, a period known as the Pax Romana began. *Pax Romana* is Latin for "Roman peace." During the Pax Romana, which lasted about 200 years, goods moved freely within Rome's far-reaching borders. In Rome the people had bread to eat each day, thanks to shipments of North African wheat. They could cook in pots made from Spanish copper. Wealthy Romans ordered clothes made from Greek wool, Egyptian linen, or even Chinese silk! These goods were bought, along with pepper and pearls, by traders at markets in Asia. The Pax Romana benefited other nations, too, as Roman money and goods flowed in.

How did peace replace war in Rome? The story is a complex one. The story of Augustus and the building of a Roman empire actually begins with a leader who ruled before him.

236

THE RULE OF CAESAR

Julius Caesar (JOOL yus SEE zur) was born into a patrician family in 100 B.C. As a boy, he dreamed of becoming a Senate leader, which he did. He also served as a commander in the army.

By 59 B.C. Caesar was elected consul of Rome. The following year he became the military governor of Gaul—which today is France. There he won fame, riches, and the loyalty of a great army. Caesar could now try for his biggest goal—total control of Rome.

Civil War

In 49 B.C. Caesar and his rebel army marched into Italy. Civil war, or war between groups within one country, began. This war spilled into Egypt. There Caesar joined forces with Cleopatra (klee uh PA truh). She was the 21-year-old ruler of the Egyptian government based in Alexandria. In Chapter 8 you read about this Greek city-state on the Nile Delta.

Caesar helped Cleopatra defeat her brother, the pharaoh of Egypt. She gave Caesar money he needed to continue fighting for control of Rome. In 45 B.C. Caesar returned in triumph to Rome and made himself dictator. A dictator is someone who rules with absolute power. Government under a dictator is called a dictatorship.

A New Government

As dictator, Julius Caesar made important changes to life in Rome. He changed the way people measured time—creating the basis for the calendar we still use today. In Julius's honor the month of his birth was named "July." Caesar also gave land to his soldiers and free grain to poor citizens. He increased the number of people who could serve in the Senate. Also, he granted Roman citizenship to many people not born in Rome.

Some senators hated Caesar for ruling as a dictator. They felt he was destroying the traditions of Rome's republican government. Some began plotting to kill him. According to legend, a friend warned Caesar to "Beware the Ides (ĪDZ) of March," which is March 15. Caesar ignored the warning. On that day in 44 B.C. he arrived at the Senate, as usual without a bodyguard. There he was stabbed to death by enemies. The senators who killed Caesar believed they had saved the republic from dictatorship.

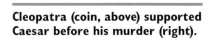

Cleopatra (coin, above) supported Caesar before his murder (right).

EMPEROR AUGUSTUS

After Caesar's death, civil war broke out once more as different groups fought for control. After 14 long years of fighting, the winner was Julius Caesar's grand-nephew and adopted son Octavian. He was just 18 years old when the fighting began. By 27 B.C. Octavian had defeated some of Rome's most experienced generals. These victories cleared the way for him to become dictator in all but name. As a sign of his new power, Octavian took the name Augustus, or "honored one." The month of August is named after this powerful ruler and general who helped to build Rome into a huge empire.

Pax Romana

Under Augustus, life throughout the Roman empire underwent great changes. Most important, his rule began the Pax Romana. During this period of peace Augustus ordered the building of new roads, buildings, and water systems. Like the emperors of China, Augustus also worked to create a single system of government and money throughout the empire.

Both the empire itself and the city of Rome now were bigger than ever. About one million people lived in the city of Rome. In the city's center the Forum now included large marble temples and government buildings. Nearby stood new theaters and public baths. New waterways called aqueducts (AK wuh duktz) were built to bring streams of fresh water into the city.

Thanks to Augustus, Romans now enjoyed police and fire protection. Even so, daily life had its unexpected dangers. Read this amusing description of Roman life. How did Rome's cramped quarters affect the way people lived?

MANY VOICES PRIMARY SOURCE

Excerpt from Satires, by Juvenal, c. A.D. 100.

To get to an urgent business call, the rich man travels by litter and the crowd has to give way as the huge contraption is hurried along over their heads—while inside he reads, or writes, or just sleeps. . . . We might get a move on but for the people in front blocking our way. . . . Someone digs me in the ribs with his elbow; someone else hits me with a sedan-chair pole. A beam catches me full in the face; someone else drops a barrel on my head. My legs are caked with mud and I'm trampled to death by huge feet and my toes are flattened by a soldier's hobnailed boot.

---

litter: a covered couch used for carrying a single passenger
sedan-chair: a chair carried on poles by two people
beam: a long piece of heavy wood

Roman aqueducts (left) brought millions of gallons of water each day to Roman cities. Modern travelers still find Roman roads in use in Europe (below).

"All Roads Lead to Rome"

Amid the crowds of people who filled the Forum each day stood a tall stone marker. Its size reflected its importance. It marked the start of all major roads leading out of Rome.

The Roman empire at its peak was crisscrossed by more than 50,000 miles of roads! Those roads—along with boats—helped to make communication, trade, and travel throughout the empire possible. Not all the roads led to Rome, of course. Many of the people and goods traveling along the stone pathways, however, either began or finished there. Rome acted like a giant magnet. Everyone in the empire felt its pull on their lives in one way or another.

Running an Empire

From Spain to Sparta, Alexandria to Jerusalem, people felt the pull of Rome through its laws. Laws were upheld by governors who also acted as judges.

The pull of Rome was even stronger through its taxes. Taxes paid by craft-workers and merchants helped to pay for the upkeep of the empire. Few people escaped paying. Every five years Rome took a census, or count, of people living in the empire.

Army units were posted far and wide to enforce Roman law, as well as to help build the empire's roads. Unlike the soldiers of the old Roman Republic, most soldiers of the Roman empire were not citizens. They were paid to serve in the army full-time. For many poor men, the army offered the best chance to earn a decent living.

Travel and Trade

One sign of the strength of the Roman government was safe travel. In the empire, the army made sure that bandits could not threaten citizens on land or sea. On the empire's roads, soldiers passed messengers carrying letters written on papyrus sheets. The Roman empire had a mail system similar to America's pony express. Every 8 miles riders would exchange their tired horses for fresh ones.

Merchants clattered along on ox-drawn carts, bringing goods like wine or dried fish to market. If their paths overlooked the sea, travelers probably saw merchant sailboats cutting through the blue waters. The cargoes might have included anything from Spanish silver to Egyptian linen.

VAST PROJECTS

The sheer size of the Roman empire united some of the world's most skilled craftworkers and engineers. They built beautiful—as well as useful—structures that reflected the empire's great wealth and power.

Throughout the empire Roman engineers built long aqueducts to bring fresh water to cities. Engineers spanned rivers with stone bridges to speed up the movement of soldiers and merchants. For cleanliness, engineers built public baths complete with heated floors. For entertainment, they created huge stadiums where **gladiators** fought animals, such as lions or bears, or each other—often

Crowds of Romans often filled the Colosseum seats (right) to watch the popular sport of chariot racing (below).

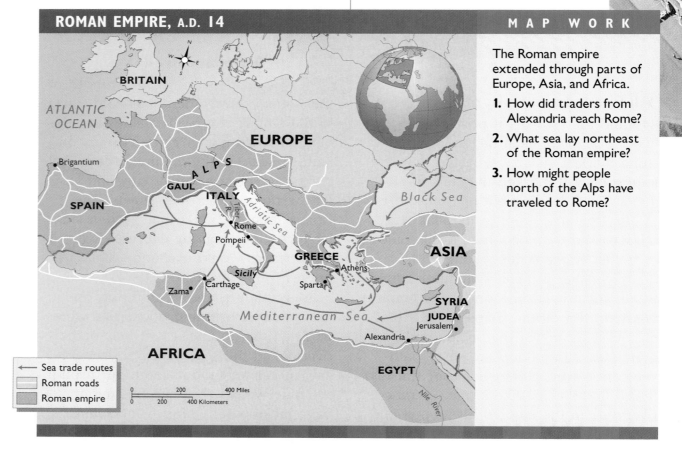

ROMAN EMPIRE, A.D. 14

M A P   W O R K

The Roman empire extended through parts of Europe, Asia, and Africa.

1. How did traders from Alexandria reach Rome?

2. What sea lay northeast of the Roman empire?

3. How might people north of the Alps have traveled to Rome?

BRITAIN

ATLANTIC OCEAN

EUROPE

Brigantium

ALPS

GAUL

ITALY

SPAIN

Tiber R.

Rome

Adriatic Sea

Pompeii

Black Sea

ASIA

GREECE

Athens

Sicily

Sparta

Zama

Carthage

SYRIA

Mediterranean Sea

JUDEA

Jerusalem

Alexandria

AFRICA

EGYPT

Nile River

← Sea trade routes
Roman roads
Roman empire

0   200   400 Miles
0   200   400 Kilometers

A Fabulous Temple

About a mile west of the Colosseum stood another Roman monument—the Pantheon. The Pantheon was just one of many temples in the city. It honored all the gods and goddesses of the Roman world.

By the time of the empire, Romans honored gods and goddesses from many parts of the world. They believed that these gods and goddesses had helped Rome to grow. For example, the Romans worshiped the major gods and goddesses of Greece, although they gave them Latin names. Many Romans also made sacrifices to Isis, the powerful goddess of Egypt, and Mithra, a Persian sun-god.

Large temples were also built to honor emperors like Augustus. Emperors of Rome were thought to become gods when they died.

to the death. Most of the gladiators were slaves. Some, however, were condemned criminals or prisoners of war. All were forced to fight in bloody contests of strength.

Many of these contests were held in the largest and most famous stadium in Rome, the Colosseum (kol uh SEE um), completed in 80 A.D. It held about 50,000 people. The Colosseum was so vast that fake sea battles were staged in it! Among the other contests that ancient Romans held in their stadiums were chariot races.

DID YOU KNOW?

How were Roman architects able to build large, lasting structures?

Roman architects mixed sand, lime, and pieces of stone and brick to make the very first cement. They used this material to bind stones and bricks into walls and foundations. Using its strength, the Romans built temples, bridges, and baths that still stand today.

Modern builders make cement in much the same way. They use it to build sidewalks, swimming pools, apartment buildings, and bridges. Perhaps some of these structures will last 2,000 years too.

Infographic

Daily Life in Pompeii

You have read about many aspects of life in the Roman empire. How did ordinary people live during the days of Augustus and later emperors? Here are a few things archaeologists have found in the Roman city of **Pompeii** (pahm PAY). You can find this city on the map on page 240. Pompeii was destroyed by the eruption of Mount Vesuvius in A.D. 79. Many artifacts have been preserved in the volcanic ash that fell on the city. What similarities can you find between items shown here and things you see every day?

Makeup Kit

Makeup kits (right) included white powdered chalk, red ocher (iron dust), and ash. Perfume was another popular item among the women of Rome.

Mosaic of Wealthy Woman

Wealthy Roman women wore different kinds of jewelry. Some also had their ears pierced for earrings.

Carbonized Bodies

Up to 13 feet of volcanic ash suddenly rained down on the city, trapping people beneath it. The ash quickly hardened, preserving the bodies.

Serving Bowls

Partly eaten meals— here eggs and hazelnuts (left and below)—were among the items in Pompeii preserved in volcanic ash.

"Beware of Dog"

Guard dogs were sometimes kept chained to a door. Signs (above) warned would-be thieves not to enter.

WHY IT MATTERS

Under Julius Caesar, and later, Augustus, Roman citizens lost some of the political rights they had once enjoyed. Yet under Augustus, Rome was also more peaceful than it had been for many years. Before his death in A.D. 14, Augustus also had made many improvements in daily life.

Around this time in a dusty town not far from Jerusalem another important development began that would affect the entire world. You will read about it in the next lesson.

✔ Reviewing Facts and Ideas

SUM IT UP

- Julius Caesar became dictator of Rome in 45 B.C. He was killed by senators opposed to his rule on the Ides of March in 44 B.C.

- Under Augustus, around 27 B.C., the Roman empire began a 200-year period of peace and active trade called the Pax Romana.

- Roman religion shared many similarities with that of ancient Greece. Romans also worshiped Egyptian and Persian gods and goddesses.

THINK ABOUT IT

1. What happened to the republican government of Rome when Julius Caesar took control?

2. What did Roman religion have in common with that of ancient Greece?

3. **FOCUS** How did life in Rome change during the Pax Romana?

4. **THINKING SKILL** What *effects* did Augustus's rule have on life throughout the Mediterranean?

5. **GEOGRAPHY** Why were roads a major lifeline for the Roman empire?

DOMES & ARCHES

How would you begin to build something? You might first look at how similar things have been built by others. That is how the ancient Romans began when they built houses, temples, and public buildings. They learned the building techniques used by other civilizations, such as the Egyptian and the Greek. Then they developed some new techniques.

Romans used arches in many of their building projects. An arch is a curved structure used as a building support.

Learning how to use arches helped Roman engineers develop a new structure. This was the dome. A dome is a curved roof that looks like a bowl turned upside down. A dome can cover a huge space without any supports.

Roman engineering is a legacy that can be seen throughout the world. Look around you to see domes and arches.

You have already read that ancient Romans worshiped the gods and goddesses represented at the Pantheon. The Pantheon is a temple with one of the largest domes ever built.

The famous Pont du Gard was built by the Romans in France. Arches help support it. The structure was once used as an aqueduct. Water flowed through a channel along the top which gradually sloped downward.

The large area covered by the Houston Astrodome (above) can seat 70,000 people—with no supports other than itself! The United States Capitol (left) has both arches and a dome.

500
B.C.
250
B.C.
A.D.
1
A.D.
100
A.D.
250
A.D.
500

BEGINNINGS OF CHRISTIANITY

Focus Activity

READ TO LEARN
What did Jesus teach?

VOCABULARY
Christianity
New Testament
Messiah
parable
apostle
bishop
pope

PEOPLE
Jesus
Peter
Paul

PLACES
Judea
Bethlehem
Nazareth

READ ALOUD

"Fear not; for, behold, I bring you good news of great joy . . . for to you is born in the city of David a Savior, who is Christ the Lord. And this will be a sign for you; you will find the babe wrapped in swaddling clothes, lying in a manger."

These words, taken from the writings of an important new religion, announce the birth of a child in the Roman empire. Despite his humble birth, this child grew up to change the world.

THE BIG PICTURE

During the rule of Augustus, Rome increased its control over Judea, the region that once had been known as Canaan. You read in Chapter 5 that many Jews had been exiled from this land and brought to ancient Babylon. Many descendants had by now returned from their exile to rebuild their towns and cities. In Jerusalem they built a new temple that stood on the remains of the one that had been destroyed long ago. Elsewhere, towering aqueducts stood as reminders of the newer, Roman rule.

Into this world a new religion, Christianity, was born. The story of its birth is told in a collection of books called the New Testament. The Hebrew Bible, which you read about in Chapter 5, came to be called the Old Testament by followers of Christianity. Together, the Old and New Testaments formed their Bible. Its words are sacred to nearly 2 billion Christians living in the world today.

THE LIFE OF JESUS

One book of the New Testament begins with an important order from Emperor Augustus that a census be taken throughout the entire empire. Augustus's order meant that all the people in the empire had to return to the towns where they were born so that they could be counted. So a Jewish carpenter named Joseph and his wife Mary set out for Bethlehem (BETH luh hem), a small town south of Jerusalem. Find Bethlehem on the map on this page. While there, the Bible says, Mary gave birth to a son, Jesus.

Jesus' Childhood

The New Testament says little about Jesus' childhood. Jesus and his family lived in Nazareth (NAZ ur uth), a tiny village in the northern hills of Judea. The New Testament does say, though, that as a boy Jesus learned a great deal about the teachings of Judaism. According to the Bible, that became clear when Jesus was 12 years old and he went to Jerusalem with his parents. They went to celebrate the Passover festival there.

When the festival was ended and they started to return, the boy Jesus stayed behind in Jerusalem, but his parents did not know it. . . . When they did not find him, they returned to Jerusalem to search for him. After three days they found him in the temple, sitting among the teachers, listening to them and asking them questions. And all who heard him were amazed at his understanding and his answers.

This passage would by no means be the last one in which the New Testament describes how Jesus amazed those around him.

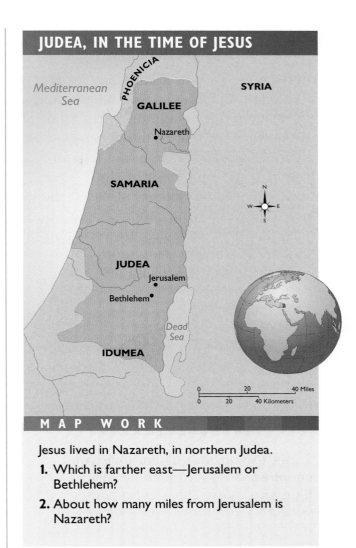

JUDEA, IN THE TIME OF JESUS

Mediterranean Sea

PHOENICIA

SYRIA

GALILEE

Nazareth

SAMARIA

JUDEA

Jerusalem

Bethlehem

Dead Sea

IDUMEA

0   20   40 Miles
0   20   40 Kilometers

MAP WORK

Jesus lived in Nazareth, in northern Judea.

1. Which is farther east—Jerusalem or Bethlehem?
2. About how many miles from Jerusalem is Nazareth?

From the age of 30 on, the Bible says, Jesus spent much of his time teaching crowds of people. Many came to hear him, the Bible says, because he healed sick people and performed many other miracles.

According to Jewish belief, the Messiah is a special leader to be sent by God in order to guide the Jewish people and to set up God's rule on Earth. The word *Messiah* in Greek is *Christos*. In time the followers of Jesus came to believe that he was the Messiah, or Christos. The people who followed Jesus became known as Christians. Their religion soon became known as Christianity.

THE TEACHINGS OF JESUS

The New Testament states that Jesus often used parables, or simple stories that contain a message or truth. Some of these stories taught the value of seeking the right path in life. Others described the greatness of God's love for all people. Still others stressed the importance of loving other people. Many of Jesus' parables are recorded in the New Testament. How does Jesus describe love in this passage?

MANY VOICES
PRIMARY SOURCE

Excerpt from the Gospel of Luke, New Testament, c. A.D. 90

I say to you that listen, love your enemies, do good to those who hate you, bless those who curse you, pray for those who abuse you. If anyone strikes you on the cheek, offer the other also; and from anyone who takes away your coat do not withhold even your shirt. Give to everyone who begs from you; and if anyone takes away your goods, do not ask for them again. Do to others as you would have them do to you.

In the Sermon on the Mount, Jesus revealed many of his most important teachings.

Twelve Apostles

Jesus' closest followers were called apostles (uh PAHS ulz). The apostles were 12 men Jesus had chosen to help him in his teaching. The Bible says they came from all walks of life. One of the apostles, Peter, had fished for a living before joining Jesus. Another, Levi, had been a tax collector for Rome. The Bible tells us that the apostles had little in common before they met Jesus. It goes on to say, however, that they became united through Jesus' teachings. The apostles helped to spread Jesus' teachings after he died.

A Growing Following

The New Testament says that while he taught, Jesus also cured many people of illnesses. Both Jews and non-Jews benefited from these miracles, the Bible says. As a result, the number of Jesus' followers grew. The New Testament states that a prophet called John the Baptist sent people to ask Jesus if he was the Messiah the Jews were

Christian church services (left) honor Jesus' life and teachings. Leonardo da Vinci's *The Last Supper* (above) shows Jesus' final meal with the twelve apostles.

waiting for. The Bible says Jesus answered:

Go and tell John what you hear and see: the blind receive their sight, the lame walk . . . , the deaf hear, the dead are raised, and the poor have good news brought to them.

Jesus' answer was made up of quotes from the Hebrew Bible.

Trouble with Rome

Jesus' growing popularity troubled many people. Some of them were afraid that he wanted to be a king and was going to set up a new kingdom on Earth. These beliefs added to the fears of the Roman governors that talk of revolt was spreading throughout Judea.

When crowds jammed the streets of Jerusalem to celebrate the Passover festival, soldiers moved in on Jesus to arrest him. After questioning Jesus, a Roman governor sentenced him to die by crucifixion (kroo suh FIK shun). The word *crucifixion* means "putting to death by hanging from a cross." Roman leaders throughout the empire commonly used crucifixion to punish slaves, rebel leaders, and others regarded as criminals.

According to the New Testament, Jesus may have been in his thirties when he died. The Bible also tells us that Jesus rose from the dead three days after he was crucified. Then he rejoined his apostles and told them again about the coming kingdom of God. Afterwards, the Bible says, Jesus rose to heaven. Today most Christians try to follow Jesus' teachings and to celebrate his renewed life and message of hope on Easter Sunday.

THE SPREAD OF CHRISTIANITY

The New Testament does not end with the story of Jesus' ascent, or rise, into heaven. It goes on to tell how Christianity spread throughout the Roman world. Leading the growth of Christianity were the apostles of Jesus.

A Christian Church

The New Testament says that after the death of Jesus, Christians scattered to cities throughout the Roman empire. There they set up dozens of Christian churches. Soon these churches drew the attention of Roman leaders. Some Roman rulers were angry at the Christians for refusing to worship the emperor. Still, the new religion continued to grow and attract followers.

According to the New Testament, the new churches included people from all ranks in life. These included the Roman commander Cornelius, the cloth merchant Lydia, and the slave Onesimus.

A church leader named Paul reminded them that

> There is no longer Jew or Greek, . . . slave or free, . . . male or female; for all of you are one in Christ Jesus.

Paul was not one of the first 12 apostles. Unlike the earliest followers of Jesus, Paul grew up in a big city, Tarsus, in what is today Turkey. Paul was well educated in both the Hebrew Bible and Greek classics. At first he was against Christianity, but later he became a Christian himself. Paul spoke in many different cities about Christianity. The New Testament says he debated with Jewish teachers in Jerusalem and with philosophers in the streets of Athens. Paul, together with other Christians, spread Christianity throughout the Roman world.

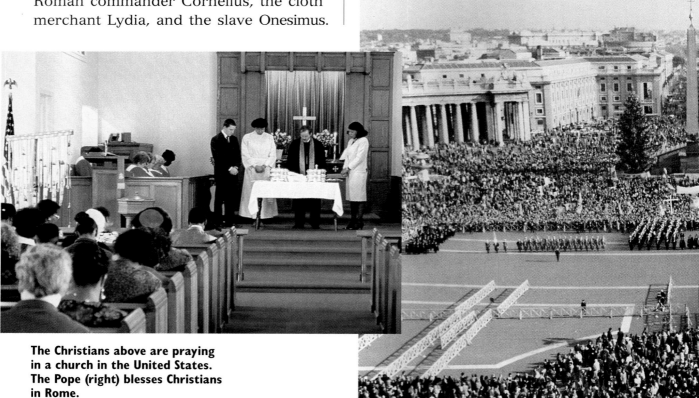

The Christians above are praying in a church in the United States. The Pope (right) blesses Christians in Rome.

Christianity in Rome

Early church historians wrote that the apostle Peter helped bring Christianity to Rome's crowded neighborhoods. Before they died, Peter and Paul helped build the framework that would make Rome's Christian community the largest in the empire. Christians call Peter the first **bishop**, or regional church leader, of Rome. Later, Christians would give the bishop of Rome the title **pope**—from the Latin word for "father." The pope today is the leader of a branch of Christianity known as Roman Catholicism.

As time passed, Christians were tortured and killed by the Roman government. Despite increasing violence against Christians, Christianity continued to flourish in Rome and elsewhere. Both rich and poor continued to be drawn to Jesus' message of love and hope.

WHY IT MATTERS

One of the most powerful supporters of Christianity was a man who became emperor of Rome. You will read about this man and the effects of his actions in the next lesson.

Since its beginnings in the hills of Judea and its spread throughout the Roman empire, Christianity has become one of the world's major religions. In chapters to come you will read about how Christianity has affected life on every continent on Earth.

Reviewing Facts and Ideas

SUM IT UP

- Christianity developed in Roman-occupied Judea during the Pax Romana.

- The life and teachings of Jesus are recorded in the New Testament of the Christian Bible.

- The New Testament says that the followers of Jesus believed that he was the Messiah.

- Two of Jesus' followers, Peter and Paul, helped to spread Christianity throughout the Roman world.

THINK ABOUT IT

1. Why, according to the New Testament, was Jesus born in Bethlehem?

2. Why were the followers of Jesus called *Christians?*

3. **FOCUS** How were Jesus' teachings rooted in Judaism?

4. **THINKING SKILL** *Make a conclusion* about the importance of the Apostles to the spread of Christianity.

5. **GEOGRAPHY** What role did the Roman empire play in the movement of Christianity throughout the ancient Mediterranean world?

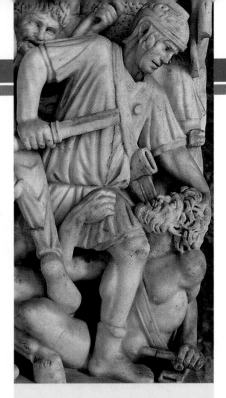

500
B.C.

250
B.C.

A.D.
1

A.D.
180

A.D.
500

THE DECLINE OF THE ROMAN EMPIRE

Focus Activity

READ TO LEARN
What contributed to the decline of Rome?

VOCABULARY
Eastern Orthodox
  Christianity
architecture
Roman Catholicism

PEOPLE
Diocletian
Constantine

PLACES
Palestine
Constantinople
Byzantine empire

READ ALOUD

About A.D. *400 Rome's emperor passed a law banning people from wearing pants or certain kinds of boots. People who broke the law faced losing all of their belongings and being thrown out of the city. Why did the emperor pass such laws about fashion? Pants were the everyday clothes of foreign soldiers whom the Romans called "barbarians." By* A.D. *400 these peoples had the power to take over the once-mighty city of Rome.*

THE BIG PICTURE

During the Pax Romana from 27 B.C. to A.D. 180, the Roman empire was by no means the only power in its area of the world. On Rome's eastern border, a new Persian empire was developing and growing. North of Rome, different groups were beginning to outgrow the heavily forested lands of northern Europe. After a while some of these people began looking toward the fertile lands within Rome's borders. Like the hunters of China's northern steppes, Europe's northern peoples began raiding the wealthy lands to their south.

Invasions from the north would eventually bring many changes to the Roman empire. The Pax Romana came to an end while new groups moved through the lands of the empire. Many Romans tried to protect themselves and their property. As fear spread, a Roman emperor made a decision that would have a tremendous impact on the Roman empire.

THE DECLINE OF AN EMPIRE

Despite its name, the Pax Romana was not a completely peaceful time in Rome's history. Revolts and border wars flared up often, but the Roman army had always managed to regain control. The Pax Romana ended when large armies from northern Europe began to invade the empire in the late A.D. 100s.

The Empire Under Attack

The northern invaders were German-speaking peoples. They were attacking a Roman empire that had become too big to control. There were increasing difficulties with communicating and collecting taxes. The army weakened, and the empire became poorer.

The raids from the north destroyed cities and farmlands. They made the empire's roads and coasts unsafe. Thieves held up travelers, and pirates hijacked ships. Trade suffered.

As time passed the raids caused life in the empire to change in almost every way. Many cities in the western empire isolated themselves behind thick new walls. In the countryside, wealthy landowners withdrew into their well-protected villas. In the west, where most invasions took place, the Roman empire was rapidly falling apart.

The Empire Is Divided

In A.D. 284 an emperor who was named Diocletian (di uh KLEE shun) came to power. Like other emperors who ruled during this time of war, Diocletian was a powerful general. He realized that the empire was simply too big to be ruled by one man, so he divided it into two main parts.

Three assistants took charge of affairs in the troubled western empire. Diocletian became head of the eastern empire. This region included the wealthy cities of Egypt, Greece, and Palestine—the Roman name for Judea. By choosing to oversee the eastern empire, Diocletian created a major turning point in Roman history. For the first time, Rome was no longer the most important city in the empire. Power was shifting from west to east.

This painting shows the northern invaders who began to attack the Roman empire in the late A.D. 100s.

A CAPITAL IN THE EAST

In 306 **Constantine** became emperor. He reunited the Roman empire under his rule. Like Diocletian, Constantine focused on the eastern half of the empire. He based the empire in a new city on the site of an ancient Greek colony named Byzantium (bih ZAN tee um). Renamed **Constantinople** (kahn stan tuh NOH pul) in his honor, it became the capital of a huge empire. The city still exists today, as Istanbul, Turkey.

The location of the new capital was perfect for many reasons. Surrounded on three sides by water, Constantinople was easy to protect. It was on major trade routes between the eastern empire and Asia. Finally, the city was far away from Rome and all its traditions of government and religion. This distance made changing the government easier.

Constantinople had an elegant marble forum and aqueducts that flowed with clear water. Thousands of fans attended events in the city stadium. Constantinople, however, not only had temples to many gods but numerous Christian churches as well.

Freedom for Christians

Earlier emperors had Christians killed for refusing to honor Rome's gods and goddesses. Constantine, however, became a supporter of Christianity.

In a dream Constantine was said to have had the night before a major battle in 312, he was told to mark the sign of the cross on his soldiers' shields. He had this done and won the battle. The cross is a religious symbol of Christians.

As a result, Constantine granted freedom to Christians. He donated

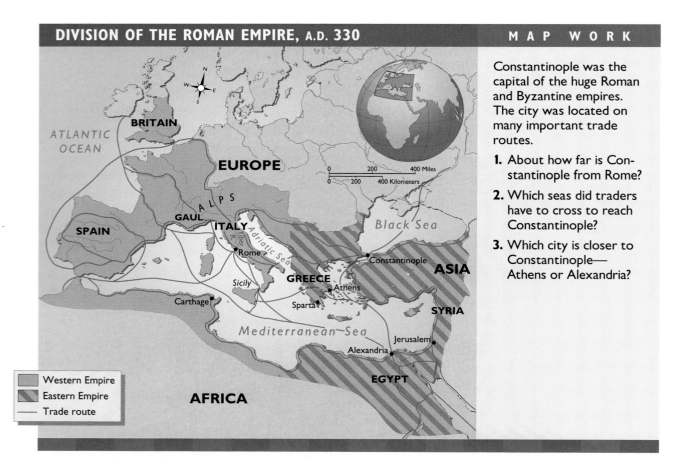

DIVISION OF THE ROMAN EMPIRE, A.D. 330

ATLANTIC OCEAN
BRITAIN
EUROPE
A L P S
GAUL
SPAIN
ITALY
Rome
Tiber R.
Adriatic Sea
Sicily
Carthage
GREECE
Athens
Sparta
Black Sea
Constantinople
ASIA
SYRIA
Jerusalem
Mediterranean Sea
Alexandria
EGYPT
AFRICA

200   400 Miles
200   400 Kilometers

Western Empire
Eastern Empire
Trade route

M A P   W O R K

Constantinople was the capital of the huge Roman and Byzantine empires. The city was located on many important trade routes.

1. About how far is Constantinople from Rome?

2. Which seas did traders have to cross to reach Constantinople?

3. Which city is closer to Constantinople— Athens or Alexandria?

Istanbul, Turkey (above), was founded by Constantine (below) as Constantinople. It lies partly in Europe and partly in Asia.

money to build Christian churches throughout the empire. He also appointed Christians to important government posts. Constantine became the first of many future rulers in Europe who saw themselves as protectors of Christianity.

End of the Roman Empire

Meanwhile the western empire continued to weaken. Northern peoples settled into more parts of the empire. In 410 their soldiers took Rome itself. In 476, Rome's last emperor was removed from the throne. The city of Rome—once all-powerful in the western Mediterranean—no longer had much influence.

The Eastern Empire Lives On

After the fall of the western Roman empire, the eastern half lived on for another 1,000 years. It became known as the Byzantine empire, in honor of its roots in the Greek city of Byzantium.

Greek culture had a large role in Byzantine life. People spoke Greek rather than the Latin of Rome. Greek as well as western Asian cultures also influenced Byzantine art and building styles. Christianity spread through the empire and influenced the life and arts as well.

Christianity in the Byzantine empire was influenced by Greek culture. As a result, Christianity developed differently than in the west. Western Christians regarded the pope as the only leader who could speak for the church. Eastern Christians did not agree. Their religion, Eastern Orthodox Christianity, would also have a deep influence on people's lives in eastern Europe and western Asia.

Even though there were differences, Byzantine civilization preserved the strong traditions of the Roman empire. Many years later, Roman laws would revive in western Europe thanks to their survival in the Byzantine empire.

THE LEGACY OF ROME

Though the western Roman empire collapsed in the 400s, many important legacies live on. You read about Roman engineering earlier. There were many others too.

Law and Government

Even before the empire was born, Romans crafted the foundations of their laws and government. That was to be their most important legacy. The basic framework of the Roman republic has often been copied. Founders of the United States were inspired by the republic's idea of having leaders serve in three branches of government. They also used the word *senate* and the idea of *veto* power.

New Languages

As the Roman empire spread, the Latin language spread as well. Long after the western empire died, many new languages grew out of Latin. Today these "Romance" languages are still spoken in western Europe and the rest of the world. They include Italian, Spanish, French, Portuguese, and Romanian.

Today even more people use the Roman alphabet. Look carefully at the chart. The Roman alphabet owed much to the Greek alphabet, which in turn grew out of the Phoenician alphabet. The Roman style of letters, though, became the base for the ones we use today. English is just one of many languages that are written with the Roman alphabet.

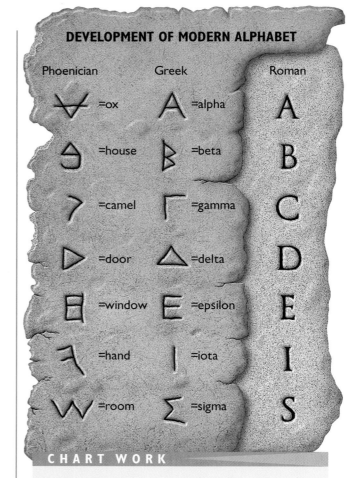

DEVELOPMENT OF MODERN ALPHABET

Phoenician		Greek		Roman
	=ox		=alpha	A
	=house		=beta	B
	=camel		=gamma	C
	=door		=delta	D
	=window		=epsilon	E
	=hand		=iota	I
	=room		=sigma	S

CHART WORK

The Roman alphabet developed from the Greek and Phoenician alphabets.

1. In what way is the Roman "A" different from the Phoenician symbol for ox?
2. Which Greek letter is similar to the Roman "E"?

Roman Buildings

As you read earlier, architecture, or the science of planning and constructing buildings, was a major legacy of ancient Rome. Roman architecture borrowed heavily from other cultures. Greek columns and Etruscan arches were parts of many Roman buildings. Yet Roman engineers developed new ideas from these old forms.

Christianity in the West

Roman language and architecture enriched the development of Christianity. Church ceremonies and writings were in Latin. Many huge churches all over Europe were built in the Roman style. Some of the grandest were built in Rome itself. Rome would be the city that would later become the leader of Christianity in western Europe. This western Christianity was later known as Roman Catholicism. Like Eastern Orthodox Christianity, Roman Catholicism has many followers today.

The remains of the Roman Forum (below), mark the site where the senate met in 27 B.C. to name Augustus emperor.

WHY IT MATTERS

The civilization of ancient Rome influenced life in the eastern Mediterranean and western Europe for centuries. As the peoples of western Europe developed a new civilization, they would carry Roman ideas with them. Eventually these ideas influenced peoples throughout the world. The story of this influence will be told in chapters to come.

Reviewing Facts and Ideas

SUM IT UP

- Invasions, tax collection problems, and other factors weakened the Roman empire in the A.D. 200s.

- In about 284 Diocletian divided the Roman empire into two parts, making it easier to rule.

- Constantine established the Byzantine empire in the east, where Christianity also became a powerful force.

- While the eastern empire continued to live on, the western empire collapsed in the 400s.

- Rome has left legacies of government, language, and architecture.

THINK ABOUT IT

1. What brought about the end of the Pax Romana?

2. How did Romans use the legacies of other civilizations? What Roman legacies affect our lives today?

3. **FOCUS** Why did the western empire finally collapse?

4. **THINKING SKILL** What _conclusions_ can you make about the changes that occurred in the Eastern Roman empire under Constantine?

5. **WRITE** Why was Constantinople a good location for the new capital?

CHAPTER 9 REVIEW

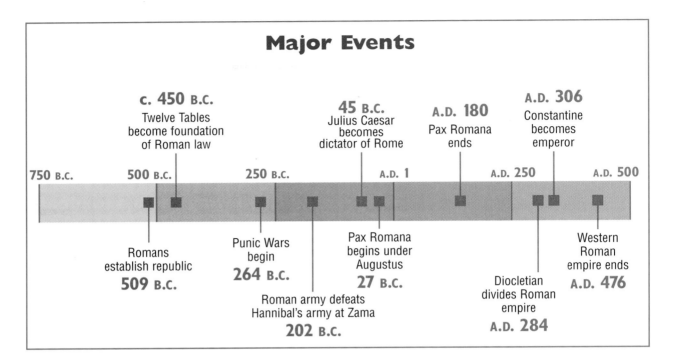

Major Events

c. 450 B.C.
Twelve Tables become foundation of Roman law

45 B.C.
Julius Caesar becomes dictator of Rome

A.D. 180
Pax Romana ends

A.D. 306
Constantine becomes emperor

750 B.C.   500 B.C.   250 B.C.   A.D. 1   A.D. 250   A.D. 500

Romans establish republic
509 B.C.

Punic Wars begin
264 B.C.

Pax Romana begins under Augustus
27 B.C.

Western Roman empire ends
A.D. 476

Roman army defeats Hannibal's army at Zama
202 B.C.

Diocletian divides Roman empire
A.D. 284

THINKING ABOUT VOCABULARY

Number a sheet of paper from 1 to 10. Beside each number write the word or phrase from the list below that best completes the sentence.

architecture   Messiah
civil war   patrician
consul   profile
dictator   representative
elevation   republic

1. Height above sea level is called _____.

2. A _____ is a war between groups inside a country.

3. A _____ is a member of a noble family.

4. In a _____ people get to choose their own government leaders.

5. A person elected to act for others is called a _____.

6. A _____ was one of the Roman leaders elected by the citizen assembly.

7. The _____ is believed by his followers to have been a special leader sent by God to lead the Jewish people.

8. A _____ is a view of something from the side or a cross section.

9. A _____ is somebody who rules with absolute power.

10. _____ is the science of planning and constructing buildings.

THINKING ABOUT FACTS

1. How did the Alps and the Apennine Mountains cause difficulty for travelers in Italy?

2. What role did Hannibal play in Roman history?

3. Why was Julius Caesar assassinated?

4. What is the New Testament? Why is it important to Christianity?

5. According to the time line above, for about how long had Rome been a republic before Julius Caesar became a dictator?

THINK AND WRITE

WRITING AN EXPLANATION

Write two paragraphs about Rome's republican government. First explain how it worked. Then compare and contrast it with Athenian democracy.

WRITING A TV REPORT

Suppose you are a television reporter sent back in time to ancient Rome to cover the assassination of Julius Caesar. Write a report that you will give on the evening news.

WRITING A COMPARISON

Write a paragraph about the decline of the Roman empire. Compare the problems of the western empire with the successes of the Byzantine empire in the east.

APPLYING GEOGRAPHY SKILLS

READING ELEVATION PROFILES AND MAPS

1. What is an elevation map? What is a profile map?

2. Look at the elevation map of Rome (Map A) on page 228 to find the elevations of the seven hills. Which hills are the highest? Which is the lowest? List the hills of Rome in order of elevation from highest to lowest.

3. Look at the profile map of Rome (Map B) on page 229. How much higher is the Palatine Hill than the Caelian Hill? How much higher is the Caelian Hill than the Tiber River?

4. Why can an elevation map show the locations of places in an area better than a profile map can? What is the advantage of a profile map?

5. Why are elevation and profile maps useful? When may they be too limiting?

Summing Up the Chapter

Copy the cause-and-effect chart below on a separate piece of paper. Then review the chapter to find at least three causes for each effect listed. After you have filled in the causes, use the chart to write a paragraph that answers the question "How did Rome grow into a great empire?"

CAUSE	EFFECT
	Rome becomes a powerful empire.
	The Western Roman empire declines.

CHAPTER 10

Ancient Arabia

THINKING ABOUT
HISTORY AND GEOGRAPHY

In this chapter you will read how early peoples lived in the deserts and mountains of Arabia. Farming, herding, and trade developed in this region. The religion of Islam spread rapidly to unite many Arabs in one belief. The civilization that followed built a glorious capital city and created many legacies that still influence people today.

300 B.C.
PETRA

Petra becomes a caravan stop for Arab traders

A.D. 622
MEDINA

Muhammad moves to Medina; Islamic calendar begins

A.D. 762
BAGHDAD

Caliph Al-Mansur founds a capital city

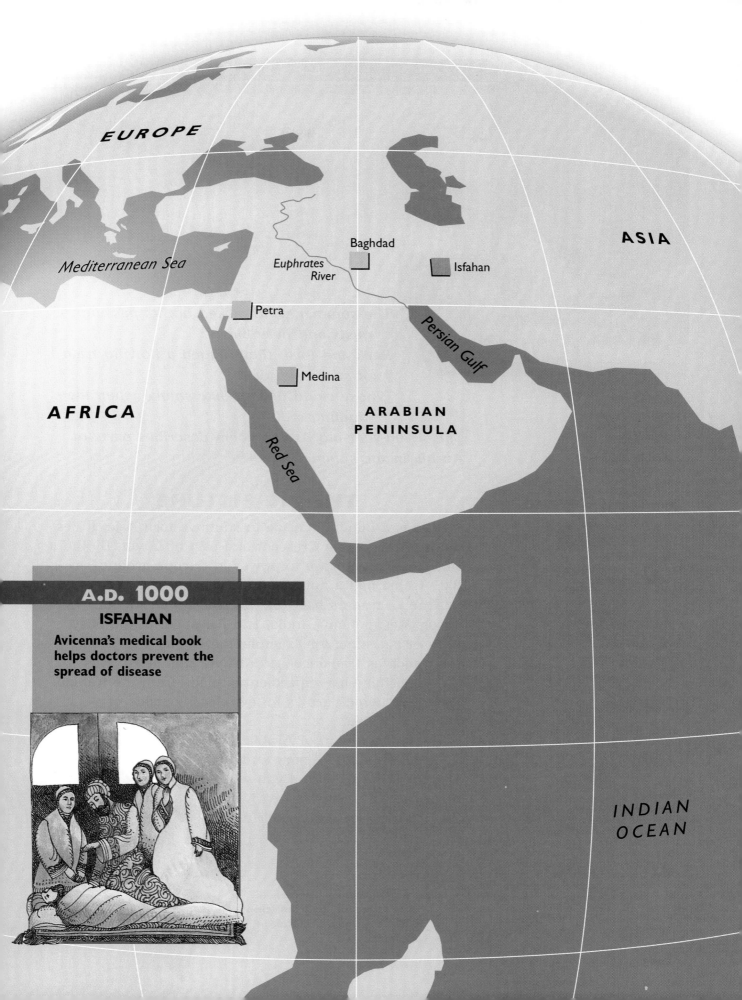

EUROPE

ASIA

Mediterranean Sea

Euphrates
River

Baghdad

Isfahan

Petra

Persian Gulf

Medina

AFRICA

ARABIAN
PENINSULA

Red Sea

A.D. 1000

ISFAHAN

Avicenna's medical book
helps doctors prevent the
spread of disease

INDIAN
OCEAN

GEOGRAPHY OF ARABIA

READ ALOUD

*The summer wind picked up, its passing
    gusts and fiery blasts.*
*Back and forth they tugged a flowing train
    of stirred-up dust*
*Whose cloud flies up like smoke when the
    kindling is lit.*

This 1,400-year-old Arabic poem describes parts of
Arabia in the summertime.

THE BIG PICTURE

Arabia is a huge peninsula in southwestern Asia. It lies
south of the Fertile Crescent and east of Egypt. By the
time Constantine rose to power in Europe around A.D.
300, Arabia had a number of flourishing civilizations.

Arabian traders had long been traveling to cities in
Egypt, Mesopotamia, India, and Palestine. In the busy
cities of Palestine, for example, merchants sold luxury
items such as frankincense (FRANG kihn sens). This
costly, perfume-like ingredient is made from the frankincense tree, which grows in few places outside of
southern Arabia.

Today the region of Arabia contains several
nations, including Yemen, Kuwait, and Saudi Arabia. In this lesson you will read
about the ways in which early people of these areas used their environment to develop thriving
civilizations.

**Dates are an important crop
of the Arabian peninsula.**

Focus Activity

READ TO LEARN
How did the people of
the Arabian peninsula
adapt to the region's
geography?

VOCABULARY
oasis
caravan

PLACES
Arabia
Persian Gulf
Arabian Sea
Red Sea
Yemen
Petra

262

THE ARABIAN PENINSULA

The Arabian peninsula is bounded by the Persian Gulf to the east. To the south is the Arabian Sea. To the west, the Red Sea almost completely separates Arabia from Africa. Find these places on the map below.

Arabia can be divided into three environmental areas. Find them on the map. The Jabal al-Hijaz (JAB al al hihj AZ) mountains rise along Arabia's west coast to its southernmost tip. The rainfall here makes agriculture possible.

Arabia's east coast is the second environmental area. It is also fertile enough for farming.

The third area covers the inner part of the Arabian peninsula. It is mostly desert. About one quarter of Arabia gets fewer than 10 inches of rain each year, and there are few rivers.

The Desert Environments

Some of Arabia's deserts contain stone cliffs. Others have huge hills of sand. The world's largest continuous body of sand is on the Arabian peninsula. This region, called the Empty Quarter, is uninhabitable. Some parts have no rain for 10 years or more. Other parts enjoy winter cloudbursts that allow desert plants to grow. All of Arabia's deserts have a lack of water and an oven-like summer heat.

Some parts of a desert are not dry. Such an area is an oasis (oh AY sis). Oases are watered by underground springs. People can grow crops in the soil of these areas. Some oases are even large enough to support towns. However, there are few oases in Arabia, and few people live in any part of the peninsula's deserts.

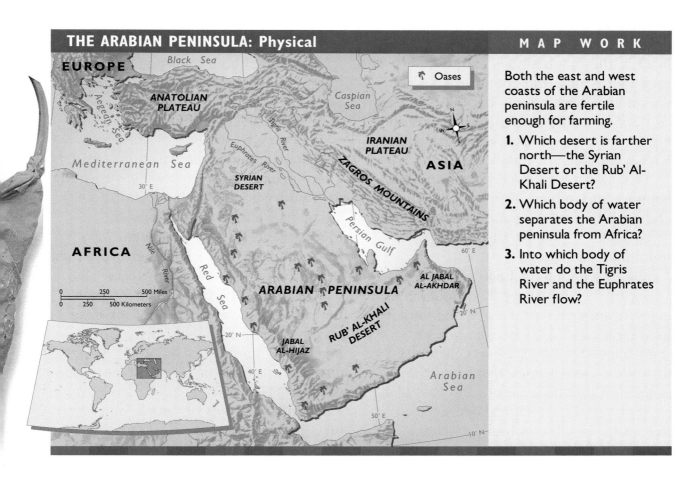

THE ARABIAN PENINSULA: Physical

MAP WORK

Both the east and west coasts of the Arabian peninsula are fertile enough for farming.

1. Which desert is farther north—the Syrian Desert or the Rub' Al-Khali Desert?

2. Which body of water separates the Arabian peninsula from Africa?

3. Into which body of water do the Tigris River and the Euphrates River flow?

PEOPLES OF ARABIA

The Arabian peninsula is named for the Arabs, the people who have lived there for over 3,000 years. The word "Arab" was first recorded around 800 B.C. It referred to the people living in northern Arabia who had domesticated the camel. Early Arabs used these animals to travel around the peninsula.

Trade caravans like the one above stopped in Petra (right), the capital of the Nabataean civilization. This temple was carved out of rock there.

Arabia's Fertile Regions

Most of the early people of Arabia lived in fertile regions. Some Arabians lived in the mountainous southwestern area that is now the country of Yemen (YE mun). These people became known as the Sabaean (suh BEE un) civilization. Find Yemen on the Atlas map on page R10 in the back of this book.

This area receives enough rainfall to support agriculture. Think about what you read in earlier chapters. What type of agriculture is most successful in mountainous regions?

Like the people in Italy and Greece, Sabaeans herded sheep and goats and grew grapes and wheat. By building irrigation canals, farmers improved their harvests. As Sabaean coastal towns developed, they began trading with the Egyptians, across the Red Sea.

Another early Arab people lived to the north, in what is today Jordan, around 300 B.C. Their kingdom was called Nabataea (nab uh TEE uh). They built their capital, Petra (PEH truh), in a place that had a large supply of water brought by aqueducts. Find Petra on the map on page 267.

Trade Across Desert and Sea

It is easy to see why Petra became an important stop on a trade route. There are no other well-watered places for hundreds of miles south of the city. Through trade with Asia and the Mediterranean, the Nabataean (nah buh TEE un) civilization grew rich. It flourished for about 400 years.

Ancient Arabs domesticated camels because they are very useful for desert travel. Camels can carry heavy loads, and go for days without water. They also provide milk to drink. Arab traders often traveled in camel caravans. A caravan is a group of people and animals traveling together. Caravans traveled along routes well known to desert

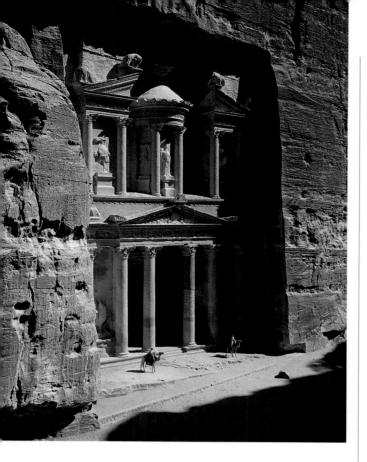

experts. Arab traders journeyed throughout the Arabian peninsula. They traded in cities of the Fertile Crescent and across the Red Sea in Egypt.

Peoples on the Move

One of the groups of people who traded in Arabia were called Bedouins (BED uh wunz). The word *Bedouins* means "people of the desert." They were family groups who lived mostly in the desert, traveling in caravans and sleeping in tents. Many Bedouin traders became wealthy and powerful, sometimes because they raided towns and other caravans.

Other peoples who often moved about were mountain herders. Like the herders of northern China, they moved to new grazing lands at different times of the year. Some went as far as the Fertile Crescent. As in China, the differences in lifestyle between herders and farmers sometimes caused conflict.

WHY IT MATTERS

The geography of Arabia presented unique challenges to the people who built civilizations in this region. The rugged mountains and water-rich oases of the Arabian peninsula received enough moisture to make farming, herding, and some city-building possible. The people who lived in Arabia's vast stretches of desert had to adapt to very harsh conditions.

Ancient Arabia was divided by geography. However, in the A.D. 600s its people would become unified under a new religion. You will read about this religion in the next lesson.

Reviewing Facts and Ideas

SUM IT UP

- While some of Arabia is desert, the coastal areas receive enough rain to support agriculture.
- Towns and trade developed in fertile regions, at desert edges, and at oases.
- Trade linked ancient Arabia with Egypt and the Fertile Crescent.

THINK ABOUT IT

1. In what ways do environments differ in various parts of Arabia?

2. How did people live in the mountainous environment of Yemen?

3. **FOCUS** How did varied geography influence the development of different cultures in Arabia?

4. **THINKING SKILL** Explain why the following statement is a *fact* or why it is an *opinion:* "The best Arabian trade routes were found in the western part of the peninsula."

5. **GEOGRAPHY** Study the map of Arabia. Which coast has more areas of high elevation?

BEGINNINGS OF ISLAM

READ ALOUD

"Allah—there is no god but He . . . Muhammad is the Messenger of Allah." These words are from the Quran (kur AHN), the most holy book of the religion called Islam. It contains the most basic teachings of Islam. In this lesson you will read about how this religion came to hold great influence on the Arabian peninsula. In time Islam would spread throughout many areas of the world.

THE BIG PICTURE

By A.D. 500 Hinduism had deep roots in the Indian sub-continent. Buddhism had spread to Southeast Asia and China. In China, Buddhism mixed with Confucian ideas. Christianity had grown around the Roman empire and spread into North Africa and Mesopotamia. Judaism, which had also grown in the eastern Mediterranean, reached as far as the oasis towns of western Arabia.

In the same region of Arabia, a new religion called Islam (is LAHM) was born. *Islam* means "submit to the will of God" in Arabic, the Arab language. Followers of Islam are called Muslims—which translates "ones who submit to God." The story and teachings of Islam have been written down in the Quran, the most important book of Islam. Its words are sacred to the more than 1 billion Muslims in the world today.

Focus Activity

READ TO LEARN
What are some of the major teachings of Islam?

VOCABULARY
Islam
Quran
Kaaba
hijra
Five Pillars
pilgrimage

PEOPLE
Muhammad
Khadija

PLACES
Mecca
Medina

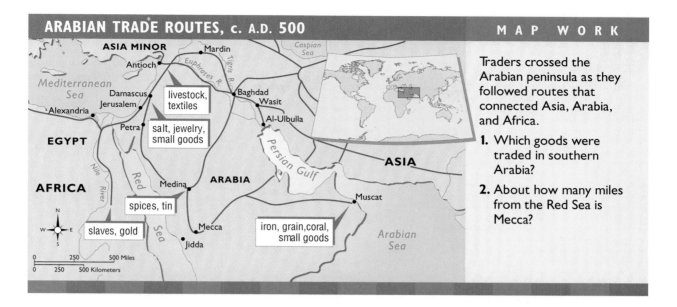

ASIA MINOR
Mardin
Antioch
Caspian Sea
Euphrates R.
Tigris R.
Mediterranean Sea
Damascus
Jerusalem
Baghdad
Wasit
Alexandria
Petra
Al-Ulbulla
livestock, textiles
salt, jewelry, small goods
EGYPT
Persian Gulf
ASIA
AFRICA
Nile River
Red Sea
Medina
ARABIA
spices, tin
Muscat
slaves, gold
Mecca
Jidda
iron, grain, coral, small goods
Arabian Sea

0 250 500 Miles
0 250 500 Kilometers

Traders crossed the Arabian peninsula as they followed routes that connected Asia, Arabia, and Africa.

1. Which goods were traded in southern Arabia?

2. About how many miles from the Red Sea is Mecca?

THE BIRTH OF MUHAMMAD

In the last lesson you read that traders had been crisscrossing the Arabian peninsula for hundreds of years. Find some of the caravan trade routes on the map on this page. By A.D. 500 traders carried goods and ideas to and from many different communities. In some towns Arab traders could buy iron tools from a Jewish craftworker or have a tooth pulled by a Christian dentist. Religious beliefs differed from place to place, as did languages and writing systems. The people in western Arabia had developed a written language, Arabic, sometime before 800 B.C. An example of Arabic writing is shown below.

According to Muslim tradition, a boy named Muhammad (mu HAM ud) was born in the oasis city of Mecca about A.D. 570. His father died before he was born. Because Muhammad's mother died not long after his birth, he was raised by an uncle who was a trader. In time Muhammad mastered the skill of leading caravans.

The writings that trace Muhammad's life say that his skills caught the eye of a wealthy widow and merchant, Khadija (ka DEE jah). On her behalf Muhammad traveled to the Fertile Crescent to trade goods. When he returned from his journey, they were married.

The City of Mecca

Muhammad's marriage to Khadija is said to have given him wealth and respect in busy Mecca, where they lived. Mecca lay on the main trading route through western Arabia. Therefore, many merchants came to do business there.

The city also attracted other visitors because of the Kaaba (KAH buh), Mecca's temple. At this time the Kaaba was like the Pantheon of Rome. It honored gods and goddesses worshiped by the people of Mecca.

A young Bedouin reads from the Quran (left). Thousands of Muslims face the Kaaba as they pray (below).

TEACHINGS OF ISLAM

According to Muslim belief Muhammad often went to a mountain cave near Mecca to pray. The writings say that one night, when Muhammad was about 40 years old, something happened that would change the history of Arabia.

Muslims believe that Muhammad received a message from Allah (ahl LAH). *Allah* is the Arabic word for God. Muhammad was told, "O Muhammad, you are the Prophet of Allah." As you learned in Chapter 5, a prophet is believed by followers to speak for God. Over many years, Allah is said to have given other messages to Muhammad.

The Prophet Muhammad

Muslim writings say that Muhammad's wife Khadija helped him greatly. With her encouragement and support,

he set out to teach people in Mecca about Allah. Over the next three years, his group of followers slowly grew.

According to tradition Muhammad aroused the anger of city leaders. They were upset because he criticized the Meccans' way of life and their belief in many gods. His disagreement with city leaders is said to have caused him and his followers to leave Mecca in 622.

Muhammad's Migration

The writings about Muhammad say that he moved over 200 miles from Mecca to another oasis town, Medina (muh DEE nuh). He gained many supporters there. Muhammad's hijra (HIHJ ruh)—Arabic for "migration"— marked a major turning point in Islamic history. The year of the hijra, 622, marks the starting point of the Islamic calendar.

Return to Mecca

Muslim scholars say that in 624 Muhammad led attacks on Meccan caravans, cutting off Mecca's source of riches. Later, with peace agreements, he is said to have won Mecca's surrender. After his victory in 630, Muhammad destroyed the statues of the gods and goddesses in the Kaaba and proclaimed Mecca a Muslim city. It is holy to Muslims to this day.

Writings state that Muhammad won the support of many Arabian communities. In 632 he is said to have spoken to his followers at Mecca. His words, taken from the Quran, were "[Muslim] believers are brothers one of another." Later that year Muhammad died.

The Sacred Book of Islam

In Islamic belief the Quran contains Allah's teachings to Muhammad. Muslims believe these words were written down soon after Muhammad's death. The most important teaching was that there was only one God in the universe—Allah. The Quran says that Allah is the God worshiped both by Christians and Jews.

We believe in God, and in that which has been sent down on Abraham . . . and that which was given to Moses and Jesus.

The Quran serves as a guide for living for Muslims, as the Bible does for Jews and Christians. Through its words, Muslims learn about Allah's teachings.

The Five Pillars of Islam

The Quran outlines five basic duties of all Muslims. The purpose of these duties—the Five Pillars of Islam—is to strengthen Muslims' ties to Allah and to other people. The first pillar is the belief in one God, Allah, and that Muhammad is Allah's prophet. The second describes the prayers Muslims offer Allah five times each day. Wherever they are in the world, as they pray, Muslims look toward Mecca, their holy city. The third pillar speaks of giving to those in need, especially the poor. The fourth instructs Muslims to fast during the holy month of Ramadan (rahm uh DAHN). From sunrise to sunset Muslims neither eat nor drink. They spend time in worship. The final pillar instructs Muslims who can afford it to visit Mecca at least once in their lives. A journey for religious purposes is called a pilgrimage.

The Quran's first chapter has important instructions. What do these words say about Islam?

MANY VOICES
PRIMARY SOURCE

Excerpt from
***The Quran*, about A.D. 650**
Chapter One, Verses 2–7.

Praise be to [Allah], The Cherisher and Sustainer of the worlds;

Most Gracious, Most Merciful

Master of the Day of Judgment.

Thee do we worship and Thine aid we seek.

Show us the straight way,

The way of those on whom Thou hast bestowed Thy Grace.

MUSLIMS AROUND THE WORLD

Muhammad's death must have caused his followers great sorrow. One said, "O men, if you worship Muhammad, Muhammad is dead; if you worship Allah, Allah is alive." Muslims then joined together to spread the message of Islam.

During the 100 years after the death of Muhammad, the Islamic community grew steadily. It spread and flourished, and by A.D. 750, followers of Islam could be found from Spain all the way to the Indus valley.

Gradually, over a period of time, nonreligious legacies spread throughout this vast region, as well. Just as the Latin language spread through the Roman empire, for example, Arabic became the common language in many Islamic lands. The different peoples who came under Islamic rule also made many important contributions to the heritage of Islam. You will read about some of these contributions in the next lesson.

Islam Today

Of the great number of Muslims in the world today, probably around 5 million live in the United States. The customs of Muslims often vary from one country to another. However, nearly all Muslims honor the end of Ramadan with a joyful feast. People wear new clothes to celebrate the beginning of the month following the long fast.

Millions of Muslims from all around the world still make the pilgrimage to the holy city of Mecca every year. Muslims everywhere view the pilgrimage as one of the most important events in their lives.

Muslims gather for worship in Cordoba, Spain (top). The end of Ramadan is celebrated by many with music and dance (right).

At home Muslim women take time to teach their children about the Quran. Muslim families have celebrations when sons or daughters memorize large parts of the Quran. Some young people go on to study Islam and other subjects at Muslim schools and colleges.

WHY IT MATTERS

The modern city of Mecca, in Saudi Arabia, is the center of a world-wide Muslim community. No matter where they may be in the world, when they pray, Muslims always position themselves to face this holy city.

For almost 1,400 years Islam has been anchored in both the life of Muhammad and the teachings of the Quran. Throughout that long stretch of time, the religion of Islam has shaped civilizations and human achievements. You will read about some of those achievements in the next lesson.

Reviewing Facts and Ideas

SUM IT UP

- According to Muslim belief Muhammad, the founder of Islam, lived from A.D. 570 to 632. Muhammad preached that there was only one God—Allah.

- Muhammad journeyed from Mecca to Medina in 622. This event is called the hijra. Muhammad went on to become a powerful leader in Medina. Later he returned and proclaimed Mecca a holy city.

- Muslims believe that the sacred book of Islam, the Quran, contains holy teachings that Muhammad received from Allah.

- The Five Pillars of Islam from the Quran instruct Muslims about how they should honor Allah in their lives.

THINK ABOUT IT

1. Why was Mecca an important religious center even before Islam was founded? Why was it an important trading city?

2. What is the most important teaching of Islam?

3. **FOCUS** How do the teachings of Islam affect the daily lives of Muslims?

4. **THINKING SKILL** According to Islamic writings, what was the main *cause* of Muhammad's *hijra*, or migration? What were some of its *effects*?

5. **GEOGRAPHY** Find the holy city of Mecca on the map on page 267. In what direction would a Muslim living in Mardin face during prayer? Estimate the distance that he or she would need to journey in making a pilgrimage to Mecca.

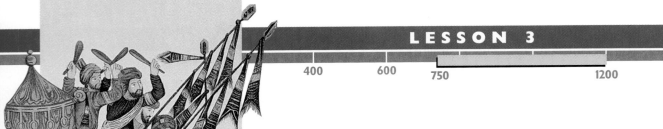

A MUSLIM CALIPHATE

READ ALOUD

Lining the docks, ships filled with Egyptian rice, Chinese dishware, Syrian glass, and Arabian pearls could be seen bobbing on the river. The roads leading to the city were crowded with farmers bringing oranges and cucumbers, and with traders carrying elegant carpets. Occasionally the government's "air-mail" service flew overhead. The service was actually pigeons that had been trained to carry letters! Even more wonders lay within the incredible city of Baghdad (BAG dad).

THE BIG PICTURE

Centuries before the founding of Baghdad, Persian rulers controlled lands north of the Arabian peninsula, from Egypt to India. By the A.D. 600s the Persian empire was in decline. As Islam developed in Mecca, Muhammad gained power on the Arabian peninsula. Leaders who ruled after Muhammad extended Islam to Persian lands and other areas. By 700 Muslim rulers controlled the Mediterranean region.

In 762 the Muslim ruler al-Mansur (al man SUR) decided to build a capital city along the Tigris River in present-day Iraq. He reportedly declared, "This is the site on which I shall build. Goods can arrive here by way of the Euphrates, Tigris, and a network of canals. Only a place like this will support the army and the general population." Not long afterwards the city of Baghdad began to take shape. The city along the Tigris quickly became the center of the Muslim civilization's greatest achievements in science, art, and architecture.

Focus Activity

READ TO LEARN
What did Muslims achieve in the city of Baghdad?

VOCABULARY
caliph
mosque
algebra
astrolabe

PEOPLE
Avicenna

PLACES
Baghdad

272

MUSLIM RULE

In the 760s Islam was just over 100 years old. Much had changed in this time. Caliphs (KAY lihfs) had been chosen to govern the land and religion of Islam. *Caliph* means "successor [to the Prophet]." The lands ruled by the caliph were called the caliphate (KAY luh fayt). As the map below shows, the caliphate expanded to western Asia and North Africa. In many places people welcomed the Muslims, who overthrew hated rulers of old. Many people became Muslims. Others did not, but they learned Arabic. An Islamic civilization united by Muslim leadership developed.

Baghdad

From the late 700s until the 1200s, Baghdad was the capital of the Muslim caliphate. One of the world's largest cities, it had about 1 million residents.

Baghdad's layout reflected the grandness of the Muslim caliphate. At the center of the city stood the caliph's huge, domed palace. Next to it rose a great mosque (MAHSK). A mosque is a place of worship where Muslims go for daily prayers.

From the center of Baghdad, four main roads went to all parts of the caliphate. Traders used these roads to bring riches from all over the caliphate and beyond.

Baghdad had an international flavor. Shoppers packed the streets where Arabian perfume, Indian pepper, African ivory, and Russian furs were among the items sold. Some shops sold only Chinese dishware, while others sold only books. Merchants had learned paper-making from the Chinese, and Baghdad's new paper mill made it possible to create many books.

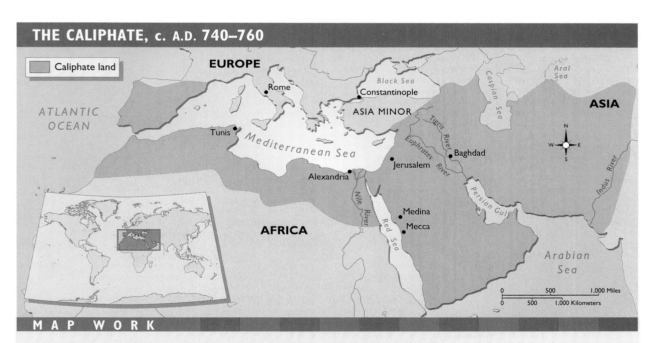

THE CALIPHATE, c. A.D. 740–760

Caliphate land

EUROPE
ATLANTIC OCEAN
Rome
Black Sea
Constantinople
ASIA MINOR
Aral Sea
Caspian Sea
ASIA
Tunis
Mediterranean Sea
Tigris River
Euphrates River
Baghdad
Jerusalem
Alexandria
Nile River
Persian Gulf
Indus River
AFRICA
Red Sea
Medina
Mecca
Arabian Sea

0 500 1,000 Miles
0 500 1,000 Kilometers

MAP WORK

Under the rule of the **caliphs**, an Islamic civilization spread throughout Arabia, North Africa, and western Asia.

1. Which rivers flowed near Baghdad?

2. Which city is closest to the Persian Gulf—Constantinople, Baghdad, or Mecca?

3. About how far is Baghdad from Mecca?

ACHIEVEMENTS OF THE CALIPHATE

Baghdad's caliphs valued education and learning. Muhammad was said to have declared, "He who travels in search of knowledge, travels along Allah's path of Paradise." As a result, the caliphs preserved works from all over the caliphate in a huge library, the House of Wisdom. There, Greek, Roman, and Indian works were translated into Arabic. Over time these works spread throughout the caliphate and the world. Arab scholars read these books on history, science, law, and mathematics. Many later developed and improved these fields of study.

Advances in Medicine

Muslim doctors studied translations of Greek medical texts and a work by a famous Muslim doctor who lived in Persia in the early 1000s. His name was Ibn Sina (IHB un SEE nuh), or Avicenna (av ih SEN uh) in Latin. Avicenna described how some diseases spread through air and water. He wrote that stress could cause stomach problems and that cancer could be fought with surgery. In time Avicenna's book became a standard medical text in many parts of North Africa, western Asia, and Europe.

The caliphate had many doctors. Some of them treated patients in Baghdad's large hospitals. Others oversaw the government's "moving hospitals." These doctors and their assistants gave free treatment to patients who lived far from Baghdad. Such traveling medical teams carried beds, medicines, and other supplies by camel.

Math and Science

When calculating doses of medicine, doctors used a simpler number system

A Muslim doctor treats a patient (above). The site of Dome of the Rock (right) is considered to be holy by both Muslims and Jews.

than that of the Romans. In the Roman system, "XVIII" was "18"—its equal in Arabic numbers. You know the Arabic number system because we use it today.

Muslim mathematicians built on the work of Hindu scholars in India. For example, they helped improve earlier mathematics methods and notation. Muslims also added greatly to the field of *al-jabr* (al JAHB ur). In English, it's algebra, a type of mathematics.

In its vast collections, the House of Wisdom had many Arabic volumes on astronomy. Astronomy, the study of the stars and planets, was of great interest to Muslims. The Islamic calendar was based on the moon's movement. Stars also helped people determine directions. Muslims used a Greek instrument, the astrolabe (AS truh layb), which they improved, to figure out position from the stars.

Places of Worship

Throughout the caliphate, mosque builders took care to follow certain standards. They had to make sure the mosque faced Mecca. Special nooks in the walls showed people the direction of Mecca. From tall towers, religious leaders could call Muslims to prayer. Walled-in courtyards held hundreds of worshipers. Beyond these basic features, builders used their imaginations to make each mosque as beautiful as possible. Many remain standing today.

The oldest Muslim monument still standing is the Dome of the Rock in Jerusalem. Built in 691, this building is not a mosque. Instead it honors the place where Muslims believe Muhammad ascended into heaven. Its Roman-style dome and Greek columns show how Muslims combined old and new ideas to create a unique style of architecture.

Where did you get that guitar?

Before A.D. 700, Arab musicians made and performed on stringed instruments. One of these was the *oud* (OOD) which has a pear-shaped body. Another favorite of Arab musicians was a similar instrument with a flat back, called the guitar. Many historians believe Arabs invented the instrument.

As the caliphate spread, Muslim musicians introduced their stringed instruments in Spain. The oud eventually developed into the lute, a popular instrument in Europe from the 14th to the 16th centuries. The Arabian guitar is the ancestor of the modern guitar that is still popular today. Can you think of any other instruments related to the guitar? Listen to a recording of a guitar.

Literature and Music

Long before Islam was born in Arabia, literature and music had been popular there. You read an excerpt from a pre-Islamic poem in the introduction to Lesson 1. Poetry remained well loved among the people of Baghdad, and its appreciation spread throughout the region at this time.

Folktales were also very popular among the citizens of Baghdad and the rest of the caliphate. Over time, favorites from Persia, India, Arabia, and other places were collected into a book called *The Arabian Nights*. The book's main story is of a wise princess named Shahrazad (shah rah ZAHD). She is married to a cruel king who threatens to kill her after their wedding. She saves herself by distracting him with tales of Aladdin and his lamp, Ali Baba and the 40 thieves, and other exciting stories.

infographic

Life in the Caliphate

During the time of the Baghdad Caliphate, Muslim control spread to parts of Europe, North Africa, and western Asia. Important cultural and scientific achievements spread as well. The stunning architecture of the Alhambra (left), a palace in Spain, is an example. What were some other achievements found in the Caliphate?

Learning

Around 1200, a Muslim teacher (below) who lived in what is today Turkey taught his students about the proper way to form sentences.

Court Life

This painting of court life (above) in what is today Iran shows the wealth of the empire. Notice the oud player on the left.

Weaving

Muslim weavers became famous for their beautiful rugs. Rugs from this region are still treasured for their excellent quality.

Design

This jar (left) may have been used to pour water or wine. Notice the expert working of the design and spout.

WHY IT MATTERS

Baghdad's caliphs ruled lands that stretched from Morocco to India. Islam established deep roots in that area. So did a rich heritage that included major achievements in the arts and sciences.

As you have read, the Arabic language developed on the Arabian peninsula. It is now the common language of most of northern Africa and of parts of western Asia. Today Muslims in many different nations are united by the legacy of Islam. People around the world share other Arabian legacies.

✔ Reviewing Facts and Ideas

SUM IT UP

- Under the caliphs who came after Muhammad, Islam spread into Asia, Africa, and Europe. For centuries the caliphs ruled from Baghdad.

- The caliphate furthered learning in medicine, math, and astronomy.

- Mosques were centers of Muslim worship throughout the caliphate and remain religious centers today.

THINK ABOUT IT

1. Which of Baghdad's trade goods came from other regions?

2. What were some of the achievements of the Muslim caliphate in medicine?

3. **FOCUS** In what ways did Islam influence life in the city of Baghdad?

4. **THINKING SKILL** Based on your study of the geography of Mesopotamia, _make a conclusion_ about the dangers of building Baghdad on the Tigris.

5. **WRITE** Write an article for a science journal describing Baghdad's House of Wisdom. How might it have helped scientists and mathematicians develop new ideas?

Legacy

map making

As the Muslim caliphate expanded, the mapping of new lands became important to the caliphs. The science of making maps is called cartography (cahr TOG ruh fee). To improve their skills, Muslim cartographers, or mapmakers, learned techniques used in earlier civilizations, such as ancient Greece. They also used their mathematical skills to develop new methods that helped make maps more accurate than earlier versions.

One technique that Muslim cartographers used was to draw lines dividing the world into different climate zones. These lines, shown on the map at right, were similar to today's lines of latitude.

Cartography is an important legacy that helps us to understand the world around us. Today, different mapping techniques can be used to show us every part of the world, from the ocean floor to the skies above us.

Muslim cartographer al-Idrisi (al IHD rih see) made this circular map of the world around 1150. The Arabian Peninsula looks different from the way you usually see it, because on this map, north points *down*!

In the 1700s sailors relied on maps similar to this one (left) during ocean voyages. Several centuries earlier, Muslim cartographers used the astrolabe (below) to estimate their position on Earth.

This colorful map is made up of photographs taken by satellites in orbit around our planet. The map shows how Earth might look from space if it were not covered by clouds! The cartographer used only photographs that contained no clouds.

GEOGRAPHYSKILLS

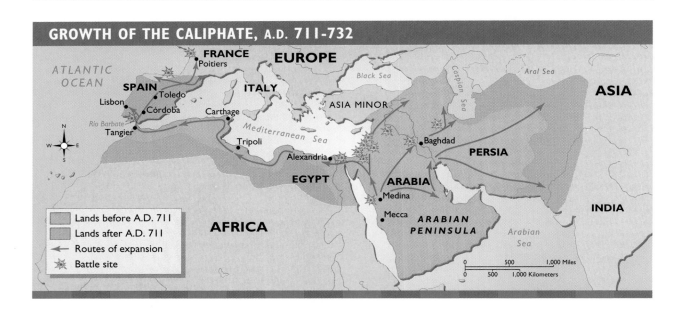

GROWTH OF THE CALIPHATE, A.D. 711-732

Lands before A.D. 711
Lands after A.D. 711
Routes of expansion
Battle site

Reading Historical Maps

VOCABULARY
historical map

WHY THE SKILL MATTERS

In A.D. 711, while the caliph extended his power throughout western Asia, he also sent an army into Europe. Before very long the caliphate controlled all the land in present-day Spain and Portugal.

One way to get a quick overview of such events is to study **historical maps**. Historical maps show information about the past. Use the Helping Yourself box on the next page to guide you in reading historical maps.

USING THE SKILL

Study the map of the caliphate's expansion into Europe on this page. Read the map title. It is an historical map because it shows places and events from the past. Notice that the map shows the names of several countries. These are included to help you locate areas and events.

In 711 the caliph's forces crossed from North Africa to Spain and defeated the army of Roderick, a Spanish king. Now read the map key. It explains a symbol that stands for caliphate battles. As you can see, the Muslim army passed Toledo (tuh LEE doh). Actually, the people of Toledo surrendered without a battle. The next year, more Muslim armies arrived. Find Poitiers (pwah TYAY) in France. Did the caliphate army fight a battle in this city?

Although the caliphate did not conquer France, Muslims ruled parts of Spain for 700 years. In that time Spanish caliphs had magnificent mosques and libraries built. The most stunning mosque, in Córdoba, still stands.

TRYING THE SKILL

The map on page 281 shows events that happened over 600 years after the caliphate victories in Spain. Refer to the Helping Yourself box as you answer questions.

At the time shown here, a Muslim, Ibn Battuta (IHB un bat TOO tuh), set out on a pilgrimage to Mecca from Tangier in present-day Morocco. Little did he know that he would travel 75,000 miles, exploring Africa, Asia, and Europe before returning home. When did Ibn Battuta travel?

Ibn Battuta saw the lighthouse at Alexandria and Jerusalem's Dome of the Rock before visiting Mecca. Baghdad followed. When did he visit Jerusalem?

After he returned to Mecca, Ibn Battuta heard tales about India. Instead of taking the shorter but riskier sea route, he went by land. Constantinople was one stop on this long journey. What city did he visit north of Constantinople? Between what years did

Ibn Battuta visit the Maldive Islands?

Later Ibn Battuta explored Muslim Spain and went by caravan far into Africa. Before Battuta died in about 1377, he recounted his travels to a scribe. As far as we know, he was the only person who had explored the world so thoroughly up to that time.

REVIEWING THE SKILL

Use the map on this page to answer the following questions.

1. What makes this is an historical map?
2. Between what years did Ibn Battuta visit the east coast of Africa?
3. Did he visit Delhi before or after Mecca? How do you know?
4. When is an historical map helpful?

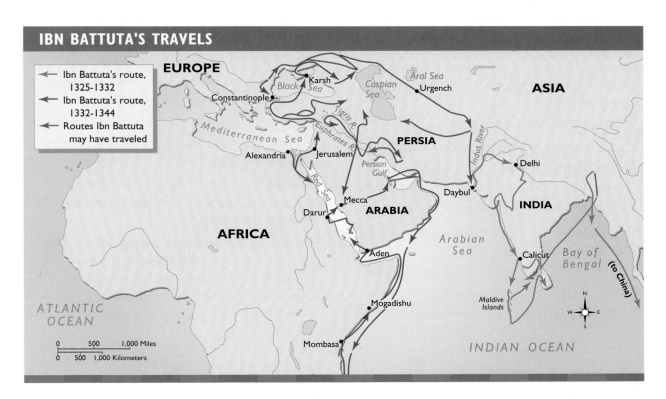

IBN BATTUTA'S TRAVELS

← Ibn Battuta's route, 1325-1332
← Ibn Battuta's route, 1332-1344
← Routes Ibn Battuta may have traveled

CHAPTER 10 REVIEW

Major Events

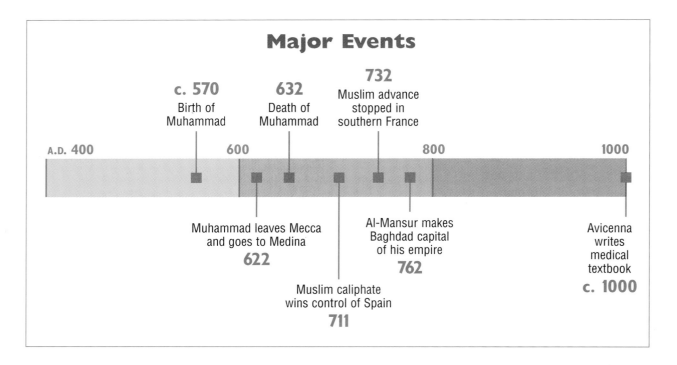

c. 570 Birth of Muhammad

632 Death of Muhammad

732 Muslim advance stopped in southern France

A.D. 400   600   800   1000

Muhammad leaves Mecca and goes to Medina **622**

Al-Mansur makes Baghdad capital of his empire **762**

Avicenna writes medical textbook **c. 1000**

Muslim caliphate wins control of Spain **711**

THINKING ABOUT VOCABULARY

Each of the following statements contains an underlined vocabulary word. Number a sheet of paper from 1 to 10. Beside each number write **T** if the statement is true and **F** if the statement is false. If the statement is false, rewrite the sentence using the vocabulary word correctly.

1. A caliph is a Muslim ruler.
2. An oasis is a Muslim place of worship.
3. The Kaaba is a temple in Mecca that was used to honor gods and goddesses.
4. The Five Pillars are part of the Kaaba.
5. A journey made for religious reasons is called a pilgrimage.
6. The Quran is a famous mosque in Cairo.
7. A caravan is a desert tent.
8. Algebra is a type of mathematics.
9. Muslims used an astrolabe to help them illustrate books.
10. Muhammad's migration from Mecca to Medina, which marks the beginning of the Islamic calendar, is called the hijra.

THINKING ABOUT FACTS

1. Who are the Bedouins? How did some of them become wealthy and powerful?
2. Why is the Quran important to Muslims?
3. What are the Five Pillars of Islam? What are their purpose?
4. What have been some of the important contributions that Muslims have made to world civilization?
5. Look at the time line above. What information do you find there that would make you conclude that Islam spread very rapidly? In what year did the Muslim caliphate gain control of Spain?

THINK AND WRITE ◄⟩

WRITING A DESCRIPTION
Write a paragraph about the geography and climate of the Arabian peninsula. Describe both the fertile and desert parts of the peninsula. Provide information about the climate of the Empty Quarter.

WRITING AN ARTICLE
Write a short article for your school newspaper about Islam. Describe its main beliefs and practices.

WRITING A LETTER
Suppose you are on a pilgrimage to Mecca. Write a letter home describing what you are doing and what you see. Describe the things that impress you the most. Provide descriptions of the art and architecture you see in Mecca.

APPLYING GEOGRAPHY SKILLS

READING HISTORICAL MAPS
1. What is an historical map?
2. Look at the historical map on page 280. What historical information does it provide?
3. What does the map on page 280 tell you about the speed and direction of Muslim expansion?
4. Look at the historical map on page 281. What type of information does it provide? How does the map show different routes of travel?
5. How are historical maps helpful?

Summing Up the Chapter

Review the chapter. Then copy the main-idea chart below on a separate piece of paper. Fill in details in each column that are connected to the main idea. After completing the chart, use it to help you write a paragraph that answers the question "What are the greatest contributions of Muslims to world civilization?"

MAIN IDEA: Islam Spread Throughout Muslim Caliphate

Geographic Setting	Teachings	Achievements

CHAPTER 11

Ancient America

THINKING ABOUT
HISTORY AND GEOGRAPHY

Some scientists believe that early peoples crossed a land bridge from Asia to North America about 30,000 years ago. From there they moved through North and South America. Some settled on the rich lands of Mexico and Central America. The time line shows that these early peoples developed agriculture and built civilizations there. One group, the powerful Maya, built many large cities, which they suddenly and mysteriously abandoned.

30,000 YEARS AGO

BERINGIA

Hunters and gatherers cross a land bridge in search of food

5000 B.C.

VALLEY OF MEXICO

Early people in Mexico cultivate corn

1000 B.C.

LA VENTA

The Olmec use waterways to transport goods

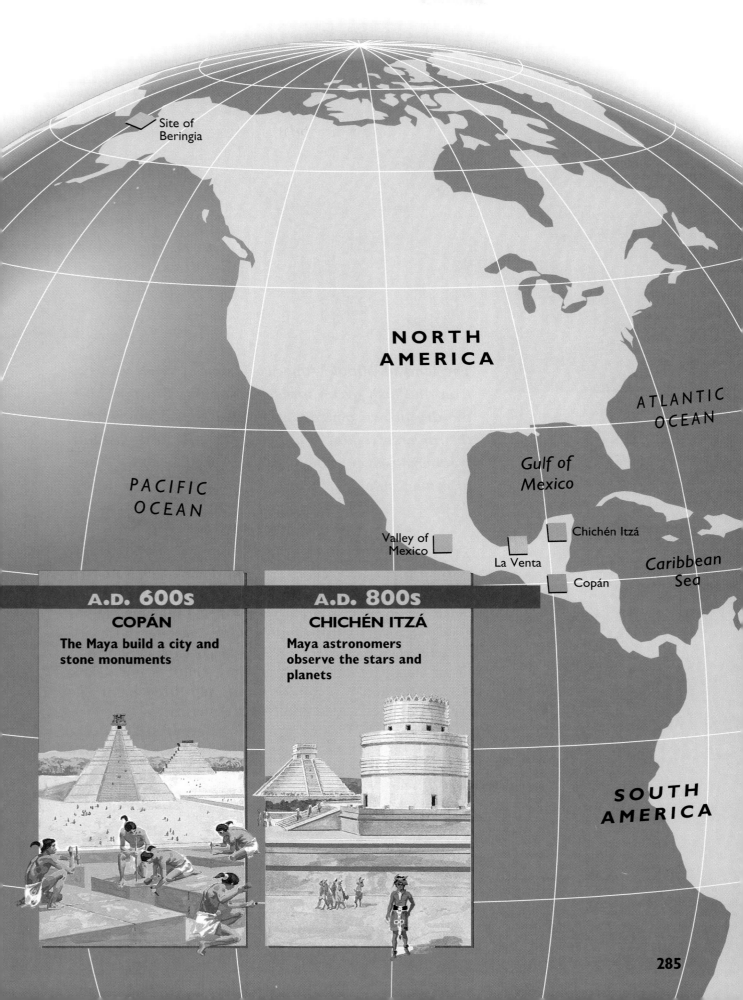

Site of
Beringia

NORTH
AMERICA

ATLANTIC
OCEAN

PACIFIC
OCEAN

Gulf of
Mexico

Chichén Itzá

Valley of
Mexico

La Venta

Caribbean
Sea

Copán

SOUTH
AMERICA

A.D. 600s

COPÁN

The Maya build a city and stone monuments

A.D. 800s

CHICHÉN ITZÁ

Maya astronomers observe the stars and planets

GEOGRAPHY OF MIDDLE AMERICA

Focus Activity

READ TO LEARN
What is unique about the geography of Middle America?

VOCABULARY
Ice Age
glacier
tropical
rain forest

PLACES
Beringia
Middle America
Central Plateau

READ ALOUD

The land of Middle America is one of great variety— from the lush green forests, dripping with rain, to the dry brown plateaus, scorched by the sun. Within this diverse region, with its icy mountain peaks and wandering river valleys, early people forged a series of remarkable civilizations.

THE BIG PICTURE

About 40,000 years ago, Earth's climate was much colder than it is today. This period of time is called the Ice Age, because ice covered nearly half of Earth's land mass. Ice formed in great sheets called glaciers that slowly spread south from the North Pole. As more water turned to ice, the level of the oceans began to drop. When the oceans sank, more land became visible. A "land bridge" we call Beringia (buh RIN jee uh) formed between Asia and North America.

Beringia was located where the Bering Strait is today. Find this area on the map on page R11. Many scientists believe that it was across Beringia that people first came to the Americas. Asian hunters probably followed herds of reindeer across the land bridge and onto the unknown continent. By 15,000 years ago, hunters and gatherers had spread throughout the Americas. In this chapter you will read about the region where the first American civilizations developed. It is called Mesoamerica, or Middle America. *Meso* is from the Latin word meaning "middle."

ENVIRONMENTS OF MIDDLE AMERICA

The early people who traveled south from what is now the United States found warmer lands of great variety. There were towering mountains, lush coastal plains, and dry plateaus. These lands also had large animal populations to hunt and ideal climates for growing food. Many early people settled in Middle America. Look at the map on this page to find this region. It included parts of what are now Mexico and Central America. Here, thousands of years ago, people developed unique cultures that included traditions of farming, religion, government, and art.

The Land of Middle America

Much of Middle America is covered by steep mountains. A large area of rolling hills, called the Central Plateau, is located in the northern part of the region. Ancient volcanoes are found in the valleys of the Central Plateau. As Earth warmed after the Ice Age, this region became home to many different kinds of animals and plants. Not surprisingly, archaeologists have also found bones of early people here. Today the Central Plateau is the location of one of the world's most populous cities, Mexico City.

The Climate of Middle America

Most of Middle America is in the tropical zone. *Tropical* refers to the area of Earth that is near the equator, between the Tropic of Cancer and the Tropic of Capricorn. Middle America has many mountains, so climate also changes with elevation.

The hottest regions, from sea level to 3,000 feet, are called *tierra caliente* (tee AIR ruh cahl YEN tay), which in Spanish means "hot land." These regions are found mostly in the low coastal plains. Here the temperature is over 80°F most of the time. The next level of elevation in Middle America, which includes the Central Plateau, is called *tierra templada* (tee AIR ruh tem PLAH dah), or "temperate land." At this elevation the climate is generally mild. The highest mountain elevations, above 6,000 feet, are known as *tierra fría* (tee AIR ruh FREE ah), or "cold land." The weather there is usually cooler than that of the other two regions.

These varying climate regions all have one thing in common—the rainy season. Almost all the rain that falls in Middle America comes between the months of May and October. Between the months of November and April, the skies are usually clear.

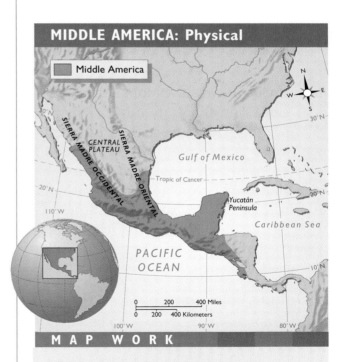

MIDDLE AMERICA: Physical

MAP WORK

Middle America has a variety of landforms.

1. Where are the highest lands found?

2. The Yucatán Peninsula is bordered by which two bodies of water?

Monkeys like these (below) are found in Middle America's rain forests. Abundant plant and animal life have provided food for the Olmec and modern peoples.

THE RAIN FOREST

One environment of Middle America gets more rain than any other. This region is the rain forest. A rain forest is a forest that receives more than 80 inches of rain per year. That's more rain than the city of San Francisco gets in four years! Most rain forests are in tropical regions. The world's tropical regions lie between the Tropics of Cancer and Capricorn.

A Unique Environment

Rain forests are home to a huge variety of plants and animals. Three-quarters of Earth's living things are found in rain forests. Writer Arnold Newman describes this unique environment:

The forest interior is a magical and mercurial [changing] place—an enchanted realm where anything is possible. . . . There are "roses" with 145-foot trunks; daisies and violets as big as apple trees . . . 18 foot cobras . . . [and] frogs so big they eat rats. . . . The forest's climate is the key to all this.

The rain forests of Middle America are in the tierra caliente and in the tierra templada. The trees in the tropical rain forests near the Gulf of Mexico can grow 200 feet tall—about as high as a stack of 20 school buses. Here thousands of kinds of plants and animals live under the canopy, or roof, of trees.

The canopy is so thick that little sun

reaches the forest floor. In the cooler rain forests of tierra templada, clouds sometimes blanket the entire forest.

People in Middle America

The first people in Middle America probably arrived about 11,000 years ago. Small knives and arrow points have been found in the Central Plateau. These stone tools were left in caves by early hunter-gatherers. Early Americans gathered onions, squash, and avocados, and hunted rabbits and deer. Like early people in other parts of the world, they moved around in search of food.

WHY IT MATTERS

After the first people came across Beringia to North America, some moved southward to Middle America. The diverse lands of this region provided a warm climate and abundant food. These resources made Middle America ideal for human settlement. In the next lesson you will read about one of the many groups of people who created a civilization on this land.

DID YOU KNOW?

How hot WAS it?

To learn about recent changes in climate, scientists often look at written records. By studying records, such as the dates of cherry blossom festivals in Japan or harvest records in France, they can learn if a region's climate has become hotter or colder, wetter or drier, over time. The study of climate is called climatology.

The study of climates in past ages is called paleoclimatology (pay lee oh kli muh TAHL uh jee). To learn about ice ages and other big changes in climate, scientists study clues such as pollen, seeds, or soil found in rocks, fossils, and glaciers.

✔️ Reviewing Facts and Ideas

SUM IT UP

- The first people in the Americas may have come from Asia across the Beringia land bridge about 40,000 to 25,000 years ago.

- Middle America has mountains, rolling hills, and coastal plains. It also has three main climate regions defined by elevation.

- The rain forests of Middle America are unique environments with a huge variety of plant and animal life.

- The first settlers of Middle America were hunters and gatherers who lived in the Central Plateau region.

THINK ABOUT IT

1. How did a land bridge form between Asia and the Americas thousands of years ago?

2. What are the three major climate regions found in Middle America?

3. **FOCUS** What are three kinds of land areas found in Middle America?

4. **THINKING SKILL** What are three _conclusions_ that you can make about the rain forest environment?

5. **GEOGRAPHY** How might a rainy season affect the pattern of agriculture in an area?

STUDYSKILLS

Reading Climographs

VOCABULARY
climograph

WHY THE SKILL MATTERS

In the last lesson you read about the three different climate zones that are found in Middle America. They are tierra caliente, tierra templada, and tierra fría. Climate in these zones is largely determined by elevation, or the height of the land above sea level. Other factors that can affect the climate of a place are its distance from the equator and its distance from oceans or mountains.

Since there are many things that influence climate, the climate within a large region can vary greatly. Remember that the two most important parts of climate are temperature and precipitation. In Middle America, for example, temperatures of 90°F are common in some low-lying areas. In high mountain areas, however, the temperature is usually lower, around 40°F. Also, some areas in the region receive more than 80 inches of rain each year while other areas receive less than 15 inches.

The rain does not fall evenly throughout the year in this region. As you have read, Middle America has a rainy season. This means that for part of the year the climate here is very wet and for part of the year it is very dry.

One way to learn about the climate of a place is to study a climograph of that place. A climograph is a graph that shows the temperature and precipitation in a place over a period of months.

USING THE SKILL

Look at Climograph A. Notice that it includes two graphs—a bar graph and a line graph. The bar graph shows the average monthly precipitation. The line graph shows the average monthly temperature.

Read a climograph the same way you would read other kinds of graphs. First read the title. Then read the other information below the title. This useful information will help you to compare the climates of three cities in Mexico. Next read the labels on the sides and bottom of the climograph. The left side lists precipitation and is the key for reading the bar graph. The right side lists the temperature and is the key for reading the line graph. The labels along the bottom show that time is measured in months.

Having temperature and precipitation together on the same graph can be useful. Suppose you wanted to find out in which

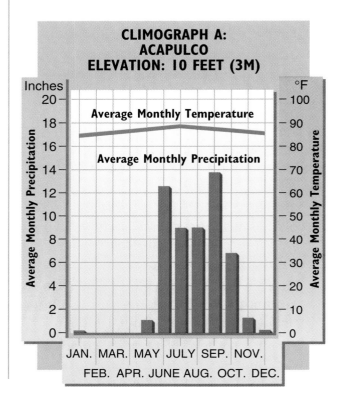

month the rainy season begins in Acapulco. By looking for a sharp increase in precipitation on the bar graph, you can tell that the rainy season begins in June. You can also see on the line graph that the average temperature in Acapulco during April, May, and June rises to about 87°F.

TRYING THE SKILL

Climographs are useful for comparing the climate of two different places. Study Climographs B and C on this page. Notice that the elevation of Mexico City and Veracruz are very different. Mexico City is in tierra templada and Veracruz is in tierra caliente. Which city would you expect to have a warmer climate? Why?

In which month does Veracruz receive the most rain? In which month does Mexico City receive the most rain? Which city receives the most rain during the month of October? How did you find this answer?

REVIEWING THE SKILL

1. What is a climograph? How can climographs be useful?

2. Which of the three Mexican cities shown has the most rainfall in August? The least rainfall during June?

3. Which city has hotter temperatures in June, Veracruz or Mexico City?

4. Suppose you were planning a vacation to Acapulco. How would using a climograph help you to plan your trip?

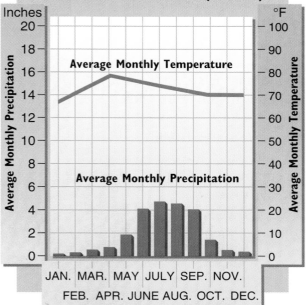

CLIMOGRAPH B:
MEXICO CITY
ELEVATION: 7,340 FEET (2,237M)

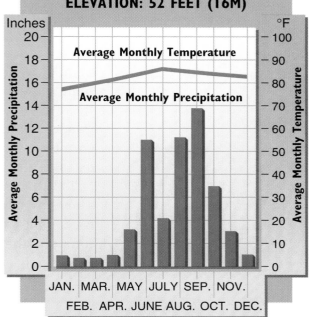

CLIMOGRAPH C:
VERACRUZ
ELEVATION: 52 FEET (16M)

THE OLMEC CIVILIZATION

READ ALOUD

In the 1860s a farmer in the Mexican state of Veracruz was clearing dense forest to build a new field for sugarcane. He came upon a large dome-shaped object which he thought was a big, upside-down pot. He called for help to uncover the mysterious object. When the "pot" was finally unearthed, it turned out to be a giant stone head nearly 5 feet high! The uncovering of this sculpture led to more excavations in the area. Slowly the story of an ancient people of Middle America began to unfold. We call these people the Olmec (OHL mek).

Focus Activity

READ TO LEARN
Who were the Olmec?

VOCABULARY
slash and burn

PLACES
La Venta

THE BIG PICTURE

In the lush rain forest along the Gulf of Mexico arose one of the earliest civilizations of the Americas. In about 1200 B.C. people here settled in communities and built remarkable buildings. Historians call these people the Olmec. In the Aztec language, Olmec means "people of the rubber country," for there were many rubber trees in the area. What the Olmec called themselves remains a mystery. They left behind no written records as far as we know. Fortunately, they did leave a rich assortment of artifacts.

This stone carving was found at La Venta.

Beneath a blanket of forest and greenery at Laguna de los Cerros (right), the remains of an ancient city may hold answers to mysteries of the Olmec.

THE OLMEC

Archaeologists believe the Olmec flourished along the Gulf of Mexico from about 1200 B.C. to 400 B.C. The area is still made up almost entirely of rain forest. Rivers cut through the forest on their way to the Gulf of Mexico. This lush environment was rich in food. Fish, turtles, ducks, wild turkeys, boars, and deer were plentiful. The forest also provided fruits, such as guava. The Olmec probably hunted and gathered, as earlier people in the region had done.

It was their success in agriculture, however, that allowed the Olmec to build a stable culture. They used a farming method known as slash and burn. In this method, farmers first cleared, or slashed, the dense jungle growth with stone axes. Then during the dry season, they burned what remained. The left-over ashes helped enrich the soil.

MIDDLE AMERICA, 500 B.C.

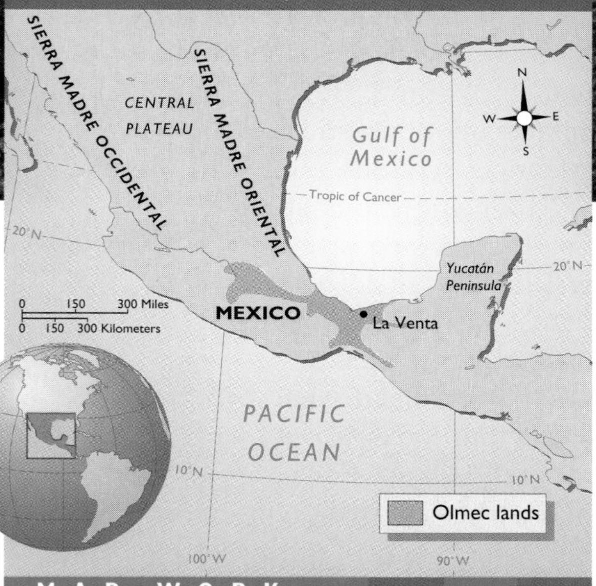

SIERRA MADRE OCCIDENTAL
SIERRA MADRE ORIENTAL
CENTRAL PLATEAU
Gulf of Mexico
Tropic of Cancer
20°N
Yucatán Peninsula
20°N
0   150   300 Miles
0   150   300 Kilometers
MEXICO
• La Venta
PACIFIC OCEAN
10°N
10°N
Olmec lands
100°W
90°W

MAP WORK

The Olmec built their civilization on the coastal plain of what is today southern Mexico.

1. To what degree of latitude is La Venta closest?

2. What landform lies to the northeast of the Olmec lands?

Like early farmers in Egypt and China, the Olmec made use of the flooding rivers to grow crops. After the summer floods deposited new soil, the Olmec planted the fertile river banks with crops. Three main crops were corn, beans, and squash.

293

LIFE IN AN OLMEC TOWN

Archaeologists have uncovered four important Olmec settlements. By about 1000 B.C. the town of La Venta had become the major center of Olmec culture. La Venta is located on a large island, surrounded by swamps and rivers, near the northern coast of what is now southern Mexico. Look at the map on page 293 to find La Venta.

The People of La Venta

In the center of what was La Venta sits a huge earthen mound, 82 feet high. This was probably the base of an Olmec pyramid. Beyond this mound are smaller mounds and a large plaza surrounded by stone pillars. In the plaza are four enormous stone heads. The largest weighs 24 tons! These heads are probably statues of Olmec rulers. Each stone head wears a hat that looks like a football helmet. Each helmet has its own symbol, which may stand for the name of a ruler.

The stone heads and other artifacts reveal interesting clues about the Olmec people. We know, for example, that the people who lived in La Venta did specialized work. Some people worked as stone carvers. They carved the gray basalt, a hard volcanic rock, into statues or into tools for grinding corn. Others carved more delicate items out of jade and obsidian, another kind of volcanic rock. These small objects probably had religious uses. Most of the Olmec, however, were farmers, and growing food was the central activity at La Venta.

The Olmec made this rubber ball (left) over 3,000 years ago. Similar balls were used in games by later cultures in Middle America.

The leaders of La Venta controlled most of the land that was used for farming. They also built stone monuments with carvings. The monuments also reminded the people of the authority of their leaders.

Olmec Religion

Artifacts and ruins in La Venta also provide us with some hints about the religious beliefs of the Olmec. Like the other people of Middle America, the Olmec practiced polytheism. They

Crafts of the Olmec

Since they lived in a warm climate, the Olmec probably wore simple, light articles of clothing. The many beads and small carvings that have been found indicate that the Olmec liked to wear jewelry. Both men and women wore bracelets, necklaces, and earrings made of jade and other beautiful stones. Some people, perhaps town leaders, wore headdresses decorated with colorful feathers and beads. These creations may have been worn for special religious ceremonies.

The Olmec collected sap from rubber trees to make rubber balls. They used these balls to play special games in open fields. For musical entertainment, the Olmec made flutes and other musical instruments out of clay and wood.

believed in more than one god, such as gods of fire, rain, and sun. Throughout La Venta archaeologists have found special altars that were used to make sacrifices to the gods. To sacrifice means to give up or destroy something for the sake of something else.

The Olmec also believed that certain animals had special powers. No animal, they believed, was as powerful as the jaguar. This rain forest cat played a central role in Olmec beliefs that remains a mystery to us. Perhaps the Olmec believed that the jaguar helped bring fertile crops. Many carvings and statues of jaguars have been found in Olmec settlements. Near the plaza at La Venta, archaeologists have discovered a large mosaic, or pattern of stones, in the image of a jaguar.

Beautiful jade carvings, like this jaguar-headed figure, have been found at La Venta and other Olmec sites.

The figure (above) is typical of the stone monuments carved by the Olmec.

Olmec Traders

Archaeologists believe that the Olmec traded with other groups of people in Middle America. Clay goods and figures made in the Olmec style have been found in places as distant from Olmec lands as central Mexico, more than 300 miles to the north. Perhaps the Olmec traded these objects for food, feathers, and animal skins. Traders would have traveled to distant settlements by foot on narrow forest paths.

WHY IT MATTERS

Around 400 B.C. Olmec civilization was gradually beginning to disappear. Historians are not certain why the culture faded. Some think that the system of agriculture began to break down from overuse of the land. La Venta and the other Olmec settlements were abandoned. Eventually thick rain forest grew up around the Olmec towns. The achievements of this early Middle American civilization lived on, however, in artifacts left behind. You are about to read of a huge civilization that developed in Middle America and built on the achievements of the Olmec.

✔// Reviewing Facts and Ideas

SUM IT UP

- The Olmec built one of the earliest civilizations in the Americas, starting around 1200 B.C.

- The Olmec developed a system of slash and burn agriculture in the dense rain forest environment.

- The Olmec were craftworkers who designed objects such as earrings, beads, and necklaces. They probably traded these objects with people in other parts of Middle America.

THINK ABOUT IT

1. In which part of Middle America did the centers of Olmec culture grow?

2. How did the Olmec create fields for growing crops?

3. **FOCUS** What clues have helped archaeologists to gain knowledge about Olmec culture?

4. **THINKING SKILL** What *effects* did the environment of the Olmec have on their system of farming? How in turn might the Olmec have affected their environment?

5. **WRITE** Suppose you were a trader who lived in Olmec times. Write a description of some of the Olmec objects that you would like to trade with other people.

CITIZENSHIP
MAKING A DIFFERENCE

The Rain Forest Treasures Trail

SYLVESTER VILLAGE, BELIZE—
The Gallon Jug Community School is located in the middle of a vast rain forest in Belize.

Near the Gallon Jug school, a trail extends into the forest. The school's 75 students helped create the trail. They call it the Rain Forest Treasures Trail, and they use it to teach visitors about the special plants and animals found in the tropical rain forest.

Tropical rain forests cover only about 7 percent of Earth's land. Yet they are home to fully half of Earth's plant species. Many rain forest plants provide medicines that have been used for centuries to treat everything from colds to deadly diseases.

Teacher Nancy Zuniga directs the school along with her husband, Julio. She explains that the trail came about because "the kids were always teaching me about this plant or that plant. They knew from their parents which plants helped soothe a burn or bring down a fever."

Dr. Rosita Arvigo, from Belize's Ix Chel tropical research center, taught students to recognize medicinal plants. Older villagers also helped the students learn the uses of many plants.

After the children and their parents cleared the trail, they located and labeled plants along the path. "Now," says student Adolio Bolaños, "we are tour guides. We take visitors on a half-hour walk on the trail. Along the way we teach them about the different plants and their uses."

Tourists and school groups from other parts of Belize come to walk the Rain Forest Treasures Trail. Adolio tells visitors that rain forests around the world are disappearing. Loggers cut down trees and ranchers clear land for cattle grazing. Now the children of the Gallon Jug school are working to protect rain forest plants and to replace trees. Adolio worries that "if people clear away the rain forest, we will not have medicinal plants. If we keep the forests, some day doctors may find new ways to use these plants to cure sicknesses. I read that somewhere in the forest there is a plant for every sickness. I hope it's true."

"The kids were always teaching me about this plant or that plant."

Nancy Hinchler-Zuniga

| 1400 B.C. | 800 B.C. | 200 B.C. | A.D. 250 | A.D. 900 | A.D. 1000 |

MAYA CIVILIZATION

Focus Activity

READ TO LEARN
What were some of the achievements of the Maya civilization?

VOCABULARY
Classic Period
maize
glyph
stela

PLACES
Copán

READ ALOUD

Throughout Middle America archaeologists have uncovered ruins of huge stone cities. They were built by a civilization of great builders, astronomers, and craftworkers. By studying the spectacular ruins of the ancient Maya (MAH yuh), archaeologists have developed a picture of a culture that dominated Middle America for almost 1,000 years.

THE BIG PICTURE

The Maya developed their civilization about 600 years after Olmec culture declined. Because most Maya books were lost or destroyed, many details of their lives remain a mystery. Stone pyramids and plazas, however, hint at the complex culture that thrived on the plains and in the valleys of Middle America. The Maya created a written language and achieved a remarkable understanding of the stars and planets. They also kept records of their work in stone carvings. This civilization developed in a region close to where the Olmec had lived.

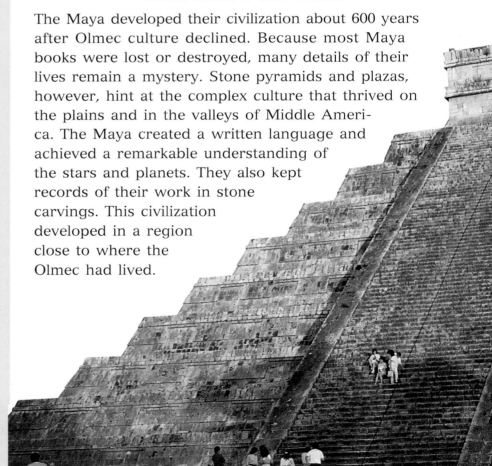

THE RISE OF THE MAYA

The Maya had lived in the southern part of Middle America as early as 1000 B.C. From the lowlands of the Yucatán (yoo kuh TAN) peninsula to the highlands of present-day Guatemala, they developed a culture based on agriculture and hunting. They had contact, no doubt, with the Olmec and other nearby groups.

Between about A.D. 250 and A.D. 900, the Maya built the richest civilization yet seen in the Americas. Historians call this period of Maya history the Classic Period. A classic period is an important time of cultural achievement for a civilization. Other classic periods often discussed by historians include those of Greece and Rome.

A Maya City

One of the great centers of classic Maya culture was Copán (ko PAHN), a city in present-day Honduras. Even today the ruins at Copán are impressive.

Among the impressive structures at Copán is the ball court. Here a fierce Maya ball game, called *pokta-pok* (POHK tuh POHK), was played. Players wore helmets and padding on their arms and legs, for the game was rough. They were not allowed to touch the five-pound rubber ball with their hands. The two teams rushed up and down the court trying to get the ball through a stone hoop. If they succeeded, they won the game. Excited spectators filled the stands and gave clothing to the winning team.

This game was part of Maya religion. You can see an illustration of a game on page 294. Those who lost were sometimes killed as a sacrifice to Maya gods. The Maya believed their gods would help them if they sacrificed something as important as a human life.

Other buildings in Copán included the tall temple-pyramids and palaces around the main plaza. These structures were built out of huge stone blocks. Since the Maya did not have wheels or work animals, all the moving and lifting was done by humans. Sometimes this work was done by enslaved people who had been captured during wars.

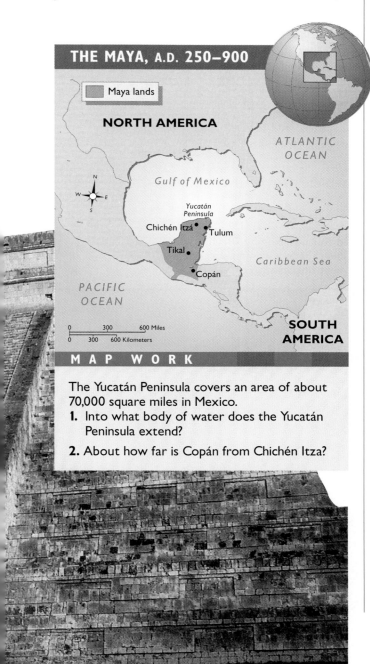

THE MAYA, A.D. 250–900

Maya lands

NORTH AMERICA

ATLANTIC OCEAN

Gulf of Mexico

Yucatán Peninsula

Chichén Itzá • • Tulum

Tikal •

Caribbean Sea

• Copán

PACIFIC OCEAN

SOUTH AMERICA

0   300   600 Miles
0   300   600 Kilometers

MAP WORK

The Yucatán Peninsula covers an area of about 70,000 square miles in Mexico.
1. Into what body of water does the Yucatán Peninsula extend?
2. About how far is Copán from Chichén Itza?

This building at Chichén Itza is the Temple of the Feathered Serpent.

LIFE IN COPÁN

At its peak between about A.D. 600 to 800, Copán was home to about 20,000 people. The region of Copán was crowded with hundreds of buildings, yet a person could have walked from one side of the city center to the other in less than ten minutes. The buildings ranged from small plaster-and-thatch houses to the huge stone pyramids that still stand today.

Copán had many visitors from nearby villages. Traders came from other Maya cities many miles away. In some ways, however, life in Copán was not so different from life for earlier Middle Americans. For example, most of the people in Copán worked as farmers.

The Most Important Crop

Agriculture was the heart of the Maya economy. **Maize** (MAYZ), or corn, was the heart of Maya agriculture. Maize was first grown in Middle America in about 5000 B.C. The cob of this early maize was tiny, about the size of a shelled peanut. When it was heated, maize exploded like modern popcorn.

Over the years Middle American farmers improved their crops of maize. It was the most important part of the Maya diet. Yum Kax, the maize god, became a significant part of the Maya religion. According to one belief, the gods created the Maya people from maize dough. The Maya performed special ceremonies for the planting and harvesting of maize.

The farmers of Copán planted other crops, too, such as beans, squash, and peppers. They also grew cacao trees, which provided chocolate—the favorite

In this painting by Diego Rivera, Maya women sort their most important crop, maize.

drink of Maya rulers. Most Maya grew avocado and papaya trees near home. They hunted for animals such as deer. Farmers and hunters sold many of their crops and products in city marketplaces.

Growing Up in Copán

Boys and girls lived very differently in Copán. When boys were in their teens, they moved out of their family homes into large group homes. There they learned to play the ball game. Boys also learned to become soldiers. Girls stayed at home, where they were strictly raised by their mothers. They learned how to cook maize and other food and how to run a household.

Maya Society

At the top of society in Copán was the king. Below the king were warriors, wealthy farmers, and merchants. As in the societies of Egypt and Mesopotamia, farmers made up the largest group. Below the farmers were slaves, who were usually prisoners taken during wars with neighboring cities.

The Religion of the Maya

Religion was very important to the Maya. They believed that the universe was made up of three levels—the upperworld of the heavens, the middleworld of humans, and the underworld of the dead. The Maya believed that their king could communicate with the upperworld. He also could bring spirits into the middleworld.

The Maya worshiped hundreds of gods. In addition to important gods such as Yum Kax, god of maize, they also believed in lesser gods. For example, hunters, poets, and beekeepers each worshiped different gods. The king and other nobles led many of the ceremonies for worshiping these gods. The Maya believed that their ancestors lived on in the upperworld.

As part of their religion, the Maya closely studied the stars and planets. The planet Venus was considered especially important. Its movement was used to make decisions about when to attack other cities. By studying the night sky, the Maya also developed an accurate calendar. This allowed them to record the exact dates of events.

The Maya, like the Olmec, carved stone figures of their gods and leaders.

MAYA WRITING

The Maya were the first people of Middle America to use a written language widely. Although almost all of their books were lost or burned by the Spanish in the 1500s, the Maya left behind a written record in stone. It is from these records as well as from other artifacts that archaeologists have been able to form a picture of what life was like for the Maya.

Unlocking Written Mysteries

Only in the last 50 years have archaeologists begun to understand the writing of the Maya. These symbols, called **glyphs** (GLIFS), are carved into the stones of Maya cities and towns. Some glyphs are like the pictures of Chinese writing and stand for objects. Others stand for sounds, as in the Roman alphabet.

At Copán the Maya built a magnificent 72-step "hieroglyphic stairway," with over 2,200 glyphs. These symbols tell the story of Copán from its beginnings until A.D. 755, when the stairway was built. Not unlike the epics of Homer in ancient Greece, this stairway recounts the heroic deeds and deaths of Maya leaders.

Maya leaders also had tall, flat stones, called **stelae** (STEE lee), carved with glyphs. These stones were put on display in the city. A stela was often used to mark an important historical event in the life of the leader. On this page you can see a stela from Copán that told about the life of the king Yax-Pac (YAKS PAK). How are these glyphs similar to Egyptian hieroglyphics?

Copán Stela A
c. A.D. 700
Stelae like this one found at Copán were carved to record important dates and events in Maya history. The Maya must have felt that stelae looked like trees, for they called them *te-tun*, or "tree-stones." Maya stelae focus only on the lives of rulers. Information about other people of the valley is more difficult to find.

Maya Math

The Maya also created a mathematical system that helped merchants keep track of goods and scribes keep track of history. This system used glyphs that the Maya developed to represent numbers. It helped the Maya to make very exact calculations.

WHY IT MATTERS

Many of the great Maya cities were abandoned in the A.D. 900s. No one knows why for sure. Some scientists believe that, like the Olmec, the Maya may have suffered crop failures. Others think that the many wars the Maya waged contributed to the decline of the civilization. Although they abandoned the cities, however, Maya people continued to live in the area.

Today the descendants of the Maya live in the highlands and lowlands of central and southern Middle America. There 4 million Maya continue many of the traditions that began hundreds of years ago. Many speak a version of the Maya language and follow ancient ceremonies of agriculture, marriage, and healing. They also grow maize and other traditional crops. Some Maya raise crops, such as coffee, that are sold around the world. Such products link the rich Maya past with the realities of today's economy.

Descendants of the Maya, like these women in Central America, continue to follow many traditional ways.

Reviewing Facts and Ideas

SUM IT UP

- The Maya built a complex civilization in Middle America from about A.D. 250 until A.D. 900.

- The Maya created large cities throughout Middle America. The cities contained temples, ball courts, and other buildings.

- Religion was an important part of life for the Maya. The Maya practiced polytheism.

- The Maya developed systems of writing and mathematics that allowed them to record important events in their history.

THINK ABOUT IT

1. What was the most important crop to the Maya?

2. What was one kind of god that the Maya worshiped?

3. **FOCUS** What are three achievements that set the Maya apart from earlier Middle American civilizations? What made Maya civilization "classic"?

4. **THINKING SKILL** _Compare_ the systems of learning of the Maya with those of ancient Greece.

5. **WRITE** Suppose you are an archaeologist exploring Maya ruins. Write a description of Copán for a magazine for sixth graders.

ASTRONOMY

Have you ever looked up into the sky on a clear night and wondered about the stars and planets? The ancient Maya must have wondered too.

Scientists have discovered that the Maya had a great interest in astronomy, or the study of stars and planets. The Maya spent much time observing the sun, moon, and the planet Venus. Using these observations the Maya were able to design a complex and accurate calendar. Like ancient Egyptians, they also predicted eclipses of the sun and moon.

People have always wanted to know what is in the sky. Astronomy continues to be an important part of scientific life. Through modern high-powered telescopes, satellites, and space shuttle missions, we continue to learn about the universe.

The United States launched the Hubble Space Telescope (right) in 1990. In 1995 it took this photo of a star being "born." The star is so far away, the light captured in this picture began its journey across space 7,000 years ago—about the time ancient Egyptians were beginning to farm along the Nile.

The Maya built this observatory (left) at Chichén Itza. Based on their studies of planets, they created a calendar. Centuries later another people, the Aztec, developed a similar calendar (above left).

CHAPTER 11 REVIEW

Major Events

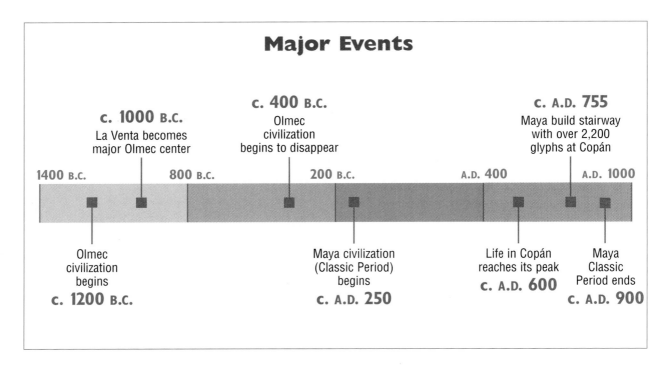

c. 1000 B.C.
La Venta becomes major Olmec center

c. 400 B.C.
Olmec civilization begins to disappear

c. A.D. 755
Maya build stairway with over 2,200 glyphs at Copán

1400 B.C.   800 B.C.   200 B.C.   A.D. 400   A.D. 1000

Olmec civilization begins
c. 1200 B.C.

Maya civilization (Classic Period) begins
c. A.D. 250

Life in Copán reaches its peak
c. A.D. 600

Maya Classic Period ends
c. A.D. 900

THINKING ABOUT VOCABULARY

Number a sheet of paper from 1 to 10. Beside each number write the word or term from the list below that best completes each sentence.

Classic Period   maize
climograph   rain forest
glacier   slash and burn
glyph   stela
Ice Age   tropical

1. A tall, flat stone carved with glyphs is a _____.

2. The Maya civilization was at the height of achievement during its _____.

3. A body of ice that inches along the land is a _____.

4. A _____ measures temperature and precipitation over a period of months.

5. The main food of the Maya was _____.

6. A _____ receives more than 80 inches of rain per year.

7. One way to clear jungle areas for farming is to _____.

8. _____ refers to the climate area near the equator where it is very warm.

9. The _____ was a period when nearly half of Earth's land surface was covered by ice.

10. A symbol called the _____ is the basis of Maya writing.

THINKING ABOUT FACTS

1. How did the Ice Age affect the history of the Americas?

2. What makes rain forests unique?

3. How did the Olmec get food? What types of food did they eat?

4. What was pokta-pok?

5. Look at the time line above. How long did the Olmec and Maya civilizations last? What may have brought them to an end?

THINK AND WRITE

WRITING ABOUT PERSPECTIVES

Write about the people who traveled between Asia and North America during the Ice Age. Describe why there was a land bridge and the reasons why people may have crossed it.

WRITING A JOURNAL ENTRY

Suppose that you have gone back about 3,000 years to live in the Olmec center of La Venta. Write a journal entry about your life there. Include details about the way you live, the work you do, and some of the interesting features of the town.

WRITING A REPORT

Write a report about the civilization the Maya built in Middle America. Describe their main achievements and the way people lived in the city of Copán.

APPLYING STUDY SKILLS

READING CLIMOGRAPHS

1. What does a climograph measure?

2. Look at the climographs on pages 290–291. Which of the three Mexican cities shown has the highest average annual precipitation? Which has the highest average annual temperature?

3. Is the rainy season the same for all three cities? If not, how is it different?

4. What can you tell about the climate of the three cities by reading the climographs?

5. How are climographs helpful?

Summing Up the Chapter

Review the chapter and copy the main idea table below on a separate piece of paper. Then place each feature listed in the correct column below. Add any additional features you find when you review the chapter. After filling in the table, use it to help write a paragraph that answers the question "What were some achievements of the early peoples in Middle America?"

MAIN IDEA: Civilizations developed in Middle America.

Features: Central Plateau; Classic Period; Copán; crafts; glyphs; La Venta; worship for Jaguar; rain forests; slash and burn; tropical climate; Yum Kax, god of maize

Geography	Olmec	Maya
Central Plateau	Copán	La Venta

UNIT 3 REVIEW

THINKING ABOUT VOCABULARY

Number a sheet of paper from 1 to 10. Beside each number write the word or term from the list below that best matches the statement.

algebra
dictator
glyph
maize
monarchy

New Testament
peninsula
philosophy
pilgrimage
republic

1. Area of land mostly surrounded by water
2. Government in which people choose their own leaders
3. Corn
4. Collection of books that describes the beginnings of Christianity
5. Branch of mathematics developed by the Arabs
6. Someone who rules with absolute power
7. Search for wisdom and the right way to live
8. Journey made for religious reasons
9. Government ruled by one person, often a king or queen
10. Mayan symbol carved into stones

THINK AND WRITE

WRITING ABOUT PERSPECTIVES

Write a paragraph comparing the perspectives of a woman from ancient Sparta and a woman from ancient Athens. How would they have viewed city laws and government? What might they have wanted to change? How were their perspectives alike? How were they different? Explain your answers.

WRITING AN ESSAY

Write a short essay about Islam as one of the world's major religions. What are its main beliefs and practices?

WRITING ABOUT CONTRASTS

Write a paragraph describing the differences between the environments of the Arabian Peninsula and Middle America. Include information about landforms and climate. Explain the challenges faced by people who have lived in these two regions. Describe how they have adapted to the environments around them.

BUILDING SKILLS

1. **Making conclusions** What is a good conclusion? Why is a conclusion stronger with more evidence to back it up?
2. **Making conclusions** Suppose you visit a distant city for a weekend. Based on what you see during the short time, give an example of a conclusion you might make about the city.
3. **Elevation maps and profiles** What are ways you could use both an elevation map and a profile map of the Alps? Explain your answer.
4. **Historical maps** Look at the historical map on page 280. Explain the information the map provides and how you found the information by using the map.
5. **Climographs** Construct a climograph that shows the monthly temperature and precipitation in your area. Compare it with the climographs of the Mexican cities on pages 290–291. Make a conclusion about how the climate where you live differs from that of Mexico.

YESTERDAY, TODAY &
TOMORROW

You have read about the achievements of great civilizations of the past. Someday future students will read about us. What do you think future historians will say our greatest achievements were? Explain your choices. How are our achievements different from those of the past?

READING ON YOUR OWN

Here are some books you might find at the library to help you learn more.

SPIRIT OF THE MAYA: A BOY EXPLORES HIS PEOPLE'S MYSTERIOUS PAST
by Guy Garcia

Kin, a twelve-year-old descendant of the ancient Maya, gains pride in his ancestry when he discovers clues to the secrets of his society.

TALES FROM ANCIENT GREECE
Retold by Pamela Oldfield

This collection of nine myths captures the adventures of Greek heroes and heroines.

PYRAMID OF THE SUN, PYRAMID OF THE MOON
by Leonard Everett Fisher

This book tells the story behind the pyramids of Teotihuacan and the Toltec civilization.

UNIT PROJECT

Perform a Scene About Life in Ancient Times

1. With your group, choose an ancient civilization from this unit.
2. Research some additional information about the civilization. Your school or local library can provide the information you will need.
3. Then write a scene that includes a character for each group member. You might tell what daily life was like in the civilization or about an event that affected the civilization.
4. Make sure each group member has several lines.
5. Next make costumes out of paper or material. Create scenery using paints and oaktag.
6. Finally, perform the scene for your class.

SUIT OF ARMOR, ITALY;
ROSE WINDOW, THE CATHEDRAL
OF NOTRE DAME, FRANCE;
INCA KNIFE, PERU

World Regions in Transition

"To no one will we deny, or delay, rights or justice."

from the *Magna Carta*
See page 327.

WHY DOES IT MATTER?

The idea of protecting people's rights was just beginning to develop in the period covered in this unit. Many of the ways of life that we think of as "modern" began in the years between about A.D. 600 and A.D. 1600. In fact, many historians call this period the Middle Ages because they think of it as being between ancient and modern times. During these years, religious ideas spread and developed in Europe, Africa, Asia, and the Americas. These ideas affected the arts, science, and the ways people viewed the world and their place in it.

MODEL OF MING DYNASTY SHIP, CHINA

PORTRAIT OF QUEEN ELIZABETH I, ENGLAND; GOLD MASK, BENIN

311

Adventures with
with
NATIONAL GEOGRAPHIC

City in the Sky

High in the Andes mountains, the Inca built a spectacular city. It had houses and stairways of stone, and terraced fields for growing crops on the steep slopes. But war came. The city was abandoned. The houses sat empty for four centuries. Forest plants engulfed the buildings. Then, in 1911, local people led American explorer Hiram Bingham to the site. After struggling through gorges and up mountainsides, he reached the ruins. "The sight held me spellbound," he declared. Later, he returned to Peru to begin clearing and excavating the city. Archaeologists are still exploring Machu Picchu today.

GEO JOURNAL

You stumble upon an empty city hidden in the mountains. Write a telegram announcing your discovery.

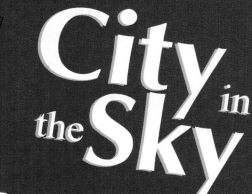

CHAPTER 12

Cultures of Medieval Europe

THINKING ABOUT HISTORY AND GEOGRAPHY

In the period called the Middle Ages, most Europeans lived, worked, and worshiped in farming communities. During this "Age of Faith," Christianity spread throughout Europe. At the same time, rulers and nobles struggled for power. At the end of the Middle Ages came a time of great creativity in the arts, sciences, and religion.

ATLANTIC OCEAN

1095
ROME
Pope Urban II calls for Crusades to Jerusalem

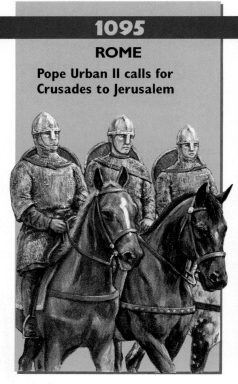

ABOUT 1200
CHARTRES
Craftworkers build a magnificent cathedral

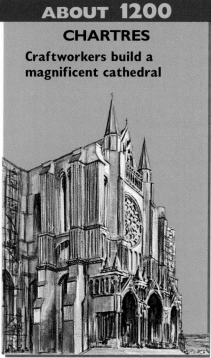

1215
ENGLAND
King John signs the Magna Carta

ASIA

ENGLAND

Wittenberg

Chartres

EUROPE

Florence

Rome

Black Sea

Mediterranean Sea

Red Sea

AFRICA

1503

FLORENCE

Leonardo da Vinci paints the *Mona Lisa*

1517

WITTENBERG

Martin Luther posts his 95 Theses

Focus Activity

READ TO LEARN
What effects did the waterways of Europe have on the development of civilizations there?

VOCABULARY
temperate
deforestation
navigable

PLACES
Eurasia
North Sea
North European Plain
Seine River

GEOGRAPHY OF EUROPE

READ ALOUD

"The great rivers and the strange number of canals . . . do not only lead to every great town, but almost to every village, and every farm-house in the country; and the [countless number] of sails are seen every-where coursing up and down upon them."

These words were written by an English man named William Temple, after he visited the Nether-lands 300 years ago. Like others before and after him, he was fascinated by the many rivers and canals throughout Europe.

THE BIG PICTURE

You have already studied the geography of two parts of Europe—Greece and Italy. The Netherlands, often called Holland, is a small present-day country in northern Europe. In this chapter you will learn more about the European continent and its history.

Next to Australia, Europe is the world's smallest continent. Europe, however, connects with Asia to create the world's largest landmass, called Eurasia. Find the Ural (YUR ul) and Caucasus (KAW kuh sus) mountains on the map on the next page. They are considered to be the border between Europe and Asia.

In Europe you can find some of the most unusual features of geography—from spouting geysers in Iceland to huge glaciers in the Alps. Waterways are an important part of Europe's geography. Much human activity here has been shaped by rivers and canals, seas and bays, and harbors and channels.

EUROPE

Europe is shaped like a big peninsula jutting westward off Eurasia. The continent has many peninsulas and islands. Europe also has a long, jagged coastline. It is surrounded by the Atlantic Ocean, the Mediterranean Sea, the North Sea, and the Baltic Sea. The Scandinavian peninsula, located in the north, has narrow inlets called fjords (FYORDZ) where the sea surges in between cliffs.

The climate of Europe is temperate, or mild, because of the winds that blow over the warm currents of the ocean. Even some lands near the Arctic Circle are relatively temperate. Extreme temperatures are found mostly along the border with Asia and on the peaks of the Alps.

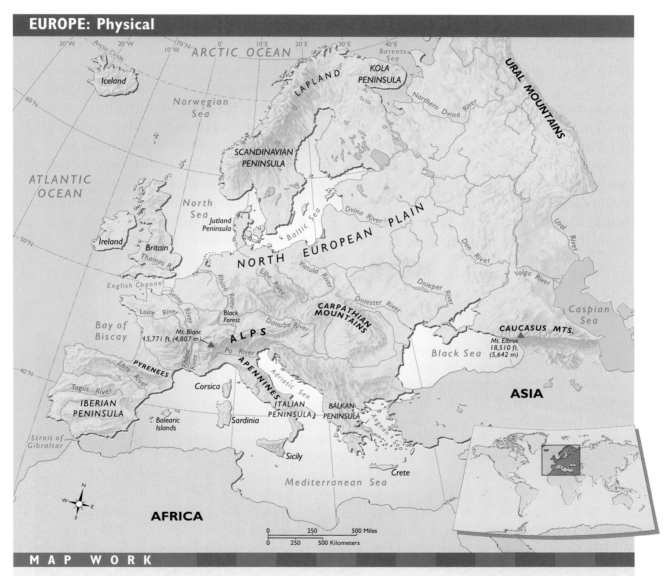

EUROPE: Physical

MAP WORK

The geography of Europe is varied. The continent has mountainous areas, plains, and rivers.

1. Which mountains separate the Iberian Peninsula from the rest of Europe?

2. Which is farthest north—the Aegean Sea, the Baltic Sea, or the Black Sea?

3. Which is the highest mountain in Europe?

LAND AND WATER

The land and water of Europe are rich in natural resources. These resources have helped to make Europe a wealthy and productive region.

From Forests to Farmland

Two thousand years ago most of Europe lay under a blanket of dense forest. One group of Roman explorers is said to have walked through forests from Poland to France without ever seeing sunlight! Europeans began to clear forests to make room for farms and cities, especially after about A.D. 1100. The process of clearing forests is called deforestation. It has happened in many places around the world throughout history.

After forests were cleared, Europeans could farm more land. The most fertile farmland in Europe is found in a region called the North European Plain. Look at the map on page 317 to see this region. A long growing season helps farmers to grow crops like wheat in the plain's rich soil. In southern countries, like Greece and Spain, oranges and olives are grown.

Bounty from Rivers and Seas

Much of the European continent is within 300 miles of the sea. The jagged coastline creates natural harbors that help to protect boats. For these reasons, it is no surprise that fishing has always been important to the European economy. Fish are especially plentiful in the North Atlantic. Today nearly a third of all fish caught in the world come from waters around Europe.

Europe's rivers are also important to the economy. Over 2,000 years ago, Europeans began using river power to turn waterwheels that ground wheat. Traders transported goods on Europe's many long, navigable (NAV ih guh bul) rivers. Navigable rivers are deep

Today people still fish the waters near Iceland and herd cattle in mountainous Switzerland.

EUROPE AT A GLANCE

	Total Land Area	4,032,000 sq. miles 10,443,000 sq. km
	Highest Mountain	Mt. Elbrus, Russia 18,510 feet (5,642 m)
	Longest River	Volga River, Russia 2,194 miles 3,531 km
	Largest City	Moscow, Russia Population 8,769,000
	Current Population	707,000,000
	Percent of World Population	13%

GEO FACT

Though many of Europe's forests have been cleared, there are still large forests in Northern Europe. One of them is the Black Forest of Germany. This region gets its name from the dark fir and spruce trees covering its mountainsides. Many German fairy tales tell of the creatures of the Black Forest.

CHART WORK

The chart provides information about the size and geography of Europe.

1. What is the largest city in Europe? What is its population?

2. How did the Black Forest get its name?

enough for boat travel. One important navigable river is the Seine River. Paris, France, one of Europe's largest cities, grew alongside the Seine River. Europeans have developed thriving economies by using rivers for power and transportation.

European engineers created more waterways by building canals. In fact, it is possible to travel by boat from the English Channel in the west to the Ural Mountains in the east. Locate these features on the map on page 317.

WHY IT MATTERS

Rivers and coasts were very important in the growth of European cultures. Waterways provided power and helped to make transportation and trade possible. Remember, though, that Europeans added to their natural river system.

Europe's rivers and coasts still affect the way people live. They are used for transport. The fishing trade helps feed millions of Europeans.

In upcoming lessons, you will read how Europeans used their continent's resources to build civilizations.

Reviewing Facts and Ideas

SUM IT UP

- Europe, Earth's second-smallest continent, has a long, jagged coastline.

- Closeness to the sea has had important effects on Europe's climate and economy.

- Europe's rivers and seas are great sources of fish. Waterways are also used for transportation and power.

THINK ABOUT IT

1. What makes the climate of Europe temperate?

2. Name a trade that has always been important to the European economy.

3. **FOCUS** How did the waterways of Europe affect life there?

4. **THINK** Explain why the following statement is a *fact* or why it is an *opinion*: "Europe's navigable rivers help in the transport of goods."

5. **GEOGRAPHY** Find the island of Corsica and the English Channel on the map on page 317. Trace two possible sailing routes between these places— one by sea and one by river. Which route is longer? How much longer?

THE MIDDLE AGES

READ ALOUD

"Woe to thee, Rome, that thou art crushed and trodden down by so many peoples; who has been seized by a northern king, and thy folk slaughtered and thy strength brought to nothing."

These words were written around A.D. 900 by a monk after an attack on Rome. The invaders were from England.

THE BIG PICTURE

Following the end of the western Roman empire around A.D. 500, Europe entered a new era of history. This period became known as the Middle Ages. It lies between the Roman period and about the 1400s.

The Roman empire left behind many legacies, including the Latin language and a large network of roads. The Christian religion also continued to grow and spread. However, the breakdown of Roman rule brought great changes for the people of Europe. Many small kingdoms developed.

Along with changes in government, the end of the Roman empire also brought about economic changes in Europe. Trade declined, after which ownership of land came to mean wealth and power. Large estates owned by wealthy nobles were called manors. Workers, called serfs, became bound to work on the manors. Serfs had little more freedom than slaves. Unlike slaves, however, serfs could not be bought or sold.

Focus Activity

READ TO LEARN
What was life like in Europe during the Middle Ages?

VOCABULARY
Middle Ages
manor
serf
feudalism
lord
vassal
fief
guild
Magna Carta

PEOPLE
Charlemagne
William the Conqueror
King John I

PLACES
Aachen
Normandy
England

320

THE FRANKISH EMPIRE

Of the many small kingdoms in western Europe, one rose to great power in the 700s. This kingdom, ruled by a people called the Franks, was based in present-day France. You may remember from Chapter 9 that this region was the place the Romans called Gaul. The Franks built an empire that was the largest and richest in Europe since Roman times. Find it on the map.

A Powerful Ruler

The greatest leader of the Franks was called Charles the Great, or Charlemagne (SHAHR luh mayn). He conquered lands in southwestern parts of what is now France and in Italy and Germany. Charlemagne was a Christian. As his armies spread across Europe, they also spread Christianity.

Charlemagne's biggest achievement came in 800, when he arrived with his army in Rome. The leader of the Roman Church, Pope Leo III, placed a golden crown on Charlemagne's head and declared him Emperor. For a while, it appeared to western Europeans that the old Roman empire had risen again.

Charlemagne's Court

Charlemagne set up his capital in the city of Aachen (AH khun) in what is today Germany. His court became a lively political and cultural center.

Charlemagne was very tall for his time—over 6 feet. He loved to ride horses and swim in a pool he had built at Aachen. Perhaps most remarkably for his time, he also loved learning.

During the Middle Ages books were scarce and very few people could read. Charlemagne filled his court with scholars, poets, and musicians. One scholar at Charlemagne's court wrote this about the emperor:

You know very well how sweet is arithmetic in its reasoning, and how pleasant is a knowledge of the heavenly stars in their courses. And yet how rare it is to find a man who takes the trouble to know these things!

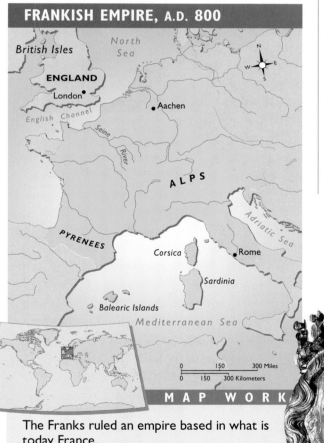

FRANKISH EMPIRE, A.D. 800

British Isles

North Sea

ENGLAND

London

Aachen

English Channel

Seine River

ALPS

PYRENEES

Corsica

Rome

Adriatic Sea

Sardinia

Balearic Islands

Mediterranean Sea

0   150   300 Miles
0   150   300 Kilometers

MAP WORK

The Franks ruled an empire based in what is today France.

1. Which Mediterranean islands were part of the Frankish empire?

2. About how many miles was the city of Aachen from Rome?

Charlemagne established a school at his palace where scholars collected and copied Roman works.

321

LIFE IN THE MIDDLE AGES

During the Middle Ages, the manor was almost a world within itself. Some manors were so large that they included several villages as well as many acres of farmland. Often things that were needed were grown or made right on the manor. This meant that money was not needed to buy goods. It also meant that most people seldom left the manor during their entire lives.

Starting around A.D. 800 a system called feudalism developed in Europe. Feudalism is a way of organizing and governing society, based on land and service. Like the laws of ancient Rome, feudalism required that people behave in certain ways.

Lords and Ladies

At the top of feudal society was the noble, called the lord, who owned the manor. The lord had total control over his manor. In some parts of Europe, the lord also had to serve a king.

The lord's wife was the lady of the manor and was in charge of castle affairs. When the lord was away, she often led the defense of the castle if it was attacked.

As you can see on the diagram, the lord's castle was the center of all activity on the manor. The castle served both as a house for the lord's family and as a fort to protect the manor in case of attack.

The Lord's Vassals

Manor lords chose nobles who did not own land to serve as vassals. Vassals took an oath of loyalty to the lord, pledging to serve him. In return, the lord gave each vassal a fief (FEEF). A fief was usually a separate manor. The vassal often did not own his fief, but he had authority over its serfs. Next to the lord, vassals were the most powerful people in feudal society.

The lady of a manor ran daily affairs, while knights defended the lord and his lands.

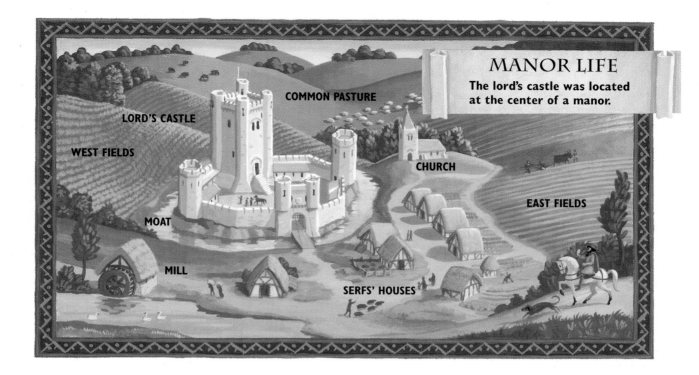

MANOR LIFE
The lord's castle was located at the center of a manor.

LORD'S CASTLE

WEST FIELDS

COMMON PASTURE

CHURCH

EAST FIELDS

MOAT

MILL

SERFS' HOUSES

The most important duty of a vassal was to serve as the lord's knight. Knights were soldiers who protected the manor. Sometimes they traveled with their lords to fight in distant lands.

A Knight's Training

The son of a noble began preparing for knighthood when he was young. First he learned to ride and care for horses. At the age of seven he left home to live and train in a knight's household. There he learned to behave with courtesy and to handle small weapons.

From the ages of 15 to 20, the young noble began to ride into battle alongside the knight. After this experience he was ready to become a knight himself. In a special ceremony he knelt before a lord and was declared a knight.

Life of a Serf

In Europe during the Middle Ages, only about one person in a hundred was a noble. Most Europeans were serfs or village craftworkers. Craftworkers were free, but they had to follow the rules of the nobles.

Serfs were given some land to farm for themselves, but they had to work the lord's land too. Serfs also had to pay rents and taxes to the lord. They even had to ask the lord's permission to get married.

Serfs usually lived in small one-room houses with a fire in the center for cooking and warmth. The whole family slept in one large, straw bed. Most shared their houses with animals. One observer said, "The livestock use the same entrances as the people, and they are not far from sleeping together."

Life was short and difficult—few serfs lived past the age of 40. Most people married while they were in their early teens. Serfs' lives revolved around work in the manor fields. Everyone, including young children, gathered wheat and picked vegetables. The village church bell rang every hour and signaled breaks for meals.

GROWTH OF TOWNS

Around A.D. 1000 Europe's economy began to change. The nobles began to spend less time in battle and more time on the manors. Nobles increased their farmlands, clearing forests and draining swamps. This created crop surpluses for the manor lords. Towns developed to provide a marketplace for the surpluses.

European traders exchanged goods like grains, wool cloth, and wine for spices and silk from Asia and Africa. They also used coin money for the first time since the days of ancient Rome.

With more to eat, people lived longer and the population grew. So did the towns. By the 1200s many towns had become crowded and dirty. Houses were so close that upstairs neighbors could shake hands across the street. Many serfs saw towns as places where they could escape from the manors. They came to the towns because they said the "air was freer." In fact, serfs could win their freedom if they remained in a town without being caught for a year and a day.

Much trading took place in towns like Rothenburg, Germany (left). Food brought to town from manors was sold in busy markets (below).

Town Craftworkers

The narrow town streets were lined with shoemaking, saddle making, and other craft shops. Most shops were family-owned businesses on the ground floor of a house. The father might have been an expert craftsman, or master. He ran the business while his wife and children helped. If her husband died, the wife often took over the business.

Traders and craftworkers organized themselves into groups called **guilds** (GILDZ). Each craft, such as carpentry, had its own guild that made rules about quality and prices. The guild also set the path by which an apprentice, or a beginner craftworker, became a master.

Europe's Cities

Some towns, such as London, grew into cities. In 1175 one London resident, William fitz Stephen, wrote:

Among the noble and celebrated cities of the world, London, the capital of the kingdom of the English, extends its glory farther than all others and sends its wealth and [goods] more widely.

Not everyone agreed that London was a glorious city. Some people thought that London was very dangerous. One trader from France who visited there said,

> If you go to London pass through it quickly ... Every evil or [vicious] thing that can be found anywhere on earth you will find in that one city.

Carcassonne, a town in southern France, was protected by three rows of stone walls. The French restored the town beginning in the 1800s.

Popular Songs

Some of the people passing through Europe's towns and cities during this time were traveling musicians. These people of the 1100s and 1200s were called troubadours (TROO buh dawrz) and minstrels (MIN strulz). Troubadours and minstrels wrote and performed songs about love and life for Europe's nobles. These traveling musicians usually accompanied themselves on the guitar or lute. You may remember that both instruments had been introduced to Europe by Arab musicians in the 700s.

Although many troubadour songs praised the idea of love, some of them were funny. This song, by a woman troubadour named Isabella, tells about a man she once loved.

> Elias Cairel, you're a phony
> if I ever saw one,
> like a man who says he's sick
> when he hasn't the slightest pain.
> If you'd listen I'd give you good
>   advice:
> go back to your [home] and don't
> dare pronounce my name again.

Minstrels often had to wander from court to court looking for work.

CONQUERORS AND KINGS

The growth of towns and trade had greatly changed the economy and social life of Europe by the 1200s. At the same time, western Europe's political life was also undergoing developments.

Invasions from the North

At the end of Charlemagne's reign, in the early 800s, mainland Europe had come under attack by people from the north. These invaders were called Vikings, or Norsemen. The name Norsemen means "Northmen." The Norsemen sailed from Scandinavia in search of riches and land. For hundreds of years they made surprise attacks across Europe. Their invasions were part of the reason that the Frankish empire fell apart after Charlemagne's death.

By 900 some Norsemen began setting up villages around the mouth of the Seine River. Find this region on the map on page 321. These Norsemen became known as Normans. The region in which the Normans settled was called Normandy. The Normans adopted Christianity, the French language, and many Frankish customs.

Normans Invade England

In 1066 Norman forces crossed the English Channel and conquered the Anglo-Saxon people of England. The Norman leader became known as William the Conqueror.

William, the first Norman king of England, established a strong and well-organized rule in England. As a result, Norman and English cultures blended. In fact, the English language we speak today comes from a mix of French and the language of the Anglo-Saxons.

These Viking chess pieces were carved from walrus ivory.

The Power of English Kings

One of the kings who ruled England after William was King John I. King John was crowned in 1199. Like other kings before him, he tried to increase his power over England's lords. John demanded money from the lords to pay for wars. He also claimed the power to imprison a person without a trial.

In 1215 a group of lords took action to limit the king's power. They wrote a charter, or legal document, which stated that they had certain rights, such as the right to a fair trial. This charter was called the Magna Carta, which means "great charter" in Latin.

With the support of their knights, the lords forced the king to sign the Magna Carta. Some of the laws are shown on the next page. Which one guarantees that even the king would have to follow the laws?

Excerpts from the Magna Carta, by the lords of England, 1215.

We have granted to all free men of our kingdom for us and our heirs forever, all the liberties written below.

No widow shall be forced to marry so long as she wishes to live without a husband.

A free man shall not be fined for a small offense.

No sheriff, or anyone else, shall take horses or wagons of anyone without permission.

No freeman shall be taken, or imprisoned, or banished, or in anyway injured, except by the law of the land.

To no one will we sell, to no one will we deny or delay, rights or justice.

All merchants shall be safe and secure in leaving and entering England . . . both by land and by water, for buying and selling.

All these customs and liberties . . . shall be observed by all men of our kingdom.

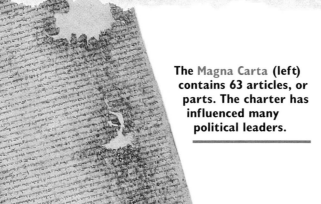

The Magna Carta (left) contains 63 articles, or parts. The charter has influenced many political leaders.

WHY IT MATTERS

The Magna Carta was a beginning toward limiting the power of a ruler by law. It gave rights mainly to nobles. Eventually, it would serve as an example of rights for all people. As you will read in the next lesson, the Christian Church also had great effects on the lives of Europeans during the Middle Ages.

✓ Reviewing Facts and Ideas

SUM IT UP

- Charlemagne, a king of the Franks, built an empire in Europe in the 800s.
- The manor was the center of life for most Europeans in the Middle Ages.
- In the late Middle Ages towns grew and trade expanded.
- Normans, a people from Scandinavia, invaded many parts of Europe and eventually conquered England.
- King John I was forced to sign the Magna Carta in 1215, protecting certain rights of England's nobles.

THINK ABOUT IT

1. What did vassals promise to a lord under feudalism? What did the lord give in return?

2. What was the purpose of guilds in European towns?

3. **FOCUS** How was life different for serfs and town residents during the Middle Ages?

4. **THINKING SKILL** What *effects* did the Magna Carta have on the relationship between England's lords and kings?

5. **WRITE** Suppose you are a visitor to a manor during the Middle Ages. Write three daily journal entries about what you see at the manor.

THINKINGSKILLS

Determining Point of View

VOCABULARY
point of view

WHY THE SKILL MATTERS

In the last lesson you read about some of the different people who made up European society in the Middle Ages—lords and ladies, serfs and craftworkers, troubadours and minstrels. All these people had different roles in society, with different jobs, rights, and duties. They also had different points of view.

A point of view is the position from which someone looks at the world. It is shaped by his or her background, concerns, likes and dislikes, interests, and fears. A person's point of view helps shape his or her opinion on many things. Different people often have different points of view about the same subject. No one point of view presents any subject completely and accurately. In a classroom for example, a teacher's point of view is usually different from a student's point of view. To understand information completely and accurately, you must look at it from a variety of points of view. Determining the point of view of a writer also helps us to understand more about the information.

USING THE SKILL

One way to determine a person's point of view is to look carefully at a statement that he or she has made. The person's focus, the words he or she uses, and the opinions expressed reveal his or her point of view.

The poem you will read was written during the Middle Ages. First identify the subject. The first line tells you that the writer was writing about his lord. Apparently his relationship to the lord was very important. As you read the poem, try to find clues that tell how the writer felt about his lord. These clues will help you to determine his point of view and who he was.

> If my dear lord is slain, his fate I'll
> share.
> If he is hanged, then hang me by his
> side.
> If to the stake he goes, with him I'll
> burn;
> And if he's drowned, then let me
> drown with him.

One clue that you might notice right away is the word *dear*. This word tells the reader that the writer cared very much about his lord. Other phrases also show that the writer felt that the lord was very important. In fact, the writer was willing to die with him. What kind of person wrote this poem? A knight? Why do you think that he held these strong feelings and opinions? Remember that a knight was a lord's vassal. He pledged to

The Bayeaux Tapestry, embroidered in the 1100s, is a Norman record of their invasion of England in 1066.

serve his lord. This poem shows *loyalty*, one of the most important qualities for a knight to have. Can you think of another word that describes this knight's point of view?

TRYING THE SKILL

Now read the following announcement that Charlemagne sent to all the lords in his empire. Remember that Charlemagne was a ruler of the Franks during the Middle Ages. As you read this announcement, use the Helping Yourself box to help you determine Charlemagne's point of view.

You must arrive at Strassfurt with your men on June 18, complete with supplies, so that you will be able to proceed from there in any direction in which you may be ordered to go.

What are some key words or phrases in this announcement that tell how Charlemagne felt about the lords? How was Charlemagne's point of view about the lords different from the knight's in the earlier example? How can you tell?

REVIEWING THE SKILL

1. What is a point of view?

2. What shaped the knight's point of view toward his lord? Explain your answer.

3. Suppose you were a lord. How would you view your knights? How would you view Charlemagne? Describe and explain your point of view.

4. Why might learning about various points of view be important in a democracy?

THE CHURCH IN THE MIDDLE AGES

Focus Activity

READ TO LEARN
How did Christianity affect life in Europe?

VOCABULARY
monastery
nun
convent
cathedral
saint
Crusade
plague

PEOPLE
Benedict
Francis of Assisi
Pope Urban II

PLACES
Chartres

READ ALOUD

The overwhelming majority of people in Europe in the Middle Ages were Christian. In fact, Europe was a large part of what the Christians called Christendom—or "kingdom of the Christians." At the center of this "kingdom" was the Christian Church based in Rome. The Church leader was the Pope, who was as powerful as any king or lord.

THE BIG PICTURE

During the Middle Ages Christianity spread throughout the entire continent of Europe. Kings, such as Charlemagne, brought Christianity to conquered lands. In other places, such as Ireland, priests brought the new religion. Eventually Christianity became central to life for almost everyone in Europe. People even measured a simple act like boiling an egg by the length of time it took to say a certain prayer.

Not all Europeans were Christian, however. Jews had lived in villages and towns throughout Europe since the early days of the Roman Empire. Muslims had come to Spain around A.D. 700. In this lesson you will read how the Christian Church in Rome affected Europe during the Middle Ages.

AN "AGE OF FAITH"

The growth of Christianity in Europe happened gradually. Over time most people of other religions began to accept the Christian faith. Eventually Christian belief grew so strong that the later Middle Ages became known as the "Age of Faith."

Life in Monasteries and Convents

For several centuries, life in Europe revolved around religion. Some men, called monks, devoted their lives to religion. They lived in communities called monasteries. Women who vowed to devote their lives to religion were called nuns. Their communities were called convents. Many people entered convents and monastaries at a young age and stayed until death. In no place was faith stronger.

An Italian monk named Benedict wrote the first plan for monasteries in the A.D. 500s. Monks had to obey the head monk, who was called the abbot. Here are some of Benedict's rules:

No one, without permission of the abbot, shall presume to give, or receive, or keep as his own, anything whatever: neither book nor tablets, nor pen: nothing at all.... All things are to be common to all.

Monasteries and convents, like manors, were churches, farms, homes, and schools all rolled into one. Most monks and nuns spent much of the day in prayer. They also farmed and studied, and made wine, medicines, and craft goods.

Monasteries served as centers of learning in the Middle Ages. Most monasteries had a scriptorium, or a room for making books. Since no printing press existed, all books were carefully copied by hand. Monks wrote books of prayer and poetry. They also copied old Greek and Roman texts. These beautifully decorated books are called manuscripts. Some had such value that they were chained to desks. Today they are important records of ancient life and the Middle Ages.

In addition to praying, monks often spent time making illustrated books.

THE ROMAN CHURCH

For years there had been tension between the Pope in Rome and other Christian leaders in Constantinople. In 1054 these tensions led to a split in the Christian Church. The Church based in Constantinople was called the Eastern Orthodox Church. The Church based in Rome later became known as the Roman Catholic Church.

At around the same time as the split in the Christian Church, towns began to grow in size and wealth. Townspeople expressed their religious beliefs by building grand churches, or cathedrals. Skilled craftworkers created windows for the cathedrals out of pieces of colored glass. These stained-glass windows often showed scenes from Christian writings.

A Magnificent Cathedral

Suppose you are a traveler to Chartres (SHAHRT), France, in 1260. The road is narrow and muddy. As you emerge from the thick forest, you see the spires of the town's magnificent cathedral rising high into the sky.

Chartres Cathedral took about 36 years to build. Many workers never saw their cathedrals completed. Some took more than 400 years to build. Many cathedrals still stand as one of the great legacies of the Middle Ages.

Saints and Pilgrimages

Another way that Christians showed their devotion was through pilgrimages. Europe's Christian pilgrims traveled great distances to Rome or Jerusalem. Jerusalem was and is a holy city to Jews, Muslims, and Christians.

During the Middle Ages, pilgrims also traveled to shrines, or special buildings that had been built for saints.

The Cathedral of Notre Dame in Paris is known for its tall spires and many stained-glass windows (right). Sometimes knights on pilgrimage were women (below).

Saints are women and men considered to be especially holy.

One of the most honored saints of the Middle Ages was Francis of Assisi. He lived from about 1181 to 1226. Francis devoted his life to serving the poor and sick in Italy. His followers came to be called Franciscans.

The First Crusade

In 1095 Pope Urban II called for Christians throughout western Europe to make a pilgrimage to Jerusalem. He also urged the pilgrims to capture Jerusalem from the Seljuk Turks, who were Muslim. Thousands of Europeans responded to the Pope's call. This journey to gain control of Jerusalem was the first Crusade. Those who went were called Crusaders.

As they marched through Europe, the Crusaders attacked others who were not Christian. They raided Jewish communities in France and Germany. One shocked Christian wrote:

They should have traveled their road for Christ. Instead they turned to madness and shamefully, cruelly cut down the Jewish people in the cities and towns through which they passed.

About 100,000 knights, priests, and other pilgrims left for the "Holy Land," as the Crusaders called the land around Jerusalem. The Crusaders battled against Turkish armies even before they reached Jerusalem. The Crusaders suffered such great hunger and sickness that half died before they reached Jerusalem in 1099.

For two days the Crusaders attacked Jerusalem, killing many Muslims and Jews. The Crusaders captured Jerusalem, which would remain in Christian hands for about 100 years.

Links to ART

Design a Stained-Glass Window

The art of making stained-glass windows developed in western Europe during the Middle Ages. These windows are made of pieces of glass joined by strips of lead. At first the windows were small. By the 1200s, though, stained-glass windows were larger and had different shapes.

Many stained-glass windows in churches and cathedrals tell stories. Such windows helped people who did not know how to read to learn Bible stories.

Draw a design for a stained-glass window that you would like to see at the entrance of your school. As examples, look at stained-glass windows in churches and other buildings in your community. Then draw a sketch of the design and pieces of colored glass.

END OF THE MIDDLE AGES

Other Crusades took place over the next 200 years, but most of these failed. Despite their failure the effects of the Crusades were felt far beyond the Holy Land. Find the Crusade routes on the map on this page. As you can see, the Crusaders often passed through the Italian port cities on their way to the Holy Land. With more people passing through, trade began to grow in these cities. The Crusaders also returned to Europe, bringing products and new knowledge from Asia and Africa.

By the end of the Crusades in 1291, Europe had changed in many ways. With changes in Europe's economy, the system of feudalism was gradually breaking down.

"Most Terrible of Terrors"

One of Europe's cities bustling with activity was Siena, Italy. Here trade flourished and the people had been building a great cathedral since the 1100s. This cathedral remains unfinished to this day, however. Its construction was halted in 1348, when a plague struck Western Europe. A plague is a terrible disease that spreads quickly. This plague was caused by bacteria that was spread by rats and fleas. At that time, however, no one knew what caused the sickness. They just knew terrible misery and sadness. This plague, which was later called the Black Death, wiped out one third of the western European population. In Siena, two thirds of the people died. One man from that city described the horrible effects that the Black Death

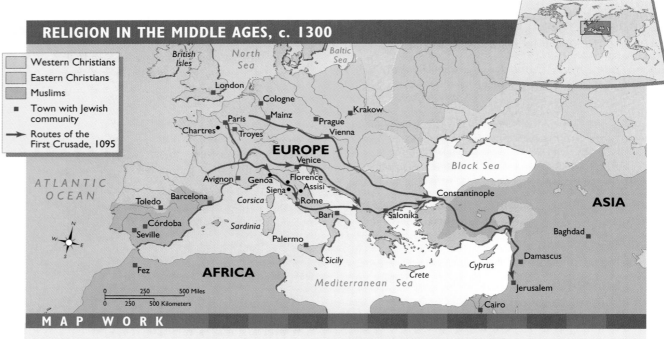

RELIGION IN THE MIDDLE AGES, c. 1300

Legend:
- Western Christians
- Eastern Christians
- Muslims
- ■ Town with Jewish community
- → Routes of the First Crusade, 1095

Map labels: British Isles, North Sea, Baltic Sea, London, Cologne, Krakow, Mainz, Paris, Prague, Chartres, Troyes, Vienna, EUROPE, Venice, Black Sea, ATLANTIC OCEAN, Avignon, Genoa, Florence, Assisi, Constantinople, ASIA, Barcelona, Siena, Corsica, Rome, Toledo, Bari, Salonika, Baghdad, Córdoba, Sardinia, Seville, Palermo, Damascus, Cyprus, Fez, AFRICA, Sicily, Crete, Jerusalem, Mediterranean Sea, Cairo

0 250 500 Miles
0 250 500 Kilometers

MAP WORK

Crusaders traveled throughout Europe on their way to Jerusalem.

1. Which towns east of Constantinople had a Jewish community?

2. Where did more Muslims live—in Europe or in northern Africa?

3. Which city did Crusaders pass through after they left Vienna ?

These Crusaders are preparing to sail from Italy to Jerusalem.

had on people who became infected with the disease:

> The plague began in Siena in May, a horrible and cruel event. They died almost immediately . . . they would swell up under the armpits and drop dead while talking. People brought members of their own household to the ditches as best they could, without priest or holy ceremony or ringing of bells. Nobody wept for the dead, since each was awaiting death; and so many died that everyone thought the end of the world had come.

Towns in France flew black flags from church towers to warn travelers of the plague. Nearly 130 years would pass before the plague was completely gone from Europe.

WHY IT MATTERS

Today the Roman Catholic Church and the Eastern Orthodox Church continue to be important to the lives of many Christians around the world. Some men and women still live in monasteries and convents. The splendid cathedrals of the Middle Ages remain as well. These creations of technology, imagination, and faith stand as stunning reminders of the achievements of the Middle Ages.

Reviewing Facts and Ideas

SUM IT UP

- The Christian Church had a great influence on the lives of Europeans during the Middle Ages.
- Christians in Europe built magnificent cathedrals for worship.
- Monasteries across Europe served as centers of faith and learning.
- During the first Crusade, beginning in 1095, Christians conquered Jerusalem.
- In 1348 a plague struck Europe, killing one out of three people.

THINK ABOUT IT

1. What rule did Benedict give about property for monks?

2. For Pope Urban II, what was the main purpose of the Crusades?

3. **FOCUS** Why are the Middle Ages known as the "Age of Faith"?

4. **THINKING SKILL** Read the quote by the Christian writer on page 333. What shaped this person's *point of view*? What might have been the point of view of a Crusader?

5. **GEOGRAPHY** Study the map on page 334. What city was a stop along all Crusade routes shown? What empire ruled this city?

THE RENAISSANCE

READ ALOUD

"This is the supreme, marvelous truth of man. He can be that which he wills to be. God the Father endowed man, from birth, with the seeds of every possibility and every life."

These words are by Pico della Mirandola (PEE koh DAYL luh mee RAHN doh lah), an Italian scholar of the 1400s. He expressed a powerful new way of thinking that arose in Europe as the Middle Ages came to an end.

THE BIG PICTURE

Out of the misery of the Black Death came new ideas that stirred Europe. Starting around 1350 enthusiasm for art, literature, and trade increased throughout northern Italy. This was the beginning of a period called the Renaissance (REN uh sahns), from the French word meaning "rebirth." Many Europeans saw this time as a rebirth of the classical periods of Greece and Rome. Although the Renaissance began in Italy, within a century it had spread to the rest of Europe.

The Renaissance was a time of great creativity. Central to the ideas of the Renaissance was a powerful interest in humanism (HYOO muh niz um). Humanism meant concern with human interests and values. People in the Middle Ages had often turned their thoughts toward the "next world," or heaven. People of the Renaissance were still usually very religious. However, they began to focus more on what people could achieve in this world.

Focus Activity

READ TO LEARN
What were some major achievements of the Renaissance?

VOCABULARY
Renaissance
humanism
patron

PEOPLE
Lorenzo Medici
Petrarch
Michelangelo
Leonardo da Vinci
Nicolaus Copernicus

PLACES
Florence

RENAISSANCE IN ITALY

Of course, the Renaissance did not happen overnight. Europeans did not wake up one morning and start a new era. Change came first to the city of Florence, in northern Italy. Why did the Renaissance begin in Florence?

The Glory of Florence

As you read in the last lesson, growth in trade, partly caused by the Crusades, benefited Italian cities. By 1400 Florence had become one of the richest cities in Europe. Find this city on the map on page 334. Traders from Florence journeyed to the towns of France and to the port cities of the Black Sea. They also traveled to Asia and Africa, returning with spices and silks. Florence was a busy craft-producing city. People worked in about 200 shops, turning out enormous amounts of woolen cloth.

Lorenzo the Magnificent

One of the wealthiest families in Florence was the Medici (MED ih chee) family. The Medicis gained great wealth through banking and trading. Although Florence had become a republic around 1300, by the 1400s the Medicis had gained control. The most famous member of the family was Lorenzo Medici. He came to power in 1469. Some considered him a tyrant—an all-powerful and often unjust ruler. One Florentine, however, said, "If Florence was to have a tyrant, she could never have a better or more delightful one."

Lorenzo Medici was a patron, or supporter, of the arts. He loved poetry and painting. Before long, scholars and artists flocked to Florence, where they were paid by Lorenzo to pursue their work. The city was soon bursting with art and learning, and its leader became known as "Lorenzo the Magnificent."

Lorenzo Medici (right) made Florence a powerful city in the late 1400s.

ARTS AND IDEAS

As you have read, the Renaissance was a time of looking back to achievements of earlier civilizations. During the 1300s humanists began to search the Italian countryside for Greek and Roman artifacts. They found examples of classical cultures such as manuscripts, coins, and statues to study for ideas.

European scholars, especially scientists, also learned from Arab scholars. As you read in Chapter 10, scholars in Baghdad preserved and developed Greek, Roman, and Indian scientific knowledge. As trade between Europe, Asia, and Africa grew during the Crusades, goods and knowledge spread.

The Power of Words

One of the earliest Italian humanists to study classics—works of literature from ancient Greece, Rome, and Arabia—was Petrarch (PEE trahrk). Petrarch was a poet who lived from 1304 to 1374. He loved learning, and he read every book he could find. Petrarch believed the classics were better than any works written later.

Petrarch became the most celebrated poet in all of Europe. He once described his love of writing as follows:

> *There is no lighter burden, nor more agreeable, than a pen.... As there is none among earthly delights more noble than literature, so there was none more lasting, none gentler or more faithful.*

Renaissance Artists

Artists as well as poets learned from ancient Romans and Greeks. One of the greatest Renaissance artists was Michelangelo. He used many classical ideas—such as balance of form—in his paintings, sculptures, and architecture.

You can see his *David* at the beginning of this lesson.

A very famous painter of Italy was the humanist Leonardo da Vinci (lee uh NAHR doh duh VIHN chee). He lived from 1452 to 1519. Like Michelangelo, Leonardo da Vinci was a painter, sculptor, and architect. However, Leonardo da Vinci was a scientist, engineer, and musician as well. Da Vinci's interests and talents were as broad as the Renaissance itself.

Leonardo da Vinci, the Painter

As a child, Leonardo da Vinci showed great ability in drawing. When he turned 15, his father took him to study with the greatest painter in

Mona Lisa, **by Leonardo da Vinci, is one of the most famous paintings in the world.**

Florence. Leonardo painted with such skill that his teacher put down his own paintbrushes and never picked them up again. Before long, Leonardo was invited to set up his studio in the garden of his patron, Lorenzo Medici.

Da Vinci loved the world of Florence. He would sometimes follow interesting townspeople for a whole day and then paint them from memory. Leonardo da Vinci's careful observation helped him create paintings that were so realistic they surprised viewers.

Da Vinci drew this portrait of himself. He also made many sketches of his inventions such as a flying machine (below).

Leonardo da Vinci, the Inventor

Besides painting, da Vinci also kept hundreds of notebooks in which he wrote down all kinds of new ideas. Da Vinci always wrote backward to keep his ideas secret. He made plans for a submarine and a machine gun. He wrote this plan for a parachute:

If a man has a tent made of linen, of which the holes have all been stopped up, and it is 20 feet across and 20 in depth, he will be able to throw himself down from any great height without sustaining any injury.

Leonardo da Vinci studied carefully the flight of birds. His close observation helped him to design a flying machine. Four hundred years would pass before a human actually flew. Leonardo da Vinci's love of knowledge inspired future artists and inventors.

Earth, Sun, and Stars

In a small town in Poland, a young man named Nicolaus Copernicus (kuh PUR nih kus) studied books of Greek and Arab astronomy. He observed the night sky with a simple telescope and carefully recorded the positions of the stars he saw.

In 1514 Copernicus made a startling discovery. Earth seemed to orbit around the sun, once each year. This was a new idea. Since people first tracked the stars and moon, they believed that Earth was the center of the universe. Many European leaders, including officials of the Church in Rome, found this new theory unacceptable. They felt it went against Church teachings, which put Earth at the center of the universe. It was not until after Copernicus died that his book was published. It was called *On the Revolutions of the Heavenly Spheres.* Copernicus's ideas about the universe greatly changed our knowledge of astronomy.

Infographic

Spread of the Renaissance

As you have read, the Renaissance began in Florence, Italy, around 1350 and later spread throughout Europe. Artists, writers, and scientists often traveled to different Europeans cities to study and work. How might exchanging ideas have led to achievements?

> " All the world's a stage, And all the men and women merely players. "
>
> by William Shakespeare

Clock

This clock and its decorated cover were made in France around 1540. Powered by a coiled spring, the clock was portable.

El Greco "A View of Toledo"

El Greco was a Greek who studied art in Venice. He settled in Toledo, Spain, and painted many scenes of life in that city.

Tempietto

Donato Bramante designed Tempietto, a temple in Rome. Completed in 1502, the temple has features of classical architecture such as columns.

Caterina Van Hemmessen

Painters in Europe often painted themselves, as in this self-portrait by a German woman.

WHY IT MATTERS

The Renaissance was a time of looking back to the classical achievements of Greece, Rome, and Arabia. It was also a time of looking forward, for much remained to be discovered.

Though the Renaissance began in Italy, it soon spread to the rest of Europe. The Renaissance brought about changes to many old ways of thinking. For this reason, historians often call it the beginning of the modern age.

In the next lesson you will read about the spread of new ideas into the Roman Catholic Church.

✔// Reviewing Facts and Ideas

SUM IT UP

- The Renaissance began in Italy, where an interest in humanism first developed.
- In Florence wealthy patrons like Lorenzo Medici supported artists and scholars.
- Renaissance scientists studied Greek, Roman, and Arab texts, and made new discoveries about the world.

THINK ABOUT IT

1. What did the people of the Renaissance mean by *humanism*?

2. How did Florence become one of the richest cities in Europe?

3. **FOCUS** How did Renaissance achievements reflect both the past and their own time?

4. **THINKING SKILL** Make and explain at least two *generalizations* about Renaissance thinkers.

5. **WRITE** Look at one of the Renaissance artworks in this lesson. Write a paragraph explaining what you like or dislike about the art.

400   700   1000   1300 1450   1600

THE REFORMATION

READ ALOUD

"Here I stand; I can do no other. God help me. Amen."

These words were spoken in the 1500s by a German monk named Martin Luther. Luther had spoken out against the Church in Rome. Church leaders had called upon Luther to take back his criticisms. Luther's beliefs were too strong, however. He refused to back down.

THE BIG PICTURE

As humanism gained popularity among Europe's artists and scholars, people began to question everything around them. They studied books and started schools in an effort to find answers to their questions. Nicolaus Copernicus, you may recall, questioned the old belief that Earth was the center of the universe. The Renaissance had shaken many of Europe's established traditions and beliefs.

At the same time some Christians began to be concerned. They thought that some Renaissance artists and scientists had gotten too far away from their religious teachings. These Christians said that many artists and scientists were too worldly, or concerned about this world. Many also felt that the Church in Rome had become too worldly and rich. A few Christians began to question the authority of the Pope.

Focus Activity

READ TO LEARN
What changes did the Reformation bring to Europe?

VOCABULARY
indulgence
reform
Reformation
Protestantism
armada

PEOPLE
Erasmus
Martin Luther
Johannes Gutenberg
King Henry VIII
Queen Elizabeth I
William Shakespeare

THE CHURCH OF ROME

By 1500 the Roman Church had become the most powerful institution in Europe. The Pope claimed authority over all of Europe's rulers. The Pope's power also brought great wealth to the Roman Church. Like the government of the Roman empire, the Roman Church taxed the people of Europe. Some of this money was spent on works of art.

Questions of Faith

Starting around 1500, humanists such as Erasmus (ih RAZ mus) began to criticize the Roman Church. He especially questioned the Church policy concerning indulgences (ihn DUL juns ez). An indulgence is a pardon, or forgiveness, from the Church. During the Middle Ages, some people began to pay to be forgiven by the priest for acting against Christian teachings. Erasmus believed that the indulgences were wrong. He hoped to reform, or change, the Roman Church.

In Wittenberg, Germany, the sale of indulgences also made a monk, Martin Luther, angry. He felt that the money, often given by people who were poor, should not be spent on the building of Saint Peter's, a great cathedral in Rome.

In 1517 Luther wrote 95 Theses (THEE seez), or statements, of protest. He placed this list on a Wittenberg church door. Luther had no idea that this simple act would soon shake beliefs across the entire continent.

Read the excerpts from Luther's Theses. How did he suggest that the Church pay for building Saint Peter's?

Excerpt from the 95 Theses, written by Martin Luther in 1517.

*Out of love and **zeal** for truth and the desire to bring it to light, the following theses will be publicly discussed at Wittenberg under the chairmanship of the Reverend Martin Luther.*

*Before long all the churches, palaces, walls, and bridges of Rome will be built out of our [indulgence] money. . . . We Germans can not attend Saint Peter's. Better it should never be built than that our **parochial** churches should be **despoiled**. . . . Why doesn't the pope build the **basilica** out of his own money?*

---

zeal: eagerness
parochial: local
despoiled: robbed
basilica: cathedral

Martin Luther studied law before he became a monk in 1505.

A CALL FOR REFORM

Martin Luther's 95 Theses in Wittenberg started a movement called the Reformation (ref ur MAY shun). This movement brought reform to the Church in Rome. It would also lead to another division of Christianity.

Spreading the Word

News of Luther's bold action in Wittenberg spread with the help of a recent invention. In 1448 a man named Johannes Gutenberg (yoh HAHN uhs GOO tun burg) had built a printing press. It used metal letters called movable type to spell out words on a page.

Before 1448, each page had to be hand-carved. Now that letters could be moved around, printing was cheaper and easier as well as faster. Gutenberg's press could print 300 pages a day. By 1500 several million books had been printed in Europe!

The new invention helped spread Luther's criticisms of the Roman Church and a translation of the Bible. In those days almost everything was printed in Latin. Luther wrote in German, which helped to unite many German-speaking people on his side.

Division of the Roman Church

In 1520 Pope Leo X (the Tenth) ordered that Luther's books be burned, but Luther did not stop his protest. A visitor from Rome reported: "All Germany is up in arms against Rome."

Although the leaders of the Roman Church in Rome wanted Luther punished, German rulers protected him. By this time their loyalty to their homeland had become stronger than their loyalty to the Pope. These rulers also hoped to keep taxes intended for Rome.

In 1529 the break in the Roman Church became permanent. Luther's followers were now called Protestants, because they protested against the Roman Church. Western Christianity was divided in two—Protestantism (PROT uh stun tiz um) and Roman Catholicism.

The Protestant Church

The indulgence issue was not the only Church policy with which Protestant leaders disagreed. These leaders taught that monasteries and convents were unnecessary. Protestants also thought that church decorations and services should be simpler. They worked to spread translated Bibles and have church services in local languages.

Johannes Gutenberg built the first printing press out of a device used to press grapes and cheese.

In time, new Protestant leaders arose, such as John Calvin in Switzerland. Calvin founded a separate Protestant group called the Calvinists. The new Protestant groups did not agree on every issue, but they were united in their refusal to follow the Pope.

Roman Catholic Reform

Even before the Protestants split from the Roman Church, Catholic leaders had begun making reforms. Between 1545 and 1563 a group of Catholic leaders met in the city of Trent, Italy. They ordered that parts of church services should be in the language of the people of a country, not just in Latin. They also tried to see that the Church's money was spent more carefully. These reforms helped to strengthen the Roman Catholic religion. Some critics, such as Erasmus, decided not to leave the Catholic Church.

During the 1500s most people in Germany, Scandinavia, Holland, and Switzerland became Protestant. As you can see on the map on this page, most of Spain, Italy, and France remained Catholic. Tensions between Protestants and Roman Catholics increased.

England's Break With Rome

At this time of religious conflict, a new ruler brought religious change to England. This ruler was King Henry VIII. Henry was building a strong monarchy, or a government ruled by a king or a queen.

At the beginning of his rule in 1509, Henry supported the Roman Church. His view, however, changed in 1527. Henry, who had one daughter, wanted a son to inherit his throne. His wife, Queen Catherine, was unable to have more children. So the king asked the

CHRISTIANITY IN WESTERN EUROPE, c. 1560

Legend:
- Roman Catholics
- Lutherans
- Calvinists
- Anglicans
- Eastern Christians
- Mixture of Catholics, Lutherans & Calvinists
- — Present-day boundaries

MAP WORK

By 1560 many different Christian groups had formed. Followers of these groups were spread throughout western Europe.

1. In which country was the Anglican religion common?
2. Which religion was most widespread?

Pope to give him permission to divorce the Queen. The Pope refused.

Henry VIII stated that the Pope did not have authority over the English monarchy. He then took control of Church land and cut off payments to Rome. Henry started a new Protestant church, the Church of England, also called the Anglican Church. With control over England's church, Henry's monarchy became more powerful.

England's Queen Elizabeth I (below) stands on a map of her empire. England defeated the Spanish Armada (right).

QUEEN ELIZABETH I

In the years following the split with the Catholic Church, England was torn by religious differences. During this troubled time, Henry VIII's daughter, Elizabeth, came to the throne. In 1558 she became Queen Elizabeth I. Not only did the queen face conflict at home, but also there were threats of invasion from mainland Europe. Despite these problems, Elizabeth became one of the most powerful and popular monarchs England has ever known.

The Elizabethan Age

Under Elizabeth the anger between England's Protestants and Catholics cooled. London bustled with business and trade. Also during this time, the Renaissance arrived in England. Elizabeth enjoyed poetry and plays. Some-times she watched the performances of a young writer and actor named William Shakespeare. Shakespeare was one of the greatest writers in the English language. You will learn more about him in the Legacy on page 348.

The Spanish Armada

Elizabeth hated war and worked hard to keep her country at peace. In 1588, however, Elizabeth faced the threat of a war with Spain.

The Spanish hoped to gain control of Atlantic trade routes. They also hoped to return England to the Catholic faith. Under King Philip II, Spain had gathered a huge and powerful fleet, called an armada, of 130 warships. They prepared to attack England.

Queen Elizabeth assembled her troops and delivered a stirring speech. How do you think the troops reacted?

MANY VOICES
PRIMARY SOURCE

Excerpt from Queen Elizabeth's speech to her troops during the battle with the Spanish Armada, 1588.

*Let tyrants fear. I have always so behaved myself that, under God, I have placed my **chiefest** strength and **safeguard** in the loyal hearts and good will of my **subjects**; and therefore I am come.... to live or die amongst you all, and to lay down for my God and for my kingdom and for my people, my honor and my blood, even in the dust. I know I have the body of a weak and feeble woman, but I have the heart and stomach of a king, and a king of England too, and think **foul scorn** that ... Spain, or any prince of Europe should dare to invade the borders of my **realm**.*

---

chiefest: greatest
safeguard: protection
subjects: people of the kingdom
foul scorn: badly
realm: kingdom

Battle at Sea

With only 90 ships, England's fleet was smaller than the Spanish Armada. However, the English ships were faster and had better guns. This battle for the seas took place in the English Channel. After nine days the Spanish Armada was badly beaten. Not one English ship was sunk. Many Spanish ships escaped, only to be wrecked in a violent storm. Only half of the Spanish Armada made it back to Spain. England continued to build its fleet. The country would soon become the greatest naval power in the entire world.

WHY IT MATTERS

By 1600 the unity that had brought Europe together under the Roman Church had broken apart. The Pope was no longer the most powerful leader in Europe. Kings and queens began to act in the interest of their own countries. In coming years, these kingdoms would extend their power to places beyond Europe—to Africa, the Americas, and Asia.

The Christian Church remained split. Of the almost 2 billion Christians in the world today, over 1 billion are Roman Catholics. Almost 400 million are Protestants. In the United States alone, there are 59 million Roman Catholics and 90 million Protestants.

Reviewing Facts and Ideas

SUM IT UP

- In 1517 Martin Luther put the 95 Theses on a church door in Germany.

- Luther's actions led to the Reformation. The Western Christian Church soon split into the Protestant and Roman Catholic Churches.

- Under Elizabeth I, England's culture and power flourished.

THINK ABOUT IT

1. What were indulgences? What did Martin Luther think about them?

2. What reforms did the Protestant and Catholic Churches make in the 1500s?

3. **FOCUS** How did the Reformation affect the unity of Europe?

4. **THINKING SKILL** What was the *point of view* of Queen Elizabeth toward Spain in her speech to her troops?

5. **GEOGRAPHY** Study the location of England and Spain on the map on page 345. Why did both countries need a powerful navy?

THE ART OF LANGUAGE: SHAKESPEARE

The Granger Collection

Many people today take a break from their routines to see a movie or a play. If you lived in London during the Elizabethan Age, you might have gone to a play by one of the greatest writers of all time, William Shakespeare. His plays are still performed today.

Born in England in 1564, Shakespeare went to work in London. He became an actor, poet, playwright, and part-owner of the Globe Theater in London.

Shakespeare's plays and poems show a deep understanding of people's thoughts and feelings. He wrote about subjects and ideas that are still important to audiences and readers today.

The genius of Shakespeare's works has also greatly influenced the English language. He is credited with inventing familiar phrases such as "catch cold" and "bump."

Before his death in 1616, Shakespeare had a successful career. However, his audiences could not have guessed how lasting his legacy would be.

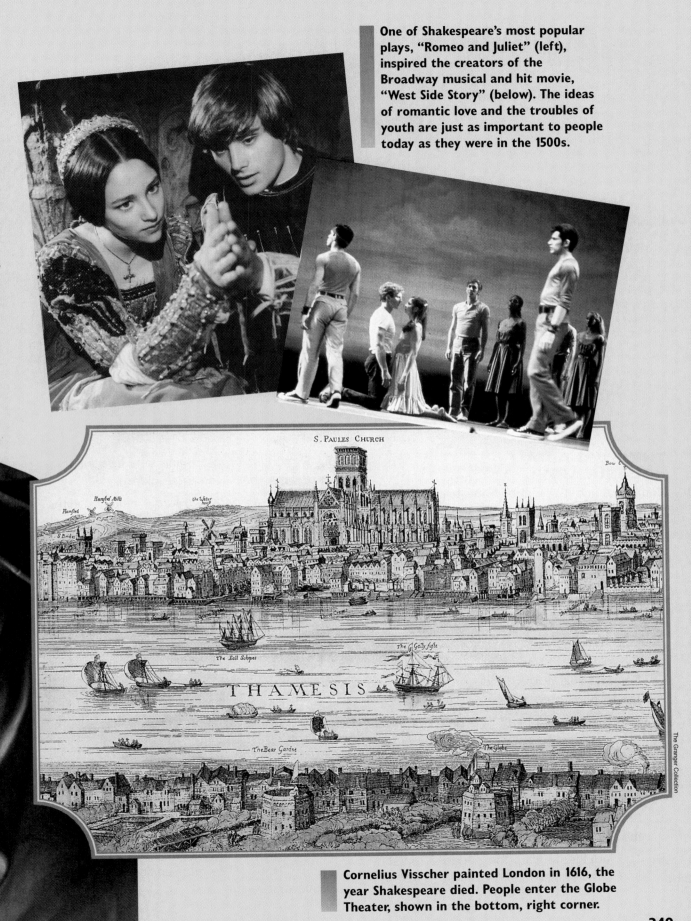

One of Shakespeare's most popular plays, "Romeo and Juliet" (left), inspired the creators of the Broadway musical and hit movie, "West Side Story" (below). The ideas of romantic love and the troubles of youth are just as important to people today as they were in the 1500s.

S. PAULES CHURCH

THAMESIS

Cornelius Visscher painted London in 1616, the year Shakespeare died. People enter the Globe Theater, shown in the bottom, right corner.

CHAPTER 12 REVIEW

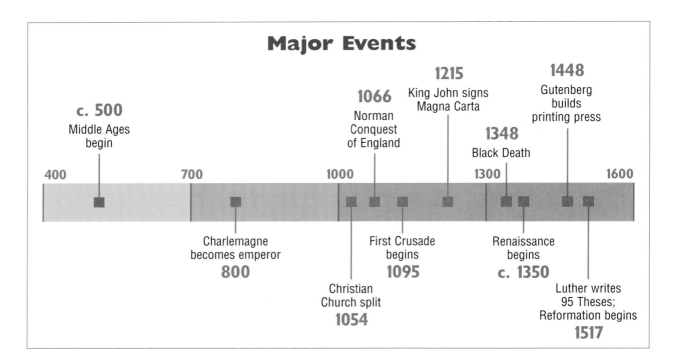

Major Events

1215
King John signs
Magna Carta

1448
Gutenberg
builds
printing press

1066
Norman
Conquest
of England

c. 500
Middle Ages
begin

1348
Black Death

| 400 | 700 | 1000 | 1300 | 1600 |

Charlemagne
becomes emperor
800

First Crusade
begins
1095

Renaissance
begins
c. **1350**

Christian
Church split
1054

Luther writes
95 Theses;
Reformation begins
1517

THINKING ABOUT VOCABULARY

Number a sheet of paper from 1 to 10. Decide whether the underlined word or term in each of the following statements correctly completes the sentence. If the word or term is correct, write **C** beside the number. If the word or term is incorrect, write **I** and then write the word or term that correctly completes the sentence.

1. A <u>patron</u> is a wealthy or influential supporter of art and artists.

2. <u>Feudalism</u> is a pardon or forgiveness from the Pope.

3. <u>Renaissance</u> is a way of organizing and governing society based on land and service.

4. A <u>guild</u> was a group of traders or craftworkers in a medieval town.

5. Protestantism was an attempt to <u>reform</u> the Roman Catholic Church.

6. The <u>indulgence</u> was the period of artistic and cultural rebirth.

7. A <u>monastery</u> is a place where monks devote their lives to religion.

8. A <u>fief</u> was part of a lord's manor given to a vassal to manage.

9. The period when many people lived on manors owned by lords is called the <u>Middle Ages</u>.

10. <u>Deforestation</u> is the clearing of forests to make room for farms and cities.

THINKING ABOUT FACTS

1. How did serfs live?

2. What was the Black Death?

3. What did Copernicus learn from observing the sky?

4. What major changes in the Christian Church did you read about in this chapter?

5. According to the time line above, how long after the beginning of the Renaissance did the Protestant Reformation begin? How were the Renaissance and Reformation different?

THINK AND WRITE

WRITING AN EXPLANATION

Write a paragraph about feudalism. Identify lords, ladies, vassals, and serfs and explain their roles in feudal society.

WRITING AN INTERVIEW

Suppose you could go back into the Middle Ages and interview a monk or a nun. Write at least three questions you would ask the person and the answers you think he or she might give.

WRITING A LIST

Make a list of three complaints some people had about the Roman church that led to the Protestant Reformation.

APPLYING THINKING SKILLS

DETERMINING POINT OF VIEW

1. What is a point of view?

2. What point of view do you think the lord of a manor might have toward his serfs? What point of view might a serf have toward the lord?

3. Reread the words of Petrarch on page 338. What is his point of view about writing? Why do you think he had that point of view?

4. How did the points of view of Protestant and Catholic leaders differ during the Reformation?

5. Why is it important to the study of history to be able to understand different points of view?

Summing Up the Chapter

Review the chapter. Then copy on a separate piece of paper the flow chart shown below. Using what you learned in the chapter, fill in the remaining events. Then use the chart to write a paragraph that answers the question "What led to the decline of the feudal system?"

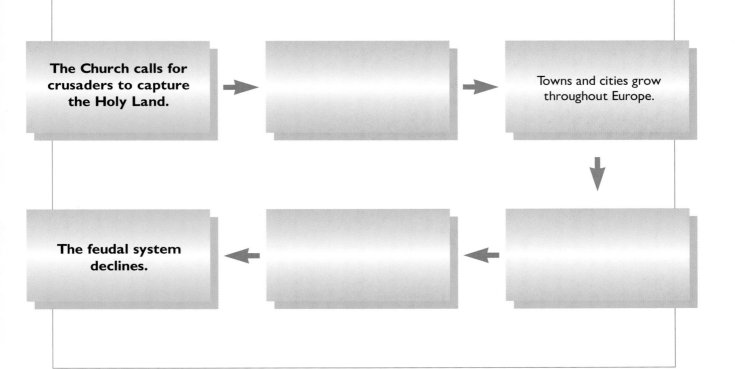

The Church calls for crusaders to capture the Holy Land. → → Towns and cities grow throughout Europe.

The feudal system declines. ← ←

CHAPTER 13

Empires and Cultures of Africa

THINKING ABOUT HISTORY AND GEOGRAPHY

The stories of Africa's cultures often take place on the continent's fertile grasslands. Following the time line, see how civilizations developed in different parts of the continent. The great amounts of gold and other trade goods in Africa made these civilizations wealthy. As different peoples came into contact, new religious and cultural traditions were born.

ATLANTIC OCEAN

1200
LALIBELA
Ethiopians carve magnificent churches out of solid rock

1300
TIMBUKTU
An important trade center develops in West Africa

1324
MALI
King Mansa Musa makes a pilgrimage to Mecca

EUROPE

■ Mali ■ Timbuktu

Red Sea

Lalibela ▫

AFRICA

1350
ZANZIBAR
Swahili cultures develop along Africa's east coast

1400
GREAT ZIMBABWE
A civilization in South Africa develops an important gold trade

Zanzibar ▫

Great
Zimbabwe
▫

GEOGRAPHY OF AFRICA

READ ALOUD

"The last rays of the sun filtered through a shredded lacework of clouds . . . the group of mud-walled houses and the dry grass, still scorched by the heat of noon, now swam in the red waters of the setting sun. . . . It was an afternoon in mid-October, at the end of the season of rains."

West African author Sembene Ousmane (sem BAY nee oos MAH nee), from the country of Senegal, wrote these words describing the end of one day in Africa. Throughout this huge continent, and throughout history, the sun—along with rain and vast stretches of grassland—has shaped the pattern of millions of lives.

THE BIG PICTURE

Africa is larger than the United States and all of the countries of Europe put together. The history of this enormous continent is long and varied. In Chapter 3 you read about the early people who lived in places like Border Cave. Then in Chapter 4, you read about one of the most powerful civilizations of the ancient world, ancient Egypt.

Civilization in Egypt, you may recall, was made possible by the "gift of the Nile." The Nile River provided both water and fertile soil in a dry environment. Several other life-giving rivers flow through Africa. Africa also has deserts, rain forests, and vast plains. This great variety has presented special challenges and opportunities for the many peoples of the continent.

Focus Activity

READ TO LEARN
How did the savanna of Africa affect the people that lived there long ago?

VOCABULARY
savanna

PLACES
Mount Kilimanjaro
Sahara Desert
Sahel
Niger River
Zambezi River
Great Rift Valley
Red Sea

AFRICA

As you can see on the map, the equator runs through the middle of Africa. Mountains rise along Africa's eastern and northern edges. Snow lingers year round on Mount Kilimanjaro. In the Sahara Desert, though, temperatures can reach a sizzling 136°F! This is the world's largest desert. Dry grasslands of the Sahel (SA hihl) form a narrow belt along the Sahara's southern edge. *Sahel* is an Arabic word that means "shore." Find the Sahel on the map.

The Niger River and the Zambezi (zam BEE zee) River water thirsty lands. The Great Rift Valley extends nearly 3,000 miles, from the Mozambique Channel to the Red Sea.

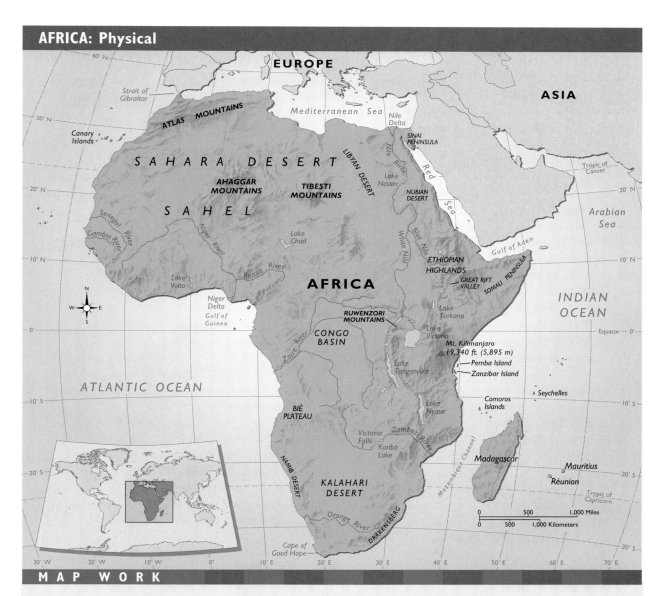

AFRICA: Physical

EUROPE

ASIA

Strait of Gibraltar

Mediterranean Sea

Nile Delta

ATLAS MOUNTAINS

Canary Islands

SINAI PENINSULA

Tropic of Cancer

SAHARA DESERT

LIBYAN DESERT

AHAGGAR MOUNTAINS

TIBESTI MOUNTAINS

Lake Nasser

NUBIAN DESERT

Arabian Sea

SAHEL

Red Sea

Senegal River

Niger River

Lake Chad

White Nile

Blue Nile

Gulf of Aden

Gambia River

Benue River

ETHIOPIAN HIGHLANDS

SOMALI PENINSULA

Lake Volta

AFRICA

GREAT RIFT VALLEY

INDIAN OCEAN

Niger Delta

Gulf of Guinea

RUWENZORI MOUNTAINS

Lake Turkana

Lake Victoria

Zaire River

CONGO BASIN

Mt. Kilimanjaro 19,340 ft. (5,895 m)

Pemba Island

Zanzibar Island

Lake Tanganyika

Seychelles

ATLANTIC OCEAN

Comoros Islands

BIÉ PLATEAU

Lake Nyasa

Victoria Falls

Zambezi River

Madagascar

Mauritius

NAMIB DESERT

Kariba Lake

Réunion

Tropic of Capricorn

KALAHARI DESERT

Mozambique Channel

DRAKENSBERG

Orange River

Cape of Good Hope

0   500   1,000 Miles
0   500   1,000 Kilometers

MAP WORK

The varied geography of Africa includes dense rain forests and empty deserts where rain may not fall for years at a time.

1. Which desert is found on the southwestern coast of Africa?

2. In which direction would you travel to go from the Tibesti Mountains to Lake Victoria?

3. What major river runs to the east of the Libyan Desert?

THE GRASSY PLAINS

Grassy, tree-dotted plains called savannas cover a large area of Africa. This area is about the size of the entire United States. Savannas cover most of southern Africa and the region between Ethiopia and Senegal.

The savannas have a dry season and a rainy season. During the dry season, savanna grasses turn brown and the ground dries and cracks. This quickly changes, though, when the rainy season arrives. Author Bessie Head describes the effect of rain on the savanna of Botswana, in southern Africa.

Before the first rains fall, it gets so hot that you cannot breathe. Then one day the sky just empties itself in a terrible downpour. After this, the earth and sky [come] alive and there is magic everywhere. . . . With just a little rain everything comes alive all at once; over-eager and hungry. . . . Crickets and frogs appear overnight in the pools around the village: there is a heavy, rich smell of breathing earth everywhere.

New grass and leaves sprout up across the savanna, providing a welcome feast for antelopes, zebras, and giraffes. The rains also bring needed water for crops and domestic animals.

Early Farmers

Africans began farming the savanna about 4,000 years ago. They domesticated grains called millet and sorghum (SAWR gum). These grains grew well in the thin, dry soil of the savannas. Both crops grew so quickly that they were ready for harvest before the dry season set in. Best of all, millet and sorghum contain vitamins, protein, and other nutrients needed for a healthy diet.

Modern equipment is used to harvest wheat on Kenya's savanna. Zambian women grind grain traditionally.

AFRICA AT A GLANCE

Total Land Area	11,704,000 sq. miles 30,312,999 sq. km
Highest Mountain	Mt. Kilimanjaro, Tanzania 19,340 feet (5,895 m)
Longest River	Nile River 4,160 miles 6,671 km
Largest City	Cairo, Egypt Population 6,052,832
Current Population	706,000,000
Percent of World Population	13%

GEO FACT
More than half of Africa receives less than 20 inches (51 cm) of rain each year. In parts of the Sahara and Namib deserts, rain may not fall for six or seven years in a row. On the other hand, the rain forests of the Congo River Basin and the coastal region of western Africa receive more than 80 inches (203 cm) of rain each year.

CHART WORK

Africa is a continent of contrasts.

1. What, according to the chart, is one of Africa's greatest contrasts?

2. Which is Africa's longest river? How long is it?

These crops—along with okra, peas, and other vegetables—became the fuel for growing civilizations throughout Africa. The crops remain important today.

People and the Environment

In ancient times farmers set fire to the savannas and nearby areas to clear the land for farming or to make room for the growth of new grass for the herds. New grasses caused savannas to spread. Many historians believe that grasslands now ripple where forests once stood.

WHY IT MATTERS

The landforms of Africa are vast and varied. So are the continent's climate and bodies of water. All of these factors have affected the way Africans have lived. Ancient Africans farmed on the savannas. So do many Africans today.

Many people have worked to preserve and protect these important regions. Some savannas have become protected areas on which thousands of wild animals roam and feed.

You have learned how farming traditions shaped Africa's environment. In the next lesson you will read about a civilization that created unique religious legacies in a rocky environment.

Reviewing Facts and Ideas

SUM IT UP

- Africa's many climate regions range from the snow-covered top of Mount Kilimanjaro to the Sahara, the world's largest desert.

- Savannas cover much of southern Africa and are home to wildlife.

- Farmers began growing millet and sorghum about 4,000 years ago.

THINK ABOUT IT

1. What parts of Africa have hills and mountains?

2. What is the Sahel? Where is this region located?

3. **FOCUS** How have Africa's savannas shaped the lives of the people who have lived on them? How have people affected the savannas?

4. **THINKING SKILL** What are some *effects* of rainfall on the savanna?

5. **GEOGRAPHY** In what ways do people interact with the savanna environment in Africa?

THE KINGDOMS OF ETHIOPIA

READ ALOUD

It began with a cliff some four stories high. From the hard red stone, workers carved out a massive block. The carvers then hollowed out the block and gave it windows and doors. They carved elegant arches, columns, and designs into the rock. The stone cliff slowly turned into a beautiful church. Such carving took place in the 1200s, in the highlands of Ethiopia.

THE BIG PICTURE

While castles and churches were being built in Europe during its Middle Ages, communities and kingdoms in Africa flourished as well. One of them developed a rich culture in northeastern Africa, near the tip of the Arabian peninsula.

In Chapter 4 you read that the Egyptian pharaoh Hatshepsut sent trading ships to the wealthy kingdom of Punt. Punt may have been located in the present-day country of Ethiopia. You also read that ancient Egypt's army conquered Kush, located in what is now Sudan. Egypt, Punt, and Kush were just three of the early civilizations of northeastern Africa. In this lesson you will read about other kingdoms that developed there.

This painting of apostles is in a stone church in Ethiopia.

Focus Activity

READ TO LEARN
How did kingdoms develop in what is today Ethiopia?

PEOPLE
Queen Amanishakhete
Lalibela

PLACES
Ethiopia
Kush
Aksum

CIVILIZATIONS IN NORTHEASTERN AFRICA

When Egyptian civilization declined, Kush became an independent kingdom. Kushite kings based their government at Meroe (MER oo ee), a city along the banks of the Nile.

The Kingdom of Kush

From about 500 B.C. to A.D. 150, Kush's rulers controlled a large trade network. This network stretched east to Arabia, north to the Mediterranean, and southwest toward the center of Africa.

Meroe's ruins give some clues to what life in Kush was like. There are remains of grand palaces, temples, and pyramid-shaped tombs. These remains show Kush's rulers had great wealth. Some of that wealth was found inside the tomb of Queen Amanishakhete (ah mahn uh SHAHK huh tee).

Queen Amanishakhete ruled Kush around 27 B.C. Archaeologists found gold bracelets, chains, rings, and statues within her tomb. The large amount of gold found in the tomb shows the richness of the Kush kingdom. The jewelry's beauty shows the skill of Kush's craftworkers.

The Kingdom of Aksum

By A.D. 350 the kingdom of Kush and its capital city had weakened. Historians are uncertain about the events that led to the decline of Kush. They know that Kush was conquered in 350 by Aksum, a powerful kingdom to the southeast.

Aksum was located high in the hills and mountains of what are today Eritrea and Ethiopia. Find Aksum on the map. Like Meroe, Aksum gained power and wealth by controlling important cities and trade routes. Traders traveled to the port city of Adula on the Red Sea.

There ships unloaded treasures from Arabia, Egypt, and India. People bought goods with gold coins or ivory.

Christianity in Africa

Many of Aksum's coins were stamped with signs of the Christian cross. Aksum's rulers became supporters of Christianity around A.D. 300. This early date makes ancient Ethiopia's Christian Church among the oldest in the world.

Christians in Ethiopia developed some beliefs that differed from those of Christians in Rome. For example, Ethiopians did not look to the Pope as their religious leader. Instead, Christians in Ethiopia follow a leader called a patriarch (PAY tree ark). Today nearly half of all Ethiopians are Christians.

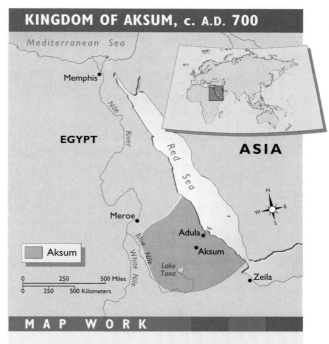

KINGDOM OF AKSUM, c. A.D. 700

Mediterranean Sea

Memphis

EGYPT

Nile River

Red Sea

ASIA

Meroe

Adula

Aksum

Blue Nile

White Nile

Lake Tana

Zeila

Aksum

0   250   500 Miles
0   250   500 Kilometers

MAP WORK

Trade thrived in cities within the kingdom of Aksum. Many traders crossed the Red Sea.

1. In which direction did Aksum's traders travel to reach the Red Sea?
2. About how far was Meroe from Adula?
3. Which rivers flowed along the western edge of Aksum?

A NEW KINGDOM

Aksum's trading success came to an end around A.D. 700. The kingdom suffered when the growing Baghdad caliphate took control of all shipping on the Red Sea. The loss of this important source of trade and wealth caused Aksum's economy to weaken. Bronze coins began to replace the more valuable gold coins. Around A.D. 900 Aksum stopped making coins altogether. By that time, the capital of the kingdom had been moved to more fertile lands farther south. Then Aksum's rulers were overthrown by local nobles called the Zagwe (ZAHG we).

Churches Carved in Rock

The Zagwe nobles, like the rulers of Aksum, supported Christianity. The most powerful Zagwe king, Lalibela (LAH lee be lah), ruled Ethiopia from about 1185 to 1225. During his rule, workers carved 11 stone churches in Ethiopia's new capital city. The city was named Lalibela to honor the king.

Day after day, year after year, people of the city probably heard sounds of clanging and chipping. Stoneworkers from as far away as Palestine and Egypt came to work on the projects. Their different languages must have been heard throughout the city.

Rock churches carved from huge pieces of stone still stand in Lalibela (left, below). Some of the services (far left) in Christian churches there and in other parts of Ethiopia follow traditions that developed under the Zagwe rulers.

Historians believe that each church in Lalibela was designed to look like a famous earlier church in Aksum. Some of the churches in Aksum had wooden beams jutting from the buildings. Lalibela's stonecutters carved out similar structures in stone. Since many of the churches were carved out of a single piece of stone, the stoneworkers had to be very careful. One slip of the chisel could result in a mistake that could not be corrected!

WHY IT MATTERS

The churches of Lalibela show the importance of Christianity in ancient Ethiopia. They also brought fame and honor to their builder, Lalibela. While little is known about the Zagwe kingdom, the stone churches have provided clues about the people of Zagwe.

The Zagwe kingdom of Ethiopia was only one of many that developed in Africa. In the next lesson you will read about a rich and powerful empire in western Africa. It grew at about the same time as the Zagwe kingdom.

✓ Reviewing Facts and Ideas

SUM IT UP

- Between 500 B.C. and A.D. 150, Kush grew wealthy from trade across the Mediterranean, in Arabia, and farther south in Africa.

- In A.D. 350 Kush was conquered by Aksum, a powerful trading state to the south. Christianity took root in Africa around this time.

- After 1100, Zagwe kings such as Lalibela created stone churches.

THINK ABOUT IT

1. How were Kush and Aksum similar? Describe one way in which the kingdoms were different.

2. Why were the churches of Lalibela so unusual and difficult to build?

3. **FOCUS** How was trade important to civilizations in ancient Ethiopia?

4. **THINKING SKILL** What _effects_ did the loss of Red Sea trade have on the kingdom of Aksum?

5. **WRITE** Write a short paragraph explaining what the artifacts in the tomb of Queen Amanishakhete reveal about Kush civilization.

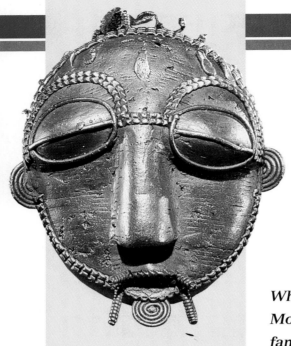

EMPIRES OF WEST AFRICA

Focus Activity

READ TO LEARN
What resources helped the empires of West Africa to grow wealthy and powerful?

VOCABULARY
supply
demand
griot

PEOPLE
Sunjata
Mansa Musa

PLACES
Ghana
Mali
Timbuktu
Songhai
Morocco

READ ALOUD

What did jewelry and coins from such places as Morocco, Spain, and the storage rooms of the Medici family in Florence have in common? The answer is African gold. From 900 to 1500 most gold in western Asia and Europe came from the rich mines of West Africa. The resources from these mines would shape life throughout the Eastern Hemisphere—most of all in Africa—for hundreds of years.

THE BIG PICTURE

As new kingdoms grew in northeastern Africa, other civilizations developed on the savannas of western Africa. These civilizations flourished while Baghdad's caliphs ruled a vast area in western Asia and northern Africa. At the same time, the Renaissance and Reformation swept through Europe.

As you read in Lesson 1 of this chapter, the savannas were a challenging environment for raising crops. Farmers could usually raise the sorghum, millet, and other crops that people needed for food. They could not, however, grow a very important item—salt. Salt was important because it could be used to prevent food from spoiling in warm climates. In parts of western Africa, salt actually became worth its weight in gold! Gold was another important item in West Africa. Much gold was bought and sold in the region's trade centers. Trade routes grew because of the need for salt and gold. These trade routes linked the empires of West Africa with the rest of Africa, Asia, and Europe.

In the Ghana empire, people sold salt in solid blocks. In some African towns, salt is still sold in the same way (left). Other trade goods included spoons, boxes to hold gold dust, and shells (below).

GHANA: AN EARLY EMPIRE

By the 700s the empire of Ghana was already a major power in Africa. Ghana was located at the southwestern edge of the Sahara, between the Senegal and Niger rivers.

The "Land of Gold"

In the 700s Muslim traders from northern Africa first began arriving in Ghana. What they saw amazed them. One trader, named al-Bakri, described the king's court in Ghana's capital city, Kumbi Salei (KOOM bee sah LEH).

Behind the king stand ten helpers holding shields and swords decorated with gold; and on his right are the sons of his vassal kings, wearing splendid garments and with gold woven in their hair. At the door of the pavilion are dogs guarding him. Round their necks they wear collars of gold and silver.

Ghana's merchants were allowed to handle only gold dust. Nuggets of gold were kept by the king. Al-Bakri explained the reason for this practice. If all of Ghana's gold was allowed into the marketplace, he wrote, "the people would [collect] gold until it lost its value."

By keeping gold scarce, Ghana's kings followed an important rule of economics called supply and demand. Supply is a quantity of some good, product, or resource. Demand is people's desire for that particular item. According to the rule of supply and demand, items that are plentiful in supply do not have high value—because they are easy to get. Items that are scarce, however, are high in value—because they are *not* easy to get. By keeping gold scarce, Ghana's kings kept its demand—and price—high.

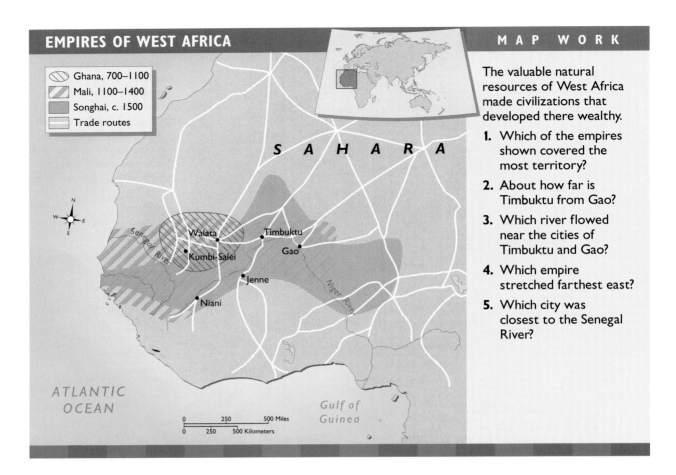

Ghana, 700–1100
Mali, 1100–1400
Songhai, c. 1500
Trade routes

S A H A R A

Walata
Kumbi-Salei
Timbuktu
Gao
Jenne
Niani
Senegal River
Niger River

ATLANTIC OCEAN

Gulf of Guinea

0   250   500 Miles
0   250   500 Kilometers

The valuable natural resources of West Africa made civilizations that developed there wealthy.

1. Which of the empires shown covered the most territory?

2. About how far is Timbuktu from Gao?

3. Which river flowed near the cities of Timbuktu and Gao?

4. Which empire stretched farthest east?

5. Which city was closest to the Senegal River?

THE RISE OF MALI

Ghana's kings controlled western Africa's gold supply for over 500 years. Eventually, though, other empires began challenging Ghana's power. According to traditional African stories, all but one prince in an empire called Mali (MAH lee) were killed.

Sunjata (sahn JAH tah) was spared because he was disabled and seemed harmless. The stories say that Mali's enemies, including Ghana, made a deadly mistake by misjudging Sunjata. He conquered his old enemies and all of Ghana as well. Sunjata died in 1255, but Mali continued to grow after his death. Look at the map to see how large Mali was at its peak in the 1300s.

From Mine to Market

Like Ghana, Mali grew very rich by controlling the gold trade. In the 1300s gold became more valuable than ever. Gold was mined in tunnels and pits throughout western Africa. Miners dug dirt and rock out of the ground.

Women sifted the gold dust. Grains they found were then poured into hollow feather quills or other containers and transported to Mali's market cities.

One of these cities was Timbuktu (tim buk TOO). It was located at a crossroads of major trade routes, near the Niger River. Timbuktu also bordered the Sahara and was a final stop for caravan routes that crossed the desert.

In Timbuktu's busy markets, farmers sold vegetables and grains. Some bargained over the price of gold, salt, and North African horses. Other traders settled the price of enslaved prisoners. Most of the enslaved people would be taken to Europe and Northern Africa.

Infographic

Timbuktu

Timbuktu grew as a trading center near the great bend of the Niger River. Located at the end of Arab trade routes that crossed the Sahara, Timbuktu was the site of much cultural exchange during the Mali and Songhai empires. How did cultural influences combine in Timbuktu?

Religion

Arab Muslims brought Islam to West Africa. The Sankore Mosque was built in 1325 while Mansa Musa ruled Mali.

Trade

The trade that flourished between Africans and Arabs continues in Timbuktu today. While salt remains a popular item, many other goods are also bought and sold.

Architecture

This 1830 watercolor shows how both Arab and African building styles were used in Timbuktu. Traditional African buildings are rounded and Arab-style structures are square.

LIFE IN THE EMPIRES

In the early 1300s the best horses and goods were bought by a Mali king called **Mansa Musa**. During Mansa Musa's reign, from 1312 to 1337, Mali was at its peak of wealth and power. Mansa Musa ruled with great authority. Nevertheless, he recognized at least one power as being greater than himself: Allah. The religion of Islam had been spreading throughout western Africa ever since the first Muslim traders arrived there in the 700s.

In 1324 Mansa Musa fulfilled one of the Five Pillars of Islam. He made a pilgrimage to Mecca. During the year-long journey, the king gave away gifts of gold to rich and poor people alike. How does the following excerpt, by a northern African writer, reflect Mansa Musa's power?

From the writings of Al-'Umari, about 1337-1338.

*W*hen the king of this kingdom comes in from a journey an [umbrella] and a **standard** are held over his head as he rides, and drums are beaten and guitars and trumpets well made of horn are played in front of him.... When one whom the king has charged with a task or assignment returns to him he questions him in detail about everything which has happened to him from the moment of his departure until his return. Complaints and appeals against **administrative oppression** are placed before this king and he delivers judgment on them himself. As a rule nothing is written down; his commands are given **verbally**.

standard: flag
administrative: governmental
oppression: unjust power
verbally: by speaking

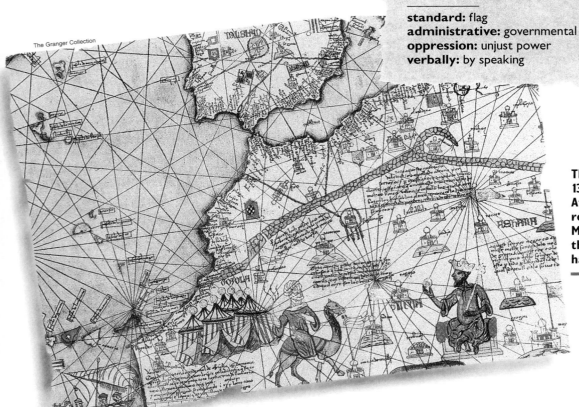

The Granger Collection

This map made in 1375 shows West African trade routes. Find Mansa Musa in the bottom right-hand corner.

This figure of an archer from Mali was found near the Niger River.

The Songhai Empire

As Mansa Musa ruled Mali, a small eastern territory called Songhai (SOHNG hi) was growing strong. In the next 150 years, Songhai rose to take Mali's place as the most powerful empire in western Africa. The empire of Songhai lasted from about 1490 until 1590.

Like the kings of Ghana and Mali, Songhai kings were all-powerful rulers. Among the most important assistants to the kings were griots (GREE ohs). Griots are people who tell stories that describe historical events. Such stories are told again and again so people can learn about the past. Kings also made use of scribes. Scribes wrote official documents in Arabic.

WHY IT MATTERS

In 1591 the Songhai empire collapsed when it was attacked by an army from the north. This army used guns against the arrows and spears of the Songhai empire. The army came from the African country of Morocco. Morocco had long had trading ties with West Africa. Its leader wanted to gain complete control of this trade and perhaps of the gold mines as well.

The great demand for gold affected life for many people in West Africa. Gold played a part in the lives of the miners who recovered it, the traders

who brought it to market, and the kings who used it to bring glory to their rule. Africa's gold was also in demand in Europe. Gold coins in Venice and Florence helped pay for the great art projects of the European Renaissance.

The empires of western Africa were not the only civilizations to spread African wealth to far-off places. In the next lesson you will read about busy port cities on the continent's east coast. Those cities had contact with places as far away as China.

✓/ Reviewing Facts and Ideas

SUM IT UP

- The empire of Ghana lasted from before 700 until around 1200. It was nicknamed the "land of gold."
  - The empire of Mali ruled from about 1240 to 1400. Timbuktu became a major center of trade.
- Mansa Musa ruled Mali between 1312 and 1337. Islam spread in West Africa during this time.
- The empire of Songhai lasted from about 1490 to 1590. Oral historians, or griots, and scribes kept records of events in the empire.

THINK ABOUT IT

1. What did Sunjata do to build the empire of Mali?

2. How were griots and scribes important to rulers of the Songhai empire?

3. **FOCUS** What role did the gold trade play in West Africa's empires?

4. **THINKING SKILL** Explain the *effects* produced when Ghana's kings kept gold scarce in the marketplace.

5. **GEOGRAPHY** How might the Niger River have been important for trade in West Africa?

GRIOTS
AND ORAL HISTORY

During the time when empires ruled West Africa, griots told stories and sang songs for traders, villagers, and kings alike. These special stories and songs described the history, beliefs, and traditions of African families and of the land. They became the oral history, or spoken record of events, of Africa.

Because many people could not read a written language, they depended upon the spoken words of the griots. African kings depended on griots to help keep people informed about happenings in the empire. In time the singing and speaking skills of the griots became an important West African legacy.

That legacy continues today. Modern griots tell African history and traditions to people around the world. Some have become teachers and historians. Others perform before audiences in order to entertain as well as educate.

Griots in ancient Africa told stories that taught people their history. Griots often know hundreds of events by heart.

Some griots travel around the world telling the stories of their cultures. Many wear traditional clothing styles that griots have worn in Africa for more than 700 years.

The griot uses a *kora* during his performance. A kora is a hand-crafted instrument that is traditionally used by griots. Each year thousands of people attend performances in which griots tell stories about history, cultural traditions, and current events.

369

GEOGRAPHYSKILLS

Reading Distribution Maps

VOCABULARY
distribution map
population density

WHY THE SKILL MATTERS

In the last lesson you learned that West Africa's earliest known empires developed between the Senegal and Niger rivers. Some 25,000 people lived in Timbuktu, making it one of the region's biggest cities. Thousands more lived in the towns and villages that developed on the nearby savannas and in forests.

Today much has changed in western Africa. The region's population as a whole has grown. So has the Sahara Desert, partly as a result of human interaction with the environment. The once-productive heartland of Ghana's empire, for example, is now part of the desert.

Looking at a distribution map can help you see how such changes have affected where people live in Africa today. A distribution map is a special purpose map. It shows how one particular feature is spread over an area. The maps on these pages show current population density in Africa. Population density is the number of people living in a given amount of space. Distribution maps can also show such features as climate, land use or products, or the languages that are spoken in an area.

Traders bargain at a busy market in Burundi.

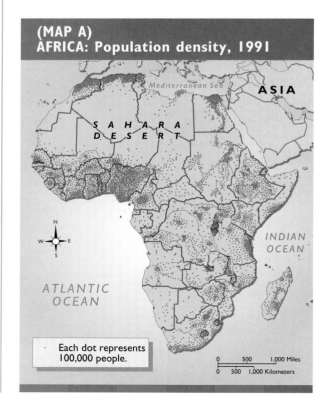

(MAP A)
AFRICA: Population density, 1991

Mediterranean Sea

ASIA

SAHARA DESERT

ATLANTIC OCEAN

INDIAN OCEAN

Each dot represents 100,000 people.

0   500   1,000 Miles
0   500   1,000 Kilometers

USING THE SKILL

Study Map A. The title tells you that the map provides information about population density in Africa. The map key shows that each dot on the map represents 100,000 people. The closer together the dots, the more dense is the population. The more spread out and fewer the dots, the less dense is the population. The great bend of the Niger River is one of the most populated areas in West Africa. This is shown by the large number of dots in that area.

TRYING THE SKILL

Distribution Map B on this page shows the population density of the continent of Africa in another way. How many people per square mile live near the coast of present-

day Ghana? How many people per square mile live near the Nile River delta?

REVIEWING THE SKILL

Use the map on this page to answer the following questions:

1. How do you know this is a distribution map?

2. Which city has more people, Nairobi or the western coastal city of Abidjan?

3. Which region has a higher population density today, the Sahara Desert or eastern lands along the coast of the Indian Ocean? How do you know?

4. What kind of distribution map could help you to better understand life in your own community?

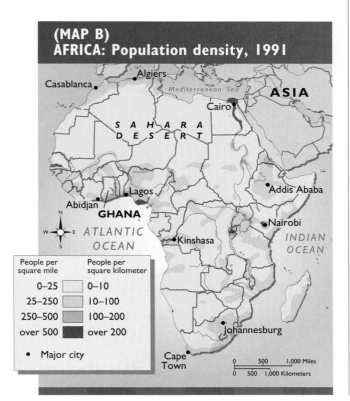

(MAP B)
AFRICA: Population density, 1991

People per square mile	People per square kilometer
0–25	0–10
25–250	10–100
250–500	100–200
over 500	over 200

• Major city

About 1.2 million people live in Harare, Zimbabwe's capital.

AFRICA'S EASTERN COAST

READ ALOUD

The king of the city of Kilwa had a palace with over 100 rooms and a maze of courtyards. He even had an eight-sided pool built into a cliff overlooking the blue waters of the Indian Ocean. The immense palace was just a small part of the great wealth in eastern Africa during the 1300s. That wealth was the result of trade.

THE BIG PICTURE

Before A.D. 1100 the kingdom of Ghana was at its peak. Another powerful African civilization was growing some 2,500 miles to the east of Ghana. Actually, this civilization's villages, towns, and cities were closer to the Indus River valley of Asia than they were to the Niger River of western Africa. Yet the African civilizations had important things in common. For example, their many languages were rooted in an ancient language called Bantu. Both civilizations also profited from trade within Africa and with other continents.

In the last lesson you read that West African gold was transported to northern Africa and Europe. There it was made into coins. In eastern Africa, gold was shipped to cities in Arabia, India, and China. So were elephant tusks, which are the material called ivory.

Focus Activity

READ TO LEARN
What was life like in the trading cities along the coast of the Indian Ocean?

PLACES
Mombasa
Zanzibar
Mogadishu

Ivory from East Africa was used to make this jeweled lion. It was worn on the arm.

372

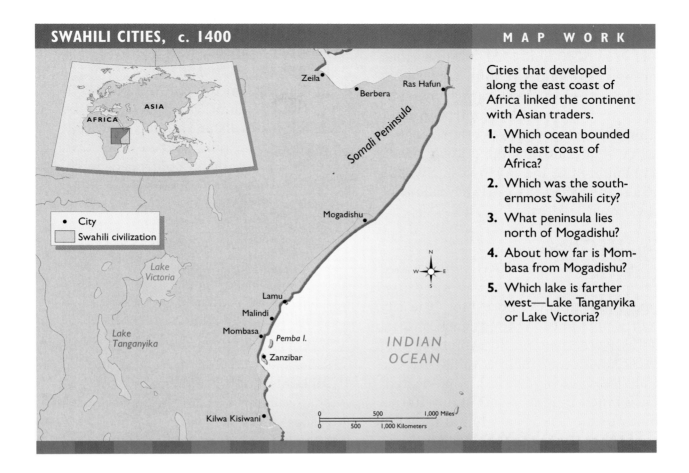

Zeila

Berbera

Ras Hafun

ASIA

AFRICA

Somali Peninsula

- City
- Swahili civilization

Lake Victoria

Mogadishu

Lake Tanganyika

Lamu

Malindi

Mombasa

Pemba I.

Zanzibar

INDIAN OCEAN

N W E S

Kilwa Kisiwani

0 500 1,000 Miles
0 500 1,000 Kilometers

Cities that developed along the east coast of Africa linked the continent with Asian traders.

1. Which ocean bounded the east coast of Africa?

2. Which was the southernmost Swahili city?

3. What peninsula lies north of Mogadishu?

4. About how far is Mombasa from Mogadishu?

5. Which lake is farther west—Lake Tanganyika or Lake Victoria?

TRADE ALONG THE INDIAN OCEAN

The coastal cities of eastern Africa linked Africa to Asia. For hundreds of years, boats loaded with trade goods sailed the Indian Ocean. In the coastal cities, merchant-sailors from Asia eagerly bought African goods.

Many of the goods were brought from further inland. These goods included gold, leopard skins, rhinoceros horns, and ivory. Demand for East African ivory in Asia was high. This ivory was softer and easier to carve than West African ivory. Arabian craftworkers made chess pieces from ivory. Chinese used it to make beautiful artwork and containers.

In the coastal markets, African merchants were able to buy goods from Asia and other places. Metal tools, fine pottery, cloth, glass containers, and wheat were in great demand in the coastal cities of Africa.

The "People of the Shore"

Over time, some of the foreign merchants settled in Africa's eastern coastal cities. Many were Arab Muslims. They made important contributions to the civilization that became known as Swahili. *Swahili* means "people of the shore" in Arabic. Many Arabic words also became part of the Swahili language. Settlers from Arabia also shared the traditions of Islam with the Swahili people. Islam became an important religious heritage for many Africans in the busy port cities that developed on the east coast.

LIFE ALONG THE COAST

Between 1000 and 1500, Swahili cities grew in size and strength. Like the trading cities of West Africa, Swahili cities grew when they controlled important trade routes. Cities often declined when that control slipped away. Unlike the empires to the northwest, Swahili cities and villages were each ruled by their own leaders.

Swahili Cities

Mombasa (mom BAH suh), located on an island of present-day Kenya, was one important trading center. The city had a port and crowded markets. Many ships were attracted to Mombasa each season. Another main Swahili city, Zanzibar (ZAN zuh bar), was located on a much bigger island about 100 miles to the south, in what is today the country of Tanzania (tan zuh NEE uh).

Mogadishu (mohg uh DISH oo), in present-day Somalia, was one of the largest of the coastal cities. Find Mogadishu on the map on page 373.

The people of Mogadishu lived by farming and fishing. Some used sailboats to transport gold to other trading centers. Mogadishu controlled much of Africa's gold trade from about 1000 to 1300. On days when the wind was still, the sailors sang songs. They often sang this one as they worked.

> *Plunge in the paddles,*
> *Plunge in the paddles,*
> *If the sail is against the mast,*
> *Plunge in the paddles.*

For much of the year Mogadishu's sailors shared their port with the larger sailboats that brought cargo and merchants from Asia. In the city's marketplaces, foreign merchants bought load after load of ivory, gold, and leopard

Sculpted elephant tusks arch over a main street in Mombasa, Kenya (above). The illustration (left) shows Mombasa during the 1300s.

skins. They also purchased tortoise shells, tools, and glass.

WHY IT MATTERS

Today some important legacies of early Swahili civilization remain in the countries of East Africa. Swahili has become the common language of Tanzania, Kenya, Zaire, and Uganda. Old Swahili ports such as Mombasa and Zanzibar still ship goods around the globe.

Once-powerful cities like Mombasa, however, are not as strong as they were long ago. The decline of these cities was a result of conflicts that broke out in the 1500s. These conflicts took place between Swahilis and newcomers to eastern Africa. You will read in Chapter 16 about how those newcomers came to explore Africa's east coast.

DID YOU KNOW?

What trade good from Zanzibar is commonly in demand today?

In the 1400s Zanzibar was known for its ivory, tortoise shells, and other goods. Today Zanzibar is the world's largest producer of tiny flowers from a special kind of evergreen tree. The unopened buds of these flowers are dried, then sold to buyers across the world. After being shipped and packaged, some of these buds eventually make their way into the spice sections of your local grocery stores. You will find them under the name "cloves." Cloves are used as spice in cooking.

✓✓ Reviewing Facts and Ideas

SUM IT UP

- Many eastern African coastal cities grew as a result of trade with Asian countries across the Indian Ocean.

- The coastal cities of Mogadishu, Mombasa, and Zanzibar were enriched by trade in ivory and gold.

- Eastern Africa's earliest Arab settlers contributed to Swahili civilization in the areas of language and religion.

- Swahili cities flourished mainly between 1000 and 1500, when a period of conflict began.

THINK ABOUT IT

1. Why was eastern African ivory a valuable trade item? What other items were traded in the coastal cities?

2. In what ways did Muslim Arabs who settled on Africa's eastern coast contribute to Swahili culture? Describe an important legacy of the Swahili civilization.

3. **FOCUS** How did life in Mogadishu reflect the importance of trade in Swahili cities?

4. **THINKING SKILL** Name one major *cause* for the settlement of Arabs in eastern Africa. Describe two *effects* of their settlement there.

5. **GEOGRAPHY** In what ways did the people of Africa's coastal cities interact with their environment?

GREAT ZIMBABWE

READ ALOUD

Around 1400 a powerful city surrounded by stone walls was located in a hilly region south of the Zambezi River. The city had covered passages that led through different sections within the walls.

One section of the city was once known as "the house of the great woman" by later neighbors. Who was that woman? What role did she play in the city? So far, the answers to those questions have remained unknown. They are just a few of the unsolved mysteries that surround the southern African civilization known as Great Zimbabwe.

THE BIG PICTURE

In the last lesson you read about wealthy cities that developed along the eastern African coast. These cities grew rich from trade in ivory, gold, and other goods. Much of the gold came from inland mines to the west, in present-day Zimbabwe.

Farming and herding villages had existed here for hundreds of years. Over time historians believe one village won control over the region's gold trade. During the 1300s this community grew in power.

Historians know very little about this community. Its people left behind no oral traditions or written documents. Historians are even unsure about the meaning of its name: Great Zimbabwe. In the Shona language, *Zimbabwe* can mean either "houses of stone" or "honored houses." By closely examining artifacts left by the peoples of Great Zimbabwe, however, archaeologists and historians have learned something about this community.

Focus Activity

READ TO LEARN
What effects did the growth of Great Zimbabwe have on southern Africa?

PLACES
Great Zimbabwe
Sofala

THE PEOPLE OF GREAT ZIMBABWE

Between bare granite hills and rolling, tree-filled savannas are the ruins of Great Zimbabwe. Early farmers and herders made use of the region's fertile areas. Farmers raised crops year after year. Herds of cattle, sheep, and goats lived on nearby savannas.

People built their villages and cities near these areas. Craftworkers made jugs and other containers from clay. These pieces of pottery helped people cook, carry water, and collect grains. Pottery fragments in the area show that the community of Great Zimbabwe grew between about 1000 and 1500. During that time people built houses with walls that were made of mud. Archaeologists have found holes that held the main poles of the houses. They have also found the remains of thick stone walls. The walls, they say, were built around the city in the 1300s. What life was like within those walls, though, is a mystery.

Walls of Stone

For the people of Great Zimbabwe, of course, the stone walls and buildings of their city were not new and different. In fact, in southern Africa at the time, over 100 other stone towns are known to have existed. The walls of Great Zimbabwe, however, were by far the biggest. Many historians believe that trade helped make the construction of these walls possible. Who was responsible for building the walls around the growing city?

Great Zimbabwe's kings probably ordered workers to make the city's walls. To do this, stoneworkers used a material that was very close at hand. They used huge granite rocks that lay in and around the city to build the walls. Many of these rocks were larger than several homes put together. Workers heated sheets of the stone, then cracked them into pieces that had straight edges. Next they cut the stones into brick-sized pieces. The work was hard. Workers stacked the granite bricks to form walls as high as 30 feet. The heavy weight of the stones held the walls in place.

This carved bird was found in an area used for ceremonies.

GREAT ZIMBABWE, c. 1400

Great Zimbabwe

AFRICA

Lake Nyasa

Zambezi River

Sofala

Madagascar

KALAHARI DESERT

Phalaborwa

INDIAN OCEAN

0   300   600 Miles
0   300   600 Kilometers

MAP WORK

Great Zimbabwe was located in a fertile area that was rich in natural building materials.

1. Great Zimbabwe was located east of which desert?

2. Which river flowed to the north of Great Zimbabwe?

3. About how many miles did traders from Great Zimbabwe have to travel to reach the Indian Ocean?

THE CITY ON A HILL

Historians believe that most of the stone walls of Great Zimbabwe surrounded the large homes of the ruling families. Were the walls meant to keep something in—or out? The walls may have been built to keep the city safe from attack by other cities and villages. Or they may have given extra privacy to the lives of Great Zimbabwe's leaders. Maybe the walls reflected their great power in the community. There is no way to know for certain. Historians can only guess at what their lives may have been like. It is likely, however, that many of these ruling families became powerful by trading gold.

Controlling the Gold Trade

Some of southern Africa's richest gold fields are located around Great Zimbabwe. Sometime in the 1300s Great Zimbabwe began to trade with an important Swahili coastal city called Sofala. Miners probably worked hard to increase the gold supply that was brought to Sofala. They probably brought gold from the mines back to Great Zimbabwe. There, workers used a special furnace to melt the gold. Melted gold then was reshaped for shipment.

Great Zimbabwe's powerful families grew wealthy from the increase in the flow of gold among the mines, the city, and Sofala. Artifacts show that they used some of their new wealth to buy loads of glass beads, cloth, and pottery from China and Persia.

Most people, however, still used locally made pottery to carry water or for cooking. Metalworkers in the city coiled gold wire into bracelets for their customers. The people who lived in Great Zimbabwe liked to wear the gold and beaded jewelry they created. The city's metalworkers also made iron hoes and axes for farmers. Farmers used those tools to raise millet and sorghum at the edges of Great Zimbabwe. Those grains, along with milk and meat, were important items in the daily diet of the city's residents. During the period in which Great Zimbabwe thrived in the

Great Zimbabwe (above) was a main trading center for 400 years. Today Harare (left) is the business center in the country of Zimbabwe.

early 1400s, about 18,000 people lived in the community. This meant that farmers and herders worked hard to provide food for the people of the walled city.

For reasons unknown to historians, Great Zimbabwe began to decline in the late 1400s. Most of its residents left and moved to other regions. Did too much farming wear out the land around the city and create hardship? Did some natural catastrophe happen? Archaeologists and historians are working to learn more about Great Zimbabwe. Even so, they may never be able to answer these questions.

WHY IT MATTERS

Events after Great Zimbabwe was abandoned are not such a mystery. In the late 1490s a small European ship sailed past Sofala. It was the first one ever to do so. In its wake would come many changes for all of Africa.

Meanwhile, a new group of peoples began to farm and trade in southern Africa. Today these distant relatives of the people of Great Zimbabwe continue to live in Zimbabwe, the country that is named after the ancient city.

✓/ Reviewing Facts and Ideas

SUM IT UP

- Information about Great Zimbabwe is limited due to a lack of oral traditions and written documents.
- The city thrived in the 1300s and 1400s, due in part to its control of local gold trade routes.
- Great Zimbabwe's trade in gold tied it to Swahili cities and to Asia.

THINK ABOUT IT

1. What purposes might the walls of Great Zimbabwe have served?

2. Why was the coastal city of Sofala important to the growth and strength of Great Zimbabwe?

3. **FOCUS** How did Great Zimbabwe's involvement in the gold trade affect life in the city?

4. **THINKING SKILL** Based on your reading, make a _conclusion_ about why Great Zimbabwe's wealthy families may have needed the protection of the stone walls. Explain how you made your conclusion.

5. **GEOGRAPHY** How did the people of Great Zimbabwe make use of raw materials when they built their city?

CHAPTER 13 REVIEW

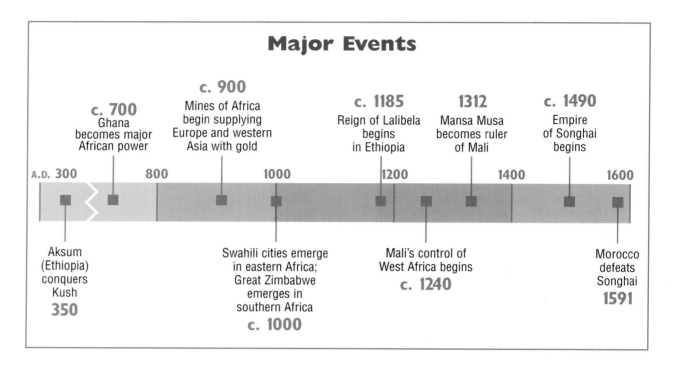

Major Events

c. 700
Ghana becomes major African power

c. 900
Mines of Africa begin supplying Europe and western Asia with gold

c. 1185
Reign of Lalibela begins in Ethiopia

1312
Mansa Musa becomes ruler of Mali

c. 1490
Empire of Songhai begins

A.D. 300   800   1000   1200   1400   1600

Aksum (Ethiopia) conquers Kush
350

Swahili cities emerge in eastern Africa; Great Zimbabwe emerges in southern Africa
c. 1000

Mali's control of West Africa begins
c. 1240

Morocco defeats Songhai
1591

THINKING ABOUT VOCABULARY

Number a sheet of paper from 1 to 5. Beside each number write the word that best matches the statement.

demand   savanna
griot   supply
Sahel

1. A grassy plain dotted with trees
2. The people's desire for an item or service
3. A quantity of available goods, products, or resources
4. The dry southern edge of the Sahara
5. A person who tells stories that describe historical events

THINKING ABOUT FACTS

1. What is the world's largest desert?
2. How long is the Great Rift Valley?
3. How much of Africa is covered by savannas? What is the weather like on the savannas?

4. What grains have Africans been growing on the savannas for 4,000 years?
5. How did the ancient kingdom of Kush become wealthy?
6. How long did the empire of Ghana last? What did Ghana's kings do to keep the value of gold high?
7. According to the time line above, when did Mansa Musa become ruler of Mali? What important change took place in West Africa about that time?
8. Name three important Swahili cities. What two important products did they trade with Asia?
9. What was Great Zimbabwe? Why don't we know more about it?
10. According to the time line above, how many years were there between Aksum's conquest of Kush and the beginning of the Songhai empire? Name three African states that arose during that time.

THINK AND WRITE

WRITING A DIARY
Suppose you are Queen Amanishakhete of Kush. Write a diary entry about some of the things you did today.

WRITING A TRAVEL BROCHURE
Imagine you are a travel agent who wants to interest people in Timbuktu. Write a brief brochure about the city's history so people will want to visit it.

WRITING A DESCRIPTION
Write a paragraph describing the Swahili civilization of eastern Africa. Include information about Swahili cities and about trade on the Indian Ocean.

APPLYING GEOGRAPHY SKILLS

READING DISTRIBUTION MAPS
1. What is a distribution map?
2. What information do the two distribution maps on pages 370 and 371 provide?
3. What other features might distribution maps of Africa and West Africa show?
4. Look at Map B on page 371. Which is more densely populated, Timbuktu or Accra?
5. Why is a distribution map useful?

Summing Up the Chapter

Copy the main idea map below on a separate sheet of paper. Then review the chapter and fill in information for each region. After you complete the diagram, write a paragraph that answers the question "What helped to make ancient Africa diverse?"

Ethiopian Kingdoms

Swahili Cities in East Africa

Civilization and Cultures Flourished in Sub-Saharan Africa

West African Empires

Southern Africa

CHAPTER 14

Empires and Cultures of Asia

THINKING ABOUT
HISTORY AND GEOGRAPHY

For centuries, Asia has been home to many civilizations. The time line and map show where some of them developed. Asian peoples between A.D. 1100 and A.D. 1650 used trade and military power to increase their influence. Many also constructed buildings that remain among the world's finest architectural achievements.

Constantinople

AFRICA

1100s	1279	1453
ANGKOR	**BEIJING**	**CONSTANTINOPLE**
Suryavarman II builds Angkor Wat	Kublai Khan conquers and unites China	Turks conquer the Byzantine empire

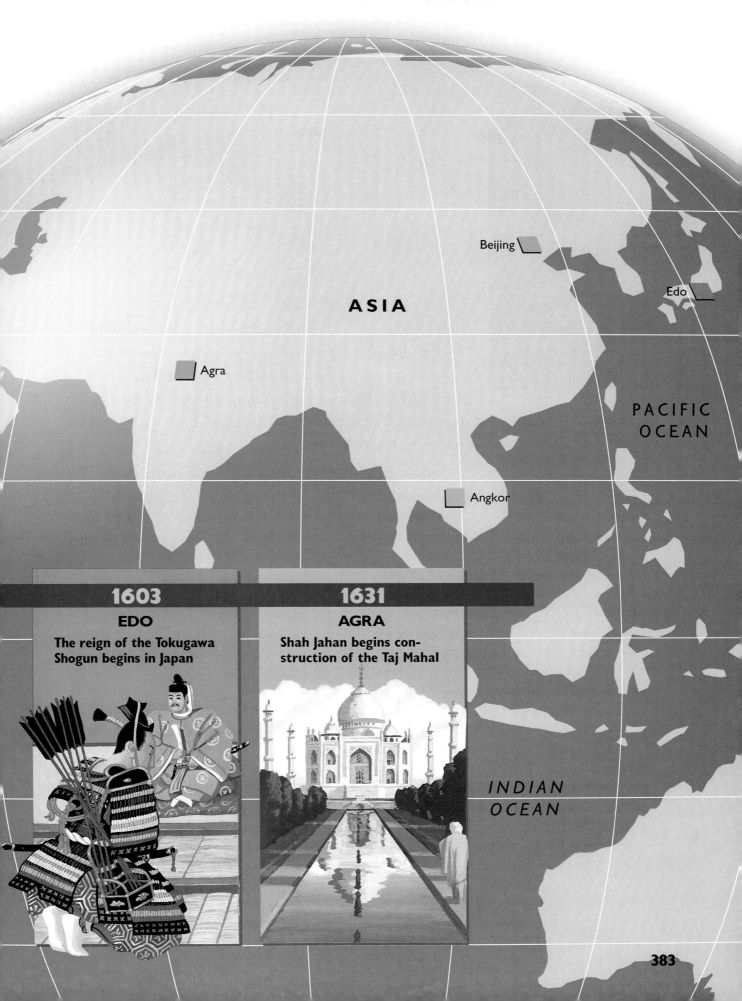

Beijing

Edo

ASIA

Agra

PACIFIC
OCEAN

Angkor

1603

EDO

**The reign of the Tokugawa
Shogun begins in Japan**

1631

AGRA

**Shah Jahan begins con-
struction of the Taj Mahal**

*INDIAN
OCEAN*

Focus Activity

READ TO LEARN
How do the Himalayas affect the geography of Asia?

VOCABULARY
archipelago
monsoon

PLACES
Himalayas
Mount Everest
Tibetan Plateau
Gobi Desert

GEOGRAPHY OF ASIA

READ ALOUD

"The summer sun, who robbed the pleasant nights, and plundered [stole] all the water of the rivers, and burned the earth, and scorched the forest trees, is now in hiding; and the autumn clouds, spread thick across the sky to track him down, hunt for the criminal with lightning flashes."

Indian poet Amaru, writing in Sanskrit, described India's yearly change of seasons over 1,000 years ago. This change is a big event for many people across Asia. Many, in fact, depend on it for their lives.

THE BIG PICTURE

Asia is the world's largest continent. It stretches from Saudi Arabia and Turkey in the west to the eastern parts of China and Japan. Asia has many regions. The continent is made up of areas called North, West, Central, South, Southeast, and East Asia. Each of these regions has a great variety of people and environments. Asia includes many climates, landforms, peoples, and histories. Some of the ancient Asian civilizations you have already read about include Harappa, Mesopotamia, and Shang China.

A thin strip of land in northeastern Egypt is considered Asia's border with Africa. The Ural mountains separate North Asia from Europe. Asia has more mountains than any other continent. It also has the highest mountains. Not surprisingly, mountains greatly affect life on the continent. You will read about the world's highest mountain range in this lesson.

ASIA

The **Himalayas** (him uh LAY uz) and neighboring mountains make up the heart of Asia. Many of the world's highest peaks are here, including the tallest of all—**Mount Everest**. The Himalayas form the southern border of the vast **Tibetan Plateau**. This plateau is a high mountain plain where more than a half dozen of the continent's powerful rivers begin. Locate the Tibetan Plateau and the Himalayas on the map below.

Asia has several island chains off its shores. One of these chains is Japan. Find it on the map. Japan forms an **archipelago** (ahr kuh PEL ih goh). *Archipelago* is the word for such a group or chain of islands.

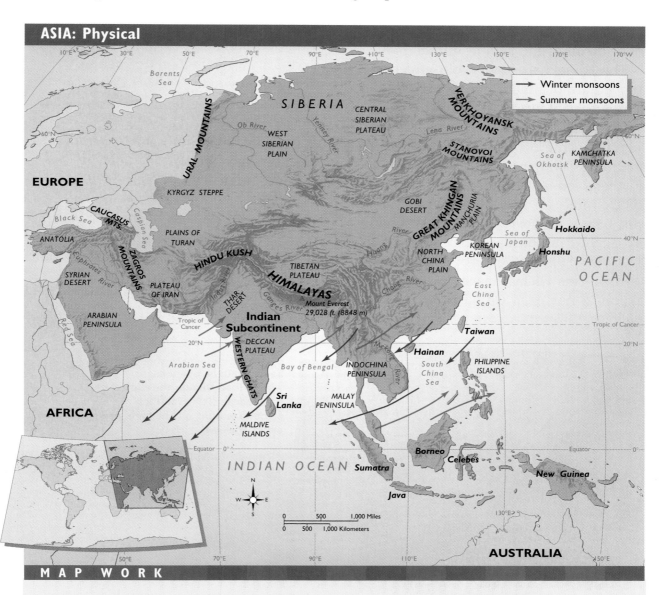

ASIA: Physical

Winter monsoons
Summer monsoons

MAP WORK

Asia is a land of extreme contrasts in geography. In addition to the highest mountains in the world, it has vast plains and deserts.

1. What mountain ranges border the Gobi Desert to the east and northeast?

2. What other deserts are in Asia?

3. What major river runs through the eastern part of the Indochina Peninsula?

A WALL OF MOUNTAINS

Himalaya means "snowy range" in Sanskrit. This vast range stretches across central Asia for 1,500 miles. Many of the peaks are over 25,000 feet high. Their immense heights form the world's highest natural wall.

The Himalayas and neighboring mountain ranges form a towering wall that divides India and Nepal from Tibet and China. The barrier makes movement through the region difficult.

The Himalayas have a big effect on the climate of much of Asia. They block clouds that blow north from the Indian Ocean. This causes large amounts of rainfall on the ocean-facing sides of the mountains and small amounts on their northern sides. In Cherrapunji, India, for example, an average of 38 feet of rain falls each year! By contrast, only a few inches fall on the other side, Tibet. Even less falls in the Gobi (GOH bee) Desert. This rocky, nearly treeless region in northern China is almost twice the size of Texas.

Monsoons

Plenty of rain is usually good news for Asia's many farmers. Throughout much of South Asia, though, most rain falls during only one season. The rest of the year remains dry. Rain clouds are brought to the region by seasonal winds called monsoons.

An Indian leader named Indira Gandhi once remarked, "for us in India scarcity [shortage of resources] is only a missed monsoon away." What she said is true for millions of people throughout Asia. Farmers count on the monsoons to bring water for their crops.

In India the months of November through May remain dry and, toward the end, intensely hot. During these months dry winter monsoons blow across South Asia from the northeast. From about June through October, however, moisture-bearing winds from the southeast and southwest sweep across the continent. These winds are the summer monsoons. Farmers joyfully

Rains brought by monsoon winds flood Dhaka, the capital of Bangladesh (left). In Tibet camps are built on the high, drier plains (below).

ASIA AT A GLANCE

	Total Land Area	16,992,000 sq. miles 44,009,000 sq. km

	Highest Mountain	Mt. Everest, Nepal 29,028 feet (8,848 m)

	Longest River	Chang River, China 3,915 miles 6,300 km

	Largest City	Tokyo, Japan Population 8,112,000

	Current Population	3,389,000,000
	Percent of World Population	61%

GEO FACT
Giant pandas live in bamboo forests in the high elevations of southwestern China. The bearlike animals eat bamboo shoots. Because there is often a shortage of bamboo for the pandas to eat, panda numbers are limited. In the late 1980s scientists estimated that only about 600 pandas were left in the wild.

CHART WORK

The chart provides information about the size and geography of Asia.

1. What is one condition that contributes to the limited population of the giant panda?

2. What percentage of the world's population lives in Asia?

---

greet the huge sheets of rain brought by summer monsoons that water their rice, sorghum, millet, and chickpeas, among other crops.

As long as the rain-bearing monsoon runs its normal course, farmers can count on successful harvests. An Indian proverb, however, warns "if the sky fails, the earth will fail." If too much rain falls, as often happens in some regions, flooding may result in loss of life and property.

WHY IT MATTERS

From the chart on this page you can see that Asia has a large population. People in the many regions of Asia have adapted to the great variety of geographical features on the continent.

Some of these features—mountains, river valleys, and monsoons—helped create rich farmland on which people could live. In the following lessons you will read about some of the people who lived in these different environments.

✓ Reviewing Facts and Ideas

SUM IT UP

- Asia, the world's largest continent, has more mountains than any other. These mountain ranges include the awesome Himalayas.

- The Himalayas block clouds blowing north from the Indian Ocean. As a result, large amounts of rain fall south of the mountains while little falls to the north.

- Seasonal winds called monsoons affect many Asians' lives. Important crops depend on rain the summer monsoons bring each year.

THINK ABOUT IT

1. Why are monsoons important to farmers in South Asia?

2. How does the Tibetan plateau affect other regions of Asia?

3. **FOCUS** How is life in Asia affected by the Himalayas?

4. **THINKING SKILL** What _conclusions_ can you make about life in Asia from the information in this lesson? On what facts did you base your conclusions?

5. **GEOGRAPHY** Look at the map on page 385. What major rivers begin on the Tibetan Plateau?

387

THE OTTOMANS

READ ALOUD

"In Baghdad I am the shah [king], in Byzantine realms the caesar, and in Egypt the sultan; who sends his fleets to the seas of Europe, North Africa, and India."

These words were written by a leader named Süleyman, who headed one of the world's biggest empires in the early 1500s. His capital was not Baghdad, nor was it a new city. Rather it was a city that had once been the capital of the Eastern Roman empire. That city was Constantinople.

THE BIG PICTURE

The city once known as Constantinople is located in present-day Turkey. Now called Istanbul, the city crosses two continents. It extends across both sides of the Bosporus Strait, which separates Asia from eastern Europe. Anatolia, as Turkey was known during the Byzantine empire, has been home to some of the world's oldest civilizations. In Chapter 3 you read about the prehistoric city of Catal Huyuk, which thrived there over 8,000 years ago. In Chapter 9 you learned about the Roman emperor Constantine. He built Constantinople and its many Christian churches around A.D. 330.

For 1,000 years after Constantine built this city, the Byzantine empire remained a center of Christianity. In the 1300s, though, Anatolia was settled by a people called Turks. The Turks were Muslims from Central Asia. Within 150 years the Turks had made the city of Constantinople the capital of a new Turkish-led empire.

Focus Activity

READ TO LEARN
What was life like in the Ottoman empire?

VOCABULARY
sultan
grand mufti

PEOPLE
Osman
Süleyman
Sinan

PLACES
Istanbul
Anatolia

388

AN EXPANDING EMPIRE

In 1301 Turkish warriors rallied behind a leader named Osman (OHZ mahn). He led them to their first major victory against the Byzantine empire. In honor of Osman's great skill as a leader, his followers called themselves "Osmanlis." In the next 150 years the "Osmanlis" became known as Ottomans. Their growing empire eventually surrounded the city of Constantinople.

The Battle for Constantinople

In 1453 Constantinople had the strongest defense of any city in Europe. It was surrounded on three sides by the sea. Attackers had to break through massive stone walls to get inside the city. Moats and ditches were built between the walls. Defenders could shoot from the tops of these walls.

The Ottoman empire also had strengths, though. Ottoman soldiers had the newest and largest cannons in Europe. These cannons hurled half-ton cannonballs more than a mile.

In the pre-dawn hours of May 29, 1453, the Ottomans fired heavily on the walls of Constantinople. Before the morning was over, Constantinople had fallen into Ottoman hands. After more than 1,000 years, the Byzantine empire was no more.

The Christian rulers of Europe, who once waged crusades against Islam, now had Muslim neighbors to the east. Those neighbors would be a powerful force in Europe for years to come.

Leadership of the Empire

When Constantinople became the new capital of the Ottoman empire in 1453, the Turks called the city Istanbul. This name comes from a Greek word meaning "in the city." Istanbul remained the empire's center until 1918. Today it is the largest city in Turkey.

During the 500 years of Ottoman rule, sultans, or supreme rulers, governed the empire. They passed control to their oldest or favorite sons. Religious leaders called grand muftis interpreted the laws of Islam and applied them to life in the Ottoman empire.

The Mosque of Süleyman is a striking sight in the landscape of Istanbul.

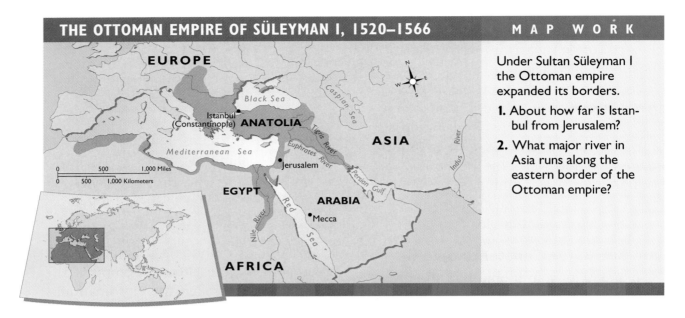

EUROPE

Black Sea

Istanbul (Constantinople)   ANATOLIA

Caspian Sea

Mediterranean Sea

Tigris River

Euphrates River

ASIA

Indus River

Jerusalem

Persian Gulf

EGYPT

Nile River

Red Sea

ARABIA

•Mecca

AFRICA

0   500   1,000 Miles
0   500   1,000 Kilometers

Under Sultan Süleyman I the Ottoman empire expanded its borders.

1. About how far is Istanbul from Jerusalem?

2. What major river in Asia runs along the eastern border of the Ottoman empire?

THE AGE OF SÜLEYMAN

Between 1520 and 1566 the Ottoman empire reached its peak under Sultan Süleyman (SOO lay mahn). As you can see from the map, Süleyman's empire sprawled over three continents. It included Jerusalem.

Life in Istanbul

If "all roads led to Rome" during the Roman empire, all routes in the Ottoman empire—whether on sea or land—led to Istanbul. Coffee flowed into the city's coffeehouses from southern Arabia. Ships from Egypt brought rice and African gold. Butter, cheese, grain, and wheat, which helped feed the Ottoman army, were shipped across the Black Sea from present-day Ukraine, along with Russian furs.

Jews who had fled persecution in Spain now lived and worked in the city. So did Christians from all over Europe. Jews, Christians, and other non-Muslims worshiped freely in Istanbul.

At times Istanbul's non-Muslim merchants did business in the vast outer coutyard of Süleyman's palace. There they blended with the thousands of guards, weavers, armor-makers, horse-tenders, and gardeners who worked for the sultan. Few, however, could enter the beautiful, walled-off garden and palace beyond the courtyard. The sultan lived and worked within these walls, along with his grand mufti and advisors, court musicians, painters, and poets. Almost all of Süleyman's assistants, soldiers, and closest advisers were slaves.

Government workers chose boys who were 8 or older to be slaves at the palace. The boys were trained to do many jobs. Some became craftworkers, surgeons, and architects.

One of the boys drafted into service, Sinan (suh NAHN), was the son of an Anatolian stoneworker. After years of training he became Süleyman's chief architect. He designed dozens of libraries, hospitals, and colleges for the sultan. Sinan also built buildings for Süleyman's wife, Hürrem Sultan. Among these buildings were a school for orphans and a soup kitchen for the poor. Sinan's greatest achievement was the mosque he designed for Süleyman. It still stands in the center of Istanbul.

WHY IT MATTERS

The battle for Constantinople in 1453 marked an important turning point in world history. It brought to an end the Byzantine empire and its 1,000-year-old link with ancient Rome. That battle also caused the center of Eastern Orthodox Christianity to give way to the Islam of the Ottoman empire.

Under Süleyman, the Ottoman empire grew and prospered on three continents—Europe, Asia, and Africa. A large mix of goods came to Istanbul from the empires' vast lands. Many different peoples came to Süleyman's capital as well. Enslaved youths from all over the empire rose through the ranks to carry out the sultans' laws.

The Ottoman empire lasted until 1922. Soon after the empire dissolved, the Turkish Republic was formed. Today the legacy of the Ottoman empire lives on. It can be found in the people and the grand mosques of southeastern Europe and Istanbul.

DID YOU KNOW?

How did Süleyman's gardens change life in the Netherlands?

Süleyman, like most sultans, loved flowers. His favorites included flowers that European visitors had never seen before—tulips, named after the Turkish word for "turban." A turban is a Muslim head-covering that is made by wrapping material around the head.

In the 1560s Austria's ambassador to Süleyman's court gave a handful of tulip bulbs to a Dutch gardener. When they bloomed, the rare flowers sparked a huge demand. In the early 1600s one bulb could fetch the price of an entire home or business! As time went on, prices dropped, but Dutch farmers continued to grow the turban-like flowers. Today the Netherlands is the world's largest producer of tulips.

Reviewing Facts and Ideas

SUM IT UP

- The Ottoman victory at Constantinople in 1453 ended the Byzantine empire and began a new era of Muslim rule in part of Europe.
- The Ottomans renamed the city of Constantinople, calling it Istanbul.
- The Ottoman empire was governed by leaders called sultans.
- During Süleyman's rule Istanbul drew products and peoples from across the empire. Non-Muslims were allowed to worship freely.

THINK ABOUT IT

1. Who was Sinan? What were some of the buildings he designed?

2. Why was Constantinople a difficult city to conquer? What role did technology play in its defeat in 1453?

3. **FOCUS** How did Süleyman's palace in Istanbul affect life in the city?

4. **THINKING SKILL** Why was the battle for Constantinople a disaster from the _point of view_ of the Byzantines? Why was it a triumph in the eyes of the Ottomans?

5. **WRITE** Write a paragraph explaining why the fall of Constantinople was an important event in history.

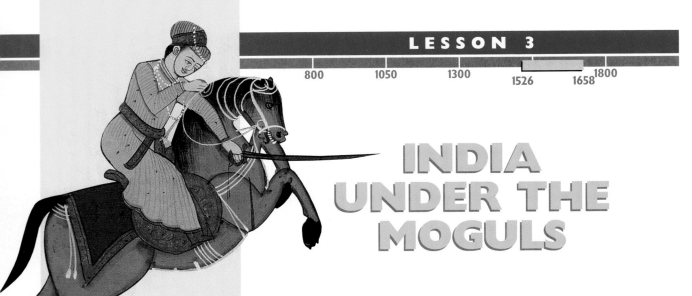

INDIA UNDER THE MOGULS

Focus Activity

READ TO LEARN
Who were the Moguls and what did they achieve?

PEOPLE
Akbar
Shah Jahan
Mumtaz Mahal

PLACES
Agra
Taj Mahal

READ ALOUD

In 1543 a prince was born in a desert near the Indus River, where his parents were on the run from enemy leaders. In his youth he became an expert hunter. He also battled what may have been seizures and a reading disorder. At the age of 13 he became ruler of his father's battered territory in India. This prince, whose name meant "Great" in Arabic, would build a powerful empire.

THE BIG PICTURE

A powerful new empire began when Muslims from Central Asia began moving onto the Indian subcontinent. In Chapter 6 you read that Aryan princes gained control over much of the Indian subcontinent around 500 B.C. In the thousand years that followed, Hindu traditions became deeply rooted in India. Hindu rulers were challenged, however, by Muslim conquerors. By A.D. 1200 the fertile lands of the Indus plain had come under Muslim control.

The new sultans of the plain made Islam the law of the land. Hindus were called upon to pay a special tax, which cost ordinary workers as much as a month's wages. By law Hindus could no longer build any new temples. These and other rules caused anger among the large Hindu population. The result was more war, rather than peace. However, a new prince was about to bring big changes to the Indian subcontinent.

THE MOGUL EMPIRE

The conquerors you read about in the Big Picture were called Moguls. The Moguls were originally from Central Asia and may have been related to the Turks. In 1526 Moguls invaded the Indus plain. Within three years the Moguls controlled much of northern India. The map on this page shows you the region where the Moguls ruled. India's Mogul empire would grow even bigger during its 235-year rule. At one time it would cover most of the Indian subcontinent. Much of that growth would take place under Akbar, the ruler whose name meant "Great" in Arabic.

Akbar's Achievements

As you read in the Read Aloud, Akbar was made ruler of the Mogul empire when he was just 13. The year was 1556—when workers were completing Süleyman's mosque in Istanbul and shortly before Elizabeth I became queen of England.

At the age of 19, Akbar led an army into battle for the first time. Over the next 43 years he and his army fought many wars to expand the Mogul empire. During that time Akbar almost never lost a battle, and his fame as a brilliant commander grew.

Akbar offered no mercy to those who opposed him. At the same time he worked hard to improve life for those under his rule. He created a unified money system so that business would run smoothly throughout the empire. He varied the amount that farmers had to pay in taxes, based on how

fertile their land was. Akbar also ordered government workers to build new canals and wells to help farmers.

Akbar's major changes, though, affected Hindus, the majority of people in India at that time. The changes helped to create a remarkable period of unity and power in Indian history.

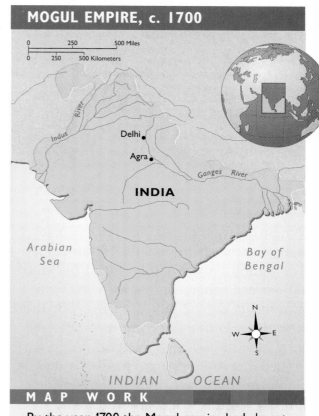

MOGUL EMPIRE, c. 1700

0   250   500 Miles
0   250   500 Kilometers

Indus River
Delhi
Agra
Ganges River
INDIA
Arabian Sea
Bay of Bengal
N W E S
INDIAN   OCEAN

M A P   W O R K

By the year 1700 the Mogul empire had almost covered the entire Indian subcontinent.

1. What geographical features were near the Mogul empire's northern borders?

2. About how far is Delhi from Agra?

Tiger hunting was a favorite sport of Akbar.

Today only official buildings like the Hall of Public Audience (left) remain in Fatehpur Sikri. Akbar had the city built in 1570.

AN ERA OF HARMONY

When he was 20, Akbar married the daughter of an important Hindu leader. The young emperor then hired his wife's father and other Hindus to work with him in his capital city of Agra. For the first time, Hindus became top officials in a Muslim-led government.

In 1579 the emperor passed a law that won him even more support among Hindus. That law did away with the tax that earlier Muslim leaders had forced all non-Muslims to pay. Akbar also allowed Hindus to build temples once more. These acts showed that the new emperor wanted Hindus to be treated more fairly under Mogul law.

Akbar himself had a strong interest in other religions. He had a special building constructed at his palace where Muslims, Hindus, Christians, and other religious leaders could meet and explain their beliefs. It is said that Akbar would pace back and forth on walkways above the building floor, listening to those sitting below. At times he would toss out questions that sparked heated debates.

The Leader's Interests

In addition to learning from such debates, Akbar learned from books in his library. The library included custom-made translations of Hindu, Persian, Arabic, and Greek classics. Since he could not read, Akbar had someone read to him every day. His legendary memory helped him to remember most of what he heard.

Akbar also loved the beauty of arts and crafts. He paid fortunes to bring Asia's best painters, poets, musicians, and craftworkers to his palace. During the day he often visited the palace's 100 workshops. There experts made carpets, curtains, weapons, jewelry, and paintings, among other things. It was not uncommon to see the emperor hammering iron, shaving camel hair, or discussing painting. At night musicians played for him and sometimes he joined in on drums.

Akbar oversaw the creation of many new buildings. Under his direction workers built several huge forts and new palaces.

In this painting an artist captured the creation of one of Akbar's palaces in Fatehpur Sikri. What does the painting tell you about how buildings were made in Akbar's time?

MANY VOICES
PRIMARY SOURCE

Painting from Mogul India depicting the building of Fatehpur Sikri, 1570

This painting is one of a series illustrating a biography of Akbar by his closest assistant. It shows ordinary people working together to create a lasting legacy of the Mogul empire.

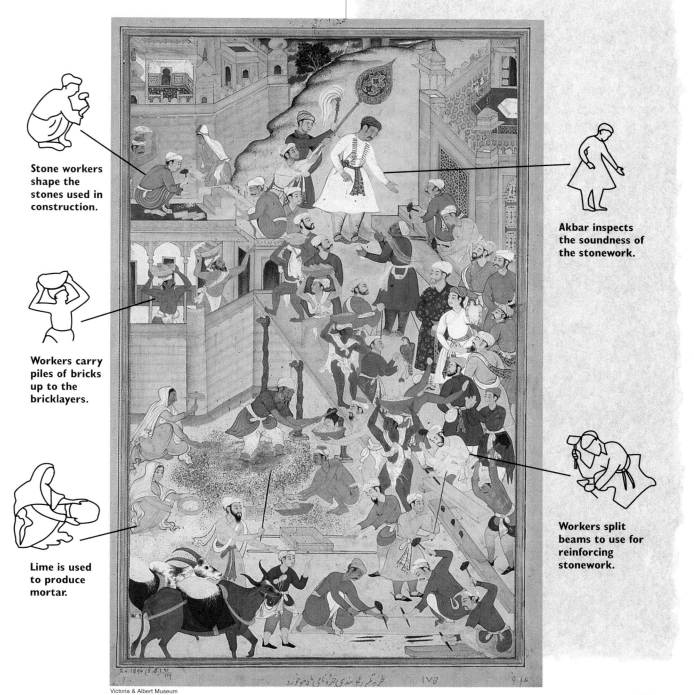

Stone workers shape the stones used in construction.

Workers carry piles of bricks up to the bricklayers.

Lime is used to produce mortar.

Akbar inspects the soundness of the stonework.

Workers split beams to use for reinforcing stonework.

Victoria & Albert Museum

SHAH JAHAN

In 1605 Akbar died at the age of 63. As his legacy, he left behind one of the wealthiest and most powerful empires in the world at that time.

Akbar's grandson, Shah Jahan (SHAH juh HAHN) ruled the Mogul empire from 1628 to 1658. His name meant "Emperor of the World" in Arabic. In addition to expanding the empire, Shah Jahan spent immense fortunes constructing spectacular objects and buildings. His throne alone cost twice as much to make as the palace of Akbar in which it sat! The throne took seven years to build and was made of diamonds, pearls, rubies, and other jewels set in gold.

The Taj Mahal

The tomb Shah Jahan had made for his wife, Mumtaz Mahal (mum TAHZ mah HAHL), or "Chosen One of the Palace," was even more amazing. Mumtaz Mahal died during childbirth in 1631. The grief-stricken emperor ordered his chief architect and thousands of workers to build a special tomb for her in Agra. No expense was spared. When it was completed nearly 20 years later, the Taj Mahal stood as one of the most beautiful buildings ever made.

The white marble dome of the Taj Mahal rises some 20 stories from the ground. Passages from the Koran elegantly carved over each gateway

describe the paradise said to await all Muslims upon death. In this way the Taj Mahal honors not only the life of Mumtaz Mahal and her husband, but also the beliefs of Islam.

Trading With Europe

The Taj Mahal was one of the costliest buildings ever built under Mogul rule. One reason Shah Jahan could afford to spend so much on it was because trade in India was booming as never before. India's cotton fabric now clothed many people in Asia and even Africa and Europe. For the first time, spices and silks were sold directly to eager merchants from Portugal, England, and the Netherlands. In Chapter 19 you will read about how Europeans took part in Indian life.

The Mogul empire is known for its beautiful jewelry and the Taj Mahal (left), built by Shah Jahan in honor of his wife (far left).

WHY IT MATTERS

During the 1500s and 1600s, the rulers of the Mogul empire united most of the Indian subcontinent under one government. That government in turn benefited from India's growing trade with the rest of the world. Akbar also changed life in India by passing laws that promoted harmony between the Hindu majority and India's small but powerful Muslim population. By this time, Hinduism had spread to other regions of Asia, especially Southeast Asia. You will read about its influence there in the next lesson.

Reviewing Facts and Ideas

SUM IT UP

- By 1200 India's Indus plain was controlled by Muslims who had arrived from central Asia.

- Akbar expanded the large and wealthy Mogul empire. He gave Hindus rights which had been denied them by other Mogul leaders.

- Akbar's grandson Shah Jahan built the Taj Mahal in honor of his wife and the religion of Islam.

THINK ABOUT IT

1. What was the Mogul empire?

2. Why was it helpful to the Mogul empire that Akbar was a strong military commander?

3. **FOCUS** How did Akbar's rule affect Hindus in the Mogul empire?

4. **THINKING SKILL** Describe the main _cause_ that led Akbar to construct a special building for religious meetings. What is one _effect_ this building might have had on life in India?

5. **WRITE** Write a paragraph describing the Taj Mahal.

THE KHMER OF SOUTHEAST ASIA

Focus Activity

READ TO LEARN
What cultures influenced the Khmer of Southeast Asia?

PEOPLE
Jayavarman II
Suryavarman II

PLACES
Mekong River
Tonle Sap
Angkor
Phnom Penh

READ ALOUD

The stone temple enclosed an area the size of 370 football fields. Its walls were covered with carvings of famous Hindu stories. At its center rose five towers shaped like the buds of water lilies. On the first day of spring, visitors standing at the temple's west gate could see the sun rise directly over the highest tower. This was fitting since the name of the temple's patron meant "one protected by the sun."

THE BIG PICTURE

The temple described above is called Angkor Wat (ANG kawr WAHT). Today it is a tourist attraction in the country of Cambodia. Some 700 years ago, however, it was the center of a great kingdom in Southeast Asia.

About 2,000 years ago, Indian merchants stopped at various places in Southeast Asia. The peninsula region of Southeast Asia includes what are now Vietnam, Cambodia, Thailand, Myanmar, and Laos. Some stopped at the mouth of the Mekong (MAY KAHNG) River, a highway of ships and goods since ancient times. Chinese merchants and diplomats also came, bringing their own traditions. As a result, Indian traditions of Hinduism and Buddhism began to take root in Southeast Asia.

Many civilizations were enriched by Chinese and Indian traditions. One of those, along the Mekong, was the Khmer (kuh MER) Kingdom. It occupied present-day Cambodia. Angkor Wat, built in the 1100s, was one of many amazing structures in the Khmer kingdom.

LIFE ALONG THE MEKONG

The Mekong, like many of the world's great rivers, provides needed water and silt to farmers of Southeast Asia. During the monsoon rains, torrents of rainwater fill the Mekong to overflowing. In fact, so much water pours into the river that a branch of it starts to flow *backward* into Tonle Sap (tahn LAY SAP) or "Great Lake." When the rains end, that branch of the Mekong flows forward again and the Tonle Sap returns to its normal size. Locate the Mekong and Tonle Sap on the map.

About 2,000 years ago, Khmer farmers were already using floods along the Mekong and Tonle Sap. Plentiful silt and water allowed them to grow large rice crops. Along with fish, rice became a mainstay of Khmer meals.

Farmers and God-Kings

A food surplus made it possible for a complex civilization to grow in Cambodia. Like their counterparts in ancient Egypt and medieval Europe, Khmer farmers often worked on land owned by religious or government officials. The rice, fruits, vegetables, and livestock that farmers raised fed temple workers, craftworkers, and nobles as well.

Much of the surplus supported the head of Khmer society, the king. The Khmer believed that their king was not only all-powerful, but a living god as well. One of Cambodia's first kings, Jayavarman II (jah yah VAHR mahn), ruled in the 800s. He, like many Khmer kings to come, observed Hindu traditions and claimed to be a human form of the god Shiva.

Khmer, whether farmers or nobles, were expected to do their part to support their god-king. In local markets women sold rice, fish, and fruits like bananas. Like other workers, they gave some of their goods to the king as taxes. Military leaders promised:

> *We will not revere another king. . . . If there is a war, we will strive to fight and disregard life, with all our soul, in devotion to the king. . . . The reward of those who are devoted to their masters, may we obtain it from this world into the next.*

Kings, in return, built canals and roads in the kingdom. Canals watered the fields, producing better crops. Roads provided better means of transportation. Kings also led troops in war and judged disputes.

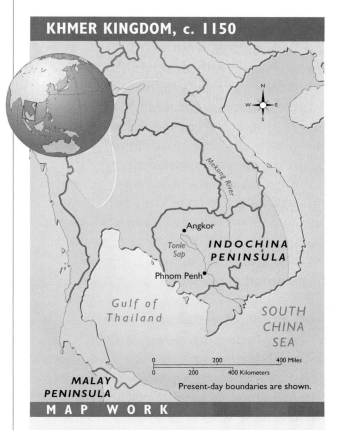

KHMER KINGDOM, c. 1150

MAP WORK

Trade and travel routes helped the cultures of southeast Asia to grow.

1. The Mekong River empties into which body of water?

2. On which peninsula is Phnom Penh located?

A CAPITAL CITY

Between 800 and 1200, Khmer forces expanded the borders of their kingdom into present-day Vietnam, Laos, and Thailand. The map on page 399 shows the territory of the Khmer. This expansion made the kingdom rich. In the early 1100s the king was Suryavarman II (sur yuh VAHR mun). He used a large part of this wealth to build a temple in the capital city of Angkor, on the north shore of Tonle Sap. You read about this temple, Angkor Wat, at the lesson's beginning. *Angkor* means "holy city" in the Khmer language.

Angkor Wat was the biggest temple built by the Khmer up to that time. Like the pyramids of ancient Egypt, it was built with thousands of stones from distant sources. Farmers working as laborers loaded the heavy stones onto boats Stones were transported about 20 miles on canals. Architects designed the temple so that, in the spring, the sun shone on the walls, which told Hindu stories about the world's creation. At year's end, by contrast, the sun highlighted scenes that described death.

The Walls of Angkor Thom

One of the boys who watched Angkor Wat being built was the king's great-grandson, the future Jayavarman VII. When he became king in 1181, Jayavarman VII set out to create an even grander complex than his great-grandfather's. His Angkor Thom (ANG kawr TAWM) became just that. In 1296 a Chinese diplomat named Zhou Daguan visited the city. He wrote this description:

The city walls are approximately 2.5 miles in circumference. They have five gateways and each gate is a double one. On the outer side of the wall is a great moat. On either side of the moat's bridges are 54 stone gods like "stone generals;" they are gigantic and terrible to look at.

At the center of the city stood a large temple. This one honored Buddhist, rather than Hindu, beliefs. In this respect Jayavarman VII differed greatly from his forefathers. Over time many Khmer would adopt Buddhism as their religious belief. Today, as a sign of this change, Angkor Wat itself contains Buddhist as well as Hindu statues, and the people of Cambodia are mostly followers of Buddhism.

Angkor Wat (above) was built by the Khmer in the 1100s. Many of the statues at the temple (left) represent both Hindu and Buddhist figures.

The Decline of Angkor

The great building projects of Angkor drained Khmer resources. So did the constant wars that Khmer kings waged against neighboring kingdoms. Their strongest enemies were kingdoms that were in what are today Vietnam and Thailand. Jayavarman VII won control over both kingdoms, but they broke free of Khmer rule after his death. In the 1430s Thai soldiers attacked Angkor itself. The city was abandoned shortly thereafter. Khmer rulers moved their capital to a site farther south along the Mekong. Later the kingdom would become known as Kampuja and its capital as Phnom Penh (puh NOM PEN). It remains Cambodia's capital city today.

WHY IT MATTERS

The Khmer are just one of the many peoples who built a lasting civilization in the monsoon environment of Southeast Asia. As a reminder of their ancient heritage, today's Cambodians have put an image of Angkor Wat at the center of their flag. Each time they salute their flag, Cambodians honor the special blend of traditions that makes their country unique.

✓// Reviewing Facts and Ideas

SUM IT UP

- The Khmer kingdom of Southeast Asia was located along major shipping routes between India and China. For this reason, Indian and Chinese traditions became part of life in the Khmer kingdom.

- Khmer kings were considered to be living gods who deserved great power and respect.

- In the 1100s and 1200s, Khmer kings ordered the construction of great buildings and temples in the capital city of Angkor.

THINK ABOUT IT

1. Why was the Mekong River important to life in early Cambodia?

2. Explain why an advanced civilization was needed to build a place like Angkor Wat.

3. **FOCUS** How did Angkor Wat reflect what—or who—was most important to the Khmer?

4. **THINKING SKILL** What would you do to determine the *credibility* of the description of Angkor Thom quoted on page 400?

5. **GEOGRAPHY** How did monsoons affect life in early Cambodia?

GREAT EMPIRES OF CHINA

READ ALOUD

The walls that Shihuangdi and the Qin dynasty built along China's northern border were meant to protect against invaders. In the 1200s, though, these walls did little to stop a fierce group of conquerors. These invaders from the grasslands north of China had conquered much territory in Asia. Then they focused their might on the biggest prize of all: China.

THE BIG PICTURE

In the 1100s—while the Khmer were building Angkor and Europeans were fighting the Crusades—China was prospering as never before. Chinese farmers began to grow a new kind of rice developed by the Khmer and their neighbors. They were able to grow more of this rice in less time, especially in southern China's warm and wet climate. Huge surpluses were shipped to faraway cities using a system of canals that kept water flowing for hundreds of miles.

Port cities such as Guangzhou (GWAHNG JOO)—later known as Canton—linked China to international trade. In those busy cities people made new kinds of printed books, paintings, compasses, and large ships that could carry as many as 500 people.

All of this was threatened in the 1200s, when invaders from the north set out to take over China. China's ancient border walls could not stop them. These invaders were called Mongols. They were herders and horse-riding experts from the grassy steppes north of China. Sheep provided much of what they needed. The Mongols also depended on trade for goods such as cloth and weapons.

Focus Activity

READ TO LEARN
How did the Mongols affect life in China?

VOCABULARY
Grand Canal

PEOPLE
Genghis Khan
Kublai Khan
Marco Polo

PLACES
Beijing
Forbidden City

NORTHERN INVADERS

In 1209, Mongol leader Genghis Khan (JENG gihs KAHN) united Mongol communities to conquer China, their main source of supplies. The Mongols rode south into China. They were helped by Chinese military leaders who joined their side after being defeated. When Genghis Khan died in 1227 he controlled almost all of northern China.

Kublai Khan

In 1252 Genghis Khan's grandson Kublai Khan (KOO bli KAHN) invaded southern China. After 27 years, all of China yielded to Kublai Khan's rule. China's Mongol rulers were called the Yüan dynasty. How would Mongols, who lived neither on farms nor in cities, govern a land of both?

Kublai Khan's answer was to have Mongols oversee China's already vast government. Kublai Khan made tax collection easier, though, by establishing paper money. The world's first all-paper money system made things easier on people's pockets. One note replaced about 8 pounds of coins!

Kublai Khan also oversaw the expansion of the Grand Canal. This canal had been built many years earlier to connect the Huang and Chang rivers. With Kublai Khan's expansion, it connected the new capital city, Beijing (BAY JING), with cities over 1,000 miles to the south. The Grand Canal is still used for shipping today.

Kublai Khan assigned soldiers to protect merchants traveling on the ancient Silk Road that connected Asia with Europe. You will read more about the Silk Road and one man who traveled on it, Marco Polo, in the Infographic on page 406.

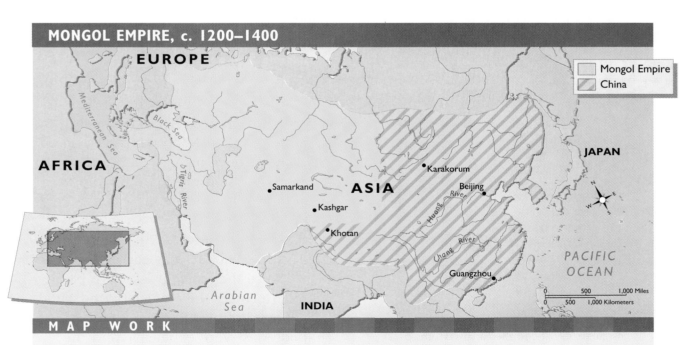

MONGOL EMPIRE, c. 1200–1400

Mongol Empire
China

EUROPE
Mediterranean Sea
Black Sea
AFRICA
Tigris River
Samarkand
ASIA
Kashgar
Khotan
Karakorum
Beijing
Huang River
Chang River
Guangzhou
JAPAN
PACIFIC OCEAN
Arabian Sea
INDIA

0   500   1,000 Miles
0   500   1,000 Kilometers

M A P   W O R K

In the 1200s the Mongol empire extended west into eastern Europe.

1. Which river flowed near the westernmost Asian boundary of Mongol lands?

2. About how far from Beijing is the mouth of the Tigris River?

3. Which cities in the empire were *not* in China?

THE MING DYNASTY

After Kublai Khan's death in 1294, Mongol control over China began to weaken. Terrible floods along the Huang River, famine, and disease added to the country's distress. In 1368 the Mongols were driven out by rebel Chinese forces. Chinese rulers once again came to control China. The Ming Dynasty had begun.

Cultural Expansion

During the Ming dynasty's 276-year history, China prospered. Between 1417 and 1420 almost one million people worked to build the Forbidden City in Beijing. Stoneworkers and carpenters built almost 1,000 stately palaces, libraries, temples, and gardens. Ming emperors lived and ruled from within the walls of this city. Outside the poor

MING CHINA, 1368–1644

- Ming China
- Great Wall
- Grand Canal

0   400   800 Miles
0   400   800 Kilometers

Huang River
Beijing
Yellow Sea
Chang Jiang
Hangchow
East China Sea
Guangzhou
PACIFIC OCEAN
South China Sea

M A P   W O R K

Ming rulers expanded the canal system to increase trade.

1. To which sea did the Grand Canal link Beijing?
2. The Great Wall extended along which of China's borders?

sang to passersby, asking for money. You can see one of their songs on the next page.

When the Forbidden City was completed, China's best porcelain, silk, and paintings were sent to fill its palaces and kitchens. The Ming government controlled thousands of porcelain workshops. They produced blue-and-white dishes that became world-famous. The government also controlled silk workshops. In those shops women and children over the age of 10 worked to produce China's valuable silk cloth.

Many of these luxury products went to the emperor's palace. Still more were bought by foreign merchants. Some merchants brought goods home along the Silk Road. Others shipped their goods from port cities like Guangzhou.

In 1405 large ships were built to take Ming officials on trading expeditions. The largest ship was about 400 feet long! Ming ships reached East Africa.

Looking Inward

With the new ships, China was well on its way to becoming the world's greatest sea power. That changed in the late 1400s, when Ming concerns shifted northward once again. Fears of another Mongol invasion grew. Ming emperors focused China's resources on the Great Wall as protection. They strengthened and extended the walls Shihuangdi had built almost 2,000 years earlier.

Because their resources were being used to protect their borders, the Ming abandoned efforts in shipbuilding. Expeditions were expensive and the Ming government was not interested in expansion. By the year 1525 it had given up all efforts in sea travel. China's interests turned inward for the next several centuries.

Fung Yang Song

Chinese Folk Song
Arranged by Marilyn Davidson

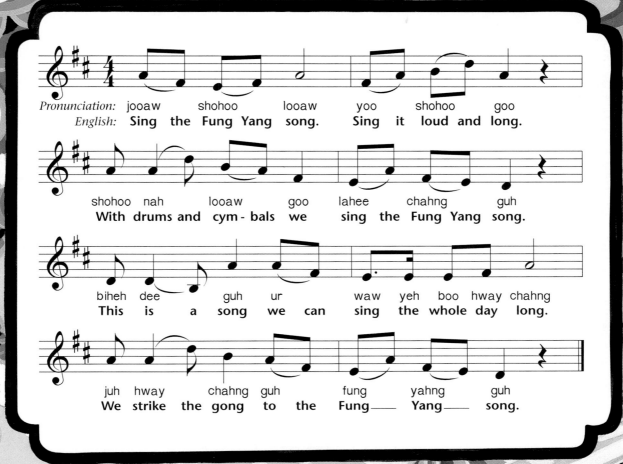

Pronunciation: jooaw shohoo looaw yoo shohoo goo
English: **Sing the Fung Yang song. Sing it loud and long.**

shohoo nah looaw goo lahee chahng guh
With drums and cym - bals we sing the Fung Yang song.

biheh dee guh ur waw yeh boo hway chahng
This is a song we can sing the whole day long.

juh hway chahng guh fung yahng guh
We strike the gong to the Fung   Yang   song.

405

Infographic

Trade on the Silk Road

In the 13th century a Venetian explorer named Marco Polo traveled the entire route of the Silk Road, from Constantinople to Khanbalik, China. As he traveled, he kept records of the places he visited and the things he saw. The Silk Road provided a route for merchants and traders to transport goods. What are some of the items Marco Polo saw and described in his travels along the Silk Road?

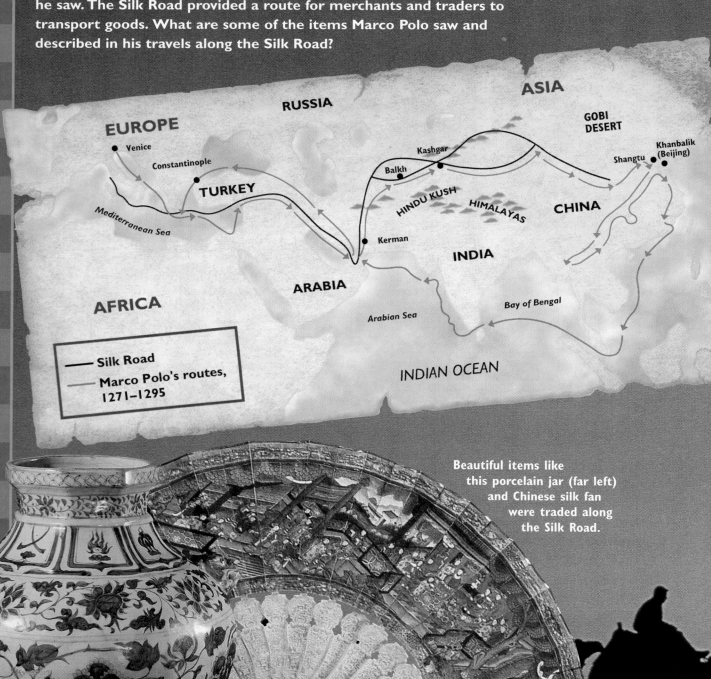

EUROPE
- Venice
- Constantinople

RUSSIA

ASIA

GOBI DESERT

TURKEY

Mediterranean Sea

Kashgar
Balkh
HINDU KUSH
HIMALAYAS
CHINA
Shangtu
Khanbalik (Beijing)

Kerman

ARABIA

INDIA

AFRICA

Arabian Sea

Bay of Bengal

INDIAN OCEAN

Legend:
— Silk Road
— Marco Polo's routes, 1271–1295

Beautiful items like this porcelain jar (far left) and Chinese silk fan were traded along the Silk Road.

This artwork shows Marco Polo trading goods.

66 **The strangest and most valuable things come from [China] and other provinces.... At least 1,000 cartloads of silk are sent [here] every day.** 99

66 **The Great Khan's subjects are perfectly willing to be paid in paper money since with it they can buy anything, including pearls, precious stones, gold, and silver.** 99

WHY IT MATTERS

Between the 1200s and 1500s, China underwent many changes. The Mongol invasions hurt once-bustling cities. Under Kublai Khan, though, China's cities and trade grew once again. In the Ming dynasty that followed, China became even stronger.

Wherever its trade goods went, China's ideas and traditions soon followed. China's influence was especially strong in the chain of islands that lay to the east. Those were the islands of Japan, which will be the focus of the next lesson.

✔ Reviewing Facts and Ideas

SUM IT UP

- Genghis Khan began the Mongol invasion of China in the 1200s.
- Kublai Khan ruled by using China's ancient government system. He also started the world's first all-paper money system and made the Silk Road safer for travel.
- Trade, cities, and sea travel grew under the early Ming dynasty. With the threat of foreign invasion, Ming emperors focused on defense projects such as the Great Wall.

THINK ABOUT IT

1. Why did Mongols invade China?

2. What did Kublai Khan do to govern China? Why might he have wanted to protect travelers?

3. **FOCUS** How did Kublai Khan improve life in China?

4. **THINKING SKILL** Make at least two _conclusions_ about the importance of trade in Ming China. On what facts did you base each conclusion?

5. **GEOGRAPHY** How did the Grand Canal affect movement in China?

THINKINGSKILLS

Queen Elizabeth I (left) and Ghengis Khan were powerful leaders who ruled vast empires.

National Portrait Gallery, London

The Granger Collection

Making Generalizations

VOCABULARY

generalization

WHY THE SKILL MATTERS

In the last lesson you read about Genghis Khan and the Mongols' rise to power in China. You have also read about other leaders and how they came to rule—Alexander the Great, Sunjata, and Elizabeth I, to name a few. If you compare their histories, you might notice certain similarities. As a result, you might make a general statement about what things are necessary for people to become powerful leaders.

If you did so, you would be making a generalization. A generalization is a broad statement of observation applied to different kinds of examples. A generalization shows how all of the examples are connected by a single concept or idea.

Why are generalizations useful? Sometimes things that seem very different on the surface are actually similar underneath. A generalization helps you to see similarities you otherwise might have missed.

Of course, generalizations can be helpful only if they are supported by facts. Use the Helping Yourself box to guide you in making generalizations.

USING THE SKILL

Suppose you wanted to make a generalization about how people become powerful leaders. To start, you might choose three leaders to serve as your examples. Say that you chose Genghis Khan, Sunjata, and Alexander the Great.

Your next step would be to compare and contrast your examples. The *differences* between the examples might catch your attention first. Genghis Khan was a horseman from the steppes of central Asia, living in the 1200s. Sunjata also lived in the 1200s, but on the savannas of western Africa. Alexander the Great, meanwhile, grew up over 1,000 years earlier than these leaders on the rocky shores of northern Greece.

To make a generalization about powerful leaders, think about what features or qualities the leaders may have shared. These features will support the generalization you make. One thing these three rulers had in common was command of strong military forces. You may recall that, by making the most of their armies, each of the rulers won control over many people and vast stretches of land.

More than one generalization could be made about this topic. Based on these facts, though, one possible generalization might be: Many leaders gain power as a result of control they have over a strong military force.

- **A generalization is a statement of observation that can be applied to different kinds of examples.**
- **Decide on a topic to make a generalization about.**
- **Choose examples and facts that give you material from which to build a generalization.**
- **Create a broad statement based on your examples.**

TRYING THE SKILL

You just made a generalization about leaders' rise to power. Now try making a generalization about how leaders can use their power to develop strong governments. Remember that common features will support the generalization you make.

Use as your examples the rules of Akbar, Elizabeth I, and Caesar Augustus. You may recall that Akbar faced religious conflict. Elizabeth I and Augustus were challenged by threats of war when they came to power. Akbar used his power to bring peace and religious tolerance to India. Elizabeth I faced down the Spanish Armada while England enjoyed the Renaissance. Augustus brought the Pax Romana to ancient Rome. How did their actions win these rulers special popularity, thereby strengthening their governments? What generalization can you make from these three examples?

REVIEWING THE SKILL

1. What is a generalization?

2. Suppose you made the following generalization: "Strong government results when leaders address the greatest needs of their citizens." Is it supported by the three examples in the Trying the Skill section? Why or why not?

3. What generalization can you make about leaders today? What facts did you use to support your generalization?

4. How can generalizations help us to learn more from history?

FEUDAL JAPAN

READ ALOUD

"Nothing is more important than duty. Second in importance comes life, and then money." To writer Muro Kyuso, who lived almost 300 years ago, these words described life for a certain group of people in Japan. They were Japan's soldiers.

THE BIG PICTURE

As you read in Lesson 1, Japan is located in the Pacific Ocean east of mainland Asia. Its four main islands form a 2,000-mile-long archipelago. This arc stretches from Russia in the north toward the Korean Peninsula in the south. From ancient times Chinese and Korean people moved to the islands of Japan. They brought Confucian teachings with them. Immigrants from Korea also introduced Buddhism to Japan around A.D. 550, along with China's writing system and new forms of art.

These immigrants arrived in a region that already had ancient traditions of its own. Most important was the Japanese religion called Shinto (SHIN toh), or "the way of the gods." According to Shinto belief, everything on Earth has a spirit of its own, including the land and such crops as rice. As in ancient Greece, Japan's farmers tried to ensure good harvests by offering prayers before planting or harvesting. The most important prayers, though, were offered by Japan's emperor. The emperor's family was believed to be descended from the Shinto sun goddess.

In time Shinto, Buddhism, and Confucianism blended together in Japan to form a unique way of life. All Japanese were believed to be part of one big family, whose head was the emperor. As in all families, each member had duties to fulfill. Not all duties were the same, and not everyone had equal rank, as you will see.

Focus Activity

READ TO LEARN
What changes did the shoguns make in feudal Japan?

VOCABULARY
Shinto
shogun
samurai

PEOPLE
Yoritomo
Tokugawa Ieyasu
Lady Murasaki Shikibu

PLACES
Edo
Tokyo
Kyoto

A FEUDAL SYSTEM

The ruler of Japan was the emperor. However, powerful families fought for control over Japan's mountains and plains. One family won the long, fierce struggle for power in 1192. The emperor made the leader of this struggle, Yoritomo (yawr ee TOH moh), Japan's first shogun, or military commander. Yoritomo changed the way Japan was governed. While the emperor headed Japan in name, the shogun ruled the country as military dictator.

Samurai Warriors

Life in Japan, like life in Europe at this time, was shaped by a type of feudalism. Lords controlled large pieces of land, which were worked by farmers. Protecting the lords and their lands were soldiers called samurai. They believed their main duty was to remain loyal to their lord. "Nothing is so important in a warrior as loyalty," wrote one samurai in the 1400s.

Although lords held great power in their regions, they were considered vassals of the shogun. Lords had to serve the shogun. This service could mean providing rice or samurai for war. In return the shogun granted new lands or privileges to lords.

The shogun, his lords, and their samurai formed the upper part of Japan's social pyramid. Below them were farmers, craftworkers, and merchants. These commoners—non-nobles— had to show utmost respect to those above them in society. Whenever a lord and his samurai passed through a village, servants shouted "Down! Down!" This signal prompted commoners to fall face-down on the ground in respect. Those who did not do so risked death.

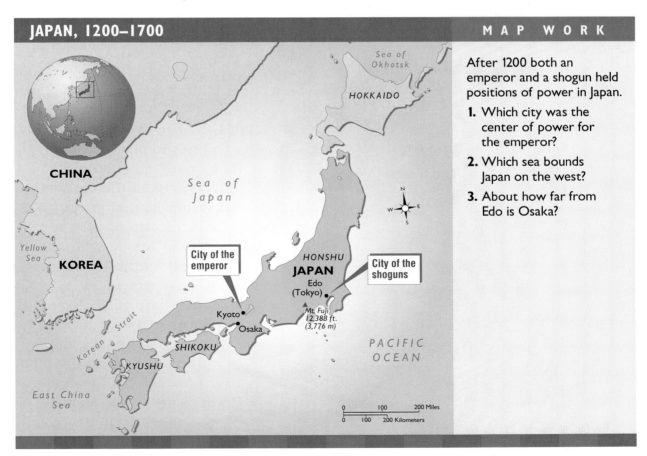

JAPAN, 1200–1700

MAP WORK

After 1200 both an emperor and a shogun held positions of power in Japan.

1. Which city was the center of power for the emperor?

2. Which sea bounds Japan on the west?

3. About how far from Edo is Osaka?

TOKUGAWA SHOGUN

Shoguns like Yoritomo were very powerful. However, they were not always strong enough to keep lords from rebelling and seizing more land for themselves. Remember, Japan is a very long archipelago. For this reason, keeping control over Japan's dozens of powerful lords proved almost impossible. By the early 1500s the shoguns had lost much of their power.

In 1603, though, the emperor made Tokugawa Ieyasu (toh koo GAH wah ee yeh YAH soo) Japan's ruler. Under the Tokugawa, Japan became not only unified but remained at peace for over 200 years. How did the Tokugawa leaders achieve what no one else had been able to do?

A samurai wore the decorated headdress and cloak shown. Samurai also carried two swords.

Ruling Japan

The Tokugawas became the unchallenged masters of Japan by ordering massive changes in society. To prevent rebellion, only samurai could own weapons. Lords who opposed the Tokugawa leaders were stripped of their lands. Those lands amounted to half the farmable land in Japan. These lands were given to loyal vassals.

Most importantly, all lords had to live in the Tokugawa capital city of Edo (ED oh), or what is today Tokyo. There the shogun's assistants could keep a close watch on the lords, making sure no rebellions were planned. Every two years the lords could return to their towns. Their wives and children, however, had to stay in Edo to insure that the lords would return.

Lords oversaw most everyday affairs in Japan, including collecting taxes from commoners. The lords were not taxed, but were expected to contribute whenever a new national road or castle was built. Lords had to prove their loyalty to the shoguns by giving them many gifts. Lords who did not risked the chance of losing land or privileges. The lords also had to obey strict rules about everything, from what kind of silk they wore to how many servants they had. These rules forced the lords to spend lots of money. Without plenty of money, no lord would have the resources to wage a war against the shoguns.

Life in Villages and Cities

One road that Japan's lords helped pay for connected Edo with the emperor's capital city of Kyoto (KYOH toh). In time its 300-mile length became crowded with the shogun's servants carrying messages from the shogun to the emperor. Merchants also used the road on their way to market, as did lords traveling to and from Edo.

As the lords traveled with their servants and samurai, they passed through a Japan that was steadily changing. Peace had brought boom times. In farming villages, people leveled forests to clear new farmland. With improved irrigation more rice, cotton, and other crops could be grown. Village shrines and temples were also being expanded. Many of them started schools where children could study reading, writing, arithmetic, and religion.

More and more, older children of farmers were leaving their villages. They left to live in Japan's growing towns and cities. Some found work as servants or laborers on building projects. Others became maids in the homes of samurai families.

Development of Edo

No other city grew as big or as fast as Edo. After 1603 more than 200 lords and their families moved into stately city homes. These households required the services of thousands of maids, cooks, and other servants. Etsu Sugimoto described the maids who worked in her family's kitchen:

> Here the air was filled with the buzz of work mingled with chatter and laughter. In one corner, a maid was grinding rice for tomorrow's dumplings; another was making padded scrub-cloths out of an old kimono; . . . and a little apart from the others sat another whirling her spinning wheel.

Servants searched the city's markets each day for fresh goods. While the lords and samurai spent money to satisfy the shogun, merchants became rich. Some became far richer than many lords.

413

A FLOURISHING CULTURE

New traditions were being born in the heart of Edo. Actors playing in a new form of drama called Kabuki packed Edo's theaters each night. Their plays dealt with samurai heroes and ordinary people, often torn by love or by struggles between duty and freedom.

New technology also made book printing easier than ever before. Merchants carried huge stacks of books on their backs. Books were rented for next to nothing. Some people read adventure stories about the golden age of the samurai. Others read love stories or classics like Lady Murasaki Shikibu's *The Tale of Genji* (GEN JEE), from around the year 1000. It is thought to be the world's first novel. In this excerpt, the main character decides on a way to solve his problems.

For Genji life had become an unbroken string of problems. He must consider what to do next. If he went on pretending that all was well, then even worse things might lie ahead.

Genji thought of the Suma coast [near present-day Kobe]. People of great value had once lived there, he was told, but now it was deserted, save for the huts of fishermen. According to his attendants, however, Suma was known to be the home of one mysterious resident: a puppet. And the puppet had powers to make human beings a joyful lot.

Genji thought to himself, "Soon, I shall make the journey to Suma. Soon, a wonderful puppet shall rest on my arm. Soon, I shall turn to a puppet and gain the gifts of friendship and joyfulness."

This painting (right) shows a scene from *The Tale of Genji*. Today actors continue to perform Kabuki drama.

The Closing of Japan

The Tokugawa shoguns kept an iron-handed grip over life in Japan for over 200 years, between 1603 and 1867. During this time Japan had almost no contact with other countries. Like the emperors of Ming China, the shoguns of Tokugawa Japan saw outside influences as threats to their rule. Their response was to seal off their borders. Lords were forbidden to have any foreign contact or to build ships. Throughout most of its history, Japan had grown from contacts with the outside world; now it remained isolated.

WHY IT MATTERS

Japan was one of the few countries in Asia to remain largely untouched by outside forces in the 1600s and 1700s. Even without the benefits of international trade and movement, though, life in Japan continued to grow and change. Most importantly, feudal society changed as lords moved to Edo.

Samurai no longer fought wars but instead often held desk jobs. Drawn to new economic and cultural opportunities, farmers set off for growing towns and cities. A new age had begun in Japan. That age, however, would be jolted in the 1800s, as foreign ships came to challenge Japan's closed borders. You will read about where the ships came from and why in Chapter 17.

✓ Reviewing Facts and Ideas

SUM IT UP

- The Japanese religion of Shinto was changed by the arrival of Buddhism and Confucianism. Together they formed the belief that Japan was like a family, with the emperor as head.

- Feudal society in Japan was run by a military leader called a shogun.

- The Tokugawa shoguns held power for over 200 years. They forced lords to live in Edo and also shut off Japan to outside influence.

THINK ABOUT IT

1. Describe Japan's social pyramid during feudal times.

2. Why was the order for lords to move their families to Edo so important to Tokugawa rule?

3. **FOCUS** How did life change for people in Japan under shogun rule?

4. **THINKING SKILL** How might Tokugawa history support this _generalization_: "Strict rule can bring positive results."

5. **GEOGRAPHY** How did Japan's sheer length affect the early shoguns' ability to keep order in the country?

PRINTING AND Calligraphy

Do you remember how difficult writing seemed when you first learned to do it? You probably practiced drawing letters over and over. Then you began to learn to write words and sentences.

Japanese of feudal times also worked hard at their writing. They used brush strokes similar to painting. They developed their written language, which they borrowed from the Chinese, into an art form called calligraphy (kuh LIHG ruh fee).

Advances in printing technology brought this art to many people. Printing made it possible for many people to own beautifully written works of art.

Calligraphy is still an important part of education for many Asian students. This Chinese girl practices her writing at school.

The woman in this Japanese print (above) is writing a letter using a calligraphy brush. The scroll (left) shows the following Japanese poem, titled "Waiting for the Cuckoo." The calligraphy, handwritten by the poet Yoshimasa, is still admired for its beauty.

Oh, cuckoo, crying for thy mate
Up in the sky, on mine own part,
I wait for thee tonight
With my whole heart.

417

CHAPTER 14 REVIEW

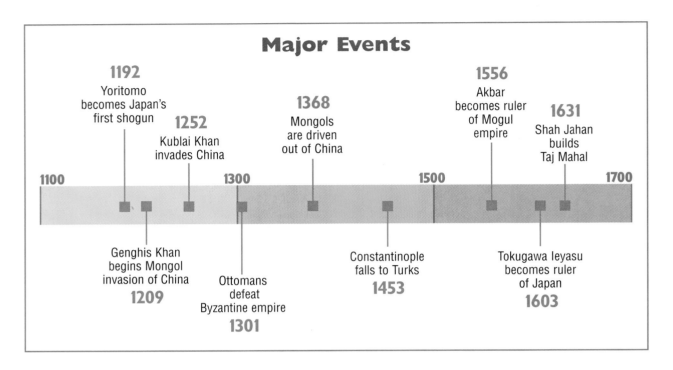

Major Events

1192 Yoritomo becomes Japan's first shogun

1252 Kublai Khan invades China

1368 Mongols are driven out of China

1556 Akbar becomes ruler of Mogul empire

1631 Shah Jahan builds Taj Mahal

1100 — 1300 — 1500 — 1700

Genghis Khan begins Mongol invasion of China **1209**

Ottomans defeat Byzantine empire **1301**

Constantinople falls to Turks **1453**

Tokugawa Ieyasu becomes ruler of Japan **1603**

THINKING ABOUT VOCABULARY

Number a sheet of paper from 1 to 5. Beside each number write the word or term from the list below that best completes each sentence.

archipelago
Grand Canal
samurai
shogun
sultan

1. _____ were soldiers used by Japanese lords.

2. A _____ is a supreme ruler of a Muslim state.

3. _____ is a word meaning "a chain of islands."

4. The name of the human-made waterway in China that connects the Huang and Chang rivers is the _____.

5. A _____ was a military commander who governed Japan.

THINKING ABOUT FACTS

1. What Asian rivers begin on the Tibetan Plateau?

2. Who was Sinan and what were his accomplishments?

3. What did Akbar do to strengthen the Mogul empire in India?

4. Why was the Taj Mahal built?

5. What is Angkor Wat?

6. Why did the Mongols invade China?

7. Who was Kublai Khan? How did he govern China?

8. What was the effect of the Tokugawa dynasty on Japanese history?

9. What was the most significant achievement of Lady Murasaki Shikibu?

10. According to the time line above, how long after Ghengis Khan invaded China were the Mongols driven out?

WRITING A NEWS ARTICLE

Suppose you are a newspaper reporter sent back in time to cover the fall of Constantinople. Reread page 389. Then use the information to write an on-the-scene report about what happened.

WRITING A COMPARISON

Write a comparison of the Mogul empire in India and the Mongol empire in China. How were they similar? How were they different? Include the contributions made by Akbar and Kublai Khan.

WRITING DESCRIPTIONS

Write one paragraph each about two of the following places: (1) Taj Mahal, (2) Angkor Wat, and (3) the Forbidden City.

APPLYING THINKING SKILLS

MAKING GENERALIZATIONS

1. What is a generalization?

2. Review Lesson 2. Explain how using the example of the Mogul emperor Akbar helps to support this generalization: "Effective rulers make the people they govern feel they are being treated fairly."

3. Make a generalization about what is required to become ruler of a large area. Use information from this and other chapters you have read.

4. What generalization can you make about the ways rulers of the past governed? Use as examples the rulers you chose for number 3.

5. Why are generalizations useful?

Summing Up the Chapter

Copy the main-idea chart below on a separate sheet of paper. Then fill in each column with information from the chapter. When you have completed the chart, use the information to write a paragraph that answers the question "What contributions did peoples of Asia make to civilization?"

MAIN IDEA: Powerful civilizations were built in Turkey, India, Cambodia, China, and Japan.

Country	Dynasty	Rulers	Capital Cities	Achievements
Turkey				
India				
Cambodia				
China				
Japan				

CHAPTER 15

Empires and Cultures of the Americas

THINKING ABOUT HISTORY AND GEOGRAPHY

In this chapter you will read about civilizations that developed in North America and South America. Follow the time line to see how empires developed in what are today Mexico and Peru. The peoples of these empires built unique and powerful civilizations. Near the Great Lakes of North America, Native Americans became skilled farmers who traded across a wide area.

1325
TENOCHTITLÁN

The Aztec build a city in the Valley of Mexico

1350
CUZCO

The Inca develop a wealthy and productive civilization in Peru

1400
ANDES MOUNTAINS

The Inca fertilize crops to feed an expanding empire

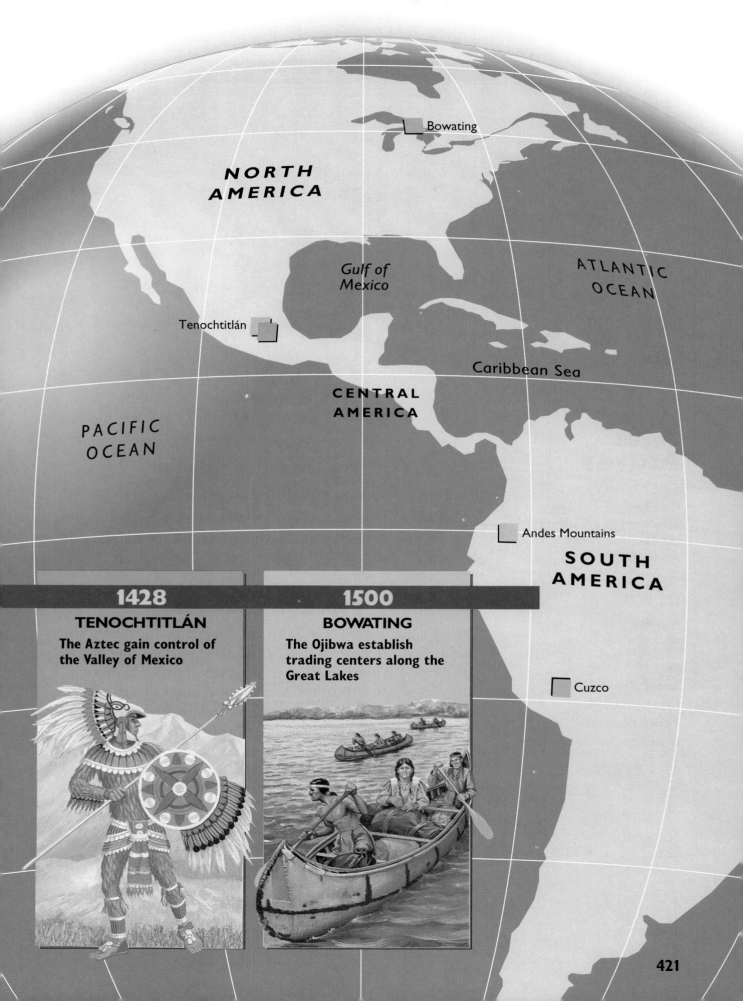

NORTH AMERICA

Bowating

Gulf of Mexico

ATLANTIC OCEAN

Tenochtitlán

Caribbean Sea

PACIFIC OCEAN

CENTRAL AMERICA

Andes Mountains

SOUTH AMERICA

Cuzco

1428

TENOCHTITLÁN

The Aztec gain control of the Valley of Mexico

1500

BOWATING

The Ojibwa establish trading centers along the Great Lakes

GEOGRAPHY OF THE AMERICAS

Focus Activity

READ TO LEARN
How have mountains affected the growth of civilizations in the Americas?

VOCABULARY
tundra
isthmus
timberline

PLACES
Andes Mountains
Great Lakes
Rocky Mountains
Canadian Shield

READ ALOUD

"Here at the top of the continent, I felt that the Americas 'belonged' to me in a way that they belonged to no one else. . . . The fog's curtain slowly lifted. . . . This was the end. Great sobs shook my frame, and my tears mingled with frozen dust."

These words were written in 1976 by the Englishman George Meegan. Over a period of seven years, he walked from the southern tip of South America all the way north to the Arctic Ocean.

THE BIG PICTURE

Pulling his belongings in a cart, Meegan climbed up the Andes Mountains and down to the steamy rain forests of Central America. He also traveled across Mexico's dry deserts and through the Great Plains of North America. He walked along the shores of the Great Lakes, up and over the Rocky Mountains, and across the tundra, or treeless plain, of Alaska. After 19,000 miles, Meegan had crossed both North and South America—the two continents that form the Western Hemisphere.

Many civilizations have developed in the Americas during the past 10,000 years. Among the earliest of them, as you may recall, were the Olmec and the Maya of Middle America. In this lesson you will read about the geography of the Americas and the ways in which some people adapted to it.

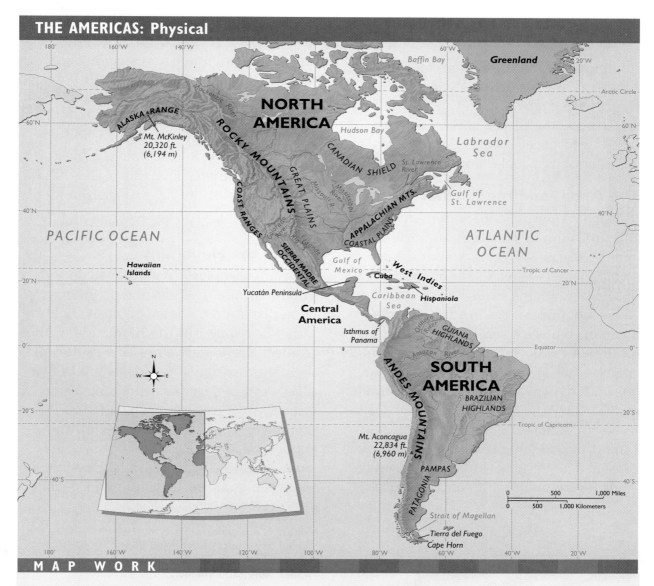

THE AMERICAS: Physical

MAP WORK

The Americas have many physical features.

1. Which mountain range extends along the western part of South America?

2. Which oceans bound the Americas?

3. Which are the two largest gulfs in the Americas?

4. Where are the Great Plains located?

5. In which mountain range is Mt. McKinley located?

THE AMERICAS

Many physical features in the Americas were shaped by glaciers during the Ice Age. The Canadian Shield is a huge rocky region in northern Canada where soil was removed by glaciers. Their crushing weight also carved the basins of the Great Lakes. When the Ice Age ended about 15,000 years ago, glaciers melted and filled the basins with water.

Melting glaciers also caused the ocean levels to rise. At the southern tip of Central America, rising waters covered land, leaving only an isthmus (IHS mus) between the continents. An isthmus is a narrow strip of land that connects two larger land masses.

MOUNTAINS OF THE AMERICAS

Climbing the tall mountains of the Americas was an exhausting part of George Meegan's journey. The mountains are some of the spectacular features—and great resources—of the continents that make up the Americas.

The Andes and the Rockies

North America and South America are similar in at least one important way. A great wall of mountains stretches along the western side of each continent. Huge plains extend to the east of these mountains. The Andes Mountains in South America make up the longest mountain range in the world. The range spans 4,500 miles. Mount Aconcagua (ak un KAH gwuh), the tallest mountain in the Americas, towers to 22,834 feet.

North America's Rocky Mountains extend over 3,000 miles, from Texas to Alaska. They are not quite as tall as the Andes. Mountain goats and bighorn sheep live on the steepest peaks above the timberline. Above this imaginary line on a mountain, trees cannot grow. Below the timberline, mountain lions and bears can be found living in forests of fir and spruce trees.

Like the Himalayas in Asia, the Andes and the Rockies have a great effect on climate. They have also influenced ways of life, transportation, and the history of civilizations.

Life in the Mountains

Many peoples have adapted to mountain life. In fact, one of South America's most advanced early civilizations developed in the highlands of the Andes. Early peoples of this region built irrigation systems and developed effective ways of fertilizing the soil. They found ways to farm crops such as maize, peppers, and potatoes on the slopes of the Andes. They also built rope bridges to make travel possible between some of the mountain peaks.

Hiking is a popular activity in the Rocky Mountains (left). Reed boats are used on Lake Titicaca in the Andes Mountains (below).

THE AMERICAS AT A GLANCE

Total Land Area	16,236,000 sq. miles 42,051,000 sq. km

Highest Mountain	Mt. Aconcagua, Argentina 22,834 feet (6,960 m)

Longest River	Amazon River 4,000 miles 6,437 km

Largest City	Mexico City, Mexico Population 10,263,275

Current Population	757,000,000
Percent of World Population	14%

GEO FACT
Northern Canada and Alaska make up part of the Arctic tundra. The climate of the tundra is so cold that the ground from 1 to 5 feet below the surface stays frozen all year. During the summer, the surface of the tundra thaws and moss and wildflowers grow.

CHART WORK

The Americas are rich not only in resources, but also in plants and minerals.

1. What is the longest river in the Americas?

2. How does the climate of the Arctic tunda affect the ground?

In North America's Rocky Mountains, early peoples had more difficult lives. Longer winters than those in the Andes, and less fertile soil, made farming a greater challenge.

WHY IT MATTERS

From the windy tip of South America to the icy rivers of Alaska, the Americas provide a 10,000-mile span of varied geography. Every possible climate zone can be found here, including polar, temperate, and tropical. Many physical features, such as North America's Grand Canyon and South America's Amazon River, which flows through the world's largest rain forest region, make these continents unique.

A study of this great land is incomplete, however, without meeting the people who live here. You have already read about the ancient civilizations of the Olmec and the Maya. Soon you will read about later peoples who lived in other parts of the Western Hemisphere.

✓ Reviewing Facts and Ideas

SUM IT UP

- Glaciers shaped much of the land of North America.

- The Isthmus of Panama connects North America and South America.

- The Andes Mountains and the Rocky Mountains are the two major mountain ranges of this region.

- North and South America contain a variety of landforms and climates.

- Early peoples of the Andes region built irrigation systems and developed ways of growing maize, peppers, and potatoes on the mountain slopes.

THINK ABOUT IT

1. How were the Great Lakes formed?

2. What is the timberline?

3. **FOCUS** How have mountains affected the growth of civilization in the Americas?

4. **THINKING SKILL** How might mountains such as the Andes and Rockies have *effects* on trade?

5. **GEOGRAPHY** Use the map on page 423 to determine at what degrees of latitude and longitude Lake Superior is located. At about what latitude is the Amazon River located?

THE AZTEC EMPIRE

Focus Activity

READ TO LEARN
How did the Aztec build an empire?

VOCABULARY
chinampas
tribute
Triple Alliance
codex

PLACES
Tenochtitlán
Valley of Mexico
Lake Texcoco

READ ALOUD

"The great city has many broad streets, though among these are two or three main ones. Of the remainder, half of each is hard earthlike pavement, and the other half is by water, so that the people leave in their canoes or barks, which are of wood hollowed out, although some of them are large enough to hold comfortably five persons. The residents go for a stroll, some in canoes and others along the land, and keep up conversations."

This is a description of a city in Middle America made by a Spanish soldier in 1519. The soldier was greatly impressed by the beautiful city and the people who lived there—the Aztec.

THE BIG PICTURE

As you have read, Middle America was the scene for the development of two great ancient civilizations—the Olmec and the Maya. As time passed, these civilizations lost their power. Other peoples carried on their traditions of farming and building. In the 1400s the Aztec built an empire that rivaled the achievements of the Maya hundreds of years earlier. The center of Aztec culture and power was the great capital city called Tenochtitlán (te noch tee TLAHN).

At the time the Spanish soldier observed it, Tenochtitlán was probably larger than any other city in the world. Today one of the world's largest cities, Mexico City, is located in the same area. That area is a fertile valley where the great drama of the Aztec unfolded.

THE AZTEC SETTLE IN MIDDLE AMERICA

According to legend, the Aztec, who called themselves *Mexica*, journeyed for years in Middle America, searching for a place to settle. In the 1100s the Aztec came to the Valley of Mexico. They were among many newcomers there seeking a home. In this high valley surrounded by mountains are several lakes. About 1325 the Aztec arrived at the shores of Lake Texcoco (tay SKOH koh).

The Aztec saw an island in the center of the lake. On that island, their historical accounts state, they received a sign. An eagle flew from the sky, perched atop a cactus, and began eating a snake. The Aztec took this to mean that they should build a city on the island. The Aztec named the city Tenochtitlán. *Tenochtitlán* means "place of the prickly pear cactus" in the Aztec language, Nahuatl (NAH wah tul).

Creating Farmland

At first Tenochtitlán was no more than a collection of reed huts surrounding a temple. Although their land was poor, the Aztec soon developed a system of agriculture similar to the ones used by other peoples of the area. They carved canals through the marshland. In the lake they piled up the lake's soil to make smaller islands. Most of these islands were about the size of a football field. These human-made islands, were known as chinampas (chin AHM pahz). Chinampas were held in place by wooden stakes and the roots of willow trees. Some chinampas actually floated. They could be moved from one part of the lake to another!

By carefully planting different crops year round, Aztec farmers created a constant supply of squash, tomatoes, chili peppers, and flowers. The most important crop, maize, was grown mostly in fields on the lake shore.

Building a City

Although three out of four Aztec worked as farmers, many worked at other jobs in Tenochtitlán. Some people worked to make stone buildings that gradually replaced the reed huts. Others built three long bridges, or causeways, that connected the island to the lake shore. Although most people lived in one-room stone or mud houses, Aztec rulers lived in grand palaces surrounded by luxurious gardens. A Spanish soldier described one of these palaces: "I walked until I was tired and never saw the whole of it." That palace even had its own zoo!

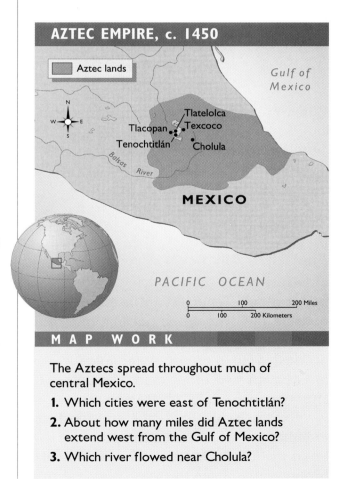

AZTEC EMPIRE, c. 1450

Aztec lands

Gulf of Mexico

Tlatelolco
Texcoco
Tlacopan
Tenochtitlán
Cholula

Bolsas River

MEXICO

PACIFIC OCEAN

0   100   200 Miles
0   100   200 Kilometers

M A P   W O R K

The Aztecs spread throughout much of central Mexico.

1. Which cities were east of Tenochtitlán?

2. About how many miles did Aztec lands extend west from the Gulf of Mexico?

3. Which river flowed near Cholula?

GROWTH OF AN EMPIRE

When the Aztec first arrived in the Valley of Mexico, they had to pay tribute, or taxes, to the rulers of nearby cities. This tribute was usually a part of their crops, which people carried by boat and on foot from Tenochtitlán to the other cities.

The Triple Alliance

Before long, though, tribute was pouring into Tenochtitlán instead of pouring out. The Aztec became one of the most powerful groups in the Valley of Mexico. In 1428 the Aztec joined forces with two other cities, Texcoco and Tlacopan (tlahk oh PAHN). They formed the Triple Alliance and worked together to strengthen their power. Soon the Triple Alliance gained control of the entire Valley of Mexico.

By 1450 Aztec power spread beyond the mountains surrounding the Valley of Mexico. Under the leadership of the Aztec ruler Ahuítzotl (ah WEE soht ul), the armies of the Triple Alliance conquered areas west to the Pacific Ocean and south to what is today Guatemala. Equipped with wooden shields and sharp stone spears, the Aztec army caused great fear among the peoples of Mexico.

One Aztec poet described the great respect paid to soldiers who died in battle, writing "There is nothing like death in war." Soldiers preferred, however, to capture enemies as prisoners. These prisoners were sacrificed to honor the Aztec god of the sun, Huitzilopochtli (weet si loh POHCH tlee). To sacrifice means to kill in a religious ceremony. The Aztec believed that only human blood could nourish the sun god.

The tribute the conquered cities paid brought the Aztec great wealth. Workers brought more than one million loads of food for tribute to the Aztec capital each year. Tenochtitlán grew until it reached a population of about 150,000 people.

Governing the Empire

Like those of many other cultures you have read about, the Aztec social pyramid was made up of several levels. At the top was the emperor, who held great political and religious power. He was the richest person in Tenochtitlán. He also led the Aztec army. The emperor was worshiped by the Aztec people, who believed he had godlike powers. The emperor even had a special color—turquoise. No one else was allowed to wear clothing of this color.

Below the emperor were nobles and government workers. Nobles were in charge of running the Aztec empire. They made sure tributes were paid, temples were built, and streets were swept. Nobles also planned wars.

The majority of the population made up the family groups called *calpulli* (kahl POOL lee). *Calpulli* means "groups of houses" in Nahuatl. In Tenochtitlán there were 20 different calpulli. Each had its own leaders and was settled in a different part of the city. Each also had its own temple, school, and farm-land. Members worked as farmers, craftworkers, merchants, and soldiers.

Near the base of Aztec society were poor farmers. They were among the poorest members of society, since they owned no land and had to work for others. Below the farmers were slaves. Only about 2 percent of the people in Tenochtitlán were enslaved. Most slaves were captured outside Aztec lands and brought to the capital by merchants. Slaves had no freedom and had to do whatever work their owners told them to do. Unlike those in most other cultures that practiced slavery, the children of Aztec slaves were free and could make choices about their lives.

This mosaic serpent was made to be worn on the chest. The serpent was a god to the Aztec.

AZTEC CIVILIZATION

By 1500 the city of Tenochtitlán bustled with trade and learning. Aztec doctors made more than 1,000 medicines from plants. Plants were used to heal wounds, reduce fevers, and cure stomachaches. Predicting eclipses and the movements of planets, Aztec astronomers built on Maya knowledge of the heavens. Craftworkers created beautiful feather headdresses, gold and copper jewelry, ceramic storage jars, and woven cloth.

The Great Temple

From birth until death, from morning until night, religion played a central role in the lives of the Aztec. The center of religious life in Tenochtitlán was the temple district. This district was located where three main streets came together. Here stood temples to

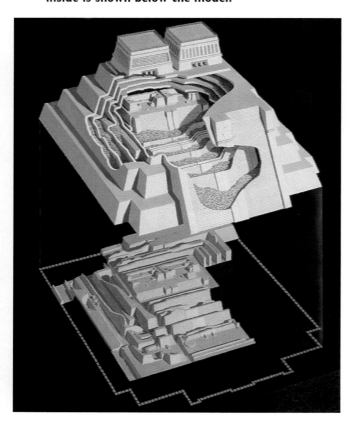

This model shows the outside of the Great Temple at Tenochtitlán. The inside is shown below the model.

different gods, homes for men and women priests, schools for young priests, and ball courts. Rising as high as an eight-story building was the Great Temple. Aztec built this temple to honor Huitzilopochtli, their sun god, and Tlaloc (TLAH lohk), their rain god.

Two staircases, decorated with carved and painted sculptures, led up to the top of the temple platform. It was here, on two massive stone blocks, that special priests sacrificed thousands of war prisoners every year.

Aztec Writing

In addition to performing temple ceremonies, priests kept a calendar that was used to predict the future. Some kept records using a special Aztec system of writing. Colorful pictures and symbols were drawn on a long folded sheet of paper. Each of these folded sheets was called a codex (KOH deks). Two or more of these sheets were called codices (KOH dih seez). Codices contained information about the history, religion, government, and science of the Aztec. Few

The codex (far left) shows the god of spring. A statue of the god of flowers and song is at left.

remain because the Spanish destroyed most Aztec records in the 1500s.

The Aztec also had a strong oral tradition. People memorized many poems, songs, and speeches. Poems were often recited on special occasions, accompanied by drums and flutes. This is an Aztec poem:

An emerald fell to the ground,
and a flower was born; this is your
    song!
Whenever you sing your songs here
    in Mexico
the sun shines eternally [forever].

WHY IT MATTERS

Within only a hundred years, the Aztec built one of the most powerful empires in the Americas. Farming techniques and efficient government helped the empire to grow and run smoothly. Constant warfare brought many enemies under Aztec rule. In 1521 the Aztec fell to the European kingdom of Spain.

Aztec people and many of their traditions survived. Food such as maize, Aztec crafts, and even the Nahuatl language are all part of Mexican culture today. The name *Mexico* comes from the name the Aztec called themselves. Even the flag of Mexico celebrates the Aztec legacy. At its center the flag shows the Aztec symbol of an eagle with a snake in its beak.

✔ Reviewing Facts and Ideas

SUM IT UP

- The Aztec first settled in the Valley of Mexico in about 1325.
- The Aztec built a powerful empire centered at Tenochtitlán.
- The Aztec gained much knowledge in medicine and astronomy and created beautiful buildings and works of art.

THINK ABOUT IT

1. Why did the Aztec settle in the Valley of Mexico?

2. How did the people of nearby cities help make Tenochtitlán wealthy?

3. **FOCUS** How did the Aztec expand their empire to areas beyond the Valley of Mexico?

4. **THINKING SKILL** Make a *conclusion* about how the people of conquered villages were treated in the Aztec empire. Explain how you reached your conclusion.

5. **WRITE** Write a paragraph describing one major achievement of the Aztec. Explain why that achievement was important for the Aztec civilization.

GEOGRAPHYSKILLS

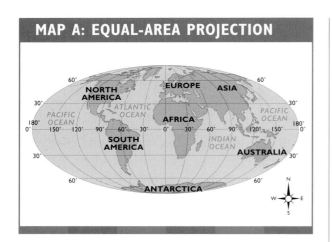

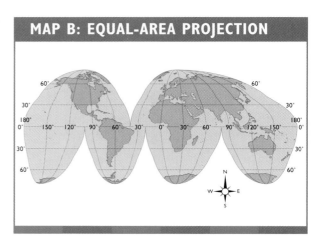

Using Map Projections

VOCABULARY

distortion
projection
equal-area projection
mercator projection
polar projection

WHY THE SKILL MATTERS

Only one tiny map fragment remains from Aztec times, but most historians believe that the Aztec commonly used maps. Maps would have been an important tool for keeping track of the widespread Aztec empire.

Today some maps are more accurate than others. Maps that show the entire world vary greatly in accuracy. Since Earth is a sphere, cartographers must stretch or cut parts of the globe, making it fit onto a flat map. This stretching and cutting causes distortion—errors that make the map less accurate.

When cartographers create a map of Earth's entire surface, they must use a projection. A projection is a way of showing parts of Earth on a flat map.

USING MAP PROJECTIONS

One of the most common types of map projections is the equal-area projection. An example of this projection is shown on Map A. This map is especially useful for comparing sizes of land masses. However, it distorts the shapes of land. Distances between places at the edges of this map are distorted. It is also difficult to find north and south on this map, because these directions curve along meridians.

Map B is another kind of equal-area projection. The shapes on Map B are more accurate than the shapes on Map A. However, the cuts in this map make it very difficult to tell the distances between places.

Another kind of world map, the mercator projection, is shown on Map C. This projection was invented by a Flemish mapmaker in the 1500s. Near the equator there is little distortion and sizes are accurate, too. However, as you move farther from the equator, sizes become more distorted.

Polar projections are used to show the area around the North Pole or the South

432

Pole. Most polar projections show only half the globe or less. Map D shows a polar projection of the North Pole. Sizes and shapes near the center are accurate. Near the edges, however, there is distortion.

Polar projections like Map D are used by pilots flying over the North Pole. The shortest distance between two points on a polar projection is a straight line.

TRYING THE SKILL

Suppose you are traveling on a long trip through the Americas. You want to use a map that will accurately show the distances you have traveled and how far you still have to go. Which kind of projection would you select? Would you have any use for a polar projection on this trip?

REVIEWING THE SKILL

1. Why do all flat maps of the world have some distortion?

2. Where does distortion occur on a mercator projection map?

3. Look at the Atlas map of the world on page R18. Which type of projection is used for this map?

4. In what ways is a flat map better than a globe? In what ways is a globe better?

5. Why are there many different kinds of map projections?

MAP C: MERCATOR PROJECTION

MAP D: POLAR PROJECTION

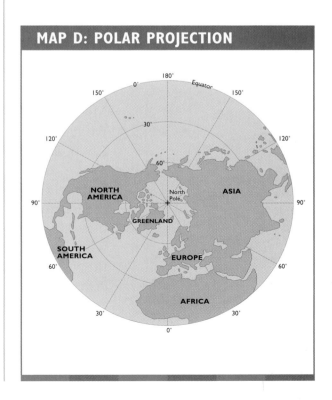

433

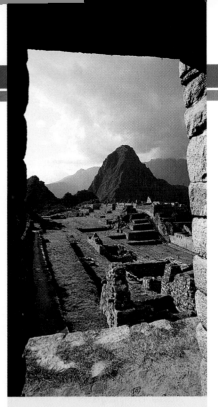

THE INCA EMPIRE

READ ALOUD

I am rich in silver

I am rich in gold.

These words come from an Inca poem. They cele-brate the wealth of the Inca civilization, which devel-oped in the Andes Mountains of South America. In these mountains the Inca found the large amounts of metal and minerals that made their empire rich. They also found a place to develop traditions that made their culture rich as well.

THE BIG PICTURE

While the Aztec were extending their rule beyond the Valley of Mexico, another culture was expanding in the mountains of South America. This people, known as the Inca, built an empire along the Andes Mountains. The empire stretched from what is today Ecuador to central Chile. This distance is about equal to the distance from New York City to the Panama Canal. At its peak the Inca empire had about 12 million peo-ple. Although they had little contact with the Aztec, the Inca, too, worshiped the sun, depended on maize as a major crop, and organized a strong army. Like the Aztec to the north, the Inca also created a system of government in their empire. In many other ways, however, the Inca were unique in the Americas and in the world.

Focus Activity

READ TO LEARN
What were some of the major achievements of the Inca?

VOCABULARY
terrace
quipu

PEOPLE
Pachakuti Inca

PLACES
Cuzco
Machu Picchu

434

THE RISE OF THE INCA

The Inca empire rose out of a small village called Cuzco (KOOS koh) in a fertile valley in what is today Peru. About 1200 the Inca settled at Cuzco to grow maize and other crops. At first the word *Inca* was the name for the ruler. Later the word applied to all of the people. When drought reduced the amount of fertile farmland, the Inca took over their neighbors' land. During the 1300s the Inca ruled most of the Cuzco Valley and demanded tributes from the other people living there.

Building an Empire

In 1438 a ruler called Pachakuti (pah chah KOO tee) Inca greatly extended the Inca borders. Soon the Inca controlled land west to the Pacific Ocean and south to the area of Lake Titicaca. Find the Inca lands on the map on this page. The Inca army seemed unstoppable in its quest to conquer new areas. In the Inca language, the word *Quechua* (KECH oo uh) means "to fight" and "to enjoy oneself."

Pachakuti became known as Sapa Inca, or Supreme Inca. As emperor, Pachakuti set about organizing the new land he controlled. He forced conquered people off their land. Then he allowed people who

This poncho was made of feathers by an Inca craftworker. It was worn during Inca ceremonies.

were loyal to the Inca to settle there. Pachakuti appointed governors in each region. People from all corners of the empire were required to do jobs for the government. Men built roads and raised crops; women made cloth.

Pachakuti also spread the Inca religion throughout the empire. Their religion was based on the worship of an ancient Inca god called Viracocha. According to Inca beliefs, this god had appeared in the emperor's dream during a war. Conquered people were forced to worship Viracocha and provide offerings of food. However, the Inca also let people continue to worship their own gods, as well.

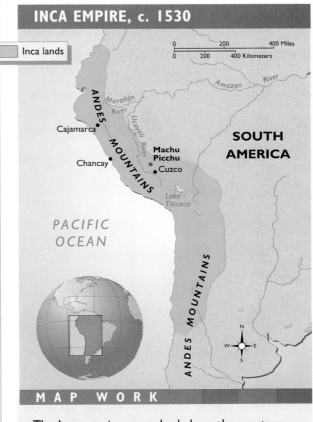

INCA EMPIRE, c. 1530

Inca lands

ANDES MOUNTAINS
Marañón River
Ucayali River
Amazon River
Cajamarca
Machu Picchu
Chancay
Cuzco
Lake Titicaca
PACIFIC OCEAN
SOUTH AMERICA
ANDES MOUNTAINS

MAP WORK

The Inca empire stretched along the western edge of South America.

1. Which city was located along the Ucayali River?

2. About how far is Lake Titicaca from Machu Picchu?

435

CHILDREN OF THE SUN

After his victory Pachakuti built a temple with a gold sculpture of the god Viracocha. This temple was located in the city of Cuzco. The most important temple in Cuzco, though, honored Inti, the sun god. In the center of this temple was a huge golden sculpture of the sun, decorated with precious stones. The Inca considered Inti to be their parent and often called themselves "Children of the Sun."

Life in Cuzco

Cuzco served as the center of government, religion, and trade in the Inca empire. The temples and government buildings at the center of Cuzco were constructed of stone blocks. These blocks fit together so well that it is impossible to put a knife between them!

Beyond the main plaza lived the emperor and wealthy nobles. These people were easy to recognize by the special headbands and earrings they wore. One of the first Spanish soldiers to visit the city was impressed by Inca building skill. He wrote the following description in the 1500s:

Cuzco is large enough and handsome enough to compare to any Spanish city. Most of the houses are of stone; others have stonework only halfway up; many are of adobe [clay bricks] and all are regularly built. The streets, all stone-paved and straight, cross each other at right angles, and have each a stone-lined water channel running down the middle. The city is placed on high ground, and many houses cling to the slopes above and many can be seen on the flat lands below.

The Inca were skilled at building with stone (left) and at farming, as the codex (below) shows.

Outside Cuzco, workers and farmers lived in small mud huts with high windows. Also outside the city were many government storage buildings. Some contained food, such as maize, dried fruit, or salt. Others contained neat piles of beautiful wool and cotton cloth. There was even a building just to hold the feathers of hummingbirds, which were used as decoration for clothing.

Inca Agriculture

Every year the Inca emperor, followed by a group of nobles, traveled to a field outside Cuzco and dug up the ground with a plow made of pure gold. This act signaled the importance of agriculture to all of Inca society.

Inca farmers grew potatoes, maize, and peppers. They adapted their farming methods to the geography of different parts of the empire. In hilly areas they built terraces, level platforms of earth that climbed each hill like a staircase. In rocky areas Inca farmers dug huge pits 20 feet deep. Farmers enriched the soil by placing fish in the pits. In dry areas the Inca brought water through a system of canals and aqueducts. One stone aqueduct crossed nearly 500 miles to bring water from a faraway mountain lake.

Although all farming was done by human labor, the Inca did raise animals for other uses. They used llamas as pack animals to carry many trade items through the empire. The best wool came from wild sheep. Only the nobles were allowed to wear the fine wool from these sheep. The Inca also hunted deer for food and clothing.

As in the past, llamas are still used to carry goods in the Andes Mountains.

DID YOU KNOW?

How did the Inca keep records of trade throughout the empire?

Although the Inca did not have a written language, they developed a method for recording important matters. The Inca used special cords called quipus (KEE pooz). A quipu was about 2 feet long and had threads of different colors hanging from it. White threads stood for silver, yellow stood for gold, and red stood for war. By tying knots in the string, a quipu keeper could record trade items, battles, or births and deaths in a village.

437

The Inca used decorated knives (below) in ceremonies at places such as Machu Picchu (above).

TRAVELING THROUGH THE EMPIRE

Nothing was more important to keeping the empire together than the huge network of roads. The Inca built more than 19,000 miles of roads—over some of the most rugged landscape in the world. One Spanish visitor wrote this report in the 1500s:

> I believe there is no account of a road as great as this, running through deep valleys, high mountains, banks of snow, torrents of water, living rock, and wild rivers. Through some places it went flat and paved; it was dug out of steep rock in the mountains; it passed with walls along rivers, and had steps and resting spots in the snow.

Important quipu messages were carried through the empire by runners. Messengers stopped every few miles to pass on messages to the next runner. Huge armies and long trade caravans made up of hundreds of llamas also traveled along the useful stone highways.

A City in the Clouds

Roads connected all corners of the empire, but some places were still difficult to reach. One road wound high into the mountains north of Cuzco, through stone tunnels and along steep cliffs. The road ended on a mountaintop, at a town called Machu Picchu (MAHCH oo PEEK choo). Machu Picchu is so far from other towns that it was forgotten until an American

This girl from Peru wears traditional clothing suited to the cool climate of the Andes.

explorer named Hiram Bingham came across it in 1911.

Bingham found stone ruins of buildings, walls, and terraces at the mountaintop location. No one is sure why Machu Picchu was built or why it was forgotten. Some historians think that it may have been a special religious town, similar to a European monastery. There Inca may have worshiped at shrines. Many historians believe the town was built around 1438 by the Inca ruler Pachakuti, who wanted a place to worship. Another possibility is that the town was used as a fortress during war.

WHY IT MATTERS

The lost city of Machu Picchu is just one of many mysteries that surround the Inca. When Spanish soldiers conquered the Inca empire in the 1500s, they destroyed many Inca treasures. Fortunately, many quipu records remain, and some Spanish soldiers wrote down their thoughts about this civilization.

The few gold artifacts that remain show the skill of Inca craftworkers. Stone roads and city walls are evidence of great building knowledge. The songs and poems recorded by Spanish conquerors give a hint of the Inca's rich oral tradition. The language of the Inca is kept alive by millions of people today. People who speak Quechua still live in the Andes region of Peru. Through these sources historians can still get a sense of the brilliant culture created by the "Children of the Sun."

Reviewing Facts and Ideas

SUM IT UP

- The Inca built a huge empire in the Andes Mountains in western South America.
- The Inca capital of Cuzco was the center of government, religion, and trade in the empire.
- Inca farmers used terraces and irrigation to grow crops.
- The vast Inca road system helped unite the empire. Roads allowed easy travel for armies, merchants, and messengers.

THINK ABOUT IT

1. Why did the Inca call themselves "Children of the Sun"?

2. How did terraces help the Inca expand their agriculture?

3. **FOCUS** List three major achievements of the Inca.

4. **THINKING SKILL** _Compare_ the Inca empire with the Aztec empire. How were they similar? How were they different?

5. **GEOGRAPHY** Describe two ways in which the Inca interacted with their environment.

EARLY PEOPLE OF NORTH AMERICA

READ ALOUD

In summer the Ojibwa (oh JIHB wah) lived by the waters of Lake Superior. When summer changed to autumn, they moved to the marshes where wild rice grew. They left the marshes before the heavy snows fell, living now near the herds that could be hunted. In spring sap flowed in the maple trees, and the Ojibwa came to collect it.

Like many of the peoples of North America, the Ojibwa moved their villages each season. This way of living allowed them to use many of the resources of their environment.

Focus Activity

READ TO LEARN
How did the Ojibwa make use of their northern forest environment?

VOCABULARY
diversity
Three Fires Council
wigwam

PLACES
Bowating

THE BIG PICTURE

As you have read, North America and South America were home to many peoples before the arrival of Europeans. These peoples and their descendants are called Indians. Tremendous diversity has always existed among these peoples. Diversity refers to differences. Peoples who lived in what is now the United States, and their descendants, are also called Native Americans. All of these peoples had many things in common, but each group adapted to its environment in unique ways.

Around 1400, in the Great Lakes region of North America, a group of Native Americans called the Ojibwa learned to make use of the forest environment. The Ojibwa harvested wild rice, collected maple sap in the forest, and developed many cultural traditions based on the changing seasons of their region.

PEOPLE OF THE WOODLANDS

About 500 years ago nearly all the land east of the Mississippi River was thick forest. The Native Americans who lived here used the forest as a source of fuel, tools, shelter, and food. The forest provided such things as wood and maple syrup. One group of Native Americans, the Seneca, praised the forest in this poem about the sugar maple tree:

> To The Tree:
> O we share your scents,
> You the forests!
> We beg you
> To continue as before,
> The flowing waters of the maple.

The Ojibwa

Among the other woodland groups living in the eastern part of North America was the Ojibwa. The Ojibwa lived in the Great Lakes area of what are today Canada and the United States. The Ojibwa called themselves *Anishinabe* (ahn ish uh NAH bee), which means "original people."

According to their traditions, the Ojibwa once lived near the mouth of the St. Lawrence River, near the Atlantic Ocean. They migrated to the Great Lakes region about 500 years ago. There the Ojibwa settled along the eastern end of Lake Superior, which they called Kitchigami. A tremendous lake, with cold, deep waters, Kitchigami was an object of wonder and worship for the Ojibwa.

Villages at the Shore

The Ojibwa lived in villages of a few hundred people each. Many of these villages were scattered along the shores of Kitchigami and on the north shore of the peninsula between Lakes Huron and

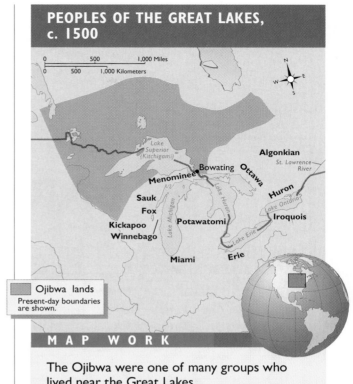

PEOPLES OF THE GREAT LAKES, c. 1500

Ojibwa lands
Present-day boundaries are shown.

MAP WORK

The Ojibwa were one of many groups who lived near the Great Lakes.

1. On which side of Lake Superior was the village of Bowating located?
2. Near which lake did the Winnebago and Miami groups live?

Michigan. Some of the larger villages served as trading centers. One trading center was the village of Bowating (BOH ah tihng). *Bowating* means "place at the falls." This village was located on an island in the river that connects Lake Superior and Lake Huron. As you can see on the map on this page, Bowating was centrally located for people who depended on boat travel.

Two neighboring Native American communities—the Potawatomi and the Ottawa—joined the Ojibwa to form the Three Fires Council. This council was a league, or cooperative group. Its main purpose was trade. People traveled among communities, bringing their trade goods in bark canoes. At what time of day does canoe travel take place in the song on the next page?

CYCLE OF THE SEASONS

To make the best use of their environment, the Ojibwa followed the cycle of the seasons. This meant that the Ojibwa moved with the change of seasons during the year. In each village families built dome-shaped houses they called wigwams. The Ojibwa made these houses by placing sheets of birch bark and cattail reeds over a frame of wooden poles. Families could roll up the birch bark sheets, leaving the wood frame behind.

Summer and Fall

The Ojibwa settled near a lake during the summer months. However, they often traveled as far as 50 miles away to find food. Men fished in the lakes and rivers and hunted in the surrounding forests. Women and children gathered nuts and berries. They also grew corn, beans, and squash.

To relax, the Ojibwa sometimes played a game called *baggataway*. Villages competed against each other to drive a ball over a goal line, using sticks with nets attached. Today a modern version of this game, lacrosse, is still played in many parts of the United States and in Canada.

When fall came, the Ojibwa moved near the marshes and ponds where wild rice grew. There women and men worked together to harvest the rice. Men used poles to push birch bark canoes through the shallow lakes and streams. Women used special sticks to knock rice grains into the canoes. The Ojibwa also worked to spread wild rice to new areas.

Winter and Spring

During winter the Ojibwa moved to areas where they could hunt. To travel through the deep snow of their long winter season, they wore snowshoes and used toboggans, or sleds. The Ojibwa hunted deer, moose, bear, and fox. They used bows and arrows, spears, and special traps that dropped logs or other heavy weights on animals. Meat was roasted or boiled and then smoked so that it could be stored. The skins from animals were tanned and then sewn into clothing and moccasins.

In spring the Ojibwa moved to an area where many sugar maple trees grew. The Ojibwa collected the maple sap in birch bark buckets and then boiled it down to make maple sugar. This sugar was used to flavor rice, fish, and other food. The Ojibwa moved on to their summer villages after maple sugar season ended. They carried the maple sugar with them in containers decorated with pictographs. Pictographs are drawings of symbols that are used as a writing system. In fact, the name *Ojibwa* comes from a term that means "those who make pictographs."

People of the Great Lakes region still make products from maple sap.

Infographic

Cultural Regions of North America, c. 1500

- ☐ Arctic
- ☐ Subarctic
- ☐ Eastern Woodlands
- ☐ Southeast
- ☐ Plains
- ☐ Northwest Coast
- ☐ California
- ☐ Basin and Plateau
- ☐ Southwest
- ☐ Northern Mexico
- ☐ Central America
- ☐ Middle America
- ☐ Caribbean

Inuit

Inuit

Inuit

Haida

Cree

Micmac

Ojibwa

Ottawa

Penobscot

Walla-Walla

Nez Percé

Crow

Menominee

Huron

Iroquois

Mohawk

Mohegan

Hupa

Lakota

Winnebago

Kickapoo

Pomo

Cheyenne

Powhatan

Chumash

Hopi

Navajo

Pueblo

Zuni

Shawnee

Cherokee

Comanche

Cochimi

Choctaw

Seminole

Huichol

Taino

Toltec

Aztec

Maya

Zapotec

Hupa girls and women used shells and feathers to decorate their clothing. They wore necklaces like this one made of abalone and clam shells.

Native North Americans

Native North Americans lived in all parts of the continent. Many different groups lived in each of the cultural regions shown on the map. They made distinctive types of jewelry and clothing. Why might these items have been important to the different groups?

Young Menominees wore beaded bags (above right) that were sometimes called Friendship Bags because they were given as gifts. The Aztec wore jewelry like this gold pendant (right). Other Aztec items were made of beautiful stones or crystals.

WHY IT MATTERS

The arrival of Europeans in North America in the 1600s brought great change for the Ojibwa and other Native American groups. Wars, disease, and European settlement all took a tremendous toll on the Ojibwa and their way of life. Still, the Ojibwa survived, and they continued many of the traditions of their people.

Today nearly 200,000 Ojibwa live in the Great Lakes region of the United States and Canada. Gerald Vizenor, an Ojibwa writer, recently described his feelings about his homeland:

> The land is everything to me. The land is part of my language, part of the way I perceive [become aware of] the world. The water, the trees, the smell of pine, the smell of autumn, the smell of wet leaves in the spring. It is all part of my imagination, part of my dreams.

Today the Ojibwa continue to follow important cultural traditions. This Ojibwa dance group is performing at a Native American harvest festival in Wisconsin.

Reviewing Facts and Ideas

SUM IT UP

- The woodlands of North America provided many resources for the Native Americans who lived there.

- The Ojibwa settled around the area of Lake Superior about 500 years ago.

- The Ojibwa moved with the seasons to hunt, fish, farm, and harvest food in different places.

- Many Ojibwa continue to live in the Great Lakes region and carry on their cultural traditions.

THINK ABOUT IT

1. According to tradition, from where did the Ojibwa migrate when they settled near Lake Superior about 500 years ago?

2. Why did the Ojibwa travel to different areas throughout the year?

3. **FOCUS** How did the Ojibwa use forest resources to make their homes?

4. **THINKING SKILL** What _conclusions_ can you make from the fact that wigwams were easily taken apart?

5. **WRITE** Create a calendar that describes what the Ojibwa did during each season of the year.

CHAPTER 15 REVIEW

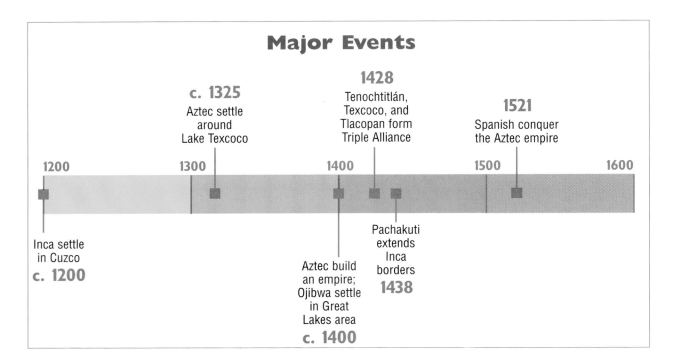

Major Events

1428
Tenochtitlán, Texcoco, and Tlacopan form Triple Alliance

c. 1325
Aztec settle around Lake Texcoco

1521
Spanish conquer the Aztec empire

1200　1300　1400　1500　1600

Inca settle in Cuzco
c. 1200

Aztec build an empire; Ojibwa settle in Great Lakes area
c. 1400

Pachakuti extends Inca borders
1438

THINKING ABOUT VOCABULARY

Each of the following statements contains an underlined vocabulary word or term. Number a sheet of paper from 1 to 10. Beside each number write **T** if the statement is true and **F** if the statement is false. If the statement is false, rewrite the sentence using the vocabulary word or term correctly.

1. Great <u>diversity</u> existed among various Native American peoples.

2. <u>Wigwams</u> were made by placing sheets of birch bark and cattail reeds over a frame of wooden poles.

3. The islands the Aztec made in a lake for farming were called <u>quipus</u>.

4. The Aztec had to pay <u>tribute</u> to the rulers of nearby cities when they arrived in the Valley of Mexico.

5. A <u>codex</u> is a weapon used by Ojibwa warriors.

6. Inca farmers planted crops on <u>terraces</u> that climbed up hills like stairs.

7. <u>Chinampas</u> was the name of the corn eaten by the Ojibwa people, who lived in the Great Lakes region.

8. During the last part of his seven-year walk from the southern tip of South America to the Arctic Ocean, George Meegan walked across the warm, swampy <u>tundra</u> of Florida.

9. North America and South America are connected by an <u>isthmus</u>.

10. A <u>timberline</u> separates Native American villages.

THINKING ABOUT FACTS

1. How did the Ice Age glaciers affect physical features of North America?

2. Describe the Aztec system of writing.

3. What role did Pachakuti play in Inca history?

4. What was the Three Fires Council? Why was it formed?

5. According to the time line above, how long did the Aztec empire last?

WRITING A LETTER

Suppose you are George Meegan in 1976 and you have just finished your seven-year walk across the length of the Americas. Write a letter to a friend about your journey.

WRITING A SUMMARY

Write a paragraph summarizing the achievements of the Aztec civilization.

WRITING A DESCRIPTION

Write a paragraph describing how the Ojibwa of the Great Lakes region adapted to their forest environment.

APPLYING GEOGRAPHY SKILLS

USING MAP PROJECTIONS

1. What is a map projection?

2. Maps A and B on page 432 both show equal-area projections. What are some of the advantages and disadvantages of each map?

3. Place a ruler between North America and South America on Map C. Then find a globe and use a string to measure the same straight-line distance. Explain why that line would look curved on Map C.

4. Compare Maps A and D on pages 432–433. If you were exploring the North Pole, which map would you bring with you? Why?

5. Why are map projections useful?

Summing Up the Chapter

Copy the word map below on a separate sheet of paper. Review the chapter to find at least two pieces of information to support each topic in the word map. When you have filled in the map, write a paragraph that answers the question "What made the Aztec, Inca, and Ojibwa civilizations similar and what made them different?"

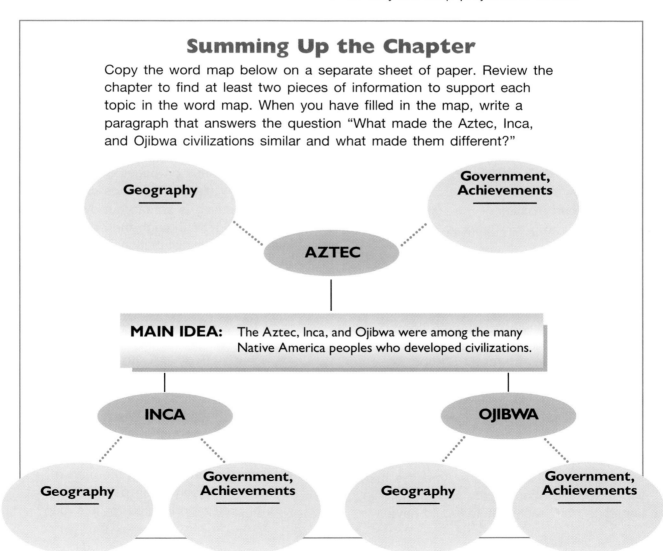

Geography

Government, Achievements

AZTEC

MAIN IDEA: The Aztec, Inca, and Ojibwa were among the many Native America peoples who developed civilizations.

INCA

OJIBWA

Geography

Government, Achievements

Geography

Government, Achievements

UNIT 4 REVIEW

THINKING ABOUT VOCABULARY

Number a sheet of paper from 1 to 10. Beside each number write the word or term from the list below that best matches the definition.

diversity
feudalism
grand mufti
griot
isthmus

monarchy
monsoon
navigable
savanna
shogun

1. A grassy, tree-dotted plain
2. A seasonal wind
3. A military ruler of Japan
4. Can be traveled by ships
5. A way of organizing and governing society based on land and service
6. A government by king or queen
7. A religious leader responsible for interpreting Islamic law
8. Made up of or showing different kinds
9. A narrow strip of land that connects two larger land masses
10. A special African storyteller and oral historian

THINK AND WRITE

WRITING ABOUT PEOPLE

Write about somebody you read about in the unit—Michelangelo, Queen Amanishakhete, Kublai Khan, Lady Murasaki Shikibu, or Pachakuti Inca, for example. Discuss the person's achievements and his or her importance in history.

WRITING ABOUT PERSPECTIVES

Choose two of the empires or civilizations in Europe, Africa, Asia, and the Americas that you have read about. Write about what someone from each culture would have thought about war. What might they consider to be important reasons for going to war? Explain why there might be differences in their perspectives.

WRITING AN EXPLANATION

Write two paragraphs about the rise of empires in West Africa. Explain how the area's natural resources played a role in the development of trade. Describe the effects of this trade on the people living in the area. Include facts about powerful rulers who led the empires.

BUILDING SKILLS

1. **Point of view** Reread the section about the fall of Constantinople on pages 388–389. Explain different points of view about the event. For example, how might a Turkish historian describe the fall of the city? How might a Byzantine historian describe it?

2. **Distribution maps** Look again at the population maps on pages 370–371 to review how distribution maps can show how something is spread out over an area. Then look through the book for at least two other distribution maps. What do they show?

3. **Making generalizations** From what you already know about the growth of civilizations, make a generalization about the types of environment civilizations require. What are some exceptions to your generalization?

4. **Making generalizations** Make a generalization about students. What do they have in common that would allow you to generalize about them as a group?

5. **Map projections** Look at the map of Marco Polo's journey on page 406. What kind of projection is used for this map?

YESTERDAY, TODAY &
TOMORROW

Civilizations in Europe, Africa, Asia, and the Americas had very different cultures and languages. Today mass communication is helping people around the world understand each other better. Do you think people in different civilizations will be more similar in the future? Do you think someday everybody will speak the same language? Explain your answers.

READING ON YOUR OWN

Here are some books you might find at the library to help you learn more.

THE SILK ROUTE: 7,000 MILES OF HISTORY
by John S. Major
The dangerous journey of China's most precious cloth during the years A.D. 618–906.

KNIGHTS IN ARMOR
Edited by John D. Clare
A well-illustrated overview of the lifestyle and role of the knight during the Middle Ages.

ALL OF YOU WAS SINGING
by Richard Lewis
This is a retelling of an Aztec myth.

UNIT PROJECT

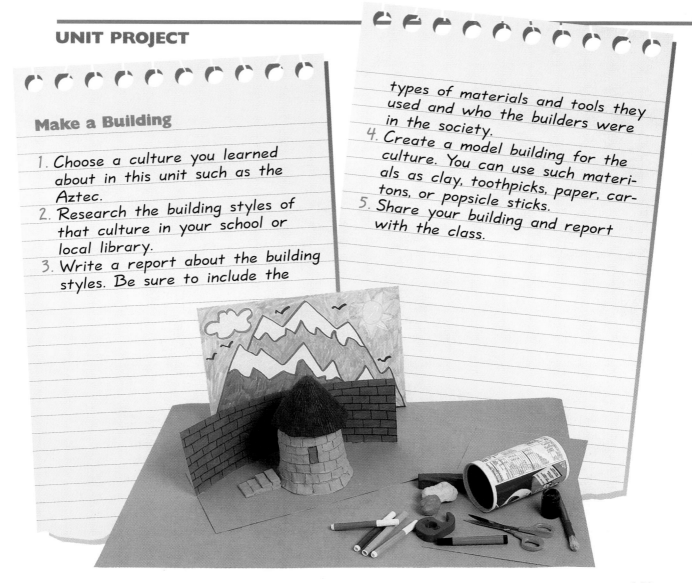

Make a Building

1. Choose a culture you learned about in this unit such as the Aztec.
2. Research the building styles of that culture in your school or local library.
3. Write a report about the building styles. Be sure to include the types of materials and tools they used and who the builders were in the society.
4. Create a model building for the culture. You can use such materials as clay, toothpicks, paper, cartons, or popsicle sticks.
5. Share your building and report with the class.

INCA MASK, PERU;
GOLD AND SILVER
COINS, SPAIN;
PAINTING OF
FRENCH REVOLUTION

Dawn of the Modern World

"Knowledge shall be sought throughout the world."

from the Charter Oath
See page 511.

WHY DOES IT MATTER?

These words, from a Japanese document of 1889, express a yearning for new ideas and knowledge. During the period you will read about—when our modern world was just beginning to take shape—new ways of thinking spread among many peoples.

People began to learn more about the world around them. European explorers sailed to the Western Hemisphere, charting new courses and coming into contact with peoples of the Americas. Scientists learned about Earth and its position in the solar system. They invented new technologies. The changes that resulted created a world of new ideas and challenges.

STEAM LOCOMOTIVE, UNITED STATES

GALILEO'S ROOM, ITALY; EXPLORER'S COMPASS, EUROPE

451

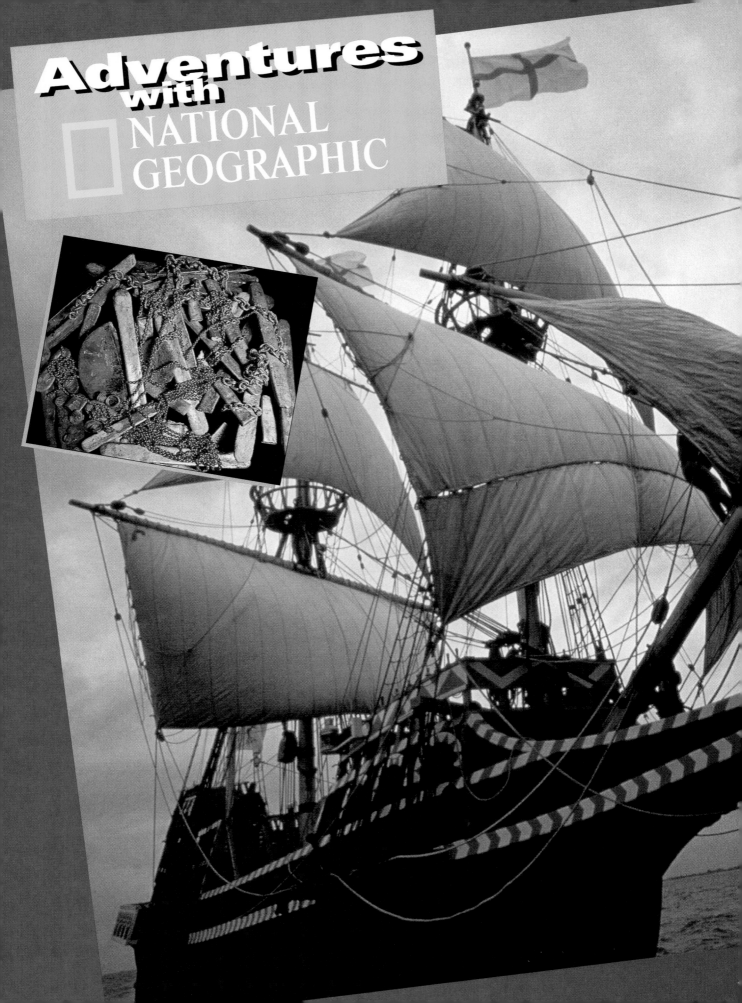

Adventures with

NATIONAL GEOGRAPHIC

Golden VOYAGE

Today, a reproduction of the *Golden Hind* sails off the coast of England. Four hundred years ago, the real *Golden Hind* carried explorer Francis Drake from England around the world. Surviving violent storms, Drake rounded South America and headed up its western coast. Along the way, he picked up a fortune in treasure—by raiding Spain's South American ports. Three years after his departure, Drake returned to England. Queen Elizabeth was so pleased by his feat—and by the treasure he brought home—that she knighted him right on the deck of the *Golden Hind*.

GEO JOURNAL

You're Queen Elizabeth's speechwriter. Compose a speech to welcome Drake home.

CHAPTER 16

European Expansion

THINKING ABOUT
HISTORY AND GEOGRAPHY

The story of European movement into the Western Hemisphere begins in the late 1400s. Explorers were able to sail to distant lands as a result of new technology. Following the time line, you can see how the explorers encountered civilizations in the Americas that were thousands of years old. This meeting began an exchange of goods, ideas, and people that changed the shape of history.

1519

VALLEY OF MEXICO

Moctezuma watches the Spanish approach the Aztec capital

1520

STRAIT OF MAGELLAN

Ferdinand Magellan sails around the southern tip of South America

1535

LIMA

Francisco Pizarro founds the city of Lima as the capital of Peru

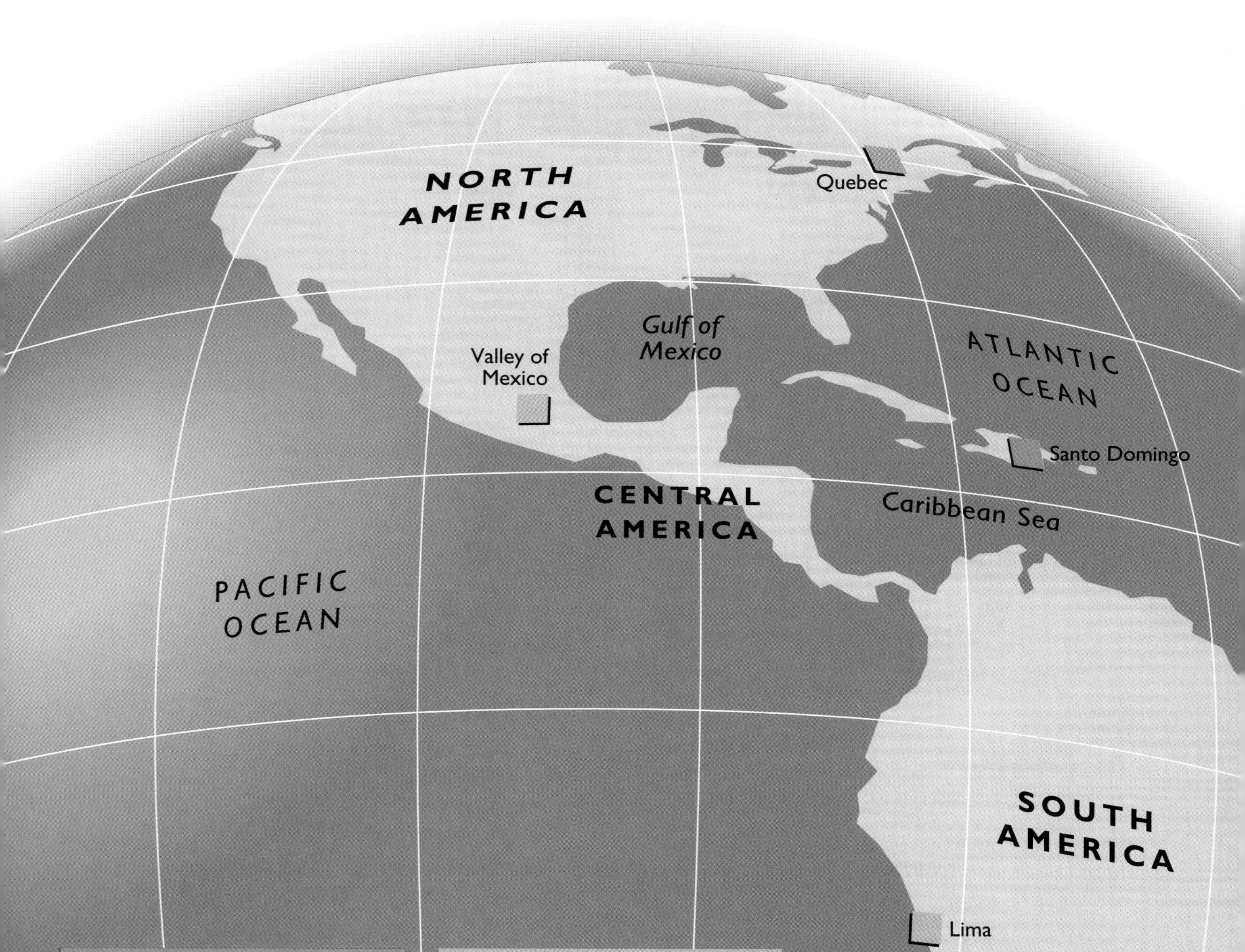

NORTH
AMERICA

Quebec

Gulf of
Mexico

ATLANTIC
OCEAN

Valley of
Mexico

Santo Domingo

CENTRAL
AMERICA

Caribbean Sea

PACIFIC
OCEAN

SOUTH
AMERICA

Lima

1600

SANTO DOMINGO

Enslaved Africans work on sugarcane plantations

1608

QUEBEC

Samuel de Champlain establishes a settlement for France

Strait of Magellan

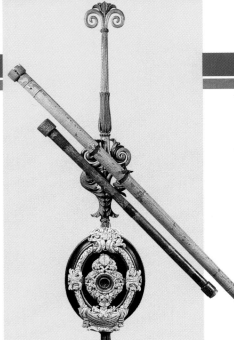

TVBVM OPTICVM VIDES GALILAEI INVENTVM ET OPVS,QVO SOLIS MACVLAS
ET EXTIMOS LVNAE MONTES,ET IOVIS SATELLITES,ET NOVAM QVASI
RERVM VNIVERSITATE PRIMVS DISPEXIT A.MDCIX.

Focus Activity

READ TO LEARN
What were the achievements of Galileo Galilei and Isaac Newton?

VOCABULARY
geocentric
heliocentric
telescope
gravity
scientific method

PEOPLE
Galileo Galilei
Isaac Newton

THE BEGINNING OF MODERN SCIENCE

READ ALOUD

In the early 1600s Galileo Galilei (gal uh LAY oh gah lee LE ee) used a new invention, the telescope, to look into space for the first time. He saw more stars than he could count. He wrote:

"Upon whatever part of the galaxy the telescope is directed, a crowd of stars is immediately presented to view. Many of them are rather large and quite bright, while the number of smaller ones is quite beyond calculation."

THE BIG PICTURE

Around 1500 Europeans were expanding their influence in other parts of the world. Explorers were making new connections between Europe and other continents. In the cities of Renaissance Italy, artists such as Leonardo da Vinci were painting the world around them in exciting new ways. As you read in Chapter 12, the Christian world was changing as well.

Scientists, too, began to take a fresh look at the world around them. Until this time most Europeans' understanding of the universe and how it worked came from ancient times. Most people believed that the universe was geocentric (jee oh SEN trihk), or centered around Earth. This view seemed to make sense. After all, it was the sun that seemed to "rise" and "set" each day, while Earth seemed not to move. In the early 1500s, however, a challenge to this belief would excite and disturb many Europeans.

NEW VIEWS

At this time scientists were talking about the ideas of Polish scientist Nicolaus Copernicus. In Chapter 12 you read that Copernicus suggested that Earth is not located at the center of the universe. He put forth a heliocentric (hee lee oh SEN trihk), or sun-centered, view. In this view, Earth and other planets move in orbits, or paths, around the sun. The heliocentric view caused a great stir. Was it really possible that Earth—and the people who lived on it— were not at the center of all things?

Copernicus spent much time studying the night sky. He also spent a great deal of time doing mathematics. Copernicus and many other scientists saw astronomy as a kind of mathematics. Astronomy is the science that deals with the sun, moon, stars, and planets. Scientists' ideas began to change when a new way of actually *seeing* the stars was invented. That invention was the telescope, which made faraway things appear close. As you will read, the telescope first became a useful scientific tool in the hands of Galileo Galilei.

Observing the World

Galileo was born in 1564 in the Italian city of Pisa, famous for its Leaning Tower. Like Copernicus, Galileo became interested in mathematics. Everywhere he looked, Galileo saw mathematics as part of daily life. A hailstorm made him wonder, do large hailstones fall faster than smaller ones? Ancient Greek thinkers such as Aristotle said that they do, because large hailstones are heavier than smaller ones. Yet when Galileo carefully watched hail falling from the sky, he thought Aristotle might have been wrong. A new age of testing ideas through observation had begun.

Galileo learned a great deal by looking closely at the world around him. In a cathedral one day, he saw an oil lamp swinging in a draft. Galileo made careful notes about the swinging lamp. Other inventors used Galileo's ideas to create clock pendulums. A pendulum is a weight hung so that it can swing back and forth—much like the oil lamp Galileo noticed!

Copernicus (right) studied the sky and made drawings of planets orbiting the sun (below).

The Granger Collection

Galileo (below) often worked on his **telescope** and other instruments in his room in Florence, Italy (left).

The Granger Collection

EXPERIMENTS AND INVENTIONS

Not long after he observed the swinging lamp, Galileo went on to study and to teach. Though he loved his new work as a teacher, he did not earn much money. So Galileo tried to come up with ideas for useful items that he could sell. He created the world's first thermometer. A thermometer measures temperature. It was 22 inches long and filled with water. No one had much use for the thermometer in the late 1500s, so it did not seem important then.

Galileo came up with a very successful device, however, in 1609. He learned that a maker of eyeglasses had invented an instrument that made distant things seem close. Galileo quickly made some changes and created his own model of a telescope. He gained wealth and success when he gave a telescope to the ruler of Venice. Commanders of the ruler's navy used the telescope for looking at far-off ships.

A Look into Space

The telescope brought changes to Galileo's life—and to the world—in another way. One night Galileo looked at the moon through the telescope. He expected to see the smooth surface that the ancient Greeks and many others had described. Instead, he saw that the moon was "rough and uneven, covered everywhere, just like Earth's surface, with huge mountains and deep valleys."

Galileo now began to study the sky carefully, night after night. He realized that it was far more complex than most people had ever realized. Far more stars existed than anyone had ever dreamed! Galileo discovered that another planet, Jupiter, also had moons orbiting it—just as the moon orbits Earth. Earth itself appeared to be slowly spinning, and moving around the sun.

Galileo began to think that the long-held belief that Earth was at the center of the universe was wrong. His studies supported Copernicus' heliocentric idea.

Galileo made his findings public in 1610. At the time, it was as if a "new" universe had been discovered. Anyone could see it simply by looking through a telescope. Some people were shocked and surprised. Others, especially Church leaders, were angry.

Science and the Church

Leaders of the Catholic Church prepared to put Galileo on trial. They said that his views went against the Church's teachings. Earlier scientists had been sentenced to death because they wrote about heliocentric ideas.

Galileo, who was Roman Catholic, faced great danger. In 1633 the 69-year-old scientist was arrested and brought to Rome for trial. There Galileo was strongly advised to take back what he had said about the place of the sun in the universe.

Threatened with torture, Galileo finally stated, "I do not hold this opinion of Copernicus." Galileo was then taken back to his home in northern Italy. For the rest of his life, he was not allowed to leave his home. Galileo never publicly upheld the heliocentric view again. Before he died in 1642, though, he wrote:

> *I have two sources of comfort—first, that in my writings there cannot be found the faintest shadow of disobedience towards the Holy Church; and second, the truth of my own conscience, which only I and God in Heaven thoroughly know. And He knows that in this cause for which I suffer, none have spoken with more religious devotion or with greater enthusiasm for the Church than I.*

How have telescopes changed since Galileo's time?

Galileo's first telescope was about as long as his arm. It was made only of a tube and two-inch lenses.

By contrast, the Hubble Space Telescope, launched in 1990, is over 43 feet long. It uses mirrors over 7 feet wide and has a tangle of wires 26,000 miles long! The Hubble Telescope travels around Earth at a distance of 380 miles above the planet's surface. From there, the Hubble Telescope can spot stars *trillions* of miles away. Here's another way to put it: The Hubble could spot the punctuation mark at the end of this sentence from a mile away, or a dime from 20 miles away!

The Work of Isaac Newton

In the same year that Galileo died, Isaac Newton was born in the countryside of England. Newton grew up to become one of the world's giants in science. In fact, he built on Galileo's scientific legacy.

According to one story, the young Newton found a key to unlock these mysteries one day in 1675, when an apple fell on his head. The apple's fall from a tree led him to study the force of gravity. Gravity is the force that pulls things toward Earth. Newton calculated that the same force that pulls a falling apple toward Earth also pulls at the moon. Instead of falling to Earth's surface, the moon is kept moving in a circular path around the planet. Newton's study of gravity helped scientists in the late 1600s understand how a heliocentric universe actually worked.

WHY IT MATTERS

European discoveries in science had many results. They led to a new understanding of humanity's place in the universe and how that universe worked. Improvements in technology came about as well. For example, ship captains could now use telescopes to see faraway land, or to quickly spot enemy ships on the way. The pendulum clock helped people to measure time accurately.

European interest in learning about the natural world had another important result. It led to the development of what is called the scientific method. The scientific method is a way of questioning and studying things that occur in nature. With this method, an idea must be thoroughly tested before it is accepted as true. This is what Galileo did when he carefully studied the motions of the stars and planets. His experiments, and the work of other scientists, led Europe and the rest of the world into a new age of science. Scientific advances in astronomy, medicine, and other fields continue to have great effects on the way we live and view the world.

This is a reconstruction of a clock part invented by Galileo. The swinging pendulum causes the gears to move.

✔ Reviewing Facts and Ideas

SUM IT UP

- Most Europeans in the Middle Ages shared the ancient Greeks' belief that the universe was geocentric, or centered around Earth.

- In the early 1600s, Galileo Galilei built on the heliocentric, or sun-centered, ideas of Copernicus.

- Galileo's findings clashed with Catholic teachings. The Church supported geocentric ideas.

- Isaac Newton's studies of gravity in the late 1600s helped scientists to learn how a heliocentric system might work.

THINK ABOUT IT

1. How did the scientific method help both Galileo and Newton in their work?

2. Why was Newton's work with gravity important?

3. **FOCUS** How did scientists like Galileo and Newton change the way people thought about the world?

4. **THINKING SKILL** Explain some different *points of view* people held about the universe in the 1500s. What might account for each of these?

5. **WRITE** Write a paragraph explaining how science affects the way we live today.

CITIZENSHIP
MAKING A DIFFERENCE

Making History in Space

NOORDWIJK, THE NETHERLANDS—Like Galileo and Newton, modern scientists and explorers want to learn more about unexplored areas. Shortly after the year 2000, the European Space Agency will work with the United States, Russia, and Japan to put an international space station into orbit. The station, called Alpha, will be home to humans for long periods of time. Using Alpha as a base, 21st-century astronauts will both study and explore space.

French engineer Jean-Francois Redor (JAHN fran SWAH RAY dohr) works at the agency's offices in Noordwijk. There he and scientists from 14 European nations design and launch spacecraft.

Redor and his team have the important job of making *Alpha* a place where humans can live in space. "We are designing and testing life support systems for the spacecraft," Redor explains. "Life support is everything that has to do with making sure that the environment inside the spacecraft is safe for humans. The air must be breathable and the water drinkable. Human and kitchen waste must be stored or recycled."

Although the work Redor does is designed to help people survive in space, this research is already helping us on Earth. An air filter developed for use in space can be used in hospitals, office buildings, and airplanes to remove pollutants and odors from the air. New life support systems may allow submarines to remain underwater for longer periods.

New systems are providing solutions for the problems caused by animal waste on Earth. Redor explains, "We are learning how to recycle waste products and carbon dioxide on space ships using harmless bacteria. The bacteria convert the waste into simple plants that can be used as food." In Belgium and France, pollution from animal waste is a serious problem. According to Redor, "The systems we are working on for the space mission will help chicken and cattle farmers reduce the pollution their animals cause." Farmers will be able to recycle these wastes. Redor and other Agency researchers are finding space-age answers to some Earthly problems.

"The systems we are working on . . . will help . . . farmers reduce the pollution their animals cause."

461

AN AGE OF EXPLORATION

READ ALOUD

"They sent out a small boat in order to find the cape of the other sea, and they came back at the end of the third day and told how they had seen the cape of the great sea. And the Captain General wept with joy. And they named that cape Cape Desire because they had desired it for so long."

This description was written by a passenger on a ship captained by Ferdinand Magellan (muh JEL un). In the middle 1400s few Europeans had traveled far into the Atlantic Ocean. By 1520, though, European sailors were regularly crossing the Atlantic. One sailor, Magellan, was about to sail into the great Pacific Ocean. His goal was to sail around the world.

THE BIG PICTURE

In the middle 1400s the Aztec empire and its capital city, Tenochtitlán, were at the height of power and influence in Mexico. Across the Atlantic Ocean in western Africa, meanwhile, gold was flowing north from Mali to the coastal cities of North Africa. Cities in Italy were becoming rich from trade with Asia.

Soon trade would link these different parts of the world more closely. Already goods were moving between Asia, Africa, and Europe. However, the route to Asia was very long and expensive. In order to buy spices and other goods, European merchants would have to find another way to reach Asia. That search would bring the two hemispheres—East and West—into contact.

Focus Activity

READ TO LEARN
How did European explorers bring distant parts of the world into contact with each other?

VOCABULARY
caravel
strait

PEOPLE
Prince Henry
Bartholomeu Dias
Vasco da Gama
Christopher Columbus
Ferdinand Magellan

PLACE
Strait of Magellan

TRAVEL FOR TRADE

European trade with Asia started to grow thanks largely to Marco Polo's travels on the Silk Road. In 1295 Polo returned to Venice from China. Not long after, his tales of the Silk Road and China became widely known. Polo's accounts made many Europeans want to take part in trade with Asia. Trade along the Silk Road thrived for more than 100 years afterward.

One of the most profitable goods to bring home was pepper. Since people did not have refrigerators, meat quickly spoiled unless it was preserved with salt. The salt, however, gave the meat a flavor that many people did not like. Europeans found that adding pepper made meat taste much better. Pepper became a very popular item.

A journey along the Silk Road sometimes took years to complete and was expensive. Yet those who returned could make as much as 60 times the amount they had spent making the journey. For this reason, some European leaders spent huge sums of money on the search for quicker, cheaper routes to Asia.

The Search for a Shorter Route

Prince Henry of Portugal was one leader who supported the search for such routes. He became known as Henry the Navigator. Henry lived between 1394 and 1460. He wanted to find a sea route to the gold mines of western Africa. He provided money and help to Europe's finest sailors, mapmakers, and shipbuilders. These people improved the compass, updated maps, and simplified the astrolabe, which you read about in Chapter 10.

Most important, the people working with Prince Henry designed a new kind of boat called a **caravel** (KAR uh vel). Caravels combined the smooth bodies of European sailing ships and the three-sided sails of Arab boats. These sails allowed boats to sail into the wind. Earlier captains usually had to direct their ships wherever the wind was blowing. Now, for the first time, European ships could go in almost any direction their captain wished. You can see a type of caravel on page 462.

The Granger Collection

Prince Henry helped navigators improve the compass. Italian sailors used this compass (right) around 1580.

EXPLORING AROUND THE WORLD

In 1469, nine years after Prince Henry died, Portuguese sailors became the first Europeans to reach the coast of western Africa. In 1488 a Portuguese captain became the first to sail around the southernmost tip of Africa, the Cape of Good Hope. This captain was Bartholomeu Dias (bahr tu lu MAY u DEE ush), whose achievement marked a turning point in the search for a new route to Asia. By sailing around Africa, Dias had discovered a possible sea route from Europe to the East.

Nine years later another Portuguese captain set sail for Asia. Vasco da Gama led a voyage that attempted to complete the trip around Africa to Asia. His success in reaching the coast of India made him the first European ever to sail so far east. Da Gama returned to India in 1502, bringing a navy to conquer rich port cities for Portugal. This began a period of European rule on the Indian subcontinent that would last for more than 400 years.

Across the Atlantic

Another explorer, Christopher Columbus, set out in 1492 to reach Asia by traveling in the opposite direction—west. Columbus did not reach Asia. However, as you will read in the next lesson, his voyage had tremendous effects on both Spain and the Americas.

The wealth of Asia's spice-rich lands continued to draw Europeans. In 1519 Spain sent Ferdinand Magellan on a westward journey to Asia. Neither Magellan nor anyone else had ever led such a voyage. Magellan was trying to sail around the whole world!

Magellan and his crew made their way through a strait at the tip of South

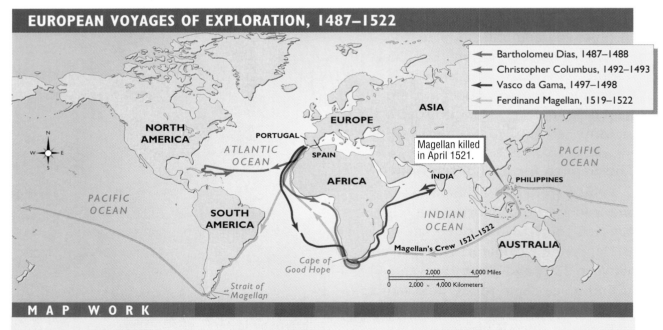

EUROPEAN VOYAGES OF EXPLORATION, 1487–1522

← Bartholomeu Dias, 1487–1488
← Christopher Columbus, 1492–1493
← Vasco da Gama, 1497–1498
← Ferdinand Magellan, 1519–1522

Magellan killed in April 1521.

Magellan's Crew 1521–1522

MAP WORK

Beginning in the late 1400s, Europeans raced to find the shortest sea route to Asia.

1. Which explorer sailed along the east coast of Africa?

2. Which voyage did not reach the southernmost tip of Africa?

3. Which explorer sailed for the longest period of time?

Ferdinand Magellan studied astronomy and navigation for two years before leaving Europe with a fleet of five ships in 1519.

America. A strait is a narrow channel, or body of water, between two larger bodies of water. Find the Strait of Magellan on the map. After sailing through this strait, Magellan reached the calm waters of an ocean he called the *Pacific*, or "peaceful," Ocean.

For Magellan and his crew, the voyage on this ocean was anything but peaceful. Lack of food left the crew eating dust made from the wood on board and the leather from their gear to survive. In the Philippines, Magellan himself was killed in battle. The crew sailed on, finally reaching ports in Asia and then, in 1522, Spain. They were home at last after a three-year journey around the world.

Of 238 men and 5 ships that set out with Magellan, only 17 men and 1 ship returned. That single ship's cargo, or load, paid for the whole voyage, with money left over.

WHY IT MATTERS

New technology, together with human courage, added greatly to western Europe's knowledge of the world in the late 1400s and early 1500s. As ships sailed new sea routes again and again, different regions became more closely linked through trade and communication. Such links led to further exploration—and conquest. You will read about exploration and conquest in the Americas later in this chapter.

✓// Reviewing Facts and Ideas

SUM IT UP

- To find a cheaper route to Asia, Europeans explored sea routes south around Africa or west across the Atlantic Ocean.

- Portugal's Prince Henry helped develop the caravel.

- In the 1480s and 1490s, Portuguese explorers Bartholomeu Dias and Vasco da Gama discovered a route to Asia by sailing around Africa.

- Ferdinand Magellan set sail on a voyage around the world in 1519.

THINK ABOUT IT

1. How did the caravel help European explorers?

2. Why did Europeans want to find new routes to Asia?

3. **FOCUS** What were two major changes brought about by Europe's explorers in the 1400s and 1500s?

4. **THINKING SKILL** Make a *generalization* about the qualities explorers such as Dias, Da Gama, and Magellan must have needed to be successful.

5. **GEOGRAPHY** Describe some of the difficulties explorers faced in trying to reach Asia by sea.

The Granger Collection

EUROPEANS IN THE AMERICAS

Focus Activity

READ TO LEARN
How did the empires of the Americas fall to Spain?

VOCABULARY
Line of Demarcation
conquistador
missionary
convert
hacienda

PEOPLE
Pedro Álvarez Cabral
Hernando Cortés
Moctezuma
Francisco Pizarro
Atahualpa

PLACES
Hispaniola
Cuzco
New Spain
Peru
Mexico City
Lima

READ ALOUD

The commander of the exhausted men drew a line in the sand and challenged, "Here, you return to Panama to be poor; there, you may go on to Peru to be rich. Choose which best becomes you as good Spaniards!"

All but one man crossed the line in the sand with the commander, Francisco Pizarro (frahn SEES koh pih ZAHR oh). They went on to gain great fortunes at the expense of one of the world's largest empires—the Inca empire.

THE BIG PICTURE

Growth and change were taking place all around the world in the late 1400s. In western Africa the markets of Timbuktu were growing within the Songhai empire. China's Ming rulers were adding to the Great Wall, as Chinese workers produced more and more porcelain, a fine hand pottery, and silk. In the Americas, meanwhile, both the Aztec and Inca empires were growing larger than any civilizations that had yet developed in the Western Hemisphere.

In 1492, Christopher Columbus crossed the Atlantic Ocean, opening up the Americas to European exploration. Within 40 years the Atlantic Ocean had become a vast highway crisscrossed by ships filled with people, trade goods, and treasure. Most of this traffic was controlled by just two European countries—Spain and Portugal. Though these countries were small in size, their power stretched across the globe.

EUROPEAN CLAIMS

In Lesson 2 you read that, in the late 1400s, Europe's race for new routes and territories was on. Portugal and Spain were in the lead. Their leaders believed that they had the right to claim whatever lands they explored. In 1494 the leaders of Spain and Portugal met to divide the lands of the Americas. They agreed upon an imaginary line, called the Line of Demarcation, across a map. Look at the map to see how this line affected claims in the Americas.

In 1493, Columbus had crossed the Atlantic for a second time. He brought more than 1,000 people with him to the island he called Hispaniola (his pun YOH luh). The Spanish were not coming simply to trade or explore— they meant to stay and colonize.

Portugal soon made its own claim in the Americas. Pedro Álvarez Cabral (PAY droh AHL vah rayz kuh BRAHL) set sail for India in 1500. A storm blew his ships west. So began a 300-year period of Portuguese rule in Brazil.

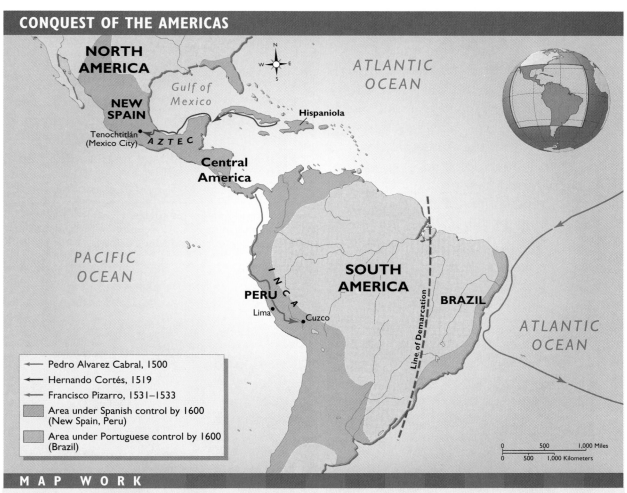

CONQUEST OF THE AMERICAS

NORTH AMERICA

Gulf of Mexico

NEW SPAIN

Tenochtitlán (Mexico City)

AZTEC

ATLANTIC OCEAN

Hispaniola

Central America

PACIFIC OCEAN

INCA

PERU

Lima

Cuzco

SOUTH AMERICA

Line of Demarcation

BRAZIL

ATLANTIC OCEAN

← Pedro Alvarez Cabral, 1500
← Hernando Cortés, 1519
← Francisco Pizarro, 1531–1533
Area under Spanish control by 1600 (New Spain, Peru)
Area under Portuguese control by 1600 (Brazil)

0   500   1,000 Miles
0   500   1,000 Kilometers

MAP WORK

The Line of Demarcation divided control of lands in the Americas.

1. Which European power controlled Aztec and Inca lands?

2. Which explorer sailed to the east coast of South America?

3. About how far from the Line of Demarcation was Cuzco?

4. Which explorer reached Tenochtitlán?

THE CONQUISTADORS

Beginning in the early 1500s, Spain sent more men to explore and make claims in the Americas. These conquistadors (kon KEES tuh dawrz), or "conquerors," soon defeated the Aztec and Inca empires and took control of their lands and resources.

Cortés and the Aztec

Conquistador Hernando Cortés (er NAHN doh kawr TAYS) and over 500 soldiers arrived in 1519 in the area that is now Mexico. Cortés had already lived in Spain's Caribbean colonies. He had heard stories of a powerful inland empire. This was the Aztec empire.

With the help of translators who knew both Spanish and the Aztec language, Cortés soon learned about the Aztec people. He was especially interested to learn that the Aztec empire had a great amount of gold.

After Cortés landed on the coast of Mexico, messengers of the Aztec ruler, Moctezuma (mahk tuh ZOO muh), watched his movements. These messengers told the emperor that Cortés and his men were coming to the capital of the empire, Tenochtitlán.

When the Spaniards arrived in the city, Moctezuma welcomed them as guests. That welcome eventually proved the downfall of both Moctezuma and the Aztec empire. With the help of Indians who turned against the Aztec, the conquistadors kidnapped and killed Moctezuma. After a war that ended in 1521, Cortés destroyed Tenochtitlán and conquered the Aztec empire.

Pizarro and the Incas

Ten years after Cortés conquered the Aztec, another conquistador prepared to invade Inca lands. Recall that these lands were located to the south, in the Andes Mountains. Francisco Pizarro (fran SEES koh pih ZAHR oh), like Cortés, was a military leader who had

Hernando Cortés (below right) led a large Spanish force in the conquest of Tenochtitlán, shown in the painting (below).

CONQVISTA DE MEXICO POR CORTES..7

spent some time in the Americas. He too had heard stories of a kingdom filled with treasure.

Pizarro began his conquest of the Inca empire in 1531. The Inca were just ending a civil war that left Atahualpa (ah tah WAHL pah) emperor. As Atahualpa and his army traveled to the Inca capital of Cuzco (KOOZ koh), they heard news of some 160 strangers marching along a nearby coastal road. Meanwhile, Pizarro learned that Atahualpa was nearby. The conquistadors made their way to Atahualpa's camp. There, they were amazed to see the large number of tents that housed the new emperor's army.

The Death of Atahualpa

That night, Pizarro and his men talked about what they should do when they met with Atahualpa the next day. One soldier later wrote:

Few slept, and we kept watch in the square, from which the camp fires of the Indian army could be seen. It was a fearful sight. Most of them were on a hillside and close to one another: it looked like a brilliantly star-studded sky.

Pizarro chose to set a trap for the emperor and the thousands of Inca who would come with him to the meeting. During the meeting, the conquistadors captured Atahualpa. In exchange for his freedom, the emperor offered to fill the room in which he was held prisoner once with gold and twice with silver. The Inca honored Atahualpa's part of the bargain. Pizarro, nevertheless, ordered the emperor's death. Many bloody battles between the Spanish and the Inca followed. By 1535 much of the 3,000 mile-long Inca empire had fallen to the conquistadors.

This Inca codex, created in 1565, shows a battle between the Spanish and the Inca.

The Spread of Spanish Control

By the 1540s conquistadors had claimed land for Spain from what is today Kansas almost to the tip of South America. Spain's rulers divided this enormous area into two colonies, called New Spain and Peru.

New Spain stretched from southern Central America northward into what is now the southwestern United States. Its capital, Mexico City, was built over Tenochtitlán. The colony of Peru—today the name of a country—included most of South America except present-day Brazil. Peru's capital was the coastal city of Lima, built by Pizarro in 1535.

The street plan of Lima showed what life was like in the Americas under Spanish rule. Lima boasted majestic churches and a university. At the center of town stood the homes of Peru's most powerful citizens. Many of these people had been conquistadors like Pizarro. Top government jobs were held by men who were from Europe or had only European heritage. Neither Indians nor *mestizos*, people of both Indian and Spanish heritage, could get such jobs.

This cathedral (left) in Lima is on the site of a church built by the Spanish in 1535. Churches are also found in Peru's rural areas.

LIFE IN SPANISH AMERICA

By the late 1500s it seemed nothing in Spanish America was as powerful as the Catholic Church. Most people who came to the Americas from Spain, whether conquistadors or craftworkers, were Catholic. Among them were **missionaries**, or people who worked to make others see the truth of their religion. Their main goal was to **convert**, or win over to Catholicism, the millions of Indians in the Americas.

Missionaries often achieved their goal through teaching. They built churches and schools throughout the colonies. Missionaries educated many Indians in the subjects that Europeans learned about. All schools—including the university—in New Spain and Peru were run by priests and nuns. At times though, the goal to convert Indians was achieved by force.

Indians at Work

Almost half of all Spaniards in the Americas lived in major cities like Lima or Mexico City. Most of the Indians, however, continued to live in the countryside. Many were forced to work on **haciendas** (hah see EN duz) owned by Spaniards or the Catholic Church. *Hacienda* is Spanish for a large area of land used for agriculture.

Like the feudal manors of Europe, haciendas were like small towns. Indian families lived and worked there to raise wheat, grapes for wine, cattle, and other products that were sold in colonial cities. Although such products brought large profits to hacienda owners, Indians received low wages. To feed themselves, Indian workers raised corn and beans on small plots of land set aside for their use.

Indians also provided another source of wealth in Spanish America—silver. By law all Indian men had to spend some time working in the silver mines of Peru and New Spain. Men who had to carry the precious metal had the worst job of all. They worked in darkness, with candles tied to their foreheads or little fingers for light. Carriers hauled as much as 300 pounds of silver at a time. Accidents often happened on what was sometimes a 60-story climb to the mine entrance.

Illness Strikes the Indians

Accidents and overwork caused many Indian deaths. Disease, however, caused an even greater number. Indians had no resistance to, or ability to overcome the effects of, several of the germs that caused diseases in Europe. Historians believe that in the 50 years following conquest, smallpox and measles were among the diseases that caused the most deaths. In those 50 years New Spain's Indian population may have fallen from about 25 million people to under three million. Peru's decreased from perhaps nine million people to under two million.

Hacienda owners, and those who ran the mines, saw a rapid drop in the number of available workers. They soon came up with a new source for cheap workers—enslaved Africans. You will read more about slavery in the Americas in the next lesson.

These children are a few of the more than five million people who live and work in Lima today.

WHY IT MAT

In 1519, on the eve of Her journey into Mexico, the A empires controlled vast str land in the Americas. By th end, their lands had been conquered and many monuments destroyed. Many Indians died of disease or overwork.

In the place of the Indian empires, Spanish conquistadors created a new civilization with ties to Spain and Portugal. Many European legacies exist today in the Americas, including languages and the Catholic religion. Legacies of the Aztec and Inca continue, as well. These can be seen in customs, language and, most importantly, people.

Reviewing Facts and Ideas

SUM IT UP

- In 1521 Hernando Cortés conquered the Aztec empire for Spain. Francisco Pizarro brought Spanish rule to the people of the Inca empire after 1531.

- Life for Indians in Spanish America was shaped by missionaries, mining, and farm work. Millions died from disease and overwork.

THINK ABOUT IT

1. What is a conquistador?

2. How did Pizarro gain control of the Inca empire?

3. **FOCUS** How did Spain's conquest of the Americas affect Indians there?

4. **THINKING SKILL** Support or deny the _generalization:_ "One person can change the world." Use evidence in the lesson.

5. **WRITE** Write a paragraph describing some ways in which Spain might have had trouble controlling its colonies in the faraway Americas.

THINKINGSKILLS

Analyzing the Credibility of a Source

VOCABULARY

credibility

WHY THE SKILL MATTERS

In the 1500s news of conquistadors in the Americas spread throughout Spain. Many Europeans learned about the Americas from sources such as books, reports, and letters. Did such sources give them honest and accurate information?

Being able to determine the credibility, or believability, of a source is an important skill. People use many types of sources to learn about unfamiliar things. How can we know which we can believe, and which, perhaps, are less believable?

The most important task in determining the believability of a source is learning as much about the author of the source as possible. Is he or she considered an expert on the source's topic? Does he or she have something to gain by giving false or distorted information? Does she or he have a reputation for being accurate?

USING THE SKILL

Consider an example. In the early 1500s, a Spaniard traveling through the Aztec empire might have written a letter to family members at home. It might have included this description of an Aztec city:

The city is built on islands in a lake. The people here eat food such as bread, corn, and fish. There is a market in this city, and the people buy and sell jewelry made of gold, silver, and stones. Around the city are beautiful valleys, where the people cultivate the land.

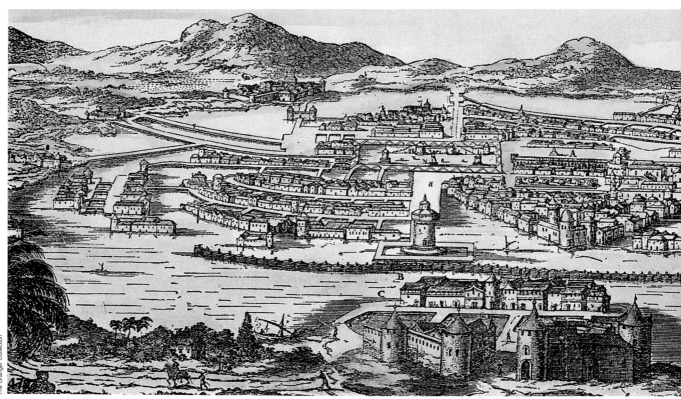

The Granger Collection

Is this a credible source about life in an Aztec city? To find out, apply the steps in the Helping Yourself box. Did the writer have firsthand experience viewing the empire? Did he have any reason not to tell the truth? This Spaniard did see the empire himself, and probably would not lie to a family member. This source is probably credible.

TRYING THE SKILL

Now consider a second example. Suppose a person who has never been to the Americas has decided to explore the Aztec cities he has heard about. The first-time explorer writes this letter to a friend:

I am planning to sail across the ocean because anyone who does so is likely

to become very rich! Gold is for the taking in the cities, and the land is so fertile that farming is little work at all. Silver and shining jewels litter the hills and valleys. If you are willing to provide funds, you can join this expedition.

Is this source less or more believable on the topic of Aztec life than the explorer who visited an Aztec city? Why?

REVIEWING THE SKILL

Use the Helping Yourself box to help you answer the questions below.

1. What makes a source less or more credible?

2. Why is an expert on a subject likely to be a credible source?

3. What did you consider when you determined whether the first-time explorer was credible?

4. How can analyzing the credibility of a source help you in the study of history?

Roswell Museum

This artwork (far left) shows Mexico City, built by the conquistadors on the site of Tenochtitlán.

473

The Granger Collection

1400   1505   1789

AFRICANS IN THE AMERICAS

Focus Activity

READ TO LEARN
How did slavery develop in the Americas?

VOCABULARY
sugarcane
plantation
Middle Passage
triangular trade

PEOPLE
Olaudah Equiano

PLACES
West Indies
Caribbean Sea
Santo Domingo

READ ALOUD

"Among the poor chained men, I found some from my own nation, which in a small way eased my mind. I asked what was to be done with us? They told me we were to be carried to the white people's country to work for them."

An African named Olaudah Equiano (AHL uh duh ih kwee AH nah) (left) wrote about his experiences in 1789. He was a captive on a slave ship bound for the Americas.

THE BIG PICTURE

The islands known as the West Indies were explored by Christopher Columbus in 1492. Later, ships loaded with silver from Lima and Mexico City sailed among these islands in the Caribbean Sea on their way back to Spain. In the early 1500s, Europeans began to establish colonies in the West Indies. The colonists learned that the region's tropical climate was ideal for growing sugar-producing plants. Enslaved persons were used to produce sugar for European markets.

You have read about slavery many times in this book. Nearly all the ancient empires in every part of the world kept people as property and forced them to work without pay. In the 1500s, however, a new form of slavery, based on an enormous demand for labor, took hold in the Americas. Millions of Africans were forced to lead harsh and difficult lives as slaves. Slavery in the Americas also had far-reaching effects on trade. This new form of slavery would create suffering as well as wealth for people on both sides of the Atlantic Ocean.

WEST INDIAN COLONIES

The first West African slaves were brought to Spanish colonies in the Caribbean about 1505. Many were brought to Santo Domingo, a settlement in what is today the Dominican Republic. Santo Domingo had been established by the Spanish just nine years earlier, in 1496. You can see other European colonies on the map.

The islands' warm climate was perfect for growing sugarcane. Sugarcane is a tall grass with a thick, woody stem. It is a source of sugar. Many Europeans in the West Indies set up sugarcane plantations, or large farms. The region's Arawak Indians worked the plantations. However, like the Inca of South America, many Arawak soon died from diseases brought by the Europeans. Many were also killed in conflicts with the Spaniards.

Slavery in the Colonies

To take the place of the Arawak workers, enslaved people were brought from Africa to the colonies. Between 1500 and the middle 1800s, more than nine million Africans were shipped to the Americas.

Most West Africans who became slaves were kidnapped during surprise attacks led by European, Arab, and African traders. Captives were sold to other traders who would send them across the Atlantic Ocean to the West Indies. During the voyage across the Atlantic, captured Africans experienced many hardships. This part of the journey to the Americas became known as the Middle Passage. Captives were chained in crowded sections of ships. They were often given spoiled food and unclean water. Large numbers did not survive the voyage.

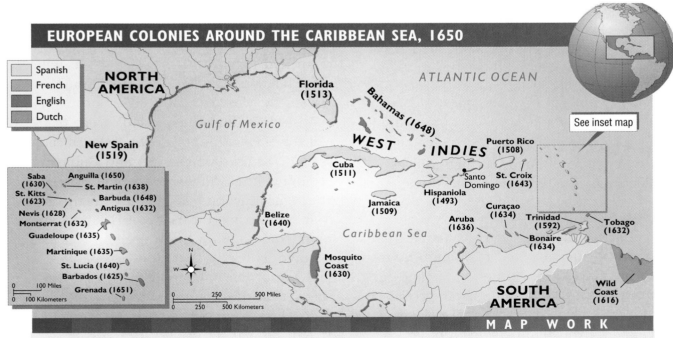

EUROPEAN COLONIES AROUND THE CARIBBEAN SEA, 1650

Spanish
French
English
Dutch

NORTH AMERICA
Florida (1513)
ATLANTIC OCEAN
Bahamas (1648)
Gulf of Mexico
WEST INDIES
New Spain (1519)
Puerto Rico (1508)
Cuba (1511)
Santo Domingo
St. Croix (1643)
Hispaniola (1493)
Jamaica (1509)
Belize (1640)
Curaçao (1634)
Trinidad (1592)
Tobago (1632)
Aruba (1636)
Bonaire (1634)
Caribbean Sea
Mosquito Coast (1630)
SOUTH AMERICA
Wild Coast (1616)
See inset map

Saba (1630)
Anguilla (1650)
St. Martin (1638)
St. Kitts (1623)
Barbuda (1648)
Nevis (1628)
Antigua (1632)
Montserrat (1632)
Guadeloupe (1635)
Martinique (1635)
St. Lucia (1640)
Barbados (1625)
Grenada (1651)
100 Miles
100 Kilometers

250 500 Miles
250 500 Kilometers

MAP WORK

By 1650 most of the islands of the Caribbean Sea had been claimed as colonies by European powers.

1. Which power claimed the largest land area in the Americas?

2. Which European power claimed Nevis?

3. About how far from Jamaica is Puerto Rico?

4. Which island is the largest in the Caribbean?

This painting shows slaves on a sugarcane plantation in Antigua bringing stalks from the field and preparing them for boiling.

PLANTATIONS AND THE SUGAR TRADE

Plantation owners depended on the hard work of enslaved Africans for success. Slaves cleared forests for planting. They hoed the soil and kept fields clear of weeds. At harvesttime they cut sugarcane all day in the hot sun. They also rushed the sugarcane stalks, or stems, to plantation mills. There liquid could be pressed out and boiled. During boiling, tiny crystals of sugar formed. Slaves filled barrel after barrel with the sugar.

The Atlantic Routes

Barrels of sugar were valuable trade goods. Sugar allowed plantation owners to buy expensive clothes, food, and furniture. Most important, sugar profits enabled planters to buy more slaves. Owners exported, or sold to other countries, sugar. Enslaved Africans were imported, or brought from other lands. This exporting and importing of sugar and slaves tightly linked plantations to the rest of the world.

Ships loaded with sugar traveled from the West Indies to Europe. Some returned to the West Indies loaded with fine furniture or cloth. Many, though, sailed to West Africa. There, European guns, cloth, and other goods were traded for slaves. Ships carrying slaves then sailed for the West Indies and English colonies in North America. The routes between Europe, Africa, and North America formed a triangle. For this reason, trade among these regions was known as the triangular trade.

One of the millions of Africans purchased in the triangular trade was Olaudah Equiano. He was kidnapped when he was 11 years old and sold in 1756. Read the following short piece from his autobiography, the story of his life. How was Equiano treated on the slave ship? How does he describe the way Africans lived in Jamaica?

Excerpt from
The Life of Olaudah Equiano,
written by himself, 1789.

The first object which saluted my eyes when I arrived on the [African] coast, was the sea, and a slave ship, which was then riding at anchor, and waiting for its cargo. . . . I was soon put down under the decks, and there . . . , with the **loathsomeness** *of the* **stench**, *and crying together, I . . . wished for the last friend, death, to relieve me. . . .*

I found Jamaica to be a very fine, large island. . . . There (were) a vast number of Negroes here, whom I found as usual, **exceedingly imposed** *upon by the white people, and the slaves punished as in the other islands. . . . When I came to* **Kingston**, *I was surprised to see the number of Africans who were assembled together on Sundays. . . . Here each different nation of Africa meet and dance after the manner of their own country.*

---

loathsomeness: quality of being hateful or disgusting
stench: odor
exceedingly: to a large degree
imposed: to have had unfair demands made upon one
Kingston: a large town in Jamaica

WHY IT MATTERS

The civilization developed by Europeans in the West Indies affected not only that region but also the whole world. The demands of working on a sugarcane plantation cost the lives of thousands of Arawak Indians. Those Indian workers were replaced by enslaved people taken from their homes in Africa. Sugar from the plantations, and slaves themselves, became valuable and important goods in a triangle of trade that involved the West Indies, Europe, and Africa. By the 1800s the fortunes made in the sugar trade helped to make islands in the West Indies among the wealthiest and most powerful in the world. In time, as you will read in Chapter 17, those enslaved persons who made sugar plantations successful would fight for their own freedom.

✓ Reviewing Facts and Ideas

SUM IT UP

- The warm climate of islands in the West Indies was perfect for growing sugarcane.

- Sugarcane plantations in the West Indies depended on enslaved Africans for success.

- Between 1500 and the middle 1800s, more than nine million Africans were shipped to the Americas as slaves. They had been kidnapped from their homes and brought to slave ships.

- Trade of sugar, European goods, and slaves linked the West Indies, Africa, and Europe in the triangular trade.

THINK ABOUT IT

1. How did trade link the West Indies with other parts of the world?

2. How did many Africans become slaves?

3. **FOCUS** Why did slavery develop on sugarcane plantations in the West Indies?

4. **THINKING SKILL** Analyze the *credibility* of Olaudah Equiano as a source of information about slavery. What steps will you follow?

5. **GEOGRAPHY** Why was sugarcane a successful crop in the West Indies?

1400   1497   1800

A EUROPEAN COLONY IN CANADA

Focus Activity

READ TO LEARN
How did the French establish a colony in North America?

PEOPLE
John Cabot
Samuel de Champlain

PLACES
St. Lawrence River
Quebec
New France

READ ALOUD

"There are many white bears, and likewise there are infinite fish, sturgeons, salmon, very large soles a yard in length, and many other kinds of fish, and the greatest of them are called Baccalaos [codfish]."

Explorer John Cabot wrote this description of wildlife he saw along the eastern coast of what is today Canada. Cabot was the captain of the first English ship to arrive in North America. He arrived in 1497, just five years after Columbus's first Atlantic journey.

THE BIG PICTURE

In Lesson 2 you read about Europeans' search for a new route to Asia. Navigators from several European nations began sailing north along the east coast of North America. They were looking for a passage that would lead them through the continent.

John Cabot, an Italian who sailed for England, was among the first to explore the eastern coast of what is today Canada. Almost 30 years later, explorers sent by France arrived. These explorers also hoped to discover a passageway, or route, to Asia. Instead, they found a land rich in natural resources, civilizations, and such waterways as lakes and rivers.

The explorers claimed these lands for France and started a colony. Farther south, the English formed 13 colonies. In time the French and English would fight for control of North America's lands and resources.

THE ST. LAWRENCE RIVER VALLEY

By the early 1500s European fishers crowded the waters off Newfoundland Island to harvest boatloads of cod. This fish was so popular that it was nick-named "beef of the sea." Cod was pre-served with salt and cut into thick, flat pieces. It was a valuable trade item in European ports. Europeans who sailed west to fish the cold waters of the western Atlantic had the chance to make a great deal of money.

Other Europeans began trading with Indians along the St. Lawrence River for animal furs. They also were drawn by the opportunity to make a profit. The St. Lawrence River connects Lake Ontario, one of the Great Lakes, with the Atlantic Ocean. Find the St. Lawrence River on the map.

When French fur traders arrived in the region in the 1600s, there were large numbers of fox, lynx, and otters in the St. Lawrence Valley. Europeans paid almost any price for clothes made with the fur of these animals. Demand soared even higher for beaver fur. A new fashion in hats required the use of the waterproof inner layer of a beaver's fur.

A Trading Post

Because France want-ed to remain involved in the growing fur trade, explorer Samuel de Champlain was sent to set up a trading post and settlement. In 1608 he established Quebec (kwi BEK) near the mouth of the St. Lawrence River. Quebec was located at an ideal spot for overseeing trade and travel on the river. Most important, Quebec was in an area where the Algonkian (al GAHNG kee un) lived. These Native Americans were France's first supplier of furs.

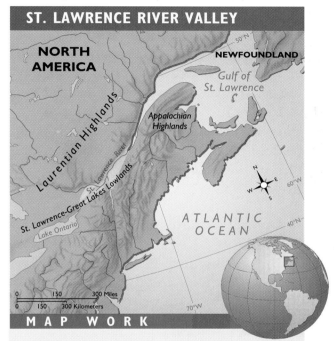

ST. LAWRENCE RIVER VALLEY

NORTH AMERICA

NEWFOUNDLAND

Gulf of St. Lawrence

Laurentian Highlands

Appalachian Highlands

St. Lawrence River

St. Lawrence-Great Lakes Lowlands

Lake Ontario

ATLANTIC OCEAN

0 150 300 Miles
0 150 300 Kilometers

MAP WORK

The French living along the St. Lawrence River farmed its valleys and traded goods for a living.

1. Which highlands are located west of the St. Lawrence River?

2. About how far from the Gulf of St. Lawrence is Lake Ontario?

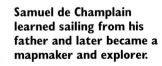

Samuel de Champlain learned sailing from his father and later became a mapmaker and explorer.

LIFE IN EASTERN CANADA

Not long after he settled Quebec, Champlain met the Huron. These Native Americans lived northwest of Lake Ontario. The Huron raised corn and other crops and fished and hunted in nearby lakes and forests. The Huron were also expert traders, exchanging corn for furs and other goods with other Native American communities along the northern shores of the Great Lakes.

In the 1620s the Huron began to trade with European settlers. Huron traders brought thousands of beaver furs to the French trading posts to exchange for European goods.

A Colony Called New France

During the next 100 years, New France, France's colony in North America, grew. French traders traveled rivers and lakes in Native American-style canoes. Meanwhile, newcomers from France settled in the St. Lawrence River valley and began to grow wheat. In summer they traveled to Quebec by boat. When the river froze in winter, they rode sleds over its surface. At Quebec's trading post they could buy boots, tools, and clothing.

As New France expanded to the Great Lakes and the Mississippi River valley, conflicts developed with both Native Americans and colonists from Great Britain. In 1753 Britain sent military forces to the Ohio River valley. The soldiers were led by a young man named George Washington. His job was to protect British claims to the area, also claimed by France. The fighting that broke out led to war. The French and their Indian supporters fought the British.

This war is known as the French and Indian War. In Europe it is called the Seven Years' War. France was defeated and lost control over its vast colony in North America.

Look at the map on the next page to see early European claims in North America at this time.

The Granger Collection

Canada's Indians (above) traded with the French in Quebec, still a center of business and culture.

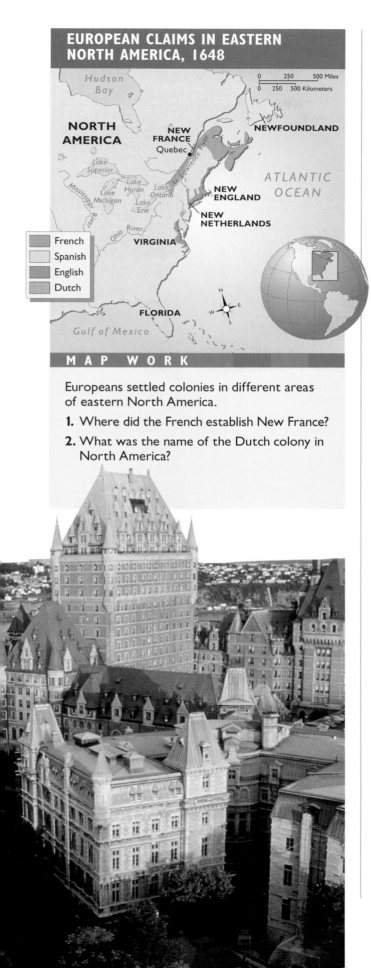

NORTH AMERICA

NEW FRANCE
Quebec

NEWFOUNDLAND

Hudson Bay

Lake Superior

Lake Huron

Lake Michigan

Lake Ontario

Lake Erie

Mississippi River

Ohio River

NEW ENGLAND

NEW NETHERLANDS

ATLANTIC OCEAN

VIRGINIA

FLORIDA

Gulf of Mexico

0   250   500 Miles
0   250   500 Kilometers

- French
- Spanish
- English
- Dutch

M A P   W O R K

Europeans settled colonies in different areas of eastern North America.

1. Where did the French establish New France?

2. What was the name of the Dutch colony in North America?

WHY IT MATTERS

For over 150 years wealth poured into France from its North American colony in the forms of fish, fur, and other goods. After the French and Indian War, these riches were directed to Britain. England now controlled a large eastern part of North America. However, the French who settled Quebec continued to follow many of their own customs. For example, they continued to speak the French language. Meanwhile, Spanish colonies in Middle America and South America were thriving. Would these colonial powers continue to succeed in the Western Hemisphere? Only time would tell.

Reviewing Facts and Ideas

SUM IT UP

- Plentiful supplies of fish and fur became the major source of wealth in New France.

- The St. Lawrence River was an important transportation route for traders in New France.

THINK ABOUT IT

1. What role did fishing play in the early growth of New France?

2. Who participated in the fur trade in North America? What goods were traded?

3. **FOCUS** How and why did France establish a colony in the St. Lawrence River valley?

4. **THINKING SKILL** What was one *cause* for the great demand for beaver fur in Europe? What *effects* did it have on life in North America?

5. **GEOGRAPHY** How was the St. Lawrence River important to the growth of New France?

CHAPTER 16 REVIEW

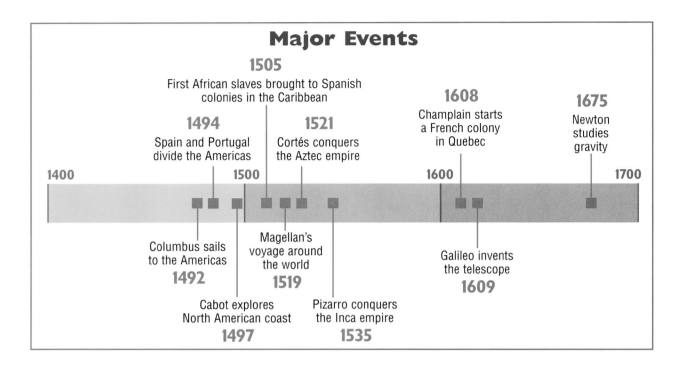

Major Events

1505
First African slaves brought to Spanish colonies in the Caribbean

1608
Champlain starts a French colony in Quebec

1675
Newton studies gravity

1494
Spain and Portugal divide the Americas

1521
Cortés conquers the Aztec empire

1400   1500   1600   1700

Columbus sails to the Americas
1492

Magellan's voyage around the world
1519

Galileo invents the telescope
1609

Cabot explores North American coast
1497

Pizarro conquers the Inca empire
1535

THINKING ABOUT VOCABULARY

Number a sheet of paper from 1 to 10. Beside each number write the word or term from the list below that best completes the sentence.

caravel
conquistador
credibility
geocentric
Line of Demarcation

Middle Passage
plantations
scientific method
strait
telescope

1. The _____ was a voyage that captured Africans were forced to make.

2. Galileo's invention of the _____ allowed him to study the sky more closely.

3. A _____ is a narrow waterway that connects two larger bodies of water.

4. The Portuguese ship that allowed explorers to sail into the wind was the _____.

5. Thoroughly testing an idea before accepting it as true is the _____.

6. Large farms in the West Indies where sugarcane was grown were called _____.

7. Somebody who can not be believed has lost his or her _____.

8. A _____ was a military person sent to the Americas to explore and gain land for Spain.

9. In 1494 Spain and Portugal drew the _____ to divide lands in the New World between them.

10. _____ means "centered around Earth."

THINKING ABOUT FACTS

1. What was Isaac Newton's main contribution to science?

2. What did Portuguese explorers accomplish in the New World?

3. How did colonial trade link the West Indies to other parts of the world?

4. What did Samuel de Champlain accomplish? How have his achievements continued to affect Canada?

5. According to the time line above, which were the first two European countries to colonize the Americas?

WRITING AN ESSAY

Write a short essay about differences between Spanish and French colonies in America. Describe the regions that the Spanish and French colonized. Mention what each country gained from its settlements. Also describe the way the colonists interacted with Native Americans.

WRITING BIOGRAPHICAL PARAGRAPHS

Write a paragraph about two of the following people: (1) Galileo (2) Henry the Navigator (3) Magellan (4) Cortés.

WRITING ABOUT PERSPECTIVES

Write about the different perspectives Native Americans and Europeans had toward each other in the 1500s. What do you think each thought of the other one? What do you think they might have found strange? What do you think they might have found appealing?

APPLYING THINKING SKILLS

ANALYZING THE CREDIBILITY OF A SOURCE

1. What is a credible source?

2. To analyze the credibility of a source, what three things should you find out?

3. Reread the account of Olaudah Equiano on page 474. Do you find it credible? Why or why not?

4. Give an example of an account of the trip slaves were forced to make from Africa that would be less credible than Equiano's.

5. In what ways will this skill be helpful to you as a student?

Summing Up the Chapter

Copy the main-idea pyramid below on a separate sheet of paper. Then review the chapter to find information to finish filling in the pyramid. When you have filled in the pyramid, use the information to answer the question "What were the main accomplishments of European scientists and explorers from the 1400s to the 1600s?"

Europeans from the 1400s to the 1600s made important discoveries in science and exploration.

European explorers colonize the Americas

European scientists make important discoveries

Cortés - Mexico

CHAPTER 17

Revolutions Change the World

THINKING ABOUT HISTORY AND GEOGRAPHY

In this chapter you will read about revolutions that changed the lives of people around the world. Follow the time line and the map to find out when and where these changes occurred. Some happened very quickly while others took longer. In each case, people's lives were changed, with effects that are still felt today.

PACIFIC OCEAN

1789
PARIS, FRANCE
French citizens storm the Bastille

1810
DOLORES, MEXICO
Miguel Hidalgo calls on Mexicans to fight for freedom

1821
CARABOBO, VENEZUELA
Simon Bolívar defeats the Spanish army

NORTH
AMERICA

Tokyo

Dolores

Gulf of
Mexico

ASIA

Manchester

ATLANTIC OCEAN

Paris

EUROPE

Carabobo

SOUTH
AMERICA

AFRICA

INDIAN
OCEAN

1824

MANCHESTER, ENGLAND

Workers form unions to demand shorter hours and better pay

1868

TOKYO, JAPAN

The Meiji era begins

THE FRENCH REVOLUTION

Focus Activity

READ TO LEARN
What conditions led to the French Revolution?

VOCABULARY
absolute monarchy
divine right
revolution
estates
aristocracy
peasants
Declaration of the Rights of Man and of the Citizen
Reign of Terror

PEOPLE
Louis XVI
Marie Antoinette
Maximilien Robespierre
Napoleon Bonaparte

PLACES
Versailles
Paris
Bastille

READ ALOUD

"Can you not hear in your hearts the voices of the citizens who died? Can you not see all the nations of the world, all the generations present and future, waiting until you show them whether the King has the right to murder citizens and groups without punishment; whether a monarch is a god whose actions must be blessed or a man whose crimes must be punished."

The words above were spoken by Jean Mailhe (MAY yuh) in France in 1792. As a member of the newly elected National Assembly, Mailhe was calling for the execution, or killing, of the king.

THE BIG PICTURE

Just four years earlier King Louis XVI held firm control over his kingdom. France was an absolute monarchy. This means that the king had complete power to govern. His title, "Louis, by the Grace of God, King of France," showed the belief in his divine right. Divine right was a belief that a monarch's authority came from God. Now, in a sudden turn of events, the king faced the judgment of people he once ruled.

Throughout the continent, a system of rule based on the power of monarchs, nobles, and church leaders had been in place for centuries. Unhappiness with this system, however, was leading the people of France closer to a revolution. A revolution is a sudden or great change. The revolution in France would upset the old system of government and change Europe.

486

AN AGE OF DISCONTENT

In many ways France in 1789 was not much different from France in the Middle Ages. Although feudalism no longer existed, most people still worked the land. By 1789, however, the population had been divided into three estates, or social classes. The chart on this page shows France's three estates.

The Three Estates

The First Estate was made up of the Catholic clergy. The clergy consists of people who perform religious services. About 130,000 of France's 26 million people belonged to the clergy. The wealthy Catholic Church owned nearly 15 percent of France's land and paid no regular taxes.

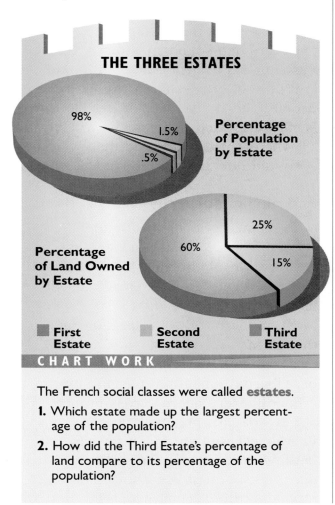

THE THREE ESTATES

98%
1.5%
.5%

Percentage of Population by Estate

Percentage of Land Owned by Estate

25%
60%
15%

■ First Estate   ■ Second Estate   ■ Third Estate

CHART WORK

The French social classes were called estates.

1. Which estate made up the largest percentage of the population?

2. How did the Third Estate's percentage of land compare to its percentage of the population?

Aristocracy (ar uh STOHK ruh see) made up the Second Estate. The aristocracy included members of noble families. In the late 1700s nobles owned about 25 percent of the land in France. Most of them did not pay taxes. Although most nobles were rich, they had little power in government. In fact they were unhappy that the king held all political power in France. Even the richest nobles could not make laws.

The vast majority of people, nearly 98 percent, belonged to the Third Estate. This group included merchants and lawyers as well as craftworkers and peasants. Peasants are farm workers. A few members of the Third Estate were rich. Most, however, were poor.

Although many peasants owned land, they often did not have enough to support themselves and their families. One traveler described a seven-year-old peasant girl as "terribly ragged, if possible worse clad than if with no clothes at all." The different members of the Third Estate had two things in common. They paid taxes and had no say in how they were governed.

This cartoon from 1789 shows the First and Second estates riding on the back of the Third Estate.

487

A STRUGGLE FOR LIBERTY

By the late 1770s the French had been greatly influenced by the American Revolution. One French noblewoman said,

The American cause seemed our own; we were proud of their victories, we cried at their defeats, we tore down bulletins and read them in our houses. None of us reflected on the danger that the New World could give to the Old.

France had given millions of dollars to support the American colonies in their war against the British. This expense, as well as the cost of the king's lifestyle, drained money from the French government. By 1789 there was no money left.

The Revolution Begins

King Louis XVI hoped to raise more money by taxing the nobles, or the Second Estate. The nobles refused. They demanded a meeting of the Estates General. The Estates General was a group made up of representatives from each of the three estates.

The Estates General met near the king's palace in Versailles (vair SIGH) in May of 1789. Members of the Third Estate wanted equal rights. They did not like being the least powerful group in France. A priest described the dissatisfaction of the Third Estate:

What is the Third Estate? Everything. What has it been up 'til now in the political order? Nothing. What does it desire to be? Something.

Soon the members of the Third Estate began meeting to write a constitution. They formed a new law making body, called the National Assembly. The French Revolution had begun.

Storming the Bastille

Struggle for power between the estates and the king developed so quickly that rumors began to fly. One rumor was that the king was sending troops to break up the National Assembly. On July 14, 1789, about 800 people gathered in Paris, the capital of France. They marched to the big stone prison fortress called the Bastille (bas TEEL). They hoped to get weapons there to defend themselves. As people surrounded the prison, someone fired a cannon into the crowd.

Nearby, a citizen named Pierre Hulin convinced a group of 60 soldiers to help the crowd. "Do you not hear the cannons? Parisians are being slaughtered like sheep. Will you not march on the Bastille?" he said.

Although 98 people died, the marchers and soldiers captured the Bastille. This event became an important symbol of revolution to the French people. The anniversary of Bastille Day is still celebrated in France every July 14. The event also showed that even the army did not support the king.

End of the Monarchy

In August of 1789 the National Assembly issued a statement called the Declaration of the Rights of Man and of the Citizen. This statement called for fair taxation and freedom of religion. Most important, the Declaration said that all men were "born and remain free and equal in rights." Soon shouts of "Liberty! Equality! Fraternity [brotherhood]!" were heard across France.

Crowds also began singing a song, *La Marseillaise* (lah mahr say YEZ). It became France's national anthem. What does the song tell you about the point of view of the French people?

NEW RULERS IN FRANCE

The old France was gone. A new democratic government was rising in its place. The king was still leader of the government, but the National Assembly now had most of the power. In 1791 King Louis XVI was forced to approve the Declaration of the Rights of Man and of the Citizen.

After approving the Declaration, King Louis, Queen Marie Antoinette (muh REE an twuh NET), and their family tried to escape. They left Paris disguised as a family of tourists. They had not gone far, however, before someone recognized the king from his picture on money. The man tipped over a cart of furniture on a bridge to block the family's escape. Soldiers soon arrived and returned the royal family to Paris. In 1792 the monarchy was abolished and France became a republic.

The Reign of Terror

The change from a monarchy to a republic was not smooth for France. The Assembly angered many people by taking all land away from the Catholic Church. Priests who did not support the revolution lost their churches.

Maximilien Robespierre (MAX ih mihl yen ROHBZ pee air), a Revolution leader, became the most powerful man in the new government. He waged a war against enemies of the revolution by executing suspects. This period of cruelty became known as the Reign of Terror.

Robespierre's weapon was a machine, the guillotine (GEE oh teen),

Marie Antoinette (above), Queen of France and wife of Louis XVI, was beheaded in 1793. The guillotine (below) killed thousands during the revolution.

with a steel blade that chopped off people's heads. In January 1793 King Louis XVI was tried and executed by guillotine in a public square in Paris. Queen Marie Antoinette's execution by guillotine followed in October.

Aristocrats and nobles were targeted for death. However, it seemed no one was safe from the threat of execution. People feared execution for such "crimes" as giving sour wine to soldiers or weeping at the murder of a family member. When the Reign of Terror came to an end in 1794, about 25,000 French citizens had been killed. One of them was Robespierre himself.

The Revolution Ends

The time has come when people would ask for bread and be given corpses.

The woman who wrote this statement lived during the Reign of Terror.

She summed up the disappointment that many people felt. Five years of revolution and bloodshed left many people hoping for peace and stability.

In this environment, the army gained more and more power. A 26-year-old general named Napoleon Bonaparte (nuh POH lee un BOH nuh pahrt), from the island of Corsica, became extremely popular. His success in a French war against Italy won him great support. When he returned to Paris in 1799, one newspaper reported: "Everyone is thrilled" by his victory.

Five years later, the young general had gained control of the new French Republic and crowned himself Emperor Napoleon I. Barely 10 years after the execution of Louis XVI, France had another absolute ruler. The French Republic was over.

After making himself emperor of France in 1804, Napoleon set out to conquer lands across Europe.

WHY IT MATTERS

Napoleon expanded French power across Europe. His armies conquered Holland, Germany, Italy, and Belgium, bringing new riches to the French.

Although France once again had a monarch, many of the changes that had come with the Revolution remained. For example, the old system of three estates was gone forever.

Napoleon's vast empire collapsed in 1815. The French began again to build a republic. They picked up many of the ideas that had fueled the revolution 25 years earlier. After the fateful events in France in 1789, the world would never be the same again. From India to Turkey to South America, the ideas of "Liberty, Equality, Fraternity" sparked national freedom movements around the world.

Reviewing Facts and Ideas

SUM IT UP

- Before the Revolution French society was divided into three "estates."

- The French Revolution began in 1789.

- Robespierre's Reign of Terror brought fear and disorder to France.

- Napoleon Bonaparte created a huge European empire.

THINK ABOUT IT

1. Who made up the Three Estates?

2. Why was a meeting of the Estates General called in 1789?

3. FOCUS List three reasons for the discontent among many French people before the Revolution.

4. THINKING SKILL What *effects* did the American Revolution have on France?

5. WRITE As a member of the Third Estate, write a paragraph describing changes you would like to see.

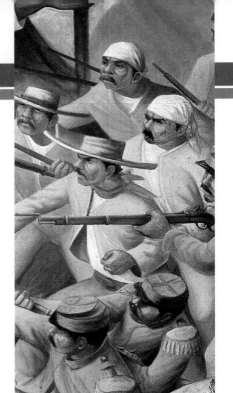

INDEPENDENCE IN THE AMERICAS

READ ALOUD

"We are threatened with the fear of death, dishonor, and every harm; there is nothing we have not suffered at the hands of . . . Spain."

Simón Bolívar (see MOHN boh LEE vahr) wrote these words in a letter in 1815. He went on to free his native Venezuela and several other South American nations from Spanish rule. Freedom from Europe was a goal that inspired many people of the Americas.

THE BIG PICTURE

In the year 1800 the United States was the only independent country in the Americas. Yet the desire for independence was felt in colonies throughout the Western Hemisphere. Events in faraway places helped feed these desires. The American and French Revolutions caused others in the Americas to think about gaining their own rights. Many Spanish colonists said, "I am not a Spaniard, I am American." These feelings spread throughout Latin America. Latin America is a cultural region south of the United States that was strongly influenced by Spain, Portugal, and France.

Europe's costly wars with Napoleon made it possible for colonies to take control of their own governments. A period of 300 years of European rule in the Americas was ending. By 1830 North and South America were made up almost entirely of independent nations.

Focus Activity

READ TO LEARN
How did European colonies in the Americas gain independence?

VOCABULARY
Latin America
mestizo
confederation

PEOPLE
Toussaint L'Ouverture
Miguel Hidalgo
José María Morelos
Agustín de Iturbide
Simón Bolívar
José de San Martín

PLACES
Hispaniola
Dolores
Venezuela

A SPIRIT OF FREEDOM

Although each colony in Latin America was unique, all had some things in common. For one, they felt that European nations were taking advantage of them. Europeans took minerals and crops, but gave little in return.

People born in the Latin American colonies struggled to grow crops or to work in mines for other people. Like the English colonists of North America, Latin Americans also had to pay taxes without having a voice in their government. One popular song expressed the Latin American colonists' viewpoint:

> *If anyone wants to know*
> *Why I go shirtless*
> *It's because of the taxes*
> *Of the king.*

Revolution in the Caribbean

The first rumblings of independence began on the large Caribbean island of Hispaniola (hihs pun YOH luh). Although Columbus had claimed Hispaniola for Spain in 1492, France controlled the western part of the island. In the French colony, called Saint Domingue (san duh MANG), enslaved Africans grew coffee and sugar on plantations.

When the French Revolution broke out across the Atlantic, distant cries of "Liberty, Equality, Fraternity" echoed in Saint Domingue. In 1791 a group of about 100,000 slaves rose up against plantation owners. This group was led by Toussaint L'Ouverture (too SAN loo ver TYUR). L'Ouverture believed that slavery was wrong. He and other former slaves forced the French to abolish it throughout Saint Domingue. In 1796 L'Ouverture took control of the colony's government.

In 1802 Napoleon Bonaparte tried to regain control of Saint Domingue. He sent a huge army to restart the practice of slavery on the island. This time L'Ouverture began a revolution to drive the French out completely.

Although L'Ouverture was captured and taken to France, the revolution became the first successful slave revolution in history. From it, the independent country of Haiti was born on Hispaniola in 1804.

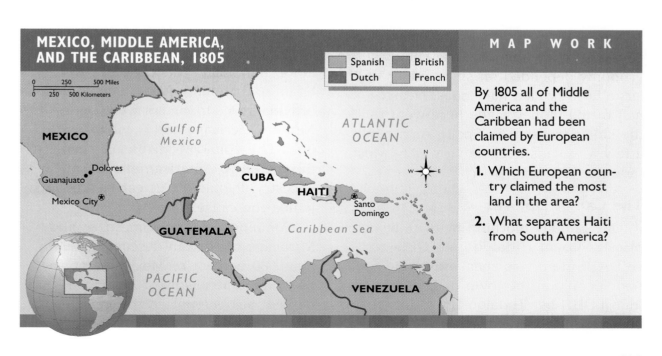

MEXICO, MIDDLE AMERICA, AND THE CARIBBEAN, 1805

Spanish | British
Dutch | French

0   250   500 Miles
0   250   500 Kilometers

MEXICO
Gulf of Mexico
ATLANTIC OCEAN
Dolores
Guanajuato
Mexico City
CUBA
HAITI
Santo Domingo
GUATEMALA
Caribbean Sea
PACIFIC OCEAN
VENEZUELA

MAP WORK

By 1805 all of Middle America and the Caribbean had been claimed by European countries.

1. Which European country claimed the most land in the area?

2. What separates Haiti from South America?

This painting by Mexican artist José Orozco shows Miguel Hidalgo rallying Mexicans to fight for independence from Spain.

REVOLUTION IN MEXICO

Six years after independence in Haiti, the bells of freedom began ringing in Mexico as well. The Spanish grip on New Spain, or Mexico, weakened when Napoleon conquered Spain in 1808.

Mexico was the richest of Spain's colonies. Remember that the colony's economy depended on silver mines and large farms called haciendas. Nearly half of the money made here went to the king's treasury in Spain. As a result, a few Mexicans became very rich. Most, though, were very poor.

The Call of Dolores

One Sunday morning in 1810, a priest, Miguel Hidalgo (mih GEL ee DAHL goh) was speaking to the poor people in the town of Dolores (duh LOHR us). Hidalgo felt a duty to improve life for Mexicans. He called upon his listeners to sweep the Europeans from office and create a better government. In this stirring speech, now known as *The Call of Dolores*, Hidalgo encouraged the local people to "recover from the hated Spaniards the land stolen from your forefathers."

The response to Hidalgo's speech was explosive. His words fueled a revolution that called for freedom from Spain and equality for all people. Most of Hidalgo's supporters were poor Native Americans and mestizos (mes TEE zohz). Mestizos are people of mixed Native American and European ancestry. People of African descent also joined the cause.

Combined, the poor mestizos and Mexicans of African descent made up about 80 percent of Mexico's population. Some Mexicans of European descent also supported the movement for independence.

A Setback

The angry crowd in Dolores arrested Spanish officials and destroyed Spanish haciendas. The number of revolutionaries swelled to 25,000, and Hidalgo's army captured the nearby city of Guanajuato (gwah nuh HWAH toh). As they moved on toward Mexico City, another 60,000 people joined in the march. Hidalgo called for equality for all groups. He also declared the end of slavery and the unfair taxes that the people had to pay the Spanish government.

Hidalgo's army never reached Mexico City. The Spanish army pursued the rebels, captured Hidalgo, and executed him in 1811. All hope for the Mexican war of independence seemed lost.

After Hidalgo's death, another priest, named José María Morelos (ho SAY muh REE uh moh RAY los), carried on the revolution. Morelos led a small army in central Mexico. He fought strong Spanish forces for several years. In 1813 Morelos called Mexico's first national congress and declared the colony's independence from Spain. In 1815, like Hidalgo before him, Morelos was captured and killed by Spanish soldiers.

An Independent Mexico

One of the soldiers who had fought against both Hidalgo and Morelos soon came to power. Agustín de Iturbide was an officer in the Spanish army. In 1821 Iturbide issued the *Plan de Iguala* (PLAHN day ih GWAH luh). It described his own ideas about Mexico.

All inhabitants of New Spain, without any distinction between Europeans, Africans, and Indians, are citizens of this monarchy. . . . Behold the sweet chain that unites us; consider the bonds of friendship, interdependence of interest, education, language, and harmony of feelings. . . . The time has arrived . . . that our union should emancipate [free] America without need of foreign help. At the head of a brave and determined army, I [declare] the Independence of Northern America.

Finally, 11 years after Miguel Hidalgo rang the bell at his church in Dolores, Mexico was independent. However, Hidalgo's dream of liberty and equality for all Mexicans was lost. In 1822 Iturbide declared himself Emperor of Mexico. Five months later he dismissed the congress Morelos had started. Many years would pass before all Mexicans were given a say in their government.

This huge monument was built in honor of José Morelos.

INDEPENDENCE MOVES

The forces of liberty soon pressed upon other parts of the Americas. Beginning in 1810 the Spanish-speaking colonies of South America began to revolt. Brazil, ruled by Portugal, was not far behind. Far to the north, in Canada, other changes were coming.

The Liberator of South America

The driving force behind independence in South America was Simón Bolívar. Bolívar was born into one of the richest families in Venezuela. He had read books by French writers explaining ideas of freedom. Liberty and equality served as the main goals of his struggle. Bolívar offered the hope of freedom from colonial rule to all people who joined his cause.

Bolívar spent ten years struggling to free his homeland from Spain. In 1821 a decade of leading armies through the rain forests and mountains of South America finally paid off. Bolívar's forces defeated the Spanish army in Venezuela. In a speech to his troops Bolivar said:

But we cannot rest. Other obligations await us. And when our native land is entirely free, we shall go to fight the Spaniards in any part of America where they are in control, and we shall throw them into the sea. Freedom shall live protected by our swords!

Bolívar carried the revolution further into South America, freeing the areas now known as Colombia, Bolivia, Panama, Ecuador, and Peru from Spanish rule. His actions won him the nick-

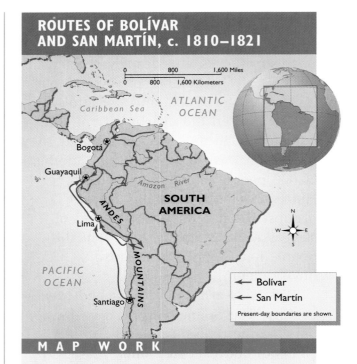

ROUTES OF BOLÍVAR AND SAN MARTÍN, c. 1810–1821

MAP WORK

Bolívar and San Martín won independence for many of the lands of South America.

1. Which of these two liberators traveled farther south in South America?

2. How far is Santiago from Lima?

Simón Bolívar, a Venezuelan soldier, liberated much of northern South America.

name "Liberator of South America."

From the southern part of the continent came another liberator. His name was José de San Martín (ho SAY day sahn mahr TEEN). San Martín led revolutions in Argentina and Chile. Find his route on the map on this page.

Changes in Canada

Canada did not experience violent revolution. Instead, the people of the Canadian colonies changed their government slowly. Remember that the British took control of this land after winning the French and Indian War

Parliament in Ottawa is the center of Canada's government.

in 1763. The British created four colonies there: New Brunswick, Nova Scotia, Upper Canada, and Lower Canada.

One by one these colonies became provinces, each with its own leaders. A province is similar to a state. Upper Canada later became Ontario and Lower Canada became Quebec. Still, Britain remained in control.

In 1867 the provinces formed a confederation, or a group of provinces under one central government. This new confederation was called the Dominion of Canada. Canada was now united and free to govern itself, although the king or queen of Great Britain remained the highest ruler.

WHY IT MATTERS

The 1800s brought great change to both North and South America. Sometimes the change came peacefully, as it did in Canada. Often, however, people had to fight for their freedom.

With liberty came responsibility. The young countries were now able to make decisions for themselves. Faraway kings and queens no longer took a large share of wealth. However, it was still difficult for the new nations to build strong economies. Often a few rich families controlled the country's land and money.

The peasants of Mexico often said their revolution "placed the same rider on a new mule." They meant that one group of rulers usually just replaced another. Although the colonies were free, freedom and equality for all people remained a distant promise.

Reviewing Facts and Ideas

SUM IT UP

- In 1804 Haiti became the second independent country in the Americas, after the United States.
- Miguel Hidalgo led Mexicans in a revolt against Spain in 1810, triggering a movement of independence.
- Mexico became independent from Spain in 1821.
- Simón Bolívar and José de San Martín liberated much of South America from Spanish rule.

THINK ABOUT IT

1. How did Haiti gain independence?

2. From which social classes did Hidalgo gain most of his support?

3. **FOCUS** How did events in Europe influence the fight for independence in American colonies?

4. **THINKING SKILL** What steps would you take to *determine the credibility* of the quote by Iturbide on page 495?

5. **WRITE** Suppose you are a reporter recording the early events of the war of Mexican independence. Write a list of questions you could ask Miguel Hidalgo about his actions and his hopes for the future.

THE UNITED STATES
CONSTITUTION

As you know from studying United States history, people in our country fought a revolution earlier than the ones in France and Latin America that you have read about. When the founders of our country wrote the Constitution in 1787, they made sure to protect the freedoms they had just won.

Because the United States had the first written constitution in the world, other countries used it as a model for their own constitutions. Many Latin American countries were especially influenced by the United States Constitution. In Costa Rica all citizens are considered equal before the law and can state political opinions freely.

In another part of the world, India's constitution protects freedom of religion, the right to assemble peaceably, and other rights. These freedoms have been guaranteed in the United States for over 200 years.

The first part of the United States Constitution states the goals and freedoms that the colonists sought. These students are looking at the Constitution in Washington, D.C.

A woman in India votes in elections that are protected by the nation's constitution. A politician (below) speaks openly to the press in Costa Rica. Free press is guaranteed in both of these countries.

Like the constitutions of India and Costa Rica, the Japanese constitution protects freedom of the press. Here a reporter prepares a news broadcast.

The Granger Collection

THE INDUSTRIAL REVOLUTION

READ ALOUD

"From this foul drain the greatest stream of human industry flows out to fertilize the whole world. From this filthy sewer pure gold flows."

This is how French writer and historian Alexis de Tocqueville (a LEKS ihs dih tawk VEEL) described Manchester, England, in 1835. A revolution was taking place in Manchester and other European cities. This revolution did not cause the bloodshed that had taken place in France and Latin America. It did, however, permanently change the lives of people around the world.

THE BIG PICTURE

Before 1700 the most important event across Europe every year was the harvest. Most people lived and worked the land in rural areas. Many never traveled more than ten miles from their villages.

From 1700 to 1800, however, rural life throughout Europe began to change. New farming methods and technology—such as iron plows, crop rotation, and fertilizers—made farms much more productive. Europe's population exploded, nearly doubling to 190 million by 1800. No change, however, had as many effects as the one that began in England in the 1700s. The Industrial Revolution was a period of time when great technological advances changed the way goods were made and the ways people lived. Industry became the focus of economic activity. Unlike national revolutions, this revolution was felt around the world.

Focus Activity

READ TO LEARN
What changes were brought about by the Industrial Revolution?

VOCABULARY
Industrial Revolution
textile
factory
middle class
working class
socialism

PEOPLE
John Kay
James Hargreaves
Richard Arkwright
Edmund Cartwright
James Watt
Karl Marx

500

THE GROWTH OF INDUSTRY

The Industrial Revolution started in Britain, spread across Europe, and reached the United States. It began in Britain for a number of reasons. British laws allowed people to start businesses, protect their property, and earn money. Britain also had a stable government and a rich supply of the raw materials coal and iron.

Work in the Country

The Industrial Revolution did not happen all at once. Industry first appeared in the countryside. Peasants produced thread and cloth on spinning wheels and looms in their homes. Peasants worked the fields in the summer. Then in the winter they spun yarn and made textiles. A textile is a cloth fabric that is either woven or knitted.

This type of work soon became an important source of income for rural families. As one Irish traveler observed:

The poor people spin a good deal of wool, and weave it into flannel for their own wear.

The Textile Boom

By the middle 1700s a growing population created more demand for textiles. New machines were invented that could make textiles more quickly and cheaply. Some of these machines are shown in the Infographic on page 503. They were expensive and too big to fit in a farmer's two-room cottage. Merchants built large buildings, called factories, to house new machines.

Most of these new machines were made for weaving cotton. Cotton does not grow well in the cold, wet climate of Britain. However, it is cheaper than wool and has many uses. In the 1700s Britain became part of the triangular trade you read about in Chapter 16. The British found a vast source of cotton in the colonies of North America.

Soon a brisk trade developed. Raw cotton was shipped from America to the mills of Britain. Finished textiles were then shipped to Africa and traded for enslaved persons. Captured Africans were sent to work as slaves on cotton plantations in British colonies in America. British cities such as Liverpool soon became centers of textile manufacturing and shipping.

Before factories started, families made textiles at home (right). A hand-operated spinning wheel (above) was used to make thread.

Victoria & Albert Museum

501

Ironworks produced large amounts of iron needed for railroads and other new inventions.

THE SPREAD OF INDUSTRY

The Industrial Revolution began mostly with cotton textiles. It soon included many textiles. The Industrial Revolution widened to cover other goods as well. In Britain coal and iron mines provided raw materials used to build machines and power factories.

The Iron Horse

No new machine created as much interest as the locomotive. These steam-powered railway engines hissed, belched, and squeaked along Britain's iron rails. The first passenger railroad, between Stockton and Darlington, opened in 1825. Within 15 years, more than 1,000 miles of track crisscrossed Europe. By 1870 the railroad had cut the travel time from London, England, to Edinburgh, Scotland, from 4 days to 12 hours! In 1888 the railroad, nicknamed the "iron horse," linked Europe from Calais, in France, to Istanbul. Passengers and goods could reach more distant places in less time than ever before.

More Products for Sale

As factories hummed and railroads chugged, the number of products people could buy increased. A pamphlet called *The Results of Machinery* gave one example in 1831:

> *Two centuries ago not one person in a thousand wore stockings; one century ago not one person in five hundred wore them; now not one person in a thousand is without them.*

This description was an exaggeration, since many workers could not even afford shoes. However, it shows an important change in the economy. Before the Industrial Revolution began, most people lived on farms that provided them with food and clothing. By 1800 about 20 percent of the population lived in cities.

The people who did move from farms to cities now worked in factories and were paid wages. New factory workers used this money to buy food, cotton clothing, and other goods.

Infographic

Inventions of the Industrial Revolution

New machines and new sources of power drove the Industrial Revolution forward. Each of the machines shown here was invented in Britain. The effects of these inventions on industry and on people's lives soon spread throughout Europe and the Americas. How did each invention make a later one possible?

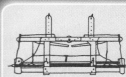

Flying Shuttle

John Kay invented the flying shuttle in 1733. This simple wooden device had yarn attached. It replaced the hand loom, allowing weavers to work twice as fast.

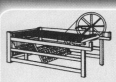

Spinning Jenny

Because weaving was so much faster, the demand for yarn increased. In 1765 **James Hargreaves** invented the spinning jenny, a machine that allowed workers to spin 16 spindles of yarn at once.

Water Frame

Richard Arkwright invented the water frame in 1769. This waterpowered device made even better thread for fabrics than the spinning jenny did.

Power Loom

An invention that made use of the yarn and thread that were being produced so quickly was **Edmund Cartwright's** power loom. Although this machine only became common in factories in the early 1800s, it speeded up the production of textiles tremendously.

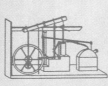

Steam Engine

James Watt perfected a steam engine in 1769. This machine, more than any other, gave a boost to the Industrial Revolution. By using coal as fuel, the steam engine provided a steady and unlimited source of power to run factory machines and later inventions like the steam locomotive.

A NEW SOCIAL PYRAMID

As the economy of Britain shifted from farms to factories, British society changed too. The middle class became more important as cities grew larger. The middle class was made up of business people, including merchants, lawyers, factory owners, and bankers. Although they did not have land or political power, the middle class increased trade and manufacturing. Some members of the middle class became rich.

The biggest group in British society was the working class. These men and women were mostly farmers who left farms to work in towns and cities. The rural lives they left behind were often difficult. However, many workers found life in the cities was sometimes worse.

Working Conditions

Working hours in the textile factories and mines were long and the conditions dangerous. Unlike farming or traditional craft work, factory work was boring and repetitive. One writer described what it was like:

They work fourteen hours per day, including the hour for dinner; the door is locked in working hours, except half an hour at tea time; the workpeople are not allowed to send for water to drink in the hot factory: and even the rain water is locked up, by the master's order, otherwise they would be happy to drink even that.

Many children worked in the narrow, wet, underground tunnels of the mines. Children as young as four years of age also worked in factories. Although children had always worked on farms, the conditions of the factories were severe. A French writer described a group of people leaving work, including

. . . young children, in greater numbers than the women, just as dirty, just as haggard, covered with rags which are thick with oil splashed over them as they toiled at the loom.

This painting (left) contrasts the middle class and the working class. Children often pulled carts through the narrow tunnels of coal mines (above).

An Idea for Change

Conditions in factories led many workers to organize. They formed organizations called unions. Weak at first, these organizations were outlawed by the government until 1824.

Karl Marx, a German philosopher living in England, wrote about the workers. In *Das Kapital* he wrote, "The [workers] have nothing to lose but their chains; they have the world to gain." Marx believed that those who owned property became rich while those who did not remained poor. The solution, he felt, was for workers to own the factories.

Marx believed that the world was entering a new economic period when workers would rise up and take control. In time, Marx wrote, there would be no social classes, and government would disappear. Many people in Europe became interested in some of his ideas, which became known as socialism. Much later, in Russia, these ideas would form the basis of a new type of government.

WHY IT MATTERS

Thousands of years ago people experienced an economic revolution—agriculture. Farming meant that people no longer had to hunt and gather to meet their needs. The Industrial Revolution was another revolution that changed the way people met their needs.

The Industrial Revolution did not bring sudden change, as the French Revolution did. The term "Industrial Revolution" was not even used by the people who lived through it. Still, industry created new cities, bustling with activity and spewing clouds of smoke.

The Industrial Revolution spread from its birthplace in Britain throughout Europe and the Western Hemisphere. It would eventually change most of the planet. As these incredible changes took place, there would be no going back.

Reviewing Facts and Ideas

SUM IT UP

- The Industrial Revolution began in Britain in the middle 1700s.
- New inventions in textile manufacturing led to the building of factories.
- The middle class gained much money and power during this period.
- Life for the working class was frequently difficult, with low wages and poor working conditions.
- The Industrial Revolution spread from Britain to Europe and the Americas.

THINK ABOUT IT

1. What work did peasants do in their homes before factories were built?

2. What was the first product of the Industrial Revolution?

3. **FOCUS** List some good and bad effects of the Industrial Revolution.

4. **THINKING SKILL** How might the *point of view* of a working class person differ from that of a middle class person?

5. **GEOGRAPHY** How might the invention of the steam engine allow factories to be built anywhere?

GEOGRAPHYSKILLS

Using Cartograms

VOCABULARY

Gross Domestic Product
cartogram

WHY THE SKILL MATTERS

The Industrial Revolution had a great impact on the economy of Great Britain and eventually on the entire world. As more countries built factories and trade increased, the economies of the whole world became connected. A price increase on cotton in the Americas, for example, affected textile factories and buyers of textiles throughout the world.

To understand these effects it is important to be able to measure and compare economic information. Suppose that you want to learn about a country's gross domestic product, or GDP. GDP is the total value of goods and services produced by a country during a certain period, usually one year. You might look up a country's GDP on an economic table.

Suppose you want to compare the GDPs of different countries. You could use a cartogram. A cartogram is a special kind of map used to present economic and other kinds of information. Cartograms are especially useful for comparing information about many countries.

USING THE SKILL

Most maps show the shapes of land as they look from above. You read about the different ways map makers project these shapes onto flat surfaces in the Using Map Projections Skills Lesson, on page 432. Physical maps, political maps, and historical maps all show countries or continents in relation to their actual size. On a cartogram, however, the size of a country is not related to the country's physical size, but rather to the information that is being compared. For example, on a cartogram showing populations of countries, China would appear as the biggest country on the map. This is because China has the largest population in the world.

The cartogram on this page shows the GDP of all of the countries in the world. The larger a country appears on this map, the greater is the value of all the goods and services produced by its economy. We see on political maps that Russia is the largest country in physical size. Does Russia also have the greatest GDP?

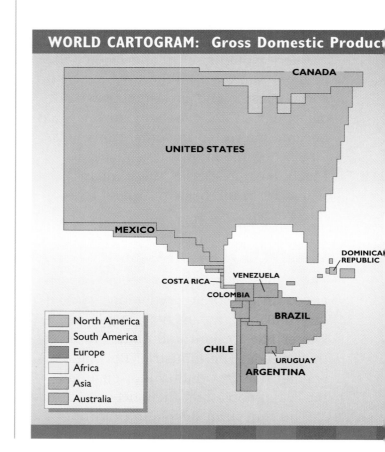

WORLD CARTOGRAM: Gross Domestic Product

CANADA
UNITED STATES
MEXICO
DOMINICAN REPUBLIC
COSTA RICA
VENEZUELA
COLOMBIA
BRAZIL
CHILE
URUGUAY
ARGENTINA

North America
South America
Europe
Africa
Asia
Australia

TRYING THE SKILL

In the last lesson you read that the Industrial Revolution began in Great Britain and then spread throughout Europe and to the Americas. You will read in the next lesson that it also spread to Japan. The influence of the Industrial Revolution is still felt today. For example, many of the countries with the greatest GDPs were among the first to build factories over 100 years ago. Which country has the largest GDP in the world?

Which regions have countries with smaller GDPs? Why do you think this is so?

REVIEWING THE SKILL

1. How are cartograms different from other kinds of maps?

2. How are cartograms useful for comparing countries?

3. Look at the cartogram on this page. Which country has the second-largest GDP?

4. Britain was the birthplace of the Industrial Revolution. Does this country still have the world's biggest GDP? Is its GDP greater or smaller than Germany's?

5. What other kinds of information could be presented in a cartogram?

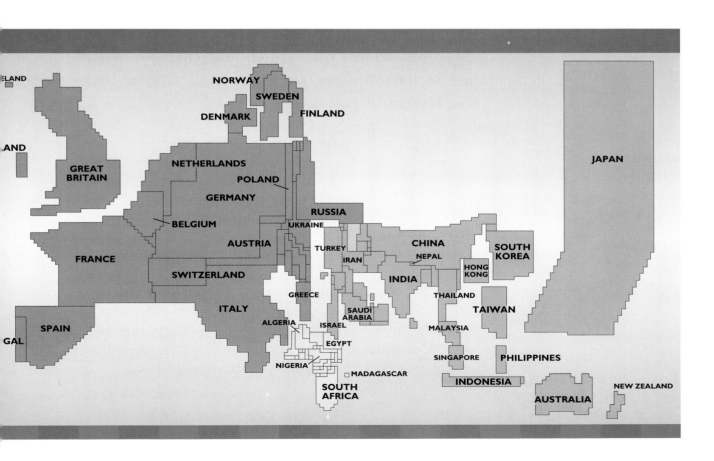

THE RISE OF INDUSTRIAL JAPAN

READ ALOUD

"We recognize the excellence of Western civilization. We value the Western theories of rights, liberty, and equality; and we respect Western philosophy and morals. . . . Above all, we esteem Western science, economics, and industry. These, however, ought not to be adopted simply because they are Western; they ought to be adopted only if they can contribute to Japan's welfare."

This statement was written in a Japanese newspaper in 1889. It expressed the feelings of many Japanese citizens at that time.

THE BIG PICTURE

In the 1630s, as you read in Chapter 14, the Tokugawa shogun had closed Japan to Western influences—influences of Europe and the United States. Only one Western ship was allowed to enter Japan each year. Japanese could not, under punishment of death, travel outside the country.

By the middle 1800s Western nations had adopted a policy of imperialism. Imperialism is the extension of a nation's power over other lands by military, political, or economic means. It was at this time, in the 1850s, that Japan was forced to reopen its borders.

Focus Activity

READ TO LEARN
How did Japan change during the Meiji Restoration?

VOCABULARY
imperialism
Meiji Restoration
bureaucracy

PEOPLE
Matthew C. Perry
Meiji

PLACES
Tokyo

OPENING A CLOSED COUNTRY

After the 1630s almost every foreign ship that sailed to Japan for any reason was turned away. Although many ships from Europe and the United States sailed near Japan, few made contact with the Japanese.

Arrival of the Western Fleet

By the 1850s, however, the foreign pressure on Japan to reopen its borders increased. Many Western nations were seeking markets for new, factory-made goods. The United States, especially, wanted to sail its ships to Japan. During this time many American ships crossed the Pacific to hunt whales for oil. Japan would provide a perfect resting stop for these ships. The United States was also expanding its trade with China. Japan was located along the sea routes from California to China's ports.

In 1853 the United States government sent four warships to Japan. They were commanded by Commodore Matthew C. Perry. Perry carried a letter from President Millard Fillmore. The letter said that the United States wanted to be friends with Japan. "But no friendship can long exist," warned the letter, "unless Japan ceases to act toward Americans as if they were her enemies." Perry said he would return the next year for a response. Perry returned to Japan in 1854. This time he sailed eight warships into Edo bay. The Japanese realized they could not match the firepower of these ships and agreed to meet with Commodore Perry.

Japanese leaders agreed to open two ports to American ships. The ships could stop at these ports to pick up supplies as they crossed the Pacific. Britain, France, Russia, and Holland also made trade agreements with the Japanese after Perry opened the door to trade with Japan.

The Granger Collection

The arrival of Matthew Perry (left) pushed Japan to negotiate a trade agreement with the United States.

The emperor Meiji (above) moved to the imperial palace (left) in Tokyo after the shogun was overthrown in 1868.

THE MEIJI RESTORATION

The opening of Japan to foreign trade shook Japanese society. Many leaders opposed the shogun's agreements with Western countries. They believed Japan was giving too much away. A few Europeans and Americans living in Japan were attacked and killed.

A New Government

In 1868 the disagreement with the shogun grew into a revolt. Leaders of several samurai groups took over the shogun's palace in Kyoto. They returned control of Japan to the emperor, who had long been powerless in the Tokugawa government. Since the emperor's name was Meiji (MAY JEE), this event is known as the Meiji Restoration. While the uprising was really a revolution against the shogun, it was called a restoration because power was restored to the emperor.

The new Japanese government began to adopt foreign ways of governing. The feudal system was abolished. Lords became regional governors for the new central government. Lords also had to give all of their land to the emperor in exchange for money.

A modern army was created, and the samurai lost their special right to carry swords. Many samurai had to look for jobs as farmers or merchants. The emperor moved from Kyoto to what had been the shogun's palace in Edo. Edo was renamed Tokyo, which means "eastern capital" in Japanese.

Although the emperor was now the official head of Japanese government, leaders called ministers made most decisions. They controlled a large bureaucracy. A bureaucracy is a large organization that runs the daily business of government. The new central government issued a declaration called the Charter Oath. This document declared that all Japanese would be given a say in their government. It also stated that old customs would be abandoned and "knowledge shall be sought throughout the world." In 1889 Japan had a new constitution and a parliament called the Diet (DIE et). The island nation was entering a new era.

Changes in Japan

This was not the first time that Japan looked to the outside for new ideas. Buddhism from China and Korea, and Confucianism from China, had been important parts of Japanese culture for centuries. Now, to learn about Western cultures, the Japanese government sent hundreds of students to the United States and Europe. Most studied such subjects as shipbuilding and navigation that would make Japan stronger. Some studied medicine and other subjects that would help Japanese people.

The Japanese government paid foreigners for expert advice on building railways, running factories, and sailing steamships. By 1889 telegraph lines and railroads linked all major cities. On steamships built in new shipyards, Japan began to export silk and tea to Europe and the United States. The first factories made silk textiles, but soon cotton mills were also built.

As contact with other cultures continued, styles of dress changed too. People began to wear suits or dresses instead of Japanese-style kimonos. In 1873 one person reported that he had seen a man wearing a samurai outfit in Tokyo. The man was stared at because his clothes seemed so strange. The samurai hairstyle, with hair pulled up on top, quickly went out of style. The new government built buildings in Western styles of architecture. Some people even began to eat beef and other Western foods.

These changes broke down many Japanese feudal customs. For example, the strict separation between social classes became blurred. A foreign visitor described the attitude of many farmers:

In the old days the farmer did not complain; he thought his lot could not be changed. He was forbidden to adopt a new calling and he was restricted by law to a frugal way of living. Now farmers can be soldiers, merchants, or officials, and can live as they please. They begin to compare their standard of living with that of other callings.

Links to ART

From East to West

The flow of information between Japan and the West ran in both directions. Many artists in Europe and the United States became interested in Japanese art, particularly the colorful prints called Ukiyo-e. Artists such as Vincent van Gogh, Claude Monet, and James Whistler adapted many of the colors and styles of these prints. In fact, the French coined a term— *japonisme* (jap oh NEEZ mah)— to describe this use of Japanese artistic styles.

You can find art books in your library showing paintings by the artists listed above. Find also Japanese woodblock prints, such as the one by Hiroshige on page 514. How were European and Japanese styles similar and how were they different?

EXPANSION OF JAPAN

Japan changed quickly because of the Meiji Restoration. The country soon became a military and economic power. Between 1883 and 1912 an increase in Japanese exports more than doubled world trade. In the 1890s Japanese leaders began to change unequal trade treaties they had signed years before.

Through all these changes Japan grew stronger and kept its own identity.

Military Activity Overseas

Japan soon began to show its power overseas. In 1894 Japan invaded Korea, which had long been occupied by China. China demanded that Japan remove its troops. Japan refused. Soon, Japan controlled most of the Korean Peninsula and the surrounding seas. Japan continued its push into Asia, attacking the Chinese mainland. In 1895 a treaty gave Japan control of Korea as well as the island of Taiwan.

In 1904 Japan entered into war against another neighbor—Russia. The most important battle of this war was in the stormy seas of the Tsushima (tsoo SHEE muh) Straits, which are part of the Korean Strait. There, Japan's navy destroyed the powerful Russian

GROWTH OF JAPAN, 1870-1905

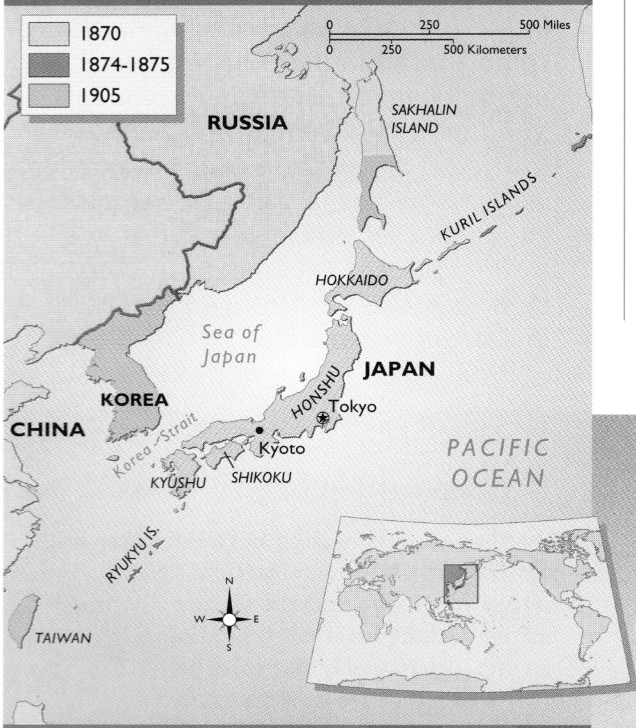

1870
1874-1875
1905

0   250   500 Miles
0   250   500 Kilometers

RUSSIA
SAKHALIN ISLAND
KURIL ISLANDS
HOKKAIDO
Sea of Japan
JAPAN
HONSHU
KOREA
Tokyo
CHINA
Korea Strait
Kyōto
KYŪSHU   SHIKOKU
PACIFIC OCEAN
RYUKYU IS.
TAIWAN
N W E S

M A P   W O R K

Japanese wealth and military power led to expansion into neighboring territories.

1. In which direction did Japan expand?

2. What body of water separates Japan from Korea?

Today bullet trains (right) run the length of the main Japanese island, Honshu.

navy. The war was costly for both sides, but the Japanese victory caused the rest of the world to notice Japan's new strength. When the two countries signed a peace treaty in 1905, Japan gained land from Russia on the Asian mainland as well as half of Sakhalin Island. Look at the map on page 512 to see new lands controlled by Japan.

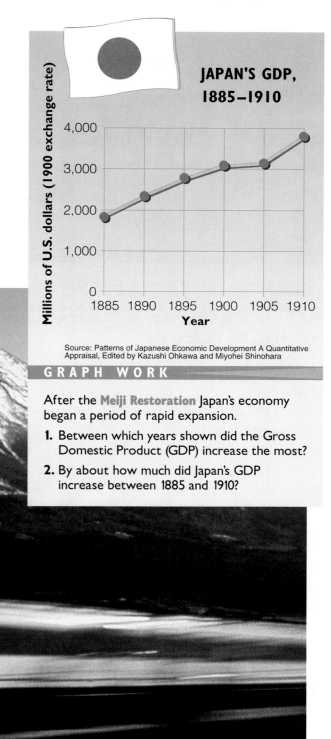

JAPAN'S GDP, 1885–1910

Millions of U.S. dollars (1900 exchange rate)

Year

Source: Patterns of Japanese Economic Development A Quantitative Appraisal, Edited by Kazushi Ohkawa and Miyohei Shinohara

GRAPH WORK

After the Meiji Restoration Japan's economy began a period of rapid expansion.

1. Between which years shown did the Gross Domestic Product (GDP) increase the most?

2. By about how much did Japan's GDP increase between 1885 and 1910?

WHY IT MATTERS

The Emperor Meiji died in 1912, bringing to an end a remarkable era in Japanese history. During his nearly 50-year reign, Japan emerged from two centuries of isolation and feudal rule. It grew to become the most powerful military and economic force in Asia.

Japan's expansion did not end with the Meiji era. The small island nation grew even more powerful. When most of the world went to war in the 1940s, as you will read in Chapter 18, Japan played a major part in the conflict.

✓ Reviewing Facts and Ideas

SUM IT UP

- In 1854 the United States forced Japan to reopen to outside trade.

- In 1868 the Meiji Restoration created a new central government, with the Emperor as its head.

- Japan rapidly modernized, borrowing many ideas from other cultures.

- By the 1890s Japan had become a powerful industrial country and began to expand into mainland Asia.

THINK ABOUT IT

1. Why did Japan have so little contact with the outside world under the Tokugawa Shogun?

2. How did Commodore Perry force Japan to begin trade with the West?

3. **FOCUS** What did Japan do to interact with the countries of the West?

4. **THINKING SKILL** In what ways did the establishment of a new government in 1868 _affect_ Japan's relationship with other countries?

5. **GEOGRAPHY** How did Japan's island location help it first become isolated and later become industrialized?

CITIZENSHIP
VIEWPOINTS

This woodblock drawing of Perry arriving in Shimoda, Japan, was made by Hiroshige in 1855.

1853: WHAT DID THE JAPANESE THINK ABOUT OPENING THEIR COUNTRY TO THE WEST?

In July 1853, as you read in the last lesson, Commodore Matthew Perry sailed into Edo Bay and demanded that Japan be opened to trade with western nations. His arrival added urgency to a debate that had been going on in Japan for years.

Many Japanese people said that opening the country was too great a risk. They felt that their nation should maintain its own culture, without Western influences. A scholar named Fujita Toko wrote that once foreign ideas took hold there would be no way to restore Japanese traditions.

Japanese Lord Ii Naosuke believed that Japan should strengthen and protect itself by setting aside some of its feudal customs and learning from the West. He explained that the technology of Western nations made them strong enough to overpower Japan.

A Japanese writer stated that Japan should remain isolated. As you will read in the second viewpoint, he favored attacking Westerners who were in Japan.

Read and consider three viewpoints on this issue.

Three DIFFERENT Viewpoints

1 LORD II NAOSUKE
Feudal lord, Excerpt from a letter, 1847

The condition of foreign states is not what it once was: they have invented the steamship and introduced radical changes in the art of navigation. They have also built up their armies to a state of great efficiency and are possessed of war implements of great power and precision; in short, they have risen to be imposing powers. If we cling to our outdated systems, heaven only knows what mighty calamity may befall our empire.

"... our outdated systems ..."

2 AIZAWA SEISHISAI
Writer, Excerpt from *New Proposals,* 1825

Second-rate leaders, thinking only of easy peace, let the foreigners go unchecked. . . . They make the situation worse through half-hearted inaction. If, instead, the government issues orders to the entire nation to smash the foreigners whenever they come into sight and to treat them openly as our nation's foes, everyone high and low will push forward to enforce the order. This is a great opportunity. It must not be lost.

"... treat them openly as our nation's foes ..."

3 FUJITA TOKO
Scholar, 1849

Why should we not be able to defend our land against the invaders, though our defenses are not quite what we wish them to be? If once permitted, foreigners will soon try to win the hearts of the common people. If we suddenly find ourselves with the minds of our people loosened, our defenses neglected, the foreign religion *(Christianity)* gaining ground, what remedy would there be to reverse this awful state of things?

"... foreigners will soon try to win the hearts of the common people."

BUILDING CITIZENSHIP

1. What was the viewpoint of each person?
2. In what ways were some of the viewpoints alike? In what ways were they different?
3. What viewpoints might people have on this issue today?

SHARING VIEWPOINTS

Discuss what you agree with or disagree with about these viewpoints. Discuss why you think each speaker might feel as he did. Then as a class, write a statement that all three of the speakers might have agreed with in the Japanese debate over the opening of their country.

CHAPTER 17 REVIEW

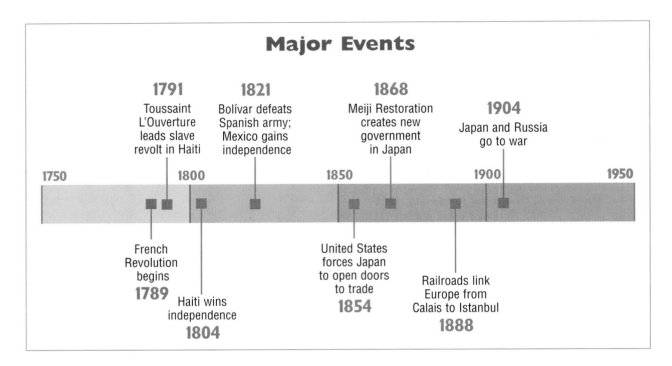

Major Events

1791
Toussaint L'Ouverture leads slave revolt in Haiti

1821
Bolívar defeats Spanish army; Mexico gains independence

1868
Meiji Restoration creates new government in Japan

1904
Japan and Russia go to war

1750   1800   1850   1900   1950

French Revolution begins
1789

Haiti wins independence
1804

United States forces Japan to open doors to trade
1854

Railroads link Europe from Calais to Istanbul
1888

THINKING ABOUT VOCABULARY

Number a sheet of paper from 1 to 10. Beside each number write the term from the list below that matches the statement.

absolute monarchy   Latin America
aristocracy   mestizo
bureaucracy   middle class
cartogram   revolution
Industrial Revolution   socialism

1. A large organization that runs the daily business of government

2. The period of rapid industrial and technological growth that began in England in the 1700s

3. The region south of the United States influenced by Spanish and Portuguese culture

4. A form of government in which a king or queen has complete power

5. A special map used to present economic and other kinds of information

6. A system of society based on ideas of Marx in which workers would own and control all property

7. A social class that includes merchants, lawyers, bankers, and business owners

8. A person of mixed Native American and European ancestry

9. A social class made up of nobles and their families

10. A sudden or great change

THINKING ABOUT FACTS

1. What role did the Estates General play in triggering the French Revolution?

2. What effect did Simón Bolívar have on South American history?

3. What were the main ideas of Karl Marx?

4. What part did Commodore Perry play in opening Japan to trade?

5. What does the time line above suggest about the possible influence of the French Revolution on events in Haiti and Latin America?

THINK AND WRITE ◀ ▭ ▷

WRITING AN ANALYSIS

Write a paragraph about the Industrial Revolution. Describe both the progress it brought and the social problems it created.

WRITING A JOURNAL ENTRY

Suppose you were alive during the French Revolution. Choose one event: (1) the meeting of the National Assembly (2) the storming of the Bastille or (3) the execution of the king and queen. Write a journal entry about what you saw or know happened.

WRITING AN EXPLANATION

Describe the changes that took place in Japan during the 50-year reign of the Emperor Meiji. Reread pages 510–511. Then write a short essay about the reasons behind the emergence of Japan from two centuries of isolation and feudal rule.

APPLYING GEOGRAPHY SKILLS

USING CARTOGRAMS

1. What is a cartogram?

2. Look at the cartogram on pages 506–507. Name in order the ten countries with highest GDPs. On which continents are they located?

3. According to the cartogram, which five countries in Africa have the highest GDPs? Is Algeria's GDP greater or less than Singapore's?

4. Is India's GDP greater or less than Argentina's? Than the United Kingdom's? Than South Africa's?

5. Why are cartograms useful?

Summing Up the Chapter

Copy the cause-and-effect chart below on a separate sheet of paper. Review the chapter and fill in at least two effects for each cause listed. When you have filled in the information, use it to answer the question "What important changes came about because of revolutions in Europe, the Americas, and Japan?"

CAUSE		EFFECTS
French Revolution	As a Result →	
Latin American Revolutions	As a Result →	
Industrial Revolution	As a Result →	
Meiji Restoration	As a Result →	

UNIT 5 REVIEW

THINKING ABOUT VOCABULARY

Number a sheet of paper from 1 to 10. Decide whether the underlined word in each of the following statements correctly completes the sentence. If the word is correct, write **C** beside the number. If the word is incorrect, write **I** and then write the correct word to complete the sentence.

confederation

convert

divine right

heliocentric

Meiji Restoration

missionary

Reign of Terror

sugarcane

textile

Triangular Trade

1. The belief that a monarch's authority came from God was called <u>divine right</u>.

2. <u>Reign of Terror</u> is the name of the trade that developed between England, Africa, and North America in the 1600s.

3. To <u>convert</u> people is to win them over to one's point of view or beliefs.

4. The <u>Meiji Restoration</u> was the return to the throne of a Japanese emperor during a revolt against the shogun.

5. Enemies of the French Revolution were executed during a period called the <u>Triangular trade</u>.

6. <u>Sugarcane</u> is a tall grass with a thick, woody stem that contains the liquid source of sugar.

7. The <u>missionary</u> view, developed by Copernicus, Galileo, and Newton, states that the sun is the center of the universe.

8. A <u>textile</u> is a group of states that join together under a central government.

9. A <u>heliocentric</u> is a cloth that is woven or knitted.

10. A <u>confederation</u> tries to make other people see the truth of his or her religion.

THINK AND WRITE

WRITING ABOUT PERSPECTIVES

Suppose you were an African who crossed the Atlantic on a slave ship. Describe how your perspective would be different from an African who had never left home.

WRITING AN INTERVIEW

Suppose you could interview one person you read about in this unit. Write down your questions and his or her answers.

WRITING A PAMPHLET

Write a pamphlet explaining the reasons for the French revolution.

BUILDING SKILLS

1. **Analyzing credibility** How would you determine the credibility of the statement made by the woman who lived during the Reign of Terror? Look back at page 490.

2. **Analyzing credibility** Reread the excerpt on page 502. What does the point of view expressed suggest about the author?

3. **Analyzing credibility** Reread the two quotations on page 504. What is the point of view of these writers and how does it differ from the quote on page 502?

4. **Using cartograms** Look at the cartogram on page 506. Find three places in the world where rich and poor countries are located near each other.

4. **Using cartograms** The cartogram on page 506 shows the GDP of countries but *not* the average wealth of people in each country. Explain how people in a country with a relatively high GDP, like China, might actually be poorer than people in countries with lower GDPs but also fewer people. What kind of cartogram would give an accurate picture of the relative wealth of people in each country?

YESTERDAY, TODAY & TOMORROW

History has shown that some changes are brought about rapidly through revolution. Others are more gradual. What important changes do you think are taking place today? What changes do you think will take place in the future? What do you think the world will be like centuries from now? Explain your answers.

READING ON YOUR OWN

These are some books you might find at the library to help you learn more.

EXPLORER
by Rupert Matthews
This visual history with background information takes you from ancient to modern times through land, sea, air, and space.

THE INDUSTRIAL REVOLUTION
edited by John D. Clare
This illustrated book helps trace the technology that grew out of the Industrial Revolution.

THE MEIJI RESTORATION AND RISE OF MODERN JAPAN
by Monique Avakian
This book details Japan's transformation to a modern industrial and military power.

UNIT PROJECT

Make a Famous People Game

1. First each partner will choose six names from the unit. Then each player will write each name on a separate index card. Choose the people together to avoid repeating names.
2. Next each partner will write a fact about each of the people named on six additional cards. For example, if you choose Marie Antoinette, your fact might be that she was the queen of France until the French Revolution.
3. To play, mix the 24 cards and lay them face-down. Take turns turning over two cards. Your goal is to match each person with his or her correct fact. If you don't turn up a name with a matching fact, turn the cards face down again. If you turn up two matching cards, keep them and take another turn. The player with the most cards at the end wins.

WAR POSTER,
GREAT BRITAIN;
WAR PLANE, WWII;
ATOMIC EXPLOSION

BRITONS

"WANTS"
YOU
JOIN YOUR COUNTRY'S ARMY!
GOD SAVE THE KING
Reproduced by permission of LONDON OPINION

F. W. DE KLERK AND
NELSON MANDELA,
SOUTH AFRICA

A Century of Conflict

"This cruelty too will end."

from *The Diary of Anne Frank*
See page 546.

WHY DOES IT MATTER?

A young girl, Anne Frank, wrote these words during a war that affected the entire world. In this, the second World War, as well as in the first World War, new weapons and fighting techniques caused tremendous loss of life.

Other struggles affected nations in the 1900s. Democratic beliefs and human rights were challenged. Colonies around the world struggled to gain independence.

As Anne Frank hoped, and as millions around the world continue to hope, conflicts have been giving way to greater peace, freedom, and cooperation. The technology that caused destruction has also been a source of life. New medicines and techniques have enabled people to live longer, more healthful lives. New ways of sharing information have also linked the whole world. People today share ideas that will shape the present and the future.

ANNE FRANK; MOHANDAS GANDHI

521

Adventures
with
NATIONAL
GEOGRAPHIC

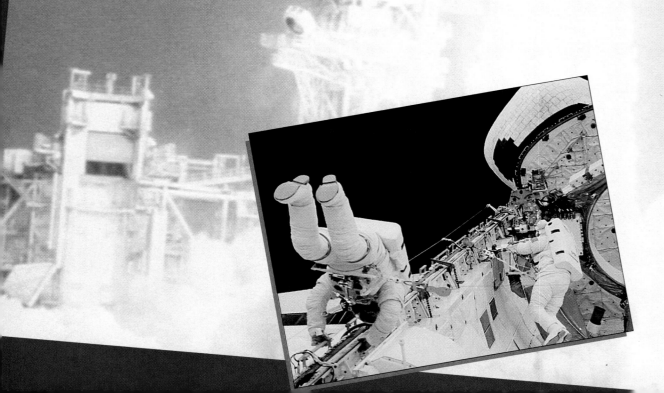

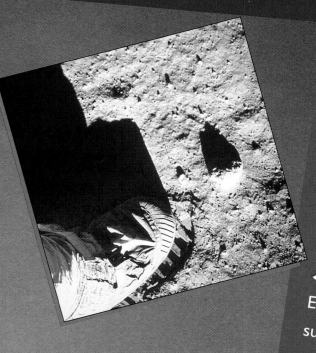

The Last Unknown Place

A human being's foot leaves an imprint on the moon. A blue and white planet—our Earth—appears over the horizon of a gray lunar surface. The space shuttle blasts away from Earth, carrying astronauts who will live and work in space for days at a time. Throughout history, people have experienced the urge to explore. In this century, that urge takes us far beyond our own atmosphere. But the courage and imagination needed for exploration today are the same as they were for the first human beings who set their eyes on the horizon and started out for unknown places.

GEO JOURNAL

Write an application to become an astronaut. What qualities do you have that would make you a good one?

CHAPTER 18

A World at War

THINKING ABOUT HISTORY AND GEOGRAPHY

The twentieth century has been a time of great change and conflict. Old ways of governing were overthrown in many parts of the world. Two world wars were fought with weapons of great destruction. When the fighting ended, two superpowers with opposing goals sought to influence other nations. Follow these events on the map and on the time line.

AFRICA

1914
SARAJEVO, AUSTRIA-HUNGARY

World War I begins after Franz Ferdinand is killed

1917
ST. PETERSBURG, RUSSIA

Protesters end the rule of Russia's monarchy

1934
RUIJIN, CHINA

Communists begin their 6,000-mile Long March

ARCTIC
OCEAN

Normandy

St. Petersburg

Berlin

EUROPE

Sarajevo

ASIA

Ruijin

1944

NORMANDY, FRANCE

Allied forces successfully invade Europe during World War II

1961

BERLIN, EAST GERMANY

East German police build a wall between East and West Berlin

INDIAN
OCEAN

THE "GREAT WAR"

READ ALOUD

"I saw the ship go down. There was this huge lovely liner, and as I watched one [smokestack] went [under] and then the other and the other until the ship was gone and the sea was calm, and all you could see was bodies, and wreckage of furniture and everything that had been in the ship floating in the water."

This was how Alice Lines remembered the 1915 German submarine attack on the *Lusitania*, a ship crossing the Atlantic. The ship carried many American passengers. Lines was one of the few survivors. The 1,198 people who died were victims of an international conflict, the "Great War."

THE BIG PICTURE

The sinking of the *Lusitania* angered many people in the United States. Two years after that event, the country entered a war that had already involved many nations of the world. What forces and events led to the war?

In Chapter 17 you read about vast changes that swept through the world in the late 1700s and 1800s. Factories were built during the Industrial Revolution. Overland travel sped along with the help of railroads. Steamships crossed the Atlantic Ocean in just six days.

Countries such as Britain, Germany, and France grew economically because of the Industrial Revolution. The populations and military strength of many European countries also increased. This growth brought with it many new problems. European leaders wondered which countries would continue to strengthen. Which ones would eventually become the most powerful nations?

Focus Activity

READ TO LEARN
In what ways did nationalism affect the events leading to World War I?

VOCABULARY
nationalism
alliance
Central Powers
Allied Powers
armistice
League of Nations
Treaty of Versailles
World War I

PEOPLE
Franz Ferdinand

PLACES
Sarajevo
Serbia

EUROPE AT THE TURN OF THE CENTURY

In the early 1900s Europe was like a huge jigsaw puzzle. The "pieces" were nations. Some, such as Britain and France, had existed for centuries. Others, such as Italy and Germany, had been unified only in the 1800s.

In many of these European nations, a feeling of unity had grown among peoples who spoke the same language and shared a common history and culture. These feelings developed into the force that is known as nationalism (NASH uh nuh lihz um). Nationalism is a strong loyalty to one's own country and culture. Those who are influenced by nationalism want their countries to be more powerful than any others.

By the early 1900s nationalism had grown stronger in Europe. So had tensions between neighboring countries. To prepare for the possibility of war, countries trained large armies and formed alliances (uh LI un sez). An alliance is an agreement between countries that ties their interests together. Members of an alliance, called allies, pledge to defend each other if any of them are attacked.

Two Shots that Started a War

On June 28, 1914, Archduke Franz Ferdinand, the heir to the throne of Austria-Hungary, visited Sarajevo (sar uh YAY voh). This city had come under his empire's control. Sarajevo, capital of a region called Bosnia, shared ties with Serbia, a nearby kingdom. Many Serbian nationalists thought that Sarajevo and Bosnia should be part of Serbia. Some of them decided to send a message to the archduke's government.

As Ferdinand and his wife Sophie drove through Sarajevo, someone threw a bomb at them. The archduke knocked it away and the bomb exploded behind them. A wrong turn, however, took them in front of another Serbian nationalist. This man used a gun. He fired twice, killing them both.

Austria-Hungary, backed by Germany, declared war on Serbia in July. Serbia was aided by its ally, Russia. Russia's allies, France and Britain, also came to Serbia's aid. A British leader described Europe on the brink of war: "The lights are going out all over Europe. We shall not see them lit again in our lifetime." By August 1914 the "Great War" had begun.

Archduke Franz Ferdinand and his wife Sophie were killed by a Serbian nationalist as they rode through Sarajevo. This photo shows them preparing for the ride.

Central powers
Neutral states
Allied powers

NORWAY
SWEDEN
North Sea
DENMARK
Baltic Sea
GREAT BRITAIN
NETHERLANDS
BELGIUM
GERMANY
RUSSIA
ATLANTIC OCEAN
LUXEMBOURG
FRANCE
AUSTRIA-HUNGARY
SWITZERLAND
RUMANIA
Adriatic Sea
PORTUGAL
ITALY
SERBIA
BULGARIA
SPAIN
MONTENEGRO
ALBANIA
GREECE
Mediterranean Sea
OTTOMAN EMPIRE
0   150   300 Miles
0 150 300 Kilometers

The map shows how Europe was divided at the start of the "Great War."

1. Which nations made up the Central Powers?

2. Which neutral states bordered France?

3. Which of the Allied Powers were located east of Germany?

NATIONS AT WAR

As you can see on the map, Austria-Hungary, Germany, and their allies became known as the Central Powers. Serbia, Russia, France, Britain, and others were called the Allied Powers.

The Central Powers had some military success in the fall of 1914. Their armies forced their way deep into France and Russia. The Allied Powers, however, had a greater number of soldiers and more supplies. They were better equipped to survive a long war.

The Battlefront

Over the next four years the battlefront in France hardly changed. The battlefront, or front, is the place where opposing armies fight. Millions of soldiers died trying to push the front east or west. During many battles at the front, generals stuck to old-style war techniques. These ways of fighting were no match for the deadly technology now being used in war. Machine guns and poison gas could kill hundreds of enemy soldiers in a short time.

All across France, soldiers on both sides dug maze-like dirt trenches, or ditches, for protection. Soldiers camped in the trenches while waiting for orders. Bombs exploded nearby and bullets whizzed overhead. In winter, rain filled the trenches with puddles and mud. In summer, the heat and dust were almost unbearable. The worst times, though, were when the soldiers were ordered to go "over the top." This phrase meant climbing out of the trenches and into enemy machine-gun fire. How did one British soldier describe fighting at the front?

Excerpt from an interview with British soldier, Charles Quinnell, about the Battle of the Somme in 1916.

I gave the order "advance—up the ladders—over the top.". . . We went through, we got halfway across and then the two machine guns found us . . . they played on us like spraying with a hose. At the finish I was the only man standing but I'm not one of those heroes who want to take on the German Army on my own and so I went to earth, I got down behind the lip of a big shell-hole. . . . The machine gun crew spotted me and they opened up on me. I ducked my head down . . . and the dirt was just spraying down the back of my neck.

shell-hole: hole caused by an explosion

The Home Front

While millions of troops served in the war, people at home did what they could to help. People who worked to support the troops were said to be fighting on the "home front." Women and men worked in factories to make bullets, bombs, and airplanes. Others volunteered to serve as nurses or ambulance drivers at the war front.

In order to save food for the soldiers, governments controlled the amount of food people could buy. In Britain, laws for restaurants stated:

Two meatless days are to be observed. No milk may be served or consumed (drunk), except by children under 10 years of age.

In Germany and eastern European countries, food prices soared. Many people ate potato peels and watery soup given out by their government.

The United States Enters the War

Conditions were better for the Allied Powers because they received supplies from the United States. These supplies were sent on ships. In 1915 German submarines sank the *Lusitania*, which was carrying war supplies. The ship's passengers included 128 United States citizens. Many died in the attack. Attacks on ships outraged leaders and citizens of the United States. So did a secret message sent by Germany to Mexico that plotted an alliance against the United States.

In April 1917 the United States declared war on Germany and the other Central Powers. Large numbers of American soldiers, as well as vast amounts of money and supplies, greatly helped the Allied Powers. As you will read on page 531, the United States used posters and slogans to help send more than 2 million troops to Europe.

Out of their trenches, soldiers near the front went fully prepared for enemy attacks.

Weapons of World War I

Nations have always made use of the latest developments in technology to produce new weapons. Some of the weapons used during World War I were not only capable of tremendous destruction, but also changed the way wars were fought. How did the weapons shown change modern war?

TANKS were armored vehicles invented by the British to cross trenches. Soldiers inside fired guns.

AIRPLANES were used to drop bombs on enemy territory. Bombs were often carried under the wings.

GAS MASKS were worn by soldiers fighting at the front for protection from poison gas.

AN END TO THE WAR

On November 11, 1918, Germany and the Allies signed an armistice (AHR muh stihs), or agreement to stop fighting. In January 1919, Allied leaders worked out terms for peace. As part of their treaty, they created the League of Nations, an international council that would work to prevent future wars. German leaders were forced to sign the Treaty of Versailles (vair SĪ) on June 28, 1919.

WHY IT MATTERS

The Treaty of Versailles caused great anger in Germany because it blamed that nation for the war. It also called for the payment of enormous fines to repair war damages. Even Ferdinand Foch, the commander of the Allied armies exclaimed, "This isn't peace! This is an armistice for 20 years!" Three months after those 20 years had passed, the nations of the world would again go to war. When that happened, the war that had been called the "Great War" became known as World War I.

Who was Uncle Sam?

Back in the War of 1812, merchant Samuel Wilson stamped "U.S." on all of his barrels headed for army troops. Wilson's workers teased him about that stamp. They said the letters "U.S." stood for his nickname, "Uncle Sam," rather than "United States." The legendary character "Uncle Sam" was born.

"Uncle Sam" became most famous in this World War I recruiting poster, which is still used today. The model for this "Uncle Sam" wasn't really anyone's uncle. He was the poster's artist, James Montgomery Flagg!

✓ Reviewing Facts and Ideas

SUM IT UP

- Nationalism was a factor that led to World War I, which was fought from 1914 to 1918.
- Modern technology played a deadly new role in the trench, sea, and air battles of World War I.
- On the "home front" women and men worked in factories, and governments controlled food supplies to make sure troops were fed.
- United States supplies and troops played an important role in helping the Allied Powers win World War I.

THINK ABOUT IT

1. What role did technology play in World War I?

2. How did people on the "home front" contribute to the war effort?

3. **FOCUS** How did nationalism play a role in the start of World War I?

4. **THINKING SKILL** Make a _conclusion_ about the impact alliances had on Europe in the early 1900s.

5. **WRITE** Read the excerpt from the interview with the soldier again. Write a letter to that soldier describing your reaction to his description of the front.

THE RUSSIAN REVOLUTION

READ ALOUD

"Peace! Land! Bread!"

This slogan summed up what ordinary Russians wanted most in the bloody, food-starved days of World War I. One group promised to give them all these things and more. Once in power, this group would transform Russia and affect the whole world.

THE BIG PICTURE

World War I was the peak of a long era of conflict and revolution. You have already read about political and industrial revolutions that rocked the world in the 1700s and 1800s. In the early 1900s, while the "Great War" still raged, yet another revolution broke out—in Russia. The Russian Revolution was an extremely important event in modern world history.

In 1900 the Russian empire stretched across parts of Europe and Asia. It included people of many different cultures. Most, though, lived in western Russia, where the land was better suited for the empire's main activity—farming. Most Russians were Christians. Muslims also lived in the empire, however, as well as many Jews.

World leaders took notice when revolutionaries overthrew Russia's leaders in 1917. Revolutionary leaders began to build a government around the ideas of Karl Marx, whom you read about in Chapter 17. The world watched and waited. What would happen in Russia? Would Russia continue to fight in World War I? How would the revolution affect other nations?

Focus Activity

READ TO LEARN
What were the causes and effects of the Russian Revolution?

VOCABULARY
Russian Revolution
tsar
strike
communism
totalitarian

PEOPLE
Alexander II
Nicholas II
Vladimir Ilyich Lenin
Josef Stalin

PLACES
Russia
St. Petersburg
Moscow
Soviet Union

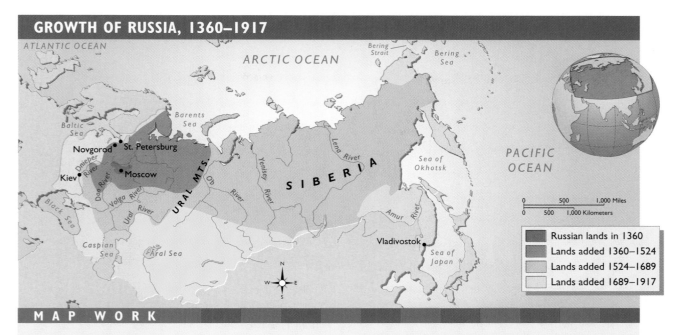

GROWTH OF RUSSIA, 1360–1917

Russian lands in 1360
Lands added 1360–1524
Lands added 1524–1689
Lands added 1689–1917

MAP WORK

Russian tsars greatly expanded their nation's lands.

1. Which city was the center of Russia in 1360?

2. In which direction is St. Petersburg from Moscow?

3. During which years did Russian lands first reach the Caspian Sea?

4. What was the eastern boundary of Russia in 1524? In 1689?

5. After what year did Russian lands extend past the Ural Mountains?

RUSSIA UNDER THE TSARS

In the middle 1800s Russia was far from being a world power. While industry changed many parts of Europe, most Russians lived much as they had during the Middle Ages.

At the top of Russia's social pyramid was the **tsar** (ZAHR), or emperor. The tsar ruled with an iron hand. Anyone who displeased the tsar might be killed or sent to prison in Siberia. Find this frozen steppe region on the map.

Beneath the tsar were a handful of rich noble families. At the bottom of Russia's social pyramid were millions of poor farmers. Their crops fed the empire.

Russian Serfs

By the late 1700s France and other European countries no longer had serfs, or farmers, bound to the land. In the early 1800s, however, most Russians were still serfs. Russian law said serfs were the property of their owners, although serfs could not be sold.

By the middle 1800s serf revolts in Russia were increasing in number. Tsar **Alexander II** began to fear a revolution. He also wanted to shift Russia's work force away from farming and toward industry. Alexander decided to abolish serfdom in 1861. To abolish means to end a practice. The Tsar said: "It is better to abolish serfdom from above than to wait until the serfs begin to free themselves from below."

In exchange for freedom and small plots of land, the freed serfs had to pay heavy taxes. Paying the taxes was difficult, since many families were given small areas to farm.

Wealthy Russians like Tsar Nicholas and army officials owned expensive items like this egg by Fabergé (right).

WORLDS IN CONFLICT

By the late 1800s Russian cities were growing. Hard times in rural areas forced many former serfs to move to the cities in search of work. By the 1890s factories and mills of the Industrial Revolution were springing up in Russia's capital, St. Petersburg.

Two Sides of a City

To poor farmers St. Petersburg was a new world. They stared in wonder at the grand winter palace of Tsar Nicholas II, who began his rule in 1894. Dozens of mansions, churches, theaters, schools, and universities lined the streets of the city. More than one million people lived in St. Petersburg.

The city also had a less spectacular side. Away from the palace and other beautiful mansions, mills and factories clustered together. Smoke from their chimneys filled the air above the overcrowded apartment buildings where workers lived.

Workers Protest

Inside the factories and mills, conditions were often grim and workers were angry. A protest in 1897 won them a shortened work day—to $11\frac{1}{2}$ hours. Factory workers protested again in 1905, shutting down the city with their strikes. A strike is a refusal to work in protest of unfair treatment.

On Sunday, January 22, 1905, thousands of striking workers marched toward the Winter Palace to speak with the tsar himself. The tsar's soldiers responded by shooting into the crowd. More than 100 people were killed. Many others were injured. The day became known as "Bloody Sunday."

A storm of revolts and strikes swept through the country after "Bloody Sunday." Tsar Nicholas II agreed to share some of his power with a new elected parliament, called the Duma. The Duma called for changes that would advance democracy and help the poor. The tsar refused. During the next nine years, Nicholas and the Duma were in constant conflict.

War and Hunger

In the years following "Bloody Sunday," unrest deepened in Russia. Things became even worse during World War I. More than a million Russian troops died on the battlefront. Some never even had guns or bullets to protect themselves, since weapons were in short supply. Most of the nation's railroads carried supplies to battle. Only a few trains were available to bring food and fuel to cities. As a result, factories and stores often closed. Many people were left without work. Goods that were already hard to get became even more scarce.

March of 1917 began as one of the coldest, snowiest months that many people in St. Petersburg could remember. The weather kept farmers and their food carts away from city markets. Within the city hungry workers lined up in the cold for hours. They hoped to spend what little money they had on small loaves of bread.

This photo from around 1900 shows workers on a farm in Russia. The lives of many Russian farmers were filled with hard work and hunger.

Revolution Begins

The skies cleared and the weather changed in time for a protest held by thousands of unhappy people. For four days, demonstrators jammed the streets of St. Petersburg. Shouts of "Down with the war!" and "Down with the government!" soon drowned out the simple cry for "Bread!"

The tsar's police called for help from soldiers who were staying in the city. Most of the soldiers, however, joined in the protest and turned on the police. With the soldiers' help the protest became a full-scale revolution against the government.

Tsar Nicholas, who was away meeting with his generals, had no idea of what was happening in his capital. By the time he set out to return home, the spirit of revolution had spread. Angry railroad workers forced his train to a standstill. On March 15, 1917, Nicholas II was forced to give up his role as tsar. Sixteen months later he, his wife Alexandra, and their children were executed. The rule of Russian tsars had come to an end. Who would rule the giant nation now?

In November 1917 soldiers marched to the Duma, where they helped the Bolsheviks gain control of government.

A NEW GOVERNMENT

After the revolution in March, the Duma chose leaders to run the country. Russia's many problems, however, continued. World War I was still underway and Russian military leaders demanded that their troops be withdrawn from the front. City workers went on striking in protest of even longer bread lines and lower wages. Many farmers, hungry and impatient for change, began seizing land for themselves.

Meanwhile a political group called the Bolsheviks was gaining strength. The Bolsheviks were led by a Russian lawyer named Vladimir Ilyich Lenin (VLAD uh meer IHL yitch LEN in). He believed that a different kind of revolution was necessary to change the government. The Bolsheviks planned a socialist revolution based on the ideas of Karl Marx whom you read about in Chapter 17. They wanted workers to control the government and own all property. Lenin promised Russians "Peace, Land, and Bread."

The Bolsheviks Take Control

With the support of the soldiers in St. Petersburg, Lenin and the Bolsheviks overthrew the Duma in November 1917. Soon after this second revolution they pulled Russian troops out of the Allied war effort. Russia began peace talks with Germany. The Bolsheviks allowed workers to control factories and farmers to use the farmland of wealthy nobles. The Bolsheviks also moved the capital of Russia south to the ancient city of Moscow.

The new Bolshevik government had many opponents. Landowners, factory owners, and nobles were losing their rights, as well as their wealth and power. Christians and different ethnic groups also opposed the government. These people led a civil war against Lenin and the Bolsheviks.

The Russian people were already battered from world war and revolution. Their suffering became even greater, however, during this new civil war. Between 1918 and 1920, millions died from disease and starvation, as well as in violent battles.

Communism

Lenin wanted to create communism in Russia. Communism is a political and economic system in which all land and all businesses are controlled by the government.

In the months before the outbreak of the civil war, Lenin wrote, the Bolsheviks had left "one foot in socialism." In other words, they had been moving slowly toward a society controlled by workers. Now, though, Bolshevik leaders took harsh steps to achieve communism in Russia.

The Bolsheviks outlawed all private property, including farms. Farmers were forced to give all of their grain to the government. Lenin replaced factory workers' committees with new managers who were controlled by the Communist Party. Citizens were called upon to serve in the military. To break people's loyalty to religion, the Bolsheviks closed churches and arrested religious leaders. Lenin insisted that all loyalty be focused on the government.

Union of Soviet Socialist Republics

By 1920 the Bolsheviks had defeated their enemies. Two years later they renamed the old Russian empire. The new nation became known as the Union of Soviet Socialist Republics, or the Soviet Union. The soviets were councils of workers and soldiers formed during the revolution.

In 1922 Lenin became ill. He struggled to return to work, but another leader in the Soviet government was growing more powerful. His name was Josef Stalin.

Paintings such as this one of Lenin (left) and political posters (above) were used to urge people to support communism and join the military.

STALIN'S RULE OF TERROR

Lenin died in 1924. Soon after, Josef Stalin became the new leader of the Soviet Union. In 1928 Stalin began working to make the Soviet Union stronger. He drew all power into the government. Stalin also created huge collective farms. Collective farms were run by the government and worked by many families. People not needed on farms were sent to work in mines and factories springing up across the nation. An economy completely controlled by government is called a command economy.

Within just 20 years the Soviet Union became one of the world's strongest industrial nations. Thousands of railroad lines crisscrossed the country, linking towns and cities that had never been connected before. Around 1900 many Russian farmers had never seen a tractor. By the 1940s Soviet factories were making more tractors than any other factories in the world.

Totalitarian Rule

People paid a huge price, however, for growth and change in the Soviet Union. Stalin used totalitarian (toh tal ih TAIR ee un) methods to rule the nation. In a totalitarian society, a dictator, often representing a single political party, controls all aspects of people's lives. Stalin and the Communist Party controlled the Soviet Union through fear and terror. For many, life was more difficult than it had been under the tsars. People were arrested for speaking their minds freely or for writing to friends in other countries. Many managers were killed because their factories or farms did not produce an expected amount. Stalin also ordered his secret police to arrest anyone who he thought challenged him in any way.

Many of those arrested were religious leaders. Their followers were forced to worship secretly or face arrest themselves. Stalin had more than 15 million people killed or sent to prison camps in Siberia. Almost half of them were Ukrainians. Many starved because the collective farms failed to produce enough food. Large numbers of people were sent to camps where religious

Stalin (below left) forced thousands of people to work on collective farms (below). Despite much hard work, many collective farms failed.

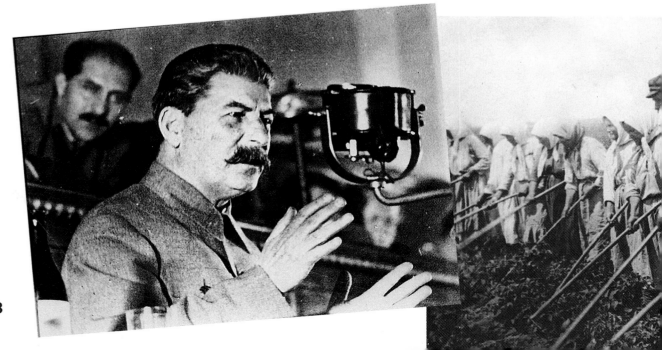

leaders, teachers, workers, and others Stalin considered "enemies of the people" were imprisoned.

Oil, iron, timber—all the resources of the Soviet Union's new industry—were in great supply in Siberia. Since few people lived there, Stalin used political prisoners to help collect the resources.

One women's camp had the job of cutting down trees. One of the prisoners, a teacher, described the camp this way:

The cold and the hunger; the hunger and the cold. This must have been the blackest, the most [deadly], the most evil of all my winters in the camps.

WHY IT MATTERS

In the early 1900s life changed dramatically in Russia during a period of revolution. Many of the changes that took place became the foundation of a communist system of government. For this reason, the Russian Revolution is also known as a communist revolution. One of the revolution's many effects was the formation of the Soviet Union.

Revolutionary leaders had promised "peace, land, and bread." Under the communist government, however, most people in the Soviet Union had none of these things. Millions were killed and sent to prison camps in Siberia by Josef Stalin. Stalin used totalitarian methods to rule the nation.

For many, suffering worsened when the Soviet Union and many other countries became involved in another world conflict. To the west of the Soviet Union, a dictator in Germany was making plans that would lead to war.

Reviewing Facts and Ideas

SUM IT UP

- Millions of serfs under Russia's tsars lived in poverty. The abolition of serfdom in 1861 gave farmers a limited amount of freedom.

- The Russian Revolution began in 1917 as a revolt against World War I, the tsar, and poor working and living conditions. Seven months later Lenin and the Bolsheviks seized control, bringing communism to the country they later renamed the Soviet Union.

- Under Stalin, the Communist Party controlled the Soviet Union using totalitarian methods.

THINK ABOUT IT

1. What were the policies of the Soviet Union regarding religious beliefs and practices?

2. Define the term *communism*.

3. **FOCUS** How were the governments led by Tsar Nicholas II and Josef Stalin similar? How were they different?

4. **THINKING SKILL** Describe Josef Stalin's _point of view_ about the need to totally control the economy of the Soviet Union.

5. **GEOGRAPHY** Why might Stalin have chosen Siberia as a site for prisons?

WORLD WAR II

READ ALOUD

"I pray to Almighty God that He shall spare the nations the terrible sufferings that have just been [forced] on my people. . . . Are [you] going to set up the terrible precedent of bowing before force?"

In 1936 Ethiopian emperor Haile Selassie (HĪ lee suh LAS ee) appeared before the League of Nations to protest Italy's invasion of his African country. The League, however, did not come to Selassie's aid. Ethiopia would not regain its independence for nearly five years. During much of that time, the world was once again plunged into war.

THE BIG PICTURE

After the signing of the Treaty of Versailles, the countries that had fought in World War I turned to their own affairs. In the last lesson you read about the communist revolution in Russia. In 1922, the dictator Benito Mussolini and his Fascist (FASH ihst) party rose to power in Italy.

The Fascists believed in a powerful leader, totalitarian government, and an extreme form of nationalism. They supported a government whose goals they thought to be more important than those of individual people. This type of government came to be known as fascism. In some places fascism also came to mean hatred of certain ethnic groups.

After Italy took control of Ethiopia in 1936, Mussolini joined forces with another fascist dictator, Adolf Hitler of Germany. The people of nearby nations began to see that fascism was a serious threat to peace.

Focus Activity

READ TO LEARN
What conditions led to the outbreak of World War II?

VOCABULARY
fascism
inflation
depression
propaganda
World War II
Axis
Allies
concentration camp
Holocaust

PEOPLE
Adolf Hitler
Winston Churchill
Franklin Roosevelt
Anne Frank

PLACES
Pearl Harbor
Normandy

GERMANY AFTER WORLD WAR I

In 1919 Germany began to live by the conditions of the Treaty of Versailles. The treaty stripped Germany of land and forced it to pay huge fines.

To meet these expenses the German government began printing large amounts of paper money. Before long Germany had printed so much money that it began to lose its value. The result was a period of inflation, or rising prices. Huge amounts of money were needed even to buy necessities such as food. By 1923 inflation had made German money practically worthless, and people's savings were gone.

In that year a bitter ex-soldier named Adolf Hitler led an attack against the German government in the state of Bavaria. Although the attack failed and Hitler was jailed, many Germans supported his actions. His followers were known as the Nazi (NAHT see) party.

Fascism in Germany

By the early 1930s, Germany and much of the world suffered a depression (di PRESH un). During a depression, fewer goods are produced, prices drop, many people lose their jobs, and money is hard to get.

During these hard times Hitler used propaganda (prahp uh GAN duh) to convince Germans that their nation could once again become powerful. Propaganda is the spreading of certain ideas or attitudes that have been exaggerated or falsified to advance a particular cause.

Hitler's propaganda spread the false idea that the Germans were a "master race," meant to rule the world. The Nazis wrongfully blamed Germany's Jews, along with the Treaty of Versailles, for the depression that was devastating the country. Promising to raise Germany back to glory, Hitler once again tried to gain control in 1933. This time he succeeded.

Hitler ruled as a fascist dictator, forming an alliance with Mussolini in Italy. He and the Nazis stirred up hatred against Jews. In five years the Nazis' plans would lead to the largest war in history.

Hitler (left) used propaganda methods to convince Germans that Germany would become powerful. His followers raised their arms and shouted "Hail Victory!"

A SECOND WORLD WAR

In 1938 Hitler ordered Nazi troops to occupy neighboring Austria. With this command, Hitler knowingly broke the rules of the Treaty of Versailles. Then, in March 1939, Hitler seized control of Czechoslovakia. After years of trying to avoid war with Germany, the leaders of Britain and France promised to defend Hitler's next target—Poland. Europe was on the brink of war once again.

The German Advance

World War II began in Europe on September 1, 1939. On that day German tanks began a *blitzkrieg* (BLIHTZ kreeg), or "lightning war," in Poland. Hitler and Josef Stalin, whom you read about in Lesson 2, had recently signed a friendship treaty. With the help of the Soviet Union, Germany defeated Poland within weeks. Britain and France declared war on Germany but had not been able to defend their ally, Poland.

Eight months later German forces turned west. Hitler's armies quickly overran Belgium. They went on to seize Paris by June 1940. Hitler's fighting method of blitzkrieg was proving very effective. Germany had beaten France—a major world power—in only six weeks! With much of France under German control, Hitler made Britain the next Nazi target.

Many areas in London (left) were destroyed during the Battle of Britain. People often found their homes reduced to rubble by nightly bombings (above).

The Battle of Britain

The British people prepared for the worst. The country's leader, Prime Minister **Winston Churchill**, declared:

We shall fight on the seas and oceans, we shall fight with growing confidence and growing strength in the air, we shall defend our island, whatever the cost may be. . . . We shall never surrender.

Two months later, in August 1940, the Battle of Britain began. For almost a year German planes bombed the island nation every night. The British air force fought back. Although many sought safety in underground shelters, more than 12,000 British people were killed in the fighting. Despite the cost Britain did not surrender. The nation stood firm, as Churchill had predicted.

Weather Plays a Part

In June 1941 Hitler ended the bombing of Britain. Germany had lost more than 2,000 planes, along with their crews. Having failed in Britain, Hitler decided to break his treaty with Stalin. He ordered his armies to turn east and invade the Soviet Union. The Germans began what was to become a three-year struggle for control of major Soviet cities and supply centers. Millions of Soviet soldiers and civilians died during the struggle.

The Soviet Union now became an ally of Britain. In spite of their political differences, the British welcomed the Soviets in the fight against their common enemy, the Nazis. By November 1941 German troops were very close to one of their goals: the Soviet capital, Moscow. Soviet armies fought to defend their capital and their country. The German troops were finally stopped, however, by a deadly northern winter. On December 6, the near-frozen Germans began to retreat. It would not be the last time nature played a part in the outcome of the war.

An Attack on the United States

War had begun earlier in Asia than it had in Europe. Japan had hoped to create an empire with an endless supply of raw materials and labor for industry. By 1931 Japanese forces had invaded northern China. Later Japan conquered about one quarter of China and some islands off the coast of South Asia. Find the region of Japanese expansion on the map on pages 544–545.

In 1940 Japan formed an alliance with Germany. The conquests and the alliance created tension between Japan and the United States, which was against Japan's continuing expansionist policy. Japan was determined to stop the United States from involvement in its expansionist plans.

On December 7, 1941, Japan launched an attack without any warning or declaration of war. The target was the United States naval base at **Pearl Harbor**, Hawaii. More than 2,000 people died in the attack. The United States was now involved in World War II.

President **Franklin Roosevelt** declared war on Japan on December 8, 1941. Three days later, on December 11, Germany and Italy declared war on the United States. Japan, Germany, Italy, and their other allies were known as the **Axis**. The **Allies** included Britain, France, the Soviet Union, the United States, and China, among others. The United States had to fight Japan in Asia and Germany and Italy in Europe and Africa. As in World War I, United States forces would be very important to the Allied war effort.

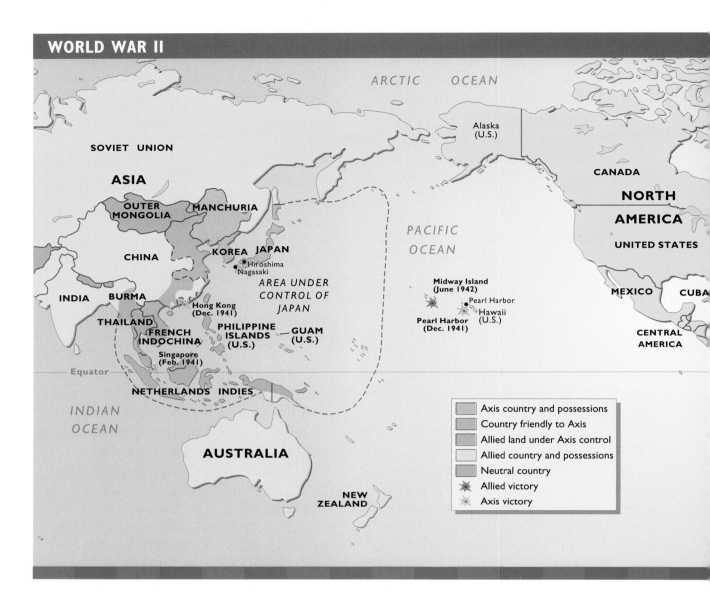

ARCTIC OCEAN

Alaska (U.S.)

SOVIET UNION

ASIA

OUTER MONGOLIA   MANCHURIA

CANADA

NORTH AMERICA

UNITED STATES

CHINA   KOREA   JAPAN
Hiroshima
Nagasaki

PACIFIC OCEAN

INDIA   BURMA

AREA UNDER CONTROL OF JAPAN

Hong Kong (Dec. 1941)

THAILAND
FRENCH INDOCHINA

PHILIPPINE ISLANDS (U.S.)

GUAM (U.S.)

Singapore (Feb. 1941)

Equator

NETHERLANDS INDIES

Midway Island (June 1942)

Pearl Harbor
Hawaii (U.S.)

Pearl Harbor (Dec. 1941)

MEXICO   CUBA

CENTRAL AMERICA

INDIAN OCEAN

AUSTRALIA

NEW ZEALAND

	Axis country and possessions
	Country friendly to Axis
	Allied land under Axis control
	Allied country and possessions
	Neutral country
	Allied victory
	Axis victory

"THE LONGEST DAY"

For three years the United States, Britain, and other Allies fought the Nazis in Europe and North Africa. In that time, the Soviet Union struggled to push back and destroy the German invaders on its soil. Finally, Allied leaders prepared to put a risky plan into action. On the night of June 5, 1944, the Allies would begin a surprise invasion of Axis-held France. If they succeeded, Germany would be surrounded on three sides—west, east, and south. The Allies' code name for this operation was D-Day.

Allied leaders prepared their forces to land on the beaches of Normandy, France, at dawn on June 6. They would reach shore while the tide was low so that German weapons on the beach would be open to attack. Months earlier, weather experts had concluded that the best conditions for an attack would exist between June 5 and 7. On June 4, though, a terrible storm raged across the English Channel. Would nature stop the biggest sea invasion in history?

The storm actually helped the Allies. German commander Erwin Rommel believed that the Allies would not

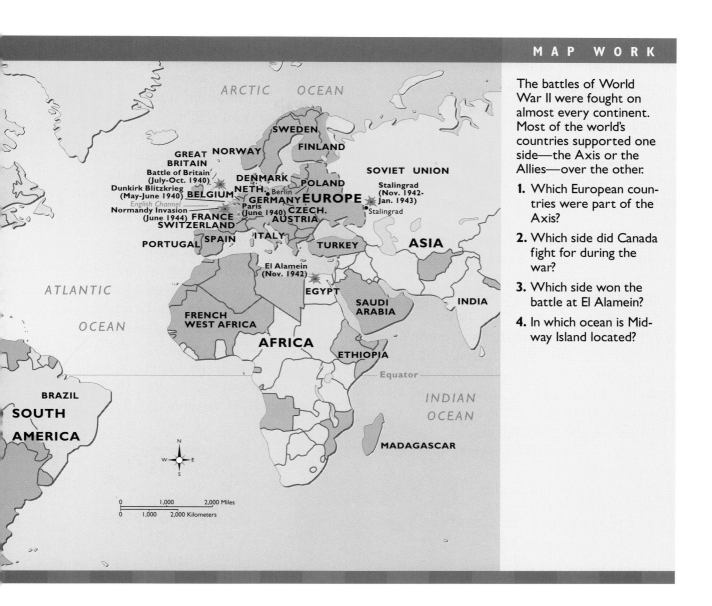

ARCTIC OCEAN

SWEDEN
NORWAY
FINLAND
GREAT BRITAIN
Battle of Britain (July-Oct. 1940)
Dunkirk Blitzkrieg (May-June 1940)
English Channel
Normandy Invasion (June 1944)
DENMARK
NETH.
BELGIUM
Berlin
GERMANY
Paris (June 1940)
POLAND
EUROPE
CZECH.
AUSTRIA
SOVIET UNION
Stalingrad (Nov. 1942-Jan. 1943)
Stalingrad
FRANCE
SWITZERLAND
SPAIN
ITALY
TURKEY
ASIA
PORTUGAL
El Alamein (Nov. 1942)
EGYPT
SAUDI ARABIA
INDIA
ATLANTIC OCEAN
FRENCH WEST AFRICA
AFRICA
ETHIOPIA
Equator
INDIAN OCEAN
BRAZIL
SOUTH AMERICA
MADAGASCAR

N
W E
S

0 1,000 2,000 Miles
0 1,000 2,000 Kilometers

The battles of World War II were fought on almost every continent. Most of the world's countries supported one side—the Axis or the Allies—over the other.

1. Which European countries were part of the Axis?

2. Which side did Canada fight for during the war?

3. Which side won the battle at El Alamein?

4. In which ocean is Midway Island located?

invade during such weather. He traveled home to Germany for a few days, just when D-Day arrived. The Allies attacked. Over 11,000 Allied planes dropped bombs and over 2,700 ships unloaded almost 200,000 men onto the beaches of Normandy. Find Normandy on the map.

Afterwards, an Allied soldier said D-Day seemed like "the longest day" of his life. At the end of that day, allied forces held the beaches. The Allies would now begin to push the Axis powers east across Europe and west from the Soviet Union.

On D-Day Allied soldiers gained control of the German-held beaches in Normandy, France, then moved inland to free Paris.

THE END OF THE WAR

Less than a year after D-Day, Allied forces closed in around Germany. With the Soviet army already in the German capital of Berlin, Adolf Hitler killed himself to avoid capture on April 30, 1945. One week later, on May 7, 1945, Germany surrendered. Japan's leaders, however, refused to give up the struggle for power.

United States leaders considered using a newly developed bomb against the Japanese. Invading Japan could lead to many deaths on both sides. Could the tremendously powerful atomic bomb bring about Japan's surrender? On August 6, 1945, the United States dropped the first atomic bomb ever used in warfare on the Japanese city of Hiroshima (hihr uh SHEE muh). Most of the city was destroyed in seconds, and at least 80,000 people died.

Japan did not surrender. Three days later the United States dropped another atomic bomb on the city of Nagasaki (nah guh SAH kee). Japan surrendered on August 14, 1945. The most terrible war in history was finally over.

The Terrible Effects of Fascism

In the days before their defeat, German and Japanese commanders rushed to hide evidence of their concentration camps. Concentration camps are places where people are imprisoned because of their heritage, religious beliefs, or political views. Prisoners in Japanese and Nazi concentration camps were tortured and often killed. Millions of others were murdered as well.

The Nazis murdered about 6 million Jews, or two-thirds of Europe's Jewish population, in concentration camps or by execution squads. These people, including women, children, and elderly people, had committed no crime. They were not soldiers. They were killed for no other reason than that they were Jewish. This deliberate destruction of human life is called the Holocaust (HOL uh kawst). About another 6 million people, among them Gypsies, Poles, Russians, and Slavs were also murdered in Nazi concentration camps.

One of the millions of young Jews who died in the camps was 15-year-old Anne Frank. She and her family spent two years hiding in the Netherlands before Nazi soldiers captured them. What did Anne Frank believe about people and about the future? Do you find her point of view surprising?

MANY VOICES PRIMARY SOURCE

Excerpt from
The Diary of Anne Frank,
July 1944.

It's really a wonder that I haven't dropped all my ideals, because they seem so absurd and impossible to carry out. Yet I keep them, because in spite of everything I still believe that people are really good at heart. I simply can't build up my hopes on a foundation consisting of confusion, misery, and death. I see the world gradually being turned into a wilderness, I hear the ever approaching thunder, which will destroy us too, I can feel the sufferings of millions and yet, if I look up into the heavens, I think that it will all come [out] right, that this cruelty too will end, and that peace and tranquility will return again.

Children like these brothers at the Auschwitz concentration camp were imprisoned by the Nazis. Prisoners in the camps were often tortured and killed.

WHY IT MATTERS

World War II was the largest war in history. Unlike World War I, which had been fought mostly in Europe, World War II took place in Europe, Asia, Africa, and the islands of the Pacific. While many battles took place on land, there were sea battles on the world's oceans, as well. The war left as many as 50 million people dead. Many millions more would be affected by its horrors throughout their lives.

People once again began to adjust to peace after a world war. It was not always easy. Destroyed roads, bridges, homes, and cities around the world had to be rebuilt. There were other serious problems, too.

Leaders of the United States and Western Europe feared the communist government of the Soviet Union. Soon the two most powerful Allies, the United States and the Soviet Union, would become bitter enemies. You will read about their conflict later in the chapter.

Reviewing Facts and Ideas

SUM IT UP

- In the 1930s Nazi leader Adolf Hitler used propaganda to convince many Germans that their nation could return to its former power.

- A world depression in the 1930s caused suffering in many nations and helped to bring about the rise of fascist dictators, such as Hitler.

- The Nazis murdered about 6 million Jews in concentration camps. This became known as the Holocaust. There were also some 6 million other victims of the Holocaust, including Gypsies, Poles, Russians, and Slavs.

- Japan attacked and conquered parts of Southeast Asia and the Pacific. After Japan attacked Pearl Harbor, the United States entered World War II. The war came to an end after the United States used two atomic bombs on Japanese cities.

THINK ABOUT IT

1. How did the United States help the Allied war effort?

2. Why was D-Day an important battle?

3. FOCUS How did Hitler use the problems created by inflation, the depression, and unemployment to make himself dictator of Germany? How did he use this power to bring about World War II?

4. THINKING SKILL List three _facts_ and one _opinion_ about fascism.

5. GEOGRAPHY What role did the weather and time of attack play in the planning and outcome of D-Day?

GEOGRAPHY SKILLS

THE WORLD: Time Zones

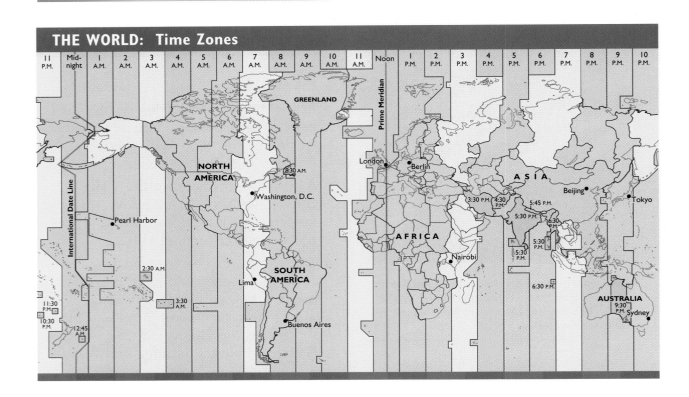

Time Zone Maps

VOCABULARY

time zone
International Date Line

WHY THE SKILL MATTERS

Just before 8 A.M. on December 7, 1941, Japanese warplanes began bombing the United States naval base at Pearl Harbor, Hawaii. What time was it in Washington, D.C.? You can figure out the answer by reading a time-zone map.

Not everyone in the world is on the same time schedule. In fact, the world is divided into 24 time zones. Time zones were created by scientists in the 1800s to standardize

timekeeping throughout the world. They based their work on the fact that Earth rotates 360° each day and that it always moves from west to east while rotating. Since Earth completes one rotation every 24 hours, the scientists divided 360° by 24. The result, 15°, is the amount that Earth rotates in one hour. Each time zone is a strip on a map about 15 degrees of longitude wide. As you can see from this time-zone map, though, some zones have been divided differently to make timekeeping easier for people living in certain regions.

USING THE SKILL

You can see Earth's 24 time zones marked in different colors on this map. As a line of reference, find the line of longitude called the prime meridian. The top of each zone tells what time it is when the time at the prime meridian is noon. Because Earth rotates eastward, zones east of the prime meridian have times that are later in the day. Zones to its west have times that are earlier in the day.

Find the zone in which Hawaii is located. Now find the zone in which Washington, D.C., is located. How many zones east of Pearl Harbor is Washington, D.C.? Since Washington, D.C., is 5 zones east, it is 5 hours ahead in time. The bombing of Pearl Harbor began at 7:55 A.M., Hawaii time, or 12:55 P.M. in Washington, D.C. President Franklin Roosevelt first received word of the bombing at 1:50 P.M., Washington, D.C., time. What time was that in Hawaii? Count west 5 zones and you know that it was 8:50 A.M., Hawaii time.

The tricky part begins when crossing the International Date Line. This is an imaginary line in the Pacific Ocean. The line marks the boundary between one day and the next. Whenever the International Date Line is crossed heading *east*, today becomes *yesterday!* Take the time difference between Japan and Hawaii, for example. Travelers from Japan add 5 hours to their watches when heading east to Hawaii. They also set back their calendars by one day! Imagine that it's 9:00 A.M. on Wednesday in Tokyo. What time and day would it be in Hawaii? It would be 2:00 P.M. on Tuesday.

What happens when travelers head west across the International Date Line? They count *backward* in the time of day, but *forward* one day. Travelers heading from Lima to Beijing, for example, would set their clocks back 11 hours, but move their calendars up one day.

TRYING THE SKILL

At 2:41 A.M. on May 7, 1945, German leaders surrendered to Allied leaders in Berlin. Thus began V-E (Victory-in-Europe) Day. What time and date was it in London when V-E Day officially began? In Tokyo?

REVIEWING THE SKILL

Use the Helping Yourself box to help determine the answers to the following questions.

1. What are time zone maps?

2. Why are time zones east of the prime meridian later than those to its west?

3. Why can crossing the International Date Line be tricky? What do travelers have to remember as they cross it heading east? Heading west?

4. What were your answers for the section above? How did you figure them out?

5. When might you need to read a time-zone map in your own life?

Airplanes like the Concorde can travel quickly through many time zones.

COMMUNISM IN CHINA

Focus Activity

READ TO LEARN
What were the causes and effects of revolution in China?

VOCABULARY
warlord
Long March
commune
Cultural Revolution

PEOPLE
Sun Yat-sen
Chiang Kai-shek
Mao Zedong

READ ALOUD

"Many times my husband told me that it was in those early days, as a poor son of a poor peasant family, that he became a revolutionary. He was determined that the [life] of the Chinese peasant should not continue to be so wretched, that little boys in China should have shoes to wear and rice to eat."

Soong Chingling (SOONG CHING LING) wrote these words about her husband, Sun Yat-sen (SUN YAHT SEN), known also as the "father of modern China." He would help start an age of revolution in China.

THE BIG PICTURE

In the early 1900s Russia was not the only country on the edge of revolution. Like Russia, China had not kept pace with the technological and economic changes that were changing western societies. Most Chinese worked as farmers, just as they had since the Han dynasty. For poor farmers, survival was a daily struggle that could be lost when a flood, drought, or big tax bill hit.

By the early 1900s, however, change had come to China. Britain had seized control of Hong Kong, and forced China to open its markets to trade. Japan had taken over the island of Taiwan. Britain and other nations also set up zones within China that were subject to their laws, rather than China's. Many Chinese disliked the way their country was being treated by European nations. Some of these people believed the time had come for another change.

THE END OF DYNASTIES

During this time of unrest, the Qing (CHING) dynasty ruled China. The Qing were Manchus. They had come from the region of Manchuria, located northeast of China. During their 267-year reign, the Manchus saw several challenges to their rule. In the late 1800s, however, unhappiness with the Manchus was perhaps greater than in the past. Many people in China called for the government to be more democratic and less influenced by other nations. Strong leaders began to call for China to change. You read about one such leader in the Read Aloud.

A Voice of the People

Sun Yat-sen was born in 1866, near the southern city of Guangzhou (GWAHNG JO). However, he lived and studied in the Hawaiian Islands when he was young. That time spent away from China helped to shape Sun's views of how life could be improved in his own country.

After returning to China, Sun devoted much of his time to trying to change the government. Sun believed that his country needed to free itself of foreign rule in order to become great again. He said society would be fairer if ordinary citizens had a voice in their government. Finally, Sun told his audiences, China needed to focus on improving agriculture and industry. Many people agreed with his message. Sun once described his goal in this way:

The real trouble is that China is not an independent country. She is the victim of foreign countries. . . . I set myself the object of the overthrow of the Qing dynasty and the establishment of a Chinese republic in its ruins.

The End of Imperial Rule

Sun and his supporters began a revolt against the Manchus in 1905. Six years later the Qing dynasty fell. It was the last of a series of dynasties that had begun ruling China more than 2,000 years earlier. On January 1, 1912, Sun Yat-sen and his Nationalist party took control of the government. They formed the new Republic of China.

Keeping the republic united turned out to be difficult. Strong local military leaders, called warlords, took advantage of China's unrest to seize power in their own areas. Nationalist forces struggled until 1927 to defeat many of the warlords. Even then it was only with the help of Chinese and Soviet communist allies that they succeeded. While Nationalist forces fought against the warlords, Sun Yat-sen died. Who would be the next leader of China?

Sun Yat-sen and Soong Chingling, his wife, helped China become a republic in 1912.

DIVIDED NATION

A Nationalist general became the next leader of the Republic of China. He was Sun's brother-in-law, Chiang Kai-shek (CHANG ki SHEK). Chiang did not want to keep lasting ties to the communist allies who had helped to defeat the warlords. Neither he nor his supporters wanted China to become communist, as the Soviet Union had. However, Communists were becoming a large political group in China. In 1927 Chiang turned on the Communists with force. A new period of civil war began in China.

The Long March

In 1934 Chiang ordered his troops to surround the Communists in southern China. The troops stopped food and supplies from getting through. Chiang hoped this plan would end the communist movement once and for all.

An army of 80,000 Communists, led by Mao Zedong (MOU DZE DUNG), broke past the Nationalist troops, however. This army began a long flight to safety in the north. The journey came to be known as the Long March. Men and women hiked and climbed almost 6,000 miles in about a year. On the map you can see the route the communists traveled in that time.

The Long March was equal to almost the entire length of a round trip across the mainland United States! During their flight the communists faced many Nationalist air attacks and battles. Also they traveled across harsh land. The marchers found it hard to cross the steep mountains. They were hungry and had little more than straw sandals for shoes. One man recalled:

As we climbed higher, we were caught in a terrible hailstorm and the air became so thin we could hardly breathe. . . . Our breath froze and hands and lips turned blue. . . .

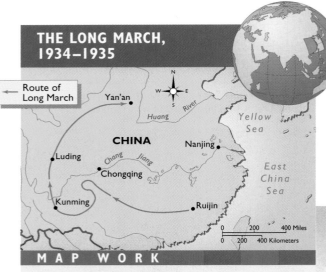

THE LONG MARCH, 1934–1935

← Route of Long March

Yan'an
Huang River
Yellow Sea
CHINA
Nanjing
Luding
Chong Jiang
Chongqing
East China Sea
Kunming
Ruijin

0   200   400 Miles
0   200   400 Kilometers

MAP WORK

Mao Zedong led the Communists on a 6,000-mile march, trying to avoid Nationalist forces.

1. Where did the Long March start? Where did it end?
2. What major river did the Communists cross?

This poster shows Mao Zedong many years after the communists took control of China.

*Those who sat down to rest . . .
froze to death on the spot.*

Those who survived the mountains faced more hardships in the rainy marshes of northern China. There, quicksand could suck people down in minutes. Finding food and clean water was very difficult.

Only about one out of ten people who began the Long March arrived at the great bend of the Huang River. There, the survivors recovered from their journey and began to spread the ideas of communism.

Enemies Cooperate—Briefly

In 1937, two years before World War II began in Europe, Japan launched a full-scale invasion of China. The Communists and the Nationalists agreed to work together to fight the Japanese. In 1945, when Japan was defeated at the end of World War II, the two parties prepared to fight each other once again.

This time the Communists had an advantage. The Nationalist government had done most of the heavy fighting against the Japanese. They were also being blamed for inflation. Remember that inflation was a problem in Germany before Hitler took power.

The Communists, meanwhile, had become very popular in rural areas. Mao and his followers talked with thousands of people. The Communists also worked with farmers, showing them ways to produce more crops.

After two years of fighting, the Communists succeeded in driving the Nationalists from mainland China. Chiang and his

On Taiwan, Chiang Kai-shek (above) and the Nationalists established a government in exile.

followers retreated to the island of Taiwan. There they continued the Republic of China in exile from the mainland. In 1949 Mao and his followers created the People's Republic of China on the mainland. It was now the Communists' turn to try to lead China.

Recovering from Civil War

In October 1949 Mao proclaimed before cheering crowds, "China has stood up!" Gone were the warlords and Nationalist leaders. Many people believed that China's new Communist leaders would bring good government and good jobs to people everywhere.

The Communists quickly set out to rebuild their war-torn nation. They provided housing, medical care, and food supplies for city workers. They supported education for all, along with equal rights for women.

The changes brought by Mao and the Communists, however, had a great price. Between 1949 and 1952, the new government took over all businesses. As in the Soviet Union, landlords had all of their property taken away. As many as one million people were killed by the Communists during the takeover.

CHINA UNDER MAO

In the early 1950s the Chinese economy was growing, but not at a pace that pleased Mao. In 1957 he announced that it was time for China to take a "Great Leap Forward." There was no telling what China could do, he said, if people pitched in and worked harder. "More, faster, better, cheaper" became the slogan of the day. Factories worked around the clock to produce more steel, the building block of industry. Families tried to help by setting up tiny steel-making furnaces in their backyards.

Commune Life

Many farmers and their families were forced to join large **communes** (KAHM yoonz). A commune is an organized community in which all members share work and resources. Mao told people that by working together they would make the land more productive. Villages were combined to form single communes of up to 20,000 people. They could not choose the crops they wanted to farm. Instead the government assigned each commune a crop to produce. People in communes were also forced to build bridges, dams, and work on other projects for the government.

Family life in the commune was very different than it had been on small farms. People were expected to put loyalty to the government and commune ahead of loyalty to their families. At first, men, women, and children each slept in separate buildings. All residents of the commune ate together in large dining halls. Commune workers were divided into teams. Each team was responsible for a particular job such as cooking the meals, hoeing the fields, or schooling the children who lived on the commune.

Instead of producing more grain, communes produced less. This happened partly because farmers were so busy doing other things, such as making steel. China, however, lacked the resources to produce the steel it needed. Also, much of the steel produced could not be used because it was made incorrectly. Few Chinese workers had been trained in the modern ways of making steel.

In time Mao's plan for China failed. As many as 20 million people may have starved to death during a famine that followed the Great Leap Forward.

A New Revolution

Some regional leaders tried to help the situation by allowing farmers to once again own and control small pieces of land. Mao accused those leaders of "copying the West." In 1966 he removed them from power and put a new plan into action.

Mao began a ten-year period called the **Cultural Revolution**. He called for the destruction of all non-communist beliefs. These included many long-held religious and cultural beliefs. Any leaders critical of Mao were punished. With

Mao Zedong's supporters wave his Little Red Book of teachings. Their banner says that they are building a new world.

government support, groups of students broke into people's homes. They destroyed Confucian books and ancient Chinese classics, as well as non-Chinese writings. Anyone with western-made clothing or a European-style haircut faced attack. Many innocent people were accused of being American spies. They were harshly punished.

One schoolgirl, Anchee Min, was forced to say her teacher was a spy. Anchee Min could not believe that her teacher, Autumn Leaves, was an enemy of China. But government leaders said that any teacher who asked students to read foreign literature was a traitor. Min later described how her teacher was treated by government officials.

Two strong men escorted Autumn Leaves onto the stage facing the crowd of 2,000 people. . . . Her arms were twisted behind her. . . . A rectangular board reading "Down with American Spy" hung from her neck. . . . Autumn Leaves kept silent. When kicked hard, she said that she had nothing to confess.

The dream of a China transformed by communism had turned into a nightmare.

WHY IT MATTERS

The Cultural Revolution ended in 1976 with the death of Mao Zedong. During Mao's 27-year rule, major changes had taken place in China. China had closed its doors to the United States and some other democratic nations until 1971. After Mao's death, though, some leaders who had been punished during the Cultural Revolution returned to power. They had new ideas for China. You will read about them in Chapter 20.

Reviewing Facts and Ideas

SUM IT UP

- In the early 1900s many Chinese felt China should be free of foreign rule and should become more democratic.

- Sun Yat-sen led a revolt that overthrew the Qing dynasty in 1911. His Nationalist Party later fought the Communists for power.

- In 1949 the Nationalists retreated to Taiwan and the Communists created the People's Republic of China.

- Mao Zedong's Great Leap Forward and Cultural Revolution brought great unrest to China.

THINK ABOUT IT

1. Why was anti-foreign feeling so strong in China in the early 1900s?

2. What were the effects of the Cultural Revolution?

3. **FOCUS** List *causes* and *effects* of the communist victory in China.

4. **THINKING SKILL** *Determine the credibility of the source* on page 552. How did you reach your conclusion?

5. **GEOGRAPHY** How might geography have played a role in helping Mao and his followers escape Nationalist forces during the Long March?

COLD WAR

READ ALOUD

"An iron curtain has descended across the Continent [of Europe]. Behind that line lie all the capitals of the ancient states of central and eastern Europe."

Winston Churchill, Prime Minister of Great Britain, said these words in 1946. He imagined an "iron curtain" that formed a dividing line between communist Europe in the East, and democratic Europe in the West. The idea of that "iron curtain" became a symbol of a new kind of war—one that would dominate world events for over 40 years.

THE BIG PICTURE

After World War II, several European countries had lost millions of people, had tremendous debts, and were in ruins. Although the Soviet Union had lost nearly 20 million people, its armies held most of Eastern Europe. Only the United States was stronger and richer than before the war. Yet about 300,000 Americans had died.

Because of their strength, the United States and the Soviet Union became known as superpowers. As you have read, the Soviet Union had a communist government. The United States supported free enterprise and democracy. A free enterprise economy, also called a market economy, is based on private ownership of land and businesses.

Tensions between the superpowers and their supporters developed into what became known as the Cold War. The Cold War was a struggle between the United States and the Soviet Union without the two nations fighting a full-scale war against each other.

Focus Activity

READ TO LEARN
How did the Cold War develop after World War II?

VOCABULARY
superpower
free enterprise
Cold War
United Nations
NATO
Warsaw Pact
Korean War
nuclear arms race

PEOPLE
Fidel Castro
Nikita Khrushchev
John F. Kennedy

PLACES
Yalta
Berlin

NEW TENSIONS

In February 1945 the end of World War II in Europe was still three months away. Allied leaders met in the town of Yalta in the Soviet Union to discuss their plans. They agreed to create a United Nations organization. This world organization would be stronger than the League of Nations. It would work to prevent future conflicts.

The Allies also agreed to divide Germany into zones that the Allies would control for a period of time. Lastly, they agreed that the Eastern European nations taken over by Soviet troops when they defeated the Nazis there should be given the right to choose their own governments.

New Alliances

The Soviet Union's leader, Josef Stalin, quickly broke the agreement at Yalta. He refused to remove his troops from neighboring countries, including Poland, Czechoslovakia, and Romania. Soviet troops forced those nations to accept communist governments.

Fearful of further Soviet expansion, nations in western Europe and North America formed NATO, or the North Atlantic Treaty Organization, in 1949.

They pledged to defend each other if attacked. The Soviet Union and the communist countries of Eastern Europe signed a similar agreement called the Warsaw Pact in 1955.

War in Korea

A year after the creation of NATO, the Cold War heated up when a conflict with weapons took place in Asia. This conflict was the Korean War. After World War II, Korea had been freed from Japanese control. The Korean peninsula was then divided into two nations. The northern nation was communist and the southern nation was democratic.

In 1950 communist North Korea invaded democratic South Korea. To prevent the spread of communism, the United States sent thousands of troops to help United Nations troops fight North Koreans. The North Koreans were aided by the Chinese. The war lasted three years without a clear victory for either side. However, North Korean troops had been forced to withdraw from South Korea. At the war's conclusion, much of the Korean landscape was devastated and four million people were dead.

Allied leaders Winston Chuchill, Franklin Roosevelt, and Josef Stalin met in Yalta in 1945 to discuss the ending of World War II.

TENSIONS BUILD UP

Korea was not the only country to be damaged by the Cold War. When World War II ended, Germany had been split. The Soviet Union was left in control of eastern Germany including the eastern part of Berlin, the capital city. Britain, France, and the United States controlled western Germany and the western part of Berlin.

By 1948 it was clear that the Soviet Union was not going to withdraw its troops from Germany. Soviet leaders established a communist government in the areas occupied by their troops. The communist part of Germany became the country of East Germany. The western part of Germany became the country of West Germany. The city of Berlin was split in the same way.

In the years that followed, thousands of East Germans who did not want to live in a communist nation moved to West Berlin. Such movement ended, however, in the early morning hours of August 13, 1961. While the people of Berlin slept, East German police built a barbed-wire fence between East and West Berlin. Over the next few days that fence became a concrete wall.

EUROPE, 1948–1989

Communist countries
Non-communist countries
— "Iron Curtain"

FINLAND
SWEDEN
NORWAY
North Sea
IRELAND
DENMARK
GREAT BRITAIN
Baltic Sea
ATLANTIC OCEAN
NETHERLANDS
EAST GERMANY
POLAND
SOVIET UNION
BELGIUM
LUXEMBOURG
WEST GERMANY
CZECHOSLOVAKIA
SWITZERLAND
AUSTRIA
HUNGARY
FRANCE
ROMANIA
PORTUGAL
SPAIN
ITALY
YUGOSLAVIA
BULGARIA
Adriatic Sea
ALBANIA
GREECE
Mediterranean Sea
0   200   400 Miles
0   200   400 Kilometers
AFRICA

MAP WORK

After World War II Europe was divided between the mostly communist eastern countries and the mostly democratic western ones.

1. Which communist countries were east of the Iron Curtain?
2. What country bordered the Iron Curtain on the southeast?

The Berlin Wall was built in 1961 to stop the flow of East Germans crossing the border into democratic West Germany.

A Divided City

The Berlin Wall divided backyards, streets, and even houses and churches. It was guarded by East German soldiers with machine guns. Escape became very difficult. Yet many people did make their way west. Some traveled in tiny tunnels or hot-air balloons. Others crossed the border hidden in coffins or secret car trunks. For every one person who made it, however, many more failed. At least 80 people were killed and hundreds more arrested while trying to leave East Berlin.

The Race to Build Nuclear Arms

A new competition between the superpowers began as Cold War tensions in Germany continued. In 1945 the United States had been the only nation with the ability to make atomic bombs. Remember the United States had used atomic bombs against Japan during World War II. By 1949, though, the Soviet Union also had these destructive weapons.

American scientists then developed the far more deadly hydrogen bomb. The Soviets matched this development a year later. The power for these weapons comes from nuclear energy. For this reason, the competition between the superpowers became known as the nuclear arms race.

In 1957 the Soviet Union's next development amazed the world. They launched *Sputnik*, a human-made satellite that orbited Earth. Scientists had come a long way since Isaac Newton first discovered how gravity held the planets in orbit. Western leaders became concerned. They were worried that *Sputnik*—and other satellites like it—could be used to launch nuclear weapons toward the West.

The Soviet Union often held military rallies like this one in Moscow's Red Square in 1988.

Preparing for Disaster

Many Americans feared that a Soviet nuclear attack could begin at any time. Students practiced what to do if a bomb exploded while they were at school. Some school principals handed out metal tags for children to wear. The tags would help them to be identified after an explosion. Thousands of families built small bomb shelters in their backyards. They stocked them with goods needed for survival.

CUBAN MISSILE CRISIS

In 1959, Cuba's Fidel Castro succeeded in establishing the first communist government in the Americas. He won the support of Nikita Khrushchev, the Soviet leader who had come to power after Josef Stalin's death in 1953. The President of the United States, John F. Kennedy, tried—unsuccessfully—to end Castro's government in 1961. In 1962 a crisis arose over this island nation.

A Nuclear Target

Khrushchev sent nuclear weapons to Cuba in the summer of 1962. By October the weapons in Cuba were ready for use. Missiles far more powerful than the atom bombs used in Japan were now just a 20-minute flight away from the capital of the United States. Millions would die if the missiles were fired.

On October 22 Kennedy told Americans of the great danger. He warned that the United States would respond to the fire of any Cuban missile with an attack upon the Soviet Union. He also ordered Soviet ships to stay out of Cuban waters or risk the start of war.

On Saturday, October 27, the crisis reached a peak. American forces around the world were on full alert. In Cuba, over 40,000 Soviet and Cuban troops checked their weapons and missiles. In Washington, D.C., hundreds of people stood outside the White House—some shouting for peace, others for war. A single Soviet ship continued on a course toward Cuba.

To many, the end of the world seemed just around the corner. An adviser to the President of the United States later recalled,

It was a beautiful fall evening . . . and I went up into the open air to look and to smell it, because I thought it was the last Saturday I would ever see.

An adviser to Khrushchev remembered,

I went and telephoned my wife and told her to drop everything and get out of Moscow. I thought [United States] bombers were on the way.

Kennedy and Khrushchev met in 1962 (above) after Castro (above right) allowed Soviet missiles into Cuba.

THE COLD WAR: GOVERNMENTS AND ECONOMIES

	Government	Economy
United States and Allies	**Democracy** Citizens elect their leaders and can influence government decisions. Rights are protected.	**Free Enterprise** Resources, property, and production are controlled by individuals and companies and the laws of supply and demand.
Soviet Union and Allies	**Communism** Totalitarian government controls nearly every aspect of people's lives.	**Command Economy** Government controls all resources and production. Citizens have little control over which goods and services are produced.

CHART WORK

The two superpowers had very different economies and ways of governing.

1. Which form of government gives citizens more rights?

2. Who controls resources and production in a command economy?

The Crisis Ends

As world leaders nervously watched and waited, Kennedy and Khrushchev reached an agreement. The United States promised not to invade Cuba. The Soviet Union's ships agreed to return home. The Soviet Union also removed its missiles from Cuba. In return the United States removed missiles based in Turkey.

The world had come dangerously close to a nuclear war. In the following year, 1963, the two superpowers signed a treaty banning most kinds of nuclear weapons testing. World leaders hoped that the treaty would reduce the chance that nuclear weapons would ever be used in war.

WHY IT MATTERS

For the next 25 years the United States and the Soviet Union continued their struggle. No part of the world was untouched by the Cold War. Conflicts between the ideas and values of communism and democracy took place around the globe. Look at the chart to compare the different systems that clashed in the Cold War. In the next chapter you will read about one such conflict in Vietnam. In the 1980s, however, Cold War tensions began to ease. You will read about that in Chapter 20.

Reviewing Facts and Ideas

SUM IT UP

- The Cold War was a struggle between the United States and the Soviet Union without the nations fighting a real war with each other.

- Josef Stalin forced some nations of Eastern Europe to accept communist.

- Communist attempts at expansion resulted in the division of Korea and Germany into separate communist and democratic nations.

- The nuclear arms race increased Cold War tensions. Nuclear war almost began after the Soviet Union placed missiles in Cuba in 1962.

THINK ABOUT IT

1. What factors led to the Cold War?

2. What was the Berlin Wall? Why was the wall such a powerful symbol of the Cold War?

3. **FOCUS** How did Cold War tensions affect the relationships between Eastern and Western nations?

4. **THINKING SKILL** What were some _causes_ of the Cuban Missile Crisis? What were some of its _effects_ on the United States and Soviet Union?

5. **WRITE** Suppose you are a journalist in Berlin at the end of World War II. Write an article describing the changes taking place in the city.

CHAPTER 18 REVIEW

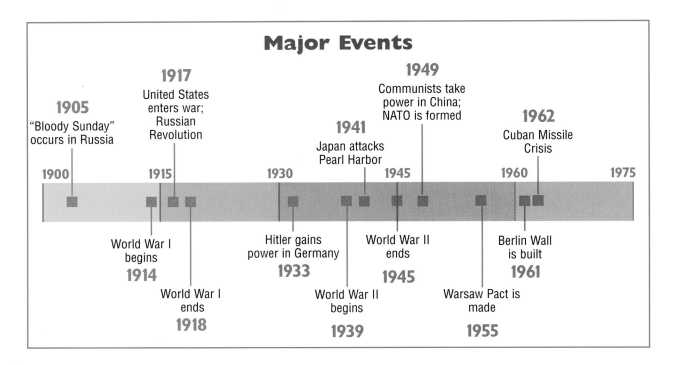

Major Events

1905 "Bloody Sunday" occurs in Russia

1917 United States enters war; Russian Revolution

1949 Communists take power in China; NATO is formed

1941 Japan attacks Pearl Harbor

1962 Cuban Missile Crisis

1900 — 1915 — 1930 — 1945 — 1960 — 1975

World War I begins 1914

World War I ends 1918

Hitler gains power in Germany 1933

World War II begins 1939

World War II ends 1945

Berlin Wall is built 1961

Warsaw Pact is made 1955

THINKING ABOUT VOCABULARY

Number a sheet of paper from 1 to 10. Beside each number write the word or term from the list below that matches the statement.

alliance   nuclear arms race
commune   propaganda
depression   superpower
fascism   totalitarian
nationalism   tsar

1. Strong loyalty to one's country and culture

2. A much stronger country than other countries

3. Exaggerated or false information used to persuade people to help advance a cause

4. Title of an emperor of Russia before the revolution

5. An agreement between countries to defend each other if attacked

6. A form of government in which a dictator controls all aspects of people's lives

7. A form of government in which the goals of a nation are more important than its individuals

8. An organized community where members share work and resources

9. The build-up of nuclear weapons by superpowers

10. An extended period of economic difficulties in a nation

THINKING ABOUT FACTS

1. How did World War I begin?

2. What was the Russian Revolution?

3. Why did Hitler gain power in Germany after World War I?

4. What was the Cultural Revolution? Why did Mao Zedong launch it? What were its consequences?

5. Look at the time line above. Which events listed after the end of World War II have to do with the Cold War? Explain.

THINK AND WRITE

WRITING AN EXPLANATION

Briefly describe the conflicts that started World War I. Then explain why the United States entered it. What factors went into changing the American policy of neutrality. How did the United States help the Allied Powers to win the war?

WRITING A COMPARISON

Write two paragraphs in which you compare Hitler and Stalin. How were they alike? How were they different?

WRITING A REPORT

Write a report about the Cold War. Describe the nuclear arms race and several of the crises and conflicts that took place during this time.

APPLYING GEOGRAPHY SKILLS

TIME ZONE MAPS

1. What is a time zone map?

2. What is the International Date Line?

3. Look at the time zone map on page 548. As you can see, Africa is larger than the United States. How many time zones cross Africa?

4. What is the time difference between the East Coast and West Coast of the United States? If you lived in San Francisco and wanted to call somebody in Boston at noon, Boston time, what time would you make your call?

5. How are time zone maps useful?

Summing Up the Chapter

Copy the sequence chains below on a separate sheet of paper. Review the chapter to find a chain of two events that led to the main event listed. When you have filled in the blanks, use the chains to answer the question "What are some of the conditions that led to the main conflicts of the twentieth century?"

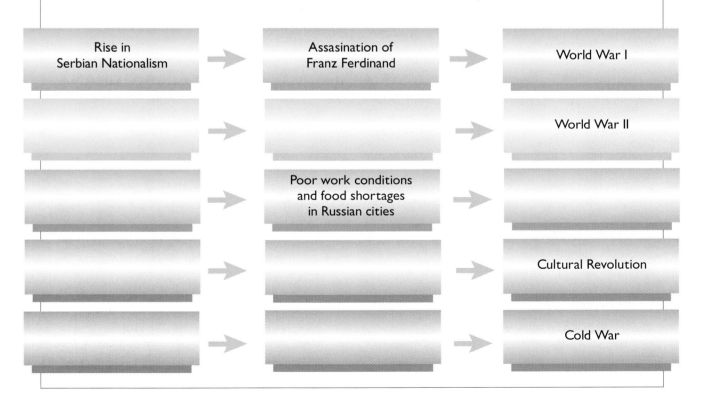

Rise in Serbian Nationalism	Assasination of Franz Ferdinand	World War I
		World War II
	Poor work conditions and food shortages in Russian cities	
		Cultural Revolution
		Cold War

CHAPTER 19

New Nations

THINKING ABOUT
HISTORY AND GEOGRAPHY

In this chapter you will read how nations in many parts of the world gained independence from colonial powers in the 1900s. In places such as Ghana and India, strong leaders led the nationalist movements that broke colonial ties. For many, though, independence brought more war.

AFRICA

Accra

1869	1940s	1957
EGYPT	**DELHI, INDIA**	**ACCRA, GHANA**
The Suez Canal is built	Mohandas Gandhi leads protests against the rule of Britain	Nkrumah declares Ghana's independence from Britain

564

EUROPE

ASIA

Egypt | Israel

Delhi

Saigon

1975

SAIGON, VIETNAM

South Vietnam falls to communist forces

1990s

ISRAEL

Israelis and Palestinians move towards peace

INDIAN OCEAN

INDEPENDENCE IN AFRICA

READ ALOUD

"You ask what the difference between colonialism and independence means to me. . . . Before white and black did not talk. But now at this moment I have the pleasure of sitting with you, a white, and I speak to you like a man. That is all we fought for, the right to respect."

Carlos Miranda spoke these words to a writer after his country, Guinea-Bissau (GIHN ee bihs OW), gained independence from Portugal in 1974. Millions of other Africans shared his feelings about the long period of European rule in Africa.

THE BIG PICTURE

The Portuguese were the first Europeans to set up colonies in Africa. They built stone forts along the West African coast in 1482. By 1900, millions of Africans had come to be ruled by Europeans. Look at the map on page 570 to see how England, France, Portugal, Belgium, Germany, and Spain carved Africa into colonies. In 1914 Ethiopia and Liberia were the only independent nations south of the Sahara Desert. In some areas European colonists set up European-style communities and profited from the continent's natural resources.

During the 1900s many Africans spoke out against the European nations that had controlled their continent. In the decades that followed World War II, Africans once again began to control their own lands and lives. In this lesson you will read about two examples of nations struggling to gain independence.

Focus Activity

READ TO LEARN

How did countries in Africa gain independence from European rule?

VOCABULARY

boycott

PEOPLE

Kwame Nkrumah
Gamal Abdel Nasser

PLACES

Accra
Ghana
Egypt
Suez Canal
Cairo

THE GOLD COAST

In 1874 the British established the colony they called the Gold Coast on Africa's west coast. The British named the colony after the gold that was plentiful in West Africa at the time. The Gold Coast is the area where the ancient African kingdoms of Ghana and Mali, which you read about in Chapter 13, were located.

As you read in Chapter 16, from the early 1500s to the middle 1800s, the Gold Coast had been a center of the slave trade. Both African and European slave traders raided villages of the region. Traders sold their captives for guns, cloth, and other goods.

Profits from Trade

Even after the British government outlawed slave trade, the Gold Coast continued to grow as an important center for British trade. By 1874, other European colonies in Africa and North America were already settled by British citizens. The Gold Coast, however, was run by fewer than 4,000 British soldiers and government officials. Profits gained in the Gold Coast were sent to Britain.

The supply of gold available in West Africa dwindled over time. The British colonists soon found a new source of income, though. The British planted cacao (kuh KAH oh) throughout large areas of the Gold Coast. The cacao tree produces seeds that are used to make chocolate. By 1920 half of the world's supply of cacao was grown in the Gold Coast.

Colonial Conflict

Many Africans in the Gold Coast had long resented British control of their land. Earlier, the British government of

Cacao beans (right) are used to make chocolate. This man in Ghana (above) is gathering dried beans.

the Gold Coast had also faced resistance from the Asante. These Africans, who lived in an independent kingdom to the north, had taken part in the slave trade along with the British and the Dutch in the 1700s. As the Asante gained wealth and power, they expanded the borders of their land. They resisted British rule until 1902.

Later, still others began to oppose British rule. Among them was a young man who studied philosophy in the United States. His name was Kwame Nkrumah (KWAHM ee en KROO muh). After leaving the United States in 1945 he wrote:

I saw the Statue of Liberty with her arm raised as if in personal farewell to me. [I said silently] "You have opened my eyes to the true meaning of liberty. I shall never rest until I have carried your message to Africa."

THE RISE OF AFRICAN NATIONALISM

When Kwame Nkrumah returned home, he found a nationalist spirit already growing in the Gold Coast. Africa's nationalist leaders wrote for newspapers and talked with people in the colonies. In response the British gave some positions in the colonial government to Africans. Nearby French colonies did the same, giving Africans control of agriculture and education.

Economic Protest

Some African leaders were happy with the way change began to take root in the colonies. Others, like Nkrumah, wanted full independence right away. Nkrumah's slogan was "Self-Government Now." He began to organize boycotts of British goods. A boycott is a form of protest in which people join together and refuse to buy goods unless their demands are met. Nkrumah also led strikes against British companies in the Gold Coast.

DID YOU KNOW?

What is the origin of the word boycott?

The word boycott was first used in the 1880s in Ireland. Ireland was then a colony of Great Britain. Captain Charles Cunningham Boycott managed a large farm for the Earl of Erne in County Mayo. He was a cruel and demanding landlord who forced the farmers living on the earl's lands to pay high rents. In 1880 many farmers refused to pay the rent that Captain Boycott demanded. Soon the word boycott began to be used to describe this and other kinds of economic protest. The word and the protest were later used around the globe.

A Big Step

In time the British governor agreed to let the people of the Gold Coast elect a prime minister. In the 1951 election, Nkrumah's party won almost all the votes in the center of Accra, the capital city. The British governor asked Nkrumah to form a government. The governor did not, however, give the government full power immediately. Control of the colony remained in British hands for six more years.

Independence at Last

On March 6, 1957, the Gold Coast became a new African nation called Ghana. The new nation was named after the ancient kingdom of Ghana, which, as you have read, ruled part of West Africa from the 700s to the 1200s.

Africans living under colonial rule in Africa were inspired by the new nation. Kwame Nkrumah, now the new nation's prime minister, said:

If we are to remain free, if we are to enjoy the full benefits of Africa's enormous wealth, we must unite to plan for the full [use] of our human and material resources in the interest of all our people.

Over the next 30 years, Africans in other nations gained control of their governments, ending European rule on most of the continent. Independence was not always won peacefully, though. Also, as in Ghana, independence did not always bring full democracy. The map on page 570 shows when each African nation gained independence from a European power.

Fight for Control of Egypt

Across the Sahara Desert, 2,500 miles northeast of Ghana, a struggle for independence was taking place in

Kwame Nkrumah, center, is shown in 1957, just after Ghana gained independence from Britain.

Egypt. The British had controlled this land since the 1880s. Britain ruled Egypt less directly than it did Ghana. Even so, the Egyptian leader had little power to govern.

British colonists in Egypt developed an economic system based on cotton. The cotton was used to supply British textile factories. More important than cotton, however, was the location of Egypt. The point where Asia and Africa meet is in the northeast corner of Egypt. There the Suez Canal Company, owned mostly by French and Egyptians, built the Suez Canal. Later the British became part of the company, and, along with the French, controlled the canal.

The Suez Canal connected the Mediterranean Sea and the Red Sea, providing a shortcut for ships sailing between Europe and Asia. British ships sailing to the British colony of India could now pass through the Suez Canal instead of traveling around Africa. The canal cut 6,000 miles from the trip.

During World War I nationalist spirit in Egypt grew. Many Egyptians were angry over British demands for men and supplies. Continued unrest led Britain to give Egyptians limited power in their government in 1922. Although Egyptians elected a parliament, Britain appointed the king, Fuad (foo AHD) I. Fuad I ruled according to the wishes of the British. Europeans continued to control the Suez Canal.

A Republic is Born

Many Egyptians were angry that they had not truly been given a voice in their government. In 1952 a group of Egyptian officers in the British army seized control of the government. The group was led by **Gamal Abdel Nasser** (guh MAHL ahb DEL NAHS ur). The officers forced the king to leave Egypt. People celebrated in the streets of the capital city, **Cairo**, singing "Raise up your head my brother, the days of humiliation have passed."

In 1956 Nasser gained control of the Suez Canal.

Today I seize the canal in the name of the people. . . . This night our canal shall be Egyptian, controlled by Egyptians!

The British and their allies sent an army to try to prevent Egypt from taking over the canal. However, governments around the world supported the Egyptians, and the British were forced to give up their claim to the canal. Finally British rule and political influence had come to an end in Egypt.

569

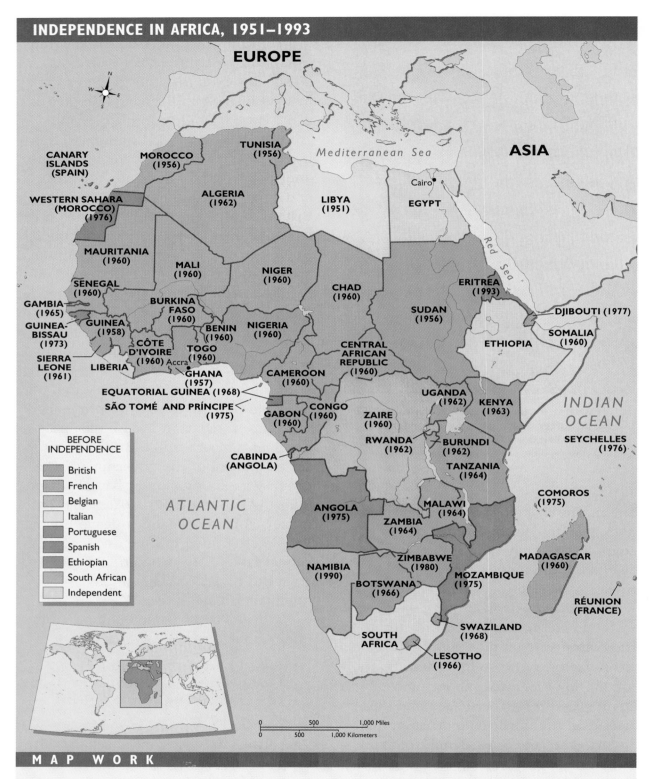

EUROPE

ASIA

Mediterranean Sea

CANARY ISLANDS (SPAIN)

MOROCCO (1956)

TUNISIA (1956)

Cairo

WESTERN SAHARA (MOROCCO) (1976)

ALGERIA (1962)

LIBYA (1951)

EGYPT

MAURITANIA (1960)

MALI (1960)

NIGER (1960)

CHAD (1960)

ERITREA (1993)

Red Sea

DJIBOUTI (1977)

SENEGAL (1960)

SUDAN (1956)

SOMALIA (1960)

GAMBIA (1965)

BURKINA FASO (1960)

BENIN (1960)

NIGERIA (1960)

GUINEA-BISSAU (1973)

GUINEA (1958)

CÔTE D'IVOIRE (1960)

TOGO (1960)

ETHIOPIA

SIERRA LEONE (1961)

LIBERIA

Accra

GHANA (1957)

CAMEROON (1960)

CENTRAL AFRICAN REPUBLIC (1960)

EQUATORIAL GUINEA (1968)

SÃO TOMÉ AND PRÍNCIPE (1975)

GABON (1960)

CONGO (1960)

ZAIRE (1960)

UGANDA (1962)

KENYA (1963)

INDIAN OCEAN

CABINDA (ANGOLA)

RWANDA (1962)

BURUNDI (1962)

TANZANIA (1964)

SEYCHELLES (1976)

ATLANTIC OCEAN

ANGOLA (1975)

ZAMBIA (1964)

MALAWI (1964)

COMOROS (1975)

NAMIBIA (1990)

ZIMBABWE (1980)

MOZAMBIQUE (1975)

MADAGASCAR (1960)

BOTSWANA (1966)

RÉUNION (FRANCE)

SOUTH AFRICA

SWAZILAND (1968)

LESOTHO (1966)

BEFORE INDEPENDENCE
- British
- French
- Belgian
- Italian
- Portuguese
- Spanish
- Ethiopian
- South African
- Independent

0   500   1,000 Miles
0   500   1,000 Kilometers

MAP WORK

Colonies in Africa gained independence from European rule beginning in 1951. Over a period of more than 40 years, many new nations emerged.

1. In what year did Tanzania gain independence?

2. Which country gained independence in 1951?

3. Which countries were formerly ruled by the Portuguese?

4. From which European country did Cameroon gain independence? Botswana?

WHY IT MATTERS

European colonies in Africa were used to produce wealth for Europeans, rather than building the economy for the benefit of Africans. Europeans also created boundaries in Africa without considering that the continent's 2,000 different peoples had lived in certain areas for centuries. Often a new boundary divided an area where a group lived. When nations became independent, the borders were often the European boundaries. Many conflicts developed as people fought for land that had historically belonged to them but was now part of another nation.

By 1995 all of Africa had thrown off European rule and gained independence. However, many problems remained for its nations—the result of years of foreign rule. In recent years, several African nations have taken steps to solve those problems. In the next chapter you will read about one large African nation and how it achieved democracy and human rights.

President Abdel Nasser of Egypt addresses a crowd in 1958. In 1952 he had won control of the Egyptian government.

✓ Reviewing Facts and Ideas

SUM IT UP

- Beginning in the 1500s several European nations established colonies in Africa.

- In 1957 the Gold Coast became the first colony south of the Sahara to gain independence. The new nation was named Ghana.

- Following several steps towards independence, Egyptians gained control of their government in 1952.

- By 1995 all European colonies in Africa had become independent.

THINK ABOUT IT

1. How did European countries gain wealth from their African colonies?

2. How did the British respond to the activities of nationalist leaders in western Africa?

3. **FOCUS** How did the country of Ghana gain its independence from Britain?

4. **THINKING SKILL** Explain two *effects* of European colonialism on Africa.

5. **GEOGRAPHY** How did the Suez Canal affect the movement of people and goods between continents?

STUDY SKILLS

Political Cartoons

VOCABULARY

political cartoon
symbol

WHY THE SKILL MATTERS

During the 1800s powerful European countries established colonies all over the world. Very often colonial powers had disagreements. People who lived in such countries as Britain and France also disagreed at times about whether their countries should establish colonies. Writers discussed these topics in magazines and newspapers.

Also during this time **political cartoons** began to appear more frequently in European magazines. Political cartoons are pictures that show an opinion about a political matter, such as a government action or an election. Political cartoons are useful historical sources. They tell the modern reader many things about cartoonists and people from the past for whom the cartoons were drawn.

USING THE SKILL

Cartoonists often use **symbols** in their cartoons to convey information. A symbol is a sign that stands for something else. For example, the character Uncle Sam is a symbol for the United States. The Statue of Liberty and the bald eagle are also symbols for the United States. Symbols provide an easy way for cartoonists to refer to a country such as the United States in a cartoon.

When you look at a political cartoon, study the symbols and try to figure out what they stand for. For example, look at Cartoon A on this page. This cartoon was published in a French magazine. The large figure is

This cartoon expresses the political viewpoint of many French who were angered by Britain's control of the canal.

John Bull, a symbol that stands for Great Britain. The smaller figures standing around John Bull are symbols that stand for other European countries.

It is also important to read any signs or captions that appear in the cartoon. In Cartoon A the words *Canal de Suez* are very important. These are the French words for Suez Canal. Remember what you read about Britain and the Suez Canal in Lesson 1.

Finally, think about the story or opinion that the cartoonist is trying to communicate. Cartoonists often use exaggeration to make their point. In Cartoon A, John Bull is much bigger than the other people. The cartoonist seems to be saying that Britain is over-exerting control of the canal.

TRYING THE SKILL

Cartoon B is from a United States newspaper. The title of this cartoon is "To France! 1917." It shows the Statue of Liberty marching with a number of soldiers. Look carefully at all of the information in the cartoon. What do you think the Statue of Liberty is a symbol for? What do you think she and the soldiers are headed off to do?

HELPING
Yourself

- **Political cartoons are useful for studying people's opinions in history.**
- **Cartoonists often use symbols to stand for something else.**
- **Study all the information to learn a cartoonist's point of view.**

Remember what you read earlier about World War I and the role of the United States in the war. How does the title of Cartoon B help you understand its meaning? What do you think the cartoon "says" about the cartoonist's feelings about Americans fighting at the battlefront in France? How can you tell?

REVIEWING THE SKILL

1. Why are political cartoons a useful source for studying history?

2. Why do cartoonists often use symbols?

3. Look at Cartoon A. How do you think an Egyptian would feel about this cartoon?

4. Look at Cartoon B. Do you think that people who lived in France would agree with the opinion of this cartoonist? Why or why not?

5. Find a political cartoon in your local newspaper. What does it tell you about how the cartoonist feels about the topic?

Political cartoons often rely on exaggerated representations or humor to express their viewpoints.

1800   1850   1874   1995 2000

NEW NATIONS IN THE MIDDLE EAST

Focus Activity

READ TO LEARN
What events led to the
Israeli-Palestinian conflict?

VOCABULARY
Zionism
anti-semitism
refugee
Intifada

PEOPLE
David Ben Gurion
Yasir Arafat
Anwar Sadat
Yitzak Rabin

PLACES
Middle East
Palestine
Turkey
Iraq
Israel
Gaza
Golan Heights
West Bank

READ ALOUD

*"The Government of the State of Israel and the . . .
Palestinian people agree that it is time to put an end
to decades of . . . conflict."*

This is the opening of the Declaration of Principles, a special treaty written in 1993. After half a century of fighting, two peoples came to an agreement: the killing must stop. What caused their conflict?

THE BIG PICTURE

Between the Mediterranean Sea and the western borders of Pakistan and Afghanistan is a region known as the Middle East. It spans all of western Asia and a small part of southeastern Europe. Find the 14 countries of the region on the map on page 576.

This region was the heart of the Baghdad Caliphate from the late 700s to the 1200s. From the 1500s until the end of World War I, the Middle East was ruled by the Ottoman empire. After 1918 Britain and France took control of most of the Middle East.

Along the western edge of the Middle East is a narrow wedge of land lying along the Mediterranean Sea. This land has had great impact on world events, and you have read about it more than once in this book. It has had many names: Canaan, Judea, Palestine, the Holy Land, Israel. Throughout history, it has been home to many peoples and cultures. In this lesson you will read about the struggle that developed between two of these peoples over a land that both claimed as their own.

A JEWISH HOMELAND

How did this struggle over the area that is today Israel develop? Part of the answer lies in the history of Zionism (ZI uh niz um). Zionism is a movement to establish a Jewish homeland, or nation. The word comes from Mount Zion, a mountain in Jerusalem.

An Ancient and Modern Hope

Modern Zionism began in the late 1800s. Its goal, in the words of a Hebrew song, was to make the Jews "a free people in our own land." Actually, the idea of a homeland for the Jewish people began much earlier. This idea began, in fact, in the time of the Diaspora. Remember from Chapter 5 that *Diaspora* means the "scattering" of the Jews from the land of Israel. This scattering began around 600 B.C., when the Babylonians conquered Judah. The Diaspora continued, but some Jews remained in the area. The Romans called it Palestine.

By the late 1800s, when modern Zionism began, Palestine was home to about 450,000 people. Most of them were Arabs. About 25,000 Jews also lived here. Most of the world's Jewish population lived outside of Palestine, in Europe and the rest of the world. However, they had never forgotten their ancient homeland. The yearly Passover seder always ends with the words: "Next year in Jerusalem!"

Troubles in Europe

The desire to return to Jerusalem grew stronger among many Jews in Europe. Feelings of nationalism had spread throughout the world since the French Revolution. Some European Jews, too, began hoping to have their own nation.

Also during this time anti-semitism grew stronger in Europe. Anti-semitism is discrimination against Jews. In Eastern European countries such as Russia and Poland where many Jews lived, Jews were often subjected to sudden, violent attacks. Many Jews left Europe for the United States and other regions, including Palestine.

These Jewish immigrants at a dock in Haifa reflect the desire of many Jews to return to the Jewish homeland and form their own nation.

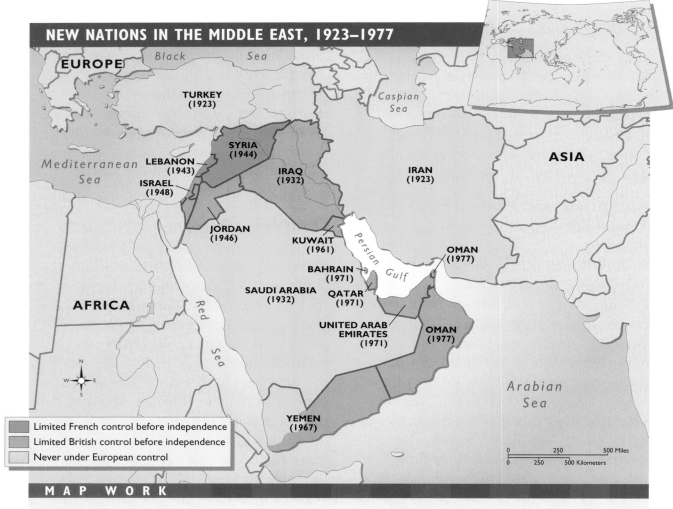

NEW NATIONS IN THE MIDDLE EAST, 1923–1977

EUROPE

Black Sea

TURKEY (1923)

Caspian Sea

SYRIA (1944)

LEBANON (1943)

Mediterranean Sea

ISRAEL (1948)

IRAQ (1932)

IRAN (1923)

ASIA

JORDAN (1946)

KUWAIT (1961)

Persian Gulf

OMAN (1977)

BAHRAIN (1971)

AFRICA

Red Sea

SAUDI ARABIA (1932)

QATAR (1971)

UNITED ARAB EMIRATES (1971)

OMAN (1977)

Arabian Sea

YEMEN (1967)

Limited French control before independence
Limited British control before independence
Never under European control

0   250   500 Miles
0   250   500 Kilometers

MAP WORK

Beginning in 1923, many nations in the Middle East became independent.

1. Which European country had limited control of Iraq before independence?

2. In what year did Qatar become independent?

3. Which nations beame independent before 1950?

CHANGES IN THE MIDDLE EAST

After the defeat of the Ottoman empire in World War I, Britain and France took over much of the Middle East. By this time, however, nationalist movements were beginning to form in the region.

In 1923 nationalists in what was left of the Ottoman empire established an independent Republic of **Turkey**. It was only the first of several new nations in the Middle East. In 1932, after a period of British rule, the people of **Iraq**

gained independence. Find these and other new nations on the map.

A Growing Population

Feelings of nationalism had been developing among both Arabs and Jews in British-controlled Palestine.

Growing numbers of Jews created tensions with Arabs who were already living in Palestine. Many Palestinian Arabs hoped to build new lives in an independent nation of Palestine. They feared that their own nationalist dreams would be lost.

World War II brought great changes to British Palestine. Many European Jews managed to escape Nazi oppression by immigrating to Palestine. After the war many survivors of Nazi concentration camps arrived in Palestine. By 1947 the number of Jews living in Palestine reached about 650,000, or about one-third of the population. The remaining two-thirds were Palestinian Arabs, most of whom were Muslims.

The Founding of Israel

After World War II the United Nations agreed to divide Palestine between Arabs and Jews. The Jews there accepted the plan. On May 14, 1948, they declared independence as the country of Israel. David Ben Gurion, a leader of the Jewish independence movement, became Israel's first prime minister.

War and Refugees

The day after Israel became an independent nation, armies from five Arab countries attacked the new nation. Jews fought to defend their new country. After more than six months of fighting, the Jews came out as victors. This war, however, was only the first of several wars that would be fought between Israel and Arab countries.

As the result of the Arab-Israeli conflict, as many as 750,000 Palestinian Arabs left Israel. Some fled out of fear. Some were forced to leave. Many settled in refugee camps in Jordan, Syria, and Lebanon. Refugees are people who have to flee their country for safety. About 600,000 Palestinians remained. Mahmoud Darwish, a Palestinian poet described his feelings about living in a homeland controlled by others:

You are my grief and my joy,
my wound and my rainbow,
my prison and my freedom.

In June 1967 war broke out again. In this conflict, the Six-Day War, Israel gained more land, including Gaza, the Golan Heights, and the West Bank. Find these areas on the map on page 578.

To gain back the land for Arabs, the Palestine Liberation Organization, or PLO, was formed in 1964. In 1968, under the leadership of Yasir Arafat, the PLO began to fight to get the land back from Israel.

The First Sign of Peace

Fighting between Arabs and Israelis continued on and off for years. Then in 1977 Egypt's President Anwar Sadat took a daring trip to Israel. For the first time an Arab leader publicly met with leaders of the Jewish nation. The Camp David agreement, signed by Egypt and Israel in 1978, established peaceful relations between those nations.

Golda Meir, Israeli prime minister from 1969 to 1974, greets Egyptian president Anwar Sadat in November 1977.

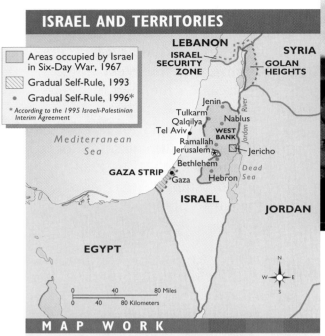

ISRAEL AND TERRITORIES

Areas occupied by Israel in Six-Day War, 1967

Gradual Self-Rule, 1993

Gradual Self-Rule, 1996*

* According to the 1995 Israeli-Palestinian Interim Agreement

LEBANON
ISRAEL SECURITY ZONE
SYRIA
GOLAN HEIGHTS
Jenin
Tulkarm
Qalqilya
Tel Aviv
Nablus
WEST BANK
Ramallah
Jerusalem
Jericho
Bethlehem
GAZA STRIP
Gaza
Hebron
Dead Sea
Jordan River
Mediterranean Sea
ISRAEL
JORDAN
EGYPT

0   40   80 Miles
0   40   80 Kilometers

M A P   W O R K

In 1993 some Palestinian areas gained self-rule.

1. Which areas were the first to gain self-rule?
2. When did Jenin gain self-rule?

Palestinians show support for their leader Yasir Arafat in September 1988.

WHY IT MATTERS

The Camp David agreement did not end the struggle between Israel and the Palestinians. In 1987 Palestinians in Gaza and the West Bank began a revolt called the Intifada (ihn te FAH duh). *Intifada* means "shaking" in Arabic. Palestinians tried to "shake off" the rule of the Israelis.

Slowly, however, hopes for peace returned to this war-torn land. PLO leader Yasir Arafat and Yitzhak Rabin (YIHT zak rah BEEN), Prime Minister of Israel, signed agreements in 1993 and 1995. You read part of the 1993 agreement in this lesson's Read Aloud. They agreed that a Palestinian homeland would be established in Gaza and the West Bank.

Peace remains a difficult goal. In 1995 an Israeli opposed to the peace process *assassinated* Yitzhak Rabin. To assassinate means to kill for political reasons. Still, hope for peace remains, as Israelis and Palestinians continue to work together to solve their decades-old conflict.

✔ Reviewing Facts and Ideas

SUM IT UP

- In the 1900s Zionist immigration to Palestine concerned Palestinians, who desired a country of their own.

- In 1948 Arab armies attacked in an unsuccessful effort to destroy the new Jewish country of Israel. Palestinian refugees fled to other Arab lands.

- An uneasy peace began in the 1990s.

THINK ABOUT IT

1. What were two reasons for the creation of the Zionist movement?

2. Why was the PLO formed?

3. **FOCUS** How did modern Israel begin?

4. **THINKING SKILL** What were two *causes* for the Israeli-Palestinian conflict?

5. **GEOGRAPHY** Why might Israel's shape make it difficult to defend?

CITIZENSHIP
MAKING A DIFFERENCE

Building Bridges to Friendship

HERZLIYA, ISRAEL—In Hebrew, the word *shalom* means both "hello" and "peace." In Arabic the word *salaam* has a similar sound and meaning. The group Interns for Peace, led by Rabbi Bruce Cohen, is helping Jews and Arabs in Israel greet each other with these words and build peaceful friendships.

Since 1976, Interns for Peace has trained over 200 Arab and Jewish volunteers to work with Arabs and Jews in schools, homes, community centers, and summer camps in Israel. The volunteers, called interns, organize projects such as building parks or planting trees.

Two 15-year-old girls, Arab Israeli Rola Gbaly (gi BALLY) and Jewish Israeli Sivan Harel participated in a project called Education for Democracy. This project pairs Jewish and Arab schools for monthly get-togethers. Sivan's and Rola's eighth-grade classes met first at Sivan's all-Jewish school in Herzliya. "The most difficult part," says Sivan, "was when we first came together. We were nervous. It wasn't just that we were meeting with new kids. It was that we were meeting with new Arab kids. We thought there would be disagreements. Then we got to know them a little and saw that they are different from us but not very different. They are children just like us."

On the second visit, Sivan's class visited Rola's school in Taibeh, Israel. There, Rola says, "we painted a peace wall." Both girls agreed that the third meeting was the best, because, says Sivan, "The conversations were like with normal friends. We didn't talk about really important things, just about daily life." Rola adds, "I tell people my age that this is a way for us to understand each other." According to Rabbi Cohen, building understanding between Arabs and Jews is the goal of all the projects. "We do not teach people to love one another, we teach understanding and tolerance."

" . . . this is a way for us to understand each other."

1800   1850   1885   1971   2000

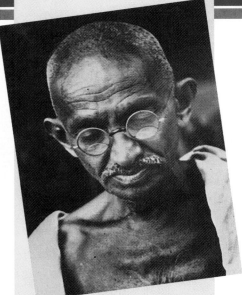

INDIA'S STRUGGLE FOR INDEPENDENCE

Focus Activity

READ TO LEARN
How did the nation of India gain independence?

VOCABULARY
Raj
civil disobedience
Green Revolution

PEOPLE
Mohandas Gandhi
Mohammed Ali Jinnah
Jawaharlal Nehru
Indira Gandhi

PLACES
India
Pakistan
Bangladesh

READ ALOUD

"The force generated by nonviolence is infinitely greater than the force of all the arms invented by man's ingenuity."

Mohandas Gandhi (moh han DAHS GAN dee) wrote these words during a period when Britain ruled his nation, India. His words describe a way of working toward independence without fighting battles that would harm and kill people. For many years Gandhi led the people of India in a largely nonviolent struggle against Britain.

THE BIG PICTURE

By the end of the 1800s Britain's empire stretched around the globe. You have already read about British colonies in the Americas, Africa, and the Middle East. Britain also controlled Hong Kong in East Asia and the island-continent of Australia. However, many British people thought one colony in particular to be "the brightest jewel in the imperial crown."

This "jewel" was India. It was exactly what Britain wanted a colony to be. The Indian subcontinent provided the British with raw materials for industry. The British introduced their way of organizing government and parts of their culture. British technologies such as the railroad helped build industry in India. Even so, as time passed, more and more Indians believed that their nation should gain independence from British rule.

COLONIAL INDIA

The story of British rule in India begins in 1600. In that year Britain's Queen Elizabeth I granted a charter to a group of English merchants. The charter gave the merchants the right to develop trade in Asia for the British government. These merchants hoped to take part in the spice trade that was controlled mostly by Dutch and Portuguese traders. Remember Europeans bought these spices to preserve meat and flavor food. In 1601 the first five English ships set sail for India. You can see India on the map on page 583.

A Powerful Trade Company

The company of merchants became known as the British East India Company. By 1700 the merchants had set up trading centers, which they called "factories," in such cities as Bombay, Madras, and Calcutta.

At the same time as the East India Company pushed farther into India, the Mogul rulers of India were losing power. The British then took part in wars that broke out between local rulers. In the 1850s, after more than ten wars within India, the Company controlled two thirds of the subcontinent. Indian princes ruled the rest of India. They were loyal to the British government. The East India Company became known as the **Raj**, which comes from a Sanskrit word meaning "king." The Raj set up telegraph lines, organized a postal service, and built railroads between the major cities.

Most Indians were not satisfied with life under the Raj. They resented foreign rule. In 1857 thousands of Indian soldiers in the British army revolted. Soon, the Great Mutiny, as it was called by the British, or the first war of independence as it was called by the Indians, spread across north and central India. Thousands of Indians and British died before Britain put down the revolt. After the war the British government took control of India from the East India Company.

This photo from the late 19th century shows British citizens in India being served by Indian servants. Many Indians resented the British rule of India.

STRUGGLE FOR INDEPENDENCE

The desire for Indian independence grew. In 1885 a group of 73 Indians attended the first Indian National Congress in Bombay. Many of the members had been educated in England. They asked that the Raj spend less of India's tax money on the army and that Indians be given important positions in the government. A few began to talk about gaining independence from Britain.

By 1905 Indian nationalism had become widespread. In that year people began to boycott British cloth. Cloth made in British textile mills and imported to India was sold cheaply. However, the British had placed a tax on Indian cloth that was sent to Britain. The tax hurt India's textile industry. Many people began wearing Indian-made cloth as a sign of national pride.

Mohandas Gandhi

Among the leaders who planned later boycotts and strikes was a young lawyer named Mohandas Gandhi. Gandhi studied law in London and then worked in South Africa to gain rights for Indians who went to live there. When he returned to India in 1915, Gandhi became an important leader in India's fight for independence.

Gandhi had three goals for India. He hoped to see the end of British rule, peace between Muslims and Hindus, and an end to poor treatment of the untouchable caste. Remember untouchables were the people at the lowest level of Hindu society.

Gandhi wore only the simplest handmade cloth and began spinning yarn in his spare time. Soon, the Indian spinning wheel became a symbol of nationalism. Because of his simple life and religious ways, Gandhi became known by the Hindi word *Mahatma*, which means "great soul."

To achieve independence in India, Gandhi believed people should practice civil disobedience. Civil disobedience is a means of protest without violence. One example was the boycott. Another was refusing to obey laws that they believed to be unjust. Gandhi said, "Mass civil disobedience is like an earthquake" and Gandhi's followers were soon shaking the foundations of British rule. Indians joined this movement by refusing to pay taxes or to buy British goods. Thousands, including Gandhi, were jailed. Even the fact that Gandhi was in prison did not stop the protest. Soon nearly all of India followed Gandhi's lead. How did Gandhi describe his work in leading India's struggle for independence?

MANY VOICES PRIMARY SOURCE

Excerpt from
The Words of Gandhi, c. 1947.

*I have nothing new to teach the world. Truth and nonviolence are as old as the hills. All I have done is to try experiments in both on as vast a scale as I could. In doing so, I have sometimes erred and learnt by my errors. Life and its problems have thus become to me so many experiments in the practice of truth and nonviolence. . . . I have not the shadow of a doubt that any man or woman can achieve what I have, if he or she would make the same effort and **cultivate** the same hope and faith.*

cultivate: to help the growth of

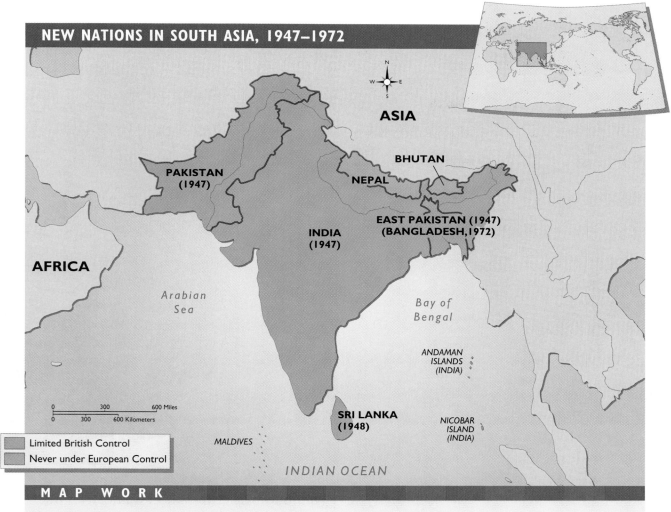

NEW NATIONS IN SOUTH ASIA, 1947–1972

ASIA

PAKISTAN (1947)

BHUTAN

NEPAL

EAST PAKISTAN (1947)
(BANGLADESH,1972)

INDIA (1947)

AFRICA

Arabian Sea

Bay of Bengal

ANDAMAN ISLANDS (INDIA)

SRI LANKA (1948)

NICOBAR ISLAND (INDIA)

MALDIVES

INDIAN OCEAN

0   300   600 Miles
0   300   600 Kilometers

Limited British Control
Never under European Control

MAP WORK

Some nations in South Asia gained independence from European rule beginning in 1947. Others had never come under European control.

1. Which nations were under British control?

2. In what year did Sri Lanka gain independence?

3. Which country became independent in 1972?

The Brink of Independence

In 1942 the Indian National Congress planned a new campaign to convince the British to leave. People shouted "Quit India" at British soldiers in India's cities. By 1947 the British were ready to give up control of India. Muslims feared that they would be treated poorly by a Hindu-led government. They demanded a separate country. On August 15, India and **Pakistan** gained independence.

Pakistan was made up of two separate areas in the northern corners of India. Many Muslims lived in these areas known as West and East Pakistan. The prime minister of Pakistan was **Mohammad Ali Jinnah** (muh HAM ud ah LEE JIHN ah). **Jawaharlal Nehru** (juh WAH hur ah NAY roo) was prime minister of India.

About ten million people moved across the border to be with people of their own faith. Nearly one million people died in violent conflicts between Hindus and Muslims. Gandhi was shot and killed in such a conflict in January 1948.

THE NEW NATIONS

Although conflicts continued between India and Pakistan, the governments of both countries set about moving their countries forward. Achieving independence had been a huge challenge, but it was only the first of many.

India's Early Years

One of the many problems faced by independent India was raising enough food to feed the country's huge population. The government worked to make agriculture more productive. New types of wheat and rice crops were developed. The new focus on agriculture throughout the nation became known as the Green Revolution.

Other changes fulfilled many of the goals of Mahatma Gandhi. The untouchable caste was officially abolished, although discrimination against untouchables continued. Also, women gained new rights. In the 1940s and 1950s women were granted the right to own property and the right to vote.

In 1966 a woman, Indira Gandhi (ihn DEE rah GAHN dee), became India's prime minister. She was the daughter of Jawaharlal Nehru. Indira Gandhi continued many of her father's plans and policies. However, she also led India in a war against Pakistan. Trouble between East and West Pakistan led to civil war in 1971. In that year the Indian army helped East Pakistan. Soon after, the leaders of East Pakistan established the new independent country called Bangladesh. The Indian subcontinent, once the "jewel in the British crown," now contained three independent nations.

Among the several programs that Indira Gandhi (left) started after she became India's prime minister in 1966, was one to make farming more productive (below).

WHY IT MATTERS

The Ganges, especially, is the river of India. . . . [It is] a symbol of India's age-long culture and civilizations, ever-changing, ever-flowing, and yet ever the same.

With these words, Jawaharlal Nehru summed up his feelings for India. He believed the flow of the Ganges River was as constant and lasting as the nation itself. Today India is the largest democracy in the world with a population of more than 900 million. Its history is long and varied. Great changes occurred in the subcontinent over the centuries. British colonialism had great effects on India in the 1800s and 1900s.

Change in India also influenced other parts of the world. As India struggled to free itself from British rule, other colonies around the world began to work toward independence, as well. Many people have been influenced by Gandhi's method of civil disobedience. In the United States, Martin Luther King, Jr., followed some of the teachings of Gandhi in the fight for civil rights. King described Gandhi with these words: "He lived, thought, and acted, inspired by the vision of humanity evolving toward a world of peace and harmony."

✓✓ Reviewing Facts and Ideas

SUM IT UP

- The British East India Company began to establish trade with India in the 1600s.

- By the middle 1800s the British government had gained control of most of the Indian subcontinent.

- Mohandas Gandhi's civil disobedience program led India to independence.

- In 1947 British rule ended and the independent nations of India and Pakistan were formed.

THINK ABOUT IT

1. Describe three changes that the British East India Company brought to the Indian subcontinent.

2. Why did Indians boycott British-made cloth in 1905?

3. **FOCUS** How did India become an independent nation?

4. **THINKING SKILL** *Compare* India's struggle for independence with the struggle of a country in Africa or the Americas. How was it similar? How was it different?

5. **WRITE** Write an editorial describing how Gandhi's teachings might or might not be useful in solving problems in the world today.

NEW NATIONS IN SOUTHEAST ASIA

Focus Activity

READ TO LEARN
How did nations in Southeast Asia gain independence?

VOCABULARY
Vietnam War

PEOPLE
Ho Chi Minh

PLACES
Vietnam
Southeast Asia
Laos
Cambodia
Burma
Thailand

READ ALOUD

In 1949 a leader named Ho Chi Minh declared the independence of his nation, Vietnam. This act followed over 100 years of colonial rule by the French. During those years many Vietnamese struggled to survive. Yet independence did not bring safety and peace to the new nation. Instead the Vietnamese continued to struggle through conflicts and war that divided the nation in many ways.

THE BIG PICTURE

Vietnam is located in Southeast Asia. In chapter 14 you read about the Khmer who lived in this region around A.D. 1000. For centuries Vietnam was invaded by neighbors such as the Khmer and the Ming of China.

In the middle 1800s, French ships began sailing into the port city of Da Nang. France established colonies in Vietnam and the neighboring countries of Laos and Cambodia. Around the same time, Britain took over parts of Burma, the westernmost kingdom in the region. Nearby Thailand remained one of the few independent areas in Southeast Asia. For about 100 years European powers would shape life for many people in the region. However, desire for the independence of the past grew very strong in Vietnam. This led to conflicts with other countries and within Vietnam.

A COLONY OF FRANCE

In 1858 the French took control of Vietnam's coast. As French soldiers moved inland, local armies slowed their progress. By 1887 France succeeded in occupying Vietnam, Laos, and Cambodia, all of which they called Indochina.

The Colonists Prosper

Vietnam was an important source of raw materials. French colonists sent tons of rice, coal, and tin to France. While the French gained wealth, many of the people of Vietnam suffered. Before the French arrived, almost every family owned some land. By 1920, however, only French colonists and wealthy Vietnamese owned land. Many people were forced to work for others. One worker wrote:

> The larger parts of our wages are taken by the supervisors and foremen . . . [and] our salaries are already too low. . . . Food prices increase every day and we have become hungrier and hungrier.

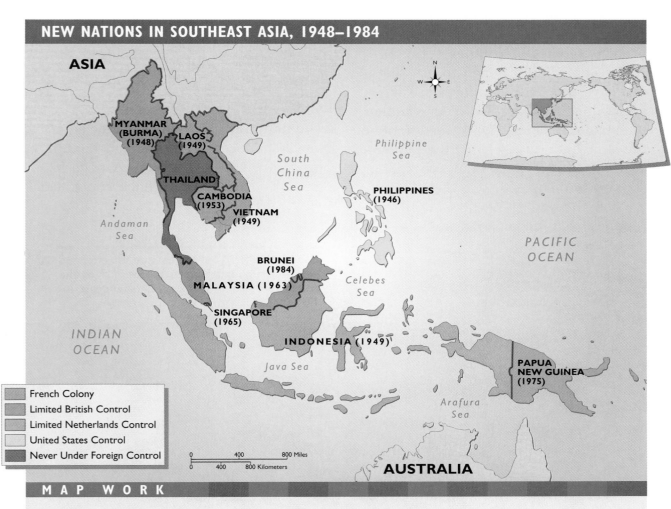

NEW NATIONS IN SOUTHEAST ASIA, 1948–1984

ASIA

MYANMAR (BURMA) (1948)
LAOS (1949)
THAILAND
CAMBODIA (1953)
VIETNAM (1949)
BRUNEI (1984)
MALAYSIA (1963)
SINGAPORE (1965)
INDONESIA (1949)
PHILIPPINES (1946)
PAPUA NEW GUINEA (1975)

South China Sea
Philippine Sea
Andaman Sea
Celebes Sea
Java Sea
Arafura Sea
PACIFIC OCEAN
INDIAN OCEAN
AUSTRALIA

French Colony
Limited British Control
Limited Netherlands Control
United States Control
Never Under Foreign Control

0 400 800 Miles
0 400 800 Kilometers

MAP WORK

Nations in Southeast Asia struggled for freedom from foreign rule. All succeeded in becoming independent.

1. Which nations became independent after 1950?

2. Which foreign power had control in the Philippines?

3. In what year did Malaysia gain independence?

FIGHTING COLONIAL RULE

In the 1920s anti-French feeling began to take shape. Many Vietnamese people formed organizations that opposed French rule. One group, the Vietnamese communists, was led by Ho Chi Minh (HOH CHEE MIHN). His goal was to create an independent Vietnam. The Vietnamese communists worked toward that goal by planning protest marches and labor strikes against the French.

Independence Is Declared

In 1940, during World War II, the Japanese captured Vietnam and other French colonies in Southeast Asia. Japan immediately began to use Vietnam's resources to support its war effort. Rice was shipped from Vietnam to Japanese soldiers who were fighting the war. Little was left for the people of Vietnam to eat. More than two million starved to death.

Near the end of World War II, Japanese rule began to crumble in Southeast Asia. In 1945 an army of Vietnamese communists, called the Viet Minh (VEE et MIHN), took action. The Viet Minh gained control of many areas of the country, especially in the northern region. By September 1945 the communists controlled nearly all of Vietnam. Ho Chi Minh declared the nation's independence and became the head of a new communist government.

The French, however, were not ready to give up their claims to Vietnam. In 1946 the French, aided by the British, went to war against the communists. After eight years of fighting, the French lost an important struggle at the town of Dien Bien Phu (dyen byen FOO). In 1954 the two sides signed an armistice. The armistice called for Vietnam to be divided in half until elections to unify the nation could be held. The elections never happened. Communists continued to control North Vietnam. A government backed by the French controlled South Vietnam.

Ho Chi Minh (left) led the communist effort to gain Vietnam's independence. France signs the treaty recognizing Vietnam's independence in 1954 (below).

From 1965 to 1973, American troops fought to try to prevent communist North Vietnam from taking over South Vietnam.

The United States in Vietnam

The armistice failed to bring peace to Vietnam. The communists wanted to unite South Vietnam with North Vietnam under their leadership. The leaders of South Vietnam, however, wanted to remain independent.

Many leaders in the United States were worried about the spread of communism from North Vietnam. By speaking out in favor of the government of South Vietnam, the United States stood firm against communism in the Cold War. American leaders wanted to keep communism from threatening democratic governments in other parts of Southeast Asia. This led the United States to take action in Vietnam. United States Secretary of State John Foster Dulles said that:

> [T]he United States should not stand passively by and see the extension of communism by any means into Southeast Asia.

War Breaks Out

South Vietnamese rebels, supported by North Vietnam, began a war against the government of South Vietnam. Later, North Vietnamese forces also moved into South Vietnam as they tried to spread communism and unite the nations.

The United States had begun to help the government of South Vietnam in 1954. The United States provided the country with money, weapons, and advisers. Then, in 1965, the United States sent troops and planes to help in the fighting. A war that became known as the Vietnam War was now raging. A million tons of United States supplies arrived in South Vietnam every month. By 1968, about half a million troops were stationed in Vietnam.

As American troops suffered losses in Vietnam, public opinion in the United States became divided. Some people believed the United States should be involved in the Vietnam War. Others, however, did not agree. In 1973 the United States began pulling its troops out of Vietnam. Two years later South Vietnam surrendered to North Vietnam. More than 58,000 Americans had died in the war. Nearly two million Vietnamese people had died.

After the **Vietnam War**, Vietnamese refugees (left) crowded into boats on a voyage to Hong Kong, where they sought freedom from communism.

FACING THE FUTURE

Vietnam faced serious problems after the war. Much of the country had been damaged by bombing and ground fighting. The communist government took control of property and businesses throughout the country after the war. Droughts and floods caused shortages of food. Planting new crops was dangerous because fields contained many unexploded bombs left from the war. Many Vietnamese were unhappy with communist government.

More than one million South Vietnamese people left their nation in overcrowded boats. They decided to risk their lives at sea to settle in free countries rather than live under a communist government. These Vietnamese eventually settled in countries throughout the world. More than 600,000 moved to the United States.

Change in Southeast Asia

Vietnam also had trouble with its neighbor Cambodia. Cambodia's communist leader, Pol Pot, had come to power in 1975 after leading a commu-

nist group against the government. During Pol Pot's rule there was a reign of terror. People were forced to leave the cities to live and work in rural camps. Educated Cambodians were considered enemies, and many of them were murdered. There was little food

and no freedom. More than one million people were killed. Many others fled the country. In 1978 Vietnamese soldiers invaded Cambodia, forcing Pol Pot and his supporters to flee. After the United Nations supervised elections in 1993, Vietnamese troops left Cambodia, and a government including different political groups took power.

WHY IT MATTERS

When Vietnam gained independence, it became one of more than 100 new nations formed since 1943. Like many of the other new nations of the world, those in Southeast Asia faced difficult problems. Over 100 years of colonial rule and 30 years of war had harsh effects on Vietnam and on the other nations in Southeast Asia.

Today Hanoi (below), Vietnam's capital, is a busy industrial center, producing textiles, chemicals, and food products.

Since the end of the war in 1975, changes have begun to occur in Vietnam. For years Vietnam depended on the Soviet Union for aid. After the Soviet Union broke up, the leaders of Vietnam, as well as other Southeast Asian leaders, began to work toward an economy that allowed more free enterprise. Foreign companies have built factories in Vietnam. In 1995 Vietnam and the United States once again began to trade and have diplomatic relations.

✓ Reviewing Facts and Ideas

SUM IT UP

- In the middle 1800s the French began to establish a colony in Vietnam. By 1887 they had influence in much of Southeast Asia.

- The colony of Vietnam provided France with many raw materials.

- After World War II the Viet Minh, led by Ho Chi Minh and others, fought for independence from France.

- The United States fought with South Vietnam against communist forces of North Vietnam until 1973.

- In 1975 Vietnam became unified, but faced economic and social problems.

THINK ABOUT IT

1. Why were many Vietnamese people unhappy under French colonial rule?

2. How did World War II change colonial rule in Vietnam?

3. **FOCUS** How did the people of Vietnam finally gain independence?

4. **THINKING SKILL** Describe the *point of view* of United States official John Foster Dulles, quoted on page 589.

5. **WRITE** Write five questions that you might ask a United States soldier who served in Vietnam.

CHAPTER 19 REVIEW

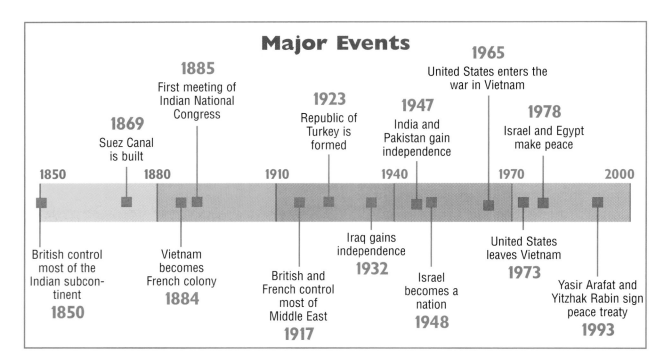

Major Events

1885 First meeting of Indian National Congress

1965 United States enters the war in Vietnam

1923 Republic of Turkey is formed

1947 India and Pakistan gain independence

1869 Suez Canal is built

1978 Israel and Egypt make peace

1850 — 1880 — 1910 — 1940 — 1970 — 2000

British control most of the Indian subcontinent **1850**

Vietnam becomes French colony **1884**

British and French control most of Middle East **1917**

Iraq gains independence **1932**

Israel becomes a nation **1948**

United States leaves Vietnam **1973**

Yasir Arafat and Yitzhak Rabin sign peace treaty **1993**

THINKING ABOUT VOCABULARY

Number a sheet of paper from 1 to 5. Beside each number write the word or term from the list below that best completes the sentence.

anti-semitism
boycott
civil disobedience
refugee
Vietnam War

1. A _____ is a person who flees his or her country for safety.

2. A nonviolent breaking of the law to protest something is called _____.

3. The _____ in Southeast Asia divided Americans against each other in the 1960s and early 1970s.

4. A _____ is the refusal to buy goods to protest something.

5. Discrimination against Jewish people is called _____.

THINKING ABOUT FACTS

1. Who was Kwame Nkrumah?

2. What role did Gamal Abdel Nasser play in Egyptian history?

3. Where did the Jews who left Russia and eastern Europe go to avoid persecution in the early 1900s?

4. How was Israel created?

5. What was the Camp David agreement? Why was it significant?

6. What was the British East India Company called? Why did most Indians dislike it?

7. Who was Mohandas Gandhi and what were his goals?

8. Why did the French colonize Vietnam, Laos, and Cambodia?

9. Who fought in the Vietnam War? What did each side hope to achieve?

10. Many new nations were created during the twentieth century. Look at the time line above and name as many newly formed nations as you can.

WRITING AN INTERVIEW

Suppose you are going to interview Mohandas Gandhi. Write at least three questions you would ask him. Then list the answers you think he might give.

WRITING A REPORT

Write a report about the Vietnam War and the disagreements it caused in the United States. Explain arguments made by opponents and supporters of the war.

WRITING ABOUT PERSPECTIVES

Write about how Zionists and Palestinian nationalists have seen the situation in the Middle East during the past 40 years.

APPLYING STUDY SKILLS

POLITICAL CARTOONS

1. What is a political cartoon?

2. Look at Cartoon B on page 573. It shows in a positive light the American decision to send troops to fight against Germans during World War I. If a cartoon on the same subject had appeared in a German newspaper, what might it have shown?

3. Review Lesson 3. Describe what political cartoons about British control of India might show. How might the British show their presence in India? How might the Indians illustrate it?

4. How might American cartoonists who supported the Vietnam War have shown it? How might cartoonists who opposed the war have pictured it?

5. Look at Cartoon B in the skills lesson again. Why are the Statue of Liberty and the American flag important to the message of this cartoon?

Summing Up the Chapter

Copy the main-idea chart below on a separate sheet of paper. Then fill in the blanks in each column with information from the chapter. When you have filled in the blanks, write a paragraph that answers the question "What are some of the new countries in this century and how were they formed?"

MAIN IDEA In this century many new countries have emerged in Africa and Asia.

Region	New Countries	Leaders
Africa		
Middle East		
South Asia		
Southeast Asia		

CHAPTER 20

A Changing World

THINKING ABOUT
HISTORY AND GEOGRAPHY

Today communication and travel around the world are easier than at any other time in history. In this chapter you will read about some of the changes that have taken place in this shrinking world. Many of the changes have resulted in more freedom and opportunities. Others have left people struggling to meet challenges.

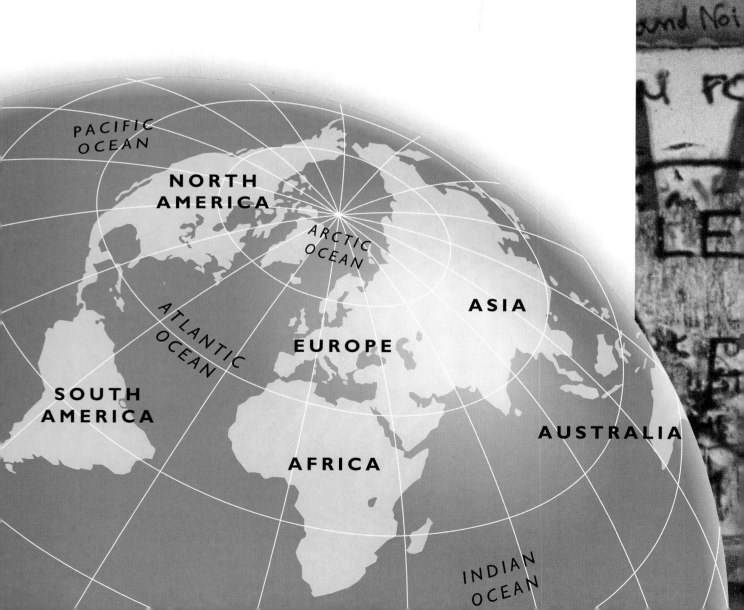

Hubertus von der Goltz

Projekt: "BALANCE"

Weg durch Deutschland

A CHANGING EUROPE

READ ALOUD

In February 1989 an East German man was shot and killed trying to escape over the Berlin Wall. Just nine months later, hundreds of East Germans gathered on and around the wall. They were there to celebrate one of the most memorable days in the twentieth century. The Berlin Wall was about to come tumbling down.

THE BIG PICTURE

By the middle 1980s the Cold War had been going on for about 40 years. During that time the United States and the Soviet Union spent huge amounts of money to develop nuclear weapons.

Each country also spent vast amounts on military struggles. In Chapter 19 you read about United States' efforts to stop the spread of communism in Vietnam. In the 1950s and 1960s, the Soviet Union used its army to crush movements for democracy in Hungary and Czechoslovakia. In the 1980s the Soviet Union invaded the South Asian nation of Afghanistan. The fighting in Afghanistan took its toll in many Soviet and Afghan lives and resources.

Problems were also growing within the Soviet Union and other Warsaw Pact countries. Government-run businesses could not provide enough food and other goods to meet people's needs. People could not discuss these problems without risking arrest. The communist system was not working well.

Focus Activity

READ TO LEARN
How has Europe changed with the fall of communism?

VOCABULARY
ethnic group
per capita income
European Union

PEOPLE
Mikhail Gorbachev
Ronald Reagan
Lech Walesa
Boris Yeltsin

PLACES
Yugoslavia
Balkan Peninsula

CHANGES IN THE SOVIET UNION

President Mikhail Gorbachev (MIHK el GAWR buh chawf) was the first top Soviet leader born and raised in Soviet society. Earlier leaders had been born before the Russian Revolution. Gorbachev's grandfather had been imprisoned as an "enemy of the people." As you read in Chapter 18, Josef Stalin jailed and killed millions in the 1930s.

As a young man Gorbachev studied law in Moscow and gained a position in the Communist party. By 1985 he had become the leader of the Soviet Union. One of his early actions was to point out the country's need for *perestroika* (per es TROY kuh), or rebuilding the failing Soviet economy. Gorbachev soon concluded however, that perestroika could not succeed without *glasnost* (GLAS nohst). Glasnost was his new policy of permission to speak freely.

The communist economy was controlled by the government. Workers had almost no voice in planning. There was little reason for them to work hard or carefully. Wages stayed much the same no matter how hard people worked. Some workers joked, "They pretend to pay us and we pretend to work."

Greater Freedom

Gorbachev believed that workers' views would change only when people had the freedom to speak up. He thought they should have some say in their government. Gorbachev said:

> *Wide, prompt, and frank information is evidence of [the government's] confidence in the people. . . . It enhances the resourcefulness of the working people.*

In the new era of glasnost, political prisoners were released. Some religious freedom was also allowed.

Soviet relations with the United States also began to improve. In 1987 Gorbachev signed a treaty with United States President Ronald Reagan. Both countries agreed to reduce nuclear weapons stockpiles. The Soviet Union also agreed to begin pulling troops out of its unpopular war with Afghanistan.

Food shortages in the Soviet Union led to long lines for food (left). Such problems caused Mikhail Gorbachev (above) to begin his policy of perestroika.

A "YEAR OF MIRACLES"

The ideas of glasnost and perestroika soon spread to neighboring eastern European nations controlled by the Soviet Union. In just one year—1989— these movements helped overturn more than 40 years of Communist rule.

Spring Thaw

In January 1989 Hungary planned its own elections. In 1956 a Hungarian revolt for more democracy had resulted in a fierce Soviet crackdown. Now Soviet troops stood by as Hungarians moved towards democracy. In May Hungarians tore down an electric fence separating Hungary from democratic Austria. In the months to come, many eastern Europeans used this hole in the "Iron Curtain" to escape to western Europe.

In Poland a workers' group called Solidarity won recognition from the government in March 1989. Eight years earlier shipworker Lech Walesa (LEK wuh LEN suh) and other Solidarity leaders had been jailed for protesting poor living conditions. Their group had been outlawed and almost disappeared under government pressure. In June 1989, however, the Solidarity party won many seats in both houses of Poland's Parliament.

Season of Fall

Still more changes took place in East Germany in the fall. Thousands of East Germans jammed city squares to demand changes in their government. East Germany's leader, Erich Honecker, ordered the army to break up the crowds. His command, however, was not followed. On October 15 Honecker stepped down. Twenty one days later East Berlin opened its gates to West Berlin.

Winter's Discontent

The "Year of Miracles," as 1989 has been called, did not end without bloodshed. In November students in Czechoslovakia protested for democracy. When they sang the American civil-rights song, "We Shall Overcome," police beat hundreds of the students. By December, however, the communist government had been overthrown. Citizens elected two new leaders. Both had served time in prison for speaking against the communist government. One year later, nearly all of eastern Europe had freed itself of communism.

Workers' rights protests in Poland, led by Lech Walesa (right), and in Romania (below) helped end communist rule in eastern Europe.

The Soviet Collapse

After the "Year of Miracles," the Soviet Union also began to change. You read in Chapter 18 that the Soviet Union's full name was the Union of Soviet Socialist Republics. Many different ethnic groups lived in its 15 republics. An ethnic group is a group of people who share a heritage of common customs, values, and language.

In 1990 and 1991, many republics broke away from Soviet control. This began with the republics of Latvia, Lithuania, and Estonia. In 1991 Russia, the biggest republic of all, held a democratic election. The Russians elected Boris Yeltsin to be their president.

These changes angered some Communist leaders. In August 1991 they tried to overthrow Gorbachev and take power themselves, moving tanks into Moscow. Before glasnost, these actions would have terrified citizens. Now, however, the Soviet people rallied behind Yeltsin, who, standing on top of a tank in Moscow, called these acts illegal. Soldiers refused to follow Communist orders. Without force to back them up, the communists had no chance of success. Yeltsin warned them:

> *You can build a throne of bayonets but you cannot sit on it for very long. There is no return to the past, nor will there be.*

Three days after it began, the revolt came to an end. Just as Yeltsin had predicted, there was no returning to the past. One by one Soviet republics declared their independence. In December 1991, Gorbachev stepped down and the Soviet Union ceased to exist. In its place stood 15 independent republics. Find these new nations on the map.

COUNTRIES OF THE FORMER SOVIET UNION

⊛ National capital

MAP WORK

Many of the republics that once made up the Soviet Union are now independent nations.

1. Which is the largest of these nations?
2. What is the capital of Ukraine?
3. Of which nation is Minsk the capital?
4. About how far is Moscow from the capital of Armenia?

AFTER THE FALL

There was much to cheer about as the Soviet Union broke apart. The Cold War had ended and the countries of the Warsaw Pact were turning toward democracy. Democracy and free enterprise had won the conflict with communism. Yet now there was much to worry about. Conflicts over nationalism and ethnic differences had replaced Cold War tensions.

Local Wars

One conflict resulting from these differences has involved the former Soviet republics of Armenia and Azerbaijan (ah zur bi JAHN). Armenia, mostly Christian, and Azerbaijan, mostly Muslim, fought a war over territory in 1993. Thousands of people left their homes as the borders shifted during the fighting.

Another place torn apart by war is the area that made up Yugoslavia until 1991. The area is part of the Balkan Peninsula, which has had a long history of ethnic and religious conflict. In 1991 Yugoslavia began to break apart. By 1992, the country had split into five separate republics. One of these republics is still called Yugoslavia. It includes Serbia and Montenegro. The other republics are Bosnia and Herzegovina, Croatia, Macedonia, and Slovenia. Find the republics on the map.

Since this breakup, many ethnic conflicts have flared in the republics. A civil war began in 1991 in Croatia between two ethnic groups, Croats and Serbs. Some of the worst fighting began in 1992 in the tiny country of Bosnia. There Bosnian Serbs, who are Orthodox Christians, and the mostly Muslim government battled for control. The fighting has had terrible effects for every group involved. Cities and towns all over the peninsula have been destroyed. Thousands of people on all sides of this war have been killed or forced to flee. In 1995, however, the region's leaders signed a peace agreement.

The war in Bosnia has left thousands of people homeless and hungry. Many refugees have fled areas of heavy fighting.

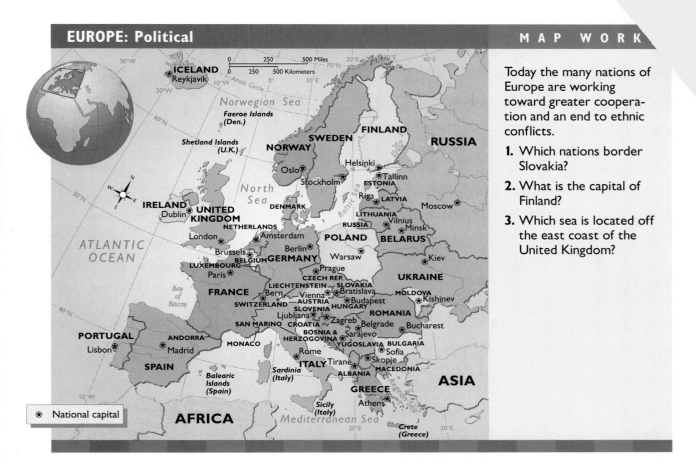

Today the many nations of Europe are working toward greater cooperation and an end to ethnic conflicts.

1. Which nations border Slovakia?

2. What is the capital of Finland?

3. Which sea is located off the east coast of the United Kingdom?

National capital

Life after Communism

Conflicts such as the one in Bosnia are among the toughest that European leaders face today. How far should nations go to help their neighbors? Ethnic conflicts in Europe and the debate over how to deal with them threaten to continue in the future. The issue is made more complicated by the reality of nuclear weapons. How can leaders be kept from using these weapons, left from the Cold War, if war breaks out?

Another concern for Europe is the continued struggle of eastern European economies. Years of communist rule left many old factories in need of complete rebuilding. Pollution from uncontrolled industry needs to be cleaned up. Costly rebuilding and repair efforts are moving along slowly, though. Today there is still a huge gap between the nations of western and eastern Europe in **per capita income**. Per capita income is the amount of money each person of a country would have if that country's total income were divided equally among its people. Look at the Infographic on page 602 to learn more about economies in Europe.

In 1995 the most powerful organization in Europe, the **European Union** (EU), agreed to consider allowing eastern European nations to join. The EU is a group of western European nations working to build a common economy throughout Europe. The EU has already broken down many barriers to trade and movement in western Europe. For example, cars and trucks can now travel freely between the nations of western Europe. German students can apply to British or French universities as easily as to colleges in their hometowns.

graphic

...y of Europe

...nd methods of
...culture have strengthened the
economies of many nations in Europe.
Look at the graph to see the gross
domestic product of five European
nations. Remember the GDP is the
total value of
goods and ser-
vices produced
in one year.
Which is
highest?

With 8.8 million people, Moscow is Europe's largest city and an important Russian economic center.

ZEHN DEUTSCHE MARK
1777–1855 Carl Friedr. Gauß
10
DD 6248255 N6

German marks

Rural-Urban Population

Rural 27 %

Urban 73 %

Coal (above) is an important natural resource for many European countries. It is used for heating and by industries. Cheese from Switzerland (below) is among many products of Europe's vast and profitable agriculture industry.

GDP: Largest Five Economies

GDP in billions of United States dollars (1993)

- 1,400
- 1,200
- 1,000
- 800
- 600
- 400
- 200
- 0

GERMANY 1,911
FRANCE 1,252
ITALY 991
UNITED KINGDOM 819
SPAIN 479

Source: The World Bank World Development Report

WHY IT MATTERS

The EU's pledge to help its eastern neighbors has raised hopes that all of Europe might someday belong to this powerful organization. Supporters see much to be gained. They hope for greater wealth and a lessened threat of war in Europe. Already, former enemies like France and Germany have become close partners through the EU.

However, many people wonder if Europe can ever be truly united. Can nationalist, ethnic, and religious conflicts—dating from at least the time of the Crusades—be set aside? Will nations allow important decisions to be made for them by an international governing body? If a time of crisis comes, will alliances between the nations hold? Only time will tell. For now the bold experiment of the EU continues to reshape life in Europe as the twenty-first century approaches.

Reviewing Facts and Ideas

SUM IT UP

- Mikhail Gorbachev's program of glasnost sparked pro-democracy movements in the Soviet Union and eastern Europe in the late 1980s.

- Communist governments throughout eastern Europe fell in 1989, called the "Year of Miracles."

- The Cold War ended when the Soviet Union ceased to exist in 1991. However, new conflicts rooted in national, ethnic, and religious differences arose in Europe.

- The European Union has created a strong partnership between many European nations.

THINK ABOUT IT

1. Why has 1989 been called a "Year of Miracles" in Europe?

2. What problems and conflicts have arisen in the Soviet Union and the nations of eastern Europe since the fall of communism?

3. **FOCUS** What are some of the challenges the European Union faces in bringing unity to all of Europe?

4. **THINKING SKILL** *Make conclusions* about how ordinary people brought about the end of the Cold War.

5. **WRITE** Use what you have learned about European history this year to explain why the European Union can be called a "bold experiment" in the continent's history.

THINKING SKILLS

Evaluating Information for Accuracy

WHY THE SKILL MATTERS

In the last lesson you read about the civil war that is raging in Bosnia. Its capital, Sarajevo, has often been bombed. Like most historical events, this conflict is complicated and difficult to understand. Many people have said many different things about this war. How will you know what to believe?

Being able to **evaluate** the **accuracy** of information is crucial to understanding history. To *evaluate* means to judge something. *Accuracy* refers to the truth of a statement. When we evaluate information for accuracy, we make a judgment about whether the information is true.

Historians constantly evaluate sources for accuracy. To reach a correct understanding of history, historians seek to use only those sources they feel are accurate. As other sources are discovered, however, historians sometimes change their interpretations of historical events. "History," in fact, is always an interpretation based on the most accurate information available. Time is one test of accuracy. Most people today might consider a particular statement to be accurate. Other information, however, may later prove that in fact something else is true.

The skill of evaluating information for accuracy combines some of the Thinking Skills presented in this book. For example, you must determine point of view and analyze the credibility of a source. Other Thinking Skills are called upon as well, such as distinguishing fact from opinion. You might want to review these skills before going on.

USING THE SKILL

Read these sources explaining events in Bosnia's civil war. The statements are from newspapers and magazines that were published in 1992. As you read, consider the following questions: What are the writers' points of view? Are the sources credible? Is the information fact or opinion?

> The situation in Bosnia has grown both more desperate and more complex.
>
> New Republic

> [Bosnia's civil war is] one of the worst . . . emergencies of our time.
>
> U.N. Chronicle

> More than 17,000 have been killed and 110,000 wounded [in Sarajevo].
>
> Time

> Residents of Sarajevo are cutting up door frames for firewood. . . . Bosnians are living on a diet of nettles [plants].
>
> U.S. News and World Report

The sources describe the situation in Bosnia as a serious one. How can you determine if this is an accurate view of the situation?

When evaluating information for accuracy, you should try to determine the author's point of view. These sources were all written by reporters whose job is to tell people about world events. Next, determine the credibility of the sources. Each of these is from an established news publication. They are likely to be credible.

You should also compare the sources to one another. When sources present similar information, we can conclude that the information is probably accurate. Remember, though, that later information may prove something different!

Last, determine which of the statements are facts and which are opinions. You will notice that the first two statements are opinions. The last two are facts that can be proved. All however, are saying the same thing: the situation in Bosnia is very bad.

HELPING Yourself

- **Evaluating for accuracy** determines which statements can be considered true.
- **Determine the author's point of view.**
- **Analyze the credibility of the source.**
- **Compare the source to other credible sources.**
- **Identify facts and opinions.**
- **Evaluate for accuracy.**

TRYING THE SKILL

Now evaluate the accuracy of this source. Its teenage author, Zlata Filipovic, lived her whole life in Sarajevo until the war forced her and her family to leave. In May 1993 she wrote in her diary:

I have another sad piece of news for you. A boy in my drama club got killed! . . . A shell fell in front of the community center and a horrible piece of shrapnel [metal] *killed him. His name was Eldin and he was a refugee from Grbavica.*

Another innocent victim of this disgusting war, another child among thousands of other children killed in Sarajevo. I feel so sorry, he was a sweet, good boy.

According to Filipovic, who are the victims of the fighting in Sarajevo? Are her statements facts, or opinions, or some of each? What does or does not give her viewpoint credibility? Make your own evaluation of whether this source is accurate.

REVIEWING THE SKILL

1. Why is it important to evaluate information for accuracy? How can you do so?

2. What did you do to determine the accuracy of Zlata Filipovic's statement?

3. How does this skill build on other thinking skills you learned about earlier in the book?

4. How can the ability to evaluate information for accuracy help you in your own life?

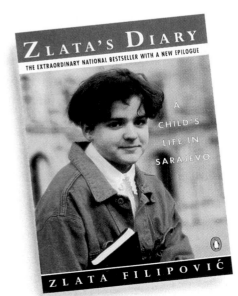

ZLATA'S DIARY
THE EXTRAORDINARY NATIONAL BESTSELLER WITH A NEW EPILOGUE

A CHILD'S LIFE IN SARAJEVO

ZLATA FILIPOVIĆ

A CHANGING AFRICA

Focus Activity

READ TO LEARN
What did South Africans do to achieve democracy?

VOCABULARY
apartheid
township
sanction

PEOPLE
Nelson Mandela
Frederik Willem de Klerk

PLACES
Cape Town
Soweto
Johannesburg

READ ALOUD

"When I walked to the voting station, my mind dwelt on the heroes who had fallen so that I might be where I was that day, the men and women who had made the ultimate sacrifice for a cause that was now finally succeeding. . . . I did not go into that voting station alone on April 27 [1994]; I was casting my vote with all of them."

Nelson Mandela wrote these words in his autobiography. Mandela and millions of other South Africans had finally voted in their nation's first democratic election.

THE BIG PICTURE

Democracy once seemed like a dream in South Africa. Europeans had ruled much of South Africa since the 1700s. Dutch settlers formed a colony at Cape Town. Find Cape Town on the map on page 607. Their descendants are called Afrikaners. Afrikaners make up 60 percent of South Africa's white population today. However, whites are only about 19 percent of the population. Most of the people are black.

The British took control from the Dutch in 1814. By 1900 Britain had established rule over all of South Africa. A large European population lived in the colony. When South Africa won full independence from Britain in 1961, the white minority continued to rule. Blacks like Nelson Mandela faced a future without freedom or a voice in government.

AFRICA: Political

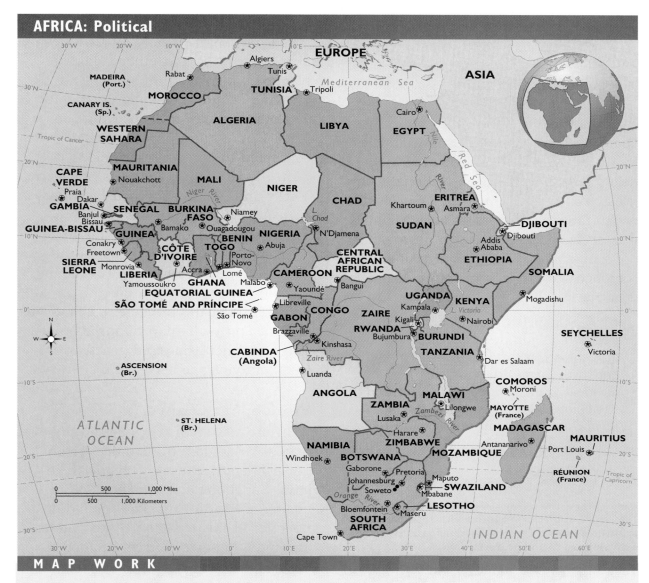

MAP WORK

More than 50 nations are found on the continent of Africa today.

1. What is the capital of Gabon?

2. Which nations border Sudan to the east?

3. Of which nation is Rabat the capital?

SOUTH AFRICA DIVIDED

Even after independence, blacks did not gain many rights or freedoms. They could not vote, own land, or move freely in the country. In 1948 white leaders created a system of laws called apartheid (uh PAHR tid). In the Afrikaans (af ri KAHNZ) language spoken by Afrikaners, *apartheid* means "apartness."

Under apartheid, millions of blacks were forced to give up their land to whites and live in townships, crowded areas for blacks in or near cities. Blacks and other nonwhites could not live or go to school in white neighborhoods. Township schools and services were of poor quality. In some cases, these services did not exist.

PROTEST AND STRUGGLE

The South African police often used force to uphold apartheid. The threat of violence did not stop many black South Africans from protesting, however. An important leader in the fight to end apartheid was lawyer Nelson Mandela. In 1960 the government banned Mandela's group, the African National Congress (ANC), along with other protest organizations. Four years later Mandela was accused of planning to destroy the government. He was put on trial and sentenced to life in jail. Before Mandela was put in jail he declared:

> *I have cherished the ideal of a democratic and free society in which all persons live together in harmony and with equal opportunities. It is an ideal which I hope to live for and to achieve. But if needs be, it is an ideal for which I am prepared to die.*

Nelson Mandela was kept in prison for 27 years.

Thousands of blacks in South Africa took part in protests against apartheid. The police often acted with violence to end protests.

Growing Tensions

During the 1960s and 1970s, sales of diamonds, gold, and other valuable resources increased. In spite of the growing economy, mining companies and other employers kept wages for black workers low. South African police continued to enforce apartheid.

In the late 1970s, tensions between blacks and police increased in South Africa. In 1976 thousands of young black students led a protest for better education in Soweto. Soweto is the name for the "South-West Townships" outside the city of Johannesburg. Police fired at the protesters, killing one student and wounding hundreds more. The bloodshed triggered years of protests and violence across the country.

Working for Change

In the 1980s countries set up sanctions against the South African government because of its apartheid laws. Sanctions are penalties placed against a nation to make it change its policies. In this case the United States and many other countries decided to boycott South African goods. In addition, South African athletes were banned from international sports events like the Olympics. World leaders hoped that these sanctions would convince the South African government to end its policy of apartheid.

The struggle for freedom continued in South Africa. Blacks often sang a song called *N'kosi Sikelel'i Afrika* (n KAW see see keh LEH lee AH free kah), or "Prayer for Africa." Groups such as the African National Congress adopted it as an anthem. What similarities can you find in the words of *N'kosi Sikelel'i Afrika* and the United States' national anthem?

N'KOSI SIKELEL'I AFRIKA
PRAYER FOR AFRICA

Words and Music by
Enoch Sontonga

Moderate

Zulu: Nkaw-see see-keh-leh lee Ah-free-kah, Mah-loo-pah-kah-nyee-soo-
English: Bless, O Lord, our coun-try Af-ri-ca, So that all may see her

pawn-daw lwah-yoh; Yeez-wah eem-ee-tahn-dah-zoh yeh-too.
glo-ry held high; Lis-ten and pro-tect us, be our guide.

1.
Nkaw-see see-keh-leh-lah, Nkaw-see see-keh-leh-lah.
Bless our moth-er Af-ri-ca. Bless our moth-er Af-ri-ca.

2.
Tee-nah loo-sah-paw lwah-yoh, Waw-zah maw-yah,_____
Bless our___ moth-er Af-ri-ca. Spir-it de-scend,_____

Waw-zah maw-yah,___ Waw-zah maw-yah, aw-yeeng, chweh-leh.
Spir-it de-scend,___ Spir-it de-scend, Spir-it de-scend, Spir-it di-vine.

Oo-see-see-keh-leh-lah. Tee-nah loo-sah-paw lwah-yoh.
Bless our moth-er Af-ri-ca. Bless our___ moth-er Af-ri-ca.

Nelson Mandela and F. W. de Klerk greeted a crowd of South Africans after Mandela became president of the nation.

AFRICA TODAY

In 1989 Frederik Willem de Klerk became the president of South Africa. De Klerk thought that the time had come for change in South Africa. In 1990 he released Nelson Mandela, then 72 years old, from prison. In 1991 De Klerk abolished most apartheid laws. As a result international sanctions against South Africa were stopped.

Even bigger changes followed in 1993. De Klerk, Mandela, and other leaders agreed that national elections should be held the following year. They would be the first in the nation's history in which all South Africans, black and white, would have the right to vote.

Despite threats of violence by extreme groups opposed to democracy, the elections were held peacefully in April 1994. Black citizens, who made up 72 percent of the total population, lined up and cast the first votes of their lives. Nelson Mandela was elected president. Members of the African National Congress won many other positions in government as well.

Life in South Africa

Democracy has put down strong new roots in South Africa. The nation, however, still faces many challenges. The challenge of overcoming the effects of apartheid will be a difficult one and will likely take years. The government is now building thousands of new homes for poor people. Many more are needed. Formerly all-white schools have been opened to students of all races. However, most black students in South Africa still attend overcrowded, poorly equipped schools.

Facing the Future in Africa

South Africa is not alone in facing such great challenges. Other African nations are also working for change. Many hope to move toward democracy after years of dictatorships and government corruption.

The greatest problem facing most African nations is poverty. As you read in Chapter 19, the economies of colonies in Africa were built to create wealth for Europe. The end of colonialism left many African nations economically weak. Now these nations are struggling to build strong businesses and develop industry. As their economies grow, African nations continue to strengthen through international trade.

One advantage for many African countries is a wealth of natural resources. Botswana produces even more diamonds each year than its neighbor, South Africa. Nigeria pumps thousands of gallons of oil each day and Algeria is rich in natural gas.

Infographic

Economy of Africa

Many African nations have gradually developed strong businesses. Because much of the continent's population is rural, agriculture has long played an important role in the economies of many of its nations. Today the gross domestic products of several nations are growing steadily. Which one has the largest GDP?

With a population of 6.6 million, Cairo is the largest city in Africa. Cairo is the center of Egypt's government as well as of its manufacturing and tourist industries.

Rural-Urban Population

Urban 31 %

Rural 69 %

South African rand

When rich deposits of gold were found in South Africa in the 1800's, mining became the center of the nation's economy. Cattle herding has long been an important economic activity in Africa. For many cultures the cattle symbolize wealth.

GDP: Largest Five Economies

GDP in billions of United States dollars (1993)

SOUTH AFRICA	106
ALGERIA	40
EGYPT	36
NIGERIA	31
MOROCCO	27

Source: The World Bank World Development Report

After years of unequal schooling for blacks, children of all races now attend classes together in South African cities.

LOOKING TO THE FUTURE

Just as Europeans formed the European Union (EU), in 1980 many southern African nations formed the Southern African Development Community (SADC). Economies of the SADC member nations are not yet as closely linked as those in the European Union. Many experts, however, believe that southern Africa's natural resources and growing democratic movements hold great promise for the economies of individual nations and for the region as a whole.

WHY IT MATTERS

It may take many years for Africans to overcome their histories of colonialism and economic problems. Yet events such as the end of apartheid and the election of a democratic government in South Africa have given many people hope. Throughout the coming years many of the peoples of Africa's diverse nations hope to continue the development of democratic governments. By gaining, protecting, and practicing new rights and freedoms, people in Africa will shape their own futures.

✓/ Reviewing Facts and Ideas

SUM IT UP

- After gaining independence from British rule, South Africa was ruled by a white minority.

- In 1994 South African apartheid ended. Black and other nonwhite citizens voted in a national election for the first time, electing Nelson Mandela president.

- Many African nations are moving to overcome years of colonialism and economic problems.

THINK ABOUT IT

1. What was apartheid?

2. Why are natural resources so important to Africa's future?

3. **FOCUS** How did South Africans succeed in ending apartheid? What did their success mean to the nation?

4. **THINKING SKILL** What was the *cause* of the Soweto students' uprising of 1976? What were some of its *effects*?

5. **GEOGRAPHY** Locate Cape Town, South Africa, on a globe. Write a paragraph explaining why Dutch settlers may have chosen this spot for a colony.

CITIZENSHIP
MAKING A DIFFERENCE

A More Equal Chance for Justice

ALEXANDRA, SOUTH AFRICA—Before they met in prison, Ashwell Zwane (zwa NAY) and Bernent Lekalakala (LEE cah la cah la) already had much in common. Both came from the black township of Alexandra. Both knew firsthand the legal and social problems people in their community faced. Both were also working to end apartheid in South Africa. Anti-apartheid activities landed each man in prison. There, Zwane and Lekalakala became friends.

During their years in prison, both saw that poor people accused of committing crimes often could not afford to hire lawyers to help them. According to Zwane, "We agreed that when we got out of prison, we would establish a center that would help people who could not afford to pay legal fees. It was our dream." In 1988, while still in prison, both started studying to become lawyers.

Lekalakala was released from prison in 1989 and Zwane in 1990. Both continued their law studies at the same university. In 1993 they graduated and talked about starting a community law center where poor people could get legal advice for free. A local business donated office space in 1994, and the Alexandra Community Law Clinic opened its doors.

About 25 people visit the clinic each day. Some need lawyers to represent them in court. Others seek advice or help in settling a conflict.

The clinic works to educate people about their rights. "People will not appreciate our new democratic system as long as they don't understand what rights it offers them," says Zwane. The lawyers often talk with high school students about their legal rights. "The law affects people's lives every day. In South Africa's new constitution, all people have legal rights. What we have to do is ensure that the poor know what their rights are and how to protect them."

" . . . all people have legal rights."

A CHANGING ASIA

Focus Activity

READ TO LEARN

How has economic growth affected the peoples of eastern Asia?

VOCABULARY

Pacific Rim

PEOPLE

Deng Xiaoping

PLACES

Japan
South Korea
Singapore
Tiananmen Square
Hong Kong

READ ALOUD

World War II left big stretches of Asia in ruins. China, Hong Kong, and other areas conquered by Japanese forces lay in shambles. Much of Japan had also been destroyed. Most buildings in its major cities had been turned to ashes by Allied bombs. People wearing rags hunted for scraps to eat. In 1946 few would have guessed that Japan and other countries of Asia would become economic giants within a few decades.

THE BIG PICTURE

In Chapter 18 you read that the Cold War began in Europe in the middle 1940s. Before long the conflict between communist and democratic governments deeply divided Asia as well. Communists took control of North Korea in 1948, mainland China in 1949, and North Vietnam in 1954. Both communist and non-communist nations throughout Asia faced similar challenges. How could they build strong governments and economies after years of war?

You have already read about Mao Zedong's attempts to meet such challenges in China. His programs, known as the Great Leap Forward and Cultural Revolution, led to some disastrous results for the Chinese people. Meanwhile, other nations in East Asia tried different methods to build stable governments and industries. Perhaps most successful of all in its efforts to rebuild after war was Japan.

THE REBUILDING OF JAPAN

Between 1945 and 1952 the United States, which occupied Japan after World War II, oversaw the rebuilding of Japan. Under United States direction, a new Japanese constitution was written. The new constitution gave Japanese women equal rights as citizens for the first time. The new constitution also stated that Japan could not go to war. United States supervision of Japan ended in 1952.

Building Japan's Economy

In Chapter 18 you read that the United States sent thousands of troops to fight in Korea between 1950 and 1953. Japan became the main United States base. At its closest point Japan is only 100 miles away from Korea. Thanks partly to the huge American military demand for everything from trucks to sleeping bags, bandages, and bootlaces, Japan's economy boomed.

After the Korean war ended, the Japanese government took steps to keep businesses growing. Schools taught business and technical skills so students would become good industrial workers. The government encouraged companies to produce goods for export. As more cash came in from trade, money was invested in new factories. More cash and new factories led to an increase in Japanese exports.

By the 1960s Japan's economy was expanding at a very fast rate. In 1950 Japan's Gross Domestic Product had been smaller than the GDP of any western country. By 1965 it had grown larger than those of Britain and France. Today the United States' GDP is still the world's largest, followed by that of Japan.

Manufacturing and shipping contributed greatly to Japan's economic expansion.

JAPAN AND THE PACIFIC RIM

The big push to industrialize made Japan wealthy. Although Japan is poor in natural resources, its workers turned imported raw materials into expensive goods. Imports such as steel and oil were used to make cars, computer parts, televisions, and cameras. The demand for these products helped make Japan one of the world's richest nations by the 1980s.

Other nations of the Pacific Rim—the ring of countries surrounding the Pacific Ocean—have grown economically as well. Look at the map to locate the Asian countries of the Pacific Rim. Among them are South Korea, Taiwan,

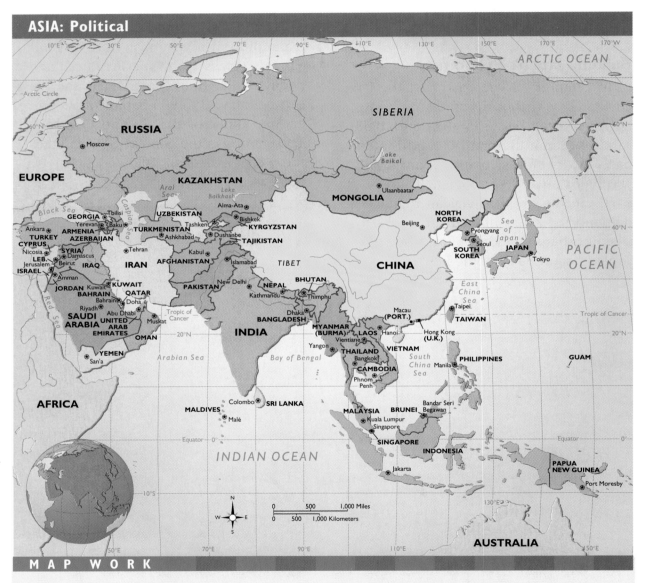

ASIA: Political

M A P   W O R K

Many Asian nations have developed strong economies based on industry. Several nations support large populations.

1. Which nations border Pakistan to the north?

2. Of which nation is Port Moresby the capital?

3. Which nations border Yemen?

The modern buildings of downtown Singapore (right) reflect the wealth of the city and its businesses.

Hong Kong, and the Southeast Asian nations of Singapore and Thailand. Also part of the Pacific Rim are Australia, New Zealand, and the islands of Oceania in the South Pacific.

The Rise of the Pacific Rim

Economic growth in the Pacific Rim has led to a shift in the power of the world's regions. For hundreds of years much of world trade and power centered around the Atlantic Ocean. The Industrial Revolution of the 1700s and 1800s brought great wealth to the United States and nations of Europe.

With the growth of Pacific Rim nations, however, a new region of wealth and power has emerged. These Asian nations have built economies that compete with those of the West.

South Korea is one example of a Pacific Rim nation that has industrialized rapidly in the last few decades. The Korean War left the nation in ruins in the early 1950s. The country quickly began rebuilding, however. Today many Korean companies build cars, electronics, and steel products.

Growth in Singapore

The tiny republic of Singapore has also become a giant in world trade. In the 1950s many people in Singapore lived on small farms or in fishing villages. Few homes had running water or electricity. Today the electronics industry provides many high paying jobs. Most people live in comfortable high-rise apartments. Many homes have televisions and other types of modern electronic equipment. Such appliances are considered luxuries throughout much of Asia.

Some people in Singapore feel that comfort has come at a high price, though. To maintain order, the government closely rules every aspect of daily life. Cameras throughout Singapore watch for people breaking laws. Some newspapers, magazines, and films are banned because they present views the government dislikes. Those who criticize the government in any way face harsh punishment. Singapore's leaders believe a tightly controlled society is more important than free speech and other democratic rights.

CHANGE COMES TO CHINA

Should jobs and the economy be more important in society than citizens' rights and freedoms? What is too high a price to pay for economic growth? People in the wealthy, capitalist nation of Singapore are not the only ones debating such questions. People in China have also been facing this complex issue.

According to legend the French leader Napoleon Bonaparte declared in the 1800s, "when China wakes, it will shake the world." Today about one out of every five people on Earth lives in China. To business leaders in other countries, China's huge population means a huge number of customers. To military planners, it means a possibly massive army. To world leaders, this population means that China's decisions could have huge effects on the rest of the world.

A Changing Economy

After the death of Mao Zedong in 1976, a power struggle began among China's top leaders. It ended when Deng Xiaoping (DUNG SHOW PING) won control of the government in 1978. Deng was a veteran of the Long March

In 1989, thousands of students (above) gathered in Beijing to demonstrate for democracy. About one month after they began, the Chinese government brought in tanks (right) to end the protests.

618

and a victim of the Cultural Revolution. When Deng gained power, his government moved away from Mao's strict style of communism.

Farmers were given more control over their work. They were allowed to sell surplus crops for profit. Mao had tried to root out everything foreign in China. Deng, on the other hand, encouraged students to study abroad. He hoped they would learn new science skills that could help China. Foreign companies began to do business in China, selling everything from airplanes to hamburgers.

A Movement For Democracy

Deng's changes led to strong economic growth. By the spring of 1989—the "Year of Miracles" in Europe—many Chinese hoped that glasnost would spread to China. In May 1989 about one million students gathered to protest for democracy in an immense square in Beijing. **Tiananmen** (TYEN AHN MEN) **Square** is at the heart of the Chinese central government area. It leads into the Forbidden City, which you read was built for China's emperors during the Ming dynasty.

Deng refused to let supporters of glasnost and democracy take over Tiananmen Square. That June the government ordered dozens of tanks into the square to destroy the democracy movement. Hundreds of student protesters were killed. Many more were wounded, and their leaders were thrown in prison. Deng succeeded in ending the democracy movement in China for the time being.

In the early 1990s Deng continued to crack down on government protesters. At the same time he welcomed more free enterprise in China. His slogan, "to get rich is glorious," started a wave of

Deng Xiaoping (above) encouraged free enterprise in China even after crushing the 1989 democracy movement.

new businesses and building in China's cities. China was moving closer to becoming a free enterprise economy. The Communist party remained in control, however, and continued to prevent democracy from increasing.

Uncertainty in Hong Kong

One place where people are especially interested in the changes in China is **Hong Kong**. This thriving city, a center for international trade, has been a British colony since the 1800s. In 1984 Britain agreed to return Hong Kong to Chinese control in 1997. The agreement also stated that China would allow the people of Hong Kong to keep their own laws and free enterprise system for 50 more years.

Even with China's promise many people in Hong Kong are concerned. They fear that democracy may be restricted under Chinese control. Many people have begun to leave Hong Kong to settle in Canada and the United States. Others are waiting to see what changes will take place in China.

Infographic

Economy of Asia

Growing economies in Asia are strengthening the political power of the countries in the region. Japan dominates the region in GDP. However, wealth in natural resources and changes toward free markets are helping to bring strong economies to other countries. Which country is second to Japan in GDP?

Japanese yen

Rural-Urban Population

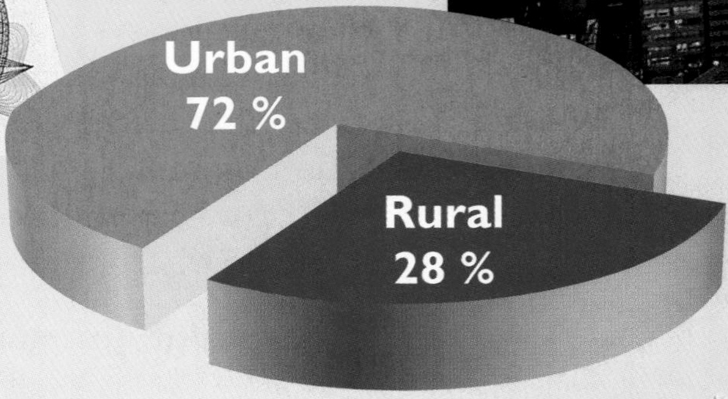

Urban 72 %

Rural 28 %

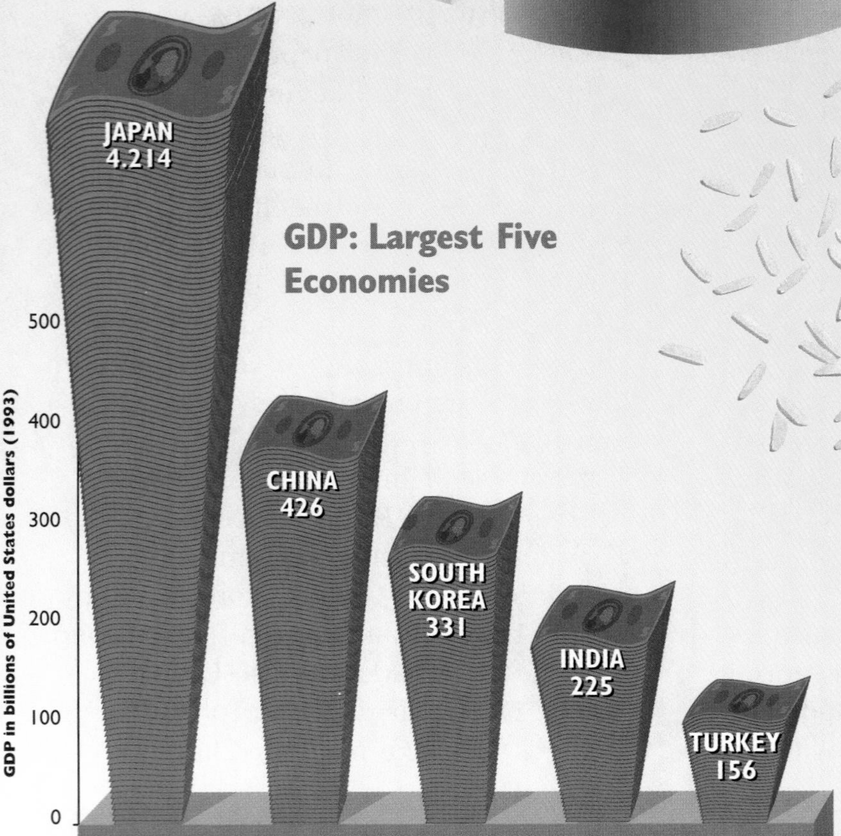

Tokyo (above) is Asia's largest city, with 8.1 million people. It is the center of economic activity in Japan and has over 80,000 factories and company headquarters.

GDP: Largest Five Economies

GDP in billions of United States dollars (1993)

- JAPAN 4.214
- CHINA 426
- SOUTH KOREA 331
- INDIA 225
- TURKEY 156

500
400
300
200
100
0

Rice (above) is a major crop in much of Asia. In India more employees work in textiles than any other industry.

Source: The World Bank World Development Report

WHY IT MATTERS

In only about 50 years, the nations around Asia's Pacific Rim have grown from areas devastated by war to major economic powers. The rapid economic growth of the nations in this region is likely to continue well into the twenty-first century. Such growth assures that the power of that part of Asia will continue to increase.

As economies develop and become more connected, whatever happens in one nation or continent will have great impact in other parts of the world. Because of this, observers around the world watch carefully to detect signs of what is in store for the most populous continent.

DID YOU KNOW?

How did Hong Kong get its name?

During the Ming Dynasty, Hong Kong shipped incense to mainland China. It was because of the sweet-smelling incense that the Chinese called the area Hong Kong. *Hong Kong* means fragrant harbor.

Until the 1800s Hong Kong was composed mainly of small fishing and farming villages. In 1842 the British won control of Hong Kong after a war with China. The first British-appointed governor of Hong Kong declared it a "free port." This term means that taxes are not collected on goods brought into the port. This advantage, along with Hong Kong's location, made it an ideal place for economic growth.

Today Hong Kong has grown into a center of banking, trade, and manufacturing. The region has over 100 banks, 4 stock exchanges, and over 38,000 factories.

✓ Reviewing Facts and Ideas

SUM IT UP

- The growing nations of the Pacific Rim make up an important new region of economic power.

- Japan's industrialization was helped by United States involvement and the Korean War. Growth was also dependent on Japanese government policies and education.

- For many Pacific Rim countries, such as Singapore, economic growth has been stressed over democracy.

THINK ABOUT IT

1. How did the Korean War affect the Japanese economy?

2. What is the Pacific Rim? Why can its growth be described as a major shift in world history?

3. **FOCUS** How has economic growth changed life for Asians since the end of World War II?

4. **THINKING SKILL** What steps would you take to *evaluate the accuracy* of the GDP graph on page 620?

5. **WRITE** Should concern about jobs and the economy have priority over the protection of individual rights? Write a paragraph describing your view of this issue.

THE CHANGING AMERICAS

READ ALOUD

"The future is the great common thread tying together Americans." To Mexican poet Octavio Paz, the "thread" that will tie people of the Americas together is not just the trade of exports and imports. It is also the free trade of ideas and cultural traditions.

THE BIG PICTURE

Earlier in this chapter you read about the great changes sweeping through Europe, Africa, and Asia in the second half of the 1900s. These include political revolutions, industrial revolutions, and a movement toward greater unity among nations. It should not surprise you to learn that change has been transforming the nations of the Americas as well.

Before World War II, the United States and Canada were the only major industrial nations in the Americas. The other nations were mainly rural. In the past Brazil imported most of its manufactured goods such as clothes and cars. Today, however, Brazilian factory workers make everything from blue jeans to armored cars. Some of their most important buyers are other nations of the Americas such as Canada and the United States.

Trade has made the nations of the Americas increasingly interdependent. This means that they count on each other to meet the needs and wants of their peoples. Agreements about trade and politics have made countries like the United States, Mexico, and Canada closer neighbors.

Focus Activity

READ TO LEARN
In what ways are the nations of the Americas working together on common problems?

VOCABULARY
interdependent
urbanization
NAFTA
bilingual
Internet

PEOPLE
Jean-Bertrand Aristide

PLACES
Brazil
Canada
United States
Haiti
Dominican Republic
Mexico
Mexico City

NATIONS OF THE AMERICAS

The Western Hemisphere includes two cultural regions. The United States and Canada make up Anglo-America. This region was influenced strongly by British culture. Latin America includes Mexico, Central America, the Caribbean islands, and South America. It was influenced by Spain, Portugal, and France.

Many Caribbean islands have gained independence from European control since the 1800s. **Haiti** in 1804 and the **Dominican Republic** in 1844 were the first. As you can see on the map, these nations are both located on one island—Hispaniola. Most Caribbean nations became independent after World War II.

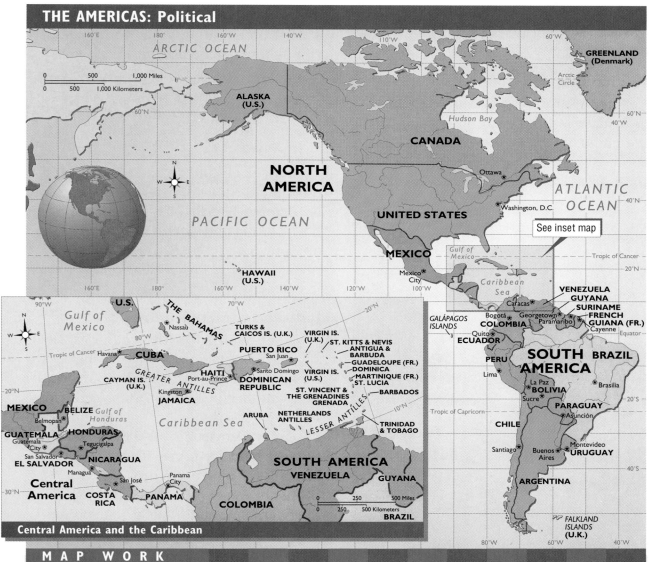

THE AMERICAS: Political

Central America and the Caribbean

MAP WORK

The two culture regions of the Americas have been shaped by European influences. Today the many nations of these regions continue to develop new and unique traditions.

1. Of which nation is Montevideo the capital? In which of the Americas is this city located?

2. Which is farther west—Mexico City or Washington, D.C.?

3. What is the capital of Jamaica?

LATIN AMERICA TODAY

Mexico, a country of 92 million people, has become one of the world's major industrial powers. It is an important producer of such items as oil, electronic goods, and cars.

Mexico's industrial revolution began during World War II. A decline in world trade left Mexico with a shortage of manufactured goods. Because of this shortage and the need for more money, Mexican leaders decided to industrialize their nation.

Mexico City

After World War II, hundreds of new factories began to fill Mexico City, the nation's capital. New jobs brought about three million people there from rural areas between 1940 and 1970.

Oil drilling (above) became important in Mexico when vast oil reserves were found.

During the 1970s oil was discovered in southern Mexico. This "black gold" helped pay for more businesses in Mexico City and other cities. By the early 1990s Mexico City had become the world's second-largest urban area—behind Tokyo, Japan.

Need for Jobs

Mexico's economic growth has created riches for a few, but has not helped all Mexicans. Many in Mexico City have a hard time finding work and housing. One woman remembered:

When we arrived in Mexico City, we lived in cardboard boxes and [searched] for food from the garbage dump. I cried. This is not what I had dreamed of.

Many thousands of Mexicans cross the United States border each year, legally and illegally. These Mexicans can go from making about $4 a day to $4 an hour. Living costs, however, are much higher in the United States than in Mexico.

Jobs and the Environment

Other Latin American countries face similar economic problems. In the 1980s Brazil's government offered poor people free land in the Amazon rain forest for farming. Thousands of families moved to this fragile environment. People set fires to clear land for crops. The rain forest land was ill-suited for growing rice or beans, however. Many people soon left their farms, though much damage had already been done to the land, the animals, and the Indians who had long lived there. This damage was then made worse by the arrival of new logging, mining, and ranching businesses.

One Brazilian scientist, Jacques Marcovitch, called for a new approach to this difficult problem:

We need strategies that are both economically productive and environmentally sound. . . . You cannot talk about ecology to people who are struggling to survive.

Today Brazil's government is working with other nations in the Americas to preserve the rain forests. Some United States companies are trying to build a demand for rain forest products such as nuts and oils. This demand helps to create jobs in the Amazon that are friendly to the environment.

Fighting the Drug Problem

Another difficult problem facing nations of the Americas is the drug trade. Farmers in Colombia, Peru, and Bolivia raise coca plants which are used to make cocaine. This illegal and dangerous drug brings little money to farmers. Most profits go to crime organizations that sell the drugs around the world. The United States has joined other nations to try to stamp out the drug trade. Their efforts include destroying coca fields and helping farmers to raise other crops.

Growth of Democracy

During much of the 1900s most Latin American countries were ruled by dictators. Dictators controlled the Caribbean nation of Haiti for almost 30 years beginning in 1957. In 1970 Chile, which had experienced dictatorship before, came under the rule of a military dictator who held power for 15 years.

In the 1980s democratic movements swept through the Americas, overturning most of the dictatorships. The people of Chile, for example, elected a new democratic government in 1988.

Two years later, Haitians elected **Jean-Bertrand Aristide** (JAHN BAIR trahnd AH rihs teed) to be their president. Military leaders ov[...] him the following year. With [...] of the United States, Aristide [...] his office in 1994.

Growing Cities

Just as in Mexico City, millions of job-seekers have moved to cities throughout Latin America. In the 1970s in Brazil, 30 million people moved from the countryside to urban areas. Find the percentage of people now living in rural and urban areas in the Americas on the Infographic on page 628.

Urbanization, or growth of cities, has brought other challenges. As you can see on the chart on this page, two out of the five largest cities in the world are in Latin America.

THE WORLD'S FIVE LARGEST CITIES

Tokyo-Yokohama, Japan	28,447,000 population / 1,089 sq. miles
Mexico City, Mexico	23,913,000 population / 522 sq. miles
São Paulo, Brazil	21,539,000 population / 451 sq. miles
Seoul, South Korea	19,065,000 population / 342 sq. miles
New York, United States	14,638,000 population / 1,247 sq. miles

Source: 1995 Information Please Almanac

CHART WORK

The world's five largest cities are located in Asia and the Americas.

1. What is the population of Tokyo-Yokohama?
2. Which city is located in Brazil?

Fiber optics (top) and other technologies have transformed our lives—from business, such as in the New York Stock Exchange (left), to medicine (above).

INTO THE FUTURE

The three largest countries of North America—the United States, Canada, and Mexico, are working to develop strong ties. In 1993 the North American Free Trade Agreement, NAFTA, went into effect. Its goal is to increase trade by lowering taxes on goods traded among these nations.

Canadian Provinces

As Canadians created closer ties with the United States, they have debated the loosening ties within their own country. In Chapter 16 you read that French explorers began the first European colony in Canada, based around the St. Lawrence River and the city of Quebec. Today that region forms a province called Quebec. Most people here are bilingual—able to speak two languages. The French Canadians, as they are called, speak both French and English, but follow French customs.

Canada's other nine provinces are rooted in the English language and British traditions. Many French Canadians want Quebec to form a separate country. After a close vote in 1995, however, Quebec has remained part of Canada.

World Role for the United States

As the remaining superpower, the United States continues to play an active role in world affairs. In 1991 the United States led an alliance of nations that sent troops to the Persian Gulf region. They forced Iraq to withdraw its troops from neighboring Kuwait. Iraq had invaded Kuwait and wanted to make it part of Iraq.

In the 1990s the United States assisted the United Nations in efforts to bring food to starving citizens in the African country of Somalia. In the last lesson you read about the civil war in Bosnia in the Balkan Peninsula. This war also brought calls for world response. Within the United States these world crises have led to heated debate. Many disagree over what the country's role in world politics should be in the future. Should it continue to act as protector of democracy and human rights as it often did during the Cold War?

New Technologies

As the United States considers its world role, it is undergoing great changes in technology at home. Scientific advances in medicine enable people to live longer, healthier lives. The average person born in the United States in 1900 lived to be only 42 years old. The average person born in this country in 1990 can expect to live more than thirty years longer, reaching 74 years of age.

Space satellites now send information back to Earth. This relay has helped scientists update their knowledge about climate and the environment. Other technological improvements have made it possible for people to communicate instantly. Fax machines and cellular phones bring the world closer together than ever before.

All of these developments are part of an "information revolution" that has changed the way we work, learn, and communicate. A big part of this revolution is the Internet. The Internet is a constantly growing group of intercon-

nected computers around the world. They are part of an "information super-highway"—new ways for people to share ideas.

The Internet had its start during the Cold War. United States technology experts began connecting government and research computers. They hoped that this link would allow the government to keep running in case of a nuclear attack. The network, which later grew into the Internet, has become one of the most important legacies of the Cold War. Instead of being used in war, it has united people around the world.

Today more than 40 million people from over 160 nations use the Internet. People can read the latest news without opening a newspaper. They can "talk" to each other without telephones or shop without going to a store. With the Internet, much of the world is no farther than a computer screen away.

Infographic

Economy of Americas

As you read, nations in the Americas are becoming increasingly interdependent. As Latin America continues to industrialize, more goods are produced that can be traded in other parts of the Americas. What importance do you think agreements like NAFTA have for North American nations?

Canadian dollars

OTTAWA 1986

Rural-Urban Populaton

Urban 72 %

Rural 28 %

Mexico City (above), with a population of 20 million, is the largest city in the Americas. Oil is a valuable resource for Mexico, Venezuela, and Colombia. Brazil grows about 30% of the world's coffee. In the United States, the world's largest coffee consumer, we drink about 400 million cups a day.

GDP: LARGEST FIVE ECONOMIES

GDP in billions of United States dollars (1993)

UNITED STATES 6,260

CANADA 477

BRAZIL 444

MEXICO 343

ARGENTINA 256

500

400

300

200

100

0

Source: The World Bank World Development Report

WHY IT MATTERS

Throughout history the world has been shaped by technological, governmental, social, and cultural change. The first agricultural revolution began over 8,000 years ago. People began to build cities and specialize in the work they did. Improvements in agriculture have continued to this day. Crops like wheat, rice, corn, and potatoes were once grown in only small parts of the world. Today these crops are grown around the globe, helping to feed millions of people.

The world's urban revolution began in places like ancient Catal Huyuk. It eventually led to the creation of large, modern cities like New York City and Buenos Aires. Political revolutions of the past few centuries brought greater democracy and sometimes, losses of freedom. The Industrial Revolution began in Britain in the 1700s. It is continuing today, reaching some parts of the world for the first time.

New technological advances continue to change the ways people live. Today the world has only just begun a new "information revolution." These advances build on earlier inventions of paper and printed books. Many everyday objects in our lives may become old-fashioned in the twenty-first century. Some people believe books and newspapers could be replaced by computers. What do you think?

It is possible that you—as a future inventor, teacher, or leader in business or government—will help influence future change. In doing so you can change history and the world.

Many students of today will become the leaders of tomorrow.

Leaders of the world's major industrial nations often meet to discuss the improvement of international trade.

WHY IS INTERNATIONAL TRADE IMPORTANT?

Every nation's economy is part of the larger world economy. Some nations are mainly exporters, others are mainly importers. Nations with rich natural resources but few factories depend on international trade for manufactured goods. For nations with few customers for their products at home, the sale of raw materials, farm crops, or manufactured goods to other countries provides money needed for growth and development.

Here are viewpoints on trade from three different countries. Ghana, in Africa, is rich in aluminum and other metals. The country needs money from international trade to develop these resources. The Asian country of Singapore buys raw materials from other nations, then processes them for sale to other countries. The fact that goods coming into Singapore are not taxed has brought much business to the nation.

Hungary, in Europe, buys oil from other nations that have processed it for use in industry. Then Hungary uses the oil to make goods for export that are needed throughout the world. Today Hungarian workers make steel, certain medicines, and cars. Consider viewpoints on world trade and answer the questions that follow.

Three DIFFERENT Viewpoints

1 **JEANNE CHENG**
Trade development official, Singapore
Excerpt from interview, 1995

Singapore, with its small land area and a population of less than three million people, has to focus on the world market and be outward-looking to achieve economic growth. As Singapore has no natural resources, it has to import industrial outputs from other countries. The key to its flourishing international trade has been its free trade policy. Almost all goods enter Singapore duty [tax] free.

"... outward-looking to achieve economic growth."

2 **GORGY KADAR**
Businesswoman, Hungary
Excerpt from interview, 1995

Hungary lacks raw materials like oil, gas, and iron. These materials must be imported for us to manufacture some of the goods we export, like buses and cars. We are a small country and we need to trade with other countries for our economy to grow. There is not enough of a market for wheat and other farm products we produce within Hungary. We must sell our surplus crops to other nations.

"... we need to trade with other nations for our economy to grow."

3 **KASSIM YAHYA**
Trade official, Ghana
Excerpt from interview, 1995

An open economy that trades with the rest of the world develops faster and is better able to improve its standard of living. Ghana has since 1983 opened its economy so that we can import goods and services, new technology, and investment capital to develop our industries. We can also export to other nations products like cacao and pineapples that we produce efficiently to earn foreign exchange for our development. Through trade, we all gain, there are no losers.

"... we all gain, there are no losers."

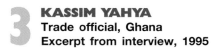

BUILDING CITIZENSHIP

1. What is the viewpoint of each person?

2. In what ways are some of the viewpoints alike? In what ways are they different? What might be the reasons each speaker has his or her viewpoint on world trade?

3. How could you find out more about how world trade affects your own community?

SHARING VIEWPOINTS

With your group, locate each of these countries on a world map and use a current world almanac to identify major exports and imports. Discuss why you think each speaker might feel as he or she does. Write two statements that all of you can agree with about the importance of global trade.

CHAPTER 20 REVIEW

THINKING ABOUT VOCABULARY

Each of the following statements contains an underlined vocabulary word. Number a sheet of paper from 1 to 10. Beside each number write **T** if the statement is true and **F** if the statement is false. If the statement is false, rewrite the sentence using the vocabulary word correctly.

1. The <u>Pacific Rim</u> is the ring of countries that surrounds the Pacific Ocean.

2. <u>NAFTA</u> is a military alliance that involves European nations.

3. The crowded areas inside or near cities in South Africa where many blacks live are called <u>townships</u>.

4. A person unable to speak more than one language is <u>bilingual</u>.

5. <u>Ethnic groups</u> have a language, customs, and a heritage in common.

6. The <u>Internet</u> is a constantly expanding network of interconnected computers around the world.

7. The system of laws once used to keep the races separate in South Africa was called <u>apartheid</u>.

8. <u>Sanctions</u> are trade agreements that countries make with each other.

9. <u>Interdependent</u> means having the ability to stand alone without getting help from other countries.

10. The amount of money each person would have if a country's total income was divided evenly among its people is called <u>per capita income</u>.

THINKING ABOUT FACTS

1. Why was 1989 considered a "Year of Miracles" in Europe?

2. How did Nelson Mandela and F.W. de Klerk transform South Africa in the first half of the 1990s?

3. What events took place at Tiananmen Square in June of 1989?

4. Who is Jean-Bertrand Aristide? What has his role been in Haiti since 1990?

5. When did the Cold War end? What helped to bring about the end? How did Europe change as a result?

6. Why did Gorbachev feel that glasnost would be an important part of rebuilding the Soviet Union's economy?

7. What are some of the economic and political problems that South Africans face now that apartheid has been abolished?

8. What changes have taken place in China under the leadership of Deng Xiaoping?

9. What do people in Hong Kong fear will happen when China takes control in 1997?

10. How does NAFTA affect North American trade? How does it affect the ties between the United States, Mexico, and Canada?

THINK AND WRITE

WRITING A JOURNAL ENTRY

Suppose you were a Russian living in Moscow in 1990. Write a journal entry about the changes taking place as the Soviet Union collapses and moves toward democracy.

WRITING A PAMPHLET

Write a pamphlet about Nelson Mandela. Describe his early work for the African National Congress. Tell about his arrest, imprisonment, and release. Then describe his election as the first president of South Africa.

WRITING ON THE INTERNET

Suppose you could send a message on the Internet to thousands of students around the world. Write a message and two answers you might receive from South America, Africa, the Middle East, or East Asia.

APPLYING THINKING SKILLS

EVALUATING INFORMATION FOR ACCURACY

1. What does evaluating information for accuracy mean?

2. Compare this skill with the skill of analyzing the credibility of a source you learned in Chapter 16 on pages 472–473. How are they similar? How are they different?

3. Choose an article from a national news magazine or newspaper. What are some of the things that had to be evaluated before the information was printed?

4. Review the account of the Vietnamese worker's conditions under the French, quoted on page 587. How would you go about evaluating this source for accuracy?

5. Why is evaluating information for accuracy important for the study of history?

Summing Up the Chapter

Copy the main idea map below on a separate sheet of paper. Review the chapter for information to complete the map. When you have filled in the main idea map, use the information to answer the question "What important changes have taken place in the world recently?"

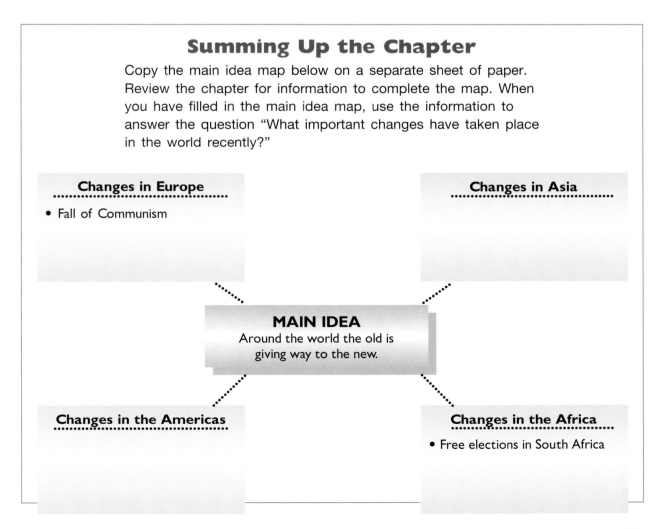

Changes in Europe
- Fall of Communism

Changes in Asia

MAIN IDEA
Around the world the old is giving way to the new.

Changes in the Americas

Changes in the Africa
- Free elections in South Africa

UNIT 6 REVIEW

THINKING ABOUT VOCABULARY

Number a sheet of paper from 1 to 10. Beside each number write the word or term from the list below that matches the statement.

armistice
communism
concentration camp
European Union
Middle East

sanctions
strike
urbanization
warlords
Zionism

1. The growth of cities
2. An organization of western European nations working to build a common economy in Europe
3. Local military leaders in China who took advantage of political unrest in the early 1900s to seize power in their regions
4. The region between the Mediterranean Sea and the western borders of Pakistan and Afghanistan
5. Penalties placed on a nation to make it change its behavior
6. A camp where people are imprisoned because of their heritage, religious beliefs, or political views
7. An agreement to stop fighting
8. The movement to establish a Jewish homeland or nation
9. A political system in which the government owns everything in the name of the workers
10. The refusal to work in protest of unfair treatment

THINK AND WRITE

WRITING AN ESSAY

Write a short essay about two or three people in the twentieth century you most admire. Describe what they accomplished and what you admire about them.

WRITING ABOUT PERSPECTIVES

The Bosnian city of Sarajevo has been at the center of conflict more than once in this century. In 1914 the assassination there of the Austrian archduke Franz Ferdinand was the spark that ignited World War I. In the 1990s the war raging between ethnic groups in the nation hit the city particularly hard. Write about the two conflicts and the links, if any, between them.

WRITING AN INTERVIEW

Choose two leaders from wars in the twentieth century. Write questions you would ask them if you could interview them. Then write the responses they might have given.

BUILDING SKILLS

1. **Time zone maps** Look at the time zone map on page 548. When it is noon where you live, what time is it in Honolulu? Montreal? Rome? Bombay? Hong Kong?

2. **Time zone maps** Explain why it is possible for somebody to fly from Tokyo on May 2 and arrive in the United States on May 1?

3. **Political cartoons** Find a political cartoon in a newspaper or news magazine. Explain what it means. How does the cartoon make its point?

4. **Political cartoons** Choose a political event that you read about in this book. Then make a political cartoon about the event. Draw simple stick figures if you like and use words to fill out the meaning of the cartoon.

5. **Evaluating information** Choose an article from a newspaper, magazine, or newsletter or take a passage from a book. How would you evaluate the information you find there for its accuracy?

YESTERDAY, TODAY & TOMORROW

The United Nations was created at the end of World War II to promote peace and help countries develop. In 1995 the UN celebrated its 50th anniversary. What role do you think the United Nations will play in the next 50 years? Do you think the United Nations should be doing more? If so, what?

READING ON YOUR OWN

These are some books you might find at the library to help you learn more.

NUMBER THE STARS
by Lois Lowry
This dramatic story tells about a family that helps a Jewish family get to safety.

GANDHI
by Nigel Hunter
This brief biography of Gandhi is accompanied by colorful photos.

NELSON MANDELA: DETERMINED TO BE FREE
by Jack L. Roberts
This biography describes the man who struggled against apartheid and became South Africa's first black president.

UNIT PROJECT

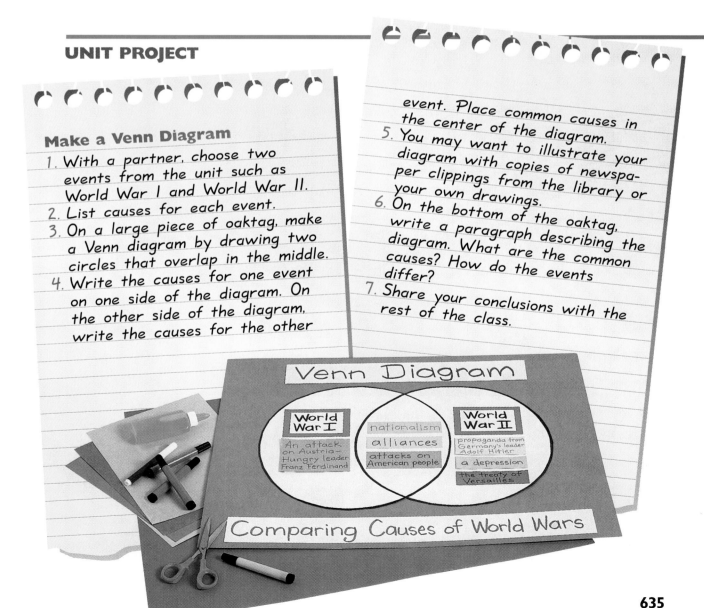

Make a Venn Diagram

1. With a partner, choose two events from the unit such as World War I and World War II.
2. List causes for each event.
3. On a large piece of oaktag, make a Venn diagram by drawing two circles that overlap in the middle.
4. Write the causes for one event on one side of the diagram. On the other side of the diagram, write the causes for the other event. Place common causes in the center of the diagram.
5. You may want to illustrate your diagram with copies of newspaper clippings from the library or your own drawings.
6. On the bottom of the oaktag, write a paragraph describing the diagram. What are the common causes? How do the events differ?
7. Share your conclusions with the rest of the class.

Venn Diagram

| World War I | nationalism | World War II |
| An attack on Austria–Hungary leader Franz Ferdinand | alliances / attacks on American people | propaganda from Germany's leader Adolf Hitler / a depression / the treaty of Versailles |

Comparing Causes of World Wars

REFERENCE SECTION

The Reference Section has many parts, each with a different type of information. Use this section to look up people, places, and events as you study.

R4   Atlas

Maps of the world, its regions, and the United States

MAP BUILDER The World: Climate
and Population R4
Europe: Political R6
Europe: Physical R7
Africa: Political R8
Africa: Physical R9
Asia: Political R10
Asia: Physical R11
The Americas: Political R12
The Americas: Physical R13
The United States: Political R14
The World: Political R16
The World: Physical R18

R20 Countries of the World

Facts about each country of the world

R36 World History Time Lines

Time lines of historical periods with events from all over the world

R46 Dictionary of Geographic Terms

An illustration showing landforms and bodies of water

R48 Gazetteer

Information about places discussed in this book

R55 Biographical Dictionary

Information about people discussed in this book

R60 Glossary

Meanings of the vocabulary words used in this book

R70 Index

An alphabetical listing with page numbers for the topics that appear in this book

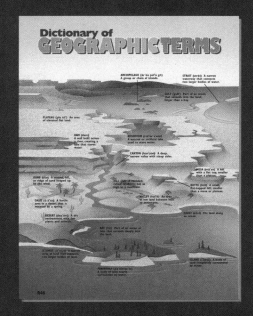

R3

Atlas

An atlas is a collection of maps. An atlas
can be a book or a separate section
within a book. This Atlas is a separate
section with maps to help you study
the history and geography
presented in this book.

MAP BUILDER
The World: Climate and Population

The map on the facing page is a special kind of map.
Each transparent overlay shows a different aspect of
the world's climate and population. You can see where
in the world similar climates exist and how climates
relate to latitude. You can also compare population
density around the world and see in which climates
people live. Start by lifting all of the transparent over-
lays and observe the base map of the continents and
oceans of the world. Then cover the base map with
the first overlay and study the climates shown. In
which climate do you live?

Allow the second overlay to cover the first and consider how climates are related to latitude. What latitude
lines divide the zones shown? What kinds of climates
are generally found nearest the equator? Finally, let
down the third overlay and compare population densi-
ties around the world. Which areas of North America
are the most densely populated? In which climates do
the fewest people live?

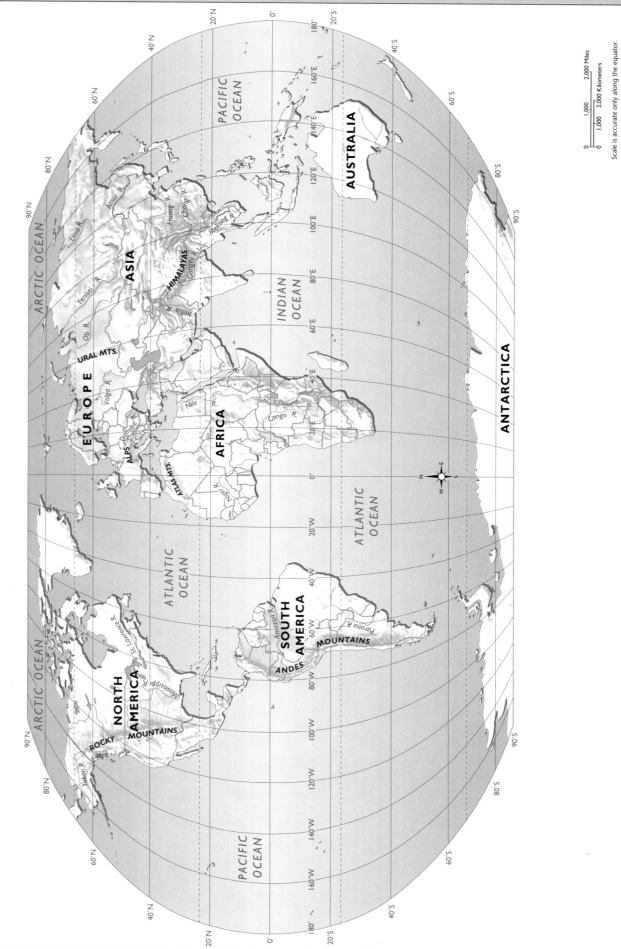

ARCTIC OCEAN

90°N

80°N

60°N

ASIA

URAL MTS.

Lena R.

Amur R.

Yenisei R.

Ob R.

Huang R.

Chang R.

Mekong R.

HIMALAYAS

Ganges R.

Indus R.

EUROPE

Volga R.

Danube R.

ALPS

ATLAS MTS.

Niger R.

Nile R.

Congo R.

AFRICA

PACIFIC OCEAN

INDIAN OCEAN

AUSTRALIA

ANTARCTICA

20°N

0°

20°S

40°S

60°S

80°S

90°S

60°E

80°E

100°E

120°E

140°E

160°E

180°

40°E

20°E

N
W · E
S

ATLANTIC OCEAN

ARCTIC OCEAN

90°N

80°N

60°N

40°N

NORTH AMERICA

ROCKY MOUNTAINS

Yukon R.

St. Lawrence R.

Mississippi R.

SOUTH AMERICA

ANDES MOUNTAINS

Amazon R.

Parana R.

ATLANTIC OCEAN

PACIFIC OCEAN

20°N

0°

20°S

40°S

60°S

80°S

20°W

40°W

60°W

80°W

100°W

120°W

140°W

160°W

180°

Scale is accurate only along the equator.

0   1,000   2,000 Miles

0   1,000   2,000 Kilometers

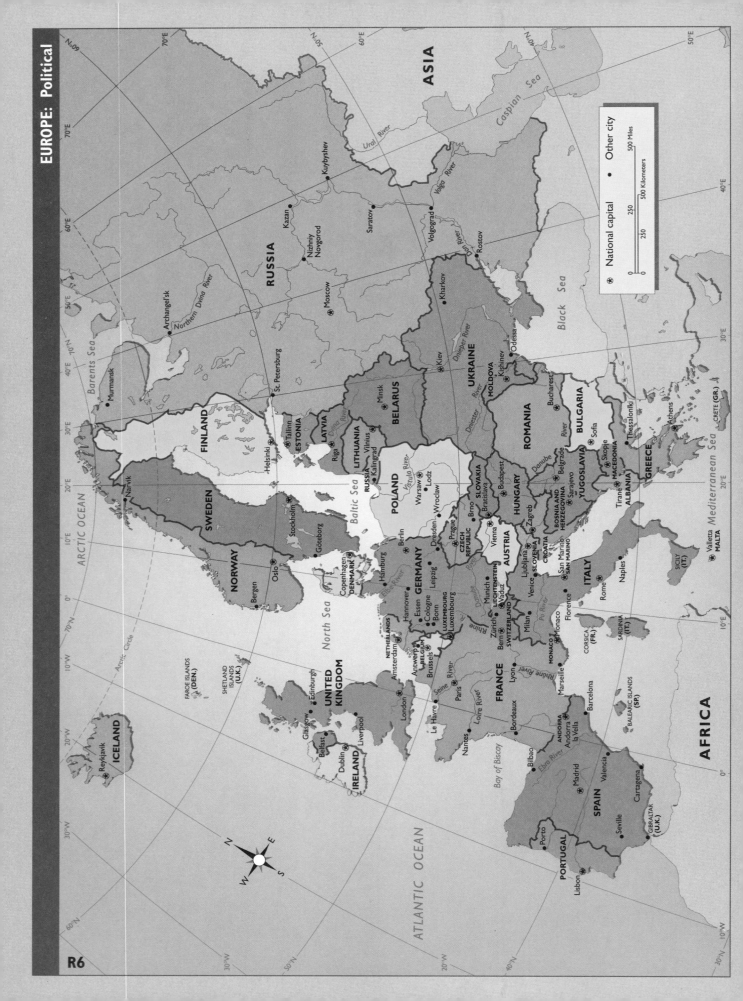

EUROPE: Political

ASIA

AFRICA

Scale legend:
- ⊛ National capital
- ● Other city

0   250   500 Miles
0   250   500 Kilometers

Water features
- Barents Sea
- Caspian Sea
- Black Sea
- Baltic Sea
- North Sea
- ARCTIC OCEAN
- ATLANTIC OCEAN
- Mediterranean Sea
- Bay of Biscay
- Ural River
- Volga River
- Don River
- Northern Dvina River
- Dnieper River
- Dniester River
- Danube
- Vistula River
- Dvina River
- Elbe River
- Rhine
- Rhône River
- Ebro River
- Loire River
- Seine River
- Po River

Countries and cities
- RUSSIA — Moscow, Kazan, Nizhniy Novgorod, Saratov, Kuybyshev, Volgograd, Rostov, Archangel'sk, Murmansk, St. Petersburg
- FINLAND — Helsinki
- SWEDEN — Stockholm, Göteborg
- NORWAY — Oslo, Bergen, Narvik
- ICELAND — Reykjavik
- FAROE ISLANDS (DEN.)
- SHETLAND ISLANDS (U.K.)
- UNITED KINGDOM — London, Liverpool, Glasgow, Edinburgh
- IRELAND — Dublin, Belfast
- DENMARK — Copenhagen
- ESTONIA — Tallinn
- LATVIA — Riga
- LITHUANIA — Vilnius
- RUSSIA — Kaliningrad
- BELARUS — Minsk
- POLAND — Warsaw, Wrocław, Lodz
- UKRAINE — Kiev, Kharkov, Odessa
- MOLDOVA — Kishinev
- GERMANY — Berlin, Hamburg, Hannover, Essen, Cologne, Bonn, Leipzig, Dresden, Munich
- NETHERLANDS — Amsterdam
- BELGIUM — Brussels, Antwerp
- LUXEMBOURG — Luxembourg
- FRANCE — Paris, Le Havre, Nantes, Bordeaux, Lyon, Marseille
- CZECH REPUBLIC — Prague, Brno
- SLOVAKIA — Bratislava
- AUSTRIA — Vienna
- SWITZERLAND — Zürich, Bern
- LIECHTENSTEIN — Vaduz
- HUNGARY — Budapest
- SLOVENIA — Ljubljana
- CROATIA — Zagreb
- BOSNIA AND HERZEGOVINA — Sarajevo
- YUGOSLAVIA — Belgrade
- ROMANIA — Bucharest
- BULGARIA — Sofia
- MACEDONIA — Skopje
- ALBANIA — Tiranë
- GREECE — Athens, Thessaloniki
- CRETE (GR.)
- ITALY — Rome, Naples, Florence, Venice, Milan, San Marino
- SAN MARINO
- MONACO
- CORSICA (FR.)
- SARDINIA (IT.)
- SICILY (IT.)
- MALTA — Valletta
- SPAIN — Madrid, Barcelona, Bilbao, Valencia, Cartagena, Seville
- BALEARIC ISLANDS (SP.)
- ANDORRA — Andorra la Vella
- PORTUGAL — Lisbon, Porto
- GIBRALTAR (U.K.)

R6

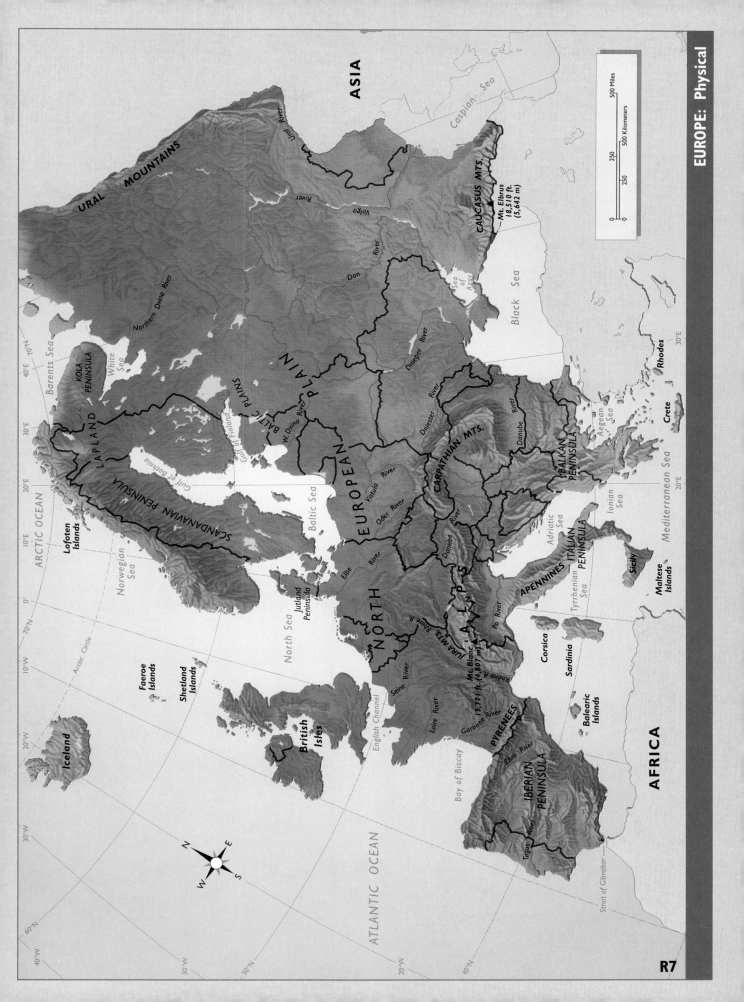

ASIA

Caspian Sea

URAL MOUNTAINS

CAUCASUS MTS.

Mt. Elbrus
18,510 ft.
(5,642 m)

Ural River

Volga River

Don River

Sea of Azov

Black Sea

Northern Dvina River

Barents Sea

KOLA PENINSULA

White Sea

Dnieper River

40°E 70°N

30°E

LAPLAND

Gulf of Finland

W. Dvina River

EUROPEAN PLAIN

BALTIC PLAINS

Dniester River

CARPATHIAN MTS.

Danube River

BALKAN PENINSULA

30°E

Rhodes

Crete

Aegean Sea

SCANDINAVIAN PENINSULA

Gulf of Bothnia

Baltic Sea

Vistula River

Oder River

Danube River

20°E

Adriatic Sea

ITALIAN PENINSULA

Ionian Sea

Mediterranean Sea

20°E

Lofoten Islands

ARCTIC OCEAN

10°E

0°

Norwegian Sea

70°N

North Sea

Jutland Peninsula

Elbe River

NORTH

ALPS

Rhine R.

APENNINES

Po River

Tyrrhenian Sea

Corsica

Sardinia

Sicily

Maltese Islands

Faeroe Islands

Shetland Islands

10°W

20°W

British Isles

English Channel

Seine River

JURA MTS.

Mt. Blanc
15,771 ft. (4,807 m)

Rhône R.

PYRENEES

Balearic Islands

Iceland

30°W

70°N

Arctic Circle

Bay of Biscay

Loire River

Garonne River

Ebro River

IBERIAN PENINSULA

Tagus River

Strait of Gibraltar

ATLANTIC OCEAN

40°N

AFRICA

N
E
W
S

20°W 30°W 40°N

250 500 Miles
250 500 Kilometers
0   250   500

R7

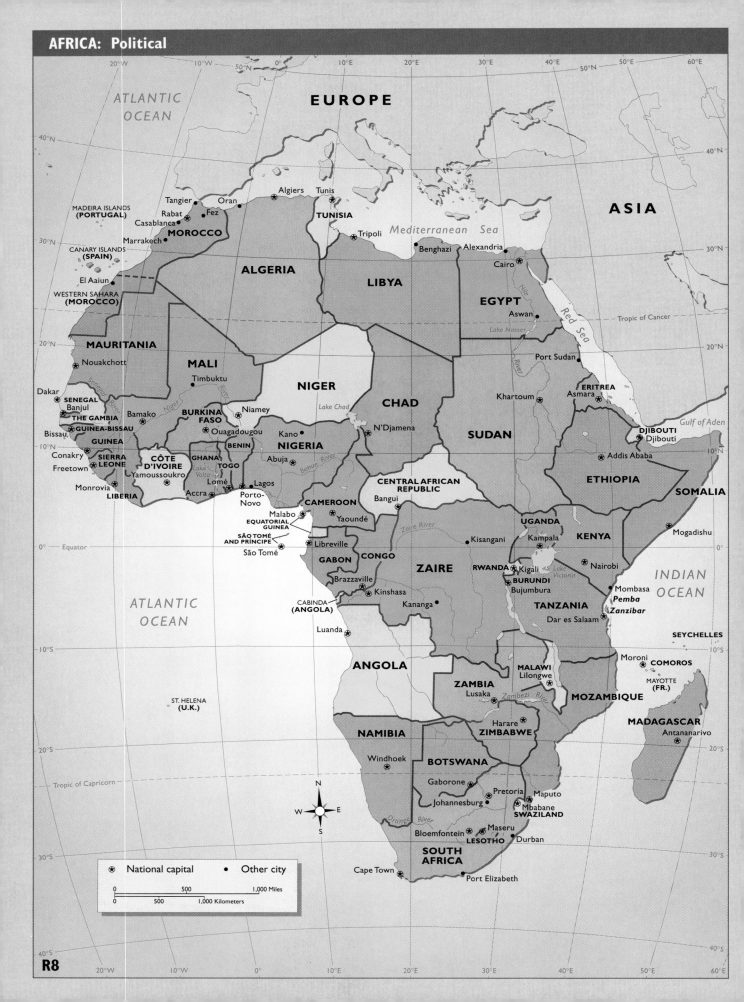

AFRICA: Political

EUROPE

ATLANTIC
OCEAN

ASIA

Mediterranean Sea

Tangier ● Oran
Algiers ● Tunis ⊛
Rabat ● Fez
Casablanca ●
TUNISIA
MADEIRA ISLANDS
(PORTUGAL)
MOROCCO
Marrakech ●
Tripoli ●
Benghazi ●
Alexandria ●
CANARY ISLANDS
(SPAIN)
Cairo ⊛
ALGERIA
LIBYA
El Aaiun ●
EGYPT
WESTERN SAHARA
(MOROCCO)
Aswan ●
Nile River
Red Sea
Tropic of Cancer
MAURITANIA
Lake Nasser
Nouakchott ●
Port Sudan ●
20°N
MALI
ERITREA
Dakar ●
Timbuktu ●
NIGER
Khartoum ●
Asmara ⊛
⊛ **SENEGAL**
Banjul
Niger River
CHAD
SUDAN
Gulf of Aden
THE GAMBIA
Bamako ●
Niamey ⊛
DJIBOUTI
Bissau ●
BURKINA
FASO
Ouagadougou ⊛
N'Djamena ●
Djibouti ●
GUINEA-BISSAU
Kano ●
GUINEA
BENIN
NIGERIA
Addis Ababa ⊛
Conakry ●
Abuja ●
SIERRA
CÔTE
GHANA
LEONE
D'IVOIRE
TOGO
Benue River
CENTRAL AFRICAN
ETHIOPIA
Freetown ●
Yamoussoukro ⊛
Lake Volta
Lomé ●
REPUBLIC
Monrovia ●
Accra ⊛
Lagos ●
Bangui ●
SOMALIA
LIBERIA
Porto-
CAMEROON
Novo
Malabo ⊛
UGANDA
KENYA
Mogadishu ●
Yaoundé ⊛
EQUATORIAL
Zaire River
Kisangani ●
GUINEA
Kampala ⊛
SÃO TOMÉ
AND PRÍNCIPE
Libreville ⊛
Nairobi ⊛
São Tomé ●
GABON
CONGO
RWANDA Kigali ⊛
INDIAN
Equator
ZAIRE
BURUNDI
Lake Victoria
OCEAN
Brazzaville ⊛
Bujumbura ●
Kinshasa ⊛
Mombasa ●
CABINDA
Kananga ●
TANZANIA
Pemba
(ANGOLA)
Zanzibar
Dar es Salaam ●
SEYCHELLES
Luanda ⊛
ATLANTIC
OCEAN
Moroni ● **COMOROS**
MALAWI
MAYOTTE
Lilongwe ●
(FR.)
ANGOLA
ZAMBIA
ST. HELENA
Lusaka ●
(U.K.)
Zambezi River
MOZAMBIQUE
MADAGASCAR
Harare ●
Antananarivo ●
NAMIBIA
ZIMBABWE
Windhoek ⊛
BOTSWANA
Tropic of Capricorn
Gaborone ⊛
Pretoria ⊛ Maputo ⊛
Johannesburg ●
Mbabane ⊛
SWAZILAND
N
Orange River
Bloemfontein ⊛
Maseru ⊛
W E
LESOTHO
Durban ●
S
SOUTH
AFRICA
Cape Town ●
Port Elizabeth ●

⊛ National capital   ● Other city

| 0 | 500 | 1,000 Miles |
| 0 | 500 | 1,000 Kilometers |

R8

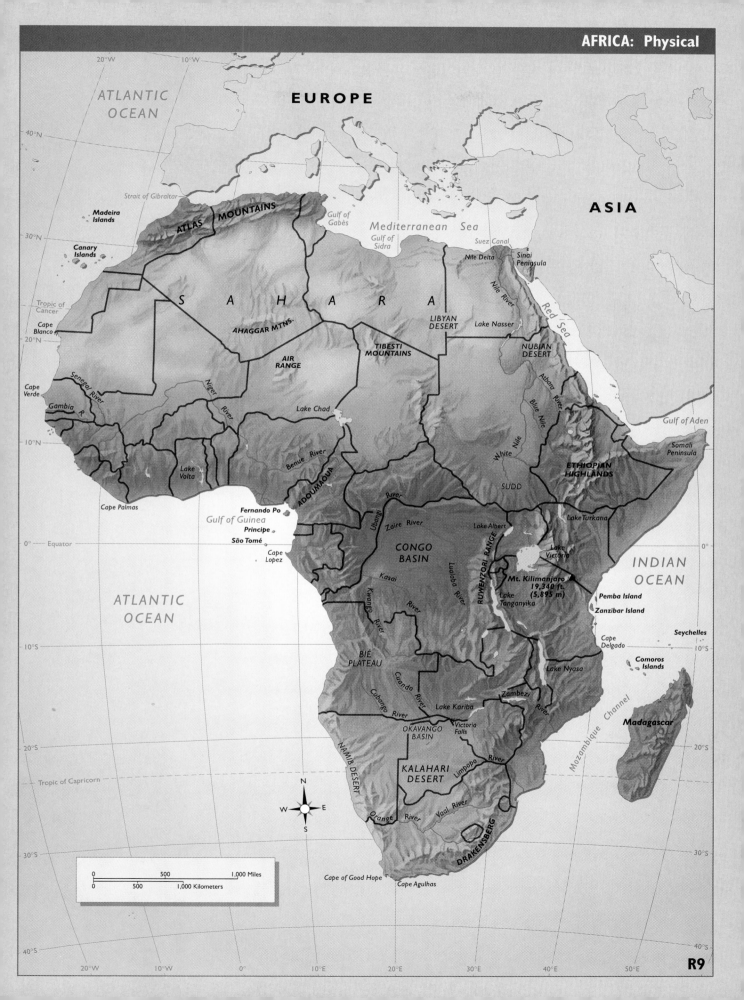

AFRICA: Physical

ATLANTIC OCEAN

EUROPE

ASIA

Madeira Islands

Strait of Gibraltar

Gulf of Gabès

Mediterranean Sea

Gulf of Sidra

Suez Canal

Nile Delta

Sinai Peninsula

Canary Islands

ATLAS MOUNTAINS

S A H A R A

Tropic of Cancer

Cape Blanco

AHAGGAR MTNS.

AIR RANGE

LIBYAN DESERT

Nile River

Lake Nasser

NUBIAN DESERT

TIBESTI MOUNTAINS

Senegal River

Niger River

Lake Chad

Atbara River

Blue Nile

Cape Verde

Gambia R.

Benue River

ADOUMAOUA

SUDD

White Nile

ETHIOPIAN HIGHLANDS

Gulf of Aden

Somali Peninsula

Lake Volta

Cape Palmas

Gulf of Guinea

Fernando Po

Principe

São Tomé

Cape Lopez

Ubangi

Zaïre River

CONGO BASIN

River

RUWENZORI RANGE

Lake Albert

Lake Turkana

Lake Victoria

INDIAN OCEAN

Equator

Kasai

River

Lualaba River

Mt. Kilimanjaro 19,340 ft. (5,895 m)

Lake Tanganyika

Pemba Island

Zanzibar Island

ATLANTIC OCEAN

Kwango River

BIÉ PLATEAU

Cuando River

Cape Delgado

Seychelles

Lake Nyasa

Comoros Islands

Cubango River

Lake Kariba

Zambezi

River

Victoria Falls

Mozambique Channel

Madagascar

NAMIB DESERT

OKAVANGO BASIN

KALAHARI DESERT

Limpopo

River

Tropic of Capricorn

Orange

River

Vaal River

DRAKENSBERG

Cape of Good Hope

Cape Agulhas

N
W   E
S

| 0 | 500 | 1,000 Miles |
| 0 | 500 | 1,000 Kilometers |

R9

20°W 10°W 0° 10°E 20°E 30°E 40°E 50°E

40°N 30°N 20°N 10°N 0° 10°S 20°S 30°S 40°S

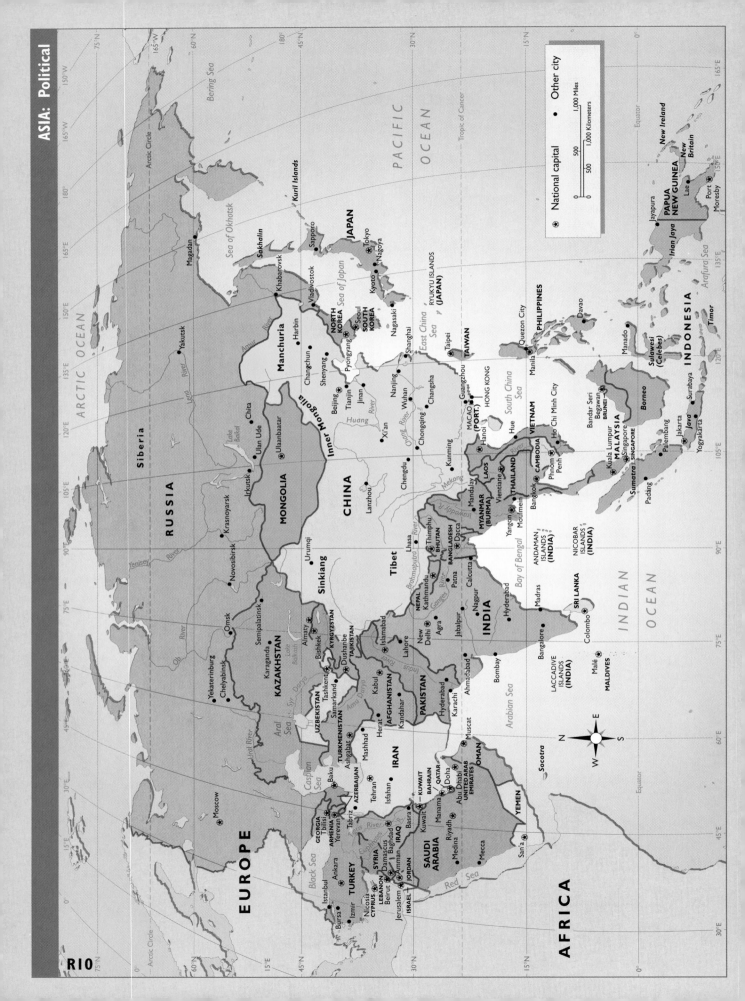

ASIA: Political

Legend:
- ⊛ National capital
- ● Other city

0 500 1,000 Miles
0 500 1,000 Kilometers

RIO

EUROPE

AFRICA

RUSSIA

Siberia

Manchuria

Inner Mongolia

MONGOLIA

CHINA

Tibet

Sinkiang

KAZAKHSTAN

UZBEKISTAN
TURKMENISTAN
KYRGYZSTAN
TAJIKISTAN
AFGHANISTAN
PAKISTAN
IRAN
IRAQ
SYRIA
TURKEY
GEORGIA
ARMENIA
AZERBAIJAN
CYPRUS
LEBANON
ISRAEL
JORDAN
SAUDI ARABIA
KUWAIT
BAHRAIN
QATAR
UNITED ARAB EMIRATES
OMAN
YEMEN

INDIA

NEPAL
BHUTAN
BANGLADESH
MYANMAR (BURMA)
THAILAND
LAOS
VIETNAM
CAMBODIA
MALAYSIA
BRUNEI
SRI LANKA
MALDIVES

NORTH KOREA
SOUTH KOREA
JAPAN
TAIWAN
PHILIPPINES

INDONESIA

PAPUA NEW GUINEA

Cities and features:

Magadan, Yakutsk, Khabarovsk, Vladivostok, Sapporo, Tokyo, Nagoya, Kyoto, Nagasaki, Seoul, Pyongyang, Harbin, Changchun, Shenyang, Beijing, Tianjin, Jinan, Shanghai, Nanjing, Wuhan, Changsha, Chongqing, Chengdu, Lanzhou, Xi'an, Kunming, Guangzhou, Taipei, Quezon City, Manila, Davao, Manado

Irkutsk, Chita, Ulan Ude, Ulaanbaatar, Urumqi, Novosibirsk, Krasnoyarsk, Semipalatinsk, Omsk, Yekaterinburg, Chelyabinsk, Karaganda, Moscow

Almaty, Bishkek, Tashkent, Samarkand, Dushanbe, Kabul, Kandahar, Herat, Mashhad, Ashgabat, Tehran, Isfahan, Baku, Tbilisi, Yerevan, Tabriz, Ankara, Istanbul, Bursa, Izmir, Nicosia, Beirut, Damascus, Jerusalem, Amman, Baghdad, Basra, Kuwait, Manama, Doha, Abu Dhabi, Riyadh, Medina, Mecca, San'a

Islamabad, Lahore, Hyderabad, Karachi, Muscat, New Delhi, Agra, Jabalpur, Nagpur, Ahmadabad, Bombay, Bangalore, Hyderabad, Madras, Colombo, Male

Kathmandu, Thimphu, Patna, Calcutta, Lhasa, Dacca, Mandalay, Yangon, Moulmein, Vientiane, Hanoi, Hue, Bangkok, Phnom Penh, Ho Chi Minh City, Kuala Lumpur, Singapore, Bandar Seri Begawan, Palembang, Jakarta, Yogyakarta, Surabaya, Padang, Jayapura, Lae, Port Moresby

Water bodies:

Bering Sea, ARCTIC OCEAN, Arctic Circle, Sea of Okhotsk, Kuril Islands, Sakhalin, Sea of Japan, PACIFIC OCEAN, Tropic of Cancer, East China Sea, RYUKYU ISLANDS (JAPAN), South China Sea, HONG KONG, MACAO (PORT.), Bay of Bengal, ANDAMAN ISLANDS (INDIA), NICOBAR ISLANDS (INDIA), INDIAN OCEAN, LACCADIVE ISLANDS (INDIA), Arabian Sea, Socotra, Red Sea, Caspian Sea, Black Sea, Aral Sea, Lake Balkhash, Lake Baikal, Equator, Arafura Sea, New Ireland, New Britain, Irian Jaya, Sulawesi (Celebes), Borneo, Sumatra, Java, Timor

Rivers:

Lena River, Amur River, Yenisey River, Ob River, Syr Darya, Amu Darya, Indus Riv., Ganges River, Brahmaputra River, Huang River, Chang River, Mekong River, Irrawaddy R., Tigris River, Euphrates River, Ural River

EUROPE

AFRICA

ARCTIC OCEAN

PACIFIC OCEAN

INDIAN OCEAN

Bering Strait

Bering Sea

Wrangel Island

ANADYR RANGE

KOLYMA RANGE

Kamchatka Peninsula

East Siberian Sea

New Siberian Islands

CHERSKIY MOUNTAINS

VERKHOYANSK MOUNTAINS

Kuril Islands

Sea of Okhotsk

Hokkaido

Sakhalin

Honshu

STANOVOY MOUNTAINS

Amur River

SIKHOTE-ALIN MOUNTAINS

Sea of Japan

Shikoku

Kyushu

Laptev Sea

Taymyr Peninsula

CENTRAL SIBERIAN PLATEAU

Lena River

YABLONOVY MOUNTAINS

MANCHURIAN PLAIN

Korea Peninsula

Yellow Sea

East China Sea

Taiwan (Formosa)

Philippine Sea

Philippine Islands

Angara River

Lake Baikal

MONGOLIAN PLATEAU

MONGOLIA

INNER

GOBI

GREAT KHINGAN MOUNTAINS

NORTH CHINA PLAIN

Huang River

QINLING MTS.

Chang River

Xi River

Gulf of Tonkin

Hainan

South China Sea

Celebes Sea

Sulawesi (Celebes)

Yenisey River

ALTAI MOUNTAINS

Turfan Depression 505 ft. (−154 m)

ALTYN TAGH

TIAN SHAN

TARIM BASIN

Tarim River

TAKLA MAKAN

KUNLUN MOUNTAINS

PLATEAU OF TIBET

Mekong River

Indochina Peninsula

Mekong River

Gulf of Siam

Malay Peninsula

Borneo

Java Sea

Java

Strait of Malacca

Sumatra

WEST SIBERIAN PLAIN

Ob River

Irtysh River

KAZAKH UPLANDS

Lake Balkhash

KIRGHIZ STEPPE

Syr Darya

KARAKORAM RANGE

HINDU KUSH

HIMALAYAS

Mt. Everest 29,028 ft. (8,848 m)

Brahmaputra

Ganges River

Indian Subcontinent

DECCAN PLATEAU

Godavari R.

EASTERN GHATS

WESTERN GHATS

Sri Lanka (Ceylon)

Bay of Bengal

Andaman Islands

Nicobar Islands

Andaman Sea

Irrawaddy R.

Kara Sea

Yamal Peninsula

Aral Sea

UST-URT PLATEAU

Amu Darya

THAR DESERT

Indus River

Laccadive Islands

Maldive Islands

Ural River

URAL MOUNTAINS

PLATEAU OF IRAN

Caspian Sea

ZAGROS MOUNTAINS

Persian Gulf

Gulf of Oman

RUB AL-KHALI

Arabian Sea

Socotra

Black Sea

Sea of Azov

ANATOLIA (ASIA MINOR)

Bosporus

Tigris River

MESOPOTAMIA

Euphrates River

SYRIAN DESERT

NAFUD

Arabian Peninsula

Gulf of Aden

Red Sea

Mediterranean Sea

N
E
W
S

Tropic of Cancer

Equator

New Guinea

Arafura Sea

Timor

Celebes Sea

500   1,000 Miles

500   1,000 Kilometers

0

0

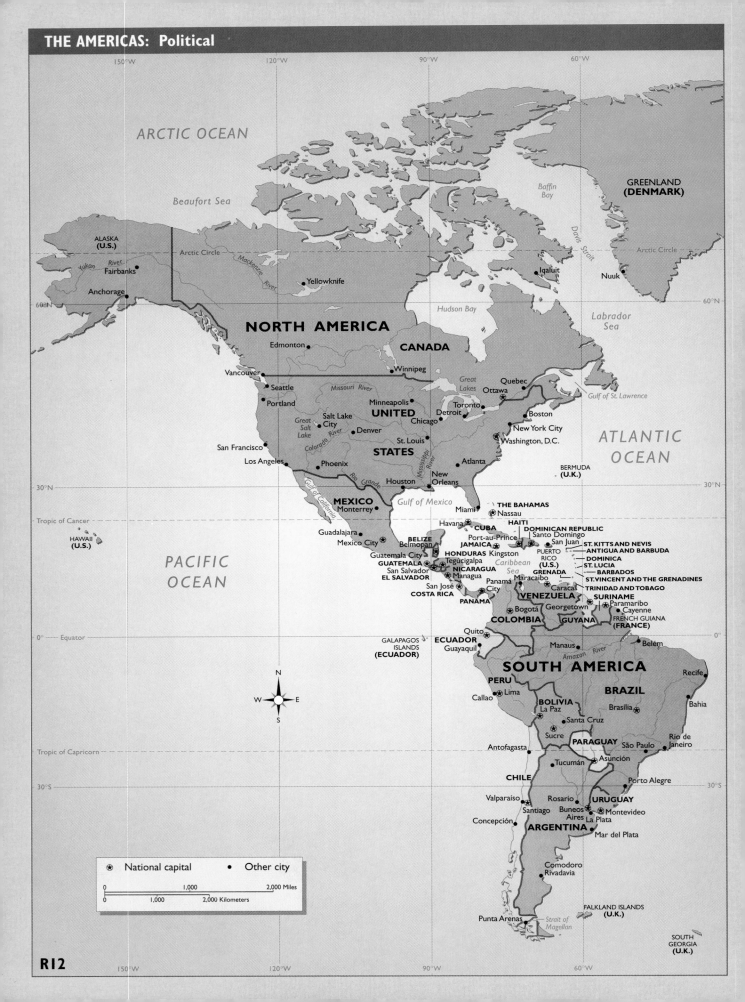

THE AMERICAS: Political

ARCTIC OCEAN

Beaufort Sea

Baffin Bay

GREENLAND
(DENMARK)

ALASKA
(U.S.)

Arctic Circle

Mackenzie River

Arctic Circle

Yukon River
Fairbanks

Anchorage

Yellowknife

Iqaluit

Nuuk

Davis Strait

60°N

Hudson Bay

Labrador Sea

60°N

NORTH AMERICA

Edmonton

CANADA

Winnipeg

Quebec

Great Lakes

Ottawa

Gulf of St. Lawrence

Vancouver

Seattle

Missouri River

Portland

Minneapolis

UNITED

Toronto
Detroit

Boston

Salt Lake
City

Chicago

New York City

Washington, D.C.

ATLANTIC
OCEAN

Great Salt Lake

Denver

Colorado River

St. Louis

San Francisco

STATES

Mississippi River

Atlanta

BERMUDA
(U.K.)

Los Angeles

Phoenix

New
Orleans

30°N

Gulf of California

Rio Grande

Houston

30°N

Tropic of Cancer

Gulf of Mexico

Miami

THE BAHAMAS

Nassau

HAWAII
(U.S.)

MEXICO

Monterrey

HAITI

HAVANA

CUBA

DOMINICAN REPUBLIC

Santo Domingo

PACIFIC
OCEAN

Guadalajara

Mexico City

BELIZE
Belmopan

Port-au-Prince

San Juan

ST. KITTS AND NEVIS

Guatemala City

JAMAICA

Kingston

PUERTO
RICO
(U.S.)

ANTIGUA AND BARBUDA

GUATEMALA

HONDURAS

DOMINICA

Tegucigalpa

ST. LUCIA

San Salvador

NICARAGUA

Caribbean Sea

GRENADA

BARBADOS

EL SALVADOR

Managua

Maracaibo

ST. VINCENT AND THE GRENADINES

San José

Panamá
City

Caracas

TRINIDAD AND TOBAGO

COSTA RICA

VENEZUELA

SURINAME

PANAMA

Bogotá

Georgetown

Paramaribo

Cayenne

Quito

COLOMBIA

GUYANA

FRENCH GUIANA
(FRANCE)

0° Equator

GALAPAGOS
ISLANDS
(ECUADOR)

ECUADOR

Manaus

Belém

0°

Guayaquil

Amazon River

SOUTH AMERICA

PERU

BRAZIL

Recife

Callao

Lima

BOLIVIA

La Paz

Brasília

Bahia

Santa Cruz

São Paulo

Rio de
Janeiro

Sucre

PARAGUAY

Antofagasta

Tucumán

Asunción

Porto Alegre

30°S

CHILE

30°S

Valparaíso

Rosario

URUGUAY

Santiago

Buenos
Aires

Montevideo

La Plata

Concepción

ARGENTINA

Mar del Plata

Comodoro
Rivadavia

| ⊛ National capital | • Other city |

0 — 1,000 — 2,000 Miles
0 — 1,000 — 2,000 Kilometers

Punta Arenas

Strait of Magellan

FALKLAND ISLANDS
(U.K.)

SOUTH
GEORGIA
(U.K.)

150°W   120°W   90°W   60°W

ARCTIC OCEAN

Queen Elizabeth Islands

Greenland

Banks
Island

Baffin Bay

Victoria
Island

Baffin
Island

Point
Barrow

Beaufort Sea

BROOKS RANGE

Mt. McKinley
20,320 ft.
(6,194 m)

Yukon
River

Davis
Strait

Arctic Circle

60°N

ALASKA RANGE

Alaska
Peninsula

Gulf of Alaska

Mackenzie
River

Great Bear
Lake

Great Slave
Lake

Hudson
Bay

Labrador Sea

Cape
Farewell

COAST MOUNTAINS

NORTH
AMERICA

CANADIAN

SHIELD

LABRADOR

Vancouver
Island

ROCKY MOUNTAINS

Saskatchewan River

Lake
Winnipeg

St. Lawrence River

Newfoundland

Snake
River

GREAT

Missouri

Great
Lakes

Gulf of
St. Lawrence

Nova
Scotia

Cape Mendocino

CASCADE
RANGE

COAST RANGES

Great
Salt
Lake

PLAINS

River

River

Ohio River

APPALACHIAN MOUNTAINS

Cape Cod

Long Island

ATLANTIC
OCEAN

SIERRA
NEVADA

GREAT
BASIN

Colorado River

Mississippi

COASTAL PLAINS

30°N

30°N

Baja California

SIERRA MADRE
OCCIDENTAL

SIERRA MADRE
ORIENTAL

Rio Grande

Gulf of Mexico

Florida Peninsula

Tropic of Cancer

Hawaiian
Islands

Gulf of
California

Yucatán
Peninsula

Straits of Florida

Cuba

WEST

Greater
Antilles

Hispaniola

INDIES

Lesser
Antilles

PACIFIC
OCEAN

Gulf of
Honduras

Caribbean Sea

CENTRAL

Lake
Nicaragua

Lake
Maracaibo

Magdalena River

LLANOS

Orinoco River

GUIANA
HIGHLANDS

AMERICA

Isthmus
of Panama

Gulf of
Panama

Rio Negro

Amazon

River

Galápagos
Islands

0°

Equator

AMAZON

BASIN

SOUTH
AMERICA

Cape
São Roque

0°

ANDES

Madeira River

MATO
GRASSO
PLATEAU

Tocantins
River

São Francisco
River

BRAZILIAN
HIGHLANDS

N

W   E

S

Lake
Titicaca

GRAN CHACO

Paraguay
River

Paraná

Tropic of Capricorn

MOUNTAINS

River

Uruguay
River

30°S

30°S

Mt. Aconcagua
22,834 ft.
(6,960 m)

PAMPAS

PATAGONIA

0   1,000   2,000 Miles

0   1,000   2,000 Kilometers

Strait of
Magellan

Falkland
Islands

South
Georgia

Tierra del Fuego

Cape Horn

150°W

120°W

90°W

60°W

ARCTIC OCEAN

RUSSIA

ALASKA

Nome

Fairbanks

CANADA

Anchorage

Juneau ★

PACIFIC
OCEAN

70°N

180°

60°N

170°W

160°W

150°W

140°W

Arctic Circle

Yukon

River

0   250   500 Miles
0   250   500 Kilometers

CANADA

Seattle
WASHINGTON
Olympia   Spokane

Great Falls

Helena ★
MONTANA

Billings

Portland

★ Salem

Eugene

OREGON

IDAHO

Boise ★

Snake River

Pocatello

WYOMING

Casper

Cheyenne ★

40°N

Columbia

Missouri River

River

NEVADA

Great
Salt
Lake

Ogden
Salt Lake City ★

Provo

COLORADO

Denver ★

Reno
Carson City ★

San Francisco
Oakland
San Jose
★ Sacramento

UTAH

Colorado
Springs

Pueblo

PACIFIC OCEAN

CALIFORNIA

Las
Vegas

ARIZONA

Santa
Fe ★

Albuquerque

NEW MEXICO

Los Angeles
Long Beach

San Diego

30°N

Phoenix ★

Tucson

El Paso

Colorado

Rio Grande

130°W

160°W   PACIFIC   155°W
         OCEAN

Kauai

Niihau   Oahu
Honolulu ★   Molokai
         Lanai   Maui
HAWAII   Kahoolawe

Hawaii
Hilo

20°N

0   100   200 Miles
0   100   200 Kilometers

N
W   E
S

MEXICO

120°W

110°W

20°N

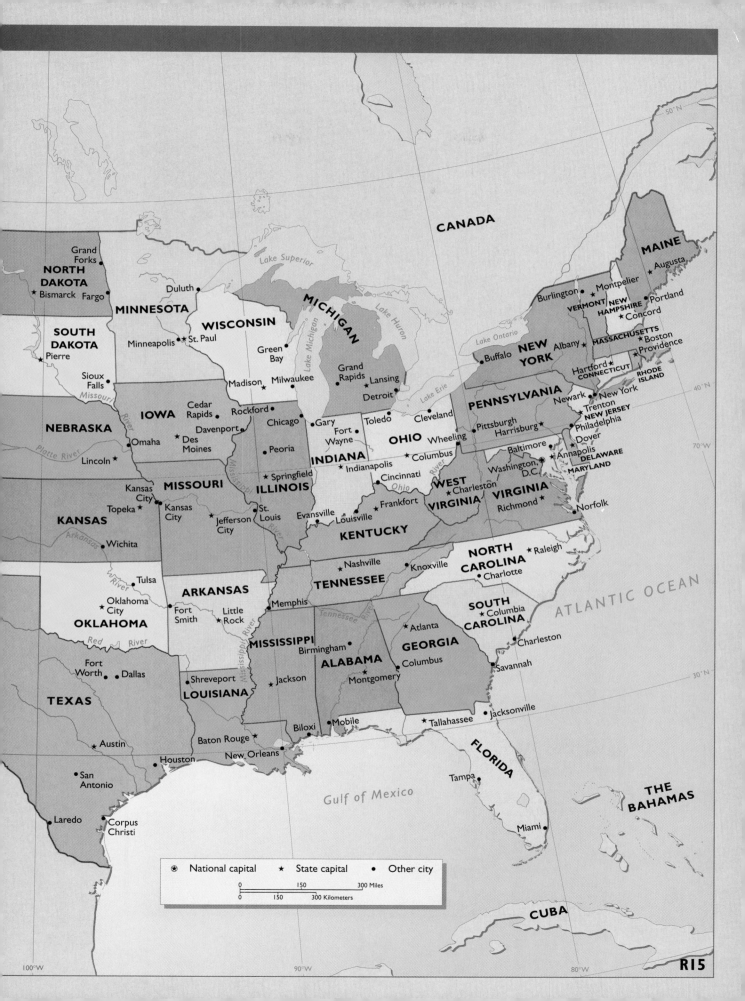

Central America and West Indies

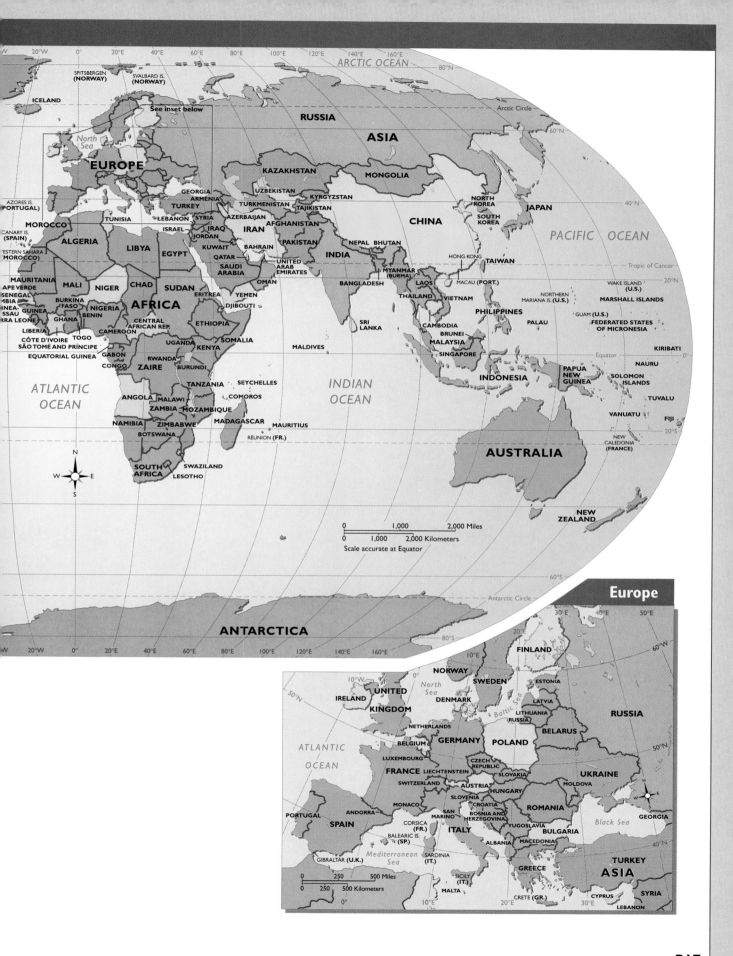

ARCTIC OCEAN

SPITSBERGEN
(NORWAY)

SVALBARD IS.
(NORWAY)

ICELAND

See inset below

RUSSIA

ASIA

North
Sea

EUROPE

GEORGIA
ARMENIA

KAZAKHSTAN

MONGOLIA

NORTH
KOREA

JAPAN

AZORES IS.
(PORTUGAL)

TURKEY

TURKMENISTAN

UZBEKISTAN

KYRGYZSTAN

TAJIKISTAN

SOUTH
KOREA

PACIFIC OCEAN

CANARY IS.
(SPAIN)

MOROCCO

TUNISIA

LEBANON
ISRAEL

SYRIA
JORDAN

IRAQ

AZERBAIJAN

AFGHANISTAN

CHINA

IRAN

ALGERIA

'ESTERN SAHARA
MOROCCO

LIBYA

EGYPT

KUWAIT

BAHRAIN

QATAR

SAUDI
ARABIA

UNITED
ARAB
EMIRATES

PAKISTAN

NEPAL BHUTAN

INDIA

MYANMAR
(BURMA)

HONG KONG

TAIWAN

MACAU (PORT.)

Tropic of Cancer

WAKE ISLAND
(U.S.)

MAURITANIA

APE VERDE

SENEGAL
MBIA

NEA-
SSAU

RRA LEONE

MALI

GUINEA

BURKINA
FASO

GHANA

NIGER

NIGERIA

BENIN

CHAD

AFRICA

SUDAN

ERITREA

CENTRAL
AFRICAN REP.

ETHIOPIA

YEMEN

DJIBOUTI

OMAN

BANGLADESH

LAOS

THAILAND

VIETNAM

NORTHERN
MARIANA IS. (U.S.)

GUAM (U.S.)

MARSHALL ISLANDS

FEDERATED STATES
OF MICRONESIA

LIBERIA

CÔTE D'IVOIRE
SÃO TOMÉ AND PRÍNCIPE

TOGO

CAMEROON

SRI
LANKA

CAMBODIA

BRUNEI

MALAYSIA

PHILIPPINES

PALAU

KIRIBATI

EQUATORIAL GUINEA

CONGO

GABON

ZAIRE

UGANDA

RWANDA

BURUNDI

KENYA

SOMALIA

MALDIVES

SINGAPORE

Equator

INDONESIA

PAPUA
NEW
GUINEA

NAURU

SOLOMON
ISLANDS

ATLANTIC
OCEAN

ANGOLA

NAMIBIA

ZAMBIA

MALAWI

MOZAMBIQUE

TANZANIA

ZIMBABWE

BOTSWANA

MADAGASCAR

SEYCHELLES

COMOROS

INDIAN
OCEAN

MAURITIUS

RÉUNION (FR.)

TUVALU

VANUATU

FIJI

NEW
CALEDONIA
(FRANCE)

SOUTH
AFRICA

SWAZILAND

LESOTHO

AUSTRALIA

N
W   E
S

0   1,000   2,000 Miles
0   1,000   2,000 Kilometers
Scale accurate at Equator

NEW
ZEALAND

Antarctic Circle

ANTARCTICA

20°W   0°   20°E   40°E   60°E   80°E   100°E   120°E   140°E   160°E

FINLAND

NORWAY

IRELAND

UNITED
KINGDOM

North
Sea

SWEDEN

DENMARK

ESTONIA

LATVIA

LITHUANIA

RUSSIA

RUSSIA

BELARUS

ATLANTIC
OCEAN

NETHERLANDS

BELGIUM

LUXEMBOURG

GERMANY

POLAND

CZECH
REPUBLIC

FRANCE

LIECHTENSTEIN

SLOVAKIA

UKRAINE

MOLDOVA

SWITZERLAND

AUSTRIA

HUNGARY

SLOVENIA

CROATIA

ROMANIA

GEORGIA

PORTUGAL

ANDORRA

MONACO

SAN
MARINO

BOSNIA AND
HERZEGOVINA

YUGOSLAVIA

Black Sea

SPAIN

CORSICA
(FR.)

BALEARIC IS.
(SP.)

ITALY

ALBANIA

BULGARIA

MACEDONIA

TURKEY

ASIA

GIBRALTAR (U.K.)

Mediterranean
Sea

SARDINIA
(IT.)

GREECE

0   250   500 Miles
0   250   500 Kilometers

SICILY
(IT.)

MALTA

CRETE (GR.)

CYPRUS

SYRIA

LEBANON

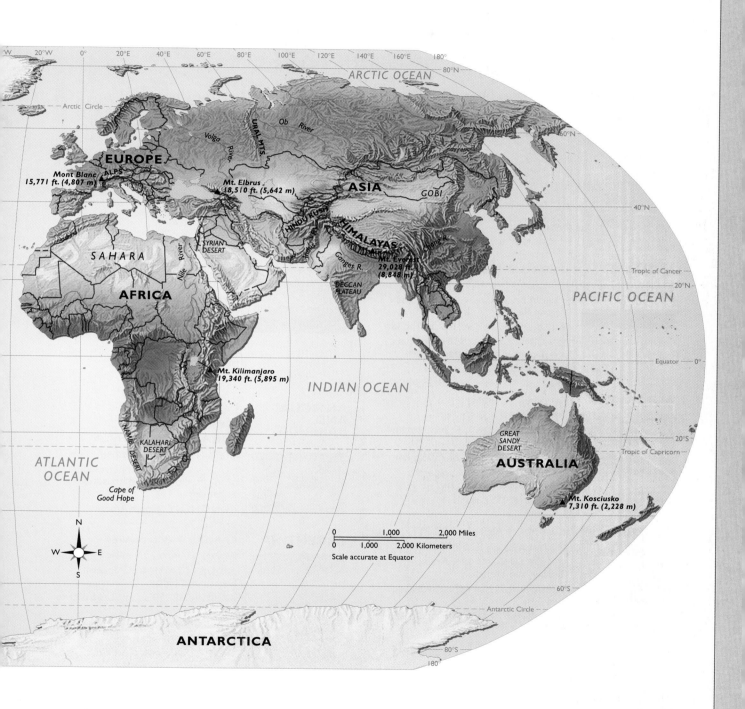

ARCTIC OCEAN

EUROPE

Mont Blanc
15,771 ft. (4,807 m)

ALPS

ASIA

GOBI

Mt. Elbrus
(18,510 ft. (5,642 m)

URAL MTS.

Volga River

Ob River

SAHARA

Nile River

SYRIAN DESERT

HINDU KUSH

HIMALAYAS

AFRICA

Tigris

Ganges R.

Indus

DECCAN PLATEAU

Mt. Everest
29,028 ft.
(8,848 m)

Chang R.

PACIFIC OCEAN

Tropic of Cancer

INDIAN OCEAN

Mt. Kilimanjaro
19,340 ft. (5,895 m)

Equator

NAMIB DESERT

KALAHARI DESERT

ATLANTIC OCEAN

Cape of
Good Hope

GREAT SANDY DESERT

AUSTRALIA

Tropic of Capricorn

Mt. Kosciusko
7,310 ft. (2,228 m)

N
W   E
S

0   1,000   2,000 Miles
0   1,000   2,000 Kilometers
Scale accurate at Equator

Antarctic Circle

ANTARCTICA

80°S

180°

20°W   0°   20°E   40°E   60°E   80°E   100°E   120°E   140°E   160°E   180°

Arctic Circle

80°N

60°N

40°N

20°N

20°S

60°S

COUNTRIES of the WORLD

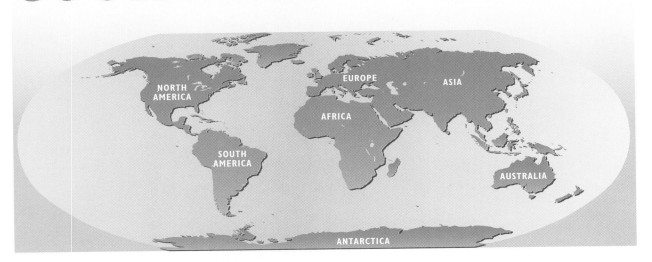

NORTH AMERICA

EUROPE

ASIA

AFRICA

SOUTH AMERICA

AUSTRALIA

ANTARCTICA

AFGHANISTAN

CAPITAL ★ Kabul

POPULATION: 16.9 million

MAJOR LANGUAGES: Pashtu and Afghan Persian

AREA: 251,773 sq mi; 647,500 sq km

LEADING EXPORTS: fruit, carpets, wool, cotton, and precious gems

CONTINENT: Asia

ALBANIA

CAPITAL ★ Tiranë

POPULATION: 3.4 million

MAJOR LANGUAGES: Albanian and Greek

AREA: 11,100 sq mi; 28,750 sq km

LEADING EXPORTS: minerals, asphalt, electricity, and oil

CONTINENT: Europe

ALGERIA

CAPITAL ★ Algiers

POPULATION: 27.9 million

MAJOR LANGUAGES: Arabic, Berber, and French

AREA: 919,592 sq mi; 2,381,740 sq km

LEADING EXPORTS: oil and natural gas

CONTINENT: Africa

ANDORRA

CAPITAL ★ Andorra la Vella

POPULATION: 64,000

MAJOR LANGUAGES: Catalan, French, and Castilian Spanish

AREA: 174 sq mi; 450 sq km

LEADING EXPORTS: tobacco products and furniture

CONTINENT: Europe

ANGOLA

CAPITAL ★ Luanda

POPULATION: 9.8 million

MAJOR LANGUAGES: Portuguese and Bantu

AREA: 481,352 sq mi; 1,246,700 sq km

LEADING EXPORTS: oil, diamonds, gas, and coffee

CONTINENT: Africa

ANTIGUA AND BARBUDA

CAPITAL ★ St. John's

POPULATION: 65,000

MAJOR LANGUAGE: English

AREA: 170 sq mi; 440 sq km

LEADING EXPORTS: petroleum products, clothing, and household appliances

CONTINENT: North America

ARGENTINA

CAPITAL ★ Buenos Aires

POPULATION: 33.9 million

MAJOR LANGUAGES: Spanish, English, and Italian

AREA: 1,068,299 sq mi; 2,766,890 sq km

LEADING EXPORTS: meat, grain, hides, and wool

CONTINENT: South America

ARMENIA

CAPITAL ★ Yerevan

POPULATION: 3.5 million

MAJOR LANGUAGE: Armenian

AREA: 11,490 sq mi; 29,800 sq km

LEADING EXPORTS: machinery and processed food items

CONTINENT: Asia

AUSTRALIA

CAPITAL ★ Canberra

POPULATION: 18.1 million

MAJOR LANGUAGES: English and aboriginal languages

AREA: 2,967,900 sq mi; 7,686,850 sq km

LEADING EXPORTS: wheat, coal, gold, wool, and alumina

CONTINENT: Australia

AUSTRIA

CAPITAL ★ Vienna

POPULATION: 7.9 million

MAJOR LANGUAGE: German

AREA: 32,375 sq mi; 83,850 sq km

LEADING EXPORTS: iron and steel products, and machinery

CONTINENT: Europe

AZERBAIJAN

CAPITAL ★ Baku

POPULATION: 7.7 million

MAJOR LANGUAGES: Azeri, Russian, and Armenian

AREA: 33,430 sq mi; 86,600 sq km

LEADING EXPORTS: oil and textiles

CONTINENT: Asia

THE BAHAMAS

CAPITAL ★ Nassau

POPULATION: 0.3 million

MAJOR LANGUAGES: English and Creole

AREA: 5,382 sq mi; 13,940 sq km

LEADING EXPORTS: medicine, cement, and crawfish

CONTINENT: North America

BAHRAIN

CAPITAL ★ Manama

POPULATION: 0.6 million

MAJOR LANGUAGES: Arabic, English, Farsi, and Urdu

AREA: 239 sq mi; 620 sq km

LEADING EXPORTS: oil, petroleum products, and aluminum

CONTINENT: Asia

BANGLADESH

CAPITAL ★ Dhaka

POPULATION: 125.1 million

MAJOR LANGUAGES: Bangla and English

AREA: 55,599 sq mi; 144,000 sq km

LEADING EXPORTS: textiles, jute, leather, and shrimp

CONTINENT: Asia

BARBADOS

CAPITAL ★ Bridgetown

POPULATION: 0.3 million

MAJOR LANGUAGE: English

AREA: 166 sq mi; 430 sq km

LEADING EXPORTS: sugar, molasses, and electrical components

CONTINENT: North America

BELARUS

CAPITAL ★ Minsk

POPULATION: 10.4 million

MAJOR LANGUAGES: Byelorussian and Russian

AREA: 80,154 sq mi; 207,600 sq km

LEADING EXPORTS: machinery and chemicals

CONTINENT: Europe

BELGIUM

CAPITAL ★ Brussels

POPULATION: 10.1 million

MAJOR LANGUAGES: Flemish and French

AREA: 11,779 sq mi; 30,510 sq km

LEADING EXPORTS: machinery, iron, steel, and diamonds

CONTINENT: Europe

BELIZE

CAPITAL ★ Belmopan

POPULATION: 0.2 million

MAJOR LANGUAGES: English and Spanish

AREA: 8,865 sq mi; 22,960 sq km

LEADING EXPORTS: sugar, citrus, clothing, and fish products

CONTINENT: North America

BENIN

CAPITAL ★ Porto-Novo

POPULATION: 5.3 million

MAJOR LANGUAGES: French and Fon

AREA: 43,483 sq mi; 12,620 sq km

LEADING EXPORTS: crude oil, cotton, cocoa, and palm products

CONTINENT: Africa

BHUTAN

CAPITAL ★ Thimphu

POPULATION: 0.7 million

MAJOR LANGUAGES: Dzongkha and Nepali

AREA: 18,147 sq mi; 47,000 sq km

LEADING EXPORTS: cement, cardamom, gypsum, timber, and handicrafts

CONTINENT: Asia

BOLIVIA

CAPITALS ★ Sucre (judicial) and La Paz (administrative)

POPULATION: 7.7 million

MAJOR LANGUAGES: Spanish, Quechua, and Aymará

AREA: 424,163 sq mi; 1,098,580 sq km

LEADING EXPORTS: metals, natural gas, coffee, and soybeans

CONTINENT: South America

BOSNIA AND HERZEGOVINA

CAPITAL ★ Sarajevo

POPULATION: 4.6 million

MAJOR LANGUAGE: Serbo-Croatian

AREA: 19,781 sq mi; 51,233 sq km

LEADING EXPORTS: (not available)

CONTINENT: Europe

BOTSWANA

CAPITAL ★ Gaborone

POPULATION: 1.4 million

MAJOR LANGUAGES: English and Setswana

AREA: 231,803 sq mi; 600,370 sq km

LEADING EXPORTS: diamonds, copper, and nickel

CONTINENT: Africa

BRAZIL

CAPITAL ★ Brasília

POPULATION: 158.7 million

MAJOR LANGUAGES: Portuguese, Spanish, French, and English

AREA: 3,286,488 sq mi; 8,511,965 sq km

LEADING EXPORTS: iron ore, coffee, orange juice, and footwear

CONTINENT: South America

BRUNEI

CAPITAL ★ Bandar Seri Begawan

POPULATION: 0.3 million

MAJOR LANGUAGES: Malay, English, and Chinese

AREA: 2,228 sq mi; 5,770 sq km

LEADING EXPORT: oil

CONTINENT: Asia

BULGARIA

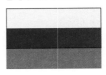

CAPITAL ★ Sofia

POPULATION: 8.8 million

MAJOR LANGUAGE: Bulgarian

AREA: 42,822 sq mi; 110,910 sq km

LEADING EXPORTS: machinery, agricultural products, and consumer goods

CONTINENT: Europe

BURKINA FASO

CAPITAL ★ Ouagadougou

POPULATION: 10.1 million

MAJOR LANGUAGES: French and Sudanic languages

AREA: 105,869 sq mi; 274,200 sq km

LEADING EXPORTS: cotton, gold, and animal products

CONTINENT: Africa

BURUNDI

CAPITAL ★ Bujumbura

POPULATION: 6.1 million

MAJOR LANGUAGES: Kirundi, French, and Swahili

AREA: 10,745 sq mi; 27,830 sq km

LEADING EXPORTS: coffee, tea, cotton, and hides

CONTINENT: Africa

CAMBODIA

CAPITAL ★ Phnom Penh

POPULATION: 10.3 million

MAJOR LANGUAGES: Khmer and French

AREA: 69,900 sq mi; 181,040 sq km

LEADING EXPORTS: rubber, rice, pepper, and raw timber

CONTINENT: Asia

CAMEROON

CAPITAL ★ Yaoundé

POPULATION: 13.1 million

MAJOR LANGUAGES: English and French

AREA: 183,568 sq mi; 475,440 sq km

LEADING EXPORTS: coffee, cocoa, petroleum products, and timber

CONTINENT: Africa

CANADA

CAPITAL ★ Ottawa

POPULATION: 28.1 million

MAJOR LANGUAGES: English and French

AREA: 3,851,798 sq mi; 9,976,140 sq km

LEADING EXPORTS: automotive products, timber, and natural gas

CONTINENT: North America

CAPE VERDE

CAPITAL ★ Praia

POPULATION: 0.4 million

MAJOR LANGUAGES: Portuguese and Crioulo

AREA: 1,556 sq mi; 4,030 sq km

LEADING EXPORTS: fish, bananas, hides, and skins

CONTINENT: Africa

CENTRAL AFRICAN REPUBLIC

CAPITAL ★ Bangui

POPULATION: 3.1 million

MAJOR LANGUAGES: French and Sango

AREA: 237,362 sq mi; 622, 980 sq km

LEADING EXPORTS: coffee, diamonds, timber, cotton, and tobacco

CONTINENT: Africa

CHAD

CAPITAL ★ N'Djamena

POPULATION: 5.5 million

MAJOR LANGUAGES: French and Arabic

AREA: 495,755 sq mi; 1,284,109 sq km

LEADING EXPORTS: cotton, cattle, textiles, and fish

CONTINENT: Africa

CHILE

CAPITAL ★ Santiago

POPULATION: 14.0 million

MAJOR LANGUAGE: Spanish

AREA: 292,259 sq mi; 756,950 sq km

LEADING EXPORTS: copper, fish, metals, and minerals

CONTINENT: South America

CHINA

CAPITAL ★ Beijing

POPULATION: 1,190.4 million

MAJOR LANGUAGES: Mandarin and local Chinese dialects

AREA: 3,705,396 sq mi; 9,596,960 sq km

LEADING EXPORTS: manufactured goods, footwear, toys, and crude oil

CONTINENT: Asia

COLOMBIA

CAPITAL ★ Bogotá

POPULATION: 35.6 million

MAJOR LANGUAGE: Spanish

AREA: 439,734 sq mi; 1,138,910 sq km

LEADING EXPORTS: coffee, petroleum, coal, and bananas

CONTINENT: South America

COMOROS

CAPITAL ★ Moroni

POPULATION: 0.5 million

MAJOR LANGUAGES: French, Arabic, and Comoran

AREA: 838 sq mi; 2,170 sq km

LEADING EXPORTS: vanilla, cloves, perfume oil, and copra

CONTINENT: Africa

CONGO

CAPITAL ★ Brazzaville

POPULATION: 2.4 million

MAJOR LANGUAGES: French, Kikongo, Lingala, and other African languages

AREA: 132,047 sq mi; 342,000 sq km

LEADING EXPORTS: crude oil, lumber, coffee, and cocoa

CONTINENT: Africa

COSTA RICA

CAPITAL ★ San José

POPULATION: 3.3 million

MAJOR LANGUAGES: Spanish and English

AREA: 19,730 sq mi; 50,100 sq km

LEADING EXPORTS: coffee, bananas, textiles, and sugar

CONTINENT: North America

CÔTE D'IVOIRE (Ivory Coast)

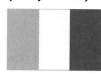

CAPITAL ★ Yamoussoukro

POPULATION: 14.3 million

MAJOR LANGUAGES: French and many African languages

AREA: 124,502 sq mi; 322,460 sq km

LEADING EXPORTS: cocoa, coffee, tropical woods, and petroleum

CONTINENT: Africa

CROATIA

CAPITAL ★ Zagreb

POPULATION: 4.7 million

MAJOR LANGUAGE: Serbo-Croatian

AREA: 21,829 sq mi; 56,538 sq km

LEADING EXPORTS: machinery, transport equipment, and other manufactures

CONTINENT: Europe

CUBA

CAPITAL ★ Havana

POPULATION: 11.1 million

MAJOR LANGUAGE: Spanish

AREA: 42,803 sq mi; 110,860 sq km

LEADING EXPORTS: sugar, nickel, shellfish, and tobacco

CONTINENT: North America

CYPRUS

CAPITAL ★ Nicosia

POPULATION: 0.7 million

MAJOR LANGUAGES: Greek, Turkish, and English

AREA: 3,571 sq mi; 9,250 sq km

LEADING EXPORTS: clothing, fruit, and potatoes

CONTINENT: Asia

CZECH REPUBLIC

CAPITAL ★ Prague

POPULATION: 10.4 million

MAJOR LANGUAGES: Czech and Slovak

AREA: 30,387 sq mi; 78,703 sq km

LEADING EXPORTS: manufactured goods and machinery

CONTINENT: Europe

COUNTRIES of the WORLD

DENMARK

CAPITAL ★ Copenhagen
POPULATION: 5.2 million
MAJOR LANGUAGES: Danish and Faroese
AREA: 16,629 sq mi; 43,070 sq mi
LEADING EXPORTS: food, machinery, and chemicals
CONTINENT: Europe

DJIBOUTI

CAPITAL ★ Djibouti
POPULATION: 0.4 million
MAJOR LANGUAGES: Arabic and French
AREA: 8,494 sq mi; 22,000 sq km
LEADING EXPORTS: hides and skins
CONTINENT: Africa

DOMINICA

CAPITAL ★ Roseau
POPULATION: 0.1 million
MAJOR LANGUAGES: English and Creole
AREA: 290 sq mi; 750 sq km
LEADING EXPORTS: bananas, soap, bay oil, and vegetables
CONTINENT: North America

DOMINICAN REPUBLIC

CAPITAL ★ Santo Domingo
POPULATION: 7.8 million
MAJOR LANGUAGES: Spanish
AREA: 18,816 sq mi; 48,730 sq km
LEADING EXPORTS: sugar, coffee, ferronickel, cocoa, and gold
CONTINENT: North America

ECUADOR

CAPITAL ★ Quito
POPULATION: 10.7 million
MAJOR LANGUAGES: Spanish and Quechua
AREA: 109,483 sq mi; 283,560 sq km
LEADING EXPORTS: oil, bananas, shrimp, and cocoa
CONTINENT: South America

EGYPT

CAPITAL ★ Cairo
POPULATION: 60.8 million
MAJOR LANGUAGES: Arabic, English, and French
AREA: 386,661 sq mi; 1,001,450 sq km
LEADING EXPORTS: oil, cotton, and textiles
CONTINENT: Africa

EL SALVADOR

CAPITAL ★ San Salvador
POPULATION: 5.8 million
MAJOR LANGUAGES: Spanish and Nahua
AREA: 8,124 sq mi; 21,040 sq km
LEADING EXPORTS: coffee, sugarcane, and shrimp
CONTINENT: North America

EQUATORIAL GUINEA
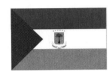
CAPITAL ★ Malabo
POPULATION: 0.4 million
MAJOR LANGUAGES: Spanish, Fang, and Bubi
AREA: 10,830 sq mi; 28,050 sq km
LEADING EXPORTS: cocoa, coffee, and timber
CONTINENT: Africa

ERITREA

CAPITAL ★ Asmara
POPULATION: 3.2 million
MAJOR LANGUAGES: Tigrinya and Arabic
AREA: 42,842 sq mi; 121,320 sq km
LEADING EXPORTS: (not available)
CONTINENT: Africa

ESTONIA

CAPITAL ★ Tallinn
POPULATION: 1.6 million
MAJOR LANGUAGES: Estonian, Latvian, Lithuanian, and Russian
AREA: 17,413 sq mi; 45,100 sq km
LEADING EXPORTS: food products, textiles, vehicles, and metals
CONTINENT: Europe

ETHIOPIA

CAPITAL ★ Addis Ababa
POPULATION: 54.9 million
MAJOR LANGUAGES: Amharic, English, and local languages
AREA: 435,186 sq mi; 1,127,127 sq km
LEADING EXPORTS: coffee, leather products, gold, and petroleum products
CONTINENT: Africa

FIJI

CAPITAL ★ Suva
POPULATION: 0.8 million
MAJOR LANGUAGES: Fijian, Hindi, and English
AREA: 7,054 sq mi; 18,270 sq km
LEADING EXPORTS: sugar, clothing, fish, gold, and lumber
CONTINENT: Islands in the Pacific Ocean

FINLAND

CAPITAL ★ Helsinki

POPULATION: 5.1 million

MAJOR LANGUAGES: Finnish and Swedish

AREA: 130,128 sq mi; 337,030 sq km

LEADING EXPORTS: paper and wood

CONTINENT: Europe

FRANCE

CAPITAL ★ Paris

POPULATION: 57.8 million

MAJOR LANGUAGE: French

AREA: 211,209 sq mi; 547,030 sq km

LEADING EXPORTS: machinery and manufactured goods

CONTINENT: Europe

GABON

CAPITAL ★ Libreville

POPULATION: 1.1 million

MAJOR LANGUAGES: French, Fang, and Bantu dialects

AREA: 103,348 sq mi; 267,670 sq km

LEADING EXPORTS: crude oil, timber, and manganese

CONTINENT: Africa

THE GAMBIA

CAPITAL ★ Banjul

POPULATION: 1.0 million

MAJOR LANGUAGES: English and Mandinka

AREA: 4,363 sq mi; 11,300 sq km

LEADING EXPORTS: peanut products, fish, and cotton lint

CONTINENT: Africa

GEORGIA

CAPITAL ★ Tbilisi

POPULATION: 5.7 million

MAJOR LANGUAGES: Georgian and Russian

AREA: 26,900 sq mi; 69,700 sq km

LEADING EXPORTS: agricultural products and machinery

CONTINENT: Asia

GERMANY

CAPITAL ★ Berlin

POPULATION: 81.1 million

MAJOR LANGUAGE: German

AREA: 137,803 sq mi; 356,910 sq km

LEADING EXPORTS: machinery and manufactured goods

CONTINENT: Europe

GHANA

CAPITAL ★ Accra

POPULATION: 17.2 million

MAJOR LANGUAGES: English and African languages

AREA: 92,101 sq mi; 238,540 sq km

LEADING EXPORTS: cocoa, gold, timber, and tuna

CONTINENT: Africa

GREECE

CAPITAL ★ Athens

POPULATION: 10.6 million

MAJOR LANGUAGES: Greek, English, and French

AREA: 50,942 sq mi; 131,940 sq km

LEADING EXPORTS: manufactured goods and food products

CONTINENT: Europe

GRENADA

CAPITAL ★ St. George's

POPULATION: 0.1 million

MAJOR LANGUAGES: English and French patois

AREA: 131 sq mi; 340 sq km

LEADING EXPORTS: nutmeg, mace, bananas, and cocoa

CONTINENT: North America

GUATEMALA

CAPITAL ★ Guatemala City

POPULATION: 10.7 million

MAJOR LANGUAGES: Spanish and Mayan dialects

AREA: 42,042 sq mi; 108,890 sq km

LEADING EXPORTS: coffee, sugar, bananas, and cardamom

CONTINENT: North America

GUINEA

CAPITAL ★ Conakry

POPULATION: 6.4 million

MAJOR LANGUAGES: French, Soussou, and Manika

AREA: 94,927 sq mi; 245,860 sq km

LEADING EXPORTS: bauxite, alumina, diamonds, and gold

CONTINENT: Africa

GUINEA-BISSAU

CAPITAL ★ Bissau

POPULATION: 1.1 million

MAJOR LANGUAGES: Portuguese and Crioulo

AREA: 13,946 sq mi; 36,120 sq km

LEADING EXPORTS: peanut products, fish, and palm kernels

CONTINENT: Africa

GUYANA

CAPITAL ★ Georgetown

POPULATION: 0.7 million

MAJOR LANGUAGES: English, Hindi, and Urdu

AREA: 83,000 sq mi; 214,970 sq km

LEADING EXPORTS: sugar, bauxite, rice, shrimp, and molasses

CONTINENT: South America

HAITI

CAPITAL ★ Port-au-Prince
POPULATION: 6.5 million
MAJOR LANGUAGES: French and French Creole
AREA: 10,714 sq mi; 27,750 sq km
LEADING EXPORTS: coffee and assembled lighting products
CONTINENT: North America

HONDURAS

CAPITAL ★ Tegucigalpa
POPULATION: 5.3 million
MAJOR LANGUAGE: Spanish
AREA: 43,277 sq mi; 112,090 sq km
LEADING EXPORTS: coffee, bananas, shrimp, lobster, and minerals
CONTINENT: North America

HUNGARY

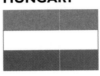

CAPITAL ★ Budapest
POPULATION: 10.3 million
MAJOR LANGUAGE: Hungarian
AREA: 35,919 sq mi; 93,030 sq km
LEADING EXPORTS: raw materials, chemicals, and consumer goods
CONTINENT: Europe

ICELAND

CAPITAL ★ Reykjavik
POPULATION: 0.3 million
MAJOR LANGUAGE: Icelandic
AREA: 39,768 sq mi; 103,000 sq km
LEADING EXPORTS: fish, animal products, and aluminum
CONTINENT: Europe

INDIA

CAPITAL ★ New Delhi
POPULATION: 919.9 million
MAJOR LANGUAGES: Hindi, English, and 14 other official languages
AREA: 1,269,342 sq mi; 3,287,590 sq km
LEADING EXPORTS: gems and jewelry, clothing, engineering goods, and fabric
CONTINENT: Asia

INDONESIA

CAPITAL ★ Jakarta
POPULATION: 200.4 million
MAJOR LANGUAGES: Bahasa Indonesian, English, Dutch, and Javanese
AREA: 741,098 sq mi; 1,919,440 sq km
LEADING EXPORTS: oil, gas, and clothing
CONTINENT: Asia

IRAN

CAPITAL ★ Tehran
POPULATION: 65.6 million
MAJOR LANGUAGES: Farsi, Turkic, and Kurdish
AREA: 636,294 sq mi; 1,648,000 sq km
LEADING EXPORTS: oil, carpets, and fruits
CONTINENT: Asia

IRAQ

CAPITAL ★ Baghdad
POPULATION: 19.9 million
MAJOR LANGUAGES: Arabic and Kurdish
AREA: 168,754 sq mi; 437,072 sq km
LEADING EXPORT: oil
CONTINENT: Asia

IRELAND

CAPITAL ★ Dublin
POPULATION: 3.5 million
MAJOR LANGUAGES: English and Irish
AREA: 27,135 sq mi; 70,280 sq km
LEADING EXPORTS: machinery, chemicals, and live animals
CONTINENT: Europe

ISRAEL

CAPITAL ★ Jerusalem
POPULATION: 5.1 million*
MAJOR LANGUAGES: Hebrew and Arabic
AREA: 8,091 sq mi; 20,770 sq km*
LEADING EXPORTS: diamonds, chemicals, and machinery
CONTINENT: Asia
*does not include the 2.3 million people and the 2,402 sq mi of the Gaza Strip and the West Bank

ITALY

CAPITAL ★ Rome
POPULATION: 58.1 million
MAJOR LANGUAGE: Italian
AREA: 116,305 sq mi; 301,230 sq km
LEADING EXPORTS: machinery, manufactured goods, cars, and clothing
CONTINENT: Europe

JAMAICA

CAPITAL ★ Kingston
POPULATION: 2.6 million
MAJOR LANGUAGES: English and Jamaican Creole
AREA: 4,243 sq mi; 10,990 sq km
LEADING EXPORTS: alumina, bauxite, sugar, and bananas
CONTINENT: North America

JAPAN

CAPITAL ★ Tokyo
POPULATION: 125.1 million
MAJOR LANGUAGE: Japanese
AREA: 145,883 sq mi; 377,835 sq km
LEADING EXPORT: machinery
CONTINENT: Asia

JORDAN

CAPITAL ★ Amman
POPULATION: 4.0 million
MAJOR LANGUAGE: Arabic
AREA: 34,445 sq mi; 89,213 sq km
LEADING EXPORTS: phosphates and agricultural products
CONTINENT: Asia

KAZAKHSTAN

CAPITAL ★ Almaty
POPULATION: 17.3 million
MAJOR LANGUAGES: Kazakh and Russian
AREA: 1,049,155 sq mi; 2,717,300 sq km
LEADING EXPORTS: oil, grain, wool, and meat
CONTINENT: Asia

KENYA

CAPITAL ★ Nairobi
POPULATION: 28.2 million
MAJOR LANGUAGES: English and Swahili
AREA: 224,962 sq mi; 582,650 sq km
LEADING EXPORTS: coffee, tea, and petroleum products
CONTINENT: Africa

KIRIBATI

CAPITAL ★ Tarawa
POPULATION: 77,853
MAJOR LANGUAGES: Gilbertese and English
AREA: 277 sq mi; 717 sq km
LEADING EXPORTS: fish, copra, and seaweed
CONTINENT: Islands in the Pacific Ocean

KOREA, NORTH

CAPITAL ★ Pyongyang
POPULATION: 23.1 million
MAJOR LANGUAGE: Korean
AREA: 46,541 sq mi; 120,540 sq km
LEADING EXPORTS: minerals, agricultural and fishery products
CONTINENT: Asia

KOREA, SOUTH

CAPITAL ★ Seoul
POPULATION: 45.6 million
MAJOR LANGUAGE: Korean
AREA: 38,023 sq mi; 98,480 sq km
LEADING EXPORTS: machinery, steel, automobiles, electronic equipment, and clothing
CONTINENT: Asia

KUWAIT

CAPITAL ★ Kuwait
POPULATION: 1.8 million
MAJOR LANGUAGE: Arabic
AREA: 6,880 sq mi; 17,820 sq km
LEADING EXPORT: oil
CONTINENT: Asia

KYRGYZSTAN

CAPITAL ★ Bishkek
POPULATION: 4.7 million
MAJOR LANGUAGES: Kyrgyz and Russian
AREA: 76,640 sq mi; 198,500 sq km
LEADING EXPORTS: metals, wool, cotton, and shoes
CONTINENT: Asia

LAOS

CAPITAL ★ Vientiane
POPULATION: 4.7 million
MAJOR LANGUAGES: Lao, French, and English
AREA: 91,429 sq mi; 236,800 sq km
LEADING EXPORTS: timber, electricity, coffee, and tin
CONTINENT: Asia

LATVIA

CAPITAL ★ Riga
POPULATION: 2.7 million
MAJOR LANGUAGES: Latvian and Russian
AREA: 24,749 sq mi; 64,100 sq km
LEADING EXPORTS: metals, oil products, timber, and dairy products
CONTINENT: Europe

LEBANON

CAPITAL ★ Beirut
POPULATION: 3.6 million
MAJOR LANGUAGES: Arabic and French
AREA: 4,015 sq mi; 10,400 sq km
LEADING EXPORTS: jewelry, clothing, metal products, and chemicals
CONTINENT: Asia

LESOTHO

CAPITAL ★ Maseru
POPULATION: 1.9 million
MAJOR LANGUAGES: Sesotho and English
AREA: 11,718 sq mi; 30,350 sq km
LEADING EXPORTS: wool, cattle, wheat, peas, and beans
CONTINENT: Africa

LIBERIA

CAPITAL ★ Monrovia

POPULATION: 2.9 million

MAJOR LANGUAGES: English and Niger-Congo languages

AREA: 43,000 sq mi; 111,370 sq km

LEADING EXPORTS: iron ore, rubber, timber, and coffee

CONTINENT: Africa

LIBYA

CAPITAL ★ Tripoli

POPULATION: 5.1 million

MAJOR LANGUAGES: Arabic, Italian, and English

AREA: 679,360 sq mi; 1,759,540 sq km

LEADING EXPORTS: oil and natural gas

CONTINENT: Africa

LIECHTENSTEIN

CAPITAL ★ Vaduz

POPULATION: 30,281

MAJOR LANGUAGE: German

AREA: 62 sq mi; 160 sq km

LEADING EXPORTS: stamps, hardware, pottery, and dental products

CONTINENT: Europe

LITHUANIA

CAPITAL ★ Vilnius

POPULATION: 3.8 million

MAJOR LANGUAGES: Lithuanian, Russian, and Polish

AREA: 25,170 sq mi; 65,200 sq km

LEADING EXPORTS: electronics, food, and chemicals

CONTINENT: Europe

LUXEMBOURG

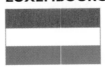

CAPITAL ★ Luxembourg

POPULATION: 0.4 million

MAJOR LANGUAGES: Luxembourgisch, German, French, and English

AREA: 998 sq mi; 2,586 sq km

LEADING EXPORTS: steel products, rubber products, glass, and aluminum

CONTINENT: Europe

MACEDONIA

CAPITAL ★ Skopje

POPULATION: 2.2 million

MAJOR LANGUAGES: Macedonian and Albanian

AREA: 9,781 sq mi; 25,333 sq km

LEADING EXPORTS: manufactured goods, machinery, and transport equipment

CONTINENT: Europe

MADAGASCAR

CAPITAL ★ Antananarivo

POPULATION: 13.4 million

MAJOR LANGUAGES: French and Malagasy

AREA: 226,656 sq mi; 587,040 sq km

LEADING EXPORTS: coffee, vanilla, cloves, shellfish, and sugar

CONTINENT: Africa

MALAWI

CAPITAL ★ Lilongwe

POPULATION: 9.7 million

MAJOR LANGUAGES: English and Chichewa

AREA: 45,745 sq mi; 118,480 sq km

LEADING EXPORTS: tobacco, sugar, tea, coffee, and peanuts

CONTINENT: Africa

MALAYSIA

CAPITAL ★ Kuala Lumpur

POPULATION: 19.3 million

MAJOR LANGUAGES: Malay, English, and Chinese dialects

AREA: 127,317 sq mi; 329,750 sq km

LEADING EXPORTS: rubber, petroleum, and electronic equipment

CONTINENT: Asia

MALDIVES

CAPITAL ★ Malé

POPULATION: 0.2 million

MAJOR LANGUAGE: Divehi

AREA: 116 sq mi; 300 sq km

LEADING EXPORTS: fish and clothing

CONTINENT: Asia

MALI

CAPITAL ★ Bamako

POPULATION: 9.1 million

MAJOR LANGUAGES: Bambara and French

AREA: 478,765 sq mi; 1,240,000 sq km

LEADING EXPORTS: cotton, livestock, and gold

CONTINENT: Africa

MALTA

CAPITAL ★ Valletta

POPULATION: 0.4 million

MAJOR LANGUAGES: Maltese and English

AREA: 123 sq mi; 320 sq km

LEADING EXPORTS: machinery, clothing, and footwear

CONTINENT: Europe

MARSHALL ISLANDS

CAPITAL ★ Majuro

POPULATION: 54,031

MAJOR LANGUAGES: English, Marshallese dialects, and Japanese

AREA: 70 sq mi; 181 sq km

LEADING EXPORTS: coconut oil, fish, live animals, and trichus shells

CONTINENT: Islands in the Pacific Ocean

MAURITANIA

CAPITAL ★ Nouakchott

POPULATION: 2.2 million

MAJOR LANGUAGES: Arabic and Wolof

AREA: 397,954 sq mi; 1,030,700 sq km

LEADING EXPORTS: iron ore and fish

CONTINENT: Africa

MAURITIUS

CAPITAL ★ Port Louis

POPULATION: 1.1 million

MAJOR LANGUAGES: English, Creole, and French

AREA: 718 sq mi; 1,860 sq km

LEADING EXPORTS: sugar, textiles, and tea

CONTINENT: Africa

MEXICO

CAPITAL ★ Mexico City

POPULATION: 92.2 million

MAJOR LANGUAGE: Spanish

AREA: 761,604 sq mi; 1,972,550 sq km

LEADING EXPORTS: oil, cotton, coffee, silver, and consumer electronics

CONTINENT: North America

MICRONESIA

CAPITAL ★ Palikir

POPULATION: 0.1 million

MAJOR LANGUAGES: English, Trukese, Yapese, and Kosrean

AREA: 271 sq mi; 702 sq km

LEADING EXPORT: copra

CONTINENT: Islands in the Pacific Ocean

MOLDOVA

CAPITAL ★ Kishinev

POPULATION: 4.5 million

MAJOR LANGUAGES: Moldovan, Russian, and Gagauz

AREA: 13,000 sq mi; 33,700 sq km

LEADING EXPORTS: wine, fur, textiles, and footwear

CONTINENT: Europe

MONACO

CAPITAL ★ Monaco

POPULATION: 31,278

MAJOR LANGUAGES: French, Monégasque, and English

AREA: 0.7 sq mi; 1.9 sq km

LEADING EXPORTS: (not available)

CONTINENT: Europe

MONGOLIA

CAPITAL ★ Ulaanbaatar

POPULATION: 2.4 million

MAJOR LANGUAGES: Khalkha Mongolian, Turkic, Russian, and Chinese

AREA: 604,248 sq mi; 1,565,000 sq km

LEADING EXPORTS: copper, livestock, and animal products

CONTINENT: Asia

MOROCCO

CAPITAL ★ Rabat

POPULATION: 28.6 million

MAJOR LANGUAGES: Arabic, Berber, and French

AREA: 172,413 sq mi; 446,550 sq km

LEADING EXPORTS: food, beverages, consumer goods, and phosphates

CONTINENT: Africa

MOZAMBIQUE

CAPITAL ★ Maputo

POPULATION: 17.3 million

MAJOR LANGUAGES: Portuguese and African languages

AREA: 309,495 sq mi; 801,590 sq km

LEADING EXPORTS: shrimp, cashew nuts, and sugar

CONTINENT: Africa

MYANMAR (Burma)

CAPITAL ★ Yangon

POPULATION: 44.3 million

MAJOR LANGUAGE: Burmese

AREA: 261,970 sq mi; 678,500 sq km

LEADING EXPORTS: timber, pulses and beans, teak, and rice

CONTINENT: Asia

NAMIBIA

CAPITAL ★ Windhoek

POPULATION: 1.6 million

MAJOR LANGUAGES: English, Afrikaans, and German

AREA: 318,259 sq mi; 824,290 sq km

LEADING EXPORTS: diamonds, metals, and livestock

CONTINENT: Africa

NAURU

CAPITAL ★ Yaren
POPULATION: 10,019
MAJOR LANGUAGES: Nauruan and English
AREA: 8 sq mi; 21 sq km
LEADING EXPORT: phosphates
CONTINENT: Islands in the Pacific Ocean

NEPAL

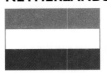

CAPITAL ★ Kathmandu
POPULATION: 21.0 million
MAJOR LANGUAGE: Nepali
AREA: 54,363 sq mi; 140,800 sq km
LEADING EXPORTS: carpets, clothing, leather goods, jute goods, and grain
CONTINENT: Asia

NETHERLANDS

CAPITAL ★ Amsterdam
POPULATION: 15.4 million
MAJOR LANGUAGE: Dutch
AREA: 14,413 sq mi; 37,330 sq km
LEADING EXPORTS: chemicals, metal products, and processed food
CONTINENT: Europe

NEW ZEALAND

CAPITAL ★ Wellington
POPULATION: 3.4 million
MAJOR LANGUAGES: English and Maori
AREA: 103,738 sq mi; 268,680 sq km
LEADING EXPORTS: lamb, wool, meat, fruit, and cheese
CONTINENT: Islands in the Pacific Ocean

NICARAGUA

CAPITAL ★ Managua
POPULATION: 4.1 million
MAJOR LANGUAGE: Spanish
AREA: 49,998 sq mi; 129,494 sq km
LEADING EXPORTS: cotton, coffee, chemicals, and foodstuffs
CONTINENT: North America

NIGER

CAPITAL ★ Niamey
POPULATION: 9.0 million
MAJOR LANGUAGES: French, Hausa, and Djerma
AREA: 489,190 sq mi; 1,267,000 sq km
LEADING EXPORTS: uranium ore and livestock products
CONTINENT: Africa

NIGERIA

CAPITAL ★ Abuja
POPULATION: 98.1 million
MAJOR LANGUAGES: English, Hausa, Yoruba, Ibo, and Fulani
AREA: 356,669 sq mi; 923,770 sq km
LEADING EXPORTS: oil and cocoa
CONTINENT: Africa

NORWAY

CAPITAL ★ Oslo
POPULATION: 4.3 million
MAJOR LANGUAGE: Norwegian
AREA: 125,182 sq mi; 324,220 sq km
LEADING EXPORTS: oil, natural gas, metals, fish, and ships
CONTINENT: Europe

OMAN

CAPITAL ★ Muscat
POPULATION: 1.7 million
MAJOR LANGUAGE: Arabic
AREA: 82,013 sq mi; 212,460 sq km
LEADING EXPORTS: fish and oil
CONTINENT: Asia

PAKISTAN

CAPITAL ★ Islamabad
POPULATION: 128.9 million
MAJOR LANGUAGES: Urdu, Punjabi, and English
AREA: 310,402 sq mi; 803,940 sq km
LEADING EXPORTS: cotton products, clothing, and rice
CONTINENT: Asia

PALAU

CAPITAL ★ Koror
POPULATION: 15,122
MAJOR LANGUAGES: Palauan and English
AREA: 196 sq mi; 508 sq km
LEADING EXPORTS: tuna and copra
CONTINENT: Islands in the Pacific Ocean

PANAMA

CAPITAL ★ Panama City
POPULATION: 2.6 million
MAJOR LANGUAGES: Spanish and English
AREA: 30,193 sq mi; 78,200 sq km
LEADING EXPORTS: bananas, shrimp, clothing, and sugar
CONTINENT: North America

PAPUA NEW GUINEA

CAPITAL ★ Port Moresby
POPULATION: 4.2 million
MAJOR LANGUAGES: Pidgin English, English, and Motu
AREA: 178,259 sq mi; 461,690 sq km
LEADING EXPORTS: gold, copper, oil, logs, coffee, and cocoa
CONTINENT: Islands in the Pacific Ocean

PARAGUAY

CAPITAL ★ Asunción

POPULATION: 5.2 million

MAJOR LANGUAGES: Spanish and Guarani

AREA: 157,047 sq mi; 406,750 sq km

LEADING EXPORTS: cotton, timber, coffee, and soybeans

CONTINENT: South America

PERU

CAPITAL ★ Lima

POPULATION: 23.7 million

MAJOR LANGUAGES: Spanish, Quechua, and Aymará

AREA: 496,225 sq mi; 1,285,220 sq km

LEADING EXPORTS: oil, copper, zinc, lead, and coffee

CONTINENT: South America

PHILIPPINES

CAPITAL ★ Manila

POPULATION: 69.8 million

MAJOR LANGUAGES: Filipino, Tagalog, and English

AREA: 115,830 sq mi; 300,000 sq km

LEADING EXPORTS: electronics, textiles, and coconut products

CONTINENT: Asia

POLAND

CAPITAL ★ Warsaw

POPULATION: 38.7 million

MAJOR LANGUAGE: Polish

Area: 120,726 sq mi; 312,680 sq km

LEADING EXPORTS: machinery, metals, chemicals, food, and fuels

CONTINENT: Europe

PORTUGAL

CAPITAL ★ Lisbon

POPULATION: 10.5 million

MAJOR LANGUAGE: Portuguese

AREA: 35,552 sq mi; 92,080 sq km

LEADING EXPORTS: machinery, cork, and paper products

CONTINENT: Europe

QATAR

CAPITAL ★ Doha

POPULATION: 0.5 million

MAJOR LANGUAGES: Arabic and English

AREA: 4,247 sq mi; 11,000 sq km

LEADING EXPORTS: oil, steel, and fertilizers

CONTINENT: Asia

ROMANIA

CAPITAL ★ Bucharest

POPULATION: 23.2 million

MAJOR LANGUAGES: Romanian, Hungarian, and German

AREA: 91,699 sq mi; 237,500 sq km

LEADING EXPORTS: metals, mineral products, textiles, and electric machines

CONTINENT: Europe

RUSSIA

CAPITAL ★ Moscow

POPULATION: 149.6 million

MAJOR LANGUAGE: Russian

AREA: 6,592,771 sq mi; 17,075,200 sq km

LEADING EXPORTS: petroleum, natural gas, wood, metals, and chemicals

CONTINENTS: Europe and Asia

RWANDA

CAPITAL ★ Kigali

POPULATION: 8.4 million

MAJOR LANGUAGES: Kinyarwanda, French, and Kiswahili

AREA: 10,170 sq mi; 26,340 sq km

LEADING EXPORTS: coffee and tea

CONTINENT: Africa

ST. KITTS AND NEVIS

CAPITAL ★ Basseterre

POPULATION: 40,671

MAJOR LANGUAGE: English

AREA: 139 sq mi; 360 sq km

LEADING EXPORTS: sugar, clothing, electronics, and stamps

CONTINENT: North America

ST. LUCIA

CAPITAL ★ Castries

POPULATION: 145,090

MAJOR LANGUAGES: English and French patois

AREA: 239 sq mi; 620 sq km

LEADING EXPORTS: bananas, clothing, cocoa, and coconut oil

CONTINENT: North America

ST. VINCENT AND THE GRENADINES

CAPITAL ★ Kingstown

POPULATION: 0.1 million

MAJOR LANGUAGE: English

AREA: 131 sq mi; 340 sq km

LEADING EXPORTS: bananas, taro, arrowroot starch, and tennis racquets

CONTINENT: North America

SAN MARINO

CAPITAL ★ San Marino
POPULATION: 24,091
MAJOR LANGUAGE: Italian
AREA: 23 sq mi; 60 sq km
LEADING EXPORTS: lime, wood, chestnuts, and ceramics
CONTINENT: Europe

SÃO TOMÉ AND PRÍNCIPE

CAPITAL ★ São Tomé
POPULATION: 0.1 million
MAJOR LANGUAGE: Portuguese
AREA: 371 sq mi; 960 sq km
LEADING EXPORTS: cocoa, copra, coffee, and palm oil
CONTINENT: Africa

SAUDI ARABIA

CAPITAL ★ Riyadh
POPULATION: 18.2 million
MAJOR LANGUAGE: Arabic
AREA: 829,997 sq mi; 2,149,690 sq km
LEADING EXPORT: oil
CONTINENT: Asia

SENEGAL

CAPITAL ★ Dakar
POPULATION: 8.7 million
MAJOR LANGUAGES: French and Wolof
AREA: 75,749 sq mi; 196,190 sq km
LEADING EXPORTS: fuels, fish, ground nuts, phosphates, and cotton
CONTINENT: Africa

SEYCHELLES

CAPITAL ★ Victoria
POPULATION: 72,113
MAJOR LANGUAGES: Creole, English, and French
AREA: 176 sq mi; 455 sq km
LEADING EXPORTS: fish, copra, and cinnamon bark
CONTINENT: Africa

SIERRA LEONE

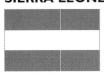

CAPITAL ★ Freetown
POPULATION: 4.6 million
MAJOR LANGUAGES: English, Mende, Temne, and Krio
AREA: 27,699 sq mi; 71,740 sq km
LEADING EXPORTS: rutile, diamonds, bauxite, and coffee
CONTINENT: Africa

SINGAPORE

CAPITAL ★ Singapore
POPULATION: 2.9 million
MAJOR LANGUAGES: Chinese, English, Malay, and Tamil
AREA: 224 sq mi; 633 sq km
LEADING EXPORTS: petroleum products, computer equipment, and rubber
CONTINENT: Asia

SLOVAKIA

CAPITAL ★ Bratislava
POPULATION: 5.4 million
MAJOR LANGUAGES: Slovak and Hungarian
AREA: 18,859 sq mi; 48,845 sq km
LEADING EXPORTS: machinery, chemicals, fuels, and minerals
CONTINENT: Europe

SLOVENIA

CAPITAL ★ Ljubljana
POPULATION: 2.0 million
MAJOR LANGUAGE: Slovenian
AREA: 7,836 sq mi; 20,296 sq km
LEADING EXPORTS: manufactured goods and chemicals
CONTINENT: Europe

SOLOMON ISLANDS

CAPITAL ★ Honiara
POPULATION: 0.4 million
MAJOR LANGUAGES: English, Pidgin English, and Melanesian
AREA: 10,985 sq mi; 28,450 sq km
LEADING EXPORTS: fish, timber, palm oil, copra, and copper
CONTINENT: Islands in the Pacific Ocean

SOMALIA

CAPITAL ★ Mogadishu
POPULATION: 6.7 million
MAJOR LANGUAGES: Somali and Arabic
AREA: 246,201 sq mi; 637,660 sq km
LEADING EXPORTS: bananas, live animals, fish, and hides
CONTINENT: Africa

SOUTH AFRICA

CAPITALS ★ Pretoria, Cape Town, and Bloemfontein
POPULATION: 43.9 million
MAJOR LANGUAGES: Afrikaans, English, Zulu and other African languages
AREA: 471,783 sq mi; 1,221,912 sq km
LEADING EXPORTS: gold, other minerals, and metals
CONTINENT: Africa

SPAIN

CAPITAL ★ Madrid

POPULATION: 39.3 million

MAJOR LANGUAGES: Spanish and Catalan

AREA: 194,884 sq mi; 504,750 sq km

LEADING EXPORTS: cars and trucks, machinery

CONTINENT: Europe

SRI LANKA

CAPITAL ★ Colombo

POPULATION: 18.1 million

MAJOR LANGUAGES: Sinhala, Tamil, and English

AREA: 25,332 sq mi; 65,610 sq km

LEADING EXPORTS: tea, garments and textiles, petroleum products, and rubber

CONTINENT: Asia

SUDAN

CAPITAL ★ Khartoum

POPULATION: 29.4 million

MAJOR LANGUAGES: Arabic, Nubian and Sudanic languages

AREA: 967,496 sq mi; 2,505,810 sq km

LEADING EXPORTS: cotton, sesame, gum arabic, and peanuts

CONTINENT: Africa

SURINAME

CAPITAL ★ Paramaribo

POPULATION: 0.4 million

MAJOR LANGUAGES: Dutch, English, and Hindi

AREA: 63,039 sq mi; 163,270 sq km

LEADING EXPORTS: rice, bananas, aluminum, and fish

CONTINENT: South America

SWAZILAND

CAPITAL ★ Mbabane

POPULATION: .9 million

MAJOR LANGUAGES: Siswati and English

AREA: 6,703 sq mi; 17,360 sq km

LEADING EXPORTS: food, sugar, wood products, and citrus

CONTINENT: Africa

SWEDEN

CAPITAL ★ Stockholm

POPULATION: 8.8 million

MAJOR LANGUAGE: Swedish

AREA: 173,732 sq mi; 449,964 sq km

LEADING EXPORTS: machinery, motor vehicles, and iron and steel products

CONTINENT: Europe

SWITZERLAND

CAPITAL ★ Bern

POPULATION: 7.0 million

MAJOR LANGUAGES: German, French, Italian, and Romansch

AREA: 15,942 sq mi; 41,290 sq km

LEADING EXPORTS: machinery, metal products, textiles, and clothing

CONTINENT: Europe

SYRIA

CAPITAL ★ Damascus

POPULATION: 14.9 million

MAJOR LANGUAGES: Arabic and Kurdish

AREA: 71,498 sq mi; 185,180 sq km

LEADING EXPORTS: oil, textiles, cotton, fruits, and vegetables

CONTINENT: Asia

TAIWAN

CAPITAL ★ Taipei

POPULATION: 21.3 million

MAJOR LANGUAGES: Mandarin, Taiwanese, and Hakka dialects

AREA: 13,892 sq mi; 35,980 sq km

LEADING EXPORTS: electrical machinery, electronic products, textiles, and footwear

CONTINENT: Asia

TAJIKISTAN

CAPITAL ★ Dushanbe

POPULATION: 6.0 million

MAJOR LANGUAGES: Tajik and Russian

AREA: 55,240 sq mi; 143,100 sq km

LEADING EXPORTS: aluminum, textiles, and cotton

CONTINENT: Asia

TANZANIA

CAPITAL ★ Dar es Salaam

POPULATION: 27.9 million

MAJOR LANGUAGES: Swahili and English

AREA: 364,900 sq mi; 945,090 sq km

LEADING EXPORTS: coffee, cotton, tobacco, and tea

CONTINENT: Africa

THAILAND

CAPITAL ★ Bangkok

POPULATION: 59.5 million

MAJOR LANGUAGES: Thai and English

AREA: 198,456 sq mi; 514,000 sq km

LEADING EXPORTS: food and machinery

CONTINENT: Asia

TOGO

CAPITAL ★ Lomé

POPULATION: 4.3 million

MAJOR LANGUAGES: French, Kabye, Ewe, Mina, and Dagomba

AREA: 21,927 sq mi; 56,790 sq km

LEADING EXPORTS: phosphates, cotton, cocoa, and coffee

CONTINENT: Africa

TONGA

CAPITAL ★ Nuku'alofa

POPULATION: 0.1 million

MAJOR LANGUAGES: Tongan and English

AREA: 289 sq mi; 748 sq km

LEADING EXPORTS: vanilla, fish, root crops, coconut oil, and squash

CONTINENT: Islands in the Pacific Ocean

TRINIDAD AND TOBAGO

CAPITAL ★ Port-of-Spain

POPULATION: 1.3 million

MAJOR LANGUAGES: English, Hindi, and French

AREA: 1,980 sq mi; 5,130 sq km

LEADING EXPORTS: oil, chemicals, and steel products

CONTINENT: North America

TUNISIA

CAPITAL ★ Tunis

POPULATION: 8.7 million

MAJOR LANGUAGES: Arabic and French

AREA: 63,170 sq mi; 163,610 sq km

LEADING EXPORTS: hydrocarbons, agricultural products, and chemicals

CONTINENT: Africa

TURKEY

CAPITAL ★ Ankara

POPULATION: 62.1 million

MAJOR LANGUAGES: Turkish, Kurdish, and Arabic

AREA: 301,383 sq mi; 780,580 sq km

LEADING EXPORTS: manufactured products and foodstuffs

CONTINENTS: Asia and Europe

TURKMENISTAN

CAPITAL ★ Ashgabat

POPULATION: 4.0 million

MAJOR LANGUAGES: Turkmen, Russian, and Uzbek

AREA: 186,400 sq mi; 488,100 sq km

LEADING EXPORTS: gas, oil, cotton, and carpets

CONTINENT: Asia

TUVALU

CAPITAL ★ Funafuti

POPULATION: 9,831

MAJOR LANGUAGES: Tuvaluan and English

AREA: 10 sq mi; 26 sq km

LEADING EXPORT: copra

CONTINENT: Islands in the Pacific Ocean

UGANDA

CAPITAL ★ Kampala

POPULATION: 19.1 million

MAJOR LANGUAGES: English, Luganda, Swahili, and Bantu languages

AREA: 91,135 sq mi; 236,040 sq km

LEADING EXPORTS: coffee, cotton, and tea

CONTINENT: Africa

UKRAINE

CAPITAL ★ Kiev

POPULATION: 51.8 million

MAJOR LANGUAGES: Ukrainian, Russian, Romanian, and Polish

AREA: 233,090 sq mi; 603,700 sq km

LEADING EXPORTS: coal, metals, grain, and meat

CONTINENT: Europe

UNITED ARAB EMIRATES

CAPITAL ★ Abu Dhabi

POPULATION: 2.8 million

MAJOR LANGUAGES: Arabic, Persian, English, Hindi, and Urdu

AREA: 29,182 sq mi; 75,581 sq km

LEADING EXPORTS: oil, natural gas, dried fish, and dates

CONTINENT: Asia

UNITED KINGDOM

CAPITAL ★ London

POPULATION: 58.1 million

MAJOR LANGUAGES: English, Welsh, and Scottish Gaelic

AREA: 94, 525 sq mi; 244, 820 sq km

LEADING EXPORTS: machinery and manufactured goods

CONTINENT: Europe

UNITED STATES

CAPITAL ★ Washington, D.C.

POPULATION: 260.7 million

MAJOR LANGUAGE: English

AREA: 3,787,319 sq mi; 9,809,156 sq km

LEADING EXPORTS: automobiles, raw materials, and consumer goods

CONTINENT: North America

URUGUAY

CAPITAL ★ Montevideo

POPULATION: 3.2 million

MAJOR LANGUAGES: Spanish and Brazilero

AREA: 68,039 sq mi; 176,220 sq km

LEADING EXPORTS: wool and meat

CONTINENT: South America

UZBEKISTAN

CAPITAL ★ Tashkent

POPULATION: 22.6 million

MAJOR LANGUAGES: Uzbek, Russian, and Tajik

AREA: 172,741 sq mi; 447,400 sq km

LEADING EXPORTS: cotton, gold, natural gas, and metals

CONTINENT: Asia

VANUATU

CAPITAL ★ Port-Vila

POPULATION: 0.2 million

MAJOR LANGUAGES: Bislama, English, and French

AREA: 5,699 sq mi; 14,760 sq km

LEADING EXPORTS: copra, beef, cocoa, timber, and coffee

CONTINENT: Islands in the Pacific Ocean

VATICAN CITY (The Holy See)

CAPITAL ★ Vatican City

POPULATION: 821

MAJOR LANGUAGES: Italian and Latin

AREA: 0.17 sq mi; 0.44 sq km

LEADING EXPORTS: (not available)

CONTINENT: Europe

VENEZUELA

CAPITAL ★ Caracas

POPULATION: 20.6 million

MAJOR LANGUAGES: Spanish and Indian dialects

AREA: 352,143 sq mi; 912,050 sq km

LEADING EXPORTS: oil, bauxite, aluminum, steel, and chemicals

CONTINENT: South America

VIETNAM

CAPITAL ★ Hanoi

POPULATION: 73.1 million

MAJOR LANGUAGES: Vietnamese, French, Chinese, English, and Khmer

AREA: 127,243 sq mi; 329,560 sq km

LEADING EXPORTS: agricultural products, oil, rice, and coffee

CONTINENT: Asia

WESTERN SAMOA

CAPITAL ★ Apia

POPULATION: 0.2 million

MAJOR LANGUAGES: Samoan and English

AREA: 1,104 sq mi; 2,860 sq km

LEADING EXPORTS: copra, cocoa, taro, and coconut oil and cream

CONTINENT: Islands in the Pacific Ocean

YEMEN

CAPITAL ★ San'a

POPULATION: 11.1 million

MAJOR LANGUAGE: Arabic

AREA: 203, 850 sq mi; 527,970 sq km

LEADING EXPORTS: oil, coffee, cotton, hides, and fish

CONTINENT: Asia

YUGOSLAVIA

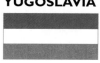

CAPITAL ★ Belgrade

POPULATION: 10.8 million

MAJOR LANGUAGES: Serbo-Croatian and Albanian

AREA: 39,518 sq mi; 102,350 sq km

LEADING EXPORTS: machinery and transport equipment

CONTINENT: Europe

ZAIRE

CAPITAL ★ Kinshasa

POPULATION: 42.7 million

MAJOR LANGUAGES: French, Swahili, and other Sudanese and Bantu dialects

AREA: 905,565 sq mi; 2,345,410 sq km

LEADING EXPORTS: copper, coffee, diamonds, cobalt, crude oil

CONTINENT: Africa

ZAMBIA

CAPITAL ★ Lusaka

POPULATION: 9.2 million

MAJOR LANGUAGES: English and about 70 Bantu dialects

AREA: 290,583 sq mi; 752,610 sq km

LEADING EXPORTS: copper, zinc, cobalt, lead, and tobacco

CONTINENT: Africa

ZIMBABWE

CAPITAL ★ Harare

POPULATION: 10.9 million

MAJOR LANGUAGES: English, Shona, and Sindebele

AREA: 150,803 sq mi; 390,580 sq km

LEADING EXPORTS: tobacco, gold, and manufactures

CONTINENT: Africa

SOURCE: population, languages, area, exports—*The CIA World Factbook*, 1994; additional information on languages—*The Europa World Book*, 1995

WORLD HISTORY TIME LINE

	BEFORE 6000 B.C.		6000–5000 B.C.		5000–4000 B.C.	
EUROPE	20,000 years ago	Hunter-gatherers paint the walls of caves near Avignon, France	6000 B.C.	Farming spreads to other parts of the continent	5000 B.C.	Farming villages appear in southern France
	10,000 B.C.	Early Europeans make tiny blades, called *microliths*, out of flint	5500 B.C.	Early pottery decorated with patterned lines is made through much of the continent	4500 B.C.	Stone axes are traded and used to clear forest land for farming
	7000 B.C.	Farming begins in southern Europe, as Greek farmers raise wheat and herd sheep and goats				
AFRICA	10,000 B.C.	People begin to build villages along the Nile River	6000 B.C.	Farmers build irrigation ditches along the Nile River	5000 B.C.	Farmers grow wheat and barley in Egypt
	8000 B.C.	People along the Nile use reed nets to catch fish	6000 B.C.	People use barbed harpoons to catch fish in Africa's rivers and lakes	4500 B.C.	Nubian artisans make pottery in what is now Sudan
	6500 B.C.	Rock paintings in the Sahara Desert show animals long gone from the region, such as buffalo, giraffes and elephants				
ASIA	8000 B.C.	Hunter-gatherers use wild rice in East and Southeast Asia	6000 B.C.	Early agriculture begins at Catal Huyuk, in what is today Turkey	5000 B.C.	First towns settled in Sumer
	7000 B.C.	Before the development of pottery, early people in western Asia make "white ware" from lime and ash			5000 B.C.	Early settlements emerge in China
					5000 B.C.	Copper used in Mesopotamia
THE AMERICAS	40,000 years ago	Asian hunters begin to cross the Beringia land bridge	5000 B.C.	Cochise and Chumash cultures develop in southwestern North America	5000 B.C.	Early maize farming begins in what is today Mexico
	15,000 years ago	People have spread throughout the Americas	5000 B.C.	Chinchorros people build settlements in what is today northern Chile	4500 B.C.	Indians use weighted nets to fish the waters of the American northwest
	7000 B.C.	Native American craftworkers use stone tools for woodworking				

R36

4000–3000 B.C.		3000–2000 B.C.		2000–1000 B.C.	
4000 B.C.	Farmers cultivate crops in the British Isles	3000 B.C.	Artisans on Crete use bronze and gold	2000 B.C.	Minoan palace civilization begins to flourish in Crete
3500 B.C.	New Stone Age period begins in western Europe	3000 B.C.	Loom weaving begins in Europe	1600 B.C.	Mycenaeans gain power in Aegean region
3300 B.C.	"Iceman" takes his last hike into the Alps	3000 B.C.	Huge stone structures built at Stonehenge, England	1500 B.C.	Minoan culture ends in Crete
		2200 B.C.	Bronze Age begins in Ireland	1400 B.C.	Mycenaean culture spreads to Greece
4000 B.C.	The sail is first used on boats on the Nile River	2772 B.C.	Egyptians create a calendar of 365 days	2000 B.C.	Kushite culture develops along the Upper Nile
4000 B.C.	Artisans make pottery in Ghana, West Africa	2600 B.C.	Pharaoh Khufu orders construction of the Great Pyramid	1550 B.C.	Egyptians defeat the Hyksos and begin the New Kingdom period
3200 B.C.	Egyptians begin to develop hieroglyphic writing	2500 B.C.	Egyptians build the Great Sphinx at Giza	1500 B.C.	Queen Hatshepsut is pharaoh
3100 B.C.	Menes unites Upper and Lower Egypt	2500 B.C.	First libraries are built in Egypt	1362–1352 B.C.	Tutankhamun is pharaoh
				1250 B.C.	Possible date of Moses' Exodus
4000 B.C.	Sumerians begin to settle in the Fertile Crescent	3000 B.C.	City-states begin in Sumer	1800 B.C.	Code of Hammurabi recorded
3500 B.C.	City of Ur founded in Mesopotamia	3000 B.C.	Plow first used in China	1700 B.C.	Babylonians conquer Sumer and more of Mesopotamia
3500 B.C.	Cuneiform writing appears in Sumer	2500 B.C.	Writing and trade begin in Indus Valley	1700 B.C.	Possible date of Abraham's journey to Canaan
3100 B.C.	Bronzework begins in Mesopotamia	2300 B.C.	Mohenjo-Daro and Harappa flourish in Indus River Valley	1700 B.C.	The Shang gain control of the Huang Valley
		2250 B.C.	Ziggurat built at Ur	1500 B.C.	Aryans migrate into Indus River Valley
3500 B.C.	Villagers in what is now Peru use the llama as a pack animal	2000 B.C.	Inuit people hunt caribou and seals in the Arctic	2000 B.C.	Andean settlements thrive in Peru
3500 B.C.	Cotton becomes an important crop in what is now Peru			1400 B.C.	Farming villages develop in Central America and southwestern North America
3500 B.C.	Haida culture begins on northwest coast of what is now Canada			1200 B.C.	Olmec civilization begins in Mexico

WORLD HISTORY TIME LINE

	1000–750 B.C.		750–500 B.C.		500–250 B.C.	
EUROPE	900 B.C.	Etruscans settle north of the Tiber River, in what is now Italy	700 B.C.	According to Roman legend, Romulus and Remus found the city on seven hills	499 B.C.	Persian Wars begin
	900 B.C.	Greek city-state of Sparta is founded	700 B.C.	Homer creates the first Greek epics	450 B.C.	Twelve Tables become basis of Roman Law
	776 B.C.	First Olympic Games are held in Greece	600–560 B.C.	Aesop tells fables in ancient Greece	431 B.C.	Peloponnesian Wars begin
			509 B.C.	Patricians take power in Rome	399 B.C.	Socrates is on trial
			500 B.C.	Greeks build the Parthenon to house statues of gods and goddesses	336 B.C.	Alexander the Great spreads Greek culture
AFRICA	900 B.C.	Nok people of Nigeria use terra cotta	700 B.C.	Iron tools made in Egypt	305 B.C.	Ptolemy II founds library in Alexandria
	900 B.C.	Kushite kingdom in Sudan thrives	671 B.C.	Assyrians overrun Egypt	300 B.C.	Kushite kingdom expands and develops extensive trade networks
	814 B.C.	Phoenician traders found colony at Carthage	600 B.C.	Nok people of Nigeria mine iron		
			600 B.C.	Carthaginian explorers sail southward from North Africa		
ASIA	950(?)–928 B.C.	King Solomon rules Israel	689 B.C.	Assyrians invade Babylonia and sack Babylon	500 B.C.	Indian traders bring Hindu ideas to Southeast Asia
	911 B.C.	Rise of Assyrian power in Mesopotamia	586 B.C.	Armies of New Babylonia conquer Judah and exile Jews	400 B.C.	Buddhism spreads through Asia
			539 B.C.	Persia's Cyrus the Great conquers Babylon and frees exiled Jews	400 B.C.	Confucius teaches about duty in China
			528 B.C.	Possible date that Siddhartha Gautama, founder of Buddhism, begins teaching in India	322 B.C.	Chandragupta founds Mauryan empire in India
					273 B.C.	Asoka spreads Buddhist teaching and religious tolerance in India
THE AMERICAS	1000 B.C.	La Venta becomes center of Olmec culture in Mexico	600 B.C.	Oaxaca culture begins to dominate Olmec civilization in Mexico	500 B.C.	Farmers in Ohio Valley construct burial mounds
	850 B.C.	Peruvians build temple at Chavín de Huantar in Andes			300–100 B.C.	City of Teotihuacán develops in Mexico

R38

New Ideas and New Empires

250 B.C.–A.D. 1	A.D. 1–250	A.D. 250–500
73–71 B.C. Spartacus leads slave revolt in Rome	**A.D. 29** Jesus' religious teachings become the foundation for Christianity	**A.D. 306** Constantine rules Roman empire
45 B.C. Julius Caesar becomes dictator of Rome	**A.D. 80** Roman Colosseum is completed	**A.D. 312** Christianity tolerated in Roman empire
27 B.C. Augustus Caesar begins Pax Romana in Roman empire	**A.D. 100** Network of Roman roads increases trade and travel through the empire	**A.D. 445** Attila the Hun attacks western Europe
		A.D. 476 Rome falls to Germanic invaders
250 B.C. Kush begins Golden Age, which lasts for about 300 years	**A.D. 238** North Africans revolt against Roman empire	**A.D. 300** Ptolemy describes Earth-centered universe
202 B.C. Roman army defeats Hannibal's army at Zama		**A.D. 300** Gold-salt trade develops in Ghana
30 B.C. Egypt becomes Roman province		**A.D. 324** King Ezana of Ethiopia becomes a Christian
		A.D. 350 Defeated by Aksum, Kushite civilization at Meroe ends
		A.D. 400 St. Augustine spreads Christianity in North Africa
250 B.C. Kingdom of Parthia emerges in eastern Persia	**A.D. 50** St. Paul spreads Christianity	**A.D. 320** Gupta empire emerges in Ganges Valley, India
215 B.C. Shihuangdi's Qin dynasty begins construction of the Great Wall of China	**A.D. 70** Romans destroy Jerusalem, beginning Jewish diaspora	**A.D. 330** Constantinople becomes new capital of Roman empire
206 B.C. Han Dynasty begins in China, adopting many Confucian ideas	**A.D. 101** Chinese invent paper	**A.D. 400** Chinese manufacture steel
	A.D. 120 Chinese invent seismograph	
	A.D. 220 Fall of Han Dynasty in China	
200 B.C. Maya culture begins to develop in Central America	**A.D. 100** Hopewell culture flourishes on upper Mississippi	**A.D. 250** Classic period of Maya civilization in Guatemala, Honduras, and eastern Mexico
200 B.C. Nazca culture begins in southern Peru	**A.D. 100–200** Oaxaca culture reaches height	**A.D. 500** Hopewell culture builds burial mounds and makes pottery and iron weapons
100 B.C. Anasazi culture emerges in southwestern United States		

WORLD HISTORY TIME LINE

	A.D. 500–750

EUROPE

A.D. 500	Middle Ages usually said to begin around this time
A.D. 529–534	Byzantine Emperor Justinian issues Codes of Law
A.D. 670	Bulgars from Russia settle near Danube River
A.D. 715	Muslims conquer most of Spain
A.D. 732	Charles Martel, king of Franks, stops Muslim advance into France

	A.D. 750–1000

A.D. 800	Charlemagne becomes emperor
A.D. 800	First castles built in western Europe
A.D. 843	Charlemagne's Frankish empire breaks up
A.D. 885–886	Vikings raid Paris, France
A.D. 900	Feudalism is widespread social and economic system
A.D. 986	Viking explorer Eric the Red founds colony in Greenland

AFRICA

A.D. 500	Kingdom of Ghana rises to power in West Africa
A.D. 640–641	Islamic leader Caliph Omar conquers Egypt
A.D. 642	Arabs build first mosque in al-Fustat, new capital of Muslim Egypt
A.D. 711	Arab empire conquers North Africa

A.D. 800	Arabs and Persians explore East African coast and set up trading stations
A.D. 800–950	Christianity continues in Ethiopia after decline of Aksum
A.D. 950–1050	Igbo-Ukwu culture thrives in eastern Nigeria
A.D. 969	Fatimid dynasty conquers Egypt and builds Cairo
A.D. 970	Fatimids build one of the world's first universities in Cairo
A.D. 970	Ghana empire flourishes in West Africa

ASIA

A.D. 552	Buddhism spreads to Japan from China and Korea
A.D. 595	Indian mathematicians use decimal system
A.D. 605–610	Sui emperors build Grand Canal in China
A.D. 610	According to Muslim sources, the date that Muhammad founds Islam in Arabia
A.D. 622	According to Muslim sources, Muhammad makes the migration, or hijra, from Mecca to Medina

A.D. 700–1100	Baghdad is capital of Arab empire
A.D. 794–1184	Heian period in Japan
A.D. 802	Jayavarman II rules the Khmer throne
A.D. 868	Chinese use wood blocks to print books
A.D. 889	Khmers build capital at Angkor, in what is today Cambodia
A.D. 907–26	Mongols conquer inner Mongolia and northern China
A.D. 970	Chinese introduce paper money

THE AMERICAS

A.D. 500	Polynesians from Southeast Asia settle in Hawaiian Islands
A.D. 600	Height of Maya civilization
A.D. 650	Teotihuacán thrives as trade center in Mexico

A.D. 900	Maya civilization in southern Mexico mysteriously collapses
A.D. 900–1000	Pueblo settlements thrive in North America
A.D. 990	Toltec people take over Maya city of Chichén Itzá in Mexico

A.D. 1000–1250

A.D. 1054	Church in Constantinople breaks with Church of Rome
A.D. 1066	Normans defeat English at Battle of Hastings
A.D. 1095	Pope Urban calls for the First Crusade
A.D. 1150	Chartres cathedral built
A.D. 1209	St. Francis of Assisi founds Franciscan religious order
A.D. 1215	King John signs Magna Carta

A.D. 1000	Bantu-speaking kingdoms emerge in southern Africa
A.D. 1000	Kingdoms in West Africa flourish from gold trade
A.D. 1100	Swahili city-states develop trade with Arabia and India
A.D. 1200	City-state of Kilwa prospers
A.D. 1235	Sunjata founds Mali empire in West Africa

A.D. 1000	Chinese perfect gunpowder
A.D. 1000	Murasaki Shikibu writes *Tale of Genji*
A.D. 1076	Muslim Seljuk Turks capture Jerusalem
A.D. 1099	Crusaders from Europe recapture Jerusalem
A.D. 1100	Samurai dominate Japan
A.D. 1100	Angkor Wat is built in what is now Cambodia
A.D. 1192	Yoritomo becomes first shogun in Japan
A.D. 1209	Genghis Khan leads Mongols to conquer China

A.D. 1000	Viking explorer Leif Erickson reaches America
A.D. 1100	Anasazi people in North America build cliff dwellings at Mesa Verde
A.D. 1200	Incas in Peru settle at Cuzco

A.D. 1250–1500

A.D. 1348–1352	Bubonic plague (Black Death) devastates Europe
A.D. 1350	Renaissance begins in Italy
A.D. 1429	Joan of Arc leads French against the English at Orléans
A.D. 1448	John Gutenberg develops the printing press
A.D. 1453	Ottomans capture Constantinople; end of Byzantine empire
A.D. 1478–1492	Renaissance art patron Lorenzo de Medici rules Italy
A.D. 1492	Columbus sails from Spain to America
A.D. 1497–1499	Portuguese explorer Vasco da Gama sails around Africa to India

A.D. 1300	Timbuktu is a major trading center
A.D. 1324	Mansa Musa, emperor of Mali, goes on pilgrimage to Mecca, Arabia
A.D. 1350	Kingdom of Great Zimbabwe thrives on gold trade
A.D. 1352–1353	Ibn Batuta writes an account of his travels across Africa
A.D. 1420	Portuguese sailors begin to explore west coast of Africa
A.D. 1488	Bartholomeu Dias sails around tip of Africa
A.D. 1490	Songhai empire begins in West Africa

A.D. 1271	Marco Polo sets out for China
A.D. 1279	Kublai Khan founds Yuan Dynasty
A.D. 1301	Osman I founds Ottoman dynasty in Turkey
A.D. 1368	Mongols are driven from China; Ming dynasty begins
A.D. 1453	Ottoman Turks conquer Constantinople, renaming the city *Istanbul*

A.D. 1300	Incas expand their empire throughout the central Andes
A.D. 1325	Aztecs found city of Tenochtitlán in what is today Mexico City
A.D. 1450	Inca city of Machu Picchu built in Peru
A.D. 1486–1521	Aztec empire at its height
A.D. 1497	John Cabot claims land in North America for England

WORLD HISTORY TIME LINE

A.D. 1500–1600

EUROPE

A.D. 1503	Leonardo da Vinci paints the *Mona Lisa*
A.D. 1517	Martin Luther nails the 95 Theses on a church door in Germany
A.D. 1519–1522	Ferdinand Magellan's crew completes sailing voyage around the world
A.D. 1534	Henry VIII of England makes himself head of English church
A.D. 1541–1564	John Calvin leads church reforms in Switzerland
A.D. 1550	Reformation spreads throughout Europe
A.D. 1558–1603	Elizabeth I reigns in England
A.D. 1588	English warships fight the Spanish Armada
A.D. 1595	William Shakespeare writes *Romeo and Juliet*

AFRICA

A.D. 1500	Songhai empire reaches height
A.D. 1575	Portugese begin colonization of Angola
A.D. 1590–591	Moroccan army overthrows Songhai empire
A.D. 1598	Dutch set up trading posts in western Africa

ASIA

A.D. 1520–1566	Ottoman empire reaches height under Süleyman
A.D. 1556–1605	Mogul emperor Akbar reforms government in India

THE AMERICAS

A.D. 1500	Pedro Cabral claims Brazil for Portugal
A.D. 1521	Hernando Cortés conquers Aztecs
A.D. 1531–1535	Francisco Pizarro conquers Inca empire
A.D. 1534	Jacques Cartier claims what is now Canada for France
A.D. 1549	Coronado conquers Zuñi pueblos
A.D. 1580	Iroquois League unites Five Nations
A.D. late 1500s	Powhatan confederacy organized

A.D. 1600–1700

EUROPE

A.D. 1609	Galileo proves the heliocentric theory
A.D. 1643–1715	Louis XIV rules France
A.D. 1653–1658	Oliver Cromwell is Lord Protector of Britain, replacing monarchy with parliamentary rule
A.D. 1682–1725	Peter the Great rules Russia
A.D. 1687	Isaac Newton publishes his "laws of gravity"
A.D. 1689	England's Parliament drafts a Bill of Rights, limiting the power of the monarchy

AFRICA

A.D. 1652	Dutch found Cape Town
A.D. 1680	Asante kingdom begins in West Africa

ASIA

A.D. 1600–1614	English, Dutch, Danish, and French East India Companies founded
A.D. 1603	Tokugawa period begins in Japan
A.D. 1603	Japan begins to restrict foreign contacts
A.D. 1627	Manchus conquer Korea
A.D. 1632–1648	Shah Jahan builds the Taj Mahal
A.D. 1644	Manchus conquer Beijing and found the Qing dynasty
A.D. 1683	Chinese control Formosa, what is today called Taiwan

THE AMERICAS

A.D. 1607	The English establish the Jamestown settlement in Virginia
A.D. 1608	French settlers found Quebec
A.D. 1610	Henry Hudson explores Hudson Bay
A.D. 1620	Pilgrims sail to Plymouth in the *Mayflower*
A.D. 1636	Puritans found Harvard University
A.D. 1664	English capture Dutch colony of New Amsterdam and rename it New York
A.D. 1681	Quaker William Penn founds Pennsylvania

A.D. 1700–1800

A.D. 1700	Industrial Revolution begins
A.D. 1769	James Watt perfects the steam engine
A.D. 1776	Adam Smith writes *The Wealth of Nations*
A.D. 1789	French Revolution begins
A.D. 1793	Louis XVI is executed
A.D. 1799	Napoleon overthrows the French government

A.D. 1720	Yoruba kingdom of Oyo prospers
A.D. 1730	More than 50,000 Africans are shipped each year to the Americas as slaves, in the Triangular Trade
A.D. 1795	British seize Cape Colony from the Dutch
A.D. 1800	Benin City becomes a center for West African slave trade

A.D. 1750	Japanese arts and commerce flourish under Tokugawa shogunate
A.D. 1750	Rice production in China increases greatly
A.D. 1770	England's Captain Cook explores eastern coast of Australia
A.D. 1784	United States begins to trade with China

A.D. 1700	Sugar plantations flourish in Caribbean
A.D. 1754–1763	French and Indian War is fought
A.D. 1775	American Revolution begins at Lexington
A.D. 1776	Declaration of Independence signed
A.D. 1781	British surrender to Americans at Yorktown
A.D. 1789	George Washington becomes first President of the United States
A.D. 1791	Toussaint L'Ouverture leads revolt against French in Haiti

A.D. 1800–1900

A.D. 1804	Napoleon crowns himself emperor
A.D. 1815	Napoleon defeated at Waterloo
A.D. 1825	The Industrial Revolution spreads to Germany, Belgium, and France
A.D. 1827	First photograph taken
A.D. 1848	Karl Marx publishes *Communist Manifesto*
A.D. 1861	Serfdom is abolished in Russia
A.D. 1895	Lumière brothers invent the film projector
A.D. 1895	Marconi invents radio

A.D. 1822	Liberia is founded as home for freed United States slaves
A.D. 1840	Zanzibar becomes a commercial center, exporting cloves and other spices
A.D. 1850	Slave trading is abolished in most countries
A.D. 1853–1856	British explorer Dr. Livingstone crosses Africa
A.D. 1867	Diamonds discovered in South Africa
A.D. 1869	The Suez Canal is opened in Egypt
A.D. 1872	Britain grants Cape Colony self-government

A.D. 1842	After a war with Britain, China is forced to open its ports to Western traders
A.D. 1853	Matthew C. Perry enters Edo Bay
A.D. 1854	United States opens Japan to trade
A.D. 1868–1912	Meiji restoration in Japan brings industrialization; capital moves to Edo, present-day Tokyo

A.D. 1804–1806	Louis and Clark explore Louisiana Territory
A.D. 1821	Bolívar frees northern South America
A.D. 1821	San Martín wins independence for Peru
A.D. 1821	Mexico wins independence from Spain
A.D. 1823	Monroe Doctrine opposes European interference in the Western Hemisphere
A.D. 1836	Texas gains independence from Mexico
A.D. 1861–1865	United States Civil War is fought
A.D. 1867	Canada's provinces unite
A.D. 1869	Transcontinental Railroad completed
A.D. 1876	Alexander Graham Bell invents telephone
A.D. 1883	Thomas Edison invents lightbulb

WORLD HISTORY TIME LINE

	A.D. 1900–1925		A.D. 1925–1950
EUROPE	A.D. 1905 — Einstein publishes his theory of relativity	A.D. 1926 — Scotland's John Logie Baird invents the television	
	A.D. 1914 — World War I begins	A.D. 1933 — Adolf Hitler rises to power in Germany	
	A.D. 1917 — Russian Revolution ends Tsarist rule and brings Communist Party to power	A.D. 1933–1945 — About 6 million European Jews are killed during the Holocaust	
	A.D. 1919 — Treaty of Versailles ends World War I	A.D. 1939 — Germany invades Poland; World War II begins	
	A.D. 1920 — League of Nations founded	A.D. 1944 — Allies land at Normandy, France on D-Day to free Europe from Hitler's advance	
	A.D. 1924 — Joseph Stalin becomes dictator of Soviet Union	A.D. 1945 — World War II ends	
		A.D. 1945 — The United Nations is created	
		A.D. 1949 — As Cold War intensifies, Western nations organize NATO	

	A.D. 1900–1925	A.D. 1925–1950
AFRICA	A.D. 1912 — The African National Congress is founded in the Union of South Africa	A.D. 1931 — South Africa gains independence from Britain
	A.D. 1914 — European powers control nearly all of Africa	A.D. 1931 — First trans-African railway completed
	A.D. 1922 — Howard Carter discovers King Tut's tomb	A.D. 1942 — Battle of El Alamein fought in Egypt during World War II
	A.D. 1923 — Ethiopia joins League of Nations	A.D. 1948 — Apartheid system begins in South Africa

	A.D. 1900–1925	A.D. 1925–1950
ASIA	A.D. 1910 — Japan invades Korea	A.D. 1931 — Japanese occupy Chinese province of Manchuria
	A.D. 1911–1912 — Manchu dynasty ends in China; Sun Yat-sen establishes a republic	A.D. 1932 — Abd al-Aziz ibn Saud unifies a new kingdom called Saudi Arabia
	A.D. 1913 — Indian poet Rabindranath Tagore receives Nobel Prize for Literature	A.D. 1934 — Mao Zedong leads Chinese Communists on the Long March
	A.D. 1920 — Mohandas Gandhi begins nonviolent protest against British rule in India	A.D. 1937–1945 — War breaks out between China and Japan
		A.D. 1945 — United States drops first atomic bombs on Hiroshima and Nagasaki
		A.D. 1947 — India and Pakistan gain independence from Britain
		A.D. 1948 — Israel gains independence
		A.D. 1949 — Mao Zedong establishes communist rule in China

	A.D. 1900–1925	A.D. 1925–1950
THE AMERICAS	A.D. 1903 — Wright Brothers make first successful airplane flight	A.D. 1929 — Great Depression begins with the New York stock market crash
	A.D. 1908 — Henry Ford produces first Model T car	A.D. 1933 — Franklin Roosevelt launches the New Deal to help end the Great Depression
	A.D. 1914 — Panama Canal opens	A.D. 1941 — Japanese bomb Pearl Harbor; United States enters World War II
	A.D. 1918 — President Wilson proposes "Fourteen Points" as a plan for lasting world peace	A.D. 1945 — United States scientists build first atomic bomb
	A.D. 1920 — Women gain voting rights in the United States	A.D. 1948–1951 — The United States' Marshall Plan helps Europe recover from the war

A.D. 1950–1975

A.D. 1955	Communist countries sign the Warsaw Pact
A.D. 1956	Eastern European countries revolt against communism
A.D. 1957	Russians launch *Sputnik* space mission
A.D. 1961	Berlin Wall is built

A.D. 1952	Egypt gains independence from Britain
A.D. 1956	Egypt takes control of the Suez Canal
A.D. 1957	Ghana gains independence from Britain
A.D. 1958	Sékou Touré used boycotts to help Guinea gain independence from France
A.D. 1964–1990	Nelson Mandela imprisoned in South Africa
A.D. 1974	Nigeria becomes leading oil producer in Africa

A.D. 1950–1953	Korean War is fought
A.D. 1960	Arab nations form the Organization of Petroleum Exporting Countries, or OPEC
A.D. 1964	Palestinians found the Palestine Liberation Organization, or PLO
A.D. 1966	Indira Gandhi becomes prime minister of India
A.D. 1965–1975	Vietnam War is fought
A.D. 1966–1969	Mao Zedong begins Cultural Revolution in China
A.D. 1970	Japan becomes second-largest economic power in the world

A.D. 1960	Martin Luther King, Jr., leads civil rights movement in the United States
A.D. 1962	The United States faces down the Soviet Union in the Cuban Missile Crisis, a tense moment of the Cold War
A.D. 1962	Jamaica gains independence from Britain
A.D. 1969	American Neil Armstrong becomes the first person on the moon

A.D. 1975–2000

A.D. 1979	Margaret Thatcher becomes first female prime minister of Britain
A.D. 1980	Lech Walesa leads a strike by Polish workers and starts the Solidarity movement
A.D. 1985	Soviet leader Mikhail Gorbachev introduces *glasnost*
A.D. 1989	Berlin Wall is torn down
A.D. 1991	Cold War ends as the Soviet Union collapses
A.D. 1991	Yugoslavia breaks up; civil war begins
A.D. 1995	The European Union agrees to consider admitting eastern European countries

A.D. 1986	Severe droughts hit Africa, especially Ethiopia
A.D. 1986	Western nations put pressure on South Africa to abolish apartheid
A.D. 1992	Foreign troops bring aid to Somalia
A.D. 1993	Apartheid ends in South Africa
A.D. 1994	Nelson Mandela is elected president of South Africa

A.D. 1978	Israel and Egypt hold peace-talks at Camp David in the United States
A.D. 1980	Iran-Iraq war begins
A.D. 1986	Corazon Aquino becomes president of the Philippines
A.D. 1989	Chinese students protest for democracy in Beijing's Tiananmen Square
A.D. 1990–1991	Persian Gulf War is fought
A.D. 1993	Palestinian and Israeli leaders sign agreement in United States for Palestinian self-rule
A.D. 1995	After signing peace agreements with the leader of the PLO, Yasir Arafat, Israel's Prime Minister Yitzhak Rabin is assassinated

A.D. 1980–1992	Civil war breaks out in El Salvador
A.D. 1987	Oscar Arias Sánchez is first Latin American to win Nobel Peace Prize
A.D. 1990–1991	United States leads fight against Iraq in Persian Gulf War
A.D. 1993	Floods in Mississippi River basin destroy homes and crops
A.D. 1995	Canadians in Quebec narrowly vote to remain a part of Canada

Dictionary of GEOGRAPHICTERMS

ARCHIPELAGO (är kə pel′ə gō) A group or chain of islands.

STRAIT (strāt) A narrow waterway that connects two larger bodies of water.

GULF (gulf) Part of an ocean that extends into the land; larger than a bay.

PLATEAU (pla tō′) An area of elevated flat land.

DAM (dam) A wall built across a river, creating a lake that stores water.

RESERVOIR (rez′ər vwär) A natural or artificial lake used to store water.

CANYON (kan′yən) A deep, narrow valley with steep sides.

MESA (mā′sə) A hill with a flat top; smaller than a plateau.

DUNE (dün) A mound, hill, or ridge of sand heaped up by the wind.

HILL (hil) A rounded, raised landform; not as high as a mountain.

BUTTE (būt) A small, flat-topped hill; smaller than a mesa or plateau.

VALLEY (val′ē) An area of low land between hills or mountains.

OASIS (ō ā′sis) A fertile area in a desert that is watered by a spring.

COAST (cōst) The land along an ocean.

DESERT (dez′ərt) A dry environment with few plants and animals.

BAY (bā) Part of an ocean or lake that extends deeply into the land.

ISTHMUS (is′məs) A narrow strip of land that connects two larger bodies of land.

ISLAND (ī′lənd) A body of land completely surrounded by water.

PENINSULA (pə nin′sə lə) A body of land nearly surrounded by water.

VOLCANO (vol kā′nō) An opening in Earth's surface through which hot rock and ash are forced out.

MOUNTAIN (moun′tən) A high landform with steep sides; higher than a hill.

PEAK (pēk) The top of a mountain.

HARBOR (här′bər) A sheltered place along a coast where boats dock safely.

GLACIER (glā′shər) A huge sheet of ice that moves slowly across the land.

CANAL (kə nal′) A channel built to carry water for irrigation or navigation.

LAKE (lāk) A body of water completely surrounded by land.

PORT (pôrt) A place where ships load and unload their goods.

TRIBUTARY (trib′yə ter ē) A smaller river that flows into a larger river.

SOURCE (sôrs) The starting point of a river.

TIMBERLINE (tim′bər līn) A line beyond which trees do not grow.

RIVER BASIN (riv′ər bā′sin) All the land that is drained by a river and its tributaries.

WATERFALL (wô′tər fôl) A flow of water falling vertically.

MOUNTAIN RANGE (moun′tən rānj) A row or chain of mountains.

PLAIN (plān) A large area of nearly flat land.

RIVER (riv′ər) A stream of water that flows across the land and empties into another body of water.

BASIN (bā′sin) A bowl-shaped landform surrounded by higher land.

DELTA (del′tə) Land made of silt left behind as a river drains into a larger body of water.

MOUNTAIN PASS (moun′tən pas) A narrow gap through a mountain range.

MOUTH (mouth) The place where a river empties into a larger body of water.

FJORD (fyôrd) A deep, narrow inlet of an ocean between high, steep cliffs.

OCEAN (ō′shən) A large body of salt water; oceans cover much of Earth's surface.

R47

Gazetteer

This Gazetteer is a geographical dictionary that will help you to pronounce and locate the places discussed in this book. Latitude and longitude are given for cities and some other places. The page numbers tell you where each place appears on a map or in the text.

A

Aachen (ä'khən) Capital of Charlemagne's empire, c. 800; a city in present-day Germany; 51°N, 6°E. (m. 321, t. 321)

Accra (ə krä') The capital and largest city of Ghana; 6°N, 0°. (m. R8, t. 568)

Acropolis (ə krop'ə lis) A hill in ancient Athens that became a religious center and meeting place; site of the Parthenon. (t. 205)

Africa (af'ri kə) The world's second-largest continent, lying south of Europe between the Atlantic and Indian oceans. (m. G5, t. G4)

Agra (ä'grə) A city in north-central India; capital of the Mogul empire around 1564–1658; 27°N, 78°E. (m. 393, t. 394)

Aksum (äk'süm) A powerful African kingdom and trading center, about 350–900, located in what is today Ethiopia. (m. 359, t. 359)

Alexandria (al ig zan'drē ə) A city in Egypt founded c. 332 B.C. by Alexander the Great; 31°N, 30°E. (m. 214, t. 214)

Alps (alps) Europe's highest mountains, extending in an arc from the Mediterranean coast to the Balkan peninsula. (m. 33, t. 33)

Anatolia (an ə tō'lē ə) Asia Minor; a peninsula in western Asia. (m. 393, t. 388)

Andes Mountains (an'dēz moun'tənz) The world's longest mountain chain, stretching along the west coast of South America. (m. 423, t. 422)

Angkor (ang'kôr) Ruined city in Cambodia; capital of the Khmer around 850–1430; 14°N, 104°E. (m. 399, t. 400)

Antarctica (ant ärk'ti kə) An ice-covered continent surrounding the South Pole. (m. G5, t. G4)

Anyang (än'yäng) The ancient Chinese capital of the Shang dynasty; 36°N, 114°E. (m. 165, t. 165)

Apennine Mountains (ap'ə nīn moun'tənz) A mountain range on the Italian peninsula. (m. 225, t. 225)

Arabia (ə rā'bē ə) A large peninsula in southwestern Asia. (m. 263, t. 262)

Arabian Sea (ə rā'bē ən sē) A body of water that lies between Arabia and India; the northwestern part of the Indian Ocean. (m. 263, t. 263)

Arctic Ocean (ärk'tik ō'shən) The body of water north of the Arctic Circle and surrounding the North Pole. (m. G5, t. G4)

Asia (ā'zhə) The largest continent, bounded on the west by Europe and Africa, on the south by the Indian Ocean, and on the east by the Pacific. (m. G5, t. G4)

Athens (ath'ənz) For many centuries the most powerful of all ancient Greek city–states; capital of present-day Greece; 38°N, 23°E. (m. 198, t. 197)

Atlantic Ocean (at lan'tik ō'shən) The body of water separating Europe and Africa from North and South America. (m. G5, t. G4)

Attica (at'i kə) A peninsula in east-central Greece on the Aegean Sea on which Athens was built. (m. 193, t. 193)

Australia (ôs trāl'yə) The world's smallest continent, bounded by the Indian and Pacific oceans; also a country. (m. G5, t. G4)

B

Babylonia (bab ə lō'nē ə) An ancient Mesopotamian empire that extended throughout the Fertile Crescent in the 1700s B.C. (m. 110, t. 112)

Baghdad (bag'dad) Capital and cultural center of the Muslim caliphate from A.D. 762 to 1100; present-day capital of Iraq; 33°N, 44°E. (m. 273, t. 272)

Balkan Peninsula (bôl'kən pə nin'sə lə) A peninsula in southern Europe, bounded by the Black, Aegean, and Adriatic seas. (m. 601, t. 600)

pronunciation key

a	at	ī	ice	u	up	th	thin
ā	ape	îr	pierce	ū	use	th	this
ä	far	o	hot	ü	rule	zh	measure
âr	care	ō	old	ù	pull	ə	about, taken,
e	end	ô	fork	ûr	turn		pencil, lemon,
ē	me	oi	oil	hw	white		circus
i	it	ou	out	ng	song		

Bangladesh (bän glə desh') A nation established in 1971 on the Indian subcontinent, and mostly surrounded by India; formerly known as East Pakistan. (m. 583, t. 584)

Bastille (bas tēl') A prison fortress in Paris that was attacked and destroyed on July 14, 1789, at the start of the French Revolution. (t. 488)

Beijing (bā'jing') The capital of the People's Republic of China; first became China's capital during the reign of Kublai Khan in the 1200s; 40°N, 116°E. (m. 403, t. 403)

Beringia (bə rin'jē ə) A land bridge that connected North America and Asia during the Ice Age; located where the Bering Strait is today. (m. 285, t. 286)

Berlin (bər lin') The capital of Germany, divided from 1945 to 1990 into West Berlin and East Berlin; 53°N, 13°E. (m. 558, t. 558)

Bethlehem (beth'lə hem) A small town south of Jerusalem where Jesus is said to have been born; 31°N, 35°E. (m. 247, t. 247)

Border Cave (bôr'dər kāv) A major archaeological site in Zululand, South Africa and home of Old Stone Age hunters and gatherers; 27°S, 32°E. (m. 47, t. 46)

Bowating (bō'ä ting) An Ojibwa village that was located on an island in the river connecting lakes Superior and Huron; 46°N, 83°W. (m. 441, t. 441)

Brazil (brə zil') The largest nation in South America, on the northeastern part of the continent. (m. 623, t. 622)

Burma (bər'mə) A nation in Southeast Asia on the Bay of Bengal; also known as Myanmar. (m. 587, t. 586)

Byzantine empire (bi'zən tēn em'pīr) The name by which the eastern half of the Roman empire became known some time after A.D. 400. (m. 254, t. 255)

C

Cairo (kī'rō) The capital of modern Egypt and the largest city in Africa; 30°N, 31°E. (m. 570, t. 569)

Cambodia (kam bō'dē ə) A nation in Southeast Asia. (m. 587, t. 586)

Canada (kan'ə də) A country in North America bordering the United States. (m. 623, t. 478)

Canadian Shield (kə nā'dē ən shēld) A large rocky plain in northern Canada that was formed by glaciers during the Ice Age. (m. 423, t. 423)

Cape Town (kāp toun) Seaport city in South Africa, settled by the Dutch in the late 1600s; 34°S, 18°E. (m. 607, t. 606)

Caribbean Sea (kar ə bē'ən sē) A sea bounded on the north and east by the West Indies, and by Central and South America on the west and south. (m. 475, t. 474)

Carthage (kär'thij) An ancient city on the north coast of Africa; 37°N, 10°E. (m. 234, t. 234)

Central Plateau (sen'trəl pla tō') A high plateau extending throughout central Mexico and bounded by high mountain ranges. (m. 287, t. 287)

Chartres (shärt) A city in northwestern France, noted for its cathedral; 48°N, 1°E. (m. 334, t. 332)

China (chī'nə) A nation in East Asia, and the most populous country in the world. (m. 616, t. 617)

Colosseum (kä lə sē'əm) A large stadium in ancient Rome where athletic events took place. (t. 241)

Constantinople (kon stan tə nō'pəl) A city established as the new eastern capital of the Roman empire by the emperor Constantine in A.D. 330, now called Istanbul; 41°N, 29°E. (m. 254, t. 254)

Copán (kō pän') An ancient city of Middle America, in what is now Honduras, that was a center of classic Maya culture; 15°N, 89°W. (m. 299, t. 299)

Crete (krēt) A Greek island in the Mediterranean Sea, southeast of Greece. (m. 193, t. 193)

Cuzco (küs'kō) A city in southern Peru; capital of the Inca empire from the 1200s to the 1500s; 14°S, 72°W. (m. 435, t. 435)

D

Dolores (də lôr'əs) A city in central Mexico where Miguel Hidalgo began Mexico's independence movement in 1810; 29°N, 108°W. (m. 493, t. 494)

Dominican Republic (də min'i kən ri pub'lik) A Caribbean nation, on the eastern part of Hispaniola, that gained independence in 1844. (m. 623, t. 623)

E

Edo (ed'ō) The former name of Tokyo, Japan; became capital under the rule of the Tokugawa shoguns in the 1600s; 36°N, 140°E. (m. 411, t. 412)

Egypt (ē'jipt) A country in northeast Africa; birthplace of ancient Egyptian civilization. (m. 570, t. 569)

England (ing'glənd) Part of the United Kingdom, on the island of Great Britain. (m. 321, t. 326)

Ethiopia (ē thē ō'pē ə) A country in eastern Africa. (m. 607, t. 358)

Euphrates River (ū frā'tēz riv'ər) A river in southwestern Asia that flows through the southern part of the Fertile Crescent. (m. 105, t. 104)

Eurasia (yù rā'zhə) A large land mass that includes the continents of Europe and Asia. (m. 317, t. 316)

Europe (yùr'əp) The continent north of Africa between Asia and the Atlantic Ocean. (m. G5, t. G4)

F

Fertile Crescent (fûrt′əl kres′ənt) A fertile region in southwestern Asia that includes the region of Mesopotamia. (m. 105, t. 104)

Florence (flôr′əns) A city in present-day Italy; one of the great centers of Renaissance art; 44°N, 11°E. (m. 334, t. 337)

Forbidden City (fər bid′ən sit′ē) A walled area in Beijing built 1417–1420, during the Ming dynasty, that contained the palaces of the emperors. (t. 404)

Forum (for′əm) The city market and meeting place in the center of ancient Rome. (t. 233)

G

Gaul (gôl) An ancient region and Roman province that included most of present-day France. (m. 240, t. 237)

Gaza (gä′zə) A territory between Egypt and Israel on the southeastern coast of the Mediterranean Sea. Controlled by Israel from 1967 to 1994, after which it began to return to Palestinian control. (m. 578, t. 577)

Ghana (gä′nə) An empire, about 400–1235, located at the southwestern edge of the Sahara Desert; a present-day country in western Africa on the Gulf of Guinea. (m. 364, t. 568)

Gobi Desert (gō′bē dez′ərt) A large desert in east-central Asia. (m. 385, t. 386)

Golan Heights (gō′län hīts) Land occupied by Israel after the Six-Day-War. 1967 (m. 578, t. 577)

Grand Canal (grand kə nal′) A canal system connecting Beijing, the Huang and Chang rivers, and cities as far south as Hangchow. (m. 404, t. 403)

Great Lakes (grāt lāks) A group of five large freshwater lakes on the border between the United States and Canada. (m. 423, t. 422)

Great Rift Valley (grāt rift val′ē) A series of cliffs and canyons caused by powerful prehistoric earthquakes that extends from Mozambique in southeastern Africa north to the Red Sea. (m. 355, t. 355)

Great Wall of China (grāt wôl əv chī′nə) A long defensive wall extending 1,500 miles (2,415 km) through northern China; built between 1300 and 1600. (m. 172, t. 170)

Great Zimbabwe (grāt zim bäb′wā) A city in southern Africa that rose to power in the 1300s through gold mining and trading; 20°S, 30°E. (m. 377, t. 376)

H

Haiti (hā′tē) A Caribbean nation, on the western part of Hispaniola, that gained independence from France in 1804. (m. 623, t. 623)

Harappa (hə ra′pə) A city of the ancient Harappan civilization, c. 2500–1600 B.C., located in the Indus Valley of South Asia; 31°N, 73°E. (m. 135, t. 135)

Himalayas (him ə lā′əz) The world's highest mountain range, forming the northern border of the Indian subcontinent. (m. 131, t. 131)

Hispaniola (his pən yō′lə) A Caribbean island settled by Spaniards in 1493; a present-day island that is divided into the Dominican Republic and Haiti. (m. 475, t. 467)

Hong Kong (häng käng) A large city and center of international trade developed as a British colony in mainland China; 22°N, 114°E. (m. 616, t. 619)

Huang River (hwäng riv′ər) [Yellow River] A river that flows from the Tibetan plateau, across northern China, and into the Yellow Sea. (m. 161, t. 160)

I

India (in′dē ə) The largest nation of the Indian subcontinent; became independent from British rule in 1947. (m. 583, t. 580)

Indian Ocean (in′dē ən ō′shən) The body of water south of Asia, between Africa and Australia. (m. G5, t. G4)

Indus Plain (in′dəs plān) A vast, dry region south of the Himalayas that is made fertile by deposits of silt from the Indus River; birthplace of the ancient Harappan civilization. (m. 131, t. 131)

Indus River (in′dəs riv′ər) A river that flows from Tibet, through the Himalayas and Hindu Kush into the Arabian Sea. (m. 131, t. 130)

Iraq (i rak′) A nation of western Asia that became independent in 1932. (m. 576, t. 576)

Israel (iz′rē əl) A country in western Asia, created in 1948 as a home for the Jews; ancient kingdom of Israelites. (m. 576, t. 577)

Istanbul (is tan bül′) Largest city in present-day Turkey; formerly the ancient city of Constantinople and later the capital of the Ottoman empire; 41°N, 29°E. (m. 390, t. 388)

J

Japan (jə pan′) An island nation off the eastern Asia mainland. (m. 616, t. 615)

Jerusalem (jə rü′sə ləm) An ancient city in western Asia; capital of present-day Israel; 31°N, 35°E. (m. 121, t. 124)

Johannesburg (jō han′əs bərg) The largest city in South Africa; 26°S, 28°E. (m. 607, t. 608)

Judea (jü dē′ə) The land in the eastern Mediterranean region populated by Jews at the time of the Roman empire. (m. 247, t. 246)

K

Kosala (kō sa'lə) An ancient kingdom in northern India where Siddhartha Gautama is said to have been born. (t. 151)

Kush (kush) An ancient kingdom in northeastern Africa, conquered by Egypt. It later regained independence and flourished through trade between c. 500 B.C. and A.D. 150. (m. 86, t. 86)

Kyoto (kyō'tō) A city in Japan; formerly the emperor's capital during the rule of the shoguns; 35°N, 136°E. (m. 411, t. 413)

L

La Venta (lə vent'ə) An ancient island town of Middle America on the east coast of what is now Mexico; center of Olmec culture in 1000 B.C.; 18°N, 94°W. (m. 293, t. 294)

Lake Texcoco (lāk tā skō'kō) A lake in what is now Central Mexico on which the Aztec built Tenochtitlán. (m. 427, t. 427)

Laos (lä'ōs) A nation in Southeast Asia, between northern Thailand and northern Vietnam. (m. 586, t. 586)

Latium (lā'shē əm) A plain on the west coast of Italy on which the city of Rome was built. (m. 225, t. 225)

Lima (lē'mə) The capital of Peru, founded by Francisco Pizarro in 1535; 12°S, 77°W. (m. 467, t. 469)

Lower Egypt (lō'ər ē'jipt) The northern part of ancient Egypt. (m. 71, t. 71)

M

Macedonia (mas i dō'nē ə) An ancient kingdom ruled by Alexander the Great that conquered Greece and the Persian empire in the 300s B.C. (m. 214, t. 213)

Machu Picchu (mäch'ü pēk'chü) The site of a ruined Inca city on a mountain in the Andes northwest of Cuzco, Peru; 13°S, 72°W. (m. 435, t. 438)

Mali (mä'lē) African empire that flourished between the 1200s and 1400s; a present-day country in West Africa. (m. 364, t. 364)

Mecca (mek'ə) An Arabian oasis city believed to be the birthplace of Muhammad; 21°N, 40°E. (m. 267, t. 267)

Medina (mə dē'nə) An Arabian oasis town to which, according to Muslim writings, Muhammad migrated in A.D. 622; 24°N, 40°E. (m. 267, t. 268)

Mediterranean Sea (med i tə rā'nē ən sē) A large, almost landlocked arm of the Atlantic Ocean touching Europe, Asia, and Africa. (m. 193, t. 192)

Mekong River (mā'kong' riv'ər) A river in Southeast Asia that flows from Tibet to the South China Sea. (m. 399, t. 398)

Memphis (mem'fis) Capital of Egypt's Old Kingdom, located on the Nile near present–day Cairo; 29°N, 31°E. (m. 76, t. 76)

Mesopotamia (mes ə pə tā'mē ə) The region between the Tigris and Euphrates rivers; birthplace of the Sumerian and Babylonian civilizations. (m. 105, t. 105)

Mexico (mek'si kō) A nation in North America, south of the United States. (m. 623, t. 624)

Mexico City (mek'si kō sit'ē) The capital and largest city of Mexico; formerly Tenochtitlán, it became the capital of New Spain after the Spanish conquered the Aztec in the 1500s; 19°N, 99°W. (m. 467, t. 469)

Middle America (mid'əl ə mer'i kə) An ancient region of North America that included southern Mexico and much of Central America. It was the birthplace of the ancient Olmec and Maya civilizations. (m. 287, t. 286)

Middle East (mid'əl ēst) A region of southwestern Asia that stretches from Turkey to Iran. (m. 576, t. 574)

Mogadishu (mōg ə dish'ü) A coastal city that dominated African gold trade between about 1000 and 1300; the present-day capital of Somalia; 2°N, 45°E. (m. 373, t. 374)

Mohenjo-Daro (mō hen'jō där'ō) A city of the ancient Harappan civilization, located in the Indus Valley; 27°N, 68°E. (m. 135, t. 135)

Mombasa (mom bä'sä) An important Swahili city-state and trading center between 1100 and 1500; the main port of Kenya on the Indian Ocean; 4°N, 40°E. (m. 373, t. 374)

Morocco (mə rok'ō) A country in northwestern Africa on the Atlantic Ocean and Mediterranean Sea. (m. 570, t. 367)

Moscow (mäs'kou) The capital and largest city of Russia; 56°N, 38°E. (m. 533, t. 536)

Mount Everest (mount ev'ər əst) The tallest mountain in the world, located in the Himalayas on the border between Nepal and Tibet; 28°N, 87°E. (m. 385, t. 385)

Mount Kilimanjaro (mount kil ə mən jär'ō) The tallest mountain in Africa, located in northeastern Tanzania; 3°S, 37°E. (m. 355, t. 355)

pronunciation key

a **at**; ā **ape**; ä **far**; âr **care**; e **end**; ē **me**; i **it**; ī **ice**; îr **pierce**; o **hot**; ō **old**; ô **fork**; oi **oil**; ou **out**; u **up**; ū **use**; ü **rule**; u̇ **pull**; ûr **turn**; hw **white**; ng **song**; th **thin**; <u>th</u> **this**; zh **measure**; ə **about, taken, pencil, lemon, circus**

Mount Olympus (mount ə lim′pəs) The highest mountain in Greece, where the ancient Greeks believed many of their gods and goddesses lived; 40°N, 22°E. (m. 198, t. 200)

N

Nazareth (na′ zə rəth) A small town in northern Judea where, according to the New Testament, Jesus grew up; 32°N, 35°E. (m. 247, t. 247)

New Delhi (nü del′ē) The capital of India and one of the most populous cities in the world; 29°N, 77°E. (m. 15, t. 15)

New France (nü frans) Colonial lands held by France in North America from 1609 to 1763. (m. 481, t. 480)

New Spain (nü spān) Spanish colony in North America including Mexico, Central America, the southwest United States and many of the Caribbean Islands from the 1500s to the 1800s. (m. 467, t. 469)

Niger River (ni′jər riv′ər) A river flowing from western Africa into the Gulf of Guinea. (m. 355, t. 355)

Nile River (nīl riv′ər) The world's longest river, which flows northward through East Africa into the Mediterranean Sea. (m. 71, t. 70)

Normandy (nôr′mən dē) A region in northwestern France on the English Channel. (m. 321, t. 326)

North America (nôrth ə mâr′i kə) The third–largest continent, located in the Western Hemisphere. (m. G5, t. G4)

North China Plain (nôrth chī′nə plān) A large, lowland region of eastern China that is watered by the Huang River; birthplace of Chinese civilization. (m. 161, t. 160)

North European Plain (nôrth yùr ə pē′ən plān) A large, fertile area that extends from the Atlantic Ocean to the Ural Mountains. (m. 317, t. 318)

North Sea (nôrth sē) A large arm of the Atlantic Ocean, between Great Britain and continental Europe. (m. 317, t. 317)

Nubia (nü′bē ə) An ancient kingdom south of Egypt. (m. 86, t. 84)

P

Pacific Ocean (pə sif′ik ō′shən) The world's largest body of water, bounded by the Americas on the east and Australia on the west. (m. G5, t. G4)

Pakistan (pak′i stan) One of two independent nations formed in 1947 on the Indian subcontinent. (m. 583, t. 583)

Palestine (pal′ə stīn) Region in southwestern Asia that became the ancient home of the Jews; the ancient Roman name for Judea; in recent times, the British protectorate that became Israel in 1947. (m. 254, t. 253)

Pantheon (pan′thē on) A large, domed temple built in ancient Rome to honor many gods and goddesses. (t. 241)

Paris (par′is) Capital and largest city of France; 49°N, 2°E. (m. 601, t. 488)

Parthenon (pär′thə non) A temple to the goddess Athena, built 447–432 B.C. on the Acropolis in Athens. (t. 205)

Pearl Harbor (pûrl här′bər) A United States naval base in Hawaii that was bombed by the Japanese in 1941, causing the United States to enter World War II; 21°N, 158°W. (m. 544, t. 543)

Peloponnesus (pel ə pə nē′səs) A mountainous peninsula in southern Greece, between the Ionian and Aegean seas. (m. 193, t. 193)

Persian Gulf (pûr′zhən gulf) A body of water east of the Arabian peninsula that separates Arabia from Iran. (m. 263, t. 263)

Peru (pə rü′) Colonial lands held by Spain in South America from the 1500s to the 1800s; present-day country in western South America. (m. 467, t. 469)

Petra (pē′trə) The ancient Arabian capital of Nabataea, in what is today Jordan; 30°N, 35°E. (m. 263, t. 264)

Phnom Penh (pə nom′ pen′) The capital of Cambodia; first became capital during the Khmer rule in the 1400s; 12°N, 105°E. (m. 399, t. 401)

Phoenicia (fə nē′shə) An ancient seafaring civilization located on the eastern shore of the Mediterranean Sea. (m. 193, t. 195)

Pompeii (pom pā′) An ancient city in southwestern Italy that was buried by the eruption of Mount Vesuvius in A.D. 79; 41°N, 14°E. (m. 240, t. 242)

Punt (pùnt) An ancient Egyptian name for an area of Africa south of Egypt. (m. 86, t. 87)

Q

Qin (chin) An ancient province in northern China that rose to power under Emperor Shihuangdi in 221 B.C. (m. 169, t. 168)

Qinling Mountains (chin′ling′ moun′tənz) A mountain range in north-central China. (m. 169, t. 169)

Quebec (kwi bek′) The first permanent French settlement in North America, settled as a trading post in 1608; the capital of the province of Quebec in eastern Canada; 47°N, 71°W. (m. 481, t. 479)

R

Red Sea (red sē) A narrow sea between Arabia and northeastern Africa. (m. 263, t. 263)

Rhodes (rōdz) A Greek island, lying east of Crete in the Aegean Sea. (m. 193, t. 193)

Rocky Mountains (rok′ē moun′tənz) A mountain range in North America that stretches from Alaska into Mexico. (m. 423, t. 422)

Rome (rōm) The former center of both the ancient Roman Republic and the Roman empire; capital of present-day Italy; 42°N, 12°E. (m. 225, t. 224)

Russia (rush′ə) A country in eastern Europe and northern Asia; the largest country in the world; a republic of the Soviet Union from 1922 to 1991. (m. 533, t. 532)

S

Sahara Desert (sə har′ə dez′ərt) The largest desert in the world, covering most of northern Africa. (m. 355, t. 355)

Sahel (sə həl′) The dry, grassy region south of the Sahara Desert, extending from Senegal to the Sudan. (m. 355, t. 355)

Santo Domingo (san′tō də ming′gō) A Spanish colony established on Hispaniola in 1496; the capital of the Dominican Republic; 19°N, 70°W. (m. 475, t. 475)

Sarajevo (sar ə yā′vō) The site of assassination that led to World War I; present-day capital of Bosnia; 44°N, 18°E. (m. 601, t. 527)

Seine River (sān riv′ər) A river that flows from eastern France northward into the English Channel. (m. 317, t. 318)

Serbia (sûr′bē ə) A country in eastern Europe. (m. 601, t. 528)

Sicily (sis′ə lē) An island in the Mediterranean Sea off the southwest tip of the Italian peninsula. (m. 225, t. 225)

Singapore (sing′ə pôr) A city and independent republic in Southeast Asia; 1°N, 104°E. (m. 616, t. 616)

Sofala (sō fäl′ə) A seaport village in eastern Mozambique; in the 1300s, an important trading center for the gold miners of Great Zimbabwe; 19°S, 35°E. (m. 377, t. 378)

Songhai (sông′hī) The most powerful empire in West Africa from about 1490 to 1590. (m. 364, t. 367)

South America (south ə mâr′i kə) The fourth-largest continent, located in the Western Hemisphere. (m. G5, t. G4)

South Korea (south kə rē′ə) A country in East Asia on the southern part of the Korean Peninsula; also a Pacific Rim nation. (m. 616, t. 616)

Southeast Asia (south ēst′ ā′zhə) A region of southern Asia bounded by the Indian and Pacific Oceans. (m. 587, t. 586)

Soviet Union (sō′vē et ūn′yən) The name commonly used for the Union of Soviet Socialist Republics, which was a country in eastern Europe and northern Asia; the largest country in the world from 1922–1991. (m. 544, t. 537)

Soweto (sə wē′tō) A black African township just outside Johannesburg, South Africa; 26°S, 28°E. (m. 607, t. 608)

Sparta (spär′tə) The largest ancient Greek city-state, located on the southern Peloponnesus; 37°N, 22°E. (m. 198, t. 198)

St. Lawrence River (sānt lôr′əns riv′ər) A river in eastern North America that flows from Lake Ontario to the Atlantic Ocean. (m. 479, t. 479)

St. Petersburg (sānt pē′tərz bûrg) A Russian port city on the Baltic Sea; formerly the capital of Russia, it was called Leningrad when Russia was part of the Soviet Union; 60°N, 30°E. (m. 533, t. 534)

Strait of Magellan (strāt əv mə jel′ən) A narrow waterway at the southern tip of South America, linking the Atlantic and Pacific oceans. (m. 464, t. 464)

Suez Canal (sü ez′ kə nal′) A canal in northeastern Egypt connecting the Mediterranean and Red seas. (m. 570, t. 569)

Sumer (sü′mər) A group of ancient city-states in southern Mesopotamia; the earliest civilization in Mesopotamia. (m. 110, t. 108)

T

Taj Mahal (täzh mə häl′) A grand tomb in Agra, India, built by Mogul emperor Shah Jahan to honor his wife. (t. 396)

Tenochtitlán (te noch tēt län′) The capital of the Aztec empire, founded around 1325 on the site of present-day Mexico City; 19°N, 99°W. (m. 427, t. 426)

Thailand (tī′land) A nation in Southeast Asia, formerly called Siam. (m. 587, t. 586)

Thebes (thēbz) An ancient city in Upper Egypt that became the capital of the New Kingdom; 26°N, 33°E. (m. 76, t. 81)

---

pronunciation key

a at; ā ape; ä far; âr care; e end; ē me; i it; ī ice; îr pierce; o hot; ō old; ô fork; oi oil; ou out; u up; ū use; ü rule, ů pull; ûr turn; hw white; ng song; th thin; th this; zh measure; ə about, taken, pencil, lemon, circus

Gazetteer

Tiananmen Square (tyen′än men skwâr) A square in Beijing, China where government troops killed hundreds of people who were demonstrating for democratic reform in 1989. (t. 619)

Tiber River (tī′bər riv′ər) A river flowing southward from north-central Italy across the Latium plain, and into the Tyrrhenian Sea. (m. 225, t. 225)

Tibetan Plateau (ti bet′ən pla tō′) A high mountain plateau in Asia. (m. 385, t. 385)

Tigris River (tī′gris riv′ər) A river in southwestern Asia that flows through the eastern part of the Fertile Crescent. (m. 105, t. 104)

Timbuktu (tim buk tü′) A trade and cultural center of the Songhai empire in the 1400s; a present-day town in the West African country of Mali; 16°N, 3°W. (m. 364, t. 364)

Tokyo (tō′kyō) The capital and largest city in Japan; formerly called Edo; 36°N, 140°W. (m. 411, t. 412)

Tonle Sap (tär, lä′ sap′) A lake in western Cambodia. (m. 399, t. 399)

Turkey (tùr′kē) A nation established in 1923 in western Asia and southeastern Europe. (m. 576, t. 576)

U

United States (ū nī′tid stāts) A nation mainly in North America consisting of fifty states, the District of Columbia, and several territories. (m. 623, t. 622)

Upper Egypt (up′ər ē′jipt) The southern part of ancient Egypt. (m. 71, t. 71)

V

Valley of Mexico (val′ē əv mek′si kō) A fertile valley between two mountain chains in central Mexico. (t. 427)

Valley of the Kings (val′ē əv thə kingz) West of Thebes in ancient Egypt, the burial place of 30 New Kingdom pharaohs; 26°N, 33°E. (m. 93, t. 88)

Venezuela (ven ə zwā′lə) A country in northern South America on the Caribbean Sea. (m. 496, t. 496)

Versailles (vâr sī′) A historic city in north-central France that contains the grand palace of Louis XIV; 49°N, 2°E. (t. 488)

Vietnam (vē et näm′) A nation in Southeast Asia that was divided from 1954 until 1975 into North Vietnam and South Vietnam. (t. 586)

W

West Bank (west bangk) An area in western Asia west of the Jordan River; controlled by Israel from 1967 to 1995, after which Palestinians gained partial control. (m. 578, t. 577)

West Indies (west in′dēz) An archipelago stretching from Florida to Venezuela, separating the Caribbean Sea from the Atlantic Ocean. (m. 475, t. 475)

X

Xianyang (shē än′yang) Capital city of the Qin dynasty during the rule of the emperor Shihuangdi; 34°N, 109°E. (m. 169, t. 169)

Y

Yalta (yôl′tə) A resort city in Ukraine; site of meeting between Franklin Roosevelt, Winston Churchill, and Joseph Stalin in 1945; 44°N, 34°E. (m. 599, t. 557)

Yemen (yem′ən) A present-day country in the mountainous southwestern area of Arabia; location of the ancient Sabaean civilization. (m. 263, t. 264)

Yugoslavia (yü gō slä′ vē ə) A nation that also included the republics of Bosnia and Herzegovina, Croatia, Macedonia, and Slovenia until 1991. (m. 601, t. 600)

Z

Zama (zä′mə) Site in northern Africa where the Roman army defeated the Carthaginian army in 202 B.C.; 36°N, 8°E. (m. 234, t. 235)

Zambezi River (zam bē′zē riv′ər) A river in southern Africa, flowing east through Zimbabwe and Mozambique into the Indian Ocean. (m. 355, t. 355)

Zanzibar (zan′zə bär) An important Swahili city-state and trading center between 1100 and 1500; an island port in Tanzania in the Indian Ocean; 6°S, 39°E. (m. 373, t. 374)

Biographical Dictionary

The Biographical Dictionary tells you about the people you have learned about in this book. The Pronunciation Key tells you how to say their names. The page numbers tell you where each person first appears in the text.

A

Abraham (ā′brə ham), 1700s B.C. Founder of Judaism who, according to the Bible, led his family from Ur to Canaan in obedience to God's command. (p. 121)

Ahmose (äm′ōs), d. 1546 B.C. New Kingdom pharaoh who drove the Hyksos out of the Nile Delta and reunited Egypt. (p. 85)

Akbar (ak′bär), A.D. 1542–1605 Ruler of the Mogul empire in India from A.D. 1556 to 1605. (p. 393)

Alexander II (al ig zan′dər), A.D. 1818–1881 Russian tsar who abolished serfdom in 1861. (p. 533)

Alexander the Great (al ig zan′dər), 356–323 B.C. King of Macedonia who conquered Greece, Persia, Egypt, and the Indus Valley; his conquests spread Greek culture throughout parts of three continents. (p. 212)

Amanishakhete (ä män ə shäk′hə tē), 100s B.C. Queen of Kush whose lavish tomb at Meroe reflects the richness of the Kingdom of Kush. (p. 359)

Arafat, Yasir (ar′ə fat), A.D. 1929– Leader of the Palestine Liberation Organization. (p. 577)

Aristide, Jean Bertrand (är′is tēd), A.D. 1953– Elected president of Haiti in 1990. (p. 625)

Aristotle (ar′ə stot əl), 384–322 B.C. Greek philosopher who was the private teacher of Alexander the Great. (p. 213)

Atahualpa (ä tə wäl′pə), A.D. 1502?–1533 The last Inca emperor, captured and killed by Francisco Pizarro. (p. 468)

Augustus (ô gus′təs), 63 B.C.–A.D. 14 First Roman emperor; won the civil war following Julius Caesar's assassination and went on to unify the empire and establish the Pax Romana. (p. 238)

Avicenna (av ə sen′ə), A.D. 980–1037 Persian philosopher and physician; wrote a medical encyclopedia that became a standard text in North Africa, western Asia, and Europe. (p. 274)

B

Ben-Gurion, David (ben gûr′ē ən), A.D. 1886–1973 Israeli prime minister from 1949 to 1953 and from 1955 to 1963; he proclaimed Israel to be a new and independent country on May 14, 1948. (p. 577)

Benedict (ben′i dikt), A.D. 480?–547 Italian monk; founder of the Benedictine order. (p. 331)

Bolívar, Simón (bō lē′vär, sē mōn′), A.D. 1783–1830 Leader of the struggle for independence in South America; his armies freed Colombia, Venezuela, and Peru from Spanish rule. (p. 496)

C

Cabot, John (kab′ət),A.D. 1450?–1498? Italian navigator and explorer in the service of England; one of the first Europeans to explore the coast of Canada. (p. 478)

Cabral, Pedro Álvarez (kə bräl′), A.D. 1467?–1520? Portuguese navigator who landed on the coast of Brazil in 1500 and claimed it for Portugal. (p. 467)

Caesar, Julius (sē′zər, jül′yəs), 100–44 B.C. Roman general who became the republic's dictator in 45 B.C. (p. 237)

Castro, Fidel (kas′trō), A.D. 1926– Cuban revolutionary leader; premier of Cuba since 1959. (p. 560)

Champlain, Samuel de (sham plän′), A.D. 1567?–1635 French explorer who founded Quebec in 1608. (p. 479)

Charlemagne (shär′lə mān), A.D. 742–814 King of the Franks from 768 to 814, and emperor of Rome from 800 to 814. (p. 321)

Chiang Kai-shek (chang′kī shek′), A.D. 1887–1975 Chinese Nationalist leader and president of Taiwan from 1950 to 1975. (p. 552)

Churchill, Winston (chûr′chil), A.D. 1874–1965 British prime minister from 1940 to 1945 and 1951 to 1955. He led Britain during World War II. (p. 542)

Cleopatra (klē ə pa′trə), 69–30 B.C. Ruler of the Egyptian government in Alexandria who backed Caesar in the civil war he waged from 49 to 45 B.C. (p. 237)

Columbus, Christopher (kə lum′bəs), A.D. 1451?–1506 Italian explorer in the service of Spain who arrived in the Americas in 1492. (p. 464)

pronunciation key

a	at	ī	ice	u	up	th	thin
ā	ape	îr	pierce	ū	use	th	this
ä	far	o	hot	ü	rule	zh	measure
âr	care	ō	old	ù	pull	ə	about, taken,
e	end	ô	fork	ûr	turn		pencil, lemon,
ē	me	oi	oil	hw	white		circus
i	it	ou	out	ng	song		

Columbus, Christopher (kə lum′bəs), A.D. 1451?–1506 Italian explorer in the service of Spain who arrived in the Americas in 1492. (p. 464)

Confucius (kən fū′shəs), 551–479 B.C. Chinese philosopher who stressed the need to respect tradition; his teachings discussed the right and wrong uses of power. (p. 174)

Constantine (kon′stən tēn), A.D. 280–337 Roman emperor who founded Constantinople as the new eastern capital of the Roman empire. (p. 254)

Copernicus, Nicolaus (kə pûr′ni kəs), A.D. 1473–1543 Polish astronomer; in 1514 he discovered that Earth and the other planets revolve around the sun. (p. 339)

Cortés, Hernando (kôr tez′, er nän′dō), A.D. 1485–1547 Spanish conquistador who defeated the Aztec in 1521. (p. 468)

D

Da Gama, Vasco (də gä′mə, väs′cō), A.D. 1460?–1524 Portuguese navigator who in 1498 sailed from Europe around Africa to Asia. (p. 464)

Da Vinci, Leonardo (də vin′chē, lē ə när′dō), A.D. 1452–1519 Italian Renaissance artist, inventor, and scientist. (p. 338)

De Klerk, F.W. (də klerk′), A.D. 1936– South African president from 1989 to 1994. He worked for a peaceful transition from the policy of apartheid to majority rule in South Africa. (p. 610)

Deng Xiaoping (dung′ shou′ping′), A.D. 1904– Chairman of the Chinese Communist Party and of the People's Republic of China. (p. 617)

Dias, Bartholomeu (dē′ash, bär tü lü mā′ü), A.D. 1450?–1500 Portuguese ship captain whose voyage around the southern tip of Africa in 1487 led to the opening of a sea route between Europe and Asia. (p. 464)

Diocletian (dī ə klē′shən), A.D. 245–313 Roman emperor who divided the empire in two and oversaw the eastern part. (p. 253)

E

Elizabeth I (i liz′ə bəth), A.D. 1533–1603 Queen of England from 1558 to 1603; the English Renaissance flourished during her reign. (p. 346)

Equiano, Olaudah (i kwē ä′nō, ōl′ə dä), A.D. 1750–1797 Enslaved African writer. In 1789 he wrote an autobiography describing his life in slavery. (p. 476)

Erasmus (i raz′məs), A.D. 1466?–1536 Dutch writer and humanist; he favored reform of the Catholic Church but came to oppose the Protestant Reformation. (p. 343)

F

Francis of Assisi (fran′sis əv ə sē′zē), A.D. 1181–1226 Italian monk who founded the Franciscan order; he devoted his life to serving the poor and sick. (p. 332)

Frank, Anne (frangk), A.D. 1929–1945 Dutch-Jewish girl who, with other Jews, hid from the Nazis from 1942 to 1944; she was found and sent to a concentration camp where she died. (p. 546)

Franz Ferdinand (franz fur′də nand), A.D. 1863–1914 Archduke of Austria whose assassination led to the outbreak of World War I. (p. 527)

Fu Hao (fü′hou′), 1100s B.C. A Chinese king's wife who led troops to war. Her tomb contained records of her life and times. (p. 166)

G

Galilei, Galileo (gal ə lā′ē, gal ə lā′ō), A.D. 1564–1642 Italian astronomer, mathematician, and physicist. His telescopes proved the sun is the center of the solar system. (p. 457)

Gandhi, Indira (gän′dē), A.D. 1917–1984 Prime minister of India from 1966 to 1977 and from 1980 to 1984. (p. 584)

Gandhi, Mohandas (gän′dē), A.D. 1869–1948 Indian political and religious leader; he supported the use of nonviolent methods to bring about change. (p. 582)

Genghis Khan (geng′gəs kän′), A.D. 1162?–1227 Mongol conqueror. At its peak, his empire included China, western Asia, and parts of eastern Europe. (p. 403)

Gorbachev, Mikhail (gôr′bə chəf), A.D. 1931– Soviet secretary general of the Communist Party from 1985 to 1990, and last president of the Soviet Union, 1990–1991. (p. 597)

Gutenberg, Johannes (gü′tən bûrg), A.D. 1400?–1468 German printer; in 1448 he invented a printing press that used movable type. (p. 344)

H

Hammurabi (hä mü rä′bē), 1800?–1750? B.C. King of the Babylonian empire; creator of the Code of Hammurabi, one of the world's oldest codes of law. (p. 112)

Han Gaozu (hän′gou′zü′), 200s B.C. A farmer-turned-general who, in 206 B.C., overthrew the Qin dynasty; he founded the Han dynasty. (p. 174)

Hannibal (han′ə bəl), 247?–183? B.C. General of Carthage who marched his army from Spain to Rome in the Second Punic War. (p. 234)

Hargreaves, James (här′grēvz), A.D. 1720–1778 English inventor of the spinning jenny. (p. 503)

Hatshepsut (hat shep′süt), 1520?–1482 B.C. One of the few women Egyptian pharaohs; organized a trade expedition to Egypt's southern neighbor, Punt. (p. 87)

Henry VIII (hen′rē), A.D. 1491–1547 King of England from 1509 to 1547 and founder of the Church of England; he broke with the Catholic Church because the pope would not grant him a divorce. (p. 345)

Henry, Prince (hen′rē), A.D. 1394–1460 Portuguese prince who directed the search for a sea route to the gold mines of western Africa. He also designed a fast, steerable ship known as a caravel. (p. 463)

Hidalgo, Miguel (ē däl′gō), A.D. 1753–1811 Mexican priest and revolutionary who led a revolt that started the Mexican war of independence. (p. 494)

Hitler, Adolf (hit′lər), A.D. 1889–1945 German dictator. He founded the National Socialist (Nazi) Party, which led Germany during World War II. (p. 540)

Ho Chi Minh (hō′chē′min′), A.D. 1890–1969 Communist leader in Vietnam who became head of the communist government in 1945. (p. 588)

Homer (hō′mûr), 700s B.C. Ancient Greek poet. (p. 200)

Iturbide, Agustin de (ē tür bē′dā) A.D. 1783–1824 Mexican soldier and leader; he won Mexican independence from Spain and became ruler of Mexico from 1822 to 1823. (p. 495)

Jayavarman II (jä yä vär′män), A.D. 800s One of the first Khmer kings of Cambodia. (p. 399)

Jesus (jē′zəs), 4? B.C.–A.D. 29? Religious leader and founder of Christianity. (p. 247)

Jinnah, Mohammad Ali (jin′ə), A.D. 1876–1948 First president of Pakistan from 1947 to 1948. (p. 583)

John I (jon), A.D. 1167?–1216 King of England from A.D. 1199 to 1216; in 1215 he signed the Magna Carta, giving more rights to British nobles. (p. 327)

Kay, John (kā), A.D. 1704–1764 English watchmaker who invented the flying shuttle used in weaving. (p. 503)

Kennedy, John F. (ken′i dē), A.D. 1917–1963 The 35th President of the United States from 1961 to 1963. He successfully negotiated the removal of Soviet nuclear missiles from Cuba. (p. 560)

Khadija (ka dē′jä), d. A.D. 619 A wealthy merchant who became the first wife of Muhammad. (p. 267)

Khrushchev, Nikita (krüsh′chef), A.D. 1894–1971 Secretary general of the Soviet Communist Party from 1958 to 1964. (p. 560)

Khufu (kü fü′), 2650?–2600? B.C. Egyptian pharaoh who built the Great Pyramid. (p. 81)

Kublai Khan (kü′blə kän′), A.D. 1215–1294 Grandson of Genghis Khan, founder of China's Yuan Dynasty. (p. 403)

Lady Murasaki Shikibu (mur ä säk′ē shē kē′bü), A.D. 978?–1026? Japanese author who wrote *The Tale of Genji*, which is thought to be the world's first novel. (p. 414)

Lalibela (lä′lē be lä), b. A.D. 1100s Zagwe king who ruled Ethiopia from about A.D. 1185 to 1225. (p. 360)

Lenin, Vladimir Ilyich (len′in), A.D. 1870–1924 Bolshevik leader and founder of the Soviet Union. (p. 536)

Livy (liv′ē), 59 B.C.–A.D. 17 Historian of the Roman Republic who wrote about the struggle between plebeians and patricians of Rome. (p. 231)

Louis XVI (lü′ē), A.D. 1754–1793 King of France from 1774 to 1792; executed during the French Revolution. (p. 486)

Luther, Martin (lüth′ər), A.D. 1483–1546 German monk and leader of the Protestant Reformation. (p. 343)

Magellan, Ferdinand (mə jel′ən), A.D. 1480?–1521 Portuguese explorer in the service of Spain; he set out to find a route to Asia by sailing around the southern tip of South America. (p. 464)

Mandela, Nelson (man del′ə), A.D. 1918– South African civil rights leader who became president of South Africa in 1994. (p. 606)

Mansa Musa (män′sä mü′sä), A.D. 1297?–1337? Emperor of Mali from 1312 to 1337, when the kingdom was at its peak of wealth and power. (p. 366)

Mao Zedong (mou′dze′dŭng′), A.D. 1893–1976 Chinese communist leader and founder of the People's Republic of China. (p. 552)

Marie Antoinette (mə rē′ an twə net′), A.D. 1755–1793 Queen of France from 1774 to 1792, who was executed during the French Revolution. (p. 489)

pronunciation key

a **at**; ā **ape**; ä **far**; âr **care**; e **end**; ē **me**; i **it**; ī **ice**; îr **pierce**; o **hot**; ō **old**; ô **fork**; oi **oil**; ou **out**; u **up**; ū **use**; ü **rule**; u̇ **pull**; ûr **turn**; hw **white**; ng **song**; th **thin**; <u>th</u> **this**; zh **measure**; ə **about, taken, pencil, lemon, circus**

Marx, Karl (märks), A.D. 1818–1883 German philosopher and economist. His ideas, called Marxism, formed the basis of communism. (p. 504)

Medici, Lorenzo (med'i chē), A.D. 1449–1492 Ruler of Florence during the Renaissance and patron of artists such as Michelangelo. (p. 337)

Meiji (mā'jē'), A.D. 1852–1912 Japanese emperor from 1867 to 1912 who led Japan into a period of rapid modernization. (p. 510)

Menes (mē'nēz), 3100? B.C. King of Upper Egypt who united Upper and Lower Egypt. (p. 75)

Michelangelo (mī kəl an'jə lō), A.D. 1475–1564 Italian Renaissance sculptor, painter, architect, and poet. (p. 338)

Moctezuma (mäk tə zü'mə), A.D. 1468?–1520 Aztec emperor defeated and killed by the Spanish conquistador Hernando Cortés in 1520. (p. 468)

Morelos, José María (mō rā'lōs), A.D. 1765–1815 Mexican priest and revolutionary who succeeded Miguel Hidalgo as rebel leader and issued a declaration of independence from Spain in 1813. He was captured and killed by Spanish soldiers in 1815. (p. 495)

Moses (mō'ziz), 1200s B.C. Prophet who led the Israelites out of slavery in Egypt. (p. 122)

Muhammad (mu ham'əd), A.D. 570?–632? Founder of Islam whose words are recorded in the Quran. (p. 267)

Mumtaz Mahal (mùm täz' mä häl'), A.D. 1592–1631 Wife of Shah Jahan, emperor of India; the Taj Mahal in Agra, India, was built in her memory. (p. 396)

N

Napoleon Bonaparte (nə pō'lē ən bō'nə pärt), A.D. 1769–1821 French revolutionary general who became Emperor Napoleon I of France in 1804. (p. 490)

Nasser, Gamal Abdel (nas'ər), A.D. 1918–1970 First President of Egypt from 1956 to 1958, and of the United Arab Republic from 1958 to 1970. (p. 569)

Nehru, Jawaharlal (nā'rü), A.D. 1889–1964 Prime minister of India from 1947 to 1964 and father of Indira Gandhi; close associate of Mohandas Gandhi. (p. 583)

Newton, Isaac (nü'tən), A.D. 1642–1727 English scientist who studied gravity. (p. 459)

Nicholas II (nik'ə ləs), A.D. 1868–1918 Last Russian tsar from 1894 to 1917. Discontent with his policies led to the Russian Revolution of 1917. (p. 534)

Nkrumah, Kwame (en krü'mə), A.D. 1909–1972 Leader in the liberation of the Gold Coast from British rule and first president of Ghana from 1960 to 1966. (p. 567)

O

Osman (äs män'), A.D. 1258–1326? Founder of the Ottoman empire. (p. 389)

P

Pachakuti Inca (pä chä kü'tē), d. A.D. 1471 Inca emperor from 1438 to 1471; he greatly extended Inca borders in 1438 and became known as Sapa Inca, or Supreme Inca. (p. 435)

Paul (pôl), A.D. 11?–67? Follower of Jesus who helped spread Christianity throughout the Roman world. (p. 250)

Pericles (per'i klēz), 495?–429 B.C. Athenian general who led Athens during the war with Sparta; he made sure that poor as well as rich citizens could take part in government. (p. 206)

Perry, Matthew (per'ē), A.D. 1794–1858 U.S. naval officer who sailed to Japan in 1853 with a demand that Japanese ports be opened to U.S. trade. (p. 509)

Peter (pē'tər), A.D. 5?–67? One of the 12 apostles of Jesus; Roman Catholics consider him to be the first pope, or bishop of Rome. (p. 248)

Petrarch (pē'trärk), A.D. 1304–1374 Italian Renaissance poet and humanist. (p. 338)

Pizarro, Francisco (pi zär'ō), A.D. 1471?–1541 Spanish conquistador who in 1532 defeated the Inca emperor Atahualpa. (p. 468)

Plato (plā'tō), 428?–347? B.C. Greek philosopher and student of Socrates. (p. 206)

Polo, Marco (pō'lō), A.D. 1254–1324 Italian merchant who traveled to China, where he lived for 17 years, at times serving as diplomat for Kublai Khan. (p. 403)

Pope Urban II (ur'bən), A.D. 1042–1099 Pope who called for the First Crusade to reclaim Jerusalem from the Muslims. (p. 332)

R

Rabin, Yitzhak (rä bēn'), A.D. 1922–1995 Prime minister of Israel who negotiated a peace plan with Palestinians in the West Bank and Gaza. (p. 578)

Robespierre, Maximilien (rōbz'pē âr), A.D. 1758–1794 French revolutionary. He sent suspected traitors to the guillotine during the Reign of Terror from 1793 until his own death by guillotine in 1794. (p. 490)

Roosevelt, Franklin Delano (rō'zə velt), A.D. 1882–1945 The 32nd President of the United States. He led the nation against the Axis powers in World War II. (p. 543)

S

Sadat, Anwar (sə dat'), A.D. 1918–1981 Egyptian president who established peaceful relations with Israel in 1978. (p. 577)

San Martín, José de (sän mär tēn'), A.D. 1778–1850 Argentine soldier who led revolutions that freed Argentina and Chile from Spanish rule. (p. 496)

Sargon (sär'gon), died 2279? B.C. King of the city-state Kish; united the city-states of Sumer to create an empire. (p. 111)

Schliemann, Heinrich (shlē'män, hīn'rikh), A.D. 1822–1890 German archaeologist and discoverer of the remains of Troy. (p. 30)

Scipio (sip'ē ō), 234?–183? B.C. Roman general who defeated Hannibal in the Battle of Zama outside Carthage, North Africa, in 202 B.C. (p. 235)

Shah Jahan (shä jə hän'), A.D. 1592–1666 Mogul emperor of India; he built the Taj Mahal in Agra, India, in memory of his wife Mumtaz Mahal. (p. 396)

Shakespeare, William (shāk'spēr), A.D. 1564–1616 English dramatist and poet; considered one of the greatest writers in the English language. (p. 346)

Shihuangdi (shē'hwäng dē), 259?–210 B.C. Chinese emperor who founded the Qin dynasty and unified China with a standardized system of writing and money; his tomb contained the famous "clay army." (p. 168)

Siddhartha Gautama (sid där'tə gô'tə mə), 563?–483? B.C. Ancient Indian religious leader known as the Buddha, or Enlightened One, who founded Buddhism. (p. 150)

Sinan (sə nän'), A.D. 1489–1588 Süleyman's chief architect; he designed more than 300 buildings, including the mosque in Istanbul. (p. 390)

Socrates (sok'rə tēz), 470?–399 B.C. Greek philosopher who discussed laws, customs, values, and religion with students; accused of urging young people to revolt, he was sentenced to death. (p. 206)

Spindler, Konrad (shpin'dlər), A.D. 1939– German archaeologist who analyzed the 5,000–year–old "Iceman" body found in the Alps in 1991. (p. 33)

Stalin, Josef (stä'lin), A.D. 1879–1953 Soviet revolutionary and dictator who ruled the Soviet Union from 1924 to 1953. (p. 537)

Süleyman (sü'lä män), A.D. 1495?–1566 Sultan of the Ottoman empire during its peak from 1520 to 1566. (p. 390)

Sun Yat-sen (sun' yät sen'), A.D. 1866–1925 Leader of the Chinese Nationalists and founder of the Republic of China in 1912. (p. 551)

Sunjata (sän jä'tä), d. A.D. 1255 King of Mali who conquered all of Ghana. (p. 364)

Suryavarman II (sur yə vär'mən), A.D. 1100s Khmer king who filled his capital city of Angkor with magnificent Hindu temples. (p. 400)

T

Tokugawa Ieyasu (tō kủ gä'wä ē yä'sü), A.D. 1543–1616 Shogun, or military commander, of the Tokugawa dynasty from 1603 to 1605; his family's shogunate kept Japan peaceful for more than 200 years. (p. 412)

Toussaint L'Ouverture (tü san' lü vər tyừr'), A.D. 1743?–1803 Haitian general; in 1802 he led a successful slave revolution, leading to the independence of Haiti in 1804. (p. 493)

Tutankhamun (tü täng kä'mən), 1371?–1352 B.C. Egyptian pharaoh who ruled from about the ages of 7 to 17; his tomb remained nearly untouched until its discovery in 1922. (p. 88)

W

Walesa, Lech (wə len'sə), A.D. 1943– Polish labor leader who became the first president of democratic Poland in 1990. (p. 598)

Watt, James (wot), A.D. 1736–1819 Scottish engineer and inventor who developed a steam engine that burned coal in 1765. (p. 503)

William the Conqueror (wil'yəm), A.D. 1027–1087 Norman king; in 1066 he defeated Harold, the Anglo-Saxon king, to become the first Norman king of England. (p. 326)

Wudi (wü'dē'), 100s B.C. Han emperor who ruled China from 140 B.C. to 87 B.C.; he set up a system of schools that prepared students for government jobs. (p. 176)

Y

Yeltsin, Boris (yel'tsin), A.D. 1931– Russian politician; in 1991 he became the first president of post-Soviet Russia. (p. 599)

Yoritomo (yōr ē tō'mō), A.D. 1147–1199 Japanese shogun, or military commander; in 1192 he attained supreme power from the emperor and ruled the country as a military dictator. (p. 411)

pronunciation key

a **at**; ā **ape**; ä **far**; âr **care**; e **end**; ē **me**; i **it**; ī **ice**; îr **pierce**; o **hot**; ō **old**; ô **fork**; oi **oil**; ou **out**; u **up**; ū **use**; ü **rule**, ủ **pull**; ûr **turn**; hw **white**; ng **song**; th **thin**; th **this**; zh **measure**; ə **about, taken, pencil, lemon, circus**

Glossary

This Glossary will help you to pronounce and understand the meanings of the vocabulary in this book. The page number at the end of the definition tells where the word first appears.

A

absolute monarchy (ab′sə lüt   mon′ər kē) A form of government headed by a ruler, or monarch, with unlimited power. See **divine right.** (p. 486)

accuracy (ak′yər ə sē) Being true or correct. (p. 604)

acropolis (ə krop′ə lis) A large hill in ancient Greece where city residents sought shelter and safety in times of war and met to discuss community affairs. (p. 197)

agora (ag′ər ə) A central area in Greek cities used both as a marketplace and as a meeting place. (p. 197)

agriculture (ag′ri kul chər) The raising of crops and animals for human use. (p. 52)

algebra (al′je brə) A type of mathematics to which Muslims made great contributions. (p. 275)

alliance (ə li′əns) An agreement between countries to work together in war or trade. (p. 527)

Allied Powers (al′īd pou′ərz) In World War I, the nations allied against the Central Powers; included Serbia, Russia, France, Britain, and the United States. (p. 528)

Allies (al′īz) In World War II, the nations allied against the Axis powers, including Britain, France, the Soviet Union, the United States, and China. (p. 543)

anti-semitism (an tē sem′i tiz əm) Discrimination against and hatred of Jews. (p. 575)

apartheid (ə pär′tīd) The government policy of strict and unequal segregation of the races as practiced in South Africa from 1948 to the early 1990s. (p. 607)

apostle (ə pos′əl) One of the 12 closest followers of Jesus, chosen by him to help him teach. (p. 248)

aqueduct (ak′wə dukt) A high, arched structure built to carry water over long distances. (p. 238)

archaeology (är kē ol′ə jē) The study of the remains of past cultures. (p. 32)

archipelago (är kə pel′ə gō) A large group of islands. (p. 385)

architecture (är′ki tek chər) The science of planning and constructing buildings. (p. 257)

aristocracy (ar ə stok′rə sē) The class of a society made up of members of noble families, usually the most powerful group. (p. 487)

armada (är mä′də) A fleet of warships. (p. 346)

armistice (är′mə stis) An agreement to stop fighting; a truce. (p. 531)

artifact (är′tə fakt) An object made by someone in the past. (p. 25)

assembly (ə sem′blē) A lawmaking body of government made up of a group of citizens. (p. 206)

astrolabe (as′trə lāb) An instrument invented by Muslims that is used to determine direction by figuring out the position of the stars. (p. 275)

Axis (ak′sis) In World War II, the nations who fought the Allies, including Japan, Germany, and Italy. (p. 543)

B

bilingual (bī ling′gwəl) Able to speak two languages. (p. 626)

bishop (bish′ əp) A church official who leads a large group of Christians in a particular region. (p. 251)

boycott (boi′kot) A form of protest in which people join together to refuse to buy goods. (p. 568)

Buddhism (bùd′iz əm) A religion founded in India by Siddhartha Gautama which teaches that the most important thing in life is to reach peace by ending suffering. (p. 150)

bureaucracy (byù rok′rə sē) The large organization that runs the daily business of government. (p. 511)

C

caliph (kā′lif) A Muslim leader who had both political and religious authority. (p. 273)

pronunciation key

a	at	ī	ice	u	up	th	thin
ā	ape	îr	pierce	ū	use	<u>th</u>	<u>th</u>is
ä	far	o	hot	ü	rule	zh	measure
âr	care	ō	old	ù	pull	ə	about, taken,
e	end	ô	fork	ûr	turn		pencil, lemon,
ē	me	oi	oil	hw	white		circus
i	it	ou	out	ng	song		

caravan (kar′ə van) A group of people and animals traveling together for safety, especially through a desert. (p. 264)

caravel (kar′ə vel) A sailing ship developed in Portugal in the 1400s that had greater directional control than earlier ships and could sail great distances more safely. (p. 463)

cardinal directions (kärd′ən əl di rek′shənz) The directions north, south, east, and west. (p. G6)

cartogram (kär′tə gram) A special kind of map that distorts the shapes and sizes of countries or other political regions to present economic or other kinds of data for comparison. (p. 506)

caste system (kast sis′təm) The social system in Hindu society in which a person's place is determined by the rank of the family into which he or she is born. (p. 144)

cathedral (kə thē′drəl) A large or important Christian church. (p. 332)

cause (kôz) Something that makes something else happen. *See* **effect.** (p. 118)

census (sen′səs) A periodic count of all the people living in a country, city, or other region. (p. 239)

Central Powers (sen′trəl pou′ərz) In World War I, the nations who fought against the Allied Powers, including Austria-Hungary and Germany. (p. 528)

chinampas (chin äm′paz) One of the floating islands made by the Aztec around Tenochtitlán for growing crops. (p. 427)

Christianity (kris chē an′i tē) A religion based on the teachings of Jesus, as recorded in the New Testament. (p. 246)

circa (sûr′kə) A Latin word, often abbreviated "c." that means "about" or "around." (p. 59)

citadel (sit′ə dəl) A walled fort that protects a city. (p. 135)

citizen (sit′ə zən) A person with certain rights and responsibilities in his or her country or community. (p. 197)

city-state (sit′ē stāt) A self-governing city, often with surrounding lands and villages. (p. 110)

civil disobedience (siv′əl dis ə bē′dēəns) A means of protest by refusing to obey a law that is considered to be unjust. (p. 582)

civil war (siv′əl wōr) An armed conflict between groups within one country. (p. 237)

civilization (siv ə lə zā′shən) A culture that has developed systems of specialization, religion, learning, and government. (p. 55)

Classic Period (klas′ik pêr′ē əd) A time of great cultural achievement for a civilization. (p. 299)

climate (klī′ mit) The weather pattern of an area over a long period of time. (p. 9)

climograph (klī′mə graf) A graph that shows the temperature and precipitation in a place over a period of months. (p. 290)

code of law (kōd uv lô) A written set of laws that apply to everyone under a government. (p. 113)

codex (kō′deks) A manuscript page such as the kind used by the Aztec to record historical, religious, governmental and scientific knowledge. (p. 430)

Cold War (kōld wôr) A term used for the battle of words and ideas that developed between the democratic nations of the West and the Soviet Union and Eastern Europe from about 1945 to 1990. (p. 556)

colony (kol′ ə nē) A territory or community that is under the control of another country. (p. 201)

commune (kom′ūn) A community in which resources, work, and living space are shared by all members of the group. (p. 554)

communism (kom′yə niz əm) A system in which the government owns all property and makes nearly all decisions for its citizens. (p. 537)

compass rose (kum′pəs rōz) A drawing on a map that shows directions. (p. G6)

concentration camp (kon sən trā′shən kamp) A place where people are imprisoned because of their heritage, religious beliefs, or political views. (p. 546)

conclusion (kən klü′zhən) A decision or opinion reached by putting together information about a subject. (p. 210)

confederation (kən fed ə rā′shən) A group of states or provinces under a central government. (p. 497)

Confucianism (kən fū′shə niz əm) In China, a system of beliefs and behavior based on the teachings of Confucius, who said that people should lead good lives by studying ancient traditions; stressed the importance of respecting one's family and ancestors. (p. 175)

conquistador (kon kēs′tə dôr) A Spanish conqueror who came to the Americas to search for gold, land, and glory. (p. 468)

consul (kon′səl) One of two elected officials of the Roman Republic who commanded the army and were supreme judges. (p. 232)

continent (kon′tə nənt) One of Earth's seven large bodies of land. (p. G4)

convent (kon′vent) A religious community in which women, or nuns, live and pray. *See* **nun.** (p. 331)

convert (kən vûrt′) To adopt or cause someone to adopt a new religion. (p. 470)

credibility (kre də bi′lə tē) Believability. (p. 472)

Crusade (krü sād′) Any of the journeys and battles undertaken by European Christians between 1095 and 1270, to win control of the Holy Land (Palestine) from the Muslims. (p. 332)

Cultural Revolution (kul′chər əl rev ə lü′shən) A campaign in China, 1966–1976, when the Communist Party under Mao Zedong called for the destruction of all noncommunist beliefs. (p. 554)

culture (kul′ chər) The way of life of a group of people at a particular time, including their daily habits, beliefs, and arts. (p. 10)

cuneiform (kū nē′ ə fôrm) A system of writing that used wedge-shaped symbols to represent sounds, ideas, and objects; developed in ancient Sumer. (p. 108)

custom (kus′təm) A way of living that people of the same culture practice regularly over time. (p. 14)

D

decision (di sizh′ən) a choice made from a number of alternatives. See **conclusion.** (p. 30)

Declaration of the Rights of Man and of the Citizen (dek lə rā′shən) A statement issued by the French National Assembly in August 1789 that all men were "born and remain free and equal in rights." (p. 488)

deforestation (dē for ə stā′shən) The process of clearing the land of forests, often to make space for farms and cities. (p. 318)

degree (di grē′) In geography, a unit of measurement that indicates the distance between lines of latitude and longitude; a unit of measurement for temperature. (p. 12)

delta (del′tə) The flat, fan-shaped land made of silt deposited at the mouth of a river. (p. 71)

demand (di mand′) In economics, people's desire for a particular item. See **supply.** (p. 363)

democracy (di mok′rə sē) A system of government in which citizens vote to make governmental decisions. (p. 199)

depression (di presh′ən) A severe slowdown in business characterized by high unemployment and falling prices. (p. 541)

dharma (där′me) In Hinduism, the laws and duties that guide the behavior of each caste member. (p. 145)

Diaspora (dī as′pər ə) The scattering of Jews to many parts of the world. (p. 125)

dictator (dik′tā tər) A ruler who has absolute power. (p. 237)

distortion (di stôr′shən) In cartography, or map-making, the unavoidable inaccuracy caused by stretching or cutting parts of the globe to fit them onto a flat map. (p. 432)

distribution map (dis trə bū′shən map) A special purpose map that shows how a particular feature such as population density is spread over an area. (p. G11)

diversity (di vûr′si tê) Differences; variety. (p. 440)

divine right (di vīn′ rīt) The belief that a monarch received authority to rule from God and therefore could not be questioned. See **absolute monarchy.** (p. 486)

domesticate (də mes′ti kāt) To train plants or animals to be useful to people. (p. 53)

drought (drout) A long period of dry weather. (p. 105)

dynasty (dī′nə stê) A line of rulers who belong to the same family. (p. 164)

E

Eastern Orthodox Christianity (ēs′tərn ôr′thə doks kris chē an′i tē) A branch of Christianity that developed in the Byzantine Empire and that did not recognize the pope as its supreme leader. (p. 255)

economy (i kon′ə mē) The way people manage money and resources for the production of goods and services. (p. 77)

effect (i fekt′) Something that happens as a result of a cause. See **cause.** (p. 118)

Eightfold Path (āt′fōld path) In Buddhism, the basic rules of behavior and belief leading to an end of suffering. See **Four Noble Truths.** (p. 153)

elevation (el ə vā′shən) Height above sea level. (p. 228)

elevation map (el ə vā′shən map) A map that shows the height of land above sea level. (p. G10)

emperor (em′pər ər) The supreme ruler of an empire. (p. 168)

empire (em′pīr) A group of lands and peoples ruled by one government. (p. 86)

equal-area projection (ē′kwəl âr′ē ə prə jek′shən) A map that is useful for comparing sizes of land masses, on which shapes at the center are fairly accurate but are very distorted at the edges of the map. (p. 432)

equator (i kwā′tər) An imaginary line circling Earth halfway between the North and South poles and dividing Earth into Northern and Southern Hemispheres. (p. G4)

erosion (i rō′zhən) The gradual wearing away of soil and rock by wind, glaciers, or water. (p. 162)

estates (e stāts′) The three social classes into which France was divided before the French Revolution, including the clergy, the aristocracy, and the common people. (p. 487)

ethnic group (eth′nik grüp) A people who share a heritage of common customs, values, and language. (p. 599)

European Union (EU) (yür ə pē′ən ūn′yən) A group of European nations working to build a common economy and create cultural ties throughout Europe. (p. 601)

evaluate (i val′ū āt) To judge. (p. 604)

expedition (ek spi dish′ən) A group of people who go on a trip for a specific reason. (p. 87)

F

factory (fak′tə rē) A building in which machines used to manufacture goods are located. (p. 501)

famine (fam′in) A widespread lack of food resulting in hunger and starvation. (p. 162)

fascism (fash′iz əm) A totalitarian government that promotes a form of nationalism in which the goals of the nation are more important than those of the individual. (p. 540)

feudalism (fū′də liz əm) Starting in Europe around A.D. 800, a system for organizing and governing society, based on land and service. See **fief, lord, vassal.** (p. 322)

fief (fēf) In the Middle Ages, a property given to a vassal in exchange for his loyalty. (p. 322)

Five Pillars (fīv pil′ərz) The five basic duties of all Muslims. (p. 269)

Four Noble Truths (fôr nō′bəl trüthz) In Buddhism, the principles that rule life and promise an end to suffering. See **Eightfold Path.** (p. 153)

free enterprise (frē en′tər prīz) The economic system of private ownership of land and businesses that allows people to make their own economic decisions and profit from their own work. (p. 556)

G

generalization (jen ər ə lə zā′shən) A broad statement of observation applied to different kinds of examples. (p. 408)

geocentric (jē ō sen′trik) Based on the idea that Earth is the center of the universe and that the sun, stars, and planets revolve around Earth. (p. 456)

geography (jē og′rə fē) The study of Earth's environment and how it shapes people's lives and how Earth is shaped in turn by people's activities. (p. 8)

glacier (glā′shər) A great sheet of ice that moves slowly over a land surface. See **Ice Age.** (p. 286)

gladiator (glad′ē ā tər) A Roman athlete, usually a slave, criminal, or prisoner of war, who was forced to fight for the entertainment of the public. (p. 240)

global grid (glō′bəl grid) Pattern formed on a map or globe by the crossing of parallels and meridians. This pattern makes it possible to pinpoint exact locations. (p. 13)

glyph (glif) A writing symbol, often carved into stone, that stands for an object or a sound. See **stela.** (p. 302)

Grand Canal (grand kə nal′) A waterway in China connecting Beijing with cities to the south. (p. 403)

Grand School (grand skül) A school begun by Confucian scholars in China that trained students for government jobs. (p. 176)

grand mufti (grand muf′tē) A religious leader of the Ottoman empire responsible for interpreting the laws of Islam. (p. 389)

gravity (grav′i tē) The force that pulls objects toward Earth and that draws planets into orbits around the sun. (p. 459)

Green Revolution (grēn rev ə lü′shən) A campaign by the government of India in the 1950s to increase agricultural productivity. (p. 584)

griot (grē′ō) An oral historian and musician who became important in western Africa in the 1500s and still carries on oral traditions today. (p. 367)

gross domestic product (grōs də mes′tik prod′ukt) The total value of goods and services produced by a country during a year. (p. 506)

guild (gild) In the Middle Ages, an organization of workers in a trade or craft that set standards and protected the interests of its members. (p. 324)

H

hacienda (hä sē en′də) A large agricultural estate owned by Spaniards or the church in Spain's American colonies. (p. 470)

harbor (här′bər) A sheltered place along a coast used to protect boats and ships. (p. 193)

heliocentric (hē lē ō sen′trik) Based on Copernicus's idea that the Earth and the other planets revolve around the sun. (p. 457)

hemisphere (hem′is fîr) One of the halves of Earth. (p. G4)

hieroglyphics (hī ər ə glif′iks) The ancient Egyptian system of writing that used symbols to stand for objects, ideas, or sounds. (p. 78)

hijra (hij′rə) The migration of Muhammad from Mecca to Medina in A.D. 622, marking the founding of Islam. (p. 268)

---

pronunciation key

a **at**; ā **ape**; ä **far**; âr **care**; e **end**; ē **me**; i **it**; ī **ice**; îr **pierce**; o **hot**; ō **old**; ô **fork**; oi **oil**; ou **out**; u **up**; ū **use**; ü **rule**, ů **pull**; ûr **turn**; hw **white**; ng **song**; th **thin**; <u>th</u> **this**; zh **measure**; ə **about, taken, pencil, lemon, circus**

Hinduism (hin′dü iz əm) The religion of India that grew out of the beliefs of the ancient Aryan peoples; it stresses that one main force connects all of life. (p. 142)

historical map (hi stôr′i kəl map) A map that shows information about the past. (p. 280)

history (his′tə rē) The story or record of what has happened in the past. (p. 24)

Holocaust (hol′ə kôst) The deliberate killing of 6 million Jews solely because they were Jewish by the Nazis during World War II. (p. 546)

humanism (hū′mə niz əm) An idea important to the Renaissance that focused on human values and what people can achieve in this world. (p. 336)

hunter-gatherer (hun′tər gath′ər ər) A person of the Old Stone Age who met needs by hunting animals and gathering plants. (p. 46)

I

Ice Age (īs āj) Any of the periods of time in the past lasting for millions of years when glaciers spread to cover nearly half of Earth's land. (p. 286)

imperialism (im pîr′ē ə liz əm) The extension of a nation's power over other lands by military, political, or economic means. (p. 508)

indulgence (in dul′jəns) A pardon or forgiveness given by the Roman Catholic Church to people who act against Christian teachings. (p. 343)

Industrial Revolution (in dus′ trē əl rev ə lü′ shən) A time when great technological advances changed the way goods were made and the ways people lived; it began in England in the 1700s and then spread throughout Europe and the United States. (p. 500)

inflation (in flā′shən) A period of rising prices. (p. 541)

interaction (in tər ak′shən) The exchange of ideas and customs among cultures. (p. 16)

interdependent (in tər di pen′dənt) Depending upon one another to meet needs and wants. (p. 622)

intermediate directions (in tər mē′dē it di rek′shənz) The directions halfway between the cardinal directions; northeast, southeast, southwest, and northwest. (p. G6)

International Date Line (in tər nash′ə nəl dāt līn) An imaginary line in the Pacific Ocean marking the boundary between one day and the next. (p. 549)

Internet (in′ tər net) A constantly growing international group of interconnected computers. (p. 627)

Intifada (in tə fä′də) The Palestinian uprising against Israeli rule that began in 1987. (p. 578)

irrigation (ir i gā′shən) The watering of dry land by means of canals or pipes. (p. 72)

Islam (is läm′) The religion of Muslims based on the teachings of the prophet Muhammad in the A.D. 600s. (p. 266)

isthmus (is′məs) A narrow strip of land that connects two larger land masses. (p. 423)

J

Judaism (jü′dē iz əm) The religion of the Jewish people. (p. 120)

jury (jur′ē) A group of citizens chosen to hear evidence and make a decision in a court of law. (p. 206)

K

Kaaba (kä′bə) A religious temple in Mecca that became sacred to Muslims. (p. 267)

karma (kär′mə) In Hinduism and Buddhism, the end result of all of a person's good and bad acts, which determines his or her rebirth. (p. 152)

Korean War (kə rē′ən wôr) A war fought between communist North Korea, aided by China, and South Korea, aided by United Nations members, during 1950–1953. (p. 557)

L

landform (land′fôrm) A feature of Earth's surface, such as a mountain range, plain, or plateau. (p. 9)

large-scale map (lärj skāl map) A map that provides many details about a small area by measuring lesser distances in small units. (p. 92)

Latin America (lat′in ə mer′i kə) The cultural region including Mexico, the Caribbean, and South America that has been strongly influenced by Spain and Portugal. (p. 492)

latitude (lat′i tüd) Distance north or south of the equator, measured by a set of imaginary lines, or parallels, that run east and west around Earth. *See* **parallel.** (p. G4, 12)

League of Nations (lēg əv nā′shənz) An international council created in 1920 by the Allied Powers to try to prevent future wars. (p. 531)

legacy (leg′ə sē) A tradition that is handed down from one generation to the next and is a valued part of people's lives today. (p. 52)

levee (lev′ē) A wall built along a river bank to prevent flooding. (p. 162)

Line of Demarcation (līn əv dē mär kā′shən) An imaginary line drawn across North and South America in 1494 to divide the claims of Spain and Portugal. (p. 467)

locator (lō′kāt ər) A small map that shows where the subject area of a main map is located. (p. G8)

loess (les) A fine, yellow soil that is easily carried by wind and rain, found in China. (p. 161)

Long March (lông märch) A 6,000-mile journey across China by 80,000 communists led by Mao Zedong, 1934–1935, to escape Nationalist forces. (p. 532)

longitude (lon′ji tüd) Distance east or west of the prime meridian measured by a set of imaginary lines, or meridians, that run north and south from Earth's poles. *See* **meridian**. (p. G4, 12)

lord (lôrd) In the Middle Ages, a noble who owned and controlled all activities on his manor. *See* **vassal.** (p. 322)

M

Magna Carta (mag′nə kär′tə) A legal document written by English lords in 1215 that stated certain rights and limited the power of the king. (p. 326)

maize (māz) Corn; a crop first grown in Middle America about 5,000 B.C. (p. 300)

Mandate of Heaven (man′dāt uv hev′ən) The belief that the Chinese emperor's right to rule came from the gods. (p. 175)

manor (man′ər) In the Middle Ages, a large self-sufficient estate granted to a lord and worked by serfs. (p. 320)

map key (map kē) A list of map symbols that tells what each symbol stands for. (p. G8)

Meiji Restoration (mā′ jē′ res tə rā′ shən) The overthrow of Japan's shogun in 1868 and restoration of power to the emperor Meiji. (p. 510)

mercator projection (mər kä′tər prə jek′shən) A map that shows accurate shapes of land masses and correct straight-line directions, but which is distorted for areas near the poles. (p. 432)

meridian (mə rid′ē ən) Any line of longitude east or west of Earth's prime meridian. *See* **parallel.** (p. G4)

Messiah (mə sī′ə) A special leader the Jewish people believe will be sent by God to guide them and set up God's rule on Earth. Christians believe Jesus to be the Messiah. (p. 247)

mestizo (me stē′zō) A person of mixed Native American and Spanish ancestry. (p. 494)

Middle Ages (mid′əl āj′əz) A period in European history between A.D. 500 and about the 1500s. (p. 320)

Middle Passage (mid′əl pas′ij) The difficult voyage made by enslaved Africans across the Atlantic Ocean to the West Indies where they were sold. (p. 475)

Middle Way (mid′əl wā) In Buddhism, a way of life, neither too strict nor too easy, that results from following the Eightfold Path. (p. 153)

middle class (mid′əl klas) During the Industrial Revolution, the new class of business people. (p. 504)

migrate (mī′grāt) To move from one place to another to live, especially a large group of people. (p. 138)

missionary (mish′ə ner ē) A person who teaches his or her religion to people with different beliefs. (p. 470)

monarchy (mon′ər kē) A government ruled by a king or queen. (p. 197)

monastery (mon′ə ster ē) A community in which monks lead lives devoted to religion. *See* **convent.** (p. 331)

monk (mungk) A man who devotes his life to a religious group, often giving up all he owns. *See* **monastery**. (p. 151)

monotheism (mon′ə thê iz əm) A belief in one God. *See* **polytheism.** (p. 123)

monsoon (mon sün′) A seasonal wind that blows across South Asia bringing dry weather in the winter and heavy rains in the summer. (p. 386)

mosque (mosk) A Muslim place of worship. (p. 273)

N

NAFTA (naf′tə) The North American Free Trade Agreement, which went into effect in 1993, allowing free trade for many goods traded between Canada, Mexico, and the United States. (p. 626)

nationalism (nash′ə nə liz əm) A strong loyalty to one's own country and culture. (p. 527)

NATO (nā′tō) The North Atlantic Treaty Organization, a military alliance formed in 1949 by nations in western Europe and North America. (p. 557)

navigable (nav′i gə bəl) Able to be traveled by boats or ships. (p. 318)

New Stone Age (nü stōn āj) The period of human prehistory that lasted from 12,000 years ago to about 6,000 years ago, during which people still depended mainly on stone tools and began experimenting with agriculture. (p. 52)

New Testament (nü tes′tə mənt) The second part of the Christian Bible, containing descriptions of the life and teachings of Jesus and of his early followers. (p. 246)

pronunciation key

a **at**; ā **ape**; ä **far**; âr **care**; e **end**; ē **me**; i **it**; ī **ice**; îr **pierce**; o **hot**; ō **old**; ô **fork**; oi **oil**; ou **out**; u **up**; ū **use**; ü **rule**, u̇ **pull**; ûr **turn**; hw **white**; ng **song**; th **thin**; <u>th</u> **this**; zh **measure**; ə **about, taken, pencil, lemon, circus**

noble (nō′bəl) A member of a ruling family or one of high rank. *See* **aristocracy**. (p. 165)

nuclear arms race (nü′klē ər ärmz rās) The Cold War competition between superpowers to develop more powerful and greater numbers of nuclear weapons. (p. 559)

nun (nun) A woman who devotes her life to religion, often living in a convent. *See* **convent**. (p. 331)

O

oasis (ō ā′sis) A well-watered area in a desert. (p. 263)

Old Stone Age (ōld stōn āj) The period of human prehistory that lasted until about 12,000 years ago, during which stone tools were the most common technology used by humans. (p. 45)

oligarchy (ol′i gär kē) A type of government in which a small group of citizens control decision-making. (p. 197)

oracle bone (ôr′ə kəl bōn) In ancient China, a cattle or sheep bone used to predict the future. (p. 167)

oral tradition (ôr′əl trə dish′ən) The passing on of history, beliefs, or customs by word of mouth. (p. 25)

P

Pacific Rim (pə sif′ik rim) The ring of countries surrounding the Pacific Ocean. (p. 616)

papyrus (pə pī′rəs) A kind of paper made from papyrus, a reed plant growing along the Nile, that the ancient Egyptians used for writing. (p. 79)

parable (par′ə bəl) A simple story that contains a message or truth. (p. 248)

parallel (par′ə lel) In geography, any line of latitude north or south of the equator; parallels never cross or meet. *See* **meridian**. (p. G4, 13)

patrician (pə trish′ən) A member of the noble families who controlled all power in the early years of the Roman Republic. (p. 231)

patron (pā′trən) A supporter of the arts. (p. 337)

Pax Romana (paks rō mä′nə) A period of peace for the Roman Empire that began with the rule of Augustus in about 27 B.C. and lasted around 200 years. (p. 236)

peasant (pez′sənt) A small farm owner or farm worker. (p. 487)

Peloponnesian War (pel ə pə nē′zhən wôr) A war fought between Athens and Sparta in the 400s B.C., ending in a victory for Sparta. (p. 208)

peninsula (pə nin′sə lə) An area of land almost entirely surrounded by water. (p. 193)

per capita income (pūr kap′i tə in′kum) The amount of money each person would have if his or her country's total income were divided equally among its people. (p. 601)

pharaoh (fâ′rō) The title used by the rulers of ancient Egypt. (p. 75)

philosophy (fə los′ə fē) The study of or search for truth, wisdom, and the right way to live. (p. 206)

physical map (fiz′i kəl map) A map that primarily shows natural features of Earth, such as lakes, rivers, mountains, and deserts. (p. G10)

pilgrimage (pil′grə mij) A journey for religious purposes. (p. 269)

plague (plāg) A terrible disease that spreads quickly and kills many people. (p. 334)

plantation (plan tā′shən) A large farming estate where mainly a single crop is grown; until the mid-1800s slaves often worked on plantations. (p. 475)

plateau (pla tō′) An area of flat land that rises above the surrounding land. (p. 105)

plebeian (pli bē′ən) A common farmer, trader, or craftworker in ancient Rome. (p. 231)

point of view (point əv vū) The position of someone toward the world or a subject, shaped by his or her thinking, attitudes, and feelings. (p. 328)

polar projection (pō′lər prə jek′shən) A map projection that shows the area around the North or South Pole. (p. 432)

polis (pō′lis) A city-state in ancient Greece. (p. 196)

political cartoon (pə lit′i kəl kär tün′) A drawing that states an opinion about a political matter. (p. 572)

political map (pə lit′i kəl map) A map mainly showing political divisions, such as national or state boundaries, cities, and capitals. (p. G9)

polytheism (pol′ē thē iz əm) The belief in many gods and goddesses. *See* **monotheism**. (p. 111)

pope (pōp) The bishop, or church leader, of Rome and head of the Roman Catholic Church. (p. 251)

population density (pop yə lā′shən den′si tē) The number of people living in a given space. (p. 370)

prehistory (prē his′tə rē) The period before events were recorded in writing. (p. 33)

prime meridian (prīm mə rid′ē ən) The line of longitude marked 0° on the world map, from which longitude east and west are measured. (p. G4)

primary source (prī′mer ē sôrs) A first-hand account of an event or an artifact created during the period of history being studied. *See* **secondary source**. (p. 26)

profile (prō′fil) In geography, a map showing a cross-section of a land surface. (p. 228)

projection (prə jek′shən) A way of placing parts of Earth onto a flat map. (p. 432)

propaganda (prop ə gan′də) The spreading of persuasive ideas or attitudes that are often exaggerated or falsified in order to help or hurt a particular cause or group. (p. 541)

Protestantism (prot′ə stən tiz əm) The beliefs of Christians who opposed, or protested against, the Roman Catholic Church in the 1500s; the beliefs of people who follow a Protestant religion today. (p. 344)

province (prov′ins) A division of land within an empire or country. (p. 169)

Punic Wars (pū′nik wôrz) A series of conflicts between Rome and Carthage in the 200s B.C., ending in a victory for Rome. (p. 234)

Q

quipu (kē′pü) A knotted cord used for record-keeping by the Inca. (p. 437)

Quran (kù rän′) The most holy book of Islam, believed to contain the teachings of Allah, or God, to Muhammad. (p. 266)

R

rain forest (rān fōr′ist) A warm, wet forest that receives more than 80 inches of rain per year. (p. 288)

Raj (räj) The period in India from the 1850s to 1947 when it was ruled by the British. (p. 581)

reform (ri fôrm′) To change. (p. 343)

Reformation (ref ər mā′shən) A movement beginning in Europe in the 1500s, to bring reform to the Roman Catholic Church, and leading to Protestantism. (p. 344)

refugee (ref yù jē′) A person who flees his or her country for safety. (p. 577)

region (rē′jən) An area with common features that set it apart from other areas. (p. 9)

Reign of Terror (rān əv ter′ər) The period 1793–1794 in revolutionary France when suspected traitors were beheaded in great numbers. (p. 490)

reincarnation (rē in kär na′shən) A Hindu belief that people move in a constant cycle of life, death, and rebirth. (p. 144)

relief map (ri lēf′ map) A map that shows changes in elevation. (p. G10)

Renaissance (ren ə säns′) A period of great cultural and artistic change that began in Italy around 1350 and spread throughout Europe. (p. 336)

representative (rep ri zen′tə tiv) A person who is elected by citizens to speak or act for them. *See* **Republic**. (p. 232)

republic (ri pub′lik) A form of government in which citizens elect representatives to speak or act for them. (p. 231)

revolution (rev ə lü′shən) The overthrow of an existing government and its replacement with another; any sudden or very great change. (p. 486)

Roman Catholicism (rō′mən kə thol′ə siz əm) A branch of Christianity that developed in the western Roman empire and that recognized the Pope as its supreme head. (p. 257)

Russian Revolution (rush′ən rev ə lü′shən) Beginning in 1917, the events leading up to the overthrow of tsarist rule and the eventual establishment of the Soviet government led by Vladimir Ilyich Lenin and the Bolsheviks. (p. 532)

S

Sabbath (sab′əth) A weekly day of rest, prayer, and study. (p. 124)

saint (sānt) A woman or man considered by a religious group to be especially holy. (p. 332)

samurai (sam′ù rī) A class of soldiers in fuedal Japan who were loyal only to their lords. (p. 411)

sanction (sangk′shən) A penalty placed against a nation to make it change its behavior, such as a refusal to buy its goods or sell it products. (p. 608)

savanna (sə van′ə) A broad, grassy, plain with few trees, found especially in large parts of Africa. (p. 356)

scale (skāl) A unit of measure on a map, such as an inch, that is used to represent a distance on Earth. (p. G7)

scientific method (sī ən tif′ik meth′əd) A way of studying things through questioning and thorough testing. (p. 460)

scribe (skrīb) A professional writer who kept records and copied letters and official documents. (p. 78)

secondary source (sek′ən der ē sôrs) A record of the past, based on information from primary sources. (p. 27)

seismograph (sīz′mə graf) A scientific instrument that could detect earthquakes hundreds of miles away, invented during the Han dynasty. (p. 177)

---

pronunciation key

a **a**t; ā **a**pe; ä f**a**r; âr c**a**re; e **e**nd; ē m**e**; i **i**t; ī **i**ce; îr p**ie**rce; o h**o**t; ō **o**ld; ô f**o**rk; oi **oi**l; ou **ou**t; u **u**p; ū **u**se; ü r**u**le; ù p**u**ll; ûr t**u**rn; hw **wh**ite; ng so**ng**; th **th**in; <u>th</u> **th**is; zh mea**s**ure; ə **a**bout, tak**e**n, penc**i**l, lem**o**n, circ**u**s

Senate (sen'it) The lawmaking body and most powerful branch of government in ancient Rome's Republic. (p. 232)

serf (sûrf) In the Middle Ages, a person who was bound to work on a noble's manor. (p. 320)

Shinto (shin'tō) A Japanese religion marked by the belief in the spirits of nature. (p. 410)

shogun (shō'gən) The ruler of feudal Japan from the 1100s to the 1800s who, although appointed by the emperor, ruled the country as a military dictator. (p. 411)

silt (silt) A mixture of tiny bits of soil and rock carried and deposited by a river. (p. 71)

slash and burn (slash and bûrn) A farming method involving the cutting of trees, then the burning of them to provide ash–enriched soil for the planting of crops. (p. 293)

slavery (slā'və rē) The practice of one person owning another person. (p. 95)

small-scale map (smôl skāl map) A map that shows a big area in less detail by measuring its greater distance in large units. (p. 92)

social pyramid (sō'shəl pir'ə mid) A diagram illustrating the divisions within a culture; usually showing the most powerful person or group at the peak and the least powerful groups at the bottom. (p. 95)

socialism (sō'shə liz əm) An economic and political system based on collective or government ownership and control of all resources and industry; also a political philosophy based on the writings of Karl Marx. (p. 505)

specialization (spesh ə lə zā'shən) Training to do a particular kind of work. (p. 55)

stela (stē'lə) A tall, flat stone, often carved with writing, used to mark an important historical event. (p. 302)

steppe (step) A dry, grassy, treeless plain found in Asia and eastern Europe. (p. 163)

strait (strāt) A narrow channel, or body of water, connecting two larger bodies of water. (p. 465)

strike (strīk) A refusal to work as a protest against unfair treatment. (p. 534)

subcontinent (sub kon'tə nənt) A large landmass that is connected to the rest of a continent. (p. 131)

sugarcane (shŭg'ər kān) A tall grass with a thick, woody stem containing a liquid that is a source of sugar. (p. 475)

sultan (sult' ən) Supreme ruler of the Ottoman empire. (p. 389)

summary (sum'ə rē) A brief statement of main ideas. (p. 172)

superpower (sü'pər pou ər) A term used for the world's strongest nations—the United States and the Soviet Union—during the Cold War. (p. 556)

supply (sə pli') In economics, the available quantity of a good, product, or resource. *See* **demand.** (p. 363)

surplus (sûr'plus) An extra supply of something, such as crops that are not needed immediately for food. (p. 55)

symbol (sim'bəl) Anything that stands for something else. (p. G8)

T

technology (tek nol'ə jē) The use of skills and tools to meet practical human needs. (p. 45)

telescope (tel'ə skōp) An optical instrument for making distant objects, such as planets and stars, appear nearer and larger. (p. 457)

temperate (tem'pər it) Mild; moderate in temperature. (p. 317)

Ten Commandments (ten kə mand'mənts) According to the Hebrew Bible, the laws God gave to Moses on Mount Sinai. (p. 123)

terrace (ter'is) A level platform of earth built into a hillside, usually used for farming. (p. 437)

textile (teks'tīl) A cloth fabric that is either woven or knitted. (p. 501)

Three Fires Council (thrē fîrz koun'səl) A league or cooperative group formed by the Ojibwa and the neighboring Potawatomi and Ottawa to promote trade. (p. 441)

timberline (tim'bər līn) An imaginary line on high mountains or in the arctic, above or beyond it trees cannot grow. (p. 424)

time line (tīm līn) A diagram that shows when events took place during a given period of time. (p. 58)

time zone (tīm zōn) A geographic region where the same standard time is used. (p. 548)

topic sentence (top'ik sen'təns) A sentence that contains the main idea of a paragraph, often the first sentence in that paragraph. (p. 172)

Torah (tôr'ə) The first five books of the Hebrew Bible containing the laws and teachings of Judaism. (p. 123)

totalitarian (tō tal i târ'ē ən) A government in which a dictator or a small group of leaders control all aspects of people's lives. (p. 538)

township (toun'ship) A segregated area where blacks in South Africa were forced to live under apartheid. (p. 607)

trade (trād) The exchange of goods between peoples. (p. 56)

Treaty of Versailles (trē′tē əv vâr sī′) The treaty that the Allied Powers forced Germany to sign at the end of World War I. (p. 531)

Triangular Trade (tri ang′gyə lər trād) From the 1500s to the mid-1800s, the triangular-shaped trade routes between the Americas, England, and Africa, which involved the buying and selling of captive Africans as well as guns, sugar, and iron goods. (p. 476)

tribune (trib′ūn) An elected leader of ancient Rome who represented the interests of the plebeians. (p. 232)

tribute (trib′ūt) A tax, often in the form of crops, paid by one ruler to another, usually to ensure peace or protection. (p. 428)

Triple Alliance (trip′əl ə li′əns) The pact that the army of the Aztec made with the forces of Texcoco and Tlacopan in 1428 in order to gain control of the Valley of Mexico. (p. 428)

tropical (trop′i kəl) Of or relating to the area of Earth between the Tropic of Cancer (23.5°N) and the Tropic of Capricorn (23.5°S). (p. 287)

tsar (zär) In pre–revolution Russia, the emperor. (p. 533)

tundra (tun′drə) A vast, treeless plain in arctic or subarctic places such as Alaska and northern Canada. (p. 422)

Twelve Tables (twelv tā′belz) The earliest written collection of Roman laws, drawn up by patricians about 450 B.C. that became the foundation of Roman law. (p. 233)

U

unification (ū nə fi kā′shən) The joining of separate parts, such as kingdoms, into one. (p. 75)

United Nations (ū ni′tid nā′shənz) An organization founded in 1945 whose members include most of the world's nations. It works to preserve world peace, settle disputes, and aid international cooperation. (p. 557)

urbanization (ur bən ə zā′shən) The growth of cities. (p. 625)

V

values (val′ūz) Ideals or beliefs that guide the way people live. (p. 16)

vassal (vas′əl) In the Middle Ages, a noble who usually was given a fief by his lord in exchange for loyalty. (p. 322)

Vedas (vā′dəz) In Hinduism, the ancient books of sacred songs on which much of its religious beliefs are based. (p. 143)

Vietnam War (vē et näm′ wôr) A civil war fought between South Vietnam, aided by the United States, and communist North Vietnam during 1954–1975. (p. 589)

W

warlord (wôr′lôrd) In China, 1912–1927, a strong local military leader who took advantage of political unrest to seize power in the area. (p. 551)

Warsaw Pact (wôr′sô pakt) A military alliance formed in 1955 by the Soviet Union and seven eastern European nations. (p. 557)

wigwam (wig′wom) A dome-shaped dwelling built by the Ojibwa and other Native Americans made of birch bark, cattail reeds, and wooden poles. (p. 443)

working class (wûrk′ing klas) People who work for wages, such as factory workers. (p. 504)

World War I (wûrld wôr) Called the "Great War" at the time, the war of 1914–1918 in which the Allied Powers defeated the Central Powers. (p. 531)

World War II (wûrld wôr) The war of 1939–1945 in which the Allies defeated the Axis powers. (p. 542)

Z

ziggurat (zig′ù rat) A large temple located in the centers of ancient Sumerian cities. (p. 111)

Zionism (zi′ə niz əm) A movement to create a national homeland for the Jewish people. (p. 575)

pronunciation key

a **at**; ā **ape**; ä **far**; âr **care**; e **end**; ē **me**; i **it**; ī **ice**; îr **pierce**; o **hot**; ō **old**; ô **fork**; oi **oil**; ou **out**; u **up**; ū **use**; ü **rule**, ù **pull**; ûr **turn**; hw **white**; ng **song**; th **thin**; <u>th</u> **this**; zh **measure**; ə **about, taken, pencil, lemon, circus**

index

This Index lists many topics that appear in the book, along with the pages on which they are found. Page numbers after an m refer you to a map. Page numbers after a p indicate photographs, artwork, or charts.

A

Aachen, 321, m321
Abbot, 331
Abraham of Ur, 121
Absolute monarchy, 486
Accra, 568
Acropolis, 197–198, 200, 205
Aegean Sea, 208, m208
Afghanistan, 597
Africa. *See also* individual countries of
 agriculture in, 356–357, 362, 378–379
 archaeology in, 45
 Christianity in, 359
 contemporary, 606–612
 economy of, 611
 Ethiopian kingdoms of, 358–361
 geography of, 354–357, m355
 Great Zimbabwe civilization of, 376–379
 independence in, 566–571, m570
 Islam in, 366, 373
 northeastern civilizations of, 359–361
 Swahili civilization of, 373–375, m373
 trade and, 359, 363–364, 367, 372–374, 376–378, 567
African National Congress (ANC), 608, 610, R44–R45
Afrikaners, 606–607
Agora, 197–198, 205, 214
Agra, 394
Agriculture,
 in Africa, 356–357, 362, 378–379
 in Americas, 293–294, 300–301, 427, 431, 437
 in Arabia, 264
 in Aztec empire, 427, 431
 in China, ancient, 162–163, 178
 in Egypt, ancient, 72–73, 77, 96–97, p72
 in Europe, 318
 in Greece, ancient, 194–195

 in Inca empire, 437
 in India, ancient, 132–133, 140
 in Mesopotamia, 105–107
 in New Stone Age, 52–57, 58, p58
 in Rome, ancient, 226
Ahmose, 85
Ahuítzotl, 428
Akbar, 392–397
Aksum, 359–361
Alaska, 422, 424–425
Alexander II of Russia, 533
Alexander the Great, 209, 212–213, 217, 409, p213
Alexandra Community Law Clinic, 613
Alexandra, South Africa, 613
Alexandria, 214–215
Algebra, 275–277
Algeria, 610
Algonkian, 479
Allah, 266, 268
Alliance, 527
Allied Powers, 528, 531, 536
Allies, 543–547, 557, 614
Alps, 32–36, 225, 316–317
Amanishakhete, Queen, 359
Amazon rain forest, 624–625
Amazon River, 425
American Revolution, 488, 492, R42–R43
Americas, the. *See also* individual countries of
 Africans in, 474–477
 agriculture in, 293–294, 300–301, 427, 431, 437
 Aztec empire of, 426–431, 434, 466, 468, 471, m427
 contemporary, 622–629
 economy of, 628
 Europeans in, 431, 466–471, 478–481
 geography of, 286–289, 422–425, m287, m423
 Inca empire of, 434–439, 466, 468–469, 471, m435
 Maya civilization of, 298–303, 304–305
 Native Americans of, 440–445, m441
 Olmec civilization of, 292–296
Analects, The, 175
Anasazi culture, R38–R41
Anatolia, 388
Andes Mountains, 422–424, 434, 439

Angkor, 400–402
Angkor Thom, 400
Angkor Wat, 398, 400–401
Anglo America, 623
Anglo-Saxons, 326
Anti-semitism, 575
Anyang, 165–167
Apartheid, 607–608, 610, 612
Apennine Mountains, 225
Apostles, 248–251
Apprentice, 324
Aqueducts, 238, 240
Aquino, Corazon, R44–R45
Arabia
 achievements of, 274–277, 341
 agriculture in, 264
 geography of, 262–265, m263
 Islam in, 266–271, 272–273, 275
 legacy of, 277, 278–279
 people of, 264–265
 trade and, 262, 264–265, 267, 273
Arabian Nights, The, 275
Arabian Sea, 263
Arabic, 267, 270, 367
Arafat, Yasir, 577–578, p574
Arawak, 475
Archaeology, 32
Archipelago, 385, 410, 412
Architecture
 African, 365
 Islamic, 275–276, 365
 Maya, 299
 in Middle Ages, 332
 Roman, 240–241, 244–245, 257
Argentina, 496
Aristide, Jean-Bertrand, 625
Aristocracy, 487
Aristotle, 211, 213, 457, p211
Armada, 346
Armenia, 600
Armistice, 531
Art
 calligraphy, Japanese, 416–417
 dance, Indian, 148–149
 drama, Greek, 206, 209
 environment and, 50–51
 Islamic, 275–277
 in Mogul empire, 394–395
 of Old Stone Age, 47
 Renaissance, 338–339
Artifact, 25, 28–29
Aryans, 138–139, 142–143, 150

Asante kingdom, R42–R43
Asia. *See also* individual countries of
 Chinese empires of, 402–409
 contemporary, 614–621
 economy of, 620
 geography of, 131, 262, 316, 372, 384–387, m385
 Japan, feudal, 410–415, m411
 Khmer kingdom of, 398–401, 586, m399
 Mogul empire of, 392–397
 new nations in, 586–591
 Ottoman empire of, 389–391, 574, 576
Asoka, R38–R39
Assembly, 206
Assyrians, R38–R39
Astrolabe, 275
Astronomy, 275, 304–305, 339, 430, 457
Aswan, Egypt, 38
Atahualpa, 469
Athena, 200, 205, 218
Athens, Greece, 197–201, 213, 218, 224, p207
Atlantic Ocean, 317, 462, 466, 476, 479, 617
Atomic bomb, 546, 559
Attica, 193
Attila the Hun, R38–R39
Augustus, Emperor, 236, 238, 243, 246–247, 359
Australia. G4–G6, 48, 617, mG6
Austria, 542, 598
Austria-Hungary, 527–528
Avicenna, 274
Axis, 543, 545
Azerbaijan, 600
Aztec empire, 426–431, 434, 466, 468, 471, m427

B

Babylon, 112–113, 125, 213
Babylonia, 112–113
Baghdad, 272–274, 277, 338, 360, 362, 574
Balkan Peninsula, 600, 627
Baltic Sea, 317
Bangladesh, 584
Bantu, 372
Bastille, 488
Bastille Day, 488
Battle of Britain, 543
Battle of El Alamein, R44, m545

Battuta, Ibn, 280–281
Bedouins, 265
Beijing, China, 403–404, 619
Belgium, 542, 566
Bell, Alexander Graham,
    R42–R43
Benedict, 331
Ben Gurion, David, 577
Beringia, 286
Berlin, Germany, 546,
    558–559, 598
Berlin Wall, 558–559, 596
Bethlehem, Judea, 247
Bible, 120–125, 246–249, 269
Bilingual, 626
Bill of Rights (1689), R42
Bishop, 251
Black Death, 334–336
Blitzkrieg, 542
"Bloody Sunday," 534–535
Bolívar, Simón, 496–497
Bolivia, 496, 625
Bolsheviks, 536–537
Border Cave, Zululand, 46–47,
    354, m47
Bosnia, 600–601, 604, 627
Botswana, 610
Bowating, 441
Boycott, 568, 582
Brazil, 467, 469, 496, 622,
    624–625
British East India Company,
    581
British Museum, 218–219
Brueghel, Pieter, 51
Buddha, 152–154, 174
Buddhism, 150–155, 266, 398,
    400–401, 410, 511
Buenos Aires, Argentina, 629
Bureaucracy, 510–511
Burma, 586
Byzantine empire, 255,
    388–389, 391
Byzantium, 254–255

C

Cabot, John, 478
Cabral, Pedro Álvarez, 467
Caesar, Julius, 237–238, 243
Cairo, Egypt, 76, 569
Calendar
    Islamic, 268, 275
    Mayan, 301, 304–305
    Roman, 237
Caliph, 273
Caliphate, 273, 574
Calligraphy, 416–417
Calvin, John, R42–R43
Cambodia, 398–399, 401,
    586–587, 590–591
Camp David agreement,
    577–578

Canaan, 121, 124, 574
Canada
    colonial, 478–481
    independence and, 496–497
    Native Americans in,
        440–441, 443, 445
    trade and, 622, 626
Canadian Shield, 423
Canals, 316, 319
Cape of Good Hope, 464
Cape Town, South Africa, 606
Caravan, 264–265
Cardinal directions, G6
Caribbean Islands, 623
Caribbean Sea, 474
Carnarvon, Lord, 88–89
Carter, Howard, 88–89
Carthage, 234–235
Cartier, Jacques, R42–R43
Cartograms, using, 506–507
Cartography, 278
Caste system, 144–146
Castro, Fidel, 560
Catal Huyuk, 53–57, 388, 629,
    p54
Cathedral, 332, 335
Catholicism, See Roman
    Catholicism
Caucasus Mountains, 316
Cause and effect, identifying,
    118–119
Census, 239
Central America, 623
Central Plateau, 287
Central Powers, 528–529
Champlain, Samuel de,
    479–480
Champollion, Jean François, 79
Charlemagne, 321, 326, 330
Chartres, France, 332
Chiang Kai-shek, 552
Chiapas, Mexico, 10–11
Chile, 434, 496, 625
China
    agriculture in, 162–163, 178
    cities in, 165–166
    Communism and, 552–555,
        614, 619
    contemporary, 614, 618–619
    education in, 176–177, 179
    empires of, 402–407
    geography of, 160–163, 169,
        386, m161
    government in, 164, 169,
        174–176, 178
    Japan and, 509, 511–512,
        543, 553
    legacy of, 180–181
    religion in, 167
    World War II and, 543
Chinampas, 427
Chinchorros culture, R36–R37
Christianity, 246–251,

254–255, 257, 266,
    320–321, 326, 330–331,
    359, 388, 390
Chumash culture, R36–R37
Churchill, Winston, 543, 556
Church of England, 345
Circa, 59
Citadel, 135
Cities. See also city-states
    in China, ancient, 165–166
    in Egypt, ancient, 97
    in India, ancient, 135–137
    in Middle Ages, 324–325
Citizens, 197, 200, 231
City-states. See also cities
    in Greece, ancient, 196–201
    in Mesopotamia, 110–111
Civil disobedience, 582, 585
Civilization
    definition of, 55
    Egyptian, 84–91
    Harappan, 135–139
    Islamic, 273–277, m273
    Maya, 298–303, 304–305
    Olmec, 292–296
    Sabaean, 264
    Swahili, 373–375, m373
civil rights movement, 585
Civil war, 237
Civil War (U.S.), R42–R43
Clark, William, R42–R43
Classic Period, Maya, 299
Cleopatra, 237
Climate, 3
Climatology, 289
Climographs, reading,
    290–291, p290–291
Cocaine, 625
Cochise culture, R36–R37
Code of Hammurabi, 113
Code of law, 113
Codex, 430
Cold War, 556–561, 589, 596,
    600–601, 614, 627
Colonialism, 566–567, 571,
    581, 585, 587
Colonies, 201
Colosseum, 241
Colossus of Rhodes, 216–217
Columbia, 496, 625
Columbus, Christopher, 464,
    466–467, 474, 493
Command economy, 538, 561
Commune, 554
Communism
    in China, 552–555, 614,
        618–619
    collapse of, 596–603
    in North Korea, 557, 614
    in Soviet Union, 537, 539
    in Vietnam, 588–590, 596,
        614
Compass rose, G6
Concentration camp, 546

Conclusions, making, 210–211
Confederation, 497
Confucianism, 175–176, 266,
    410, 511
Confucius, 174–175, 177–178
Conquistadors, 468–469
Constantine, 254–255
Constantinople, 254, 262, 332,
    388–389, 391
Constitution, U.S., 498–499
Consuls, 232
Continent, 3, G4
Convent, 331, 335
Convert, 470
Cook, James, R42–R43
Copán, 299–302
Copernicus, Nicolaus, 339,
    342, 457
Cortés, Hernando, 468, 471
Credibility of a source, analyz-
    ing, 472–473
Crete, 193
Croatia, 600
Cromwell, Oliver, R42–R43
Crusades, 332–334, 337, 402
Cuba, 560–561
Cuban Missile Crisis, 560–561
Cultural Revolution, 554–555,
    614, 619
Cultural sites, protecting,
    38–39
Culture, 4, 16–19
Cuneiform, 108–113
Customs, 14, 16
Cuzco, 435–438
Cyrus the Great, R38–R39
Czechoslovakia, 542, 557, 596,
    598–599

D

Da Gama, Vasco, 464
Dance, Indian, 148–149
Das Kapital, 505
David, King, 124
Da Vinci, Leonardo, 338–339
D-Day, 544–546
Decision, making, 30–31
Declaration of Independence,
    R42–R43
Declaration of the Rights of
    Man and of the Citizen,
    488
Deforestation, 318
Degrees, 12
De Klerk, Frederik Willem,
    610
Delta, 71
Democracy, 199, 201, 206,
    209, 210, 556, 585, 600,
    606, 610, 619, 625, 629
Democracy, representative, 17
Deng Xiaoping, 618–619, p619
Depression, 541

Dharma, 145
Dias, Bartholomeu, 464
Dictator, 237
Dien Bien Phu, Vietnam, 588
Diet, 511
Diocletian, 253
Directions
  cardinal, G6
  intermediate, G6
Diaspora, 125, 575
Distribution maps, reading,
  370–371, G11, m370,
  m371, mG11
Diversity, 440
Divine right, 486
Dolores, Mexico, 494–495
Dome of the Rock, 275, p274
Domesticate, 53
Dominican Republic, 623
Drama, Greek, 206, 209
Drought, 105
Duma, 534, 536
Dynasty, 164

E

Eastern Orthodox Church,
  255, 257, 332, 335, 391
East Germany, 558–559, 596,
  598
Economy. See also specific
  types of
  of Africa, 611
  of Americas, 628
  of Asia, 620
  of Europe, 602
Ecuador, 434, 496
Edison, Thomas, R42–R43
Edo, 412–414, 510
Education
  in China, 176–177, 179
  in Greece, 198–199, 211
  in Middle Ages, 323, 331
Egypt
  agriculture in, 72–73, 77,
    96–97
  cities in, 97
  civilization of, 84–91
  contemporary, 38, 569, 577
  daily life in, 94–99
  economy of, 77
  geography of, 70–73, m71
  government of, 76
  Jewish captivity in, 121–123
  Middle Kingdom of, 85
  New Kingdom of, 85–86, 94,
    97, 99
  Old Kingdom of, 75–77, 85
  religion in, 76–77
  Roman empire and, 253
  science in, 90–91
  trade in, 74, 77, 84–87, 134
  transportation in, 72–73,
    83–84, p83–84
Eightfold Path, 153
Einstein, Albert, R44–R45

Elevation maps, reading,
  228–229, G10, m228,
  mG10
Elgin Marbles, 218–219
El Greco, 340
Elizabeth I of England, 346,
  393, 581
Emperor, 168
Empire, 86
Empty Quarter, 263
England. See Great Britain
English Channel, 319, 347
Environment
  of Arabia, 263
  art and, 50–51
  of Middle America, 287–288
  Native Americans and,
    440–441
  regions and, 9
Equator, 12, G4–G5
Equiano, Olaudah, 476–477
Erasmus, 343, 345
Erickson, Leif, R40–R41
Eric the Red, R40–R41
Erosion, 162
Estates, 487
Estates General, 488
Estonia, 599
Ethiopia, 356, 358–361, 540
Ethnic group, 599
Etruscans, 227
Euphrates River, 104–108, 112,
  114, 130, 272
Eurasia, 316
Europe. See also individual
  countries of
  climate in, 317
  contemporary, 596–603
  Crusades in, 332–334, 337,
    402
  economy of, 602
  feudalism in, 322–323, 334
  geography of, 316–319,
    m317
  Middle Ages in, 320–327
  Reformation and, 342–345,
    362
  Renaissance and, 336–341,
    362, 462
European Space Agency, 461
European Union (EU), 601,
  603, 612
Expedition, 87

F

Factories, 501–502
Famine, 162
Fascism, 540–541, 546
Fatimids, R40–R41
Felucca, 83, p83
Ferdinand, Franz, Archduke of
  Austria-Hungary, 527
Fertile Crescent, 104–105,
  111, 114–115, 120, m105.
  See also Mesopotamia

Feudalism
  in Europe, 322–323, 334
  in Japan, 410–415, 510–511,
    m411
Fief, 322–323
First Estate, 487
Five Pillars of Islam, 269, 366
Fjords, 317
Floods, 72–73, 105, 138, 162
Florence, Italy, 337, 339–340
Forbidden City, 404, 619
Ford, Henry, R44–R45
Formosa, R42–R43
Forum, 233
Four Noble Truths, 153
France
  Africa and, 566, 569
  Canada and, 478–481
  European Union and, 603
  Frankish empire and, 321
  French Revolution in,
    486–491, 492–493
  Japan and, 509, 615
  Middle East and, 574, 576
  religion in, 345
  Vietnam and, 586–588
  World War I and, 526–528
  World War II and, 542–543,
    558
Francis of Assisi, 332
Frank, Anne, 546
Frankish empire, 321
Free enterprise, 556, 561, 600
French and Indian War,
  480–481
French Revolution, 486–491,
  492–493
Fuad, I, 569
Fu Hao, 166–167
"Fung Yang Song," 405

G

Galileo Galilei, 456–458
Gandhi, Indira, 17, 386, 584
Gandhi, Mohandas, 580,
  582–585
Ganges River, 585
Gaul, 237, 321
Gautama. See Siddhartha Gau-
  tama
Gaza, 577–578
Generalizations, making,
  408–409
Genghis Khan, 403, 409
Geocentric, 456
Geography
  of Africa, 354–357, m355
  of Americas, 286–289,
    422–425, m287, m423
  of Arabia, 262–265, m263
  of Asia, 131, 262, 316, 372,
    384–387, m385
  of China, 160–163, 169, 386,
    m161
  definition of, 8

of Egypt, 70–73, m71
of Europe, 316–319, m317
of Fertile Crescent,
  104–105, m105
Five themes of, G2–G3
of Greece, 192–193, 195,
  m193
of India, 130–131, 225, 386,
  m131
of Mesopotamia, 104–105,
  384, m105
of Rome, ancient, 224–227
Germany. See also East Ger-
  many; West Germany
  Africa and, 566
  contemporary, 596, 598
  European Union and, 603
  religion in, 345
  World War I and, 526–529,
    531, 536
  World War II and, 539–543,
    545–546, 553, 557–559
Ghana, 363, 367, 370, 372,
  567–569
Gilgamesh, 110
Glaciers, 286, 316, 423
Gladiators, 240
Glasnost, 597–599, 619
Global grid, 13, m13
Glyphs, 302
Gobi Desert, 386
Golan Heights, 577
Gold, 85, 362, 364, 367,
  372–374, 376, 378
Gold Coast, 567–568
Gorbachev, Mikhail, 597, 599
Government
  of Aztec empire, 428, 431
  of China, ancient, 164, 169,
    174–176, 178
  of Egypt, ancient, 76
  of Greece, ancient, 197, 199,
    201, 206, 209, 210, 217
  of India, 17
  of Japan, 510
  representative democracy,
    17
  of Rome, ancient, 230–233,
    235, 237, 256
Grand Canal, 403
Grand Canyon, 425
Grand Muftis, 389–390
Grand School, 176–177
Gravity, 459
Great Britain
  Africa and, 566–569, 606
  Canada and, 478, 480–481,
    497
  China and, 550
  Church of England in, 345
  Elizabethan Age in, 346–347
  India and, 580–583, 585
  Industrial Revolution and,
    501–505, 526, 629
  Japan and, 509, 615
  Middle East and, 574, 576
  Norman invasion of, 326

Southeast Asia and, 586, 588
World War I and, 526–527
World War II and, 542–544, 556
Great Lakes, 422–423, 440–441, 445, 479
Great Leap Forward, 554, 614
Great Pyramid, 80, 81
Great Rift Valley, 355
Great Sphinx, R36–R37
Great Wall of China, 170, 404, 466, m172
Great Zimbabwe, 376–379
Greece, ancient
  achievements of, 201, 209, 217, 341
  agriculture in, 194–195
  city-states in, 196–201, 213
  culture of, 200–201, 255
  economy of, 194
  education in, 198–199, 211
  empire of, 212–217, m214
  geography of, 192–193, 195, m193
  government of, 197, 199, 201, 206, 209, 210, 217
  philosophy in, 206, 209, 217
  religion in, 200, 205
  Roman empire and, 253
  trade and, 194–195, 201, 214
Greenland, R40–R41
Green Revolution, 584
Griot, 367, 368–369
Gross Domestic Product (GDP), 506–507, 602, 615
Guangzhou, 402, 404
Guatemala, 428
Guild, 324
Gulf of Mexico, 288, 292–293
Gupta empire, R38–R39
Gutenberg, Johannes, 344

H

Hacienda, 470–471
Haida culture, R36–R37
Haiti, 493, 623, 625
Hammurabi, 112–114
Han dynasty, 174, 176, 177–178, 236
Han Gaozu, 174
Hanging Gardens of Babylon, 216–217
Hannibal, 234–235
Harappa, 135, 138
Harappan civilization, 135–139, 384
Harbor, 193
Hatshepsut, 87, 358, p87
Hawaii, 543
Heian period, R40–R41
Heliocentric, 457, 459
Hemisphere, G4–G5, m65
Henry VIII of England, 345, R42–R43

Henry, Prince (the Navigator), 463–464
Herodotus, 196, 212
Herzegovina, 600
Herzliya, Israel, 579
Hesiod, 194
Hidalgo, Miguel, 494–495
Hieroglyphics, 78–79, p83
Hijra, 268
Himalayas, 131, 150–151, 160, 225, 385–386, 424
Hinduism, 15–16, 142–147, 152, 392–394, 397, 398–399, 583
Hiroshima, Japan, 546
Hispaniola, 467, 493, 623
Historical maps, reading, 280–281, G11, m280, m281, mG11
History, 24
Hitler, Adolf, 540–543, 546, 553
Ho Chi Minh, 586, 588
Holland. See Netherlands
Holocaust, 546
Homer, 200
Honecker, Erich, 598
Hong Kong, 550, 614, 617, 619
Hopewell culture, R38–R39
Huang River, 160–163, 164–166, 170, 404
Huang River Valley, 161–164, 167–168
Hubble Telescope, 305, p305
Hudson, Henry, R42–R43
Huitzilopochtli, 428, 430
Humanism, 336, 338, 343
Hungary, 596, 598
Hunter-gatherers, 46, 52–53
Huron, 480
Hydrogen bomb, 559
Hyksos, 85

I

Ice Age, 286–287, 423
Iceland, 316
Iceman, 33–37
Igbo-Ukwu culture, R40–R41
Iliad, 200
Imperialism, 508
Inca empire, 434–439, 466, 468–469, 471, m435
India
  agriculture in, 132–133, 140
  Buddhism in, 150–155
  caste system in, 144–146
  cities in, 135–137
  contemporary, 14–15, 17, 147
  geography of, 130–131, 225, 386, m131
  Hinduism in, 142–147
  independence of, 580–585
  trade in, 134, 137

Indian National Congress, 582–583
Indian Ocean, 373, 386
Indochina, 587
Indulgence, 343
Indus Plain, 131
Indus River, 130–134, 138–140, 372
Indus River Valley, 130–134, 138–140, 213
Industrial Revolution, 500–505, 526, 617, 629
Inflation, 541
Information, evaluating for accuracy, 604–605
Interaction, 16–17, 19
Interdependent, 622
Intermediate directions, G6
International Date Line, 549
Internet, 627
Interns for Peace, 579
Intifada, 578
Inuit, R36–R37
Inventions, of Industrial Revolution, 503
Iran, 201
Iran-Iraq War, R44–R45
Iraq, 105, 115, 272, 576, 627
Ireland, 330
Iron Curtain, 556, 598
Iroquois League, R42–R43
Irrigation, 72–73, 96, 106, 132
Isis, 76
Islam, 15, 266–273, 275, 366, 373, 389, 391. See also Muslims
Israel, 115, 125, 574–575, 577–578, 579
Istanbul, Turkey, 388–391, 393
Isthmus, 423
Italy
  Rome, ancient, and, 234, 237
  geography and, 224
  plague and, 334–335
  religion in, 345
  Renaissance in, 336–337
  World War I and, 527
  World War II and, 540–541, 543
Iturbide, Agustín de, 495
Ivory, 372–373, 375, 376

J

Jabal al-Hijaz, 263
Jamestown, Virginia, R42–R43
Japan
  economy of, 614–616
  feudal, 410–415, 510–511, m411
  industrialization of, 508–513
  United States and, 509, 514–515
  Vietnam and, 588
  World War II and, 543, 546, 559

Jayavarman II, 399
Jayavarman VII, 400
Jerusalem, 124, 249, 275, 332–333, 390, 575
Jesus of Nazareth, 247–251
Jews, 121, 125, 330–333, 390, 532, 541, 546, 575, 577, 579. See also Judaism
Jinnah, Mohammed Ali, 583
Joan of Arc, R40–R41
Johannesburg, South Africa, 608
John I of England, 326
Jordan, 577
Judah, 125
Judaism, 121–123, 266. See also Jews
Judea, 246–247, 249, 253, 574
Jury, 206
Justinian, Emperor, R40–R41

K

Kaaba, 267, 269
Karma, 152
Kennedy, John F., 560–561
Kenya, 374–375
Khadija, 267–268
Khmer Kingdom, 398–401, 586, m399
Khrushchev, Nikita, 560–561
Khufu, 81, 82
King, Martin Luther, Jr., 585, R44–R45
Knights, 323
Korea, 511–512, 557–558, 615
  Korean War, 557, 617
Kosala, 151
Kublai Khan, 403–404, 407
Kush, 86, 358–359
Kuwait, 262, 627
Kyoto, 413, 510

L

Lake Texcoco, 427
Lalibela, 360–361
Landform, 3
Laos, 398, 400, 586–587
Large-scale maps, 92–93, m93
Latin, 256, 320
Latin America, 4, 492–493, 623–625
Latitude, 12–13, G5
Latium Plain, 225–226
La Venta, 294–296
League of Nations, 531, 540, 557
Lebanon, 115, 577
Legacy, 50
Lenin, Vladimir Ilyich, 536–537
Leo III, Pope, 321
Leo X, Pope, 344
Levees, 162

Lewis, Meriwether, R42–R43
Liberia, 566
Lighthouse of Alexandria, 216–217
Lima, Peru, 469–470, 474
Line of Demarcation, 467, m467
Literature
in Elizabethan England, 346
Greek, 200
Islamic, 275
Japanese, 414
Lithuania, 599
Livingstone, David, R42–R43
Livy, 231
Locator map, G8
Locomotive, 502
Loess, 161
London, England, 324–325
Longitude, 12–13, G5
Long March, 552–553, 619
Lord, 322–323
Louis XVI of France, 486, 488–491
L'Ouverture, Toussaint, 493
Lower Egypt, 71, 74–76, 85, 86
Lusitania, 526, 529
Luther, Martin, 342–344

M

Macedonia, 213, m214
Machu Picchu, 438–439
Magellan, Ferdinand, 462, 464–465, p463
Magna Carta, 326–327
Maize, 300
Mali, 364, 366–367, 462, 567
Manchuria, 551
Manchus, R42–R43
Mandate of Heaven, 175
Mandela, Nelson, 606, 608, 610, p610
Manor, 320, 322
Mansa Musa, 366–367
Mao Zedong, 552–555, 614, 618–619
Maps
cardinal directions on, G6
cartograms, 506–507
comparing, 140–141
compass rose on, G6
distribution, 370–371, G11, m370, m371, mG11
elevation, 228–229, G10, m228, mG10
global grid, 13, m13
historical, 280–281, G11, m280, m281, mG11
intermediate directions on, G6
large-scale, 92–93, m93
latitude, 12–13, G5, m12–13, mG5
locator, G8

longitude, 12–13, G5, m12–13, mG5
physical, G10, mG10
political, G9, mG9
profile, 228–229, m229
projections of, 432–433
relief, G10, mG10
scales of, 92–93, G7, m92
small-scale, 92–93, m92
symbols on, G8
time zone, 548–549, m548
Marconi, Guglielmo, R42–R43
Market economy, 556
Marie Antoinette of France, 490
"Marseillaise, La," 489
Marshall Plan, R44–R45
Marx, Karl, 505, 532, 536
Mathematics
in Egypt, ancient, 90–91
in Greece, ancient, 215, 217
in Islamic civilization, 274–275, 278
in Maya civilization, 302
Mauryan empire, R38–R39
Mausoleum at Halicarnassus, 216–217
Maya civilization, 298–303, 304–305
Mayflower, R42–R43
Measles, 471
Mecca, 267–272, 275, 366, 390
Medici, Lorenzo, 337, 339
Medicine
in Aztec empire, 430
in Egypt, 90
in Islamic civilization, 274
modern, 627
Medina, 268
Mediterranean Sea, 71, 111, 192–193, 198, 201, 213, 225, 234–235, 317, 569, 574
Meiji, 510, 513
Meiji Restoration, 510, 512
Mekong River, 398–399
Memphis, Egypt, 76, 97
Menes, 75
Meridians, 13, G5
Mesopotamia
agriculture in, 105–107
Babylonians in, 112–114
city-states in, 110–111
geography of, 104–105, 384, m105
inventions of, 108, 116–117, 118–119
Judaism in, 121
legacy of, 115
religion in, 111
Sumerians in, 108–111
trade in, 111
Messiah, 247
Mestizos, 469, 494
Mexico
Latin America and, 623–624

regions of, 4–5
revolution in, 494–495, 497
trade and, 622, 626
World War I and, 529
Mexico City, Mexico, 287, 426, 469–470, 474, 495, 624–625
Michelangelo, 338
Middle Ages
Christian Church and, 327, 330–335
Crusades in, 332–334, 337, 402
feudalism in, 322–323, 334
life in, 320, 322–323
trade in, 324, 334, 337–338
Middle class, 504
Middle East, 574–578
Middle Passage, 475
Middle Way, 153
Migrate, 138
Ming Dynasty, 404–407, 466, 586
Minoan civilization, R36–R37
Minstrels, 325
Missionaries, 470
Moctezuma, 468
Mogadishu, 374–375
Mogul empire, 393–397
Mohenjo-Daro, 135–139, 143, p136
Mombasa, 374–375
Monarchy, 197, 345
Monastery, 331, 335
Mongols, 402–404, 407
Monk, 151, 331
Monotheism, 123
Monroe Doctrine, R42–R43
Monsoon, 386–387
Morelos, José María, 495
Morocco, 367
Moscow, Russia, 536, 543, 597, 622–624, 626
Moses, 122–124
Mosque, 273
Mount Aconcagua, 424
Mount Everest, 131, 385
Mount Kilimanjaro, 355
Mount Olympus, 200
Mozambique, 355
Muhammad, 267–272, 274–275
Mumtaz Mahal, 396–397
Music
in Islamic civilization, 275
in Middle Ages, 325
Muslims, 15, 266–267, 269–271, 330–333, 388, 392, 394, 397, 532, 583, 600. *See also* Islam
Mussolini, Benito, 540–541
Myanmar, 398
"My Bark Canoe," 442
Mycenaeans, R36–R37

N

Nabataea, 264
Nagasaki, Japan, 546
Napoleon Bonaparte, 491, 492–494
Nasser, Gamal Abdel, 569
National Assembly, 486, 488
Nationalism, 527, 568, 575–576, 582
Nationalists (China), 551–553
Native Americans, 440–445
NATO, 557
Navigable rivers, 318–319
Nazareth, Judea, 247
Nazis, 541–544, 546, 557, 577
Nehru, Jawaharlal, 583–585
Nepal, 386
Netherlands, 316, 345, 461, 509, 546
New Deal, R44–R45
New Delhi, India, 14–15, 17
New France, 480
New Spain, 469–471
New Stone Age, 52, 58, 74
New Testament, 246–250
Newton, Isaac, 459
New York City, New York, 629
New Zealand, 617, mG6
Nicholas II, 534–535
Nigeria, 610
Niger River, 355, 363–364, 370–372
Nile River, 70–76, 81–84, 86, 95–96, 130, 354, m71
Nineveh, 114
"N'kosi Sikelel'i Afrika," 608–609
Nkrumah, Kwame, 567–568
Nobles, 165
Nok culture, R38–R39
Normandy, 326, 544–545
Normans, 326–328
North American Free Trade Agreement (NAFTA), 626
North China Plain, 160
North European Plain, 318
North Korea, 557, 614
North Sea, 317
North Vietnam, 588–589, 614
Nubia, 84–86
Nuclear arms race, 559
Nun, 331

O

Oasis, 263
Oaxaca culture, R38–R39
Obsidian, 56
Oceania, 617
Octavian. *See* Augustus, Emperor
Odyssey, 200
Ojibwa, 440–445

Old Stone Age, 45, 48–49
Old Testament, 246
Oligarchy, 197, 199
Olmec civilization, 292–296
Olympic Games, 200–203, 608
On the Revolutions of the
    Heavenly Spheres, 339
Oracle, 167
Oracle bones, 166–167
Oral tradition, 25
Osiris, 76
Osman, 389
Ottoman empire, 389–391,
    574, 576
Oyo, R42–R43

P

Pachakuti, 435–436, 439
Pacific Ocean, 410, 428, 435,
    465, 509, 617
Pacific Rim, 616–617, 621
Pakistan, 583–584
Paleoclimatology, 289
Palestine, 253, 574–578
Pamoedjo, Hima, 51
Panama, 496
Panama Canal, R44–R45
Pantheon, 241, 244, p244
Paper, invention of, 177
Papyrus, 79, 82–83
Parables, 248
Parallels, 13, G4
Paris, France, 319, 488–491,
    542
Parthenon, 205, 218–219
Patriarch, 359
Patrician, 231–233, 235,
    236–237
Patron, 337
Paul of Tarsus, 250–251
Pax Romana, 236, 238,
    252–253
Pearl Harbor, Hawaii, 543
Peasants, 487
Peloponnesian League, 208
Peloponnesian Wars, 208–209,
    212–213
Peloponnesus, 193
Peninsula, 193
Penn, William, R42–R43
Per capita income, 601
Perestroika, 597–598
Pericles, 206, 208–209
Perry, Matthew C., 509, 514
Persian empire, 201, 204,
    212–213, 252, 272
Persian Gulf, 105, 263, 626
Persian Gulf War, R44–R45
Peru, 435, 469–471, 496, 625
Peter (Apostle of Jesus), 248,
    251
Peter the Great, R42–R43

Petra, 264
Petrarch, 338
Pharaoh, 75–76, 95
Philosophy, Greek, 206, 209,
    217
Phnom Penh, Cambodia, 401
Phoenicia, 195, 234
Physical map, G10, mG10
Pilgrimage, 269–270, 332
Pisa, Italy, 457
Pizarro, Francisco, 468–469
Plague, 334–335
Plantation, 475–476
Plateau, 105
Plato, 201, 206
Plebeian, 231–233, 235, 236
PLO (Palestine Liberation
    Organization), 577
Point of view, determining,
    328–329
Poland, 542, 557, 575, 598
Polis, 196, 214
Political cartoons, 572–573
Political map, G9, mG9
Pollution, 601
Polo, Marco, 403, 406, 463
Pol Pot, 590–591
Polynesians, R40–R41
Polytheism, 111, 295
Pope, 251, 342–344, 347, 359.
    See also individual names
    of
Population density, 370–371,
    m370–371
Portugal, 463–464, 466, 467,
    469–471, 492, 496, 566
Powhatan, R42–R43
Prehistory, 33
Primary sources, 26, 29
Prime meridian, 13, 548, G5
Profile maps, reading,
    228–229, m229
Propaganda, 541
Prophet, 122, 268
Protestantism, 344–345, 347
Provinces, 169, 497
Ptolemy II, R38–R39
Pueblo culture, R40–R41, m44
Punic Wars, 234–235
Punt, 87, 358
Puritans, R42–R43
Pyramids, 81, 216–217, p80

Q

Qin dynasty, 168, 171, 174,
    176
Qing dynasty, 551
Qinling Mountains, 169
Quebec, Canada, 479–481,
    626
Quipu, 437, 439
Quran, 266, 269

R

Ra, 76
Rabin, Yitzhak, 578, p574
Railroads, 502
Rain forest, 288, 293, 296, 297,
    425
Rain Forest Treasures Trail,
    297
Raj, 581–582
Ramadan, 269–270
Reagan, Ronald, 597
Red Sea, 263–265, 355, 360,
    569
Reform, 343
Reformation, 342–345, 347,
    362
Refugee, 577
Regions, 3–5
Reign of Terror, 490–491
Reincarnation, 144
Relief map, G10, mG10
Religion. See also Buddhism;
    Christianity; Hinduism;
    Islam; Judaism; Shinto
  in Aztec empire, 430
  in China, ancient, 167
  in Egypt, ancient, 76–77
  in Greece, ancient, 200, 205
  in Inca empire, 435
  in Maya civilization, 294–295
Remus, 226
Renaissance, 336–341, 362,
    462
Representatives, 232
Republic, 232
Revolution, 486
Rhodes, 193
Robespierre, Maximilien, 490
Rocky Mountains, 422,
    424–425
Roman Catholic Church, 332,
    335, 339, 341–347, 459,
    470, 487, 490
Roman Catholicism, 251, 257
Romania, 557
Rome, ancient
  agriculture of, 226
  architecture in, 240–241,
    244–245, 257
  empire of, 236–243,
    252–257, 320
  geography of, 224–227
  government in, 230–233,
    235, 237, 256
  legacy of, 244–245, 256–257,
    320, 341
  roads in, 239
  trade in, 226, 239
Rommel, Erwin, 544
Romulus, 226
Roosevelt, Franklin, 543
Rosetta Stone, 79, p79
Russia. See also Soviet Union
  Japan and, 509, 512–513

  Russian Revolution in,
    532–539
  World War I and, 527–528
Russian Revolution, 532–539

S

Sabaean civilization, 264
Sabbath, 124
Sadat, Anwar, 577
Sahara Desert, 355, 363–364,
    370
Sahel, 355
Saint, 332
St. Augustine, R38–R39
St. Domingue, 493
St. Francis of Assisi, R40–R41
St. Lawrence River, 479–480,
    626
St. Petersburg, Russia,
    534–536
Samurai, 411–415, 510
Sanctions, 608, 610
San Martín, José de, 496
Sanskrit, 135
Santo Domingo, 475
Sarajevo, Bosnia, 527, 604–605
Sargon, 111–112
Saudi Arabia, 262, 271
Savanna, 356
Scale, map, 92–93, G7, m92,
    m93
Scandinavia, 326, 345
Scandinavian peninsula, 317
Schliemann, Heinrich, 30–31,
    p30
Science
  in China, ancient, 177
  in Egypt, ancient, 90–91
  in Islamic civilization, 275
  modern, beginning of,
    456–460
  in Renaissance, 339
Scientific method, 460
Scipio, 235
Scribes, 78–79, 109, 367
Secondary sources, 27, 29
Second Estate, 487–488
Seine River, 319, 326
Seismograph, 177
Seljuk Turks, R40–R41
Senate, Roman, 232, 237
Seneca, 441
Senegal, 356
Senegal River, 363, 370
Serbia, 527
Serf, 320, 323, 533
Shah Jahan, 396–397
Shakespeare, William, 346,
    348–349
Shang dynasty, 164–167, 175,
    384, m165
Shihuangdi, 168–171, 172–173,
    174

Shikibu, Murasaki, 414
Shinto, 410
Shogun, 411–413, 508, 510
Siberia, 538–539
Sicily, 225, 234
Siddhartha Gautama, 150–152, 155
Siena, Italy, 334–335
Silk, making, 180–181
Silk Road, 403–404, 406–407, 463, m406
Silt, 71, 131, 160–161
Sinan, 390
Singapore, 617–618
Slavery
    in Africa, 364, 567
    in Americas, 474–477
    in Aztec empire, 429
    in Egypt, ancient, 95
    in Greece, ancient, 197–198, 206
    in Maya civilization, 301
    in Mesopotamia, 113
    in Mexico, 495
    in Ottoman empire, 390–391
    in Rome, ancient, 231, 235, 241
Slovenia, 600
Smallpox, 471
Small-scale maps, 92–93, m92
Smith, John, R42–R43
Socialism, 505
Social pyramid, 95
Socrates, 206
Sofala, 378–379
Solidarity, 598
Solomon, King, 124
Somalia, 627, R44–R45
Songhai, 367, 466
Sources
    primary, 26, 29
    secondary, 27, 29
South Africa, 606–610, 612, 613
South America, 496, 623
Southeast Asia, 586, 589–591
Southern African Develop-
    ment Community
    (SADC), 612
South Korea, 557, 617
South Vietnam, 588–589
Soviet Union. See also Russia
    China and, 552
    Cold War and, 556–561, 596
    fall of, 597, 599–600
    founding of, 537
    Stalin and, 538–539
    Vietnam and, 591
    World War II and, 542–545, 547
Soweto, South Africa, 608
Spain
    Africa and, 566
    colonies of, 469–471, 474
    England and, 346–347

exploration and, 464–465, 466–469
    Latin America and, 492–496
    religion in, 345
Spanish Armada, 346–347
Spartacus, R38–R39
Sparta, Greece, 198, 201, 204, 208–209, 224
Specialization, 55
Spindler, Konrad, 33, 37
Sputnik, 559
Stalin, Josef, 537–539, 542–543, 557, 560, 597
Stelae, 302, p302
Steppes, 163
Stonehenge, England, R36–R37
Strait, 464–465
Strait of Magellan, 465
Strike, 534
Subcontinent, 131
Sudan, 358
Suez Canal, 569, 572
Sugarcane, 475
Süleyman, 388, 390–391, 393
Sumer, 108–113
Summary, writing, 172–173
Sunjata, 364, 409
Sun Yat-sen, 550–551
Superpower, 556, 627
Supply and demand, 363
Surplus, 55, 137
Suryavarman II, 400
Swahili civilization, 373–375
Switzerland, 345
Sylvester Village, Belize, 297
Symbol, 572
Symbol, map, G8
Syria, 115, 577

T

Taiwan, 512, 550, 553, 616
Taj Mahal, 396–397, p396
Tale of Genji, The, 414
Tanzania, 374–375
Technology
    agricultural, 500
    in Catal Huyuk, 56
    communications and, 627–628
    Industrial Revolution and, 500–503
    medicine and, 627
    in New Stone Age, p59
    in Old Stone Age, 45–46, 48–49, p48–49
    war and, 528, 530
Telescope, 456–458, 460
Temperate, 317
Tempietto, 340–341
Temple of Artemis, 216–217
Ten Commandments, 123
Tenochtitlán, 426–431, 462, 468–469
Teotihuacán, R38–R41

Terrace, 437
Texas, R42–R43
Textiles, 501
Thailand, 398, 400–401, 586, 617
Thatcher, Margaret, R44–R45
Thebes, 81, 85, 92
Thermometer, 458
Third Estate, 487–488
Three Fires Council, 441
Thucydides, 209
Tiananmen Square, 619
Tiber River, 225–227, 230, 233
Tibet, 386
Tibetan Plateau, 385
Tierra caliente, 287–288, 290
Tierra fria, 287, 290
Tierra templada, 287–288, 290
Tigris River, 104–108, 130, 272
Timberline, 424
Timbuktu, 364–365, 370, 466
Time lines, reading, 58–59
Time zone, 548–549
Time zone maps, reading, 548–549, m548
Tocqueville, Alexis de, 500
Tokugawa Ieyasu, 412
Tokugawa shogun, 412–413, 415, 508, 510
Tokyo, Japan, 412, 510, 624
Toltec culture, R40–R41
Tonle Sap, 399
Torah, 123, 125
Totalitarian, 538
Township, 607
Trade
    Africa and, 359, 363–364, 367, 372–374, 376–378, 567
    in Age of Exploration, 462–465
    Arabia and, 262, 264–265, 267, 273
    Canada and, 479–481, 622, 626
    Catal Huyuk and, 56
    Egypt and, 74, 77, 84–87, 134
    Great Britain and, 581
    Greece and, 194–195, 201, 214
    India and, 134, 137, 397, 581
    international, 630–631
    Japan and, 511–513, 615
    Mesopotamia and, 111
    Mexico and, 622, 626
    in Middle Ages, 324, 334, 337–338
    Omec civilization and, 296
    Pacific Rim countries and, 617
    Rome, ancient, and, 226, 239
    triangular, 476–477, 501
Traditional economy, 178
Trans-African railroad, R44–R45

Transcontinental railroad, R42–R43
Transportation
    caravans and, 264–265
    in Egypt, ancient, 72–73, 83–84, p83–84
    railroad and, 502, 581
    in Rome, ancient, 226, 239
    wheel and, 116–117
Treaty of Versailles, 531, 541–542
Trent, Italy, 345
Triangular trade, 476–477, 501
Tribunes, 232
Tribute, 428
Triple Alliance, 428
Tropical zone, 287–288
Troubadours, 325
Troy, 30–31
Tsar, 533, 535
Tundra, 422
Turkey, 53, 388, 391, 576
Tutankhamun, 88–90, 97, p88–89
Twelve Tablets, 233

U

Uganda, 375
UNESCO, 38
Unification, 75
Union of Soviet Socialist
    Republics. See Soviet
    Union
Unions, 505
United Nations, 557, 591, 627
United States
    Cold War and, 556–559, 589, 596
    civil rights movement in, 585
    GDP of, 615
    government of, 201, 232, 235, 256
    independence and, 492
    Industrial Revolution in, 501, 617
    Japan and, 509, 514–515
    Native Americans in, 440–441, 443, 445
    neighboring countries and, 622–626
    South Africa and, 608
    World War I and, 529
    World War II and, 543–544, 546–547
Upper Egypt, 71, 74–76, 81, 85
Ural Mountains, 316, 319, 384
Urban II, Pope, 332
Urbanization, 625

V

Valley of Kings, 88
Valley of Mexico, 427–428
Values, 16
Van Hemmessen, Caterina, 340–341
Vassal, 322–323

Vedas, 143–146, 150
Venezuela, 496
Venn diagram, 635
Versailles, France, 488
Viet Minh, 588
Vietnam, 398, 400–401, 586–591, 596, 614
Vietnam War, 589
Vikings, 326
Viracocha, 435–436

W

Walesa, Lech, 598
Warlords, 551, 553
Warsaw Pact, 557, 596, 600
Washington, George, 480, R42–R43
Waterloo, R42–R43
Weapons, of World War I, 528, 530

West Bank, 577
West Germany, 558
West Indies, 474–477
Wigwam, 443
William the Conqueror, 326
Wilson, Woodrow, R44–R45
Wittenberg, Germany, 343–344
Women
  in India, 17, 584
  in Japan, 615
  in Middle Ages, 322
  in Rome, 231
Working class, 504
World War I, 527–531, 535–536, 547, 569, 574
World War II, 542–547, 556–560, 566, 577, 588, 614–615, 622–624
Wright, Orville, R44–R45

Wright, Wilbur, R44–R45
Writing, system of
  in Aztec empire, 430
  in China, ancient, 166–167, 169, p166
  in Egypt, ancient, 78–79
  in Greece, ancient, 215
  in Islamic civilization, 267
  in Maya civilization, 302
  in Mesopotamia, 108–113
  in Rome, ancient, 256
Wudi, 176–177
Wu Ding, 167

X

Xianyang, 169

Y

Yalta, 557
Yeltsin, Boris, 599
Yemen, 262, 264

Yoritomo, 411–412
Yoruba kingdom, R42–R43
Yuan Dynasty, 403
Yucatán peninsula, 299
Yugoslavia, 600

Z

Zagwe, 360–361
Zama, 235
Zambezi River, 355
Zanzibar, 374–375
Zeus, 200, 216–217
Ziggurat, 111, p111
Zimbabwe, 376–379
Zionism, 575
Zululand, 46
Zuñi, R42–R43

CREDITS

Cover: Pentagram

Maps: Geosystems

Charts and Graphs: Eliot Bergman: pp 57, 290, 291, 319, 387, 425; Hima Pamoedjo: pp 357, 487, 513, 625

Chapter Opener Globes: Greg Wakabayashi

Illustrations: Richard Cowdrey: pp. 48-49; John Edens: pp. 564-565; Joseph Forte: pp. 42-43, 102-103, 284-285, 352-353; George Gaadt: pp. 68-69, 222-223; Theodore Glazer: pp. 106; Adam Hook: pp. 80, 314-315; Patricia Isaza: pp. 602, 611, 620, 628; Hrano Janto: pp. 73, 95; David McCall Johnston: pp. 128-129, 158-159, 260-261, 442, 454-455; W.B. Johnston: pp. 109, 166; Dave Joly: pp. 17, 37, 55, 91, 107, 114, 163, 206, 275, 289, 333, 375, 391, 459, 511, 531, 568, 603, 621, 627; Robert Korta: pp. 420-421; Rudy Lazlo: pp. 216-217; Angus McBride: pp. 140-141, 484-485; Peg McGovern: pp. 36; Hima Pamoedjo: pp. 18-19, 51, 75, 365, 395, 406-407, 503, 628; Roger Payne: pp. 207; Oliver Rennert: pp. 54; Steven Stankiewicz: pp. 88-89; Robert Van Nutt: pp. 323, 405, 382-383, 524-525 Cover: i. Lee Bolton Picture Library

PHOTOGRAPHY CREDITS: All photographs are by the Macmillan/McGraw-Hill School Division (MMSD)except as noted below.

i: Mager Photo; Boltin Picture Library. iii: m. The Picture Cube; b. Gerald Champlong/The Image Bank. iv: b. P. Aventu Rier/Gamma Liaison; t. The Granger Collection. v: b. Art Resource, Inc.; t. Lee Boltin; m. Daemmrich/The Image Works. vi: t.l. Scala Art Resource; m., b. Lee Boltin. vii: b. Lee Boltin Picture Library; t. Woodfin Camp Picture Agency; b. Phillips Collection. viii: t. Robert Harding Picture Agency; m.l. Corbis/Bettmann Archives; b. Phillip Makanna/Ghost. ix: EPA Scala. x: vautier/Woodfin Camp. G2: b. Patrick Ward; t. Michael Yamashita. G2-3: Elizabeth Wolf. G3: t. David Ryan/Photo 20-20; t. Nicholas DeVore III; b. Gerald S. Cubitt; m. Susan Griggs Agency. **Chapter 1** 2: t. Suraj N. Sharma/Dinodia Picture Agency; b. Gerald Champlong/The Image Bank; m. The Picture Cube. 3: b. David L. Brill. 4: b. Grisewood & Dempsey, Ltd. 45: Adam Woolfitt. 5: b.l. Grisewood & Dempsey, Ltd.; t. Hugh Sitton/Tony Stone Images. 6: Frank Labua/Gamma Liaison. 7: t. Wang Fuchun/China Stock; m. Freeman Patterson/Masterfile; m. Thomas Kanzler/Viesti Associates; b. Thomas Mangelson/Images of Nature. 8: t.l. Earth Imaging/Tony Stone Images. 10: b.l. Less Stone/Sygma; b.r. D. Donne Bryant; m.l. D. Donne Bryant. 14: t.l. Pablo Bartholomew. 15: t.l. Dinodia. 16-17: Pablo Bartholomew. 18: t.r. courtesy Brian Lawlor; t.l. courtesy Rachel Dennis; b.l. courtesy Anna Patricia DeMartinez; b.r. courtesy Olanike Olakunki. 19: rtesy Harry Tan. **Chapter 2** 22: b. Frank La Bua/Gamma Liaison. 23: b. Gordon Gohan/National Geographic Society; m. Tom Bean/Tony Stone Worldwide; t. R. Ian llyod/Westlight. 25: m. Comstock; b. Ken Vinocur/The Picture Cube. 26: r. UPI/Corbis- Bettmann. 27: Authentic old ads. 28: l. Corbis/Bettmann; t. Uniphoto Picture Agency. 30: b.l. Robert Freck/Woodfin Camp, Inc.; m. The Granger Collection; b.r. William Kennedy/The Image Bank. 32: t.r. Uniphoto Picture Agency. 34: t.l. Paul Hanny/Gamma Liaison; t.r. Sygma. 35: b.r. Hinterleitner/Gamma Liaison; m. Rex U.S.A, Ltd. 38: t.l. Comstock. 39: t. courtesy Gustavo Araoz; m. courtesy Nancy Marzulla; b. courtesy Brenda Pavlic. **Chapter 3** 44: t.l. Pierre Boulot/Woodfin Camp. 45: b.r. Chris Johns/Tony Stone Images; b.l. AnthroPhoto File. 46: t.l. Ira Block. 47: b.l. George Holton/Photo Researchers; b.r. Erwin and Peggy Bauer/Bruce Coleman, Inc. 48: t.l. Steve Elmore/The Stock Market; t.r. Reunions des Musees Nationaux, Paris; b. Dr. Peter Beaumont/McGregor Museum, South Africa. 49: t.r., Institute of Vertebrate and Paleontology and Paleoanthropology, Beijing, China; b.r. Mark Newman/Photo Researchers. 5051: m. Gamma Liaison. 51: t.l. Boston Museum of Fine Arts/Explorer?; m. courtesy of The Trustees of the Victoria and Albert Museum; b.r. Image Bank. 52: t. Ed Malitsky/Liaison International. 53: b. Sonia Halliday Photography. 56: m., b. Dr. James Meelaart. 64: t.r. Israel Museum; t.l. The Granger Collection; m.r. The Metropolitan Museum of Art, Fletcher Fund, 1931 31.13.1; b. Gamma Liaison 65: m. Giraudon; b. Giraudon. 66: b.l. R. W. Nicholson. 66-67: Michael Yamashita, Woodfin Camp, Inc. 67: t.l. Brian Brake, Photo Researchers; m. Georg Gerster. **Chapter 4** 70: t.l. O.L. Mazzatesta/National Geographic Society. 72: b. Michael Holford/British Museum; m. Nino Mascardy/The Image Bank. 74: t.l. Superstock. 75: b. Wernher Krutein/Liaison International. 77: b. The Granger Collection; b. Louvre/Agence Photographique des Musees Nationale; l. source:Superstock/British Museum. 78: b.r. Lee Boltin; bkgnd. Brian Brake/Photo Researchers. 79: Bridgeman Art Library, British Museum/Art Resource. 82: m. Werner Forman Archive, The British Museum, London/Art Resource. 83: t.l. Giraudon; r. Paul Popper, Ltd.; b.l. Superstock. 84: t.r. Giraudon. 85: r. British Museum; t.l. Erich Lessing/PhotoEdit. 87: b. John G. Ross; t. Giraudon/Paris. 88: m. Kelvin Wilson. 89: b. Lee Boltin; t. Metropolitan Museum of Art. 90: t.l. Giraudon. 93: b. Mike Rothwell/FPG International. 94: t.r. The Granger Collection. 96: t.r. The Granger Collection. 97: b. Richard Steedman/The Stock Market. 98: l., r. The Granger Collection; m. Brian Brake/Photo Researchers. 99: b.l. Giraudon. **Chapter 5** 104: t.l. Nik Wheeler/Black Star. 108: t.l. Michael Holford/The British Museum. 111: m.r. Art Resource (Iraq Museum Baghdad); b. Nik Wheeler. 112: m.l. Baghdad Museum/Hirner Fotoarchive (Art Resource); b. Giraudon. 113: t.r. Musee du Louvre, Paris. 114-115:m. Comstock. 115: m. The Oriental Institute of Chicago. 116: m. Giraudon. 117: b.r. bicycles in Beijing, China; m. Bob Thomason/Tony Stone Images; t.r. Jerry & Sharon Austin/The Picture Cube. 118: b.l. Erich Lessing/Art Resource; b.r. British Museum. 120: t.l. The Bettmann Archive. 122: t. B.A. Stewart/National Geographic Society; b.m. Richard T. Nowitz. 123: b. The Jewish Museum. 124: t. Kay Chernush/The Image Bank; m. Zviki-Eshet/The Stock Market. 125: b. Miro Vintoniv/The Picture Cube. **Chapter 6** 130: t.l. Pramod Mistry/Dinodia. 131: b.l. Patrick Morrow. 132: t.r. Susan McCartney. 133: m.l. Ric Ergenbright; b. Charles Marden Fitch/Superstock. 135: b.r. Giraudon/Paris. 136: b. Harrison Forman; m. Jehangir Gazdar/Woodfin Camp, Inc. 137: t.r. Dilip Mehta/Contact Press. 138-139:b. George F. Mobley/National Geographic Society. 142: t.l. Lindsay Hebberd/Woodfin Camp, Inc. 142-143:b. Mike Yamashita. 144: t. Jeffrey Alford/Asia Access; m.r. Brian Vikander. 145: b. Robert Frerck/Odyssey Productions. 146: b. Arvind Garg/Gamma Liaison; m.l. Giraudon/New Dehli National Museum; m.r. Giraudon/Musee Guimet, Paris. 147: t.l. Galen Rowell. 148: m. EPA/Scala. 149: b. Ernt Jahn/Bruce Coleman, Inc.; t. Lindsay Hebberd/Woodfin Camp, Inc.; m. Scala/Art Resource, Inc. 151: t.r. The Granger Collection. 152: m.r. Hilarie Kavanagh/Tony Stone Worldwide; t. Everton/The Image Works. 153: b.r. Dinodia Picture Agency; b.l. Ric Ergenbright Photography. 154-155: Wolfgang Kaehler. 155: m. Pablo Bartholomew/Gamma Liaison. **Chapter 7** 160: t.l. Claus Meyer/Black Star. 161: (Background for Map) Wolfgang Kaehler. 162: m. Photographer Photos Co./Gamma Liaison; l. Forest Anderson/Gamma Liaison; r. Min Zhongjie/Sovphoto Eastphoto. 164: t.l. Smithsonian Institute. 165: b. James Burke/Life Magazine (c) 1961, Time Inc. 166: l. British Library/Werner Forman Archive/Art Resource, Inc. 167: t. ChinaStock Photo Library. 168: t.l. Wolfgang Kaehler. 169: b. Sovfoto/Eastfoto. 170: t.l. Xinhua News Agency; t.r. Gamma-Liaison. 171: m. Wolfgang Kaehler/Gamma-Liaison. 172-173:m. Rolan Lloyd/Westlight. 173: b.r. Wolfgang Kaehler. 174: t.l. Bibliotheque Nationale/Paris. 175: b. Bibliotheque Nationale/Superstock. 176: t.l. Anderson/Gamma Liaison. 177: b. Michael Holford. 178: b.l. Asian Art & Archaeology/Art Resource. 179: Wu Qing. 180: m. Bibliotheque Nationale/Giraudon; t.l. Xinxua/Gamma Liaison. 181: m.l. Sovfoto/Eastfoto; t. Minneapolis Institute of Arts; b.l. Sovfoto/Eastfoto. **Chapter 8** 185: b. Monica Stevenson for MMSD. 186: t.l. Werner Forman/Art Resource; t.r. Lee Boltin/Boltin Picture Library; b.l. Daemmrich/The Image Works. 186-187:b.r. Alan Beckey/The Image Bank. 187: r. Lauros-Giraudon/Art Resource. 188: b. James M. Gurney. 188-189: O. Louis Mazzatenta. 192: t.l. Rick Falco/Black Star. 194: t.l. Dimaggio/Kalish/The Stock Market; t.r. Calvin Larsen/Photo Researchers. 194-195:m. Art Resource, Inc. 195: b.r. Trireme Trust/Cambridge University, UK. 196: t.l. Robert Frerck/Woodfin Camp & Associates. 197: b. J. Pavlovsky/Sygma. 199: m.r. Michael Holford; b. Eric Lessing/Art Resource. 200: t.r. Art Resource. 201: b.l. FPG International. 202: t. Paul J. Sutton/Duomo. 202-203: Paul J. Sutton/Duomo. 203: t. Kathleen Kliskey/The Picture Cube; b. Al Tielemaus/Duomo. 204: t.l. Nimatallah/Art Resource. 205: t. David Lees; b. Harold Sund/The Image Bank. 209: t.l. Erich Lessing/Art Resource, Inc.; m. Art Resource. 210: Giraudon. 211: b. Culver Pictures. 212: t.l. Giraudon. 213: m.l. Art Resource; b.r. National Geographic Society. 215: m. Boltin Picture Library; t. Gilda Alberto Rossi/The Image Bank. 218: t. British Museum. 219: t.r., courtesy Robert Anderson; m. courtesy Martin Krause; b. courtesy Greek Tourist Board. **Chapter 9** 224: t.l. Mike Mazzaschi/Stock Boston. 226: Amanda Merullo/Stock Boston. 227: m.l. Michael Salas/The Image Bank. 230: t.l. Ronald Sheridan Photo Library. 231: b. John G. Ross/Art Resource. 233: b. Scala/Art Resource. 234-235: The Granger Collection. 236: t.r. Scala/Art Resource. 237: i. Ronald Sheridan/Ancient Art & Architecture Historical Museum of Vienna; r. Art Resource. 238-239:t. Randy Wells/Tony Stone Images. 239: m. Louis Goldman/Photo Researchers. 240-241: Elaine Harrington/The Stock Market. 240: m. Art Resource. 242: t.r. Scala/Art Resource; t.l. Erich Lessing/Art Resource; b.l. Alinari/Giraudon; b. D.L. Mazzatenta/National Geographic Society Image Collection. 243: t. Leonard Von Matt; b. Cauros/Giraudon. 244-245:m. Tone Stone Images. 245: m.r. Emory Kristof/National Geographic Society; b. David Ball/The Picture Cube; t. F.H.C. Birch/Sonia Halliday Photography. 246: t.l. Scala/Art Resource. (Sistine Chapel). 248: b. (Fra Angelico) Giraudon. 249: t. Superstock; b. Dean Conger/National Geographic Society. 250-251:b. UPI/Bettmann. 250: b. Jeff Greenberg/Photo Edit. 252: t.r. Erich Lessing/Art Resource. 253: b. Giraudon. 255: b. Giraudon; t. Allan Oddie/Photo Edit. 256: b. Marco Cristofori/The Stock Market. **Chapter 10** 262: b. The Stock Market; t.l. Robert Azzi/Woodfin Camp, Inc. 264-265:t. Superstock. 264: t. Tom Hollyman/Photo Researchers. 266: b. Eric Millette; t.l. Giraudon/Musee des Arts Africains et Doceanie, Paris. 268: t.r. Nabeel Turner/Tony Stone Images; t.l. Nicholas Devore/Tony Stone Images. 270: m. Superstock; t. Chip Hires/Gamma Liaison. 270-271:b. P. Manoukian/Sygma. 272: t.l. Michael Holford. 274: b.r. Michael Howell/Stock Boston, Inc.; l. Giraudon/Cairo National Library. 276: t.l. David Ball/The Stock Market; b. Art Resource, Inc. 276-277:m. Art Resource, Inc. 277: b. E.R. Degginger/Bruce Coleman, Inc.; t.r. Superstock. 278-279:m. The Granger Collection. 279: b. Tom Van Sant/Geosphere Project; t. Bibliotheque Nationale, Paris, France/Art Resource, Inc.; m. Giraudon. **Chapter 11** 286: t.r. Charles Hennechieu/Bruce Coleman, Inc. 288: t.l. Cindy Karp/National Geographic Society; t.r. Masterfile; b. Klaus Meyer/Black Star. 292: b. D. Donne Bryant Stock Photography; t.l. Rick Strange/The Picture Cube. 294: m. National Geographic Society. 294-295:m. National Geographic Society. 295: b. Kenneth Garrett/National Geographic Society. 296: t.l. Everton/The Image Works. 297: courtesy Nancy L. Hinchler Zuñiga. 298: t.l. Kathleen Campbell/Gamma Liaison; b. Hiro Matsumoto/Black Star. 300: b. Everton/The Image Works; m. Carolyn Schaefer/Gamma Liaison. 301: b.r. Kenneth Garrett/Woodfin Camp, Inc.; b.l. Kathleen Campbell/Gamma Liaison. 302: m. Vautier/Woodfin Camp, Inc. 303: t. Robert Freck/Woodfin Camp, Inc. 304: t. Markova/The Stock Market. 304-305:m. Ted Kaufman/The Stock Market. 305: t.r. Gamma-Liaison; m. Julian Baum/Photo Researchers. **Chapter 12** 309: b. Mager Photo for MMSD. 310: b.r. Christopher Liu/ChinaStock; t.r. Lee Boltin; t. Adam Woolfit/Woodfin Camp Inc.; b.l. Scala/Art Resource. 311: m.r. National Portrait Gallery, London/Superstock; b.r. Lee Boltin. 312-313: David Louis Olson. 312: l. Christopher A. Klein. 313: b. E. C. Erdis, Peabody Museum of Natural History; t. Robert S. Sacha. 316: t.l. Uniphoto 318: l. Bob Llewellyn/Superstock; b.r. Phyllis Greenberg/Comstock 320: t.l. Superstock 321: m. Superstock 322: m. Erich Lessing/Art Resource; b. Pascal Lebrun/Gamma Liaison 324: t.l. Zefo-Hans Adam/The Stock Market; r. Superstock 325: t. Jonathan Blair/Woodfin Camp and Assoc. 326: t.r. Michael Holford 326-327:b. Bridgeman/Giraudon 328-329:b. Giraudon 330: t.l. Evan Agostini/Gamma Liaison Int'l; m. Art Resource. 330-331:m. The Pierpont Morgan Library/Art Resource 331: b.r. Topham/The Image Works 332: l. Superstock 332-333:t. Adam Woolfit/Woodfin Camp 333: t.r. Adam Woolfitt/Woodfin Camp. 334: m. Howard Hughes/Superstock 335: t. The Granger Collection. 336: t.l. Evan Agostini/Gamma Liaison International. 337: b.l. Jim Zuckerman/Westlight; m. Scala/Art Resource, Inc. 338: b.r. Art Resource (Louvre) 339: m.r. Art Resource; t.l. Giraudon. 340: m.l. Time Museum, Rockford, Illinois; b.l. Metropolitan Museum of Art, H.O. Havemeyer Collection, bequest of Mrs. H.O. Havemeyer, 1929; m. The Granger Collection. 341: t.r. Kunstmuseum, Basel; b.r. Art Resource. 342: t.l. Photo Researchers. 343: m. Art Resource 344: b.l. Giraudon 346: t.l. Superstock. 346-347:t. Michael Holford. 348: m. The Granger Collection 349: t.l. The Kobal Collection; t.r. Martha Swope/Time Picture Syndication; b. The Granger Collection **Chapter 13** 354: t. Robert Caputo/Aurora. 356: l. Robert Caputo/Aurora; r. Alon Reininger/Contact Press Images. 358: l. Robert Caputo/Aurora; b.r. Georg Gerster/Comstock. 360: l. Wendy Stone/The Gamma Liaison Network; t.r. Robert Caputo/Aurora. 361: b. Kal Muller/Woodfin Camp & Associates. 362: t. Lee Boltin. 363: t.l. Volkmar Wentzel/National Geographic Society Image Collection; t.r. Aldo Tutino/Art Resource, Inc. 365: t.r. John Elk III/Bruce Coleman; m., m.l. The Granger Collection; b. Norman Myers/Bruce Coleman, Inc.; t. John Elk III/Bruce Coleman, Inc. 366: b.l. The Granger Collection. 367: t. Jeffrey Ploskonka/National Museum of African Art. 368: m. Marc and Evelyne Bernheim/Woodfin Camp 369: t.l., b.l. Jack Vartoogian; t.r. Jeffrey Salter. 370: l. Bruno De Hogues/Tony Stone Images. 371: m. Guido Alberto Rossi/The Image Bank. 372: t. Marc and Evelyne Bernheim/Woodfin Camp; b. Werner Forman Archive 374: b. Anne Martens/The Image Bank 376: t. Wendy Stone/ Gamma Liaison 378-379:t. James L. Stansfield/Nat'l Geographic Society. 378: b. Guido Alberto Rossi/The Image Bank. **Chapter 14** 384: t.l. Barbara Rowell. 386: l. Gamma Liaison; r. Galen Rowell 388: m. Giraudon 389: b. Superstock. 392: t.l. Superstock. 393: b.r. Superstock. 394: t.l. Christina Dameyer/Photo 20-20. 395: m. Courtesy of the Trustees of the Victoria and Albert Museum. 396: l. Air India Library; r. Dallas and John Heaton/Westlight. 397: m. Boltin Picture Library. 398: t.l. Kevin R. Morris/Tony Stone Images. 400: m. R.Ian LLoyd/Westlight. 400-401:m. Ernest Manewal/Photo 20-20. 402: m. Allan Seiden/The Image Bank. 406: b.l. SIPA Press/Art Resource; b.l. Giraudon. 407: b. Guido Alberto Ross/The Image Bank; t.r. The

Granger Collection. 408: t.l. National Portrait Gallery, London/Superstock; r. The Granger Collection 410: l. Ronald R. Johnson/Stockphotos, Inc 412: b.l. Boltin Picture Library 413: l. Fuji-fotos/The Image Works 414: l. Fukuhara, Inc./Westlight 414-415:m. Bridgeman/Art Resource 416: m. Superstock 417: r. Superstock **Chapter 15** 422: t.l. The Stock Market. 424: l. Aaron Strong/ Liaison International; r. Walter Leonardi/Gamma-Liaison. 426: t.l. Boltin Picture Library. 428: t. H. Tom Hall/ National Geographic Society. 428-429:t. Erich Lessing/Art Resource. 429: b. Boltin Picture Library. 430: b.l. Ned M. Seidler/National Geographic Society; t. Giraudon. 431: t. Art Resource, Inc. 434: t. Ric Ergenbright; b. Dallas Museum of Fine Art/Werner Forman Archive/Art Resource. 436: l. Ric Ergenbright; r. Nick Saunders/Barbara Heller/Art Resource. 437: t. Museum Fur Volkerkunde, Berlin/Werner Forman Archive/Art Resource; b. Wolfgang Kaehler. 438: t. Ric Ergenbright; b. Boltin Picture Library. 439: t.l. Bruce Coleman, Inc. 440: m. David Meunch 443: b. Greenlar/The Image Works 444: t.l. Peabody Museum/Harvard University, photo by Hille Burger; b.r. National Museum of the American Indian. 445: t.r. David Perdew/Stock South **Chapter 16** 449: b. Monica Stevenson for MMSD. 450: b. Superstock; t.r. Jonathan Blair/Woodfin Camp, Inc.; t.l. Lee Boltin; m. The Phillips Collection. 451: t.r. Eric Lessing/Art Resource; b.r. Michael Holford. 452-453: Gordon W. Gahan. 452: t. Don Kincaid. 453: t. National Maritime Museum, London; b.l. Jean-Leon Huens. 456: t.l. Museo Della Scienza, Scala/Art Resource. 457: l. Erich Lessing/Art Resource; r. The Granger Collection. 458: m.r. Erich Lessing/Art Resource; b. The Granger Collection. 460: b.l. Michael Holford. 461: b.r. European Space Agency. 462: t.l. Michael Holford. 463: m.r. The Granger Collection. 465: t.l. Michael Holford. 465: t.l. Giraudon/Art Resource. 466: t.l. The Granger Collection. 468: l. Superstock; r. Giraudon. 469: t.r. Nick Saunders/Barbara Heller/Art Resource. 470: l. Nick Nicholson/The Image Bank; r. Alon Reininger/Woodfin Camp & Associates. 471: b.l. M. Timothy O'Keefe/Bruce Coleman, Inc. 472: b. The Granger Collection. 473: b.r. Roswell Museum and Art Center; Roswell Museum. 474: t.l. The Granger Collection. 476: t. Bridgeman/Giraudon. 478: t.l. Herb Jones/Black Star. 479: b. Giraudon. 480: b.l. The Granger Collection; b. Marc Romanelli/The Image Bank. **Chapter 17** 486: t.l. Superstock. 487: b. Giraudon. 489-492: Giraudon. 494: m. Giraudon. 495: m. Byron Augustin/DDB Stock Photo. 497: m. Superstock; t.r. Hans Blohm/Masterfile. 498: m. Michael Evans/Sygma. 499: t. Gamma Liaison; m. Cindy Karp/Black Star; b. AP/Wide World Photos. 500: t.l. The Granger Collection. 501: t. Michael Holford; b. Victoria and albert Museum/Superstock. 502: t.l. Superstock 503: Josepa Szkoiddinski/The Image Bank. 504: l. Bridgeman/Giraudon; r. Granger Collection. 505: t. Superstock. 508: t.l. Robert Harding Picture Library. 509: m. The Granger Collection; b. National Portrait Gallery, Smithsonian Institution/Art Resource. 510: l. Jack Fields/Photo Researchers, Inc.; r. Lauros-Giraudon. 512: b. Wernher Krutein/Liaison International. 514: t.m. Robert Harding. 514-515: Robert Harding. **Chapter 18** 520: m. Gamma-Liaison International; b. Bettmann Archives.; t.l. c. Philip Makanna/Ghosts. 521: m. Robert Harding; The Bettmann Archives. 522: b. Sygma. 522-523: NASA. 526: t.l. Bettmann Archive. 527: b.r. Roger-Viollet. 529: Archive Photos. 530: m.r. Archive Photo; t.r. Roger-Viollet; b.l. Roger Viollet. 531: Bettmann Archive. 532: Art Resource, Inc. 534: l. PopperFoto/Archive Photos; r. Gamma-Liason. 535: b. Roger-Viollet. 536: t.l. UPI/Bettmann. 537: l. Scala/Art Resource; r. Sovfoto/Eastfoto. 538: l. Archive Photos; b. Roger Viollet. 540: t.l. Hans Wild/Time Life 541: Roger-Viollet 542: l. Archive Photos; r. Roger-Viollet 545: m. Archive Photos 546-547: Gamma Liaison 549: m. Etienne De Malglaive/Liaison International 550: m. Sovfoto/Eastfoto 551552: Roger-Viollet 553: m. Archive Photos 554: m. Sovfoto/Eastfoto 556558: UPI/Bettman 559: t.l. Sygma 560: t.r. The Bettmann Archive 561: m. Werner Wolff/Black Star 560-561:m. UPI/Bettman **Chapter 19** 567: l. Owen Franken/Stock Boston; t.l. Carrion/Sygma. 569: The Bettmann Archive. 571: t.r. Archive Photos. 574: t.l. Dennis Brack/Black Star. 575: b.r. The Bettmann Archive. 577: b.r. Sygma. 578: t.r. Allen Tannenbaum/Sygma. 579: m. Karen Wald Cohen/Interns for Peace 580: t.l. Bettmann. 581: b.r. Popperfoto. 584: l. Sygma. 584-585:m. J.Martin/Popperfoto. 586: t.l. Gamma Liaison/Wolfgang Kaehler. 588: b.r. Bettman; l. Charles Bonnay/Black Star. 589: t. Ray Cranbourne/Black Star 590: t.l. Bettman; m. Hain Edvard/Gamma Liaison International **Chapter 20** 595-596: P.Piel/Gamma-Liaison. 597: l. Peter Turnley/Black Star; r. Bouvet/Gamma Liaison. 598: m. Paul O'Driscoll/Gamma Liaison; l. Peter Turnley/Black Star 600: Igmor Zamur/Gamma Liaison. 602: t.r. Vlastinir Shone/Gamma Liaison; r. Archive Photos. 605: courtesy Zlato Filipovic. 606: t.l. Peter Turnley/Black Star 608: S.S. Balic/Sygma. 610: Reuters/Bettman. 611: t.r. Tibor Bognar/The Stock Market; b.r. Ed Lallo/Liaison International; m.r. Lawrence Hughes/The Image Bank. 612: t.l. Roy Franco/Panos. 613: courtesy Ashwell Zwane and Bernent Lekalakala. 614: t.l. Francis Li/Liaison International. 615: b.l. Tom Wagner/SABA; r. Ken Straiton/Stock Market. 617: t.r. Hirokuyi Matsumoto/Black Star. 618: m.r. P. Durand/Sygma; b.r. J. Langevin/Sygma; m.l. Bill Pierce/Sygma. 619: t.r. Liu Hueng Shing/Contact. 620: t.r. Mark Harris/Tony Stone Worlwide. 624: b.l. Richard Melloul/Sygma. 626: t.r. Jeff Titcomb/Liaison International; t.r. Stephen Derr/Image Bank. 628: t.r. Stephanie Maze/National Geographic Society. 631: t. courtesy Joanne Cheng; m. Georgey Kadar; b. Kassim Yahya. 635: b. Monica Stevenson for MMSD. End-papers: Bridgeman/Art Library.

(continued from page ii)

Acknowledgments

Extract from **Children of the World** by E. Blauer, D.K. Wright, G. Holland, B.R. Rogers. Published by Gareth Stevens, Inc., Milwaukee, WI. Reprinted by permission.
From **The Sumerians: Their History, Culture and Character** by Samuel Noah Kramer. Copyright 1963 by The University of Chicago. Reprinted by permission of the publisher.
From **Pharaoh's People** by T.G.H. James. Copyright 1984 by T.G.H. James. Reprinted by permission of The University of Chicago Press.

From **God's Country: America in the Fifties** by J. Ronald Oakley. Copyright 1986 by J. Ronald Oakley. Red Dembner Enterprises Corp., New York.
From **Television** by Michael Winship. Copyright 1988 by Educational Broadcasting Corporation and Michael Winship. Random House, New York.
From **Monsoons**, edited by Jay S. Fein, Pamela L. Stephens. Copyright 1987 by John Wiley & Sons, Inc. A. Wiley-Interscience Publication, John Wiley & Sons, Inc.
From **The Ancient Civilization of Angkor** by Christopher Pym. Copyright 1968 by Christopher Pym. A Mentor Book published by The New American Library, N.Y. & Toronto.
From **Angkor Heart of an Asian Empire** by Bruno Dagens. English translation copyright 1995 by Harry N. Abrams, Inc., N.Y. and Thames and Hudson Ltd., London. Harry N. Abrams, Inc., Publishers.
From **The Travels of Marco Polo**, a modern translation by Teresa Waugh from the Italian by Maria Bellonci. Translation copyright 1984 by Sadgwick and Jackson Limited. Facts on File Publications, N.Y.
From **The Longest Walk: An Odyssey of the Human Spirit** by George Meegan. Copyright 1988 by George Meegan. Dodd, Mead & Company, N.Y.
From **The Way of the Earth: Encounters with Nature in Ancient and Contemporary Thought** by T.C. McLuhan. Copyright 1994 by T.C. McLuhan. Simon & Schuster, N.Y. From "The land is everything." quote printed in **Native Peoples Magazine** Vol. 6, Number 3, Spring 1993, quote from Gerald Vizenor. Copyright 1993 by Media Concepts Group, Inc. Media Concepts Group, Inc., AZ.
From **Coming of Age in the Milky Way** by Timothy Ferris. Copyright 1988 by Timothy Ferris. An Anchor Book published by Doubleday, a division of Bantam Doubleday Dell Publishing Group, Inc., N.Y. The Anchor Books Edition was published by arrangement with William Morrow and Company.
From **The Diary of a Young Girl: The Definitive Edition** by Anne Frank. Otto H. Frank & Mirjam Pressler, Editors, translated by Susan Massotty. Translation copyright © 1995 by Doubleday, a division of Bantam Doubleday Dell Publishing Group, Inc. Used by permission of Doubleday, a division of Bantam Doubleday Dell Publishing Group, Inc.
From **Red Azalea** by Anchee Min. Copyright 1994 by Anchee Min. Pantheon Books, a division of Random House, N.Y.
From **China: The Long March** by Anthony Lawrence. Copyright 1986 by Intercontinental Publishing Corp., China National Publishing Industry Trading Corp. and China Photographic Publishing House. Merehurst Press, London.
From **Mme Sun Yat-sen** by Jung Chang with Jon Halliday. Copyright 1986 by Jung Chang and Jon Halliday. Penguin Books.
From **The Cold War** by Martin Walker. Copyright 1993 by Walker & Watson Ltd. A John Macrae Book, Henry Holt and Company, N.Y.
From **The Africans** by David Lamb. Copyright 1983 by David Lamb. Vintage Books, a division of Random House, N.Y.
From **Holy War: The Crusades and Their Impact on Today's World** by Karen Armstrong. Copyright 1988, 1991 by Karen Armstrong. Papermac, a division of Macmillan Publishers Limited, London.
From **Long Walk to Freedom: The Autobiography of Nelson Mandela** by Nelson Mandela. Copyright 1994 by Nelson Rolihlahla Mandela. Little, Brown and Company.
From **Zlata's Diary: A Child's Life in Sarajevo** translated with notes by Christina Pribichevich-Zoric. Translation Copyright by Fixot and editions Robert Laffont, 1994. Viking, published by the Penguin Group, Penguin Books USA Inc., N.Y.
From **Self-Made Man: Human Evolution from Eden to Extinction** by Jonathan Kingdon. Copyright 1993 by Jonathan Kingdon. John Wiley & Sons, Inc.
From **Mesopotamian Myths** by Henrietta McCall. Copyright by The Trustees of the British Museum. British Museum Publications, London.
From **Legacy of the Indus: A Discovery of Pakistan** by Samina Quraeshi. Copyright 1974 by Samina Quraeshi. Poem on pg. 8 Copyright 1974 by Salman Tarik Kureshi. John Weatherhill, Inc.
From **The Vedic Experience Mantramanjari**, edited and translated with introductions and notes by Raimundo Panikkar. Copyright 1977 by Raimundo Panikkar. University of California Press.
From **Four-Dimensional Man: Meditations Through the Rg Veda** by Antonio T. de Nicolas. Copyright 1976 by Nicolas Hays, Ltd. Nicolas Hays Ltd.
From **The Wisdom of the Buddha**, by Jean Boisselier. Copyright 1993 by Gallimard. English translation Copyright 1994 Harry N. Abrams, Inc., N.Y. Harry N. Abrams, Inc., New York.
From **The Odyssey of Homer** a new verse translation by Allen Mandelbaum. Copyright 1990 by Allen Mandelbaum. University of California Press.
From **God's Bits of Wood**, Sembene Ousmane translated by Francis Price. Copyright 1962 Doubleday & Company Inc. Heinemann Educational Books Ltd.
From **Serowe Village of the Rain Wind** by Bessie Head. Copyright 1981 by Bessie Head. Heinemann Educational Books Ltd.
From **The Search for Africa**, by Basil Davidson. Copyright 1994 by Basil Davidson. Times Books/Random House.
From **Corpus of early Arabic sources for West African history**, translated by J.F.P. Hopkins, edited and annotated by N. Levtzion & J.F.P. Hopkins. Copyright 1981 by University of Ghana, International Academic Union, Cambridge University Press. Cambridge University Press.
From "China-the End of an Era" from *The Nation Magazine* by Orville Schell. The Nation Magazine, July 17/24, 1995.